LULA

AND HIS POLITICS OF CUNNING

FROM METALWORKE

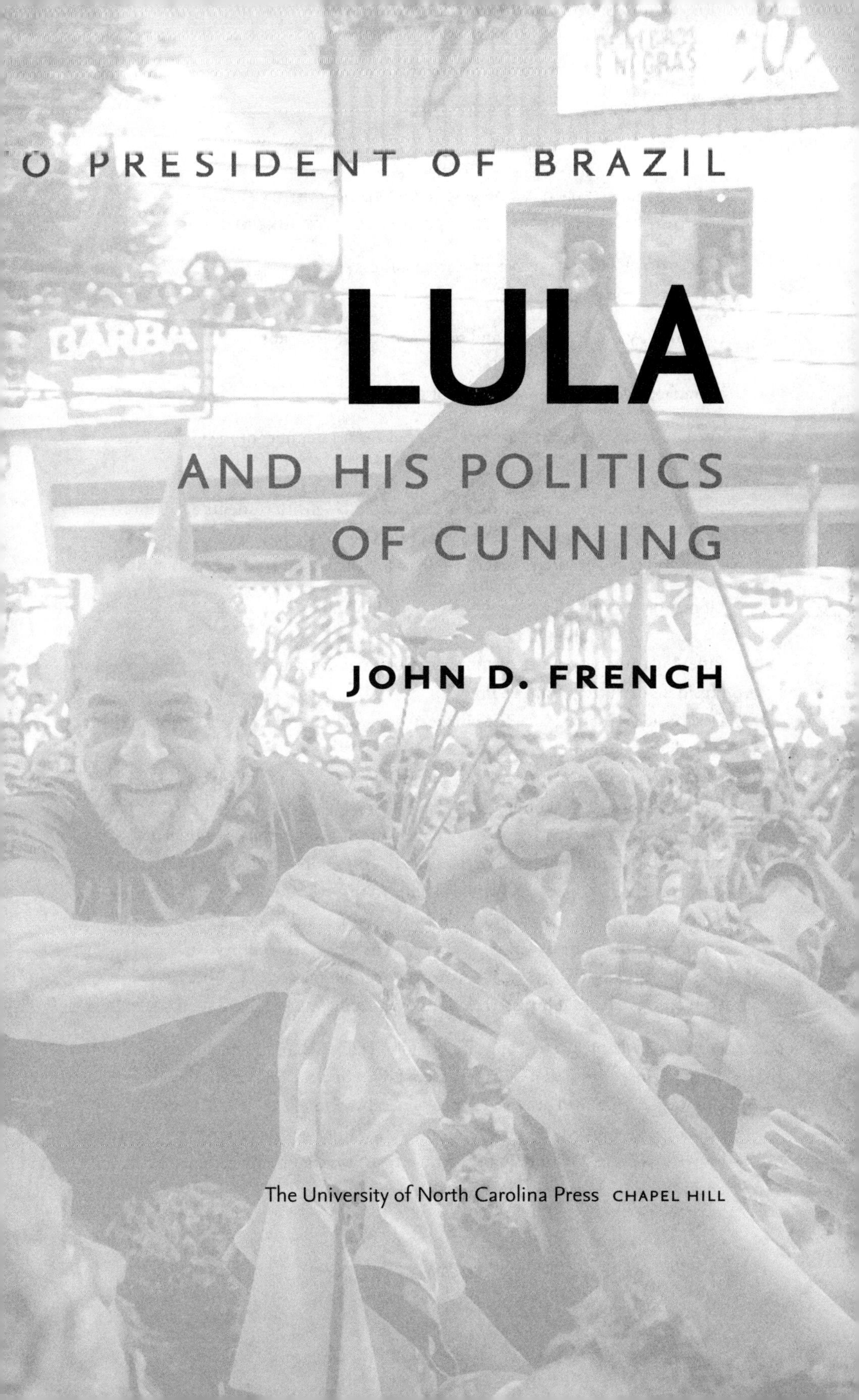

O PRESIDENT OF BRAZIL

LULA

AND HIS POLITICS OF CUNNING

JOHN D. FRENCH

The University of North Carolina Press CHAPEL HILL

PUBLICATION OF THIS BOOK WAS ASSISTED IN PART BY FUNDS FROM THE TRINITY COLLEGE OF ARTS AND SCIENCES AT DUKE UNIVERSITY.

Designed by Rebecca Evans and set in Arno and Seria Sans by
Tseng Information Systems, Inc.
Manufactured in the United States of America

The University of North Carolina Press has been a member of the Green Press Initiative since 2003.

Jacket illustration: Luis Inácio Lula da Silva dancing with students at Instituto Multidisciplinar, Universidade Federal Rural do Rio de Janeiro, December 2017. Photograph by Ricardo Stuckert; © Ricardo Stuckert and used by permission.

Library of Congress Cataloging-in-Publication Data
Names: French, John D., author.
Title: Lula and his politics of cunning : from metalworker to
president of Brazil / John D. French.
Description: Chapel Hill : The University of North Carolina Press, 2020. |
Includes bibliographical references and index.
Identifiers: LCCN 2020013710 | ISBN 9781469655765 (cloth : alk. paper) |
ISBN 9781469655772 (ebook)
Subjects: LCSH: Lula, 1945– | Presidents—Brazil—Biography. | Politicians—Brazil—Biography. | Labor leaders—Brazil—Biography. | Brazil—Politics and government—1985–2002. | Brazil—Politics and government—2003– | Brazil—Social conditions—20th century. | Brazil—Social conditions—21st century. | Brazil—History—20th century. | Brazil—History—21st century.
Classification: LCC F2538.5.L85 F74 2020 | DDC 981.06/5092 [B]—dc23
LC record available at https://lccn.loc.gov/2020013710

Portions of chapter 17 first appeared in John D. French, "Understanding the Politics of Latin America's Plural Lefts (Chávez/Lula): Social Democracy, Populism, and Convergence on the Path to a Post-neoliberal World," *Third World Quarterly* 30, no. 2 (2009): 349–70. © Southseries Inc., www.thirdworldquarterly.com, reprinted by permission of Taylor & Francis Ltd, http://www.tandfonline.com, on behalf of Southseries Inc., www.thirdworldquarterly.com.

DEDICATED TO

Marcos Andreotti (1910–1984)

Morgan James (1917–2006)

Philadelpho Braz (1926–2009)

David Montgomery (1927–2011)

Emília Viotti da Costa (1928–2017)

Jan Hoffman French

Johnnetta Betsch Cole

CONTENTS

FIGURES

LULA

AND HIS POLITICS OF CUNNING

INTRODUCTION / THE LONG VIEW

In *Lula and His Politics of Cunning*, I embrace the biographical approach that I believe is essential to understanding how Luiz Inácio Lula da Silva—a fourth-grade-educated man of the most humble origins—rose to become the thirty-fifth Brazilian president in 2003. How did Lula—a man now known around the world by just his nickname—ascend from his status as a poor rural migrant to São Paulo to become a metalworker, a union strike leader, and a radical leftist politician before finally attaining the presidency? A sui generis figure, Lula has been a star in Brazilian trade union and political life since his debut as a fiery strike leader over forty years ago. Whether loved, tolerated, or resented, Lula is familiar to all Brazilians, with his gruff voice, smiles, and boisterous good humor as well as his love of soccer metaphors and the hugs of an adoring populace. A veritable "man of the people," Lula ended his second term in 2010 with an over 80 percent approval rating, and twice Brazilian voters elected his chosen Workers' Party successor, Dilma Rousseff, to follow him as the country's leader. This stunning level of popularity in April 2009 led President Barack Obama to publicly hail Lula, when they first met, as "the most popular politician on earth."[1]

As the world's fifth-largest country, with over 200 million inhabitants, Brazil under Lula and Dilma experienced significant growth in GDP from 2005 through 2012, having been only briefly affected, in 2009, by the global financial crisis that wreaked havoc in the United States and Western Europe. Although Brazil is Latin America's most unequal country in terms of wealth distribution, the Lula-Dilma era pioneered innovative policies of inclusion and redistribution that produced a significant 10 percent drop in income inequality, with 40 million people escaping extreme poverty. As the eighth- or ninth-largest economy by GDP, the government's successes in expanding well-being and opportunity through mild but firm government intervention substantially enhanced access to social services, the consumer market, and education in the country, half nonwhite, that has the largest population of African descent outside the African continent.

By 2014, when Lula—by then a sixty-nine-year-old two-term president who was no longer in office—had helped his political party win its fourth consecutive presidential election, most Lula observers completely dismissed the man's first forty years of life as ancient history. The heights at which he had arrived

President Lula at the White House with President Barack Obama, 2009.
(Photo by Pete Souza; courtesy Barack Obama Presidential Library)

seemed to distort the narrative arc of his personal and political story, allowing the process of historical contingency to fall away. I aim, in this book, to restore all that rich and neglected personal and political history, paying close attention to the first half of his life, which explains how Lula came so spectacularly to the notice of Brazil and the world in 1979 as the charismatic leader of massive strikes under a military dictatorship. It is these early days that offer the key to understanding how Lula—the most popular president in the history of Brazil and perhaps the world—learned to act politically and came to shine both in nitty-gritty small-group interactions and as an effective communicator and trusted leader of hundreds of thousands and eventually tens of millions of Brazilians. His story will be shown to shed light on the worldview of the working poor, how radical social movements emerge, and how they can transform themselves—against the odds—into a transformative electoral politics of consistency and achievement.

In 2010, at the apex of his popularity, Lula's success seemed at times predestined—although destiny, as the Brazilian gaúcho poet Mário Quintana has observed, is often "chance attacked by a mania of grandeur."[2] In writing about

Lula, one should heed his least charitable biographer, who insists that, again and again, destiny "placed him in the right place, at the right time, and with the right person."[3] The dilemma was well captured by the literary critic Georg Lukács, who observed that "without chance, all narration is dead and abstract." "No writer," he insisted, "can portray life if he eliminates the fortuitous. On the other hand, in his representation of life he must go beyond crass accident and elevate chance to the inevitable."[4] The inevitable, in other words, must be balanced by a frank recognition that Lula's extraordinary story is about a very lucky and gifted man. As it will show, Lula's understanding of the world and his message and stratagems draw from the cunning wisdom of the weak, but he deploys them on behalf of a transformative politics of cunning capable of changing a nation.

Lula's sui generis political trajectory is best approached by analyzing the city of São Paulo from midcentury through 1980, especially its trade union arena, where his leadership was forged. This biography is the first to investigate the decisive apprenticeships that allowed Lula to become a skilled machinist and a capable, even brilliant, trade union leader. What was the configuration of dispositions, understandings, and skills that characterized this young man, and where did they come from? How did he experience the world rapidly coming into being as São Paulo industrialized? For this city's industrial workers, what was the relationship between men and machine and between men and the employers to whom they owed labor and obedience? When and how did Lula acquire the judgment needed for successful political maneuvering? And after he had acquired this, from where flowed his unusual way with words, the confidence and facility with which he spoke and the boldness with which he acted?[5]

In embracing the biographical, this book at the same time rejects an excessively individualistic narrative in which Lula's personal history displaces the history of his relationships. As Charles Payne has suggested for the US civil rights movement, excessive attention to a single individual, such as Martin Luther King Jr., not only denies the movement's bottom-up dynamics but also displaces the grassroots activists and mass following whose energies produced such a leader and gave him his stature and strength.[6] This book would fail if, in fixating on the myth known as Lula, it overlooked the thousands of his friends, allies, and admirers, the tens of thousands of rank-and-file workers, and the tens of millions of his voters. Thus, the book foregrounds the social, political, and cultural processes through which Luiz Inácio da Silva became the imagined Lula who is now the common property of all Brazilians.

As president, Lula would be celebrated as the country's preeminent symbol of social mobility, which both overestimates the man and underestimates the Brazilian people. Ignoring issues of narrative, representation, and transcendence, such accounts reflect one way that Lula can be (and is) perceived, but at the cost of liquidating the biographical individual and reducing his rise to its lowest common denominator. More importantly, this narrative of individual social mobility ignores the reasoning and feelings of the millions who made of Luiz Inácio the Lula whom all would come to know, whether they love or detest him. Such an approach implies the existence of undifferentiated "masses" who respond unthinkingly to pandering or cheap gifts like the Bolsa Família social welfare program, a view of the common people long held by Brazil's lettered elites on both the left and the right.

In this book, Lula will be treated neither in splendid isolation nor as wholly merged with his surroundings. My study is anchored, above all, in Lula's relationships with others: with his family first and foremost, especially his brother José Ferreira de Melo (better known by his nickname, Frei Chico), and the women with whom he made his life, as well as the remarkable generation of working-class baby boomers, his fellow skilled workers and trade unionists, from whom he learned as he came to practice politics. In doing so, I advance a bold new argument that Lula—and the skilled minority of blue-collar workers of which he was a part—were members of a working-class intelligentsia analogous to the ambitious young people attending the University of São Paulo (USP) at the time. By depicting the evolving relations between the lettered and the common people, this book sheds new light on how the machinist Lula and the USP sociologist Fernando Henrique Cardoso (known to Brazilians as FHC), two left-wing allies in the late 1970s, came to hold the presidency for two terms each between 1994 and 2010. Paying close attention to linguistic and cultural capital, *Lula and His Politics of Cunning* explores the ongoing and often-fraught dialogue between and among USP intellectuals and the workers who frequented the union halls of the metalworking industry in the São Paulo industrial suburbs known as ABC. This is vital because democratic change in Brazil required a painful confrontation with a profoundly authoritarian and elitist culture that exalted a highly educated and well-off minority over "ignorant" masses, lacking both confidence and knowledge, who were ultimately controlled through fear, as happened to Lula's brother in 1975.

Putting aside the sheer improbability of Lula's "log cabin" story, the deepest mystery regarding his emergence is why and how the workers of São Bernardo do Campo and Diadema, the São Paulo municipalities (*municípios*) in which Lula was based, in 1978 began three years of large-scale strikes, well-organized stoppages the likes of which Brazil had never seen before and has not seen since. Industrial militancy seemed unlikely in this world of modern factory production under a dictatorial government whose repressive apparatus worked closely with employers to snuff out opposition. Moreover, the raw material for "class consciousness" seemed lacking, given that the workforce was composed not of the classic "proletarians" of Marxist theory but of worker-migrants from rural Brazil who experienced both upward mobility and high labor turnover. Even the formal structures of union representation, which were tied to the repressive state, seemed formidable obstacles to mobilization.

This biography offers new insights—based on hitherto-unused sources, including intelligence agencies—into the extraordinary actions of the metalworkers of the São Paulo municipalities collectively known as ABC (named after the municípios of Santo André, São Bernardo do Campo, and São Caetano do Sul) and their trade unions in the 1970s. Unlike others who have discussed President Lula's life, I tackle the essential analytical question of how a mass worker insurgency emerged in ABC's metalworking industry, a world of men—along with some women, 10 percent of the workforce—who did not identify collectively as factory workers; indeed, 80 percent of them eschewed membership in the union that Lula came to lead. Lacking unity of action and a common group consciousness, ABC's metalworkers hardly seemed fruitful terrain for organizing, much less forceful, massive insurgency. Yet any serious attempt to explain Lula's subsequent trajectory has to address why these men in this place came to mass action, and what it was about Lula in particular that led to his key role(s) in these events.

I argue that Lula's rapport with rank-and-file metalworkers, forged during his five years as union president, explains why he came to be known and respected around the world. Operating in a society closed to dialogue, Lula developed a distinctive personality and approach to interpersonal relations that aimed to break through even with those of opposing views or diverging interests. Yet at the outset, even among workers, the sympathies, identification, and deep ties that emerged between Lula and ABC's workers were improbable and unexpected. Although unions were workers' legally designated representatives, their leaders had always fallen far short of achieving an effective meeting of wills with those whom they officially "represented." It was in the late 1970s that a timid new union president, finding his voice, connected viscerally with the consciousness of a large swath of his fellow workers. To the surprise of Lula, his fellow workers, and their employers, the great strikes of 1978–80 saw an extraordinary new collective actor emerge: the legendary "metalworkers of ABC." These hundreds of thousands of workers became famous for the energy, courage, and undeniable élan of their unprecedented mobilizations, which put their charismatic leader in the headlines and on TV screens globally.

Once examined closely, even the motivations behind these strikes seem mysterious. These workers in ABC, while having grievances, appreciated their well-paying jobs in modern automobile assembly and metalworking plants. Moreover, they had previously been so indifferent to politics that most had passively supported military rule after 1964, with many actively favoring the military government for delivering unprecedented GDP growth during the Brazilian "economic miracle" of 1968–74, which vastly expanded the region's factories and opportunities and thus fueled new ambitions among workers. How, then, do we explain the subsequent mass insurgency? What motivated those involved, and what was the political conjuncture that facilitated their daring? And finally, what did Lula the biographical individual have to do with it? What decisions did he make, what actions did he take, and with whom did he interact and how? What words of incitement, encouragement, and defiance did he articulate in the face of government and company repression and in the aftermath of the strikes' defeat?

Moving beyond the symbolic, this biography investigates Lula's actions during those years and their legacy, in terms of both what Lula learned and what he came to mean to those who encountered him—whether directly or through the media. The powerful bond that crystallized would reach well beyond ABC with Lula's construction in the 1980s of both a new leftist political party, the Workers' Party (Partido dos Trabalhadores; PT), and an allied trade union confederation, the Unified Workers' Central (Central Única dos Trabalhadores [CUT]), which personified the surging New Unionism. Both faced significant rivals on the left, the most important of which nationally was the leftist laborism (*trabalhismo*) of the talented politician Leonel Brizola. The Communist Left, especially the historically Soviet-aligned Brazilian Communist Party (Partido Comunista Brasileiro, PCB), also maintained a sphere of influence, with some strength in the union movement including Lula's brother Frei Chico. Even the smaller Maoist Communist Party of Brazil (Partido Comunista do Brasil, PcdoB) had support among some students, ex-students, and workers, having gained adherents from Popular Action (Ação Popular, AP), a New Left revolutionary organization founded by Catholics.

If Lula's origin was inextricably tied to a specific place and time, his triumph in the twenty-first century depended on becoming part of Brazil's rich but regionally differentiated history of labor, leftist, and electoral politics. After his ouster from the union, this new celebrity would interact ever more intensely with the many classes, factions, interests, and personalities that had emerged in a continent-sized country transformed economically by two periods of sustained industrial growth between 1957 and 1974 and politically by twenty-one years of military rule from 1964 to 1985. After an undistinguished term as federal deputy (1986–88), Lula played a singular role in the postdictatorial New Republic wracked by debt-fueled hyperinflation, economic stagnation, and political tumult, followed by a profound process of neoliberal restructuring in the 1990s. As a party and movement leader, Lula operated for two decades without holding any elected position or running for any job other than the presidency.

Why Biography and the Writing of It

The extraordinary events in ABC generated an abundance of journalistic and political coverage and a wealth of other documentation in the form of film, theater, fiction, and photography, in addition to a large and variegated body of social science research. Despite its enormous strengths, however, this formidable body of research—which broadened to encompass the New Unionism and the PT—shied away from sustained analysis of the icon of those strikes and the subsequent CUT and PT, whose presidential vote total always far exceeded those of all other PT candidates combined. For example, in his 1987 book on greater São Paulo's metalworkers, the talented Mexican industrial sociologist Víctor Manuel Durand Ponte, focusing on political economy, state-labor relations, and trade unionism, interpreted Lula as a by-product of growing identification between rank-and-file workers and their union leadership in São Bernardo. A more accurate formulation, however, is that the workers first identified with Lula and then transferred this identification, in part, to the union leadership team he headed and only later to the union as an institution.[7]

Similarly, the British sociologist John Humphrey—whose excellent work analyzed the crucial developments in mid-1970s Brazil in terms of the trade union's capacity for action, increased credibility, recruitment of shop floor militants, and so on—never discusses Lula the biographical individual; even when quoting Lula, as he often does, he frames the union president as a reflection of the union's will.[8] Humphrey adopts this approach for assessing the ABC strikes' unfolding, the very moment when Lula's fellow union directors were fully aware of his unparalleled stature and influence with the mass of workers, an influence that far exceeded their own. Among social scientists, only Margaret Keck gave pride of place to Lula as "the key figure" in the 1978–80 strikes, without whom events might have turned out quite differently. She cited his "reputed charisma," the wide respect for him in the labor movement even among his opponents, and his stature as the nation's best-known trade union leader, a man whose every action was well covered in the mass media.[9]

Curiously enough, Lula's particular role(s) and contribution(s) are also slighted in the vast literature on the New Unionism, the PT, and even his presidential campaigns, which focus on party strategy and platforms, internal ideological disputes, public opinion polls, political advertising, and voting patterns.[10] Were it not for a handful of journalistic books on several of Lula's presidential races, we would know even less about his strengths and weaknesses during grueling campaigns—both his own and on behalf of others—that involved tens of thousands of activists and millions of voters. My point is not that the existing literature, with its focus on structures, institutions, and collective behavior, is wrong or irremediably deficient. This book does argue, however, that it is time to adopt an ambitious new research focus: the biographical specificities of Lula's leadership as an illustration of how larger social structures and historical processes intersect with human agency and political praxis.[11]

Looking back at his first presidential run in 1989, it is still surprising that the inexperienced PT candidate "defeated nine national leaders from the major parties to enter the runoff election," even if the lucky Lula only beat Brizola by a nose in the first round. As a political scientist has rightly insisted, "The success of the PT in the 1989 election must not be underestimated."[12] Barely losing in the second round, he emerged as the leading presidential contender in 1994, only to fall short in the first round to FHC. Though he lost again in 1998, Lula emerged as the recognized voice of opposition to the Cardoso government, having consolidated his electoral support over the course of the decade, including among the educated minority who identified as leftist and cast for Lula a principled "vote of conscience" to signal their repudiation of the country's squalid and venal political and economic system. Yet the clear moral position of part of the PT's constituency—some spoke of the party's purism—would constitute a formidable obstacle between Lula and the presidency.

Famous at the time for its dedicated activists, the PT for two decades rejected on principle electoral alliances with any party that was not unambiguously leftist. How did the party's leaders, factions, and members come to be convinced of the need to abandon this stance and embrace ambiguity? Looking back, this recalibration of the PT's policy regarding party alliances may seem a simple matter of rational calculation, but if so, why hadn't this rational calculation occurred in 1993–94, when it would have been most useful, or in the run-up to 1998? And when the decisive change in policy did occur, why didn't this "moderation" lead to charges of selling out and thus threaten the PT's internal coherence, outrage its self-sacrificing activists, and alienate its organized leftist factions? In truth, the PT was never a party where everyone "took orders" from a single individual, even Lula, who was, party orthodoxy insisted—if not fully convincingly—simply a *companheiro* "like the rest of us," albeit a leading one.

When Lula finally reached office in 2003, the onetime socialist firebrand was charged with leading a country facing economic crisis and austerity. To most observers, it seemed unlikely that Lula, and his maturing but still radically green party, would survive the treachery at the top; the Left controlled none of the other branches of government and almost no governorships. Moreover, Lula's only prior executive experience was his five short years as union president a quarter century earlier, which hardly seemed good preparation for getting legislation passed by a Congress in which the Left was a minority or for successfully wrestling with government bureaucracies in which the president often enough seemed at best a figurehead. A president may hope to achieve many things, but how can he or she convert even a single campaign promise into effectively implemented policy and legislation? And how did Lula's success in doing so change understandings of him, both positively and negatively, among different groups of Brazilians?

Proving a quick learner, Lula was unquestionably effective, and his signature policies gained generalized assent, even among his competitors. While enhanced by his electoral support, his success depended above all on his mastery of the byzantine and often-dubious arts governing Brazil's extraordinarily opaque national political game. Needless to say, errors were indeed made, some of them crass. When the "mensalão" corruption scandal hit in 2005, the much-ballyhooed crisis decapitated the PT's leadership and led to an unprecedented prosecution and eventual jailing (in 2012) of some of Lula's key collaborators. Yet even as the crisis raged and then lingered in the media, a sufficiently robust, if changing, rapport between Lula and the national electorate allowed him to win reelection in 2006 and to get his chosen successor elected in 2010 and again in 2014. Yet less than two years later, Dilma Rousseff was impeached, and Brazil's most popular ex-president was bombarded by prosecutors, his political opponents, and the mass media as a criminal mastermind deserving imprisonment for alleged corruption. At times, such dramatic twists and turns can leave the impression that the gruffness of Lula's speaking voice is the one unifying thread among his decades in public life.

Making Sense of Lula's Success

Lula's life since 1978 has indeed been—to quote his self-promotional presidential rhetoric—a case of "never before in the history of Brazil" and, to be honest, almost anywhere else in the world. But how are we to explain his sustained success against the odds and his adept maneuvering of the government as president, for which he seemed ill-prepared due to his scant experience in elected office? Does it primarily reflect social, political, and cultural change during these decades? What role did luck play, or is something more elusive at work? And how much should we credit, alternately, Lula the biographical individual, the construction of "Lula" as a larger-than-life historical personality, and his many collaborators across the years? Surprisingly enough, these questions have not engaged mainstream "public opinion" in Brazil during the Lula era and, as we have seen, only a handful of talented journalists, media commentators, and scholars have engaged in any depth with the most distinctive figure and voice in Brazilian political history. Personal political sympathies and a familiarity that blunts curiosity no doubt plays some role in this neglect, but the key factor is the formative intellectual influence of Marxism and liberalism. Both interpretive frameworks eschew a focus on the individual as mystifying and sweep away the "subjective" in favor of objectivist abstractions such as "social class," "capitalism," "the market," or the "consumer." When such scholars brush against the Lula phenomenon (what is called *lulismo*), they also get caught up in the fraught perennial debate about "populism," which emerged from the political battles marking midcentury Brazil before the 1964 coup.[13]

The failure of mainstream journalism to take Lula seriously contrasts with the respectful attention afforded Fernando Henrique Cardoso, an ex-president who was popular with the educated public despite long polling poorly among the overall population compared to Lula—even in 2018, in the wake of the latter's arrest. This reflects the prestige that the better-off, in Brazil's wealthier areas, accord to intellectuals, with their erudite speech, modeled on the written word, as opposed to the evanescent orality of Lula's distinctive vernacular voice. Lula's "lower-class" form of speech, combined with his facile soccer analogies and rhetorical exaggerations, has long led to an underestimation of his intellectual capacity, even as he won election after election; as a man without a university degree, President Lula could never really be "one of us."

So how did educated "public opinion" explain his success after 2002? Suspicious of emotion, the educated middle and upper classes credited his electoral popularity to his connection with a "mass" audience through "charisma," which they regard as irrational. In addressing his presidential actions, centrist and even many leftist critics leaned on the term "pragmatism," easily read as a lack of principles, and suggested that his government offered little more than a face-lift to the neoliberalism of FHC's presidencies. Critics of Lula and the PT also emphasized the absence of an articulated "ideology"—not something regularly demanded of his rivals—and often advanced the dismissive claim that President Lula was never "really a leftist," as judged by their intellectual schemas. The "populist" Lula, it seemed, was at best a trade unionist, a lesser sort inclined to making deals that fell well short of political ideals. He was a man untroubled by the morally questionable bargains entailed by allying with unprincipled non-leftist politicians willing to support a PT government in exchange for access to the money and privileges of power; not without irony, it would be the upstart PT, not its inconstant allies, that were condemned as a band of pervasively corrupt racketeers by a partisan judiciary when the fight to bring the Lula-Dilma era to an end intensified after 2014.

During Lula's presidency, mainstream commentators did not take seriously the claims of the ideological Far Right, who harked back to the anti-Communism of the "good old days" of the military regime. With the end of military rule in 1985 and the dawn of the New Republic, the prevailing rules of debate gave pride of place to opposition voices such as Fernando Henrique Cardoso, the prince of Brazilian sociology, and his former leftist associates like José Serra, the Brazilian Social Democracy Party (Partido da Social Democracia Brasileira, PSDB) presidential candidate twice defeated by the PT. Yet the PSDB, even as it trended rightward, set the tone for the opposition to Lula and the PT, though more "ideological" voices were a powerful undercurrent, particularly in Brazil's dominant national newsmagazine *Veja*, with its legendary covers virulently targeting the PT and the Lula-Dilma governments. With substantial backing among the upper classes of Brazilian society, this undercurrent of far-right opposition denounced Lula as a dangerous socialist and the PT as a party of closet Marxist-Leninists participating in a subversive conspiracy directly tied to Communist Cuba, Venezuelan *chavismo*, and the Colombian guerrillas of the Revolutionary Armed Forces of Colombia (Fuerzas Armadas Revolucionarias de Colombia, or FARC) through the Forum of São Paulo (FSP), a periodic gathering of Latin America's leftist parties founded at Lula's initiative in 1990. While long underestimated, this simplistic anti-Communist rhetoric would acquire resonance and a mass base during the national political polarization that led to President Dilma's 2016 impeachment and the election of Jair Bolsonaro, an avowed supporter of the military regime, as president during the flawed and controversial 2018 contest.

For most of the Lula-Dilma era, however, mainstream journalistic and academic observers—many of whom had been sympathetic to the PT in their youth—were more likely to invoke the gap between Lula and Dilma's modest achievements and their party's early programmatic demand for profound structural transformations, if not socialism. Falling short of "real" social reform, the PT governments' redistributive policies were judged clientelist vote buying with a dash of populist demagoguery. They were quick to observe that a loud drumbeat about "workers" against "capitalists" during the PT's "heroic" early years had been replaced, in the twenty-first century, with rhetoric pitting the "common people" against the "elites." Presented thus, Lula is an unprincipled shape-shifter who had disillusioned everyone who ever believed that the PT and its project radically differed from the rest of Brazil's parties.

Those who made such a reasoned case against Lula sought to deny Brazil's first working-class president recognition as a statesman, portraying him instead as a popular, vulgar politician who had simply been lucky enough to preside over Brazil during an international commodity boom. From their superior perch, these highly educated critics were sometimes prepared to grant Lula a certain tactical talent (*esperteza*), if only to bemoan the absence of a "strategic vision" or "national project," expansive if murky lodestars popular among intellectuals. In truth, though, a vast country like Brazil could not have been governed by Lula and his chosen successor without a concept of the nation or its citizenry in all their diversity. In a society marked by radical inequalities and starkly conflicting interests, the deeper values and priorities of an elected president are revealed by his or her actions, inactions, evasions, and speech acts while exercising power. This lies at the heart of the democratic ideal: Who are we, where are we now, where have we been, and toward which horizon should we as voters set the nation's course?

This book offers a biographical interpretation of the origin, roots, and evolution of Lula's vision, values, and practice of leadership and how these played out as Lula gained in power and stature. I will argue that Lula's singular and enduring style and practice of leadership—and associated discourse—had crystallized by 1978, the year of the first strikes, and would remain unchanged over the following four decades. Here was a leader, open to dialogue but more than willing to stand up and fight when needed, who practiced an additive and transformative politics of cunning executed by creating spaces of convergence across difference. I make the case that leadership can only be understood as process and a two-way (even if asymmetrical) relationship that causally links mass consciousness and action, whether in a strike or at the ballot box.

By analyzing, in depth, the origin of Lula's actions *and* words (i.e., speech acts), *Lula and His Politics of Cunning* advances a very specific understanding of politics as relationships and leadership as embodied work done with words. After all, Lula was not authorized to rise to where he did by the social, political, or cultural order that governed Brazil. He reached the presidency through the relationships he established with the population, both above and below, through the resonance of his words, who he was, and what he came to symbolize. In penetrating the "magic" associated with the birth of Lula's charisma during the strikes in ABC, the book crafts a moving narrative of the process of self- and group-fashioning that generated a public persona who would decisively alter the following quarter century of Brazil's politics. Focusing on society as much as—if not more than—the polity, this book captures the subaltern origin of Lula's distinctive style of political leadership, from trade unionism to the presidency and beyond. In doing so, I also contribute to our understanding of the broad mix of interests, values, loyalties, and accommodations that marked the governing gestalt of the Lula-Dilma era, when Brazil represented the very heart of the leftward turns in Latin America that redefined the region's politics in the early twenty-first century. With the passage of time, what are now tentative observations will no doubt be followed by even more robust examinations of the Lula-Dilma era's long-term impact in terms of what changed, what didn't, and what it meant for whom.

1 LULA'S APOTHEOSIS

In October 2002 Brazil overwhelmingly elected as president a former metalworker and founder of a socialist party, a man whose family had left the miserable northeastern (*nordestino*) hinterland five decades earlier, only to face prejudice and hardship in the country's industrial heartland of São Paulo. The election of Luiz Inácio Lula da Silva of the Workers' Party (PT) was a clear signal that deep changes were taking place in a country marked by huge social inequalities and a contempt for manual labor engendered by almost four centuries of slavery. The fifty-seven-year-old Lula's election was not only a remarkable personal achievement for a man born into rural poverty but also a sterling tribute to the Brazilian fight to overcome the legacy of the military dictatorship that had ruled from 1964 to 1985. The amazing story of the four decades from the 1964 military coup to Lula's election can be captured in two images. Lula's 1980 police mug shot showed a subversive detained for leading a massive metalworkers' strike; his presidential portrait of 2003 depicted an older, smiling Lula who would for the next eight years command the very military men who had jailed and persecuted him.

Lula's emergence as a charismatic personality of unquestioned moral authority was linked to events between 1978 and 1980, when workers repeatedly struck the foreign-owned automobile assembly plants in the suburban ABC region of Greater São Paulo. This wave of industrial militancy, which originated among the highest-paid manual workers in Latin America, quickly spread to millions of others over the next three years. As the first mass strikes since the 1964 military coup, the ABC region's work stoppages captured the Brazilian imagination. With 1.6 million residents in 1980, this Latin American Detroit stood out as an extreme example of industrial production on a hitherto-unknown scale. The massive Volkswagen plant in São Bernardo, for example, employed between 35,000 and 40,000 workers in a single complex.

In the late 1970s, Brazil was in the opening phase of a tumultuous struggle for redemocratization, and the strikes of ABC's metalworkers not only "infused extraordinary new energy into the labor movement," as Margaret Keck has written, but also "fed the image of an increasingly powerful opposition within civil society to continued military rule."[1] The sheer scale and intensity of mobiliza-

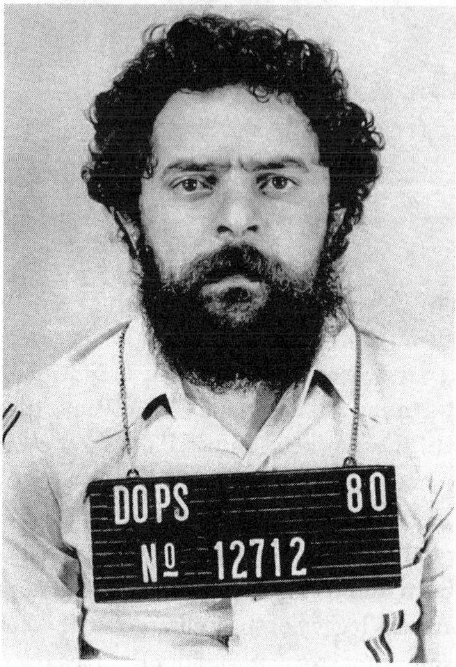

Lula's DOPS mug shot, 1980. (Courtesy President Luiz Inácio Lula da Silva)

Lula's presidential photograph, 2003. (Photo by Ricardo Stuckert)

Metalworkers at Vila Euclides with a sign comparing Lula to Jesus.
(Photo by DGABC [Reinaldo Martins])

tion in ABC excited awe. In order to accommodate the massive attendance—up to 60,000 workers—the union's general assemblies were held in a local soccer stadium. And in 1980, the workers stayed out on strike for forty-one days despite the army's occupation of the region, the closing of their union, and the arrest of its leaders.

The ABC strikes also catapulted the president of the metalworkers' union of São Bernardo do Campo and nearby Diadema to national and international prominence. "Luis Inacio da Silva is to Brazil," the *New York Times* noted in 1981, "what Lech Walesa is to Poland."[2] As strike participation reached 3 million nationwide by 1980, the charismatic thirty-five-year-old Lula came to personify the combative, grassroots-oriented New Unionism that would take institutional form in 1983 as the CUT (Central Única dos Trabalhadores, or Unified Workers' Central). In this national trade union confederation's first five years, the newly dynamized labor movement conducted the first truly national general strikes in Brazilian history. As Brazil entered a new democratic era, labor had emerged, in the words of political scientist Alfred Stepan, as the civilian group with "the greatest organizational capacity to continue to militate against those still repressive authoritarian features of the Brazilian State and Brazilian social life."[3]

Beyond his innovative contributions to labor mobilization, Lula joined with other trade union leaders in 1979 to call for the new Workers' Party, which brought labor militants together with radical activists from other social movements, especially liberation theology.[4] As New Unionism's political counterpart, the PT was an anomaly, having been built "from the bottom up." Although it did poorly in the 1982 elections (its candidates received only 3 percent of the national vote), the PT was rooted in society, in its first decade drawing its dynamism from a movement-oriented "logic of difference" that set it apart from the rest of Brazil's political parties.[5] Ideologically pluralistic, it emerged as a mass membership party that was surprisingly coherent despite a diversity that ranged from Marxist-Leninists to socially minded liberals.[6] Within the Latin American context, the PT was quickly recognized as a sui generis political experiment on the left—a unique "mutational experience," as Torcuato Di Tella put it. With the global Left in disarray after the fall of the Soviet bloc, Lula and the PT would work to bring Latin America's splintered leftist parties together in the Forum of São Paulo, which acquired broad influence well before the Left's regionwide electoral sweep in the twenty-first century's first decade.[7]

Shifting from a movement to a party leader, Lula the former trade unionist played a vital role in the popular insurgencies that swept Brazil in the 1980s. In 1984, he attended the founding convention of the Movement of Landless Workers (MST), whose dramatic land occupations made world headlines in the 1990s. And he attended the funeral of PT member Chico Mendes, the leader of the rubber tappers who was murdered in 1988 for fighting to preserve the Amazon for its residents. Serving only a single term as federal deputy (1986–88), Lula the politician preferred to travel the country spreading the gospel of popular organization, protest, and the vote. He contributed decisively, but by no means singlehandedly, to the PT's consolidation as one of the world's largest and most dynamic leftist parties in the 1990s. As they gained municipal office, the PT's elected officials pioneered grassroots "participatory budgeting" mechanisms that gained international recognition. And with the crisis of neoliberalism at the end of the 1990s, the imagination of a surging global justice movement was captured by the World Social Forum (WSF), first held in the PT-ruled city of Porto Alegre in 2001. Against the pro-globalization mantra "There is no alternative" (Margaret Thatcher's TINA), the WSF's "Another world is possible" encapsulated a renewed confidence on the left worldwide.

The PT's dynamic rise can be seen in Lula's increasing success as an electoral politician. In 1989, four years after the return to civilian rule, Lula won 16.1 percent of the vote in the first round of the country's presidential election—its first since 1960—and his vote total rose to 44.2 percent in the runoff; he lost to the favored, center-right candidate by only 5.7 percent. Lula's durable popularity at the polls was confirmed in two subsequent presidential elections. In 1994 he ran first for many months before losing in the first round to the former Marxist sociologist Fernando Henrique Cardoso, who received 54.3 percent of the vote to Lula's 27 percent. Four years later, Lula's vote total increased to 31.7 percent in his second loss to Cardoso, who this time received 53.1 percent; it went largely unremarked that support for the president had crested despite widespread acclaim for having produced economic stability by ending hyperinflation. In 2002, by contrast, Lula won 46.4 percent of the vote in the first round and 61.4 percent in the runoff, and in January 2003 he was inaugurated as Brazil's first working-class president. In 2006, Lula was reelected by similar margins, while his personally chosen successor, Dilma Rousseff, received 56.1 percent of the runoff vote in 2010 and 51.6 percent in 2014. That Latin America's greatest union leader was the region's most formidable vote getter was amply demonstrated in 2018 when the presidential candidate chosen by Lula—who had been denied his right to run, jailed, and barred from giving interviews—received 44.9 percent of the vote in the second round, against the far-right candidate Jair Bolsonaro.

Lula's 2002 election posed new but by no means unwelcome challenges for me as a scholar who has worked on ABC and its workers since 1980, the sixteenth year of military rule in Brazil. Lula's triumph was not an outcome I would have anticipated during my first visit to the country in the summer of 1980, when ABC's metalworkers had just gone down in defeat; their unions were intervened, and Lula and twelve others faced military trials (Lula was sentenced to three and a half years' imprisonment in 1981, but the sentence was later overturned). Brazil had clearly changed profoundly since then, and Lula's election was a fantastic capstone for the country's hard-won democracy. To find a meaningful equivalent in recent US history, one would have to imagine Martin Luther King Jr. being elected president in 1978, twenty-two years after the Montgomery bus boycott. Yet even this analogy understates the drama, because Lula has only a fourth-grade education—not a PhD, like King—and his impoverished background forced him into the streets at the age of eleven to work as a peddler and shoeshine and delivery boy and, from there, to a factory where, as a teenager, he lost a finger in a press.

An even closer US parallel would be if the trade unionist Eugene V. Debs, a quarter century after leading the dramatic Pullman railroad strike of 1894, had ended up in the White House in 1920 rather than in prison, eight years after he had won 6 percent of the national vote as the Socialist Party's presidential candidate.[8] Although both radicalized workers embraced socialism after imprisonment, the drama of Lula's life story dwarfs that of Debs, who was, after all, central to the heartland small-town culture of his nation.[9] Lula's family, by contrast, originated in the rural *mestiço* (mixed race) hinterlands of slaveholding northeastern Brazil. Along with his mother and six of his seven siblings, he made a two-week trek southward on the back of a truck to the hope that beckoned in São Paulo, much like the millions of black and white southerners who poured north to Chicago, Detroit, and Cleveland around World War I. And finally, unlike Debs, Silva had a Communist brother, also a trade union leader, whose arrest and brutal torture in 1975 would be the first of many decisive turning points in the life of a twenty-nine-year-old soon to be known by everyone simply as Lula.

The ability of a worker like Lula to move from the streets to the suites via the ballot box is striking from the perspective of the global North. In his sweeping world history of the twentieth century, English historian Eric Hobsbawm noted that structural change in newly industrializing countries like Poland and Brazil could "lead politics in directions familiar in the history of the First World." The strike that launched the Solidarity movement in 1978–81, he noted, was led by a "bona fide proletarian," the shipyard electrician Lech Walesa, who vaulted into the presidency of post-Communist Poland in 1990. And the strikes led by Lula, the skilled metalworker, produced a socialist-oriented "political labour-cum-people's party" analogous to the mass social democratic parties of pre-1914 Europe.[10] In 2005, Lula was joined in the ranks of Latin American presidents by Evo Morales of Bolivia, another former union leader of working-class origin. Such stories, it may be suggested, are more likely in radically unequal and riven societies like Latin America than in "richer and more homogenous and 'democratic' ones in the north with their specialized knowledge elites and developed technologies of governance."[11]

Unlike his Polish counterpart, Lula not only won reelection but also presided over a vast country with the world's fifth-largest population. During the boom years of his second term, Brazil's economy grew from the world's tenth in size to the eighth, passing the United Kingdom in 2009. A tireless world traveler, Lula worked to foster a more multipolar world based on respect for national sovereignty and social justice. An ally of Venezuela's controversial president Hugo Chávez, he championed Latin American integration and served as linchpin for the region's growing bloc of Left-led governments. While actively participating in BRIC (Brazil, Russia, India, and China) diplomacy, his government sought to unify the developing world to contest the inequities of the international trade and investment regime anchored in the World Trade Organization. Lula was especially committed to the cause of Africa and worked closely with the South African government of the African National Congress and the leaders of the continent's Portuguese-speaking countries.

Domestically, Lula's signature government programs included targeted support for the poorest of the poor on a vast scale as well as a substantial increase in the real value of the minimum wage. He also democratized access to higher education, with decisive support for affirmative action in a majority nonwhite nation. As his second term ended, his stature was buoyed by both his domestic popularity and his country's economic stability in a moment of global crisis. In 2008, the US magazine *Time* dubbed him one of the hundred people who most affected the world, while the French *Le Monde* chose him as its person of the year in 2009. That same year, the US business magazine *Forbes* ranked him thirty-third among the world's most powerful people, and the English *Financial Times* declared him one of the "fifty faces that shaped the decade." Such wide international recognition would eventually lead to Brazil being awarded the 2014 World Cup and the 2016 Summer Olympics. That Lula is a man worthy of study is clear to all, although how to execute such a study still remained uncertain.

Biography's Lies and the Emblematic Temptation

Biography has always been based on a simple lie: the individual's past is recounted in light of his future. Although biography is presented as a seamless birth-to-death narrative, the storytelling actually begins where the life ends, whether in fame or infamy. "The end is taken as the truth of the beginning," as Jean-Paul Sartre observed in a memoir of his childhood; "a young lawyer is carrying his head under his arm because he is the late Robespierre."[12] Such backward storytelling brings us Lula-as-he-becomes-who-we-already-think-we-know: a vastly popular, widely loved, and much-respected two-term president with a "demotic and larger-than-life personality."[13] In such an emblematic, even iconic, mode of narration, Lula's public life across four decades is overwhelmed by the retrospective meanings ascribed to his rise. The socioeconomic, institutional, and politico-cultural context of his life fades away, leaving a shallow story devoid of contingency and drama.

To win the presidency of any large country attracts biographers, all the more so given Lula's rise from the bottom of society to the very top of the political superstructure. Whether in potted press profiles, comic books, or a commercial biopic, Lula's trajectory came to be narrated as a tale of unprecedented social mobility fraught with symbolism. Born in a mud-and-wattle hut, Lula reached the very pinnacle of political power to reside for eight years in the "White House" of Brasília, the aptly named Palace of the Dawn. His fairy-tale ascent exemplifies the democratic promise at the heart of the cherished US "log cabin myth": that anyone's child can aspire to and achieve the presidency, no matter how humble or disadvantaged his or her origin.[14] While empowering illusions will figure in our story at the appropriate moments, along with disabling delusions, they tell us nothing about how Lula could have ever contemplated running for, much less winning, the presidency.

Lula is "not only a man, but also a myth," his British biographer Richard Bourne noted, and his extraordinary life is like "a thread running through modern Brazilian history and, most would say, for the better."[15] In treating Lula's life as fable—as the knowledgeable Brazilian journalist Paulo Markun has explicitly done—biographers have produced improbable narratives fraught with premonitions of a future destiny.[16] Even when consciously resisting the temptation, they end up referring to Lula's natural, instinctive, or intuitive "gift for leadership," which they seem to find everywhere, including his adolescent soccer playing. Ideas about his exceptional communicative capacity, if not genius and grace, are shared by his frustrated Brazilian opponents as well as his friends and admirers. In naturalizing Lula's talents, empty abstractions like "charisma" or "lulismo" are retrospectively accorded a causal role in explaining his success. Yet his actual life trajectory disproves timeless generalizations that suggest a unique gift or a stable "essence." Such approaches do little to advance our understanding of his rise to prominence in the late 1970s or the role he came to play over the following three decades.

Our understanding of Lula's origin has been decisively influenced by the research and writing of historian and journalist Denise Paraná. After serving as a staff person for his 1989 presidential campaign, she approached Lula in 1992 about doing her doctoral dissertation on his life and family.[17] With Lula's assent, she conducted one hundred hours of unstructured oral history interviews with the candidate and his surviving family members in 1993–94.[18] Her 1995 history thesis, which included these indispensable interviews, was titled "From a Culture of Poverty to a Culture of Transformation."[19] The following year it found a publisher, if not a mass audience, as *The Son of Brazil: From Luiz Inácio to Lula*.[20] A second edition, with two additional interviews, was published in 2002 as *Lula, Son of Brazil*; reprinted multiple times, it also appeared in Spanish, Italian, French, and Polish translations. Paraná reached her broadest audience in 2009 as screenwriter for *Lula, Son of Brazil*, the well-financed commercial biopic by Fábio Barreto. Although plans for a TV soap opera (telenovela) did not reach fruition, she also wrote the film's spin-off paperback aimed at "those with less financial resources and time to read."[21]

Two-thirds of Paraná's scholarly book consists of interviews with the seven surviving Silva siblings, the brother of Lula's first wife, and Lula's second wife, Marisa Letícia dos Santos. The interviews with his five nonactivist siblings and his older brother José Ferreira de Melo (known as Frei Chico) offer moving stories about the family's migration in the 1950s from the rural *agreste* in Pernambuco to the industrializing city of São Paulo. Paraná's extended oral histories with Frei Chico and Lula—which cover their personal lives, work histories, and involvement with union affairs—add considerably to the evidence from earlier interviews conducted by journalists.[22] The book's four analytical essays offer meditations on oral history, the case for using Oscar Lewis's concept of a "culture of poverty," the emergence of a "culture of transformation" in the 1970s, and the psychological dynamics of the Silva family. Lula's rise within the region's metalworkers' unions concerns her mostly for what it symbolizes: the poor breaking free from alienation and conformity. While she discusses the 1978 in-factory stoppage in which Lula played some role, the dramatic strikes directly led by Lula and his leadership team in 1979 and 1980 are barely addressed. Modest in her claims, she acknowledges that her interpretations are tentative and subject to revision in the future.[23]

Across diverse audiences, mediums, and shifting conjunctures, Paraná has deployed emblematic narrative frames in which Lula personifies a variety of collectivities, socioeconomic processes, and cultural hierarchies. She is well aware that the Silva family story, which she documented so carefully, is "in certain aspects absolutely unique and singular." It achieves "a common and universal character," she says, because of "its 'repetition' of the stories of thousands of nordestino families that migrated in search of better conditions."[24] On this level, Lula and his family stand in for the anonymous millions born in rural poverty who moved to the city, where they faced hunger, floods, and other tribulations in their struggle to survive and "make something of themselves." Their experiences, she suggests, offer a vivid portrait of "a country full of contradictions, fortunes, and miseries," a Brazil of gaps and absences, including democratic citizenship.[25]

In Paraná's depiction of the plebeian world, Lula's nonactivist siblings are "representative of the culture of poverty," only weakly aware of social class and distant from social and political claim making. Lula was part of that world until his older brother Frei Chico got him involved with union activism in 1968–69. A decisive transition, she suggests, occurs when workers break through the barriers of resignation, deference, and alienation. While they might have still suffered "economic poverty," the brothers were entering what would prove to be an emerging "'culture of transformation' [in mid- to late 1970s São Paulo] that proposed the construction of a more socially and economically democratic society."[26] "Led by his own desires, capacities, and life conditions he experienced, Lula transformed himself from an anonymous and 'alienated' worker into a great and politicized mass leader."[27] In this role, Lula "symbolizes and embodies the national working class that emerged with the 'Brazilian [economic] miracle,' which demanded better working and living conditions and mobilized in the search for democracy" that ended the Brazilian dictatorship in 1985.[28]

Paraná writes that the PT, along with other popular conquests, is "incarnated" in the figure of Lula.[29] It was during a period of multiclass struggle for democracy that Lula first emerged and won the admiration and dedicated support of a significant if minority contingent of well-educated Brazilians like herself. While Lula was in many ways a "typical peon," she says, he can be credited with a unique capacity to represent, subjectively, both the winners and the losers in Brazilian society.[30] As she closed the first edition in 1996, she felt satisfied to have vividly brought the travails of the urban popular classes to readers who knew little about them beyond what they might have picked up from their domestic help (two of Lula's sisters had been domestic servants, and his second wife's first job was working as a nanny). In the last sentences, she made a direct appeal to the conscience of this audience: the story of Lula's family offers "an original and true picture of the Brazilian nation. . . . To confront this is to encounter Brazil."[31] In 2002, a more sanguine Paraná ended on a more forceful note: Lula is a synthesis of that which is most "alive, complex, and original in the Brazilian nation"; he is indeed, she declared, "Brazil's legitimate son."[32] This religiously inflected image of Lula as "son of Brazil" gained at least symbolic validity with his 2002 presidential win.

As tools of persuasion, emblematic modes of narration have always been fundamental to members, supporters, and journalistic sympathizers of Lula and the PT. Yet Paraná's particular focus on Lula the individual was not typical of most leftist intellectuals in the 1980s and early 1990s. Steeped more deeply in Marxism, many wrote with the rhetorical grandiosity shown in the preface to the first edition of Paraná's book by her thesis codirector Osvaldo Coggiola, an exile from the Argentine terror with a French doctorate.[33] Citing Leon Trotsky, he described Lula as a result of "the startling velocity" of change as Brazil entered "fully into the world capitalist system in its monopoly phase."[34] He denounced from an Olympian perspective "the superexploitation at the service of foreign and national capital" while highlighting the "political limitations" of Lula and his generation due to the absence of a "revolutionary political tradition rooted in the Brazilian working class."[35] As a result, the objective revolutionary potential in Brazil was stymied by the ideological influence of a "politically failed but economically and socially dominant bourgeoisie." This "split and contradiction in the very life and [political] formation of Lula," he concluded, produced a "*crisis of leadership*" that would be overcome only by "a new revolutionary leap" (his preface was deleted from Paraná's second edition).[36]

Yet the PT's leadership, even at its most ideological, was forced to deploy "Lula the Brazilian everyman" (Zé Povo) in the face of the brutal exigencies of electoral competition, though at first they did so reluctantly and ineffectively. In 1982, their gubernatorial campaign pitched Lula to voters as "a worker just like you," and they improbably described him as "a typical Brazilian" in a 1989 campaign book titled *Lula: The Political Biography of a Worker.* With a cover featuring an unsmiling Lula in a hard hat, the book was written by the radical Dominican Frei Betto, a personal friend of Lula and Marisa since 1980. Betto's priorities were quite different from Paraná's. Only three pages were devoted to Lula's life before he became a trade unionist, while thirty-four dealt with union politics and the strikes with which Lula was involved; many of the twenty-two pages on the PT had more to do with the party than with Lula. Speaking to the concerns of his leftist readers, Betto assured them that there was no danger of what he called lulismo because the PT did not revolve around "a charismatic figure or electoral clientelism."[37] The PT's best-known member was simply one more companheiro, sometimes overruled in party discussions, and thus the opposite of a personalist *caudilho*—a veiled reference to the PT's key competitor, Leonel Brizola, who had inherited the mantle of *getulismo,* or the populist support for President Getúlio Vargas, who had dominated Brazilian politics from 1930 to 1954.

As a political project, the PT gradually shed the revolutionary dreams embraced by many members during the antidictatorial struggle and the troubled first decade of the New Republic after 1985. Yet even as the party evolved toward a discourse of "radicalizing democracy," a disembodied Lula still served largely to symbolize its critique of an authoritarian political order permeated by patron-client ties; bottom-up participation, an active citizenry, and an organized civil society over passive voting, clientelism, and authoritarianism; and a politics of honesty and principle, if not ideology, as opposed to politicians without ideas driven by an often-corrupt immediatism (*fisiologismo,* as it is known in Brazil). In 1989 Lula was viewed by many as a dangerous radical; his distinctive image at the time has been rightly described as that of "kind of an anti-messiah," a "factory worker from São Paulo with fractured grammar and an unmistakably proletarian appearance."[38]

The balance between politicized and personalized appeals would shift over the next three presidential races. As the dynamism of social movements ebbed with the end of inflation and the effects of neoliberal economic restructuring, the PT's forward momentum depended increasingly on winning elections, especially if they could place their man in the presidency. Lula's professionalized campaigns began to draw more heavily on political marketing to enhance and diversify forms of voter identification with him. By 2002, the centrality of "Lula the self-made man" was suggested in a campaign comic book titled *Lula: The Story of a Winner.*[39]

Once the PT was in power, control of resources allowed it to broaden Lula's mass electoral base while increasingly linking his image to a contestation of

Lula with child and father in Bahia. (Photo by Ricardo Stuckert)

existing hierarchies of status and worth, with their associated structures of feeling. The president would stand symbolically for the common people (*povo/povão*), the weak, and the poorly educated against stuffy, snobby, and well-off elites. With time, he would resonate as "representing" the periphery (residents of urban working-class and slum areas, nordestinos) as opposed to the wealthier neighborhoods, states, or regions. And even as the distance grew between where he came from and what he had become, Lula was ever more powerfully projected as a symbol of blacks, mestiços, the poor, women, and workers against prejudiced and superordinate populations, the rich, and bosses (mostly male and white). A vote for Lula was a rebuke of the haughty, the high-and-mighty, and the *doutores* (college graduates) who, as Lula always emphasized, have run Brazil for five hundred years.

Lula's presidential apotheosis reached a climax in the 2009 Barreto biopic, framed as a tale of family love and personal perseverance.[40] Pride of place was given to Lula's self-sacrificing, illiterate mother, who successfully raised eight children despite having to abandon her abusive and unfaithful husband. If they wished, viewers of the film were free to disregard trade unionism and identify with Lula as the good son who fulfilled his mother's dreams, the personification of virtues such as moderation, loyalty, selflessness, and courage. By the end of his second term, Lula's iconicity was made even more explicit in the commercial comic book *Lula: Luiz Inácio Brasileiro da Silva*, and even Richard Bourne's 2008 biography gained a new subtitle in translation: *From the Northeast to the*

Central Plateau (i.e., Brasília).[41] In 2009, the prominent Brazilian journalist Audálio Dantas, who had known Lula since the strikes of 1979–80, published a short and intimate children's book titled *The Boy Lula: The History of a Little Refugee Who Reached the Presidency of the Republic*.[42] Illustrated with nordestino woodcuts, the book's introduction described a dramatic, even bitter, childhood that, although real, can seem "almost fictional at points." Calling Lula's life a "beautiful and magnificent tale of the overcoming of obstacles [*superação*]," the book ends with the death of his mother in 1980 while he was in jail; she would never know that her youngest son would one day become president.[43]

The overwhelming focus on Lula's "impressive rise from the depths of poverty to the presidential palace" was deeply frustrating to Lula's opponents, as well as to some who had been or were PT supporters or sympathizers.[44] Politics seemed to have lost ground to crassly sentimental appeals to a poorly educated lower class that even some petistas believed was stuck in alienating marginality, if not a "culture of poverty." Consciousness-raising, class struggle, and even socialism had been replaced with the sort of storytelling that North Americans associate with the edifying tale about a certain young planter's son, his new axe, and a cherry tree. But Lula's childhood was less like Parson Weems's 1800 story about George Washington, and more like the adventures of a Brazilian Huckleberry Finn; the hardscrabble hero was a good bit more mischievous than the little boy who could not tell a lie, even if no less virtuous.[45]

The author of a 2005 French Lula biography expressed concern over such mythmaking, which reminded him of other larger-than-life Latin American presidents, such as Argentina's Juan Perón, Brazil's Getúlio Vargas, and Cuba's Fidel Castro. Christian Dutilleux's unease stemmed in part from his recognition that Lula "had himself often used his biography as a political instrument. . . . He tells the stories he wishes to tell, those that serve his ambition."[46] Despite this sensible cautionary note, this longtime Rio resident still attempted to land an interview with the busy president, although his plans came to naught. The book's claim to originality lay in its interviews with some of Lula's relatives, his companheiros in ABC, and some of the president's collaborators in Brasília. Lula's old trade union buddies, he reported, were wary of any cult around Lula, minimizing talk of his charisma; in their rendering, Lula was "a simple and sympathetic man who was faithful to himself" and who continued to live modestly in São Bernardo even after becoming famous, seeing his old friends as often as he could.[47] In the end Dutilleux's book, titled simply *Lula*, offered a sympathetic account of a man "capable of incarnating the hopes of the Brazilian Left," a "symbolic life" with great resonance for the Left internationally.[48]

If Dutilleux was mildly troubled, the PT's cult of popular biographical authenticity met a far more negative reaction among some highly educated Brazilians. In a 2005 survey titled *From Independence to Lula*, political scientist Bolívar Lamounier categorically denounced the PT's "us against them" approach to politics. For this supporter of Fernando Henrique Cardoso, the PT's polarizing posture may have originated in the Marxist-Leninist formation of many of its leaders, but it was equally objectionable in its new form as a populist demagoguery based on "a highly abstract and Manichaean vision of a country divided between two imaginary entities: the 'povo' and the 'elite.'"[49] The implicit target of criticism extended beyond Marxists to include liberation theology activists like Frei Betto, with their bottom-up fixation on the grassroots, the subaltern, and the poor (the *bases*—as in *basismo*—as the rank and file are called in Brazil). In the words of FHC in 1993, there was something regressive about "Catholic socialism's criticism of the idea of wealth," its "egalitarian utopia" slighting "the rational aspects of accumulation, productivity, and investment."[50]

After a third successive presidential defeat for FHC's party, the first critical biographical study of Lula was finally published. Unlike the outpouring of anti-Lula and anti-PT scandal books, *What I Know about Lula* was authored by a well-known conservative Brazilian journalist with impeccable credentials, José Nêumanne. As a young reporter, he had covered Lula at the very start of his union presidency in 1975, as well as during the strikes; in addition, Nêumanne had published a book on the 1989 presidential campaign of "the most famous manual worker in the history of Brazil."[51] His 2011 offering was a powerful indictment of Lula the man based on the author's personal recollections and his meditations on statements made by Lula in his many interviews. As one reviewer noted with appreciation, the author sought "to undress the man behind the myth," and Nêumanne was disparaging, even polemical, in discussing the latest of Brazil's "fathers of the Poor," linking Lula to Vargas.[52] When he challenged Lula's claims of exploitation or mistreatment by his employers, for example, he couldn't resist referring to him as the "rustic Karl Marx of Vila Carioca," the working-class neighborhood where Lula grew up.[53]

Nêumanne's apparent objective was to nullify the personal virtues being projected onto Lula through Paraná's "semiofficial biography," the Barreto biopic, and the film's associated paperback.[54] He depicted Lula the factory worker and trade unionist as self-centered and self-interested as well as disloyal to those who helped him, whether employers or fellow workers. Dismissing sanctimonious *lulista* claptrap, he charged Lula with betraying, and informing on, his fellow workers for material gain. In Nêumanne's account, Lula's pursuit of his second wife was a case of sexual harassment, and Lula had carried out a Stalin-style assassination of the reputation of Paulo Vidal, the former president of the São Bernardo metalworkers' union who had brought Lula into leadership and taught him all he knew about trade unionism. The book goes so far as to suggest that Lula was unenthusiastic about the political opening of the late 1970s and was even, in some way, a collaborator with the military, although Nêumanne wavers on this charge.[55]

What I Know about Lula veers abruptly between full-throated denunciation and passages with useful insights and balanced judgments based on the author's experience. As a professional journalist, Nêumanne knows what has to be done to nail a story down: line up the sources and evidence to make your case. However, Nêumanne's charges derive solely from forced interpretations of Lula's public statements, stories, and opinions. The truth, he wants the reader to believe, has been hiding in plain sight all along. Yet there are hints that the exposé's author is aware of his own bad faith, given that the Lula quotes he interprets so negatively are accompanied by words like "candidly," "frankly," "cynically," or "surprisingly."[56] All in all, the book is less tough-minded journalism than an expression of pique, an impression strengthened by his epigraph from Arnaldo Jabor, an early Cinema Novo filmmaker turned columnist. Writing during the run-up to the 2010 election, Jabor captured the visceral frustration of anti-petistas contending with a Teflon president who had escaped unharmed from what should have been a career-ending corruption scandal that hit Lula's government and party in 2005 by asserting that "Lula is not a politician—he is a religious phenomenon."[57]

It is not surprising that the PT's successive presidential triumphs might generate resentment, even anger, among the losers. Nor is it unexpected that intellectuals might direct their ire against the mythmaking propensities of those who orbit around the ex-Brazilian president. That their laments appeared in media unread by the very illiterates they disdained, however, suggests a powerlessness not unlike that of the Mugwumps after the US Civil War, who were horrified by the corruption of urban political machines during the Gilded Age.[58] The grievance of these Brazilian intellectuals, it appears, was having to be faced with the indignity of living in a "world allergic to critical consciousness."[59] Although the PT had lost ground within the intelligentsia by 2010, these elitist views were not yet unanimous even in São Paulo: Paraná's book, for instance, included an introduction by the distinguished literary critic Antonio Candido, a PT founder who was still a strong partisan even after the 2005 mensalão scandal.[60]

For the historian, it is hardly surprising that myths about President Lula would be elaborated for political gain, given that the founders and leaders of nations have taken their place in the modern world alongside "the mythic heroes who captivated the imagination of primitive men, the saints and knights who peopled medieval ballads and chronicles, the kings and nobles who loomed so large in the consciousness of the ancien regime." As Emília Viotti da Costa notes, it is precisely around the figure of the national patriarch where "reality and the hero, the man and the myth, are so blended and confounded that it is difficult to evaluate objectively" because "myth has beclouded reality." Yet history shows, this Brazilian historian went on, that "every class, caste, and social group has its heroes and myths" and uses them "to symbolize the dominant values of their social group." And as "social structures and values change, myths and symbols change," with new ones elaborated that in turn become part of "a fresh inventory of ideological instruments for those who struggle for power."[61] It is by no means inappropriate, in other words, that Lula's home city of São Paulo would field a samba school parade of 3,400 participants in 2012 around the theme "Behold a faithful son who does not flee from the fight. Lula, the portrait of a nation."[62]

But what about the historian's duty to unmask, undermine, or destroy myths in defense of the truth? Costa was categorical that "neither the worshipful gaze of the schoolchildren nor the equally partisan stare" of those who combat myths is appropriate for the professional historian. Our "task is neither to elevate nor to denigrate, but to analyze the relationships between a real historical individual and the larger structures that shape him and are in turn shaped by him." By doing so, we can "reduce myths and heroes to their actual proportions" by examining legends "as products of specific social needs and realities"; otherwise the historian remains trapped in their web.[63] But where does one start in the case of Luiz Inácio Lula da Silva? And what must be done to grasp what made Lula's rise possible and to better understand the deeper significance of his achievements and their impact and legacy, whether judged positively or negatively?

PART I
ORIGINS AND ROOTS

2 BEYOND THE PARROT PERCH

As Lula's second term came to an end, storytelling around the sixty-five-year-old president increasingly focused on his nordestino identity, symbolized by the makeshift trucks that carried the region's poverty-stricken residents to the promised land of São Paulo after World War II. Dubbed *pau de araras* for the wooden slats on which passengers sat like "parrots on a perch," these filthy, unregulated, and uncomfortable poor people's "buses" plied the unpaved roads linking the backlands to the big cities.[1] The term became synonymous with those who made the trip and with nordestinos as a group.

It was a thirteen-day trip on a pau de arara in 1952 that brought Lula, his mother, and his seven siblings—along with an uncle, aunt, and their grown son—to São Paulo state to join Lula's father, Aristides Inácio da Silva, and Lula's older brother Jaime in the port of Santos.[2] The Silvas were part of the southward-flowing human flood that made the pau de arara a resonant symbol, as Brazil's population, quickly urbanizing, soared from 52 to 119 million residents between 1950 and 1980. In 1950, only 21 percent of Brazilians lived in cities of more than 20,000 residents, while 58 percent of those employed worked in agriculture and mining; thirty years later, 46 percent lived in such cities, and only half as many were linked to agriculture and mining.[3] Overall, nonagricultural employment increased from 40 percent of the economically active population in 1950 to 71 percent by 1980.[4]

While the Brazilian gross national product (PIB) expanded at an average annual rate of 7.1 percent between 1947 and 1980, manufacturing grew even faster (8.5 percent), spurred by "the remarkable expansion of the durable consumer goods industry, which expanded at an average rate of 15.3 percent annually, reaching growth rates of over 23 percent annually at the expansive moments of the cycles," such as 1955–62 and 1967–73.[5] During these extraordinary decades, Brazil became internationally known as a classic case of rapid capitalist growth with growing income concentration, a society marked—as this former slave society had always been—by dramatic inequalities in land, income, and wealth distribution.[6] The sharp regional divergences were powerfully captured in Edmar Bacha and Herbert Klein's famous metaphor of Brazil as a "Belindia"—"a regionally and class defined society comparable in every way to Belgium, but

"Pau de arara" illustration by Percy Lau. (*Tipos e aspectos do Brasil* [1966])

coexisting with poorer, more rural, and more northern part of the country comparable in most respects to India."[7]

The pau de arara thus came to symbolize changes occurring so rapidly that their ramifications escaped many contemporaries. The younger generation, Bacha and Klein noted, found itself living in a modern urban society, but their parents had been born into a very different world. Even when "viewing their nation from the perspectives of an advanced industrial society," contemporary critics struggled to fully "understand the anomalies within their own world, which still exhibits many traces of its former rural and slave-bound antecedents."[8] The scene at the old North Station in São Paulo's Brás district, where legal and illegal buses unloaded their wretched passengers, emblematized Brazilian society's radical divisions and regional inequality.[9]

For some of Brazil's educated (*letrados*), the sickly *retirantes nordestinos* became a call to action, whether for charity, social reform, national development, or socialism. Yet even enlightened thinkers' reaction was marked by social distance, as was the contemporary scholarship that judged rural migrants too individualistic to play their proper role as a working class. The view from below, unsurprisingly, celebrated the saga of migration as a tribute to toughness, perseverance, and hopefulness—*teimosia*, in a word. Without denying migrants' pain and nostalgia for what was left behind, Luiz Gonzaga, the giant of the popular nordestino music that exploded on Brazilian radios after the 1940s, captured this mood in "Pau-de-arara":

When I came from the backlands
My son, from my Bodocó
My valise was a sack
and the handle just a knot
I brought only courage and luck
Traveling in a big pickup truck
I paid my dues but I got here.[10]

The dichotomy of the Northeast (tradition) and São Paulo (modernity) has proven both lasting and polyvalent in its appeal to both the superordinate and the subordinate. Backwardness could be juxtaposed negatively to progress, but an authentic Brazilian popular culture could also be contrasted to the cold artificiality of a cosmopolitan, Westernized metropolis. However productive culturally, such dualism distorts. For instance, even nonpoor nordestinos moved south to the centers of economic, political, and cultural power.[11] Moreover, millions of non-northeasterners, including many rural paulistas, were on the move, often in similar clandestine "buses," which complemented other forms of migrant transportation including regular buses, railroads (among them the famous "trem do sertão" linking Minas Gerais to São Paulo), and even travel by foot.[12]

Equating Lula with the Northeast often entails styling him a "child of the sertão," Brazil's mythic locale of abjection. Yet Lula's birthplace of Vargem Comprida, a subdistrict of what was then the município of Garanhuns, Pernambuco, is located not in the desolate sertão but in the area known as the *agreste*, sometimes called the Northeast's breadbasket. It is also hard to see Garanhuns standing in for Pernambuco as a whole, much less the Northeast, with its 29 million residents in those years. To understand Lula, his family, and his São Paulo peers demands discarding emblematic abstractions and grappling with the specificities linking the Northeast and São Paulo. Even the term *nordestino* is a by-product of the regionalist prejudice and social distance that homogenized distinct populations once outside their purported "home" regions. A Pernambucano is certainly never a *baiano* unless living in São Paulo, where nordestinos are referred to by the name of the region's state most identified with blacks. The larger analytical challenge is determining to what degree, and how, the northeastern origin of Lula's family shaped his personality as a child and young adult.

A World in Flux

In 1957, a sociologist interviewed a São Paulo metalworker who had migrated from Garanhuns, Pernambuco. The man offered a pithy judgment on his life:

"We're in a wretched state [*ruim de vida*] and if it's wretched in one spot, then you need to run and try another; only the armadillo stays in its burrow."[13] When the last of Lula's nuclear family left Garanhuns in 1952, the município had a population of 100,000, three-quarters of whom were rural, including those in the western subdistrict of Vargem Comprida, which became its own município in the early 1960s. Garanhuns is located in the agreste, a transitional zone between the wet, coastal Zona da Mata, where sugar plantations flourished, and the semiarid sertão. With adequate if uneven rainfall, the agreste was never wealthy enough to support many slaves, who made up only 4 percent of Garanhuns's 24,000 residents in 1872, 60 percent of whom were free landless laborers at a time when the region was coming out of a cotton boom dating to the US Civil War.[14]

The município's economic prospects shifted in 1887, when it became the westernmost terminal of the Recife–São Francisco railroad. The following decades brought increased production of cash crops, especially coffee (Garanhuns is its most important northeastern producer), cattle, milk, and foodstuffs. Closely associated with tenancy, these new paths to wealth ended with the Great Depression. With prices falling, the local landed elite sold parcels of land to tenants and the landless, quadrupling the number of farms between 1927 and 1950.[15]

Lula's paternal grandfather, João Grande, owned land—a substantial amount, at least in the memory of his grandchildren—as did Lula's father, Aristides.[16] They were among the thousands of *minifundistas* engaged in subsistence production who, lacking a solid basis for economic prosperity, further depressed local wages while putting existing tenancy arrangements under more stress. The post-1930 growth of small properties reflected "a perceived deterioration of the future of farming," even with a wartime boom in foodstuff production. The postwar years saw a decline in cash and subsistence crops, bringing increased out-migration and an absolute rural population decrease during the 1950s. Net out-migration, as Jason Clay emphasizes, did not result from "a single event, but rather occurred gradually," stemming from small landowners' subsistence orientation in Garanhuns.[17]

The precarious prospects for subsistence agriculturalists like Aristides figured into migration decisions, even if only to try one's luck (*tentar a sorte*) elsewhere.[18] Yet other motives might drive an individual to migrate, including, in Aristides's case, an attempt to evade family scandal.[19] When Aristides left Garanhuns abruptly a month before Lula's birth on October 27, 1945, he left with a fifteen-year-old cousin of his wife Eurídice Ferreira Melo (known as dona Lindu); the cousin's departure and pregnancy were unknown at the time. After a brief stint in Rio de Janeiro, where he injured himself, Aristides moved to

Lula at three years of age with his sister Maria in Pernambuco (first photo). (Courtesy President Luiz Inácio Lula da Silva)

Santos, where he landed a physically demanding but relatively well-paying job as a stevedore loading sacks of coffee. The whereabouts of dona Lindu's cousin Valdomira Ferreira de Góes, known as dona Mocinha, were revealed when Aristides, resplendent in new clothes, returned to Garanhuns in 1949 with two well-dressed children and dona Mocinha, once again expecting. When the visit ended, Aristides left his legal wife pregnant—with Lula's younger sister Ruth Ferreira de Mendes, known as Tiana—while allowing his second-oldest son, Jaime, to accompany him back to Santos.[20]

In a maneuver worthy of Dickens, the fourteen-year-old Jaime would later trick his illiterate father by writing a letter on his behalf to dona Lindu telling her to sell their land and belongings and join him in Santos. After the pau de arara ride with fifty or sixty others, the party of ten took a taxi from Brás, where they had disembarked in São Paulo, to Vicente de Carvalho, in greater Santos. When they arrived on his doorstep, the startled Aristides berated dona Lindu for not having brought his dog. Putting them up with a compadre, the unfaithful Aristides would demonstrate at least the minimum of respect for his milieu's gender mores by moving the recently relocated family into his main house, thus according his legal wife superior status, while moving the second family to a new place. Over the next three years, Aristides would split his time between the two households, providing for both families with the aid of the three older sons, who earned money working at a bar, a small shipyard, and a charcoal-making encampment, respectively. The two older daughters worked as maids, while the youngest sons — on arrival, Frei Chico was eleven and Lula seven — gathered wood and shellfish in the mangroves, fetched water, and did some street peddling; they also cared for Aristides's encampment when he went hunting with friends. Although it upset her husband, dona Lindu earned a pittance by selling coffee beans that had fallen on the ground back to the coffee warehouses' owners.[21]

Obsessively controlling, the illiterate Aristides was skeptical of education — especially for girls — and increasingly resented having to support two families. His children have only bitter memories of a violent, arbitrary man whom they characterize as ignorant, backward, terrible (*ruim*), and perverse. Frei Chico is the only one to openly declare hatred of his father for the beatings suffered, but all harshly criticize Aristides for the tyrannical mistreatment and verbal abuse of his wife and children. While one daughter got along well with Aristides, the most positive comments come from Vavá and Lula, who emphasize that he was extraordinarily hardworking. Yet even while crediting Aristides for "putting food on the table," Lula nonetheless described him as of "bad blood," the "gang of evil," and "way too violent," a "violence born of ignorance."[22]

The break with Aristides came after dona Lindu's eleventh pregnancy — she had already lost two children in birth in Garanhuns. She had twins, who died at home within the month while she was hospitalized with complications. Her husband's abuse worsened, and at least once he struck dona Lindu, while trying to hit Lula in the midst of beating Frei Chico. His mother, Lula recalls, "would never accept being hit by him," and soon after she told him she was leaving. When Aristides got home that night, the family was gone, having moved to a nearby shack so decrepit that it subsequently collapsed. Dona Lindu rejected Aristides's attempts to make amends, even after his siblings came from São Paulo to convince her. In 1955, she sent the oldest sons to her relatives in São Paulo city in order to land jobs that would make a move feasible. Leaving Lula, Frei Chico, and Marinete behind, she moved to São Paulo; the two boys joined her in 1956, aged eleven and fifteen; Marinete and her husband came within a year or two.[23]

As Lula put it, dona Lindu had left Garanhuns with the children "tied to her

Lula's father, Aristides da Silva, at thirty years of age. (Courtesy President Luiz Inácio Lula da Silva)

skirt," and she had done so again in leaving Santos. A single mother of eight, she faced a formidable challenge if they were to survive and thrive in the big city. The family settled in Vila Carioca, a working-class factory neighborhood with unpaved streets and poor public services. At first they stayed with an uncle, in an addition at the back of his house; their bathroom was shared with his bar, in which patrons sometimes vomited. With the older boys working, conditions improved enough for the family to rent a house on Rua Auriverde and then move to 1156 Rua Auriverde, where they lived till 1964. Like most women in her situation, dona Lindu didn't work outside the home in São Paulo; instead she washed, ironed, and took in boarders—including relatives from Pernambuco, who paid little, and dona Mocinha's son Rubens, who was being brutally beaten by his father. Eventually, she achieved a degree of stability for her brood—derived from the income of her working sons, whom Frei Chico soon joined—including the material goods, such as a two-burner gas stove, that marked a family's progress (previously they had cooked using a kerosene stove or, when it broke, a makeshift alternative).[24] Yet the new urban life would generate its own dissatisfactions, especially once memories of the *really* bad times faded and the Silvas realized that they now faced just tough times. Among the most vexing new problems in their first decade in São Paulo was the city's recurrent floods, a by-product of helter-skelter urbanization that repeatedly turned their lives upside down (fires were the only quintessential city problem that they had the luck to avoid).

The city that Lula's family entered in the mid-1950s was ground zero for Brazil's extraordinary industrial, demographic, and urban boom, which they had indirectly experienced in the fast-expanding metropolitan port of Santos, just over the Serra do Mar mountain range. With 750,000 residents in 1920, São Paulo had long been the largely agrarian nation's industrial heartland; the city's population would double by 1940 and reach 2.7 million by 1950.[25] Since the 1920s, factory development had moved down the railroad line toward Santos, due to large swathes of cheap open land. This led to São Paulo's first industrial suburbs, Santo André and São Caetano. Sparsely settled São Bernardo do Campo, not on the railroad line, developed only after the Via Anchieta highway linked the capital and Santos in 1947.

The ABC region was distinguished by its large modern factories, many established by European and US multinational corporations, especially in cutting-edge industries like metalworking. As a result, ABC's factory workforce was concentrated in larger units of production than in São Paulo município, where large enterprises were counterbalanced by numerous small shops. Thus in 1958, 39 percent of São Paulo's industrial production came from factories with more than five hundred workers, compared to 77 percent, 75 percent, and 60 percent for Santo André, São Bernardo, and São Caetano, respectively.[26] Driven by government import restrictions and fiscal incentives, São Bernardo's new automobile and truck production plants (a General Motors factory had long been located in São Caetano) began pouring out vehicles. The employment growth could be startling: the new Willys-Overland auto plant went from 569 workers in 1957 to 9,127 in 1962.[27] The state's manufacturing profile was made clear in the 1960 industrial census: São Paulo accounted for 50 percent of the national industrial workforce and 60 percent of its total wage bill—all in less than 1 percent of the national territory.[28] By the 1970s, ABC's 1,000 square kilometers produced 10 percent of Brazil's GDP, and the revenues of ABC's local governments—supported by taxes on industrial production—exceeded that of more than half of Brazil's states.[29]

Metalworking—with ABC at the center—was at the cutting edge of an industrial revolution. While Brazil produced 30,000 vehicles in 1957, production rose almost fourfold by 1960, to 110,000 vehicles; eight years after, in 1968, production had almost tripled to 280,000 vehicles.[30] São Paulo state metalworking industry employment increased by 100,000 between 1960 and 1965, with another 80,000 added by 1968, a year when these industries also employed 70,000 engineers, technicians, and administrators.[31] After a slight drop during 1963–65, vehicle production went from 280,000 in 1968 to a half million by 1971, reaching at least 1,000,000 a year from 1978 to 1980, when it peaked at 1,160,000.[32] São Bernardo was the center of this boom; the three largest factories covered by Lula's union in 1978 were auto assembly plants that employed 11,000 (Ford, which had acquired Willys-Overland), 15,000 (Mercedes-Benz), and 38,000 (Volkswagen) workers.[33]

From 1950 to 1980—the heyday of metalworking-union presidents Marcos Andreotti (1958–64) and Lula (1975–80)—came vast changes in the scale of employment in ABC. Between 1950 and 1980, workers in all branches of industry increased by 700 percent, from 50,000 to 350,000, while ABC's population expanded by 800 percent, from 215,000 to 1.6 million. Although ABC's development was particularly stormy, this mass transformation gripped the entire metropolitan region of São Paulo, whose population in 1960 (4.9 million) would more than double over the next twenty years, to 12.5 million in 1980. The economies and populations of the ABC and São Paulo municípios were tightly interwoven, with many living in one but working in the other.

The formula for São Paulo's development for most of the twentieth century was rapid urbanization fueled by a deepening industrialization that drew rural migrants from near and far. During the century's first half, the city primarily absorbed immigrants, especially of Italian descent, whether directly from Europe or, more commonly, via out-migration from the state's agricultural and plantation regions, where they were originally employed in coffee. Intrastate migration by native-born paulistas—often the children or grandchildren of immigrants—would continue to predominate, even when out-of-state migration began to increase after the 1940s, at first from Minas Gerais and then, ever more powerfully, from northeastern states after 1960. Thus, São Paulo was becoming increasingly heterogeneous—with more *negros, pardos,* and mestiços—and its popular sectors ever more representative of the country. In 1950, São Paulo state was already home to a million-plus people born in different states; despite the absence of adequate and strictly comparable data, the 1970 census showed at least 2.5 million residents who claimed to have previously lived in another state.[34]

São Paulo and its suburbs thus emerged as the quintessential geographic space where the rest of Brazil came to know each other, and paulistas, for the first time. In retrospect, it's clear that a new Brazil was coming into being in the metropolis's factories, markets, and makeshift settlements. In some respects, the story of rural–urban migration was unchanged from when Marcos Andreotti, born in 1910 in Lindóia, São Paulo, was brought to the city around World War I by his illiterate, Italian-born parents, who had earlier worked in coffee. Yet São Paulo's rural interior was a by-product of a commercial agricultural expansion that differed markedly from the subsistence agriculture practiced by so many who, like the Silvas, came from interior rural areas in the far poorer, less developed states of the Northeast and Minas Gerais. "The arrival of a small farmer [*sitiante*] from Pernambuco to São Paulo," the anthropologist Eunice Durham noted in her 1973 monograph, "involves a fundamental change in the type of labor relations," which almost signified a "passage from one socioeconomic system to another."[35]

The migratory process was spurred by an insatiable demand for *braços* (arms) in São Paulo, for industry, urban services, and agriculture. With every relative or neighbor who returned, news spread among rural folk about the promise of a better life in the city—the possibility of winning at life (*vencer na vida*) and escaping current misery (*miséria*). The point was forcefully made by Lula's brother Vavá in 1993: when "we arrived in São Paulo, you didn't have to look for work. The employer was looking for you to work for him." Frei Chico underlined the contrast with a wry comment in 1981 that he had not been born in Brazil: "One day we came to Brazil, because what is there [in the Northeast] is not Brazil."[36]

Analysts are often skeptical of the stubborn belief among migrants everywhere that streets elsewhere are, in US parlance, "paved with gold." Yet evidence from São Paulo in this period validates Vavá's optimism, echoed in many interviews that young social scientists conducted with São Paulo working people during these decades. An ingenious study of urban labor markets by a US demographer provides some statistical backing for 1970 as a "golden age" for out-of-state migrants. Late 1960s São Paulo state attracted far more interstate migration than anywhere else in Brazil, with 53 percent coming from the Northeast and 36 percent from Minas Gerais. Interstate migrants comprised 31 percent of the state's industrial labor force, divided between nordestinos (16 percent); *mineiros*, as residents from Minas Gerais are known (11 percent); and others (4 percent).[37]

Out-of-state Brazilian migrants, although far outnumbered by paulistas in industry as a whole, were concentrated in a few sectors. Their single largest source of employment was the state's booming but poorly paid construction industry, in which they constituted 56 percent of the labor force. Most strikingly, however, was that interstate migrants were disproportionately employed in what are generally considered modern industrial sectors, unlike in greater Rio, the second most important magnet for interstate migration. Compared to natives, São Paulo's out-of-state migrants were mildly disadvantaged educationally but were powerfully overrepresented in the "technologically advanced" industrial sectors, which were "more highly paid than those in which nonmigrants were concentrated." Out-of-state migrants constituted 40 percent of the total labor force in São Paulo's booming metalworking industries. It was precisely these modern sectors "that experienced the most significant demand for labor in São Paulo from 1966 through 1969" and that saw real wages and salaries grow most rapidly.[38]

Arriving in São Paulo, dona Lindu and her children entered a world where nothing was rooted or grounded, an urban, industrial environment undergoing fevered change with few preexisting communities, durable identities, or well-established structures of understanding. This stormy new urban world was experienced by all, richest and poorest, as outside their control. It was a city that never stopped expanding and changing, a city where people flowed in and out in waves; a world where even structures of power seemed impermanent; a sprawling city experienced as molten energy. It was a world in flux, continuously changing in condition, composition, and substance. The rapidly industrializing São Paulo was thus a city where luck seemed real and ambition could flourish in the decades after 1950, a place "where the different social classes were linked to each other by a similar mentality. The spirit of adventure was visible from the top to the bottom of the social scale."[39]

Winning at Life: The Silvas' Progress

As they grew from children to young adults, Lula and his closest sibling, Frei Chico, were decisively shaped by structures, rhythms, and influences that did not derive from their identities as retirantes nordestinos.[40] Ranging in age from ten to twenty-four in 1960, the Silva children lived in a world of young people with parents born in rural areas, sharing a common experience of work, leisure, and education in a metropolitan space that, whatever its frustrations, seemed full of promise. Its very growth through migration produced an unusually youthful population.

The neighborhood of factories and homes where the Silvas settled was cosmopolitan, occupied by migrants of many origins. Located within the São Paulo district of Ipiranga, Vila Carioca was by no means a nordestino ghetto.[41] In fact, Lula's first regular job, although not legally registered, was making deliveries for a nearby dry cleaner owned by a "fantastic man," either born in Japan or of Japanese descent, who playfully tried to teach his young employee his home country's language. Lula's first, short-lived girlfriend—lost due to his excessive enthusiasm for soccer—was Mitiko, a pretty Japanese girl, while the Japanese-descended Olavo was the first of his adolescent friends to purchase a car.[42]

After moving from Rua Auriverde to Vila São José, bordering São Caetano, Lula, Frei Chico, and Tiana were inseparable from the children of the family next door, headed by dona Ermínia Santos. The Santos family were subsistence agriculturalists who had left northern Minas Gerais for São Paulo state in the

The Silva family on the beach in Santos. Dona Lindu (*far left*), Tiana with wooden fish, Lula, Jaime, Zé Graxa on scooter, and Maria. (Courtesy President Luiz Inácio Lula da Silva)

same year that dona Lindu had departed Garanhuns. Before reaching the big city, they had worked in agriculture in the state's interior, a common stepping-stone for migrants that the Silvas escaped by first settling in greater Santos. The adolescent Lula's best male friend was dona Ermínia's son Jacinto Ribeiro dos Santo, a *torneiro mecânico* (machinist, metal lathe operator) who garnered the nickname Lambari from when he worked at Volkswagen. And it was Jacinto's sister Lourdes who became Lula's first wife in 1969 (Olavo was best man).[43]

These young migrants' parents were from rural areas where opportunity was scarce; their new urban milieu, while promising, could seem alien, distant, and even threatening, so they often responded with tongue-tied shyness.[44] Moreover, older men were disadvantaged even in a hot job market, given the characteristics that employers favored for the most-sought-after jobs: at least a primary-level education, youthful trainability, a capacity for consistent hard work, and obedience to the commands of the clock and the boss.[45] More likely to have not completed primary school, migrant fathers were most often hired for unskilled jobs that paid minimum wage or less and offered little in the way of security or benefits. This tended to diminish their influence in a working-class household economy in which an individual's value had a bottom line: the wages one brought in.[46] This differed drastically from the norms in the rural world, where the family patriarch's word had been law. In the case of Lambari's family, his sick father never worked, which would lead his son to playfully describe him as "a zero to the left in the good sense" in 1994; as head (*chefe*) of the family, Lambari would boldly claim to have been the one that Lula had to ask to bless his request to marry Lourdes.[47]

If fathers shrunk in the cities, sons responded with alacrity to opportunities that seemed to favor brash but savvy young men in a hurry. There was a clear hierarchy of employment preferences in an urban popular world far from being rigidly stratified (stories of bluffing one's way into jobs are legion). Given the romance of the automobile at the time, being a driver (*motorista*) was the dream of many working-class youth, including Lula.[48] But the predominant forms of informal sector activity were valued less than employment with signed working papers (*carteira assinada*); selling in the streets offered independence (*conta-própria*, working for your own account) but was unstable and netted relatively little income. As for the vast construction sector, the bulk of the jobs were for unskilled "helpers"; employment was sporadic, the pay low, and hiring often offered no labor rights.

While factory employment meant a loss of personal freedom, its most powerful attraction was its relatively dependable wages and the legal protections that it theoretically offered.[49] In terms of factory jobs, the bigger and better-paying industrial enterprises were preferred over the city's many small manufacturing plants, even though it was easier to get hired at the latter and the pace of work there was more relaxed. Recalling his time at Metalúrgica Independência in 1964, Lula told his old union mates in 2000 that it was a pleasure to work with only five others on the night shift and to count the foreman as a friend; they cooked bacon and eggs and could even nap for a few hours as long as the work got done.[50] While the demands were less intense, many of the small firms that blossomed in these years were in a precarious financial condition given the absence of a banking system equipped to provide the needed working capital. The juggling of expenses and income often led to cutting corners, including stiffing employees on payday, even if unintentionally; with high inflation, bankruptcies were common, leaving workers with wages and layoff indemnifications unpaid.[51]

The 90 percent male metalworking industry offered higher wages than other manufacturing sectors, especially the increasingly less competitive textile industry, the largest employer of female workers.[52] Within metalworking, the new automobile assembly plants stood out around 1960, as Lula recalled: "The people in the automobile industry got something like ten raises a year. They were the elite—they had houses, they were the first to buy televisions, the first to buy cars. . . . They would pass by at Christmastime loaded with boxes of toys for their kids."[53] The demands of auto work were intense and control over its execution tight, but the greater productivity of such highly mechanized plants allowed the auto companies to offer a wider range of benefits and perquisites, including medical services, cafeterias, assistance programs, and eventually, at least in São Bernardo, transportation to work. And finally, as Antonio Negro has suggested, the auto companies' self-promotion worked in parallel with the government's developmentalist propaganda—the famous "fifty years in five" of President Juscelino Kubitschek (1955–60)—to foster a sense of pride and even dignity among those lucky enough to work there.[54]

The employment profile of the five Silva brothers and the three sisters helps us place Lula's family within the topography of São Paulo's popular classes. They had many jobs, some good, others marginal, some short-term, and others sustained for years. Significantly, the family's young men avoided being sucked into the unstable, unsafe, and poorly paid construction industry, with its predictably short working lives. And if you include the husband of sister Marinete, at least four males in the immediate family worked for dozens of years in some of greater São Paulo's largest metalworking factories, such as Ford (in Ipiranga), Volkswagen, Mercedes-Benz, and Indústrias Villares. The two brothers who were not metalworkers, José Inácio da Silva (known as Zé Cuia) and Jaime, worked, respectively, as a truck mechanic—a skill in demand—and in the woodworking industry (*marcineiria*), in which paulistas predominated but which paid less. All three sisters had worked for several years as domestic servants or nannies (*empregadas, babás*), and two had worked at least briefly in one or more small factories that manufactured products such as jute and cartons. Maria Fereira Moreno, known as Maria Baixinha, had worked for six to seven years in a clinic, where she developed skill as a practicing nurse, without receiving official certification. All three stopped working once they married and had kids.[55]

Collectively, the individual achievements of the Silva siblings—especially the boys—were a triumph for their mother, guaranteeing that the migrant family she headed was making a good run at "winning at life" in the big city. Whether from out of state or within, not all rural migrants would be as successful as they were. Even at its height, the São Paulo boom would prove a bust for hundreds of thousands who embarked on the adventure only to experience a daunting, sometimes claustrophobic situation of bare survival, ongoing suffering, and recurring personal tragedy. This darker aspect of the urban working-class experience is well captured in the records (*fichas*) of an unnamed social service agency in São Paulo between 1959 and 1964, studied in a 1967 article by the geographer Armando Corrêa da Silva. He drew on a 10 percent sample of

7,274 fichas from the agency, with an overwhelmingly migrant clientele whose birthplaces included São Paulo state (30 percent), the states of the Northeast (30 percent), Minas Gerais (18 percent), and other states or foreign locales (6.5 percent). Roughly a third of the sample lived in eastern São Paulo, the zone adjacent to ABC where Lula's family lived; in 1960 the area had an estimated 1.9 million people and the município's greatest concentration of industry.[56]

Systematizing the empirical evidence, the author creatively delineated three experiences: that of the newly arrived "poor from the countryside" (*pobres do campo*), the better-established "working people" (*povo trabalhador*), and the least representative group, the "working class" (*classe operária*), which, being well established, was the smallest since it was least likely to need the agency's services. Avoiding reified, bookish categories from Marx, Silva linked dispositions and sociocultural configurations to particular ranges of occupations. Viewing migration dynamically, he presented adaptation to the city as a forced apprenticeship with a steep learning curve and marked by generational distinctions.[57] Aware of the drawbacks of ideal types, he also noted that individuals' position was subject to change over time and that different "groups," and their associated attitudinal characteristics, could be found within the same family.

Summarizing a home visit, one ficha in Silva's study ended with the following judgment: "The interested party and her husband are workers [trabalhadores] and wish to win at life [vencer na vida]." This statement epitomizes the defensive rhetorical construct through which migrants presented themselves to a wider world in which they were subaltern by birth, region, and often color. They staked their claim on a two-part basis: that they were hardworking and thus honest in character, even if unemployed or poor, and that they were no different from the rest of São Paulo's population in their drive for success.[58] With this posture they attempted to rebut the widespread stereotype of lassitude and passive suffering, which completely overlooked the burgeoning industrial revolution of which they were part.

Whether paulistas, nordestinos, or mineiros, not all who migrated to São Paulo would lodge themselves successfully in the new environment. For an individual, especially from the state's interior, failure might simply mean returning home, probably chagrined, to perhaps try again later. The stakes were far higher for nuclear families with dependents that had migrated from a greater distance. As Eunice Durham documented with sensitivity, the struggle to survive and thrive was a family project, and a kin network could provide crucial assistance at key moments, as in dona Lindu's case. While the migrant family was a flexible instrument, its cohesion and stability were always under threat, not only cyclically, as sons set up their own families, but also whenever the bonds of family interdependence weakened significantly.[59]

The most poignant disasters struck when families fell apart under stress, often occasioned by the main breadwinner's illness, accident, death, or abandonment, which was "enough to completely disorganize a family in a short period of time."[60] This befell dona Mocinha after giving birth to perhaps as many as eight surviving children with Aristides. As Lula's sister Maria Baixinha recalled, she endured years of being beaten, only to be abandoned by Aristides; she "even went hungry and had to beg to survive." "No one knows if my father was sick, crazy, or if it was just depravity itself," Maria said. In Paraná's 1993–94 interviews, the Silva siblings uniformly described Mocinha as a *coitada* or even a *coitadinha*, a "pitiful little thing." The same was said of her son Rubens, who had been tortured badly as a youth by Aristides; "today he is a coitado," Lula said of his stepbrother in 1993. "He's now working in a butcher shop . . . [but] had been a beggar" in the past and was sleeping in the streets of Santos when Lula first ran for president in 1989.[61]

Lula's mother, by contrast, was a person of courage, a fighter, in the words of Lula's second wife, Marisa. This was the personal trait most needed among the popular classes in São Paulo, whether to guarantee simple survival or to take advantage of opportunities. Unlike her onetime adolescent rival, dona Lindu had broken decisively with her abusive provider in 1955 and set off on her own despite the risks. In Marinete's words, her mother was alone in the world with eight fatherless children: "My mother didn't know how to read, my mother didn't know anything and she was living in the midst of strangers."[62] Yet over the following decade dona Lindu held a large family together in circumstances that could have easily resulted in disaster. Although her children sometimes call her a saint, she was not a superhero; she cried at times, as when the shack collapsed in Santos, and was anxious, worried, and sometimes obsessed, even angry—but she never hit her children.

While austere in her parenting style (she was never one to hug, kiss, or touch), Lula's mother demonstrated remarkable energy, determination, and skill in managing conflicts and maintaining family coherence.[63] Fresh to the big city, dona Lindu stood out from other recent migrants because she fiercely pursued a difficult objective for her two youngest sons, Frei Chico and Lula: attaining some type of professional specialization (*profissão*) in industry, the more skilled and demanding the better. We don't know how she learned of the possibility, an aspiration more common among city-born working people or better-established migrants. Indeed, it was rare enough to encounter a migrant who had "become a skilled worker [*operário especializado*] in the metalworking industry" that Durham paused to comment on one such individual in her study, which drew on interviews and investigations from 1959–60.[64]

To aspire to a formalized profession required completing primary education

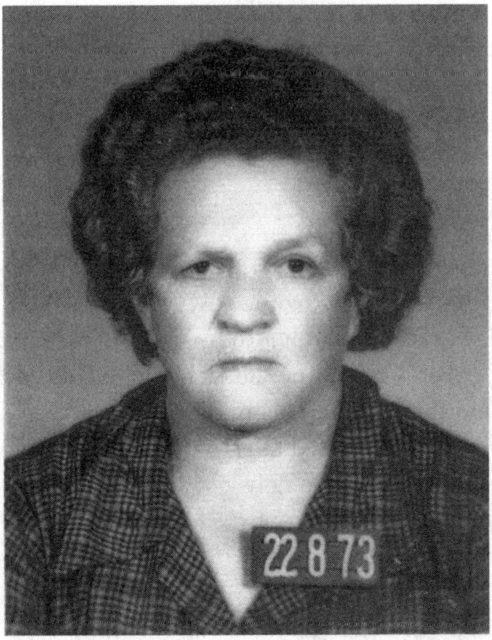

Lula's mother, dona Lindu, in 1973. (Courtesy President Luiz Inácio Lula da Silva)

at the minimum. This was fiercely pursued by almost all migrants—with the exception of those like Aristides—but was hard to achieve, given family financial constraints. It was most feasible for larger families, where the older boys' wages allowed the diversion of manpower, but only for the youngest sons, and even then it was no sure thing (dropouts were ubiquitous).[65] In the Silva family, Lula was the one who completed primary school and even part of the fifth grade before leaving to work for a dry cleaner for six months, followed by six months as an office boy at a warehouse near his house.[66]

To achieve even a complete primary school education for one son demanded "the maintenance of the discipline that regulates intradomestic relations," which was all the more difficult for a single mother; dona Lindu failed with her second oldest son, Frei Chico.[67] However, she succeeded with his younger brother, Lula. Having spotted an apprenticeship opening, she walked him to the appointment in 1960; he passed the test and interview, graduating three years later after alternating between school and factory. Lula's 1963 graduation ceremony was a conquest for the entire Silva family and a personal vindication of dona Lindu's leadership and vision.

By the standards of her time, place, and circumstances, dona Lindu was an unquestionable success in 1980, when she died from uterine cancer at the age of sixty-four.[68] She had produced hardworking, honest children without losing a single boy to criminality or daughter to prostitution. She had also placed her son in a manual working-class profession (as a torneiro mecânico), while Frei Chico achieved what Durham describes as "a semiskilled position" in industry as a welder.[69] Determination, perseverance, luck, and prayer all had their place in her family's success over her quarter century in São Paulo.

Education, Authority, and Culture

The understandings of authority and hierarchies of status entrenched among São Paulo migrants are well illustrated by examining the ABC primary school studied by Luiz Pereira between May 1958 and March 1959. This young sociologist's fieldwork in Santo André was carried out at a public school in the heavily migrant Utinga district, not far from the Vila Carioca primary school where Lula finished fourth grade in 1959. Pereira, who had taught at the school, was interested in not only the mostly female teachers' actions but also their understanding of the authority they exercised.[70] For these teachers, assiduous attendance and hard work were not enough to meet their ideal of a "good" pupil. For the school "authorities," a "good" student was above all "well disciplined," and this submission derived from "standards of behavior, values, and attitudes typical of traditionalist organizations: 'respect' in the face of adults, total obedience [*acatamento*] of their commands, reverential and even fearful interaction [with them], inhibition of the [students'] spontaneous social life . . . [and] proper 'recognition'" of the teacher's authority.[71]

The teachers studied by Pereira actually lived in São Paulo and spent only three hours a day in this "peripheral working-class residential zone" in order to earn the points necessary to transfer to better schools elsewhere. As self-described "necktie proletarians" (*proletários de gravata*), they were best understood as "an advanced beachhead of the metropolitan middle class" that nursed a range of grievances, small and large.[72] Even their commute to Santo André was a source of complaint because a recent reorganization of the railroad service (*trens de subúrbio*) abolished separate first- and second-class ticketing and seating. It is not surprising that they viewed their pupils as deviating from the appropriate "standards of submission of the good student." Teachers criticized their charges as "poorly raised," lacking in "education" (a term encompassing more than formal schooling), and failing to show the "respect" appropriate to their inferior station in life. To combat the "indiscipline" that they deemed the school's greatest problem, teachers not only routinely hit children—"for their own good," teachers insisted—but also lambasted them in class with hurtful (*injuriosas*), pejorative, and coarse (*grosseiros*) insults targeted at the "inferior socioeconomic position" of their families. As Pereira noted, the teachers especially believed in the most "direct and violent expressions of disapproval, above all physical punishments [*castigos*]." They did so even though corporal punishment was banned by the state public school system's legal *regimento*, which was, at least on paper, informed by progressive educational ideas.[73]

Although ostensibly employed in an impersonal government bureaucracy, the teachers held a patrimonial vision of the classroom as their personal domain of power. As "owners of the position" (*donos do cargo*), they brooked no interference because, as they put it, "I give the orders here" (*aqui mando eu*). In line with a seigneurial ethos dating back to slavery, their authoritarianism came with a paternalistic veneer that dictated a particularly aggressive and self-righteous posture toward inferiors. They insisted, for example, that what they did in the classroom was a personal favor to their pupils that demanded, as the appropriate response, active appreciation, total obedience, and "respect." Pereira was thus not exaggerating when he deemed students to be under "the domination of the teachers"; this treatment was extended to the parents, like dona Lindu, who were mostly illiterate or had "very little or no education," itself taken as proof of a lack of distinction and worth.[74]

The worldview of these lower-middle-class teachers—some complained about salaries insufficient to hire a domestic servant—was anchored in an understanding of society as structured in a fixed hierarchy of superimposed categories imbued with cultural and moral attributes. Thus they sharply distinguished themselves from lower-class residents and the school's menial employees (*servidores*), whom they treated like domestic servants. Whether in the classroom or walking to and from school, they publicly expressed deeply "ethnocentric judgments" derived from powerful "negative class stereotypes." They routinely contrasted their own "'elevated' style of life" with the "deficiencies" of those around them, drawing distinctions across a broad array of characteristics, including food, dress, "temperament" (*bons modos*), civic comportment, "language, amusements, health, hygiene, reading, [and] religious and moral behavior." While low wages were accorded some importance, lower-class deficiencies were understood as fundamentally moral: the absence of a "dedication to work." Misbehaving schoolchildren merely confirmed "middle-class" beliefs that these parents lacked appropriate interest in their children's future. All parents cared about, teachers complained, was landing their sons a factory job, not the more elevated goal of continued education.[75]

Pereira also investigated the relationship between the school, its personnel, and the parents, whose responses ranged from submission—by far the most common—to veiled opposition. All parents appreciated the opportunity that the school offered their children and were resigned to the features that made them uncomfortable. As one father put it succinctly, "Those who pay can make demands, those that can't owe." Fully aware of teachers' disparaging views, they responded by calling them "prideful" and "full of themselves," unlike teachers in some idealized past. Asked about inviting teachers into their homes, one resident replied bitterly that "she wouldn't come because we're poor. I wouldn't even dare! She is even disgusted by the fruits the children bring her" as gifts. In dealing with their social superiors at the school, parents adopted a strategy that Pereira described as withdrawal (*retração*): they tried as best they could to keep their children in line to avoid complications (*complicações*) that would bring contact with teachers.[76]

Some parents were dissatisfied enough to object to what they judged excessively savage physical punishments. As Pereira notes, they did not reject corporal punishment per se, viewed in the community as "an indisputable right of adult members" of a family, but they did seek to draw a line: teachers could "punish but shouldn't beat them" (*castigar pode; bater não*) or could "beat but shouldn't bruise them" (*bater, mas não machucar*). When tensions reached their height, a few parents might complain to the school's director, but most were reluctant to protest (*reclamar*) because of classroom retaliation and their belief that teachers wouldn't change even if they did complain. If sufficiently frustrated, parents felt more comfortable approaching the school's servidores, lower-class people like themselves, to vent (*desabafar*) about their child's mistreatment. Servidores told Pereira that while they occasionally alerted a teacher to a problem, they mostly did nothing because teachers disliked interference, and some were "real furies" (*danadas mesmo*).[77]

Acutely sensitive to stigma, São Paulo's working people tended to withdraw from uncomfortable situations. Feelings of inferiority and worthlessness were internalized at an early age, as can be seen from a childhood episode from Lula's life in Vila Carioca. One of Lula's brothers had pneumonia, and it was arranged for a local doctor to make a house call. When Dr. Raúl arrived and asked for a chair, Lula and his sister fled the house in shame (*vergonha*) because the family didn't yet have one; "the doctor had to do his exam standing up."[78]

All this shows how in modernizing São Paulo every encounter with superordinates was potentially threatening, especially for newly arrived residents from the countryside, and not just the Northeast, where Lula's family originated. For the rural folk (*caipiras*) from the interior of São Paulo state interviewed by José de Souza Martins, reading and writing were "irremediably identified with urban conceptions and values," a means "to defend oneself" as best one could in a world that one did not control. As a fifty-two-year-old black dependent on a small plantation, a member of an African *moçambique* dance group, concluded, "The city is great for those who have reading [*leitura*]. Those who are crude or stupid [*xucro*] have to live on the farm [*roça*]." The feeling of vulnerability created by illiteracy was compellingly expressed by a fifty-year-old landowner (*fazendeiro*) with only four months of schooling: "Many times when you go and talk to a lawyer, a judge," he will say "any old thing and you don't know what to do [*a gente fica indeciso*]."[79]

As authority figures, teachers not only peremptorily rejected students' right to dispute discipline but also reacted harshly when parents "complained about a teacher" (*se queixam do professor*), deemed a bold act of insolence (*desaforo*) from humble people contemptuously deemed "foot-scrapers" (*pé-rapados*), a term richly evocative of hierarchies going back to slavery. It referred to those so poor—especially slaves, but not exclusively so—that they had to scrape the mud off their feet because they didn't own shoes.[80] And when bold parents (*exaltados*) did complain, teachers would criticize their tattling child as a gossipy chatterbox (*linguaruda*) and impertinent meddler (*futriqueira*).[81] Yet there was evidence that an older urban world anchored in sureties of status and hierarchy was under attack in São Paulo. As documented by Pereira, parental complaints at the school were being taken up by a Santo André radio personality who criticized such injustices on his local show *Popular Voice*.[82] Given to fervent denunciations and opportunistic championing of strikes, Osvaldo Gimenez was condemned by local elites as a "populist demagogue" while gaining popular acclaim as a champion of the "little people." When this led to his election as mayor (*prefeito*), the local political class spearheaded a civic protest leading in 1961 to Brazil's first impeachment, an event trumpeted by São Paulo newspapers as a victory for morality and decency.[83] This undemocratic nullification of the popular vote was publicly protested by Andreotti and the local labor movement, even though they had not supported the Gimenez candidacy.[84]

The Intrepid in a World of Opportunity

Far more than 1,480 miles and thirteen days on a pau de arara separated the rural, sparsely settled world in which the Silvas were born from their new lives in São Paulo, at midcentury an exciting place for these new working people, its perils balanced against its great promise. Virtually uninterrupted industrial expansion—with factories avid for manpower—meant that rustic newcomers could experience a soaring of horizons. In a world in flux, energetic working people learned that anything was possible with sufficient teimosia, a Portuguese word whose meaning ranges from "persistence" to "willfulness," "stubborn obstinacy," and "fearless defiance." For Lula, *teimosia* captures what he sees as most admirable in key episodes in his mother's life. She demonstrated teimosia in 1952 when she sold the family land and household property to leave, with her children tied to her skirt, for a world she knew nothing about. Her subsequent decision to move out of her husband's house against his will illustrates the breaking of established norms of female behavior, the defiance of patriarchal authority.

Lula has repeatedly told a story about his formidable mother's first trip to São Paulo city. Needing documents for the move, the illiterate thirty-nine-year-old—four years away from Garanhuns—arrived at the bus terminal and spent an entire day wandering, unable to find her destination. Using a northeastern expression, Lula describes her as being "unharnessed" (*aredeada*) in the city, yet she persevered and eventually found her way. Lula also describes his older sister Marinete as teimosa. Forbidden by her father to see her boyfriend, a neighbor, the adolescent was struck hard in the face when Aristides discovered that she had been sneaking out; that very night, she bailed again in defiance of her father.[85] And Lula characterized himself thus in 2003: "A teimosia made me president"; "it was I who fought hard" for it in over thirty years in politics.[86]

Teimosia can apply to individuals of any social standing, but it has special resonance for those subject to structures of domination that demand obedience and consent but will settle for active deference to hierarchy; "every monkey on its own branch," as they say in Brazil. Teimosia also spurs conflict with parents and peers, not all of whom are willing to break with the defensive crouch of the weak or to display personal persistence against the odds. Thus, teimosia is also about refusing the subalterns' expected submission to "facts" of life that some regard as fate. It is to hold on to deeply held dreams—personal, familial, even political—rather than allowing one's actions to be decided by a utilitarian calculus of likely success (the crackpot realism of "penny wise, pound foolish"). At its best, teimosia for the weak is about dogged, fearless pursuit of the unlikely and improbable. It is ambition made formidable against the odds.

3 DREAMING MOBILITY

Even as Brazil's president, Lula foregrounded his profession (*profissão*) as foundational to his personal identity. It was thanks to being a torneiro mecânico, Lula said proudly in 2005, that "I went to a large firm, became a union leader, then union president, entered politics, and today I am here as president of the republic."[1] He would place this profession at the center of his self-representation in politics where it sometimes helped deflect tricky questions; when asked in 1982 whether he was a socialist or a social democrat, he would answered, "I am a torneiro mecânico."[2] Observers have treated Lula's self-identification as if it were synonymous with manual factory labor. But what are we to make of Lula's insistence that torneiro mecânico is a profession analogous to a doctor or engineer? Is this a personal conceit, or might it reflect something significant about the material and status hierarchies within the industrial world of 1960s São Paulo? To understand Lula's profession, we must turn back to the years between 1960 and 1963, when from the ages of fifteen to eighteen Lula was trained by the National Industrial Apprenticeship Service (Serviço Nacional de Aprendizagem Industrial, SENAI), as well as to the following half dozen years of employment.

Lula and Frei Chico came of age as Brazil emerged from Juscelino Kubitschek's ebullient presidency, with its extravagant promise of "fifty years of progress in five." The brothers' paths would diverge after 1960, during the reformist ferment that marked the truncated presidencies of Jânio Quadros and João "Jango" Goulart, the former the first to govern from the country's new, modernist capital of Brasília. While the two brothers were establishing themselves as professionals, careers were being launched by another group of talented young people through the new Center for Sociological Studies of Industry and Labor (CESIT), founded by Florestan Fernandes at the University of São Paulo.[3] CESIT's young director, Fernando Henrique Cardoso (FHC), would launch an ambitious program of systematic social science research into the worlds of business and labor, although its full execution was derailed by the military coup of March 31, 1964.

During the early 1960s, Lula was learning the universal machine tools that linked him to a North Atlantic industrial modernity that had forcefully arrived in São Paulo through international foreign direct investment. In parallel fashion, USP's ambitious young sociologists were mastering their craft while embracing cutting-edge international social science techniques and theories from US and French sources. The future looked promising for both groups, all the more so for CESIT's participants, who believed they were uniquely situated—like Friedrich Engels in 1840s Manchester, England—to study an industrial revolution of world historical significance. As the author of CESIT's first monograph, published in 1965, correctly noted, São Paulo was a "strategic focus for investigating industrial capitalism in the 'underdeveloped world.'"[4] This early encounter between university and factory youth, although one-sided, would yield to a more intimate but still conflicted relationship during the growing rebelliousness that roiled Brazilian schools, factories, and national Congress in 1968. In its wake, as the country moved from a civil-military regime to an open military dictatorship with Institutional Act #5 (AI-5) of December 13, 1968, Lula took his first step into the institutional machinery of trade unionism.

Arms for Industry

For Lula and his family, 1963 was a moment of triumph: he gained his SENAI diploma as a *meio-oficial* machinist and would, after some on-the-job experience, become a full holder of a profession (*ofício*). Lula recounts the thrill of this decisive moment: "To have learned a profession! . . . I was the pride of the family. I was the scientist. They felt proud that I was a machinist." The same exultation informs his account of returning home three years earlier to give his mother his first paycheck from the small screw factory where he was admitted as an apprentice at half the minimum wage. It was, he noted, as if the "cocada preta" (a coconut sweet) was his alone; "I felt like the master of the universe."[5] In these humorous, retrospective renderings, personal achievement and family pride mix with immediate material motivations and limitless youthful naïveté (the scientist!). The link between personal ambition, family advancement, and a preoccupation with status and paychecks may seem unexceptional, but they exemplify a broader dynamic for rural migrants entering the fevered industrial world of midcentury São Paulo.

How rural migrants became factory workers, whether simple operatives or skilled machinists, was the focus of CESIT's first monograph, *Work and Development in Brazil.* Defended as a doctoral thesis by Luiz Pereira in March 1965 and published in December, the book sought to understand "the skilling of labor within the expansion and consolidation of capitalism in contemporary Brazilian society."[6] How did the "common" man (*homem "comun"*), Pereira asked, become an industrial worker differentiated by skill, and with what consequences? With his fellow sociologists, Pereira was interested in how the indi-

Lula at age seventeen at his SENAI graduation. (Courtesy President Luiz Inácio Lula da Silva)

vidual, the family, and the factory operated within larger systemic dynamics and constraints. What he saw in São Paulo's emerging competitive social order was intriguing: companies contending for skilled labor, and individuals who possessed such skills competing among themselves, if less hotly, to land the jobs on offer. Anchored in an idealized conception of science, the monograph's viewpoint was from above and outside, although it made room, if slight, for the voices of those studied in the form of quotations from life history interviews aimed at the subjects' "past and present experiences" and future aspirations.[7]

In São Paulo, acquiring new skills was a pressing practical matter because of the technological densification associated with the large-scale metalworking plants in this new phase of paulista industrialization. Managers had no problem finding "arms for industry" (*braços para indústria*), as they put it, since São Paulo's labor market was flooded with migrants who gladly took the factory jobs, however poorly paid, that required only a few days (unskilled) or weeks (semiskilled) of training.[8] Using the language of SENAI's founder Roberto Mange from 1941, industry faced no shortage of "anatomical" or "diligent arms" (*braços anatómicos* or *atentos*). The need was for "thinking arms" (*braços pensantes*) to fill shop floor jobs requiring sophisticated knowledge and skills, especially with European immigration at very low levels compared to earlier in the twentieth century.[9]

São Paulo's breakneck industrial growth required not only proportionately more skilled workers but also a larger percentage with more advanced skills, especially in the new capital-intensive industries. The vocational training organization SENAI was born during a wartime industrial boom marked by especially severe shortages in the metalworking sector. Visiting fourteen years after SENAI–São Paulo's (SENAI-SP) founding in 1942, the US industrial relations specialist Robert Alexander was impressed by its premier Escola Roberto Simonsen, inaugurated in 1954 in the old industrial district of Brás. Serving as SENAI's regional headquarters, the school was named for businessman intellectual Roberto Simonsen (1889–1948), one of the organization's founders, who had been a visionary leader of the state's industrialists, a postwar senator, and a powerful advocate for national development through industrialization. Alexander described the school as "a beautiful new building that seemed to be extremely well equipped," with an emphasis on training for the metal trades.[10]

Massive new foreign investments further exacerbated the skilled worker shortage in the mid-1950s. New automobile assembly plants were built from scratch, while employment expanded in existing factories like Ford (São Paulo) and General Motors (São Caetano). Between 1957 and 1960, auto employment soared from 9,653 workers to 32,576, geographically concentrated in ABC. São Bernardo's four auto plants employed more than two-thirds of that total, with an additional 13 percent in the three factories in neighboring Santo André and São Caetano (São Paulo accounted for a fifth).[11] With its heavy use of technologically sophisticated machinery, the transport equipment industry was typical of the large-scale metalworking plants that employed a far higher percentage of skilled workers than the norm in traditional industrial sectors.[12]

Beyond the shortage of vitally important machinists, entire specializations were missing from a paulista manufacturing sector based on consumer goods, above all textiles. The case of tool and die makers (*ferramenteiros*) was especially dramatic, because no auto factory could operate without this tiny percentage of workers with even more highly specialized machining skills than "simple" torneiro mecânicos. Speaking to Pereira's team in 1963, the foreman (*mestre*) of one tool and die section spoke about the reality of very high demand and very few professionals (*oficias*). SENAI, he complained, did not even have an apprenticeship course for ferramenteiros, and he was forced into a makeshift solution: training the best of a less skilled subgroup (*ajustadores*) for this work.[13]

As an autonomous educational agency, SENAI was financed by a government-mandated tax on factory payrolls, its priorities determined by the industrialists who oversaw its operations. As Luiz Marcondes Nitsch, head of SENAI-SP's Serviço de Divulgação, indicated to Alexander, SENAI-SP officials had already concluded by the mid-1950s that surging demand could not be met solely by expanding its network of schools dedicated to three-year intensive apprenticeships producing fully certified holders of specific skills (*oficiais*).[14] With the auto industry a strategic national priority, the Kubitschek government worked with its US counterpart to ameliorate this troubling bottleneck, which included a US$4.5 million Eximbank loan to SENAI, with US$2 million destined for the training organization's operations in São Paulo, the country's industrial heartland.[15]

Thus, the majority of those with skilled positions in paulista industry would continue to gain their competency empirically, learning by doing with peers or foremen.[16] To better meet industry needs, however, SENAI-SP greatly expanded its offerings of less thorough on-the-job and short-term training programs. Between 1956 and 1960, those enrolled in "training in the workplace for minors" soared tenfold, from 1,300 in 1956 to 13,603 by 1960; the priority on training the young can be seen in the fact that only 1,137 were in similar programs for adults. The next step up were "rapid courses" in improving skills without producing certified professionals; metalworking increased its share of this program from 50 percent in 1956 to 65 percent by 1960.[17]

SENAI held firm, however, to its ideal of producing fully formed professionals for the most demanding skilled occupations, including machinists. In 1969, its standards still specified 3,000–3,500 hours of concentrated education and training.[18] The priority accorded the metalworking trades is confirmed by the completion statistics for these expensive, intensive multiyear apprenticeships (for which the student paid nothing). In 1956, metalworking accounted for half of the 1,750 completed apprenticeships but soared to 80 percent in 1960 (1,658), 285 more than the previous year.[19] The admission in 1960 of a fifteen-year-old son of an illiterate single mother would forever change the trajectory of an adolescent known in the family by his nickname, Lula.

A State of "Collective Optimism"

While SENAI's talented educators were struggling to hit a moving target, Lula's mother was trying to get a son into a SENAI apprenticeship. Her children's retrospective narratives place enormous emphasis on the pursuit's intensity. "She did everything possible to get him into SENAI," Lula's younger sister Tiana recalls; "she was forceful and really went after it so that he would achieve a profession that the others didn't have." An older sister, Maria, emphasized her mother's innumerable trips on foot to the SENAI school on 1822 Avenida Ipiranga to inquire into apprentice openings at factories. Lula said she pursued this goal at any cost, walking five miles to and from SENAI "every sainted day." Her children clearly admire their mother's teimosia, while the emphasis on the miles walked suggests a quest, ultimately fruitful. In this family storytelling, success flows naturally from the intensity of dona Lindu's hope, the energy she expended, and the determination she displayed.[20]

Narratives of underdogs succeeding are undoubtedly pleasing, but they limit our understanding of the broader social context framing a particular family's unique experience. Dona Lindu was neither alone nor exceptionally farsighted in focusing on SENAI in late 1950s São Paulo. Another illiterate mother, from nearby Santo André, expressed the same realization as follows: "Today it is necessary [for your kids] to know how to read, write, and do accounts in order to get a factory job," much less a sought-after skilled one; "those without instruction live in the dark and don't know how to converse or present themselves."[21] At SENAI, officials were accustomed to mothers stopping by to plead for their children's admission, sometimes accompanied by fourteen-year-old sons not yet eligible to become apprentices.[22] SENAI's budgetary limitations meant that the chance of success was low, since the whole setup, as Alexander noted in 1956, was "entirely inadequate for the needs which the city has."[23] In 1960, SENAI awarded only 2,000 diplomas in all industries, two-thirds of them for a growing metalworking sector that employed 250,000 workers, perhaps 40,000 to 50,000 of whom were classified as skilled.[24] It is a truism, Luiz Pereira observed, that if many "enter the struggle for social ascent, only a few will win," but this realization, he went on, did not register with the families aspiring to SENAI apprenticeships in Santo André in 1958–59. Disregarding the odds, they maintained what he called "a type of collective optimism" about their common dream.[25]

"The modern factory [*usina*] tends to intellectualize the labor force," SENAI's Italo Bologna observed, and the agency's goal was to train young men for machines that now "need more skilled people."[26] It was no longer enough to simply "know how to read," workers told Pereira's 1963 research team; many skilled positions required understanding blueprints (*desenhos*) and the "paperwork [fichas] with technical data distributed with a given work assignment."[27] Given the need for more sophisticated reading and reasoning skills, it may seem surprising that SENAI set a remarkably modest entrance requirement in terms of formal education. To be considered, the candidate had to present a diploma certifying completion of the four grades of primary school (*primário*) before moving on to an aptitude test, a physical exam, and a personal interview. Yet this minimum requirement was actually quite high in light of Brazil's abysmal educational attainment, with "only about 20 per cent of those who enter primary school" nationwide ever finishing the fourth grade.[28]

The pattern of partial, intermittent, and often incomplete primary school education among migrant families can be illustrated via the eight Silva children. The oldest had spent some time at a nearby primary school in Vargem Comprida, Garanhuns, although their schooling ended after the move to Vicente de Carvalho in greater Santos. In Vavá's words, it was either "work or die of hunger." The younger ones, including Lula, started primary school on the coast, and the youngest four—Maria, Frei Chico, Lula, and Tiana—continued attending school in Vila Carioca after the move. SENAI became an option for Lula at the age of thirteen, when he received his primary school diploma, and he went on to complete at least part of the fifth grade before taking his first regular job with a dry cleaner, followed by six months as an office boy at a warehouse.[29] Prior to this, he had hustled, like other boys his age, by combining street peddling and shining shoes with occasional odd jobs such as helping to unload trucks.[30]

SENAI used the primary school requirement solely to winnow the applicant pool before conducting their own aptitude assessment, which covered reading, writing, and math.[31] At this time in São Paulo city, the diploma itself offered no guarantee that much had been learned during those four years of schooling. In a period of stupendous in-migration and population growth, the state's public school system was entering a downward spiral felt most strongly in the expanding urban peripheries settled by migrants like the Silvas. As we have seen from Pereira's ethnography of the primary school about ten kilometers from where the Silvas lived, conducted when Lula received his diploma in 1958, the middle-class teachers, who lived far from the industrial frontier and its inhabitants, felt disdain and prejudice toward their students, most of them the children of migrants. But they felt it especially for those from Minas Gerais and the Northeast, most likely to be mestiço in origin (like Lula) and darker in skin color (unlike Lula).[32] Teacher performance was marked by frequent late arrivals, early departures, and gossiping together during class time—when they arrived at all to teach at the overcrowded and poorly equipped school. Pereira estimated that the kids in attendance received at best three of the state-mandated four hours of daily instruction.[33]

Yet the practical challenge facing SENAI was far deeper than teachers' dereliction of duty or disdainful conduct. Brazil's educational reformers, among whom were SENAI pedagogues, had long recognized that the country's schools had an overambitious and aristocratic curriculum that, even when delivered well, reflected a "strong middle-class bias . . . employing modes of expression not mastered by working-class children." This elitism made perfect sense in a former slaveholding society where education had always served to draw distinctions, not erase them. The educational system was never intended to empower the masses, and its values reflected those of "middle classes that disdain[ed] manual labor," an attitude shared by not only the lower middle class but also the popular classes, who were well aware of their social superiors' judgment.[34]

Aiming to produce an elite of lifelong skilled factory workers, SENAI's founder, Roberto Mange, knew that meeting industry needs was stymied by the "very common [Brazilian] prejudice that considers the skilled [*artifices*] of the mechanical professions as simply workers."[35] As a social scientist observed with regret, most often "those who do not share this attitude towards manual labor do not [usually] have sufficient education to become skilled laborers." This helps explain why SENAI avoided a higher cutoff for formal schooling: it risked wasting money on those likely to abandon their craft to pursue "clean," higher-status white-collar jobs.[36] The possibility of such abandonment was further facilitated by an early 1950s law making a SENAI diploma a type of high school (*colegio*) equivalency.[37] To guarantee return on investment through career longevity, SENAI's admission process included an interest evaluation "devised to eliminate students without the inclination to become a manual laborer."[38] Interviewing Lula, the staff was no doubt pleased by the attitudes inculcated by his mother, who "never talked about things like being a doctor, a lawyer. She wanted me purely and simply to be" a factory worker with a SENAI diploma.[39]

The prospects for more and better education had been among the attractions of São Paulo for migrants. Once established, the new residents showed themselves fiercely attached to the idea of schooling as the key to personal and family betterment. Their attitudes, in other words, shared nothing with Aristides's hostility to schooling as a waste of time for his children with dona Lindu. The irony, according to his sons, was that Aristides would publicly feign a literacy he didn't possess by buying newspapers to carry on the tram, although if the page didn't have pictures, he sometimes held it upside down. Dona Lindu, by contrast, was entirely representative of working-class families, who routinely made sacrifices in an attempt, not always successful, to guarantee primary school diplomas for their younger children, especially sons. It is here that we can appreciate the true measure of her achievement, because success required family cooperation and potentially fraught trade-offs. His mother, Lula says, "saw in me a chance to realize what she could not achieve for the others." As his closest brother Frei Chico, four years his senior, shared, Lula was the only one who really had the chance to study; "it was impossible for us."[40]

The household economy of families like the Silvas depended on financial contributions from all its members, especially the older brothers. This is why families with only girls faced economic difficulties, given the narrower labor market options for young women if they wished to avoid domestic service. Dona Lindu's most reliable support came from her third-oldest son, Vavá. When interviewed in 1993 by Paraná, at the time a USP graduate student, Vavá went out of his way to dispel any impression that his mother played favorites regarding educational opportunities. The youngest boy (*caçula*) was the one with the best shot at studying, he explained, and even Lula worked while at SENAI (apprentices alternated six months in school and six months in the factory, receiving half the minimum wage). Vavá's generosity of judgment is underscored by the fact that Lula's chance might be viewed as coming at a personal cost to him. During the family's first six years in the city, Vavá held a poorly paid, dirty job in a textile plant loading and unloading a cotton press. This was followed by warehouse work; only in 1965 did he land a decent job, as an unskilled metalworker at Ford Ipiranga. Looking back, his assessment is stark: there was simply "no other choice. The older ones had to work and he had to study. Someone had to make something of his life. Her desire was to have a son who was a torneiro mecânico."[41]

Lula's mother had never held a job outside the home, with or without working papers.[42] Yet it is striking that her dream for the future so closely tracked that of the working-class fathers interviewed by Pereira and his assistants in 1963. Fathers repeatedly wished a better future and happier life for their sons through the attainment of a profession. In a world they saw as changing rapidly, parents fought so that their youngest sons might, in Pereira's words, transition through skill to "the more stable 'superior' modalities of working-class life"; in doing so, the fathers affirmed "through their sons the workers they wished to be," while often indulging in ephemeral fantasies in which their sons became prestigious doutores, holders of advanced degrees such as that of a doctor or lawyer—before recognizing that "it's not possible given my [economic] state. One shouldn't even think about this."[43]

That poorer folks embraced a white-collar ideal reveals an internalization of society's governing values, which viewed those without education as inferiors condemned to stigmatized manual labor. But we must never forget that vicarious dreams of social mobility also represent a negation of one's class condition and a critique of the limits of the opportunities that São Paulo unquestionably held for those rural migrants "lucky" enough to gain a factory job. Whatever their divisions by origin or length of urban residence, workers in 1963 were well aware of their limited ability to insert themselves favorably into the labor market. Shielding themselves from hurt, they expressed their dissatisfaction most poignantly through their aspirations for their male offspring: that they might avoid the brute manual labor (*trabalho braçal*) to which fathers and older brothers were condemned.[44]

This negation encompassed their rural pasts—working with a hoe on one's small rural property (*roça*)—as well as their urban present—dead-end jobs such as the lifting and carrying of loads, through which Aristides made his living during his younger, more vigorous days. It also extended to the many other positions in which workers were treated merely as "anatomical" arms at others' disposal, the most humiliating of which was working with a broom.[45] This is why becoming a machinist seemed a utopian aspiration during the auto industry's stormy growth between the 1950s and the 1970s. Machinists' high status was attested to in a 1983 interview with a paulista metalworker identified as Durval. Born a year before Lula, he got his machinist's diploma from SENAI in 1962, when "the torneiro mecânico was a God in terms of what you heard. . . . Puxa! that guy is torneiro mecânico!" "*Everyone* was impressed," he added wryly, "although no one understood what a torneiro mecânico was much less what he did."[46] Lula has sounded a similar humorous note: he wanted a machinist job very badly but "didn't even know what" a machinist was.[47]

After recounting his mother's quest, Lula underplays his big break: "one fine day" (*um belo dia*) the opportunity emerged (*surgiu*) for him to be hired at a factory that needed to send an apprentice to SENAI (industrialists were required to sponsor a certain number based on their payroll). Hence his hiring at the Marte Screw Factory (Fábrica de Parafusos Marte), located at 337 Rua Antonio Frederico in Vila Carioca. At SENAI he "signed up, filled out the form, and went to take the test and passed." Lula would have his first factory job for a little over four years, from 1960 to 1964. In describing his first day of work at age fifteen, Lula echoes Durval's observation about popular ignorance: looking around, "everything I saw was a lathe [*torno mecânico*]. I saw a *rosquiadeira* and thought it was a lathe"; the only machine he "didn't imagine was a lathe was the lathe itself."[48]

Lula's disarming self-representation combines luck ("one fine day") with self-deprecation that avoids any hint at his own "specialness" or that he or his family might have deserved the opportunity more than others. His humility involves more than a politician's guile or a personal quirk. To openly avow being a "winner"—and to thus highlight others as losers—was seen as putting on airs, an unseemly attempt to set oneself above others. In a society permeated by patron-client ties, this popular ambivalence about individual achievement might seem to contradict the common expression "to win at life" (vencer na vida). A closer examination, however, shows that São Paulo's working people during this period used "winning at life" to express a shared aspiration, not to unquestioningly embrace an ethos of individualistic competition for success. Tiana's observation about her mother's humility is pertinent here: dona Lindu would never "step on anyone else in an effort to become more than them."[49]

As sociologist and CESIT founder Florestan Fernandes observed, midcentury São Paulo was an *emerging* competitive social order, not a fully realized one; the latter was an ideal type based overwhelmingly on individualistic norms and ideals.

A Citizen-Machinist in Training

As one of the happy ones (*felizardos*), Lula spent the next three years alternating between the Marte Screw Factory and SENAI.[50] The first two years were spent at SENAI's Avenida Ipiranga school, the last six months at the Escola Roberto Simonsen.[51] Lula was employed not by a "good factory," as workers referred to large, better-paying modern firms, but at one of the little enterprises (*fabricazinhas*) that flourished during this industrial boom. Lula was employed at a family-owned enterprise with forty to fifty workers located about five hundred meters from the Silvas.[52] Lula was on good terms with the owner, describing Miguel decades later as a friend; at the time Lula played soccer with his two sons, although Luisino and Miguelito didn't play very well, Lula adds, because they lacked the toughness and callouses formed by rough-and-tumble soccer on irregular fields (*campos de varzea*).[53]

Whatever his first impressions, Lula's initial exposure to factory work did not include the intimidation that impressed those starting at larger, more impersonal enterprises. "As a sharp and uninhibited kid [*moleque esperto*]," Lula "got along well" with everyone in this small-scale world of personal relationships. The factory's only employed minor, Lula was its "youngest little one" (*caçulinha*), who, as he observed about his own family, "always receives more care from the mother."[54] That the plant employed many northeasterners sheltered him from the latent regionalist tensions during this period of mass migration.[55] European-descended paulistas, especially longtime city dwellers, and a large swath of established skilled workers routinely called the newcomers "baianos," stigmatizing them with the name of the Northeast's "blackest" state (a term also applied to mineiros).[56] Such prejudiced teasing and humor flourished; for instance, in a 1993 interview with Paraná, Lambari, raised in the paulista interior, referred to his adolescent best friend Lula lightheartedly as a "baiano."[57]

The task ahead for the young apprentice was to master the trade of machinist, the term in US English for a new occupation that had emerged during the second industrial revolution of the late nineteenth century. It broadly designates those "who cut and shaped metal parts on machine tools" using "lathe, drill press, milling machine, shaper, or planer."[58] In Brazil, *torneiro mecânico* refers to a machinist who uses a metal lathe known in Portuguese as a *torno mecânico*. Among the most widely used universal machine tools, the lathe de-

Lula (front row, third from left) at age fifteen on a soccer team.
(Courtesy President Luiz Inácio Lula da Silva)

mands "flexibility and versatility" from its operators. To manufacture "batches and small series require the machinists who operate them to undergo extensive training, which is continually improved in the course of their professional practice long after their formal training has been completed."[59] For a newly hired fifteen-year-old, the prospect of learning the machine—its tools, settings, and quirks—was intimidating. It required knowing how to mount the raw material and to choose the proper cutting bits, the correct angles, and the appropriate speeds at which to craft a final product that met exact specifications. Errors in planning or the mishandling of the lathe might ruin the expensive raw material, cause a serious accident, or damage the machine.

The torno mecânico's importance—along with insight into SENAI's mission—is revealed by José Augusto Bezana's recollection of first meeting the revered Roberto Mange. Interrogated by the head of SENAI-SP, Bezana was asked if he knew what a lathe was, to which he replied, "I know what a wood lathe is." Dissatisfied, Mange restated his question: "And a torno mecânico?" This time Bezana admitted his ignorance, which led to an expansive commentary by Mange clearly laying out the stakes of training machinists. "Look, the important thing in a lathe is the tool [*ferramenta*]," he began, which is used "to grind the metal, and it has to be set at a certain angle. If that doesn't happen, it breaks, understand? It doesn't last. Now, it's vital to know exactly the correct angle," he went on, and "if the boy is not well educated—he could even be a good professional, know the machine [*torno*], and be capable of doing everything with it—but if he has not been educated, it could be he doesn't understand the behavior of the boss [*patrão*]." In that case, "what does he do? He could set it at the wrong angle. . . . He will break the tool, damage it [*gastar*], out of anger at the boss."[60]

Mange abruptly transitioned from the lathe to worker sabotage, common in the United States around 1900 and among ABC machinists in the 1970s.[61] He then expounded on a rationale for SENAI that he had undoubtedly rehearsed many times in convincing industrialists to support his agency (the government-mandated levy on their payroll had always aroused some resistance): "What we want is that when the man goes to the lathe he is an educated person. This is part of forming him as a professional. Because we [at SENAI] are training an elite! And if we form such an elite and provide them with a good education, in addition to a profession, its members will acquire the capacity to eventually command industry itself."[62]

Yet the machinist's professional formation did not rest solely with SENAI's classroom teachers and skilled workers turned teachers. Each apprentice also had a professional father in his factory. For Lula, it was an older black (*negro*) machinist remembered fondly by Lula for his "special preoccupation with me, helping me, teaching me, [and] treating me well." "Old man Barbosa," Lula says, acted like a real father and even shared his food.[63] Like all humans, Lula observed, Barbosa had his defects, which in his case involved a love of drinking and gambling, which led him to squander his pay betting on everything from horses and cockfights to combat between canaries (*brigas de canarios*). But all in all, he was a noble man and "first-rate machinist," in Lula's judgment.[64]

What Lula's shop floor teacher knew of his craft had been learned empirically, not through the formally structured schooling that would occupy eighteen months of Lula's life over three years. Robert Alexander laid out the daily routine of this schooling. Each morning, one group of students was "in the machine shops doing practical work; while the other part has theoretical studies. In the afternoon, the groups exchanged places. The theoretical work included Portuguese, arithmetic, sciences, history, and the technology of their industry, as well as mechanical drawing."[65] Unlike high school teachers, who had teaching school degrees (*escolas normais*), shop teachers were recruited from the factory floor, although a few employers objected to losing prized workers for this purpose.[66]

SENAI's shop floor teaching is best known for a problem-solving pedagogy called the methodical series (*serie metódico*), an inductive method that consciously avoided "abstract formulations which can severely restrict the understanding of its clientele."[67] A Brazilian social scientist in 1979 succinctly explained SENAI's "distinctive methodology based on a progressively more difficult series of practical exercises." In a course for lathe operators, for example, "the first exercise may be turning a bolt and in each subsequent exercise new operations are introduced in such a way that when the last has been completed the student will have mastered all the major techniques of the occupation. Trainees do not learn *about* lathes or their uses; they simply work with them in so-called 'methodical series.'"[68]

The SENAI experience also reached beyond the classroom. Taking shape after World War II, SENAI came to be defined by an expansive reformist mission that Mange called "education for the whole man" (*educação integral*). At his most utopian, the Swiss-born engineer argued that "the mission of SENAI. . . . is not dealing simply with the problem of vocational training" but rather "to form a citizen . . . a whole person [*homem integral*], morally, physically, and professionally . . . who is zealous [*cioso*] as to the prerogatives inherent in his human dignity and conscious of his personal and professional responsibility for the collectivity." The aim was to make learning "active and interesting" through teaching that "leads the student to think and resolve for himself the problems of real life."[69]

Through educação integral, SENAI apprentices received a broad array of services and benefits. As the flagship for the institution's richest region, SENAI-SP shows the scope of offerings when Lula was an apprentice. In 1956, the Escola Roberto Simonsen gave apprentices "two lunches during the day—milk and a sandwich—free," as well as the choice of buying a subsidized midday meal for seven cruzeiros, on which SENAI took a three-cruzeiro loss. The school also provided the students with free medical and dental consultations, paying half for any dental prosthesis; for more serious problems, SENAI arranged for treatment or an operation through an allied payroll-funded agency, the Social Service of Industry (SESI).[70] They also offered recreational activities and an active student associational life.

Looking back, Lula categorically affirms that his apprenticeship was the best period of his childhood. There was food, basketball, and table soccer. "I was taking a professionalizing course as well as the regular classes in human and exact sciences. I participated in shows. It was all a poor boy like me could dream of in life." That Lula bought in to SENAI is suggested by this fanatic soccer player's offhand admission that he allowed his playing to fall away while at school. As for punctuality, discipline, and performance, Lula had the support of his mother, who, Frei Chico observed, "stayed on top of Lula [*deu em cima do Lula*] so that he succeeded in becoming a fully formed machinist."[71]

SENAI's Nitsch would tell Alexander in 1956 that the school's teachers and administrators did not face very "many disciplinary problems," as "for the most part, the students are eager to learn [and] realize how important it is for their future careers and don't cause trouble."[72] There is evidence to suggest that this characterization was not entirely self-serving. In 1956, Alexander found students "concentrating on their work, and there was no horseplay visible."[73] But the key was the atmosphere fostered in SENAI's training programs:

> The training environment is highly structured. Minute attention is paid to every detail, ranging from the well-starched overalls to the reinforcement of values and attitudes that are functional in the everyday operation of a factory. There is no overt disciplinary control . . . but the smooth monitoring of students' time and the factory-like atmosphere create an environment that is at the same time relaxed and busy. From the first day . . . students are explicitly told what are the rules of the game and what is expected of them.[74]

This combination of a structured learning environment and a labor market favorable to SENAI's graduates helps explain the devotion that the majority of the institution's students felt toward it. At the same time, the labor market generated practical problems. Some were minor, as when in 1956 Nitsch reported that many boys didn't want to get paid less than those doing the same work in their factory. After the future wage gain promised from the diploma was explained, Nitsch said, most accepted the situation.[75] A far more serious problem was the dropout rate—which could reach as high as 40 percent. Apprentices usually quit after the second year, when the most advanced skills were about to be taught; they had learned enough by then to be much sought after by desperate employers. Although students' immediatism was criticized, SENAI officials tended to blame opportunistic employers for undermining the institution's long-term contribution to industry: the creation of fully trained professionals, not makeshift lathe operators.

SENAI as an institution was driven by and responsive to the needs and demands of the industrialists supervising its efforts. Yet the agency's functioning and intellectual elaboration were in the hands of the administrative and pedagogical cadre in charge of its day-to-day operation. Their ideal of educação integral was predicated on treating poor and working-class youth with an uncommon degree of respect and dignity. Many SENAI veterans have classified Mange and the institution as expressions of progressive humanism. After the Estado Novo dictatorship's end in 1945, they say, Mange moved from the narrow utilitarianism implied by his early schema of anatomical, diligent, and thinking arms to speak of the "student worker" (*aluno operário*).[76] The adolescent apprentice was not to be viewed as a machine, as a dependent simply because of his or her needs, as "an isolated being, lost in social atomism, or as sunk in the mass of a collectivity."[77] SENAI rejected the rigidity of established educational practice for a new approach to teaching. "It is not the teacher who is to inculcate the student with the material," SENAI's 1951 annual report declared, "but the student who should desire to acquire the knowledge, the how and why, of the practice and theory of his craft."[78] Indeed, in his last years Mange sought to create "an open, cheerful [*alegre*] school where the student lives in freedom and learns to conduct himself with self-confidence and responsibility."[79]

SENAI can be seen as a sustained attempt to create a self-conscious, collaborative working-class intelligentsia who took pride in their hard-earned skills. As Mange thought, young Brazilians turn away from industry because they fail to understand its nobility. The mechanical professions involve "manual labor intelligently executed, which required basic theoretical knowledge and reasoning, while developing spirit and character." And the skilled worker, because he feels realized (*apto ao oficio*), achieves "favorable economic conditions, loves his profession, and assumes the necessary responsibility" demanded of him.[80] SENAI, as a Brazilian social scientist observed, "develops in its trainees a taste for the occupation being learned, as well as a sense of dignity and professional pride."[81]

In an era when national development was in vogue, SENAI had a stake in winning industry the respect and prestige deserved for its contributions to Brazil's future. At its most expansive, SENAI offered a democratic vision that mid-century Brazilian elites—whether economic, political, or military—were not ready to appreciate, much less fully implement. The agency had consolidated itself between 1946 and 1964, during the unprecedented electoral democratic era now called the Populist Republic. In its fight for the future, SENAI affirmed the value, worth, and respect that the skilled manual worker, whatever his origin, was due from the wider society. For Mange, such a class benefits "industry, society, and the state." Writing before the country's twenty-one-year military dictatorship, Mange argued passionately that SENAI would provide society with men of "disciplined character, conscious of their duties and capable of fulfilling them." The elite of skilled workers, Mange dreamed, would have a healthy influence on the working classes, while the state would gain "a hardworking and orderly citizen."[82] It is hardly surprising that thirty-six years after Lula's graduation ceremony, he would still declare his three-year SENAI apprenticeship "the most important period of my life." Interviewed by fellow São Bernardo metalworkers, Lula explained why: first, he was learning a profession, and second, "it was the first time in my life that I had contact with citizenship."[83]

4 A TALE OF TWO BROTHERS

José Ferreira de Melo and Luiz Inácio da Silva, the two youngest Silva brothers, loom large in their family's story. Born in 1941 and 1945, respectively, Ziza and Lula were inseparable through adolescence; both became metalworkers and trade unionists. To avoid confusion with his oldest brother, José Inácio da Silva (b. 1936), Ziza was legally named José Ferreira de Melo but is known to all by the nickname Frei Chico (Friar Chico), coined by his union companheiros because of a premature bald spot that looked like a friar's tonsure.[1] Lula and Frei Chico, already close, discovered that they shared something else in 2011, when the sixty-six-year-old ex-president successfully underwent treatment for throat cancer and temporarily lost his hair. After long believing he was more handsome than Frei Chico, Lula was chagrined to discover that they were identical.[2]

Frei Chico comes up in Lula biographies only to explain that Lula entered trade unionism at his suggestion. We gain a deeper understanding of Lula's life, however, if we approach their relationship as a tale of two brothers, exploring what they shared and how they diverged as young working-class men in the 1960s. Compared to Lula the "good boy" (*bom moço*), Frei Chico was more independent, even a "rebel" (*revoltado*), exemplified by his decision as a seventeen-year-old to cease training to become a torneiro mecânico.[3] Looking back in middle age, Frei Chico says this 1958 decision stemmed from stupidity (*burrice*) and personal vanity. He had "the illusion of being strong [*forte*]," exercising with barbells, and "didn't like that business of standing around grinding iron"; he preferred being "a helper on a truck," so that he could be out on the streets looking at girls. This flew in the face of dona Lindu's advice; only the unquestionable authority of a "father or some other responsible person," he says, could have prevented his mistake.[4] His forceful personality is equally evident in his dissent from his family's Catholicism. Despite his nickname, Friar Chico was a skeptic since infancy, he humorously claimed in 1981: "Ever since I was little I was always half atheist. When they went to baptize me, I bit the priest and the godfather. . . . I never liked priests."[5]

Although he abandoned becoming a machinist, Frei Chico did gain certification in a skilled metalworking profession—*retificador,* which appears on his working papers. But he left that behind to become a welder, which, he explained defensively, "is a profession" but a "very unsatisfying" trade that "wears down the professional."[6] Unlike Lula, Frei Chico did not find in his profession self-realization or identity. His vocational trajectory suggests how misleading it is to assume that skilled laborers form a coherent group simply because they can be distinguished from those deemed semiskilled and unskilled. According to SENAI, a fifth of São Paulo's metalworking labor force fell within the broad swath of jobs classified as skilled in the 1960s. Yet "skilled" conceals a hierarchy marked by clear differences in status, pay, and labor market demand as well as degrees of specialization and identity. Except for a few stable professions at the very top, including machinists, skills were always in flux due to changes in industrial processes and machines, not to mention ongoing disputes about whether a given task was skilled enough to properly count as such and, if so, with what consequences. SENAI did classify welders as skilled in the 1960s—while drawing distinctions within their ranks—but they stood well below machinists, who were far closer to the smallest, most prestigious, and best-paid skilled group, the ferramenteiros.

This chapter traces Frei Chico's and Lula's distinct trajectories to illustrate behavioral contrasts that coalesced around two stereotypical figures of the worker: the "good boy" and the "rebel." These contrasting identities, as I will show, had a fundamental role to play during this historical moment in Brazil—whether in the leftist ferment of the Populist Republic's last years, from 1960 to 1964, when national unionism made great strides and leftist political parties organized to push for fundamental social reform, or in the destruction of this leftist effervescence via the March 31, 1964, coup, when workers passively accepted or even embraced the military's seizure of power. Yet both types of workers, as I will recount, set the groundwork during this time for the explosion of protest to come in 1978 from ABC's autoworkers and trade unionists.

Apprenticeship in the Class Struggle

As the Silvas' youngest boys, Frei Chico and Lula had been close from the time of the pau de arara through life in greater Santos. They remained "inseparable" as adolescents in Vila Carioca, as Lula noted. Yet there were early signs of diverging paths, even before Lula entered SENAI. Frei Chico was drawn to the "really militant" Communists he came to know in Vila Carioca in 1958. He made the point in a 1981 interview with Mário Morel, within a year of his arrest during the 1980 metalworkers' strike in ABC. The Brazilian Communist Party (Partido Comunista Brasileiro, PCB), which Frei Chico had long been connected to and eventually joined in 1971, was still illegal in 1981, so he avoided publicly avowing membership. Yet he insisted that the Communists whom he met in 1958 said what workers wanted to hear: "They really open your mind." In 1993, seven years after the PCB's legalization, Frei Chico spoke of his respect for the "strikes, agitation, and campaigns against hunger and misery . . . all headed by Communists." He and some friends began hanging out with the local Reds in bars and barbershops; he liked their talk about fighting back, ending workers' misery, and creating a world where workers were the bosses, where an effective agrarian reform meant that rural migrants no longer flooded the urban job market.[7]

Frei Chico traces his interest in politics to his father's enthusiasm for Getúlio Vargas, the populist president and "father of the poor" who defied a military ultimatum to resign by killing himself in August 1954. Since 1930, Vargas had dominated Brazilian politics, creating the country's labor legislation and government-sponsored trade unions. Although far from democratic, Getúlio (as he is popularly known) established a reservoir of goodwill among the popular classes, which was passed on—at least partly—to the more left-of-center Partido Trabalhista Brasileiro (PTB) created by Vargas in 1945. Frei Chico would have found the Communists ideal interlocutors to fan his early political interest.[8] PCB members were far from unequivocal fans of Vargas, who persecuted them, but their post-1954 strategy brought them into closer alignment with workers who idealized Getúlio and those PTB politicians who claimed his mantle, such as Juscelino Kubitschek's vice president João "Jango" Goulart and the gaúcho governor Leonel Brizola of Rio Grande do Sul. The day-to-day maneuvers of national politics were usually far removed from the lives of the popular classes—illiterates were ineligible to vote—but Getúlio's dramatic death, and the ensuing rioting and nationwide mass public mourning, registered powerfully in the lives of millions, including the Silvas.

Lula's earliest political recollections were of São Paulo's vibrant populist electoral politics. His family, he explained, were *adhemaristas*, supporters of the rotund, three-time governor Adhemar de Barros, whose popular touch and undoubted personal appeal were matched by his sticky fingers. His famous *caixinha* (cashbox) led supporters to famously joke that "he robs but get things done."[9] At the same time, Lula enjoyed watching the histrionic public speeches of Adhemar's most visceral opponent, Jânio Quadros, the eccentric former schoolteacher whose meteoric rise began with his memorable "penny against the millions" campaign for mayor of São Paulo in 1953, followed by his election as governor in 1954 and as Brazilian president in 1960. The passions that could inform São Paulo electoral politics are suggested by a story about Lula boarding a bus full of *janistas* (as Quadros's supporters were called) with an Adhemar leaflet. Lula remembers how "they made me get off, kicking and punching me, without my having understood a damn thing [*porra nenhuma*]." Jânio's renunciation of the presidency in 1961, on the anniversary of Vargas's suicide, occasioned a national crisis, and reactions among the poor, as Lula recounts, ranged from feelings of betrayal to a belief that he was forced from office because he messed with the rich.[10]

To the adolescent Lula, Frei Chico was wasting time on nonsense. Yet Lula himself was not untouched by the worker mobilizations that surged from 1957 to 1963. When his family arrived, the city's industrial districts were swept by the "Strike of the 400,000," involving hundreds of thousands of workers. And with the accelerating inflation that accompanied economic growth, discontent remained high. Lula usually encountered such labor protest as a passive participant or bystander. "My first experience with strikes," he explained, came at age fifteen. Leaving one day for work, he noticed how "the street was totally covered in graffiti." At the factory entrance, his apprehensive manager, Mr. José, spoke about the rumors of large-scale picketing; deciding that it was better to avoid trouble, he dismissed the workers. But instead of returning home, Lula got onto a small company truck with other workers and went off "to see what was happening." The younger workers, he went on, "did what the older workers ordered us to do: when we passed in front of a factory that was still working, we threw rocks at the windows." Everything was a novelty: "It was something I had only heard the older workers tell stories about."[11]

Lula reports another strike experience around this time. Numerous workers were picketing the jute factory where his sister Maria Baixinha was employed, and Lula had been sent to bring her home. The pickets, in his description, followed the established pattern for dragging companies into the strike, as they "moved along closing the factories" in their wake. On this occasion, the bosses of Maria's factory preferred to test the balance of forces by resisting. In response, "the crowd pushed over the factory wall. It was a tall wall. Everyone put their hands on the wall and started to push, push, push . . . and a big piece of it fell. With this, the factory's functionaries were freed." The pickets then formed "a Polish corridor, and as the little guys [*neguinhos*] breaking the strike left, they took a cuffing on their head, their rear end" while being jeered. His sister passed through unhurt.[12]

The third strike episode that Lula recalls involved far greater violence. As the pickets entered a small textile shop with eight or nine workers, they were met with gunfire from the owner, who hit "a companheiro in the bladder." In retaliation, the picketers threw the owner out the second-floor window; he was taken to the hospital, where Lula believes he may have died. "It was the most violent scene I had seen . . . [and] I was frightened. I thought it was a lot of violence . . . but at the same time we'd been shot at. So I thought the people were acting justly [*fazendo justice*, literally "doing justice"]." The last of the strikes Lula remembers from his childhood includes an actor central to labor relations: the forces of repression, in all their varied manifestations. On the Via Anchieta the young Lula encountered the "pickets" of the militarized police, the feared Força Pública, on horseback. Lula reports witnessing the strikers' ingenious response to the cavalrymen: the workers threw marbles onto the street, which caused the horses to lose their footing and prevented their riders from intimidating, beating, and arresting the crowd. The novelty of such a banal weapon stayed with the young Lula, who remembers the incident as an amazing adventure.[13]

Yet these passing encounters with strikes before 1964 were nothing compared to Frei Chico's path of organized trade union struggle. Lula did not belong to the union or attend its assemblies, nor did he participate in the lively mass meetings that always accompanied large strikes. What attracted Lula and many other young men was the excitement in the streets: the strike as tumult or break with normalcy (*baderna* or *farra*). The nineteen-year-old Frei Chico, by contrast, was taking a path well trodden for half a century in Brazil's industrial heartland. Successive generations of rebellious workers, almost always young and male, had been attracted to the "pleasing words" of those who fought back against bosses, stood up for workers, and didn't bend in the face of repression. During World War I, these radical workers were the anarchists made famous—or infamous, depending on your viewpoint—by the general strikes that swept through a much-smaller São Paulo in 1917 and 1919. After 1930, the activism of this tiny minority of radical workers was usually associated with the illegal PCB, which led major strikes and swept elections in the municípios of São Paulo and Santo André after 1945, during a brief period when the party was legal (by 1947 it was again outlawed and vigorously repressed). Whether from fear or conviction, the overwhelming majority of workers sensibly kept their distance from or opposed such rebels. Yet many male workers—even if only occasionally, at a distance, or secretly—experienced a certain pride in these men's virile response to those who exploited, oppressed, and humiliated their class.

The intergenerational continuity of radicalism can be seen in the career of Marcos Andreotti (1910–84), ABC's most important trade union leader before Lula. During World War I, he had been attracted to the anarchist agitators he heard in São Paulo's Praça da Sé. Like Lula, he witnessed worker ingenuity in dealing with the forces of repression: he recalls workers stringing piano wire between streetlamps, attracting the attention of the militiamen on horseback, and exulting when they were dismounted after charging into the trap. An atheist from a young age, Andreotti joined the newly formed PCB at fourteen and in the 1970s worked closely with his younger comrade Frei Chico. Andreotti's four decades of organizing included founding the Santo André metalworkers' union in 1930 and serving as its elected president for three terms from 1958 till

1964, when he was ousted during the military's massive intervention in the trade union movement.[14]

In our interviews, Andreotti offered a veteran's perspective on the apprenticeship in trade unionism and politics that Frei Chico embarked on before 1964. Based on a lifetime of shop floor organizing, Andreotti rejected a language distinguishing between "class-conscious" and "non-class-conscious" workers. For him, all workers, even those who were loyal to the boss or worked during a strike, had some level of consciousness (*consciência*) that could be raised through struggle around their felt grievances, however small or seemingly mundane. In his vocabulary, someone like Frei Chico was combative, knew he was being exploited, and "wanted to fight but didn't know where to start" or how to do so effectively. Working-class combativeness, Andreotti explained, was directed against immediate economic complaints as well as workplace conditions and treatment. The class struggle, he suggested, was most visible on the job, where shared economic and workplace grievances helped sustain among workers a unity of purpose that did not necessarily exist outside the factory gate.[15]

In Andreotti's experience, the best approach was to work in a "union way" (*sindicalmente*) with such a combative individual by helping him organize his shop mates to address shared problems.[16] Frei Chico's first lessons in organizing came as a twenty-year-old in 1960–61 while working at a small factory in Ipiranga called Metalac. The bosses adopted a new three-shift system, which meant that Frei Chico would no longer work a set shift from 7:00 A.M. to 5:30 P.M. (ten-and-a-half-hour workdays were not uncommon). Instead, he would have to rotate between three shifts with assigned hours that changed every week. It "was a pain for us single guys," Frei Chico noted, to have to work on Saturday night till 10:30 P.M. At someone's suggestion, he and his friends (*molecões*) went down to the São Paulo metalworkers' union to see if they could "win the day with an outcry [*grito*]." He began to frequent the union and got to know its leaders and functionaries, especially a great agitator named Cássio, who guided him. While the union checked the contract and labor law, Frei Chico and his friends opted for direct action: they simply decided not to show up on Saturday. This youthful act of defiance cost Frei Chico his first job.[17]

In his third metalworking job, Lula encountered a similar unwillingness on the part of employers to accommodate the social life of young adults. In 1965 he had been working for eleven months at Fris Moldu Car, an Ipiranga auto parts plant with one hundred workers, and got fired for not showing up for Saturday overtime. He had taken the money the boss provided for transportation and lunch but decided instead to go to the beach in Santos with his friends as planned. When "poor people go to Santos they don't tan," he noted wryly, and he had no defense when he showed up on Monday morning as red as a shrimp. He was fired immediately.[18] These two incidents speak to the imperatives of sociability among young adults. Yet they differ fundamentally. Frei Chico was engaged in organized struggle at Metalac involving the trade union and a group boycott. Lula's story, by contrast, related an impulsive individual decision rather than an expression of rebelliousness. Moreover, its lessons were ambiguous at best: if you're going to ditch weekend overtime, don't go to the beach, because sunburn makes it impossible to dissemble on Monday morning.

While workplace combativeness varied among individuals and groups, Andreotti emphasized that it was always more common than workers' awareness of political struggles beyond the factory involving the government.[19] Only once workers were set in motion around their economic demands, he explained, could they arrive at broader political conclusions. This was how Frei Chico progressed during the social and political ferment leading up to the 1964 military coup. Already more interested in politics than most, he followed national developments even more closely with the crisis over Jânio's renunciation of the presidency in 1961. Like other activists, Frei Chico was enthusiastic when the military veto of Vice President Goulart's inauguration was defeated. With the PTB's candidate in power, he listened avidly to the government's nightly radio program *Hour of Brazil* as promises of fundamental reforms emerged.[20] With increasing mobilization and strikes, the twenty-two-year-old Frei Chico talked up leftist heroes like governors Miguel Arrães and Leonel Brizola to Lula and his coworkers. Although obsessed with soccer rather than politics, Lula even acquired a certain admiration for the two governors after 1964 based on what he heard from a friend's father, who would talk about them as people hung out on the street corner.[21]

In the early 1960s the Brazilian labor movement achieved unprecedented organizational sophistication and capacity for mass mobilization, including the establishment of Brazil's first functioning national trade union confederation in 1961–62. The CGT (the Comando Geral dos Trabalhadores, later Confederação Geral dos Trabalhadores) even experimented with general strikes that at times involved hundreds of thousands of workers, including its first multicity political strike, in July 1962. Moreover, in 1962 the movement won through direct action and political pressure the thirteenth salary, a legally mandated Christmas bonus.

Labor also gained unprecedented influence on the most pressing and controversial issues of national life, economics, politics, and even diplomacy. Top leaders were elected to local, state, and national legislative bodies, although as members of the illegal PCB, they were often not allowed to take office (as in 1962 in São Paulo). Labor also fought boldly for the program of broad change represented by the limited but symbolically potent Reformas de Base (Fundamental Reforms) promised during Goulart's ill-fated presidency (1961–64). And finally, labor broadened its alliances to include, for the first time, important rural allies such as peasant leagues, and rural unionism spread like wildfire. Imbued with a new sense of power, the workers' movement pushed to renegotiate the populist bargain with its middle- and upper-class allies.

For a young worker like Frei Chico, all of this was exciting, and it was easy to believe the right-wing propaganda that the CGT was the nation's fourth sovereign power and its fifth (if unprofessional) army.[22] Condemning this "union-communist power" (*poder síndico-comunista*), those working toward a military coup portrayed an aggressive, even violent labor movement dominated by a minority of *politiqueros*, Communists, and *pelegos* (sellouts) who neglected workers' legitimate interests.[23] Calling for an end to corruption, subversion, and disorder, these antilabor groups criticized the "spurious organizations of political unionism" receiving President Goulart's "official and even officious support."[24]

This apocalyptic rightist rhetoric can easily be dismissed, since its proponents clearly have other motivations. Yet the Right's rhetorical choices and ability to mobilize its constituency depended on the perception, across the political spectrum, that the working class had achieved a new level of power. As two young sociologists rightly observed in 1962, the São Paulo proletariat's "social, political, and economic influence . . . has been increasing rapidly," and its "participation in decision-making—that is, its 'power'—has tended to broaden."[25] An energetic young rebel could see the future being made in front of his own eyes.

The upwelling of hope and visible social and political militancy among workers in the early 1960s was paralleled among university students, sectors of the Catholic Church, lower-level military men, and peasants and rural laborers. It was in this context that Frei Chico embraced a challenging apprenticeship in the class struggle as a union activist. Union militancy would come to define his personal identity as he built a sense of self-worth through ongoing engagement with—and combat against—authority figures who disrespected those on the bottom. Militancy provided ample room for deploying one's intelligence, daring, and cunning while requiring mastery of multiple skills and the acquisition of a broad array of knowledge, both formal and informal. It also offered a diversity of actions, ranging from one-on-one persuasion to figuring out how to get leaflets into a factory or to mobilize within one's work section without getting caught. In the streets, it included everything from agitation to joining or eventually leading strike pickets as well as knowing how to handle guards, the police, or the militia sent to disperse them. Within the union, it involved participating in assemblies and learning how to speak effectively to those attending the gatherings in the "workers' house," always full of applause and booing.

Even nonactivist workers regularly spoke up, a meaningful gesture of personal self-assertion in a world where workers were expected to walk with their heads down. The union headquarters was also a place where one could celebrate Carnival, play soccer, pursue education, or see and make friends, stepping out for a drink before or after a meeting.

Like the profession of skilled machinist, the role of union militant brought new challenges daily. Its practitioners were central to the political maneuvering around the trade union elections held every three years. Beyond the intrigue associated with assembling slates, activists decided electoral outcomes by lining up their friends' and shop mates' votes. Most slates were political compositions (to use the Brazilian terminology) designed to accommodate personalities, individual ambitions, factories, and organized political tendencies, whether clandestine or not. Moreover, one might even serve as a paid union official and thus escape the shop floor. Most importantly, union militancy gave one's life drama and meaning, the opportunity to forge intense bonds with other risk-taking males. As Andreotti would say, a man has to "make himself respected" (*fazendo-se respeitar*), and union activism, whether associated with a radical political commitment or not, allowed a working-class man to make his way, on his own terms, in a world that demeaned him. There might be a price to pay, of course, but industrial life provided little evidence that one could avoid getting screwed simply by going along with whatever the bosses wanted; that sort of submissive, unseemly behavior typified "flatterers" and "ass-lickers" (*bajuladores, puxa-sacos*).

"Rebels" and "Revolutionaries"

Workers like Frei Chico were objects of intense attention for foremen, factory managers, and the Political-Social Police (DOPS, Delegacia de Ordem Política e Social). Such union militants came up when, in 1963, Luiz Pereira's team interviewed foremen about who got laid off and why. They named "agitators," along with those committing more mundane offenses such as lateness, poor performance, or refusing to work overtime. One foreman complained about workers who "do politics [*politicagem*] in their work section by talking about strikes, wage increases, and so on. Soon enough, you'll find they've gathered a little crowd [*turminha*] around them." Another foreman stood out for his clarity and interpretive nuance. We fire people, he said, "for incapacity, for rebelliousness, for not fulfilling the requirements of their job, for influencing other workers badly with subversive ideas, or for inciting insubordination." But he went on to talk very specifically about workers like Frei Chico. "There are union members who think the union is everything," he said, hastening to clarify that they were not necessarily Communists, "just rebels [*revoltados*], and their rebelliousness messes things up [*atrapalha*], so they have to be fired." He also oddly complained that some workers used the labor laws and government-sponsored unions as weapons. Acknowledging that "the Law is a good thing" in principle, he emphasized that it was "dangerous if badly used."[26]

The bread and butter of everyday organizing is well illustrated by Frei Chico's next lesson in leading a factory struggle, one that took place in radically altered political circumstances. After his firing by Metalac, the young worker got a metalworking job in Bom Retiro before returning to Vila Carioca in early 1964 to work at Pontal, an agricultural implement firm. When he was hired, Pontal's workers were receiving good wages through a complicated system of profit sharing. Yet pay was slashed by a third with the sharp economic recession following the anti-inflationary measures of the new military regime, which had assumed power on April 1, 1964. Pontal's three hundred workers were upset that they were now being "paid shit," as Frei Chico put it bluntly in 1981. As a union activist, Frei Chico had to shape this disgruntlement into organized pressure through planning meetings at the union headquarters. At the largest gathering, union officer Orlando Malvesi encouraged the youngster to try public speaking. Trembling terribly, Frei Chico took to the microphone in front of two hundred workers, hesitated, and then took off: "I talked like the devil. I was really revolutionary. . . . I was hard-hitting [*meter o pau*]." Looking back, he admitted his performance was "shit"—when he was done, Malvesi said, "Hell, not like that, boy"—but he would learn to do better.[27]

Strikes were always difficult, but the political circumstances in 1965 meant that they were impossible, the only path forward being through the specialized courts charged with enforcing the labor laws' norms and provisions. A case was filed against Pontal; someone's name had to appear on the complaint, and in this case it was Frei Chico's. A commission of workers was named to negotiate with the company, which retaliated by firing Frei Chico for leading a strike. In doing so, Pontal avoided paying his legally mandated layoff rights. In his retrospective narrative, Frei Chico emphasized the solidarity of his fellow workers, who petitioned on his behalf and raised money to cover his salary. Yet his greatest psychological satisfaction came from his eventual triumph in the court case he filed over the firing. Since there hadn't been a strike, Pontal's action was illegal, and the company was forced to pay Frei Chico what he was due (although he was not rehired).[28]

Frei Chico was aware of what he was up against; he had stuck to his guns and could relish a small but meaningful victory when it came his way. These were discouraging times for labor activism, given the depth of organized labor's defeat with the military takeover of March 31, 1964. Among metalworkers, the coup brought police raids on the union headquarters in São Paulo, where Frei Chico was active, and in the booming industrial suburbs of ABC, all led by Communists (the Santo André union headed by Andreotti). Materials were hauled away and union leaders detained (and a few were beaten). Elected officers were replaced by government-appointed interventors, usually individuals linked to the losing anti-Communist slates in recent union elections.

Beyond weakening the unions' capacity to bargain collectively, the interventions led to the firing and flight of many activists and disrupted networks crucial to mobilization. Fear discouraged firm-level organizing, and the absence of institutional representation made it harder to mobilize labor's non-working-class allies, who had always played a vital role, whether from principle or electoral calculation. This contraction of space for public expression of discontent further weakened workers' ability to protest abuses or resist employer impositions. Over the next three years, the military regime would enact legislation—over unanimous union opposition—to further curb strikes and eliminate laws considered beneficial to workers such as the job tenure (*estabilidade*) legislation, long disliked by employers because it made layoffs more expensive.

Even before 1964, industrial and labor relations in São Paulo had been marked by ebb and flow, with periods of leniency toward labor and the Left followed by more aggressive periods of combat against "subversion." Even during the Populist Republic of 1945–64, government officials routinely used a broad array of repressive instruments without compunction and usually without any significant public objection. After all, it was easy to establish real or imagined connections between popular mobilization and illegal Communism. This spurred clandestine action, even when merely struggling for reforms or the enforcement or expansion of already existing rights (as was generally the case).[29]

What the military called a revolution after March 31, 1964, was a sharply repressive turn whose harsh realities can be illustrated by an episode at the Vemag auto plant near the Silva house in Vila Carioca. In January 1966, reaction to a half-hour stoppage by the plant's ferramenteiros was immediate. In the words of Hercules Corrêa, the clandestine Rio PCB leader assigned to the workers, "it rained police," who searched the factory section for agitators; "the justification couldn't [have been] more brutal: if it was a movement of workers, it was subversive and that was that."[30] For Vemag, a mass dismissal was impossible because ferramenteiros had a valuable skill. Yet a negotiated solution was stymied by the workers' justified refusal to publicly identify a representative. Almir Pazzianotto, the union's attorney, and the workers eventually reached an ingenious solution: workers' demands were written in the center of a piece of paper, with their names arrayed around them like pizza slices.[31] In recalling the Vemag story in his memoir, Corrêa couldn't resist a jaundiced comment on Vila Carioca's urban conditions: "The neighborhood was just a misery, dusty on sunny days and flooded when it rained."[32] In those years, as one longtime resident put it, Vila Carioca was always "a swamp full of frogs whenever it rained."[33]

In the mid-1960s, Frei Chico was teimoso in preaching organized working-class struggle in the face of disbelief, employer retaliation, and potential police trouble. In his later incarnation as a militant trade union leader, Lula would repeatedly pay tribute to Frei Chico as "the brother who influenced me more than any other because he was very militant and tried to convince us [*fazer a cabeça da gente*]."[34] But in the mid-1960s, despite his older brother's best efforts, Lula remained "totally disconnected," in Frei Chico's words, and continued to belittle involvement in union affairs, reportedly saying, "You guys are wasting your time with that union shit instead of going after girls."[35] Yet Frei Chico's path also drove a wedge between the young activist and his family. Lula explained to Altino Dantas in 1981 that while his brother was crazy for the union (*porra louca*), the sort of person who ate, slept, and breathed trade unionism all the time, "the rest of us in the family were antiunion. We believed what many workers think even today: that the union was full of thieves and untrustworthy types [*safados*] and that our brother was foolish [*bobo*]." Frei Chico's proselytism sparked an ongoing fight, as Lula related: "We would be having a family meeting, or sitting around drinking a *cachaça*, and he'd come in with: 'because the union.'" "And once he got started," Lula continued, "everyone opposed him. We'd be blasting him [*dando esporro*] because we didn't want to hear about unions."[36]

The conflict within the Silva family speaks to a central and still much-debated question about the 1964 coup: Who or what was responsible for the Left-supported government's fall from power, without resistance? To understand March 31's impact, one must grasp how much the rise of Vargas's protégé Goulart to the presidency thrilled *trabalhistas*, nationalists, Communists, and others on the left. The period from 1961 to 1964 saw a surge of mobilization for nationalist and reformist goals by workers, peasants, and students, as well as sergeants and noncommissioned officers. Full of confidence and pushing hard, these groups reached their high point at a March 13, 1964, rally in Rio de Janeiro, where Goulart pledged his presidency to the Reformas de Base and appeared onstage with trade union and leftist leaders, including trabalhistas and Communists. The rally was attended by hundreds of ABC workers mobilized by local unions.[37] The riposte from the right came a week later, on March 19, when hundreds of thousands assembled in São Paulo for the first of many "Marches with God for Liberty." Supported by São Paulo's governor Adhemar de Barros, those marching to save Brazil from Communism included William Max Pearce, the US director of the Willys-Overland auto plant in São Bernardo, and his

Brazilian-born wife; "damn proud to have been there," he told a US reporter for a business magazine article published five months later.[38]

Frei Chico still described the anti-Goulart march as his saddest memory seventeen years afterward: "I was twenty-three-years old and that march affected me profoundly. A government was doing something for the people, and the church comes along and came out against it." In the following weeks, those on the left were aware of the looming threat of a coup, but they believed it could be defeated, as in 1961, by a combination of military units loyal to Goulart and mass mobilization in the streets. The leftist national trade union confederation even issued a call for a general strike in the event of a coup attempt. But when the rebelling military units acted, as Andreotti put it dryly, attempts to organize a strike for constitutional legality completely failed. "There was no understanding on the part of the worker. So much so that here in Santo André only a single factory, Otis Elevator, stopped, but only for two hours."[39]

The story was no different in São Bernardo, where the youthful leaders in the new metalworkers' union, legally recognized in 1961, had aimed to make the union "into an organ of political struggle," unlike its counterparts in Santo André and São Paulo. While the union's president was a former textile union director, a Communist, the union was controlled by Orisson Saraiva de Castro (1925–2015), a Ceará migrant who joined the PCB at the age of twenty in 1945 and worked as a paid party organizer for the next fifteen years. Castro was sent to ABC in 1959 to help build the union and the PCB. Lacking a profession, he was initially hired at Mercedes-Benz, where he learned to be a maintenance electrician before being laid off. Hired at Termomecânica, Castro would serve as the union's secretary-general from 1961 to 1964. Allied with Santo André's veteran PCB leader Rolando Fratti, Castro believed in bold, uncompromising radicalism in the conduct of union and party affairs; in the words of the key historian of the union's foundation, he was a "man transparent in his ambitions."[40]

While moderating its political line after Nikita Khrushchev's revelations about the crimes of Joseph Stalin, in the late 1950s the São Paulo PCB also saw more open tension and conflict between Communist trade unionists and PCB functionaries. Elected union president in 1958, Andreotti banned Fratti from the union headquarters because of his attempt to hold sway in the union without being a member merely because a majority of its directors were Communists. That Andreotti prevailed over Fratti's attempt to instrumentalize the union reflects a softening of party discipline and the unusual degree of personal authority and respect commanded by Andreotti, a veteran Communist who had paid his dues in prison.[41] To Fratti and Castro, both of whom were members of the state's PCB leadership, Andreotti's stance showed a lack of "ideological rigor"; Andreotti, fifty years old at the time, was later criticized by Castro and his São Paulo counterparts as tired, old, and moth-eaten (*carcomido*). Castro, a thirty-five-year-old ex-party functionary in 1960, aggressively pursued strikes during his three years with São Bernardo's union while defying the antidemocratic restrictions on his party. He rented part of the union's offices to the PCB's newspaper to serve as a local party headquarters, a bold action in a predominantly rural and conservative município. In the bigger city of Santo André, the local Reds were more discreet, operating out of a bookstore and avoiding the local union's headquarters. Even Castro admitted errors under his leadership, including a local PCB meeting of four dozen in 1963 that, held nonclandestinely, led to a police raid in which Castro and others were arrested.[42]

The combative masculinity embraced by Castro and the young rebels he recruited to his party nonetheless betrayed insecurities. In 1986, Castro discussed why he chose not to serve as union president, placing Anacleto Potomati in that capacity instead. He said that he felt personally uncomfortable "talking with bosses, and I get nervous when I see one." In addition, there was his personal "way of being": he was "not a diplomatic man." Finally, he referenced national, regional, and racial discrimination: a visibly nonwhite nordestino, Castro believed that a paulista with an Italian name was best as president because "the bosses here are all of Italian or German origin, and when a nordestino speaks, they immediately react with racism and superiority." With a respectable ancestry, the more polished Potomati was ideal as the union's figurehead, although he lacked, Castro suggested, the audacity to "command workers" as he did.[43]

Back from exile in 1986, Castro was proud of his three years leading the São Bernardo union that by then was world famous. He regaled his petista interviewers with stories of his exploits. They asked him at one point if São Bernardo's workers had struck in 1964 against the "right-wing coup against the workers' movement." His answer no doubt disappointed them: "They didn't stop. I stayed here for two days [past the coup] and no factory struck. That's the truth." Castro managed to flee before the police arrived at their headquarters, trashed their offices, and roughed up the night watchman. Resistance in São Bernardo, however, was limited to the warning shots that Castro's group of Communists fired at the police trying to intercept the union jeep from which they were distributing leaflets calling on workers to defend Jango. Potomati was arrested, beaten up, and held for fifteen days. Castro went underground, condemned in absentia to two years in prison in 1966, and began a long series of personal and political adventures that over the next two decades would take him all around Brazil and to Bolivia, Panama, Chile, the Soviet Union, and Mozambique. This lifelong Communist still emphasizes the importance of revolutionary theory, musing in 2011 that "sometimes I ask myself what we can do so everyone will understand Marxism-Leninism."[44]

Vanguards and Masses?

March 31 revealed the stark miscalculations of those who believed that Brazil was on an irreversible path to resolving its social and democratic deficits. The coup was jarring precisely because of the extraordinary confidence of those aligned with Goulart during the Populist Republic's final years. In January 1964, the PCB's national newspaper, *Novos Rumos,* wrote that all Brazilians, "except for a small number of people on the far right, admit the need for fundamental reforms."[45] And the Santo André union newspaper trumpeted the PCB's line with a December 1963 front-page story, "The *Golpistas* [coupmakers] Are Weak." Nervous nellies were according golpistas "a force that they don't possess," the article declared; the idea that "a rightist coup might be victorious" was being used to justify the assumption by "Jango's bourgeois government" of emergency powers, opposed by a Left fearful that they might be used against them.[46] Less than five months later, a squad commanded by the local police chief descended on the Santo André metalworkers' headquarters as soon as they got word of the coup. Andreotti and eight other union leaders were arrested, the headquarters' telephones torn out, and the building occupied before the police headed to the city's other unions, finding their offices closed and leaders gone.[47]

While mobilized activists powerfully rejected the coup, the broader societal response ranged from ignorance or nonopposition to passive and even open support. The French worker-priest José Mahon, who had arrived in ABC in 1961 to assist Catholic worker movements, recalled that many felt that good might come from the change of government. While his parish was in the industrial district of Utinga, where Luiz Pereira had studied a primary school, Mahon took a job in 1964 as a skilled metalworker (*fresador,* or millwright) at Indústrias Villares in São Bernardo, where Lula would be hired in January 1966. It was from here that Mahon observed the popular reaction to the coup: "I was against it from the very first hour. . . . I never believed anything good would come from it for Brazil, but many people were willing to give the revolution and [military president] Castelo Branco a chance."[48]

Many workers were also open to the military coup, including Lula. Speaking in the 1990s, he emphasized that his rebel brother Frei Chico opposed March 31, calling it a military coup from the very beginning. But Lula said that it meant something entirely different for himself and his fellow workers than "for those who already had politics." Lula noted how at Metalúrgica Independência "the pride in the military reaching power was very great. The people had confidence in the Brazilian army . . . [and] I thought the coup was a good thing." Even among people his age, the army "was an institution with a lot of credibility, as if it was something sacred, untouchable." And the plant's older workers were quick to affirm that "everything is now going to turn out all right. They're going to fix the country and put an end to communism." Likewise, his mother, listening to the radio at home, would say that "the Army is going to fix Brazil. Now everything is going to improve." Lula suggests that this view was common, "at least among the poorest part of the population that didn't have any political consciousness."[49]

That the military's rhetoric of national salvation had appeal beyond the self-proclaimed "conservative classes" should not be surprising. The muted popular reaction reflected the distance between the symbolic promises made by President Goulart on March 13, which had excited those on the left, and the absence of effective action to control the galloping inflation eating away at working people's wages and salaries, even when minimum wages were periodically increased due to labor's political influence. After standing at 20 percent annually between 1955 and 1960, the rate of inflation rose to 35 percent in 1961 and increased every year to peak at 91 percent in 1964; it would be brought under control only through a sharp economic recession after the military regime sharply contracted government spending in its first years.[50] The problem of a "persistent and often violent rise in prices" since 1948 reflected intractable problems of inflation, shortages, and speculation well before the costly construction of the new national capital in Brasília. The crisis over Jânio's renunciation and Goulart's rise to the presidency further intensified the political and economic disequilibrium, even as the country experienced what was, on the whole, a remarkable period of accelerated economic and industrial growth.[51]

Workers in São Paulo were neither ideological, right-wing anti-Communists nor active supporters of the end of Brazilian democracy. There is no evidence, for example, that workers, labor organizations, or a sizable proportion of politicians identified with the popular classes (like those from the PTB) supported the coup or participated in the rallies that middle- and upper-class Brazilians organized to pave its way or celebrate its success.[52] Workers' indifference or passive support did not, in other words, reflect deeply held political views or even opposition to Goulart; most were well disposed to the *getulismo* from which Jango derived his standing. The workers' response is best understood as an absence of knowledge reflecting internalization of a profoundly authoritarian and elitist society's norms, with resulting personal inhibitions and self-limitations vis-à-vis politics and government. To broad sectors of this population, national-level politics was a distant world where the big shots (*grandões, cartolas*), the rich, and the letrados held sway, not people like them. This apolitical disposition prevented many from anticipating the negative consequences of the overthrow of Goulart's democratically elected government.

For those who had invested their hopes in a "Brazilian revolution," the coup was far less shocking than the weak reaction by those in whose names they had acted and spoken. The disillusionment went well beyond members of leftist organizations like the illegal PCB, the Brazilian Socialist Party, and Ação Popular (AP, Popular Action), founded by radicalized Catholic students and priests, many of whom were associated with ABC's progressive Catholic bishop, Dom Jorge Marcos de Oliveira. March 31's psychological impact was poignantly recollected in 1980 by Monsignor José Benedito Antunes, the reformist vicar of Santo André's Igreja do Carmo from 1957 to 1966: "We had a lot of confidence in the masses.... But nothing happened. It was as if it had nothing to do with them. I don't know where we went wrong."[53] "Our certainties of 1963 turned into our uncertainties of 1964."[54] This was how sociologist José de Souza Martins described the coup's emotional impact on young intellectuals drawn into the era's reformist ferment. In 1964 this twenty-six-year-old received his University of São Paulo undergraduate degree, illustrating the possibilities giving substance to São Paulo's collective optimism at the time. While his stepfather was an illiterate rural migrant, this young man "from the periphery, the factory, and a poor family" had been lucky to attend a good public school in São Caetano—with USP-trained teachers—when the state educational system was deteriorating elsewhere. Through single-minded application, he passed the USP entrance exam in 1961 and studied sociology at night while working in a factory, which he had done since the age of eleven. While his brother became a ferramenteiro, Martins indefatigably worked as a field researcher for Luiz Pereira's invaluable study of working-class social mobility published in December 1965.[55]

At USP, Martins found it "fascinating to discover that the world from which I came was the object of study" for the university's sociologists, including the dynamic Fernando Henrique Cardoso. It was a moment of intellectual excitement, he recalls, in which they tackled Marxist works like Georg Lukács's *History and Class Consciousness*, a book also mentioned by Leôncio Martins Rodrigues, a twenty-nine-year-old USP graduate student at the time. This son of a government functionary attained his USP undergraduate degree in 1961 and was one of five researchers hired by CESIT for a survey of three hundred São Paulo industrial enterprises. As Rodrigues explained in 2010, he entered USP at a time when Marxist theory had finally "left the working-class and union milieu" and begun to penetrate the academy in São Paulo. As a seventeen-year-old in 1951, he had dropped out of high school to devote five years to São Paulo's tiny Trotskyist movement, whose activist high point was its support of Quadros during his explosive 1953–54 rise. By 1956, Rodrigues had left Trotskyism behind, but his youthful revolutionary phase would prove fruitful at USP: Rodrigues was already a (disillusioned) veteran reader of Marxist-Leninist literature, while most of his student rivals were just "discovering" the working class from books.[56]

Between March and November 1963, Rodrigues researched among São Bernardo workers at Brazil's largest auto plant. Founded in 1957, the Willys-Overland factory employed 9,172 and produced a best-selling jeep in 1962. His study was conducted with company approval—a USP sociology professor was working with management—but the coup disrupted his plan to also study the three-year-old metalworkers' union led by Castro. Developed through ten open-ended interviews, his survey instrument was administered by undergraduate assistants to sixty-two workers and twenty-four ferramenteiros.[57] His resulting 1967 thesis—published in 1970 as *Industrialization and Worker Attitudes*—was based on tabulating the surveys, although the results were reported unsystematically. The thesis did include some additional comments from workers but offered nothing like the abundance of voices captured by Pereira to back up his nonquantitative generalizations. The two works also differed in spirit: Pereira was still informed by the optimistic if somewhat chastened spirit of the early 1960s, while Rodrigues's thesis was so discouraging that his adviser, Florestan Fernandes, prodded him to add at least one sentence leaving room for hope.[58]

The Populist Republic had not been rich in studies of contemporary São Paulo working-class life or opinion. The pioneering empirical work had been carried out in 1957–58 by sociologist Juarez Brandão Lopes (1925–2011), who studied the medium-size Metal Leve auto parts factory in the município of São Paulo.[59] The article is best known for its emphasis on the individualistic life strategies of these workers of rural origins and on the "absence of patterns of collective action" among them. Brandão Lopes famously described them as seeing the union not as something made *by* them but made by others *for* them. He noted how "when they mentioned the union, the workers didn't use the pronoun *us* but rather *they*," which that era's sociologists interpreted as a failure to identify with their working-class condition. The union, Brandão Lopes wrote, was solely "a means to be used for individual economic ends," especially medical, dental, and legal assistance, with the ultimate aim of escaping from being a worker.[60]

While Brandão Lopes offered nuanced ethnographic observation, Rodrigues was bold, even glib, in his generalizations about Willys-Overland's workers, a firm that would be bought and expanded by Ford in 1967. Rodrigues emphasized that they were "strongly stimulated by aspirations for social ascension and life improvements" and that they did not link their "individual perspectives with broader social and political processes."[61] Sixty percent of respondents, for example, indicated that nothing was disagreeable about their job, which led

Rodrigues to argue that they were mainly "driven by the project of social mobility," to which the job contributed.[62] Achieving individual success seemed "to offer more concrete and immediate results than collective political or trade union pressure on the part of the class as a whole."[63] Rodrigues highlighted that a third of the eighty-six workers interviewed opted for dictatorship in answering "what type of government could best speed up the country's development and elevate the living standards of the people," which led him to invoke the concept of working-class authoritarianism then being advanced by US sociologist Seymour Martin Lipset.

Unsurprisingly, Rodrigues emphasized that the vast majority of the eighty-six autoworkers saw union organization "as unnecessary, at least as an instrument of pressure against the enterprise." He reported that even unionized workers fell toward the negative end of his class consciousness scale.[64] And while finding that most workers were discontented, Rodrigues stressed that they blamed the government, not employers, bosses, or owners of the means of production.[65] Rodrigues viewed rural migrants' incorporation into the urban, industrial milieu as above all a revolution of individual social mobility; under Brazilian conditions, he concluded, one will not find "class movements based on a rejection of capitalism (as a system)."[66]

It is perhaps unsurprising that the USP sociologists of the early 1960s erected powerful structuralist explanations based on limited observations about an emerging collectivity that was to them politically and socially alien. Both Rodrigues's questions and pessimistic answers reflect images of the working class created and deployed during a moment of internal political drama for a generation of intellectuals on a mission. Whatever their political orientation, a small group of young São Paulo letrados had been drawn toward a new, little-understood "working class" during an intoxicating period of reformist ferment. Political polarization and unprecedented societal mobilization seemed to buttress talk of a Brazilian revolution, which reached its zenith with Jango Goulart's proposed Reformas de Base. Yet these same letrados blamed the working class for this revolution's dissolution. Describing the 1964 coup as "a counterrevolution in response to a prerevolution that, if not popular, was at least 'populist'"—Luiz Pereira invoked a bête noire that for letrados described the politics of a rural-origin working class. This class, superficially known, was presumed to be fodder for populism because they were devoid of class consciousness: a manipulated group that acted as a mass, not a class; a rear guard, not the hoped-for vanguard (a role students would claim for themselves in the years after the coup).

Yet the view from inside the factories, as José de Souza Martins insists, was very different. His social origins meant that for him the working class could never be the theoretical fiction it was for his fellow students of middle- and upper-class origins.[67] The Brazilian students who belonged to the educational 1 percent—only eleven children out of every thousand entering primary school would achieve a university degree—subscribed to a mechanistic linkage between class position, consciousness, and mobilization. Blind to their social distance from those they studied, these early researchers were continually surprised that the human beings they encountered, who entered factories to make a living such as it was, failed to meet their bookish ideas. These researchers consistently misinterpreted the evidence they gathered—itself shaped by the social distance they naively ignored—and drew implausibly categorical conclusions that transcended time, place, and circumstance. The newly arrived workers Brandão Lopes studied were not wrong, after all, to describe the trade unions they encountered, created and funded by the government, as made by others for them. And it was perfectly sensible for Rodrigues's respondents to possibly mask their actions by disavowing trade unions, given the fear of losing their jobs and livelihoods due to foremen, employers, and police hostile to unions. These researchers treated the intricate weave of responses offered by workers with a naive literalism rather than as layered texts needing interpretations.

An excellent example of such shortcomings can be seen in the eighty-four-line statement taken from a twenty-four-year-old unskilled nordestino assembly-line worker. For Rodrigues, this man contributes his labor to capitalist production, but his life revolves solely around his neighborhood and friendship networks: "He doesn't read newspapers, listen to radio, or watch television. He doesn't follow political events," and he values the union only as a social service agency.[68] Yet dissimulation is easily detected in this worker's discussion of trade unions with someone from a different social class. While he forthrightly admits that he has joined the union, he explains that "those with a family need it for help; we've got everything there" in terms of assistance. Highlighting that "the company doesn't like" the union, he notes that the company does discount his union dues while reiterating—in the passive voice—that "I have heard it said that the Company doesn't like people to be unionized." Aware that his union membership is an act of defiance of sorts, he follows with a disclaimer that "I only go to the union when I need a pass for a doctor. Outside of that I don't go," which suggests both his awareness of what occurs in union meetings and that fear of such activities was not enough to dissuade him from joining.[69]

Discussing his political dispositions, this assembly-line worker maneuvers with care but only weakly conceals his basic disposition toward trabalhismo. He begins by saying categorically that he abstains from voting when he can't find a good candidate but then adds that only Getúlio pleased him because he paid "more attention to workers." He coyly claims not to know whether he voted for the PTB's Jango in 1960 ("I'm not saying yes or no"), which is followed by an awareness of the era's political polarizations: "If I had to vote between Jango and [the right-wing anti-getulista Carlos] Lacerda, in that case I would vote for Jango. And between him and [ex-President] Juscelino [Kubitschek; J. K.], I'd vote for Jango. I think J. K. made a mess of things with that so-called Brasília." The strength of his pro-Jango position is clear when one actually listens to what is said.[70]

Yet Rodrigues's most striking analytical mistake is one that SENAI had long ago denounced: the educated's tendency "to lump all manual occupations together," ignoring the extent and meanings of the internal differentiation within the working class.[71] Twenty-four of Rodrigues's eighty-six interviewees were ferramenteiros, and they fit uneasily into the researcher's preconception of the working class precisely because they were, as their answers suggest, intellectuals not unlike Rodrigues and the USP undergraduates interviewing them.[72] For instance, in profiling an engine mechanic turned production inspector, Rodrigues notes the level of education and professional training of this married veteran worker—who had already worked five years in another auto plant—but links this to his consumerist desires and his wish to "abandon the working-class condition to pass into the middle strata."[73] Rodrigues describes this skilled autoworker's attitudes toward class mobilization as follows: "He rejects the union because 'its leaders are semiliterate.' In reality, he doesn't value union organization as an instrument for either making demands or providing assistance." Yet a closer examination of what this autoworker actually says in 1963 suggests a far more nuanced posture, one that will be echoed fifteen years later during the 1978 strike in São Bernardo do Campo led by a certain young union leader, Lula da Silva:

> I have never frequented the union. Or rather, I only went twice but never to return because the leaders are semiliterate; they don't know the labor laws. Union leaders should have at least *ginasio* [high school], have a course in human relations, education. The union should be on top of the situation, avoiding stupid strikes and looking for the means to educate the workers. . . . I think recourse to a strike is stupid. [But] it would be a good one if it was well led, if the workers were well instructed and avoided making a noisy tumult [*algazarras*]. Each one of us should cross our arms within the factory, without making a mess [*bagunça*].[74]

As a working-class intelligentsia, São Paulo's skilled laborers occupied a strategic position within the process of capitalist industrialization missed by several generations of sociologists who presumed that the working class was an undifferentiated whole. Indispensable to factories' running, skilled workers not only were prized by their employers but also benefited from the competition for their services, even when these workers were politically "subversive." While Andreotti and Frei Chico couldn't prevent employers from firing them, their skill, ingenuity, and persistence guaranteed that they were not unemployed for sustained periods. And the fact that the quality of one's work directly reflected professional mastery produced a strong sense of personal pride and responsibility among skilled workers. Management valued him and kept him on, Andreotti explained, because he "was always a person who met his obligations" at work. Why, I asked him, shouldn't a worker protest his exploitation by being less diligent? Admitting that some may have protested thus, Andreotti straightforwardly explained his philosophy: "As a worker, I have rights and I have duties. I meet my duties in order to demand my rights." This invocation of the reciprocal nature of workers' relationship with their employers reflected far more than Andreotti's personal philosophy; it was fundamental to his pedagogy of struggle and mobilization.[75]

Knowing full well their labor's value, the skilled workers of midcentury São Paulo did stand up for their rights and make demands on their employers. Even when unorganized, Andreotti recalls, the skilled were always more combative than the poorly paid manual laborer who experienced in his "own flesh the exploitation that capitalism carries out against the worker." The skilled were also more likely to be union members and were disproportionately represented in the PCB's ranks.[76] Despite his jaundiced portrayal, Rodrigues found skilled workers at Willys-Overland almost twice as likely as the unskilled to be unionists and far more likely to frequent the union headquarters.[77] The same was found in a 1970–71 study of an established, small metalworking plant in Santo André.[78]

Lula himself demonstrated the skilled worker's particular combativeness. At age eighteen and newly minted as a meio-oficial machinist, Lula had asked for a raise at the Marte Screw Factory. Invoking loyalty and obligation, his owner-friend Miguel responded that Lula would have to work for cheap for a bit to cover the firm's expenses for his studies. Lula pushed back, citing the injustice that an older machinist earned twice as much while producing less. When the boss remained unmoved, Lula was indignant: "Hell no, I want a raise," he reasserted, and he quit (*pedindo a conta*).[79] As one foreman told Pereira, "The firm where you learn a skill never pleases. To do better you have to change factories [after finishing your apprenticeship] because they always want to keep you there while paying less."[80]

The less skilled, by contrast, "held more tightly to their jobs and left other questions aside," in Andreotti's words. The unskilled and semiskilled acutely recognized that their jobs required little or no training and could thus be easily filled by replacements outside the factory gate. Andreotti demonstrated the skilled's indispensability in a story about Indústria Sul Americana de Metais. The plant's third electrician was fired at the urging of a Bolivian engineer. Unable to have the firing satisfactorily explained, Andreotti got the man rehired when he told the head of personnel that he'd "simply have to do his job tonight!"[81]

Unskilled and semiskilled workers lacked the sense of power and personal efficacy enjoyed by the better-paid skilled minority, fully exposed to the risks attendant to their status as proletarianized wage earners. Some in early 1960s Brazil thought this stark contrast had clear behavioral implications, evident in the currency of terms like "labor aristocracy," which some intellectuals picked up from the books they were reading. In 1963, a small pamphlet titled *How Are Strikes Made in Brazil?* confidently posited that the "highly skilled" in industry—well-remunerated workers trusted by their employers—had an "almost nonexistent class consciousness." The author, Jorge Miglioli, an enthusiastic young Marxist intellectual close to the PCB if not a member, compared such workers unfavorably to the minimum-wage-earning manual laborers, whom he described as not only more "class conscious" but also more likely to strike and to do so with constancy and intensity.[82]

The dialectic between the skilled minority and the less skilled majority was indeed fundamental to labor organizers like Andreotti, but São Paulo's social dynamics were radically different from those imagined by Miglioli (as well as some later academic researchers). Asked whether the well-paid and better-treated skilled worker would be more loyal to his boss, Andreotti emphasized that it was precisely because the skilled worker "had a better salary and a better standard of living [that] he wanted to get more . . . and knew that he could get and conquer better conditions." This generally did not inculcate a go-it-alone policy or elitist attitudes of superiority, Andreotti went on, since the skilled worker was aware that he "earned so much [which was not enough], and that the poor fellow carrying material over there earned [even] less and could feed himself less well. [Considering all this] you never asked an improvement only for yourself but sought it in the general sense."[83]

When pressed, Andreotti admitted that some foremen did try to play on average workers' resentment of skilled workers' higher pay and better conditions. Yet "it was with great difficulty," he explained, "that the [unskilled] worker embarked in that canoe, because [unionists] did a job of showing how the foremen squeezed" common workers. The pressure for production they experienced stemmed, he would explain, from the fact that foremen received, in addition to salaries, a percentage of their subordinates' production. Skilled workers like Andreotti argued that the foremen's percentage should go to those who actually did the work. Such arguments, he concluded, served as "a shock absorber" against divisive management maneuvers. Thus the alliance with the less skilled also fulfilled certain defensive needs for the skilled minority.[84]

In summarizing his conclusions from a lifetime of shop floor organizing, Andreotti advanced a philosophy of mobilization that meshes nicely with his observations about the skilled and unskilled. Workers were not moved to action by denunciations of the boss or moralistic calls to struggle; in his judgment, the biggest barrier to mobilization was their inability to believe in their own power to change things they disliked. Yet the successful mobilization of workers around their immediate demands did not, in and of itself, advance Andreotti's wider political objectives. As a Communist, Andreotti was convinced that the workers' economic and political struggles were inseparable and could be fully realized only through revolutionary regime change. Yet he knew that these views were not shared by the majority of workers, preoccupied with their own immediate problems.[85]

Andreotti saw the class struggle, in other words, as an educational process of consciousness-raising (*conscientização*) through which workers gained an increasing sense of power as they moved from smaller to more sweeping objectives. Yet doesn't an emphasis on winning modest workplace or community improvements, I asked him, produce accommodation and reformism? Wouldn't small victories within the capitalist system, by satisfying the workers' demands, disincentivize struggle? "To march toward revolution," Andreotti replied, "it is necessary to raise the people's awareness of their own force . . . and show them how to win economic and political improvements."[86]

That forward march, Andreotti insisted, should never be discounted as reformism, because "if the people are not conscious [*consciente*], not convinced of their own force, they will never make a revolution" (or anything else, for that matter). And each time a victory is gained, however small, workers learn that "dispersed they won't gain anything," and they become convinced that "united they *can* win." This growing self-confidence would in turn make it easier to organize workers for more ambitious struggles, even socialist revolution.[87] Socialism, he went on, depended on the ongoing development of workers' consciousness both during and after victory.[88] And after socialism was established, the ongoing political education of workers would be needed so that the socialism could advance and provide better laws for the worker.[89]

Basking in their newfound political prominence, the exuberant, increasingly plural Lefts of the early 1960s, with their triumphalist rhetoric, were so thrilled by the unprecedented inflow of young activists that they lost sight of the fact that the mass of the population they sought to mobilize was more like Lula than like Frei Chico. As a highly paid skilled worker, Lula was even less representative of the working class—given his status, education, and salary—than his less-well-remunerated brother, who was in a skilled but less respected profession and had not completed primary school. But Lula was more truly representative of the vast majority—whether skilled or unskilled—in his skepticism toward trade unionism and indifference toward politics, which allowed him to think a military coup might resolve the country's problems.

If the Lulas of São Paulo had been more like Frei Chico, the turbulence from 1961 to 1964 might have ended differently. If Goulart had been able to hold the loyalty of at least a sector of the army, a powerfully organized, politicized, and fully mobilized working class might have made a crucial difference. If workers en masse had shared the inclinations of its politicized activist minority, the political meaning of March 31 would have been radically different, even if the military had not split. Mass urban protests—as occurred after Getúlio's suicide—would have signaled clear opposition, and the Left would at least have gone down fighting in defense of democracy, a far less demoralizing outcome than their actual passivity when faced with the coup.

Frei Chico's and Lula's distinct trajectories illustrate behavioral contrasts that engendered stereotypes shared by workers, industrialists, and the broader society: the worker as either "good boy" or "rebel." Viewed one way, this dichotomy juxtaposed responsible collaborators with perpetually unsatisfied, recalcitrant troublemakers. From the opposing point of view, the good boys were selfish accommodationists with an eye for individual advantage, unlike the few rebels courageous enough to stand up for the weak and speak truth to power. Our examination of a "good boy" and a "rebel" from a single family suggests that we need not understand these behaviors and self-representations as dichotomous. Lula the citizen-machinist and Frei Chico the worker-citizen are part of the same story of working-class self-assertion in São Paulo. As we contemplate this diversity's implications, we would do well to first recognize that both deference and defiance are part of the behavioral and discursive repertoire of individual workers, in their performance toward those above them and as they relate to each other. Additionally, when we think of workers in motion as a social class, we are dealing with not a unitary outlook or consciousness but rather a shifting balance between, and alliances across, a range of behaviors and outlooks themselves subject to transformation once in struggle. As we will see, good boys and rebels will both have key roles to play in making history through the mass struggles of the 1970s.

5 THE CATERPILLAR AND THE MACHINE

Lula's big break came less than three years after graduating SENAI, hired in January 1966 as a machinist at Indústrias Villares.[1] Industrial and economic growth were just beginning to improve, and the hire was straightforward: "I read in the newspaper that they needed a machinist. I went there, did the test, and passed." His life changed radically: the firm not only paid well but also was "the first enterprise I worked for that was really organized."[2] The Rua Vergueiro factory in São Bernardo was part of an expanding industrial empire, founded in 1918, that famously included Atlas Elevators in São Paulo and the Villares steel company in neighboring São Caetano. Lula's new workplace consisted of a single pavilion with 530 workers producing motors, escalators, and subway parts, but over the next decade it would experience a sixfold employment increase fueled by federal government development loans.[3]

Lula's six years as a metalworker prior to 1966 had been spent in slipshod factories that shared little with Villares besides the 90 percent male workforce. This homosocial world was characterized by rituals of teasing, bullying, and male friendship, including nicknaming new hires. The choices were often creative, humorous, and usually neither arbitrary (Frei Chico did have a bald spot) nor generic (Baiano never took hold for Lula). At Villares, Lula was dubbed Taturana (caterpillar), which referred, as Lula himself explained to his former union companheiros, to his bloodshot eyes, caused by a still-existing allergy, which led his Villares workmates to speculate that he had smoked marijuana or had too much to drink the night before. A worker known as Azeitona (Olive)—who knew a lot about marijuana, Lula imagines—suggested the nickname, slang for the strongest marijuana variety.[4] Pinning "Caterpillar" on the red-eyed Lula illustrates the competitive process by which newcomers were humbled while being integrated into the group. Any effort to resist, Frei Chico noted, only made things worse.

Twenty months after his hire, Lula began to be courted—at his brother's suggestion—for an officers' slate in the February 1969 election for the Union of Workers in the Metalworking, Mechanical, and Electrical Material Industries of São Bernardo do Campo and Diadema. Lula's past biographers, who inevitably have to contend with this formidable union, have focused on his two presidential terms and neglected his earlier, six-year apprenticeship in union politics, long before he headed the massive 1979–80 Vila Euclides stadium rallies. They pass over these "silent" years of Lula's unionism—his first published interview dates from 1975—because union politics seem either inscrutable or too predictable, a government-controlled and heavily policed trade union movement purportedly dominated by either flunkies and sellouts (pelegos) or authentic, left-leaning unionists.[5] Yet it is curious that those controlling the São Bernardo union in 1968, some of whom were brought to power through government intervention in 1964, would agree to the suggestion of a leftist like Frei Chico. How did the twenty-seven-year-old acquire such influence? And why did Lula decide to accept the invitation to run, against his fiancée's wishes?

The difference between Lula and his brother traced in the previous chapter—the "good boy" and the "rebel"—should temper excessively politicized understandings of trade union life. Those who most forcefully insist on the trade union as a structure for capitalist state domination of the working class ignore its internal dynamics and the informal social processes—friendship, gossip, splits (*rixas*), betrayal, and factionalism—that permeate the union hall, where politics with a small *p* looms large, given the elections held every three years. Even after 1964, the Brazilian union leader was far from a typical government bureaucrat, although his salary was paid by an annual tax on workers' pay (*imposto sindical*). After interviewing São Paulo metalworkers' union officers, Heloisa de Souza Martins stressed in 1979 that a base-level trade unionist's success depended on pleasing not only his labor ministry superiors but also his voting members, which potentially mitigated the military regime's drive to diminish trade unions' political salience and economic role by transforming them into rigorous bureaucratic enterprises delivering social services.[6]

When Lula agreed to run for union office, discontent in cities was peaking with the military, which had seized power four years earlier. The 1968 student and labor protests exacerbated tensions between military and civilian politicians, leading to the infamous AI-5, which closed the national Congress on December 13, 1968, and initiated a regime grounded on a state of exception.[7] By Lula's April 1969 inauguration, radicalized sectors of the established Left and student movements had embraced a strategy of armed resistance that would be quickly and ruthlessly suppressed by an ever more authoritarian government. Thus, Lula began his union career under the shadow of intensified employer and government repression during Emílio Garrastazu Médici's hard-line presidency (1969–74). "When I entered the union," Lula explains, "I hadn't heard much about politics, although my brother Frei Chico followed it"; Lula believed government propaganda that its opponents were terrorists. Even when his brother explained that these purported terrorists trying to overthrow the military regime were "good people," Lula still "was afraid and half spooked."[8]

AI-5 increased the danger endured by union leaders, who routinely faced police surveillance, infiltration by informants, and even detention for leafleting on union business; in addition, they were regularly convoked by the police and other authorities to account for themselves and their union.[9] Hundreds of ABC rank-and-file activists who were leftists—or were suspected of being so—faced threats, firings, and police inquiries; several dozen experienced arrest and interrogation, a significant number were tortured, and three were killed between 1969 and 1971. This coercive environment directly affected the union: some of its activists were or had been associated with clandestine leftist groups, secretly or not so secretly. This activist core had an often-fraught relationship with elected union directors, the broader membership, and the overwhelming majority of the *categoria* who were not unionized.[10]

Unlike smaller unions in other industries, ABC's metalworkers' unions constituted a working-class public sphere existing under severe economic, political, and legal constraints without being entirely determined by them. The necessary public performance of compliance coexisted with collaboration and resistance opaque even to many directly involved in labor, industry, and government. This unionism reflected the breakdown of established political configurations on the left in both 1964 and 1968, a breakdown that would open space in the 1970s for a generation of younger workers like Lula as well as a broader array of influences, including left-moving sectors of the Catholic Church, ex-students, disillusioned ex-guerrillas, and chastened Communists.

The Trade Unionist as Winner at Life

A deeper understanding of Lula's relationship to Brazilian trade unionism has escaped analysts because they focus on concepts, processes, and abstractions—whether "class struggle," "shop floor organizing," or "authentic trade unionism"—and neglect the foibles, emotions, and logics of acting subjects with names, personalities, and ambitions. The Brazilian trade union was always far more than its bureaucratic institutional forms and should not be reduced to the vision of the lawyers who created it, the policemen who surveilled it, or the labor ministry bureaucrats and labor court judges who interacted with it. The trade unions, in their particularity, reflected the generation of workers who inhabited them. And there is no typical union experience because the union was necessarily pluralistic, articulating diverse needs, desires, and grievances, whether individually or collectively. The union was a dynamic space that shifted in relation to the political characteristics and conflicts of any given moment in the national, state, and local contest for control of the government. We need a richer understanding of the union as a social space of fully lived lives, of fun, humor, and pleasure as well as determination, suffering, and struggle. We need a differentiated, individualized understanding of the human agents who entered into and contributed to trade unionism as a legal and bureaucratic institution, constituted by a cluster of networks and with the potential to become a social movement.

Fiction possesses special strengths in depicting such nuances of working-class life—even when written with political objectives—because of its capacity to capture an unruly humanity that inevitably escapes a narrow, sterile rationalism. In *Beyond the Strike* (1978), Antônio Carlos Felix Nunes (1931–2017) does a particularly good job of bringing this capacity to bear on union activities following the 1964 coup. On March 31, the novel's protagonist, Vandelício Mascarenha, was a recently arrived twenty-three-year-old migrant from the small village of Bitolândia, four hundred kilometers from São Paulo. His experience of the coup testifies to the working class's general indifference, lamented by leftists, shared by Lula, and discussed at length in the preceding chapter. Vandelício's main thought when hearing the news on the radio was that "the factory might actually not be open tomorrow," which would give him time to fix up his rented shack, which he worried would collapse in the next rainstorm. While briefly considering the event's broader implications—"Who is going to be giving orders in the midst of this turmoil?"—he quickly returned to normal, just as the rest of his world seemed to do: "The factories opened their gates, nobody talked about stopping work, and there wasn't even an allusion to the events going on."[11]

The new military regime's 1964 union interventions were far broader than ever before in a country where trade union autonomy had never been respected. Beyond the 54 union leaders who immediately lost political rights, 761 trade unions were intervened nationwide; 301 of these were located in the southeast region, which contained the nation's most industrialized states (São Paulo, Rio de Janeiro, and Minas Gerais).[12] In this far more hostile political and industrial environment, unionists' careers were at risk as well as their families' sustenance. Most were forced into inactivity, whether temporarily or for good, but for those who stubbornly persisted, the central objective was clear: to prevent the trade union, the primary institution of the working class—with all its limitations—from falling into totally unscrupulous hands, as had happened in 1947 during the last wave of union interventions, after which the Santo André metalworkers' union (which covered all of ABC) was controlled for nine years by men such as the notorious police agent Milton Miguéis and the pistol-wielding interventor Rafael Martins, who worked with the police and factory security to persecute activists while robbing the union blind.[13] Informed by past experience, Marcos Andreotti emphasized the importance of mounting a union slate under such repressive conditions and how to do so: "We had to find individuals who had no links to the Left or who were not publicly known as leftists, or sometimes—given the difficulties of the period—we took someone who wasn't even a leftist but who was honest and hardworking [trabalhador]."[14]

Unable to prevent government intervention, working-class activists resorted to the cool nerves, determination (*garra*), and cunning that had always enabled their long-term survival. Amid systemic injustice, the only feasible strategy was to bypass (*contornar*) that which could not now be changed. Thus, activists would prepare a return to more aggressive action once the political atmosphere became more favorable, a goal to which their activism also contributed. The lived experience of such short-term strategy under the threat of repression is what Nunes traces in *Beyond the Strike*. The labor ministry's decision to regularize the intervened unions by holding elections immediately affects that novel's protagonist, Vandelício, who is invited to join a union slate.[15] For the very first time, he enthuses, "something serious was about to happen in his life," marked until then by hard work with "no substantial change in terms of salary or social position."[16]

Vandelício, an inactive union member, weighs the pros and cons of joining the slate. He wonders what had happened to the union leaders who had fled or were arrested and whether he might suffer the same fate. "Yet at the same time," he reflected, "you had to look at the positive side: the position could provide him with some advantage"—even if only the guarantee he couldn't be fired during his three years in office. But more exciting was the "possibility of making a career of it, of achieving something more for his family." As he tossed and turned that night, he felt the need—even as the man of the household—to hear what his wife thought. Reflecting patriarchal norms, her response was immediate: whatever you decide, my love.[17]

Vandelício barely knew the comrade who had invited him to join the slate, at the suggestion of the union's ousted president. He hadn't given his name but was clearly some sort of politician, because Vandelício had seen him engaged with workers at the factory gate in "long conversations, sometimes heated, in a language that was hard to understand"—at least for those like him "who had never been interested in political questions." According to Vandelício's boss, the man was an agitator whom workers should avoid. While Vandelício obeyed, he had overhead the man forewarning "knots of workers" about the military coup that would "liquidate the freedom of the unions." Such foresight convinced Vandelício that "these guys really know everything and anticipated in advance precisely how events turned out," although their call for a workers' general strike had failed miserably.[18]

When Vandelício asked why he had been chosen to run, the comrade explained that others were "politically identified, recorded as such [*fichado*] by the security organs, and thus they can't run for election." The man then affirmed his confidence that Vandelício would acquit himself well given his knowledge of union life acquired through regular attendance at assemblies—even though in fact Vandelício had attended only a few meetings, at others' insistence, and had barely paid attention or participated, simply voting with the rest to approve the union's proposal for a wage increase. Vandelício paused for a second to think about the guys who did speak with passion and even interrupted speakers; weren't they "the natural substitutes for those who fled or were politically identified?"[19]

After Vandelício agreed to stand for election, he walked into the factory ecstatic. With this show of "confidence from these strange comrades," "a great leap . . . was approaching" in his erstwhile unremarkable life: "He knew older workers, on the eve of retirement, whose whole life had been the insipid existence he had been living for the last four years. One without perspective, without flavor, without a future. You work and then you die as a worker, getting up early, a slave to your shift." Now he could escape "the destiny of his workmates" by becoming a union leader. At the first meeting regarding the election, another candidate, Jonas Anilson, known to everyone at the factory as Shorty, tried to interrupt the comrade's didactic presentation but was cut off. At the end, though, the comrade explained to Vandelício that since he wasn't part of the categoria, the candidates would have to handle the bureaucratic tasks at government offices themselves.[20]

Vandelício recognized this new world of union politics as "incompatible with the simplicity of his existence" to date, even at the level of speech: "The very vocabulary used . . . had nothing to do with the form of expression through which he and his fellow workers communicated . . . [but] had nonetheless begun to sink into his thinking . . . like a meddlesome person who makes his way into your house without being invited." These "exotic words" had some power, he found, "even though he didn't know what they each signified, as he began to pronounce them: 'Reivindicação' [demands or claims advanced], 'class consciousness,' 'arregimentacao operaria' [gathering workers together]." The contrast with his birthplace was clear: there "only a few words are in the people's heads: the words needed to fall in love, to talk about fishing, to buy *pinga* [slang for a type of cheap cane-derived alcoholic drink], rice, and beans."[21]

The union business would prove good for Vandelício, who would never have to return to the old days of poverty. Having won at life, he continued to return to Bitolândia to keep up with his buddies. Vandelício's friends, benefiting from his generosity, would engage in flattery (*puxa-saquismo*) of this new union leader and praise him in comparison to "Bororé, that arrogant black [*negro pernóstico*] who," because "he works in a factory, has a fixed salary, and has Sundays and holidays" off, thinks himself "important and forgets us." "Viva Vandelício the great!" they declared. "May God help and protect you so you can rise ever higher in this profession of . . . What it is it exactly?"[22]

The Specter of Opportunity

The author of Vandelício's adventures, the reporter Antônio Carlos Felix Nunes, had been contracted in 1971 by the São Bernardo metalworkers' union's president, Paulo Vidal, to serve as founding editor of the union's newspaper, *Tribuna Metalúrgica*, a position he held until the 1980 government intervention. When *Beyond the Strike* was republished in 1978, the union's current president, Lula—with whom Nunes had shared many a drink—blurbed the novel. The forty-seven-year-old Nunes had been immersed in unionism for twenty years, since his first job in the 1950s with *Notícias de Hoje*, the PCB's São Paulo daily.[23] In the early 1970s, this brilliant journalist invented the union's signature personality, João Ferrador, a "Zé Ninguém" (Joe Nobody) whose cheeky and humorous missives to the nation's illustrious authorities were published in *Tribuna Metalúrgica*. Given visual form during Lula's union leadership, the plucky metalworker would become the categoria's icon, with his characteristic saying, "Today I'm not okay" (Hoje, eu não tou bom).[24] A self-described independent Marxist-Leninist, Nunes used his only novel to address the specter of opportunity long haunting the Brazilian labor movement.[25] The denunciatory work's central concern was stated most clearly by Vandelício's seemingly naive friends in Bitolândia: What is a trade unionist exactly? And, Nunes would add, what should a trade unionist be?

The phantasm haunting unionists was the pelego, a redolent term that originated after Getúlio Vargas, from Rio Grande do Sul, came to power in a bloodless coup known as the Revolution of 1930. With their typical mordant wit, Rio de Janeiro residents (*cariocas*) used a term from the gaúcho world of cattle and cowboys to poke fun at the Vargas government's most striking innovation, in 1931: the country's first labor ministry, the "Ministry of Revolution," followed by laws to facilitate and fund unionization.[26] Referring originally to the sheepskin blanket placed between the horse and the saddle, *pelego* was now used by cariocas as a label for trade unionists—a new variety of government functionary in the nation's capital who, as Affonso Henriques described it, "elbowed each other in the corridors of the Ministry of Labor out of their ardent desire to flatter" officials in pursuit of personal favors.[27]

The goal behind a system of government-mandated and government-funded trade unions, according to a key policy maker in 1939, had been to foster a working-class elite that would defeat both the Communist threat and workers' "antiemployer spirit." Francisco José de Oliveira Vianna suggested that this new elite would, as responsible collaborators with the state, promote social peace by facilitating the advancement of capable workers who would rise to positions of prominence through education and acculturation.[28] As with the ideals of SENAI's Roberto Mange, a yawning chasm separated such utopian aspirations from the practical realities of government and industry, all the more so in a society permeated by patron-client ties that had only begun to become minimally democratic in electoral terms in 1945. A brilliant self-taught sociologist, Oliveira Vianna was unusual among labor policy makers because of his deep, principled commitment to a Catholic-inspired corporatist vision, authoritarian but reformist in bent. Most of the union system's architects, however, were far more cynical, and they were the ones who reached its most powerful positions and held them longest.[29] The lawyer José de Segadas Viana, a drafter of the 1943 Consolidation of Labor Laws (CLT), demonstrated this when he explained with brutal honesty in 1987 that the pelego could be said to "soften or deaden the heat of the demands of the masses and in this way permits the government to dominate" the workers. He described pelegos as professional brownnosers, men who "dive" for the carpet in the presence of powerful men and whose public displays of subservience gave pleasure to those they courted.[30]

Segadas Viana characterized all Brazilian labor leaders as pelegos, except the Communists. Tracking Vandelício's trajectory, Segadas Viana's pelego "becomes entirely subservient to power in order to obtain material advantages and above all positions, [thus] helping to fool the workers and dilute their will."[31] As a former labor minister, this profoundly conservative, anti-Communist lawyer-politician nonetheless defended the system's dependence on men driven solely by pursuit of personal advantage, especially appointments to well-paid positions in the labor judiciary.[32] There were some "good pelegos," he insisted, who helped combat Communism while serving the government as a means of contact with workers.[33] Yet in contrast to the pelego and the subversive, Segadas Viana also imagined a real union leader: a man "who has courage, [though] he may even not have culture"; who shows "selflessness, independence [*desprendimento*]"; and "has to have self-assurance [*desembaraço*], know how to speak."[34]

As a polemical term of abuse, *pelego* achieved wide currency in Brazil, although the points of reference vary widely—especially during the Populist Republic.

For industrialists, pelegos were trade unionists who made trouble, especially PTB-linked leaders during the decade when Goulart and his party controlled the Labor Ministry.[35] For anti-getulistas, pelegos were "a new parasitic class of false labor leaders" living in "the shadow of the Labor Ministry," easily manipulated tools of unscrupulous populist demagogues.[36] For the Communists, pelegos were "traitors of the working class, who live off the dirty business of helping the bosses maintain the workers in misery" in exchange for the money raised from the union tax.[37] Within the labor movement, those out of office invariably attacked those in union leadership as pelegos—until an electoral agreement was reached with one or more of them. Even Communists, distinguished as a separate group, were sometimes attacked as pelegos for the marriages of convenience they sometimes made with non-Communist labor leaders assumed to be pelegos.[38] And finally, Communists and leftists routinely used the term to stigmatize those who would not cooperate with their plans in union affairs.

All agreed, however, that *peleguismo* was most typical of the full-time union functionaries at the state federation and national confederation levels.[39] At least one step removed from local unions, these individuals were indirectly elected through a system in which weak, unrepresentative, or nonexistent unions (*sindicatos de carimbo*, or rubber-stamp unions) had a vote equal to that of stronger, larger unions with real mass memberships. This manipulated voting system had been a grievance of ABC's metalworkers' unions from the 1940s through Lula's heyday; the desire for more votes in the state federation was a factor in creating new unions in São Caetano and São Bernardo in 1957 and 1960 (represented before by an ABC-wide union based in Santo André). In 1978, Lula described these state and national entities, using a quintessentially Brazilian expression about useless sinecures, as a "cabide de emprego onde a pelegada toma conta" (a coathanger of jobs where the *pelegada* is in charge).[40]

The term *pelego* has been used so promiscuously and unreflectively as to be useless as an analytical construct.[41] Nonworkers, including radicalized students, were inclined to view all union leaders as useless, corrupt pelegos, an expression of class prejudice, social distance, and lack of knowledge. Labor activists and trade unionists were driven by other concerns, routinely criticizing pelegos—as Lula did in 1978—as an impediment to struggle, corrupted by power and molded to a system opposed to workers' interests. Pelegos, Lula went on, were those labor leaders who talk but go missing in action when the going gets tough.[42] He described his 1978 clash with Ary Campista, the infamous leader of the CNTI (Confederação Nacional dos Trabalhadores na Indústria, or National Confederation of Workers in Industry), who was ousted under Goulart but after 1964 rose to the pinnacle of the legal system as part of the Supreme

Labor Court. Campista, Lula declared, was an unprincipled *ministerialista* (a follower of the minister of labor) who would favor any government in power, whether left, right, or center.[43] As the greatest and longest-lasting Brazilian pelego, Campista was one of the few who never shied away from the term.[44] In his memoirs, an aspiring acolyte from Rio, Romulo Augustus Pereira de Souza, described Campista as a legendary, even folkloric, figure ("folclórico e lendário"). Like Segadas Viana, Campista reveled in his own clear-eyed cynicism, and assessing the aspirant's potential, he offered sage career advice: "With the authorities, you should purposefully make mistakes" when speaking because "they like that, it gives you more authenticity."[45]

Yet such criticisms miss why the pelego frightened those involved with trade unionism. The *Tribuna Metalúrgica* editor's portrayal of how a worker becomes a pelego in *Beyond the Strike* is all about what I would call the specter of opportunity that haunts the world of labor. Workers were told that the trade union would represent them and defend their interests. Yet the factory and living conditions that created the need for unions also generated, in individual workers, an intense desire to escape such conditions. One path of escape was becoming a full-time trade union leader, released from factory responsibilities and guarded against employer reprisals while in office. Every factory worker could understand the twenty-three-year-old Vandelício's excitement at joining a slate, at the very age at which Lula—who wasn't even a union member—was offered the same prospect.

Within large industrial categorias, trade unions were substantial institutions that owned real estate and were guaranteed annual government funding. Analogous to running a small business but with a higher public profile, union directorship provided status, visibility, prestige, and future possibilities, including political candidacies. Leaders got access to union cars and sometimes drivers; even more importantly, they gave orders rather than receiving them, including to individuals of a far higher status, such as the doctors, lawyers, and dentists hired to provide medical and legal assistance to members. Abundant opportunities existed for personal projection (public speaking, press coverage), and the daily routine—freed from time clocks—was more varied and infinitely less boring than factory life. Finally, the job offered cherished perks like traveling on union business, whether to lobby in the national capital or to attend trade union congresses elsewhere in Brazil or even abroad. Both Vandelício and Lula were bitten by the blue fly of ambition when contemplating union leadership. But ambition on whose behalf, and to what end? And are such motives even entirely clear to the individual in question?

A powerful incentive existed in São Paulo, an urban world teeming with opportunity, to become a full-time labor leader, especially within a large categoria. And such an aspiration need not assume the riskier path taken by Frei Chico, who became not only a rank-and-file union activist but also a shop floor organizer (unlike his brother). If the spur of personal ambition could lead some to union directorships, it could also impede the successful conduct of labor's struggle. The specter of the pelego, in other words, was linked to workers' doubts about their ability as a group to unite and act consequentially. Contemporary scholars repeatedly documented widespread cynicism, voiced in the oft-repeated observation that workers, lacking unity, were weak, easily bought, and easily fooled. For these scholars, evidence of upward mobility signaled betrayal rather than any symbolic or vicarious advancement for the group of which they were a part.

Individual ambition was thus a double-edged sword among those pouring into mid-twentieth-century São Paulo's factories. It led workers to suspect each other while suggesting that only rubes trusted so-called leaders who were really looking out only for themselves, whatever their claims to the contrary. From the workers' perspective, unions' inability to dependably resolve problems reinforced the idea that all trade unionists were useless pelegos and that searching for a real defender of workers was hopeless. Envy combined with suspicion of others' motives to produce the widespread conviction that union leaders were a bunch of crooks, in the words of the younger, antiunion Lula. An activist citing the absence of evidence for a given labor leader selling his members out did not necessarily convince: it was easy to imagine that such a person was simply sharper (*mais esperto*), waiting for the right moment to maximize his yield in pieces of silver.

Andreotti's observations about candidates' qualifications for union leadership are revealing. Reflecting on his career, he began with an anodyne statement that even potential union directors' party affiliations or political sympathies should be secondary to their devotion to "a single idea: to raise the worker's consciousness [*conscientizar*] and to organize him to fight for his rights."[46] Although a given candidate's popularity in his home factory could bring votes to the entire slate, Andreotti did not believe that popularity alone merited inclusion if the individual lacked idealism, integrity, and honesty. The metalworkers' leadership under interventor Rafael Martins had lacked any motivation or goal beyond the selfish, individualistic realities of capitalist society.[47] Yet the same Martins could dissimulate and even give a rousing speech, lend his name to mobilizations, and seemingly support the call for a strike while secretly sabotaging the effort.[48] Such duplicitous behavior—or the suspicion of it—profoundly damaged trade unionism's viability among rank-and-file workers, demoralizing even the most faithful union activists.

Andreotti always sharply distinguished between a real union leader, whether Communist or not, who fights "honestly for the collective interest of the workers," and one "fighting for his own individual interests," as the latter "will always attempt to deflect the workers from struggle so that he will be well looked on by the authorities." Those who wished "to honestly carry out the work of the union," by contrast, faced difficulties precisely because they were viewed "by the bosses and the government as dangerous elements, and thus repression is always used to remove them, in any way possible, from leadership of the union."[49] Maintaining standards of personal morality and probity mattered, Andreotti insisted, because even a well-meaning worker was easily tempted, "once he gained prominence, to distance himself from the working class." And individuals who were less than totally honest could easily manipulate their union salary and expense accounts to better themselves (even short of outright bribe taking). Workers had plenty of experience with men like Rafael Martins who "when they left or were ousted from the union were set for life."[50]

Even the appearance of self-serving action, Andreotti argued, damaged labor's cause. Shortly after his own 1958 election as president, some in the union began to maliciously suggest a connection between his new position and a refrigerator delivered to his home. Although he explained that it had been ordered on an installment plan prior to his election, Andreotti avoided further suspicion by deciding, against his wife's vigorous objections, not to buy a house as long as he held his union post—even though, given his skilled worker's salary, he could have easily built a home (common even among the region's unskilled workers). On another occasion, he turned down an apartment allotted to him at a local housing project built by the industrial workers' pension fund. Visiting it with his fellow union leader Philadelpho Braz, who lived there, he found his unit occupied; the family would be put on the street if he took it. The personal price that Andreotti and his wife paid would later in life be financially debilitating.[51]

Although he did not hold his fellow officers to this strict standard, Andreotti was determined to set an example from the outset of his presidency—he was reelected three times between 1958 and 1964, accompanied by a substantial increase in the total union electorate—and he sought to ensure that the union's expenses were rigidly controlled to prevent financial improprieties.[52] On the surface, Andreotti's emphasis on high moral standards might appear insignificant, obvious, or oddly prepolitical. In practical terms, however, he realized that any dishonesty confirmed the cynicism of workers in São Paulo, where Jânio Quadros's moralizing rhetoric (symbolized by the broom to sweep away corruption) had been enormously popular.[53] As described by Juarez Brandão Lopes, the workers' individualistic ethos of "what's in it for me"—which Andreotti preferred to call immediatism—coexisted uneasily with a weak but real sense of group solidarity.[54] Efforts to build collective action were all too easily disrupted by any suggestion that this "union business" was just another self-interested hustle. Hence the importance of honesty, dedication, and self-sacrifice, which even provided, Andreotti noted, a check on the anti-Communism propagated against him and his allies. In his words, the acceptance of Communist union leaders often had little to do with politics; Communists benefited, he recalled, from the widespread perception that they were more honest and thus less likely to make backroom deals (*conchavos*) with the bosses at the workers' expense.[55]

This cluster of class-specific meanings around the word *pelego*, which fueled Andreotti's deep concern for the moral probity of union leadership, can also be seen among the Rio textile workers interviewed in the 1970s by Vera Maria Candido Pereira. To her surprise, these workers rarely linked the pelego directly to the government, using the term to instead refer to "corrupt individuals who act only in terms of their personal interests (in general, access to ownership of real estate [*bens imóveis*] or sudden enrichment)," evidence to the workers that they were "bought by the bosses."[56] As Lula put it, the pelego-led union has a clear profile: it is the "Union of the Rubber Stamp, and the President is John Thief. In the morning he works in the market he owns while he goes to the labor court in the afternoon, where he's a lay judge. And he appears at the union at night from six to seven."[57] This, Lula insisted, was not a real trade unionist.

Like Diogenes of Sinope carrying his lamp through the streets, the world of Brazilian trade unionism had searched for an honest man, a "real trade unionist." For a cynic like Segadas Viana, this was impossible given the baseness of Brazil's subaltern raw material. But the quest for the ideal had long characterized the labor movement, especially in the big cities' large-scale industries. How did one create an ethic of honesty—while recognizing human imperfections—that could be relied on as an accepted norm for behavior? With that in hand, honest trade union leaders believed, the workers would be unbeatable, although all were aware that their local unions were far from attaining such trust from those they sought to represent.

Young, Bem de Vida, and Ready for Life's Business

Political stratagem brought into union leadership both the fictional Vandelício Mascarenha, raised in São Paulo's interior, and his Pernambuco-born counterpart Luiz Inácio da Silva. Neither was a union activist, much less a shop floor organizer; they were approached because they were unlikely to be barred by those who confused trade unionism with political subversion. Both were twenty-three years old and declaredly antipolitical. Lula, unlike Vandelício, was not even a union member and was brought to his first meeting in August 1968 by Frei Chico, as part of recruiting him for the incumbent union directors' election slate.[58]

Both young men fit within the working-class world described, as we saw earlier, by Armando Corrêa da Silva in 1967. Arrived at nineteen from rural Bitolândia, Vandelício escaped the *pobres do campo* by quickly landing a factory job, although only as a minimum-wage unskilled worker. Lula, by contrast, was already a success story, thoroughly socialized into big-city industrial and working-class life.[59] Three years after joining the city's machinists through SENAI, Lula landed a coveted job at Indústrias Villares with a much higher salary than his three earlier jobs.[60] Lula typified the labor market trajectory of SENAI graduates, who usually ended up in "large modern firms where wages and salaries" were above average and where logistical support existed to indulge the graduates' "taste for technical perfection."[61]

Avoiding reification, Corrêa da Silva argued that the working class proper was best understood as "laboring folk 'on the rise.'" Hired in large and medium-size factories, this group experienced greater employment stability and received higher, more dependably paid wages, along with regular salary adjustments for inflation. Additionally, their employers could better afford to respect the labor laws while providing greater access to medical and other assistance. These workers rose from precarious small factories "toward the better, more modern, and technically equipped enterprises," on the road to an "occupational specialization that could in time lead to a more skilled" industrial profession such as those achieved by Frei Chico and Lula.[62]

The sociocultural traits of these "modern workers" (a phrase that Corrêa da Silva himself places in quotes) were carefully distinguished from those characterizing "the more pauperized segments" of the city's popular classes. This skilled minority was decisively shaped by the prevailing "ideology of economic development and industrialization," and their "situation of relative security" allowed for "a more advanced level of consciousness." In some cases, Corrêa da Silva reported, they went "beyond the plain of purely trade union claims making" to achieve the politicized consciousness we have seen with Frei Chico. Yet Lula's "backwardness" in trade union and political terms suggests that even the skilled minority of the working class proper should be seen as a complex weave of different outlooks and awareness levels. In discussing education, Corrêa da Silva crucially highlighted how apprenticeship, whether formal or informal, produced youngsters, including the "good boys" of SENAI like Lula, who popularized the ideology of industrialization within their families and beyond. Apprenticeships could transmit not only "production techniques but [also] trade union consciousness."[63]

When Lula agreed to run for union office in late 1968, he had just completed twenty months at Indústria Villares, the break he had been looking for after six years as an apprentice, a probationary machinist (meio-oficial), and then a full machinist in São Paulo and São Bernardo, with a five-month spell of unemployment during the 1965 recession. Inaugurated as an alternate to the union's fiscal council in 1969, Lula was among the two-thirds of the twenty-four elected officials who remained on the job (*ligado a produção*) at the factory. Only in 1972 would he become a *director efetivo*, one of seven full-time directors who earned their regular salary while off the job. In total, Lula spent eleven years training to become or working as a machinist, followed by eight years—between ages twenty-seven and thirty-five—during which he shed the blue overalls known as the *macacão* (literally, "big monkey"), the mandatory uniform of industrial workers at the time.[64] Lula was elected union president in 1975 and reelected in 1978, both times without facing opposition slates.

Unlike the unskilled Vandelício, Lula's material success was already guaranteed before he ran for union office. In 1979 as union president, Lula boasted that machinists were the working class's maharajas (*marajás*) in the late 1960s and early 1970s.[65] Well into the twenty-first century, he would continue to celebrate these working-class princes even as their craft was increasingly undermined by computer-operated machine tools after 1980.[66] Before Villares, he explained, he was supporting his mother and two sisters, paying the rent, and working nights for a 25 percent differential. Then, after five months of unemployment, he landed a "job in a large factory [Villares] earning ten minimum wages because a machinist was an important profession in those days, like that of a *fresador* or a *mandrilador*." During the economic boom, he explained, he logged forty hours a month of overtime.[67]

As a privileged worker in an especially privileged industry, Lula had reason for boastfulness as someone who was indeed well-off—*bem de vida* (good of life), as they say in Portuguese. Of course, *bem de vida* was a flexible discursive metric in the conceptual vernacular of São Paulo's urban working people. Discussing his first Communion in Garanhuns, Lula's brother Vavá remembers borrowing sandals from a neighbor who was bem de vida. "He had possessions [*posses*], shoes, he had everything. We didn't have shoes. Not even slippers."[68] After arriving in Santos, Lula recalls, the family received help from godmother Jucelinha, the mother of a brother-in-law. Asked to define *bem de vida,* he said that his godmother's family was "considered rich. They had a house, the father worked as a foreman [*contramestre*] on a ship, so they were bem de vida."[69]

Enjoying a well-paid, professionally fulfilling job, Lula was flush with success and displayed neither anger toward bosses nor the aggrieved but sullen submissiveness of Vandelício. The problems Lula did confront were not perceived as deriving from exploitative structures of power, what Frei Chico had learned to call capitalism. "Those who learned in [SENAI] are always more prideful," one skilled textile worker told Luiz Pereira's team, although the man suggested they had no reason to feel superior; they did the same work as the rest.[70]

After a three-month stint at the Massari factory in São Paulo, Frei Chico in 1967 joined Indústrias Villares despite a company policy barring the hiring of relatives; the connection between the brothers was missed because of their different last names. He was laid off after six months but was subsequently hired at Carraço, a two-hundred-worker São Bernardo firm that made wagons. Coming from São Paulo with an established union reputation, Frei Chico was the type of worker who impressed Vandelício with the confidence he showed in speaking up, interrupting and participating passionately in union meetings.[71] The São Bernardo union was swept up in the general turbulence of 1967–68, which included sharpening clashes between New Left groups, often of Catholic origin, and a union leadership headed by Afonso Monteiro da Cruz, a less radical Catholic activist backed by the PCB, with which Frei Chico was aligned.

Frei Chico continued his heavy-handed proselytism toward his brother, who remained, in Frei Chico's words, as "antiunion and truly ignorant" as ever.[72] Frei Chico would harass him about attending union events, Lula complained, when he just wanted to play soccer or do something else. As he said then, "Am I going to go there to fill sausage [*encher linguica*; i.e., waste my time]? I'm staying home because it's better to watch a soap opera [*novela*]."[73] Joining would require pay deductions for dues, in addition to the involuntary union tax deducted automatically from the wages of all working within a given categoria (a source of complaint for those workers aware of it). Unskilled workers like Vandelício, especially if married, often joined the union for its medical and dental assistance. The skilled who joined were more like Frei Chico, who saw the union as a means of advancing group interests vis-à-vis employers and the state. For a well-off bachelor like Lula, the union held little interest, although once in 1967 he did stop by to inquire about the new Fundo de Garantia por Tempo de Serviço (FGTS, Guarantee Fund for Length of Service) promulgated by the government on September 13, 1966.

The FGTS, which made layoffs easier, replaced a more rigid job tenure system long complained about by employers.[74] Current workers had to choose whether to remain under the old system or to opt for the new system; the FGTS was vocally criticized by the unions, and employer pressure on individual workers was intense. His visit regarding the FGTS allowed Lula to meet Afonso Monteiro da Cruz, who left Lula furious (*puto de vida*) because he had paid more attention to a dog—a kind of mascot living in the headquarters that had been saved by the union's leaders—than to Lula.[75]

Nonmembers often stopped by union headquarters when they had a problem or inquiry. By law, the union had to provide nonmembers with legal assistance but could refuse other services, help, or advice, as did pelego-run unions seeking to discourage participation. Honest trade union leaders, by contrast, ignored the distinction, with an eye toward recruiting new members and increasing union influence. As Andreotti explained, the worker who came by, motivated by an immediate personal interest, always viewed the encounter as a test; he expected, if not victory, at least a serious engagement. If handled badly, the interaction confirmed the widespread belief that unions were useless and that their leaders were merely timeservers avoiding honest work.[76]

The Trade Union: A Complicated Thing, an Adventure

Manual workers were poorly represented in elected office in midcentury São Paulo, both before and after 1964. But there was a space in which energetic workers could make their mark politically: a trade union system that enlisted a substantial minority of factory workers, perhaps a fifth in the case of metalworkers. The electoral contests held every three years allowed those most closely involved to learn the instruments, techniques, and machinations of political life. As was true in electoral politics, the advantage always lay with those already in power—the "situation" (*situação*), as it is known in Brazil—and the union's goal in "mounting a slate" was to fill twenty-four slots in the three categories defined by the labor legislation: directors (of which there were seven full-time *efetivos* and seven alternates), members of the fiscal council (three of each), and representatives to the state-level union federation (two of each). Ideally, the final slate would have representatives from the main factories (i.e., those with the most voting members) and the key groups among the union's activists. The most visible—and overstudied—groups are those linked to various leftist organizations, who generated print material on behalf of those they supported—unlike their opponents, who operated orally and often beat these leftist groups without so much recourse to print.

The process for registering included deciding which individuals to invite (*uma indicação*) and in what order. As each deal closed, the slate's architects carefully balanced rewards for loyalty with neutralizing disappointment felt by those who fell to the wayside or were ignored (significant turnover among union officials occurred at each term's end). Ideally, one got an early lead in nailing down a broad-based slate, thus discouraging potential opponents. It was a process of political calculation, Machiavellian maneuvering, and seduction that began six to eight months ahead of the election. "Composing a slate" (*compor a chapa*) was always accompanied by speculation, murky imaginings, and self-interested storytelling, usually not captured in print. Despite all the literature on ABC's metalworkers, only the many recorded oral interviews—ten accounts by Lula and six from Frei Chico—allow us to understand part of the backstory for the February 1969 election, in which Lula first appeared on paper as a potential union officer.[77]

In 2000, Lula told an audience of ABC trade unionists that when invited to join the slate in the latter half of 1968, "I didn't want to because I was afraid. I had many doubts and went to talk with my fiancée." Lourdes played a more forceful role in Lula's decision than Vandelício's wife did in the novel. Lula has repeatedly hashed out her concerns, which illustrate the challenges of trade union involvement for working-class families. At the tiny weaving shop where Lourdes worked—an intimate setting, Lula emphasizes, where the owners, weavers, and helpers were in constant conversation—all agreed that becoming a trade union leader was a "complicated thing" and that Lula could "be persecuted and even end up in trouble with the police."[78]

This warning came to Lourdes from both the shop owners and "the older weavers," who "told her what the union movement in 1962," the year of strikes for the thirteenth salary, "was about and what happened after the coup," leaving her with a clear understanding that it was "dangerous to be a union leader." "Those who go into the union," she was told, "were fired and would never again get a job," living "the rest of their lives marginalized." The most evocative point, however, was that Lula risked "dirtying his working papers" (*sujar minha carteira profisional*). Instituted in the 1930s, the *carteira do trabalho* officially recorded one's job or skill, workplace, and length of employment. Far more than a work-related identification card, it served working people as a certificate of citizenship to be brandished with would-be employers and also the police and other government officials with whom they entered into contact.[79]

Lula freely admits that these concerns were well grounded and that he himself had doubts from the moment he was invited. As Lula put it, "I didn't want to accept. I wasn't prepared. I didn't know anything about this [union] thing"—a judgment his brother confirmed, noting that Lula "didn't even really know what a union was."[80] It would take much effort to get Lula to agree to run, and the initial courtship was conducted, unsurprisingly, by someone besides his frustrated older brother. However, Frei Chico did suggest Lula's name, and how that came about sheds useful light on the internal dynamics—formal and informal—of the São Bernardo metalworkers' union where Frei Chico had quickly gained recognition for his dedicated participation in the union's campaigns. During a year of increasingly raucous conflict, Frei Chico and those linked, directly or indirectly, to the PCB clashed with the increasingly radicalized opposition led by the AP (represented in the union directorate by José Barbosa Monteiro), with which the PCB had been tentatively aligned a few years earlier.[81]

Frei Chico was invited to run for office to both reward his dedication and cement support within the union among the surviving political arrangements (*esquemas políticas*) of the local metalworkers still linked to the PCB.

However, Frei Chico surprised them by turning down the opportunity. No doubt pleased to be asked, he faced a political difficulty, given that his factory, Carraço, was small and already had an alternate in the current union leadership, José Ferreira de Sousa (known as Zé Ferreira). The political and electoral logic was clear: a factory of 200 workers could not occupy two slots on a slate of twenty-four for an election in which 6,466 workers would vote. Although we lack any additional backstory, the invitation to Frei Chico would have meant that Zé Ferreira would have to be put off the slate. Frei Chico claims he was swayed by prospect of the older worker losing his job if deprived of the legal protection provided by his union position.[82] Whether from intraplant comity, friendship, or political miscalculation, Frei Chico felt he could not accept the offer; instead, he got fired from his firm in 1969.

Turned down by Frei Chico, the union's leaders asked him to name someone whom he trusted (*de confiança*), a way of recognizing his contribution to the union while giving him and those with whom he was linked a voice in the slate's composition. Frei Chico suggested his brother Lula, even though the latter was thoroughly antiunion. The leadership immediately grasped the compelling electoral logic set out by Frei Chico. Villares was perhaps as much as five times larger than Carraço yet had only a handful of union members. Bringing the unknown Lula into leadership thus might help build union strength in an important factory, making his nomination a risk worth taking. At a lunch the union's three top leaders took charge of convincing the young machinist: outgoing president Afonso Monteiro da Cruz, Secretary-General Mário Ladeia (leaving to run for city council), and First Secretary Paulo Vidal Neto (president on the "Green Slate" the existing leadership was assembling). The full-time union directors were only five to ten years older than Lula and were also skilled workers. With five years of union activism under their belt, they no doubt did a good job pitching the proposal. Though not at the meeting, Frei Chico speculated that "the line of argument must have been that standard pitch [*conversa de sempre*] when you want to bring someone new into the union. A new business, an adventure, you'll be able to do a lot for your companheiros."[83]

Lula became a union director not as "the result of a conscious decision," unlike those who fought to be named; in his own words, "my fight was to not enter." As Frei Chico put it, Lula came against his will (*na marra*), but in the end the leadership's pitch stuck (*a conversa colou*)—at the expense of Lourdes's misgivings. In Lula's rendering of their back-and-forth, his future wife voiced immediatist common sense against a risk she thought unwise for the man in her life. "It's not that she was conservative," Lula observed at one point. But lack of political formation—much like Lula at the time—meant that spouses and partners were often the first obstacle facing men trying to decide whether to become or continue as union leaders, an occupation inevitably gendered male.[84] At the same time, it is easy to understand her focus on the immediate issue of guaranteeing the security of a married life only just beginning, with children on the horizon.

In Lula's accounts, Lourdes forcefully expressed a clear position but believed at first that the whole thing would fade away. Once the registration date got closer, however, she got more actively concerned and threatened to call off or postpone their marriage. Lula has offered three distinct accounts of why she failed to dissuade him. The least credible is that he "convinced Lourdes of the importance of being a union director." The second is somewhat more believable: it was too late to change his mind. And the third, which sounds like a sound bite from a heated quarrel, shows Lula directly deploying his own leverage: "I'm going to do it and if you don't want me to, then let's not marry. I already gave them my word."[85]

Why did Lula proceed in the face of credible risk and loving concern? And why would loyalty to older men he barely knew prevail? It is easy to see how Lula could be impressed by these men, whose worldliness he no doubt admired. But the truth, as Lula noted frankly in his 2000 comments in ABC, was that he had already been bitten by the blue fly of ambition. Those he met in late 1968 were serious, young skilled workers quite different from his impractical older brother, with his hectoring self-righteousness. These union leaders were working in an occupation based on persuasion; they spoke to Lula not of self-sacrifice but of seizing an opportunity to broaden his world beyond Indústrias Villares. In subsequent conversations, Lula did share his own fears, expressed through Lourdes's words, but by then he was already disposed to take at face value the men's implausible assurances that being a union leader did not pose "any problem at all."[86] In truth, Lula was aware on some level, like Vandelício, that there were risks involved—manageable ones, he hoped. But what really grabbed both twenty-three-year-olds was the prospect of an intriguing opportunity within reach. The personal calculus for saying yes to joining the union slate was further strengthened by the fact that, as an alternate, Lula didn't even need to break with his established routine at Indústrias Villares; he could try out this "union business," a new adventure, even as he knew full well that it was "uma coisa complicada" (a complicated thing).

6 THE IMMEDIATISM OF EVERYDAY LIFE

In the 1960s "I didn't want to know anything at all about politics," Lula told fellow trade unionists in 2000. What interested him then was *Diário da Noite*'s soccer column, particularly coverage of the Corinthians, a famous São Paulo soccer team that he had followed since its championship win in 1954. "I just didn't have a head for anything else" at the time, he admitted.[1] His passion for soccer began as a kid, when he played all day. He was a good player, he insists, or at least better than many others, and served as inside right (*meia-direita*) on neighborhood teams such as Náutico, organized in 1962, which took its name and colors from a Pernambuco team idolized by Lula's older brother Vavá.[2] As a working machinist, he played during his short lunch break and had his union debut, twelve days after his 1969 swearing in, during a May Day game between union directors and staff. The game—which ended in a tie—pitted union "bachelors," including Lula (his marriage to Lourdes was scheduled for May 25), against their "married" counterparts, including the new union president, Paulo Vidal.[3]

Even the most single-minded São Paulo labor activists recognized that male workers devoted more thought and energy to soccer than to fighting low wages or mistreatment by employers. This was what led Marcos Andreotti, a fan but not a fanatic, to insist that labor leaders keep up with the latest soccer news. When "you arrive at the factory gate" to talk with workers, he observed, you often find yourself "in the middle of a crowd discussing soccer." In those circumstances, he continued, you can't say "'let's stop with this and talk union' because they'll leave instead of listening. So it's important to know how to enter into the discussion while gradually moving the conversation toward the terrain of [union] organization and why it's necessary."[4] As Lula has repeatedly emphasized, only after joining the union did he attain even "a little bit of class consciousness"; it would take several more years before he acquired "a certain taste" for politics. His "political apprenticeship," Lula insists, derived entirely from his union involvement, which coincides with Andreotti's assessment "that the union was the master transmission belt [*correia mestre*] in the development and politicization of the worker."[5]

Lula finally yielded to his brother's importuning in 1968–69, although the first union assemblies he attended were wracked by disputes reflecting the po-

Lula (front row, third from left) with the São Bernardo union soccer team in 1969. (Courtesy DGABC [Ademir Médici])

litical maelstrom dividing union activists, officeholders, and would-be leaders. In his recollections, Lula highlights his impressions of the raucous "internal disputes and divergences" that he witnessed as a bystander but did not yet understand.[6] At his first union meeting in mid-1968, the opposition from the floor was strong, "at least in terms of yelling." The issue under debate was minor—choosing representatives to a social welfare congress in the state's interior—but prompted a big fight, with his brother at the center. As Lula recalled, "Guys were standing up and saying—'that one is a *pelego,* he shouldn't go,'" and Frei Chico would interrupt to disagree. While being "reviled as a pelego," his brother inveighed against the opposition by calling them irresponsible crazies (*porra-loucas*).[7]

When describing these meetings, Lula never focuses on the substantive disagreements or underlying political alignments behind the sharp clashes. Rather, he describes how it felt to venture into an unfamiliar setting where the only person he knew was his brother. At the time, the conflicts seemed unnecessary and "a damned confusion." Yet Lula also makes clear that those very fights (*brigas*) helped spark his interest and left him feeling enthusiastic. He was unfazed by the threats of physical confrontation (*sair pro pau*) and reports with equanimity that some of the opposition waited after a later meeting to beat his brother up, angrier with Frei Chico than with the actual union directors whom they opposed. Lula described his decision thus: "I was so contented that I said to myself, 'this is the way I've got to go.'"[8]

It would be convenient to see the unformed Lula as responding vicariously to the rebellious spirit of 1968, a year of student rebellion, labor protest, and antimilitary defiance by civilian politicians accompanied by the first seeds of armed struggle by some of the military's leftist opponents. Yet in his retellings Lula omits 1968's dramatic high points, even though they explain the clashes that he witnessed. Although all trade unionists opposed the government's policies, intraunion conflict was driven by the year's powerful political divergences and polarizing events. In particular, May 1 saw the disruption of a legal rally in downtown São Paulo organized by a broad labor coalition that included ABC's three metalworkers' unions. In the largest mobilization since 1964, thousands of workers, labor activists, and union leaders turned out—Frei Chico attended, but not Lula—along with politicians, students, and leftist clergy such as ABC's "Red" bishop, Dom Jorge Marcos de Oliveira. The rally was interrupted straightaway by organized protesters who stoned the governor and seized and burned the stage while the humiliated politicians and "pelegos" scurried for cover. This was followed—on July 16–18—by a dramatic three-day strike in the industrial município of Osasco, in the metropolitan region's northeast, led by young union leaders linked to the May Day tumult; quickly stifled, the brief factory occupation ended with memorable images of workers surrendering to the army and police.

In recounting his first impressions of union life, Lula failed to mention the closing of the national Congress and the promulgation of AI-5 on December 13, 1968. As president in 2006, Lula explained that AI-5 had a "strong, direct, or personal impact" on those like his brother who already had political and union militancy, but "there was no big shock" for workers like himself.[9] If Lula was so distant from politics, what excited the twenty-three-year-old in what he witnessed at his first union assemblies, with their displays of pugnacity?

Breaking the story into stages, this chapter highlights elements of Lula's background and personality while using his experience between the ages of eighteen and twenty-three to explore the complexities of individual consciousness. In doing so, I distinguish between socialization, personal dispositions, and truths so well established that they stand as simple "facts" of working-class life. The chapter also offers a rich account of what the young machinist had to contend with in a world of deeply entrenched hierarchies of worth and despotic authority, whether in schools, factories, or public life. Tracing the sources of an inchoate discontent, I explain how this nonactivist worker first glimpsed perceived injustice. Disaffection with the government's economic policies had grown sufficiently by late 1967 to embolden trade unionists to publicly articulate their grievances as part of the crescendo of societal resistance ended by AI-5. The chapter ends with the complicated labor and leftist politics of 1968, a moment marked by caustic rivalries and disappointed hopes, in order to understand why workers like Lula were untouched by leftist labor leaders and activists' diagnosis of workers' problems as derived from a system of exploitation (capitalism) backed by an antilabor dictatorship with powerful foreign patrons.

Sociability, Personality, and Consciousness

Lula never directly explains what he found attractive about the public confrontations witnessed at his first union meetings. Yet when read carefully, his storytelling suggests the answer lies in the rough-and-tumble sociability of working-class manhood in São Paulo. As Lula has explained, the boys growing up in Vila Carioca lived in the streets and returned to their overcrowded homes only to sleep: "Until I was eighteen or nineteen years of age, my schedule as a youngster was to play soccer. We played all day and then at night there would be twenty or thirty boys at the corner talking about the game."[10] Other favorite diversions included "*mamona* wars," in which they used slingshots to hit one another with hard castor beans (*mamonas*). As Lula described these battles, "It was real war with guys ending up hurt. I would climb a tree with my slingshot and attack the others. If your adversary discovered you in the tree, six or seven more would come with their slingshots to hit you. And then you were lost and all you could do was cover your face and let them because if you asked them to stop, you were defeated." He also enthusiastically recalls "teams on each side of a field throwing [stones] and guys getting their heads hurt." Even soccer games often ended in physical confrontation, especially when neighborhoods played each other: "Within ten minutes a fight would ensue [*saia pau*]." This contrasted with Lula's rural birthplace of Garanhuns, where, as he noted, there weren't a lot of neighbors.[11]

Boisterous male posturing at union meetings fit easily into a world where verbal prowess and physical fighting were recognized sources of adventure, gossip, and potential triumph. Frei Chico—the family rebel, with his aggressive, macho style—and Lula—the good boy, with his less assertive personality—were differently suited for projecting themselves in such ways. Both men tell a revealing story about an incident in Santos when Lula was eight and his brother was eleven. The older boy used to go to the docks to peddle peanuts, oranges, and the tapioca and *biju* (a type of cookie) made by his mother. He brought Lula along a few times but was disappointed because he "was too timid [*tímido*] and wouldn't yell"; Frei Chico reports giving him a rap on the head (*cascudo*) in response. Lula confirms that his brother was surer of himself and yelled more loudly in pitching his wares, though he remembers the encouraging rap on the head as a "thrashing" (*esfregão*), which didn't work. Whatever the incident's level of physicality, the two brothers also differed in their retrospective evaluations of the experience. Lula concluded that street peddling would not be his life path, while his brother judged it useful for his personal development: "You have to learn how to deal with the public. Lula didn't talk at all. He was very timid."[12]

Those within and outside the Silva family confirm the contrast between Frei Chico's brassy audacity and Lula's more reserved, shy personality. Lula's insecurity helps explain his poor performance as an office boy in his second full-time job, at age fourteen. Among his tasks at the Aramazéns Gerais Columbia on Avenida Presidente Wilson was answering the phone and taking and delivering messages. This made him so nervous, Lula says, that he could never get the messages right. Luckily, he landed the SENAI slot six months later. In discussing his formative years, Lula has quoted his mother's observation that he "wasn't 'one of those who stood out the most,'" with which he agreed: "I was someone who was very, very closed [*trancada*]." This aspect of Lula's personality will likely surprise those who only know the emphatic strike leader, the insurgent party chief, or the crusading politician. Yet his comments to Paraná also suggest why he was favorably impressed by his first union assemblies. While describing himself as an inhibited child, Lula noted that the soccer field was the one place where he acted differently: "That was where I yelled, where I fought, and where I cursed."[13]

Lula was intrigued by the opportunity for personal growth offered by the union in late 1968. Unlike combative workers like Frei Chico, Lula faced little risk because elected alternates were legally protected from firing during their three years in office. Yet it would be wrong to think that his decision was devoid of broader meaning and deeper roots. As Marcos Andreotti repeatedly emphasized, a worker's decision to attend a meeting or join the union indicated greater openness to struggle, even if only in contrast to those who did not. The organizer had to get to know the individual personally and assess where he was coming from, what lay behind his decision, and where it might lead. Concerned with moving workers toward action, Andreotti approached consciousness as an empirical question—one that started with individuals—with full awareness of the diversity of outlooks among workers and their varying degrees of internal self-awareness and coherence. In this sense, individual consciousness is lodged within specific circumstances at a given time and place. When approached as a snapshot, it reflects an ever-changing mix of individual dispositions, perceptions, and relationships as they played out within the worlds of the factory, the community, and the home. For Andreotti, the organizer had to forge a relationship—a succession of encounters and snapshots—that would establish the union as a meaningful social field for struggle.

Thus consciousness for Andreotti was fluid rather than fixed, only knowable through a worker's deeds or speech acts, which provided vital evidence for understanding action taken or not taken. Yet an individual's words were neither a transparent expression of what lay within nor a stand-in for the class as a whole, errors initially made in the 1960s by some paulista social scientists and student revolutionaries. Andreotti cited workers who joined the union for mundane reasons, like needing a doctor, and whose stated views might be disconnected from, or even antipathetic to, the union as a form of class representation or struggle. Once they became members, however, they entered into "contact with unionized workers, union directors, and those who are tight with the union [i.e., its activists]," which opened the possibility that they would gain a broader "awareness of the benefits that the union" could bring. Such patient pedagogy enabled future steps that the individual might not have been able to understand or embrace at the outset.[14]

Attending a meeting or joining the union was thus the first step in a larger process of altering an individual's consciousness over time (conscientização). While Lula's decision to join the union in 1968 was not politically motivated, its political significance should not be overlooked, given that only a fifth of metalworkers belonged to the São Bernardo union that legally represented the categoria. Moreover, running for office—amid the sustained opposition of his fiancée—demanded a level of personal commitment beyond mere membership. From Andreotti's perspective, Lula's consciousness in late 1968 clearly differed from that of the mass of metalworkers, who continued to be as apolitical and vocally antiunion as Lula had been. So what underlying dynamics led to his shift in outlook?

"Facts of Life": Expectations and Etiquette

To fully understand Lula's decision to join the union, we must systematically examine his accounts of his early working life to chart how his consciousness evolved across the 1960s. To do this, we must understand that what are experienced as the facts of life do not explain workers' decisions. As an example, we might turn to a moment of pain and fear in Lula's life, when in 1964 he lost his pinky finger on the night shift at Metalúrgica Independência. Although symbolically important, this was not the turning point, then or later, leading to his unionization. Although Brazil was a world champion in industrial accidents, Lula has frankly acknowledged the role of worker carelessness in his own accident: "The screw on a press broke. I made a screw and when I went to put it in, the companheiro who operated the press was dozing and got distracted. He let go of the lever and the press closed and I lost my finger." Lula thus frames it as a matter of bad luck and avoids searing criticism of the firm, even though he waited several hours to be taken to the hospital when the plant's owner arrived at 6 A.M. Even Lula's comment about the attending doctor is understated: "Arriving at the hospital, the doctor looked at my finger and cut off the rest." (Lula has speculated that his finger could have been saved.) Lula admits to feeling ashamed, mutilated, and scarred for a number of months, even years, afterward, although such accidents were "very common among metalworkers and many were left without a finger or part of a finger. Workplace safety was almost nonexistent in that period, and guys hurt themselves a lot."[15]

Lula's brothers likewise viewed industrial accidents matter-of-factly, part of the way things were rather than a source of impassioned indignation. When interviewed by Paraná in 1993, Vavá still could not fully open or close one of his hands because of scarring from a postaccident operation around 1960. As he explained, "I went to tidy up the machine but the girl didn't see me and turned it on." The fingers of the Silvas' oldest brother, Zé Cuia, a truck mechanic, had also been "crushed in a machine," which caused his arm to swell up when it was dunked in gas or alcohol. Yet the family's champion in workplace injuries was Jaime, the second oldest brother, who used mechanized saws and shaping and planing machines. Jaime lost (wholly or partially) three fingers in multiple accidents—likely indirectly related to his chronic alcoholism—and finally stopped working after almost losing a hand. In another incident, Vavá recalls, Jaime was almost killed by the kickback from a piece of wood going through a planing machine. For the city's workingmen the lamentable state of industrial health and safety was much like the weather: there was not much one could do about it. Such injuries usually resulted in a small indemnification; Lula used his to buy land.[16]

Yet Lula's stories do point to a latent, easily missed discontent that emerged after his SENAI graduation. As an apprentice, Lula had embraced the values of professionalism, personal responsibility, self-worth, and a dedication to the common goal of industrial development and progress. He had learned that machinists were indispensable and that his certified skills gave him legitimate leverage on the job market. In his first two jobs, Lula asked for a raise and quit when the factory owners refused to entertain his request. His search for a better employer soon led him to Fris Moldu Car, but when the foreman there unilaterally assigned weekend overtime without consultation, a common practice, Lula defied him and lost his job. Yet such stories—even when Lula told them at the most radical phase of his life—were not deployed to condemn bosses or foremen as a whole; Lula recognizes, even humorously at times, that his own decisions were at the root of his losing or leaving these jobs.

Yet these undercurrents of personal discontent did not become openly articulated grievance or give rise to a strong feeling of injustice in the 1960s.[17] Looked at analytically, Lula began his career as an overconfident eighteen-year-old who believed that dialogue would yield common ground with employers. Yet once the newly minted meio-oficial entered the labor market, his expectations were dashed by cheap, arbitrary bosses who, unlike SENAI teachers, refused to treat subordinates as collaborators. Even the owners of the laughably small enterprises that first employed Lula had a hauteur associated with an unquestionable power to command. While the unskilled were too vulnerable to "talk back," the newly hired Lula was more aggressively naive than most of his fellow workers, even the skilled ones. From age eighteen to twenty, he truly believed in his right to discuss the bosses' decisions. As a result, he violated authoritarian societal expectations of crisp obedience by subordinates and active deference to those above. As the São Bernardo union's attorney explained in 1976, a policy of "yes sir, yes sir" is the "genteel" way to survive in a country where, as a self-described pelego bluntly put it in his memoirs, "those who can, command and those who are sensible obey" (manda quem pode e obedece quem tem juízo).[18]

The authoritarianism of São Paulo's factory foremen, managers, and owners dictated a strategy by subordinates that we might call de-selfing. Tamping down their feelings and muffling their desires was characteristic of all dimensions of their behavior vis-à-vis superordinates, whether in domestic service, the government, or the expanding world of factory labor. For those "at the lower levels of Brazilian society," a scholar of SENAI noted in 1979, "dealing with persons invested with authority" was "often tense and difficult."[19] There were individual exceptions, like Frei Chico, prepared to talk back to those actively disrespecting them. This small but vitally important minority was described as "combative" by the Communist organizer Andreotti and as "bad" workers by foremen and bosses, even when they knew the individual in question was untainted by Red subversion. Yet it is easy to overlook the very different type of personal assertiveness displayed by Lula during his first few years as a machinist. Emboldened by his SENAI education, Lula began his career wishing to make his feelings, complaints, and needs clear to employers who were as dismissive as the teachers studied by Pereira, for whom "'to protest' [reclamar] or 'lodge a complaint' [*dar queixa*]" was to break established norms, an "impertinence" by cheeky individuals (*atrevidos*) who didn't know their place.[20]

As a form of defeatism, the strategy of withdrawal adopted by most members of the popular classes aimed to minimize interaction with superiors by suppressing one's feelings. It is easy to see why this protective posture, adopted with primary schoolteachers, would be even more vital when the "authorities" in question controlled a family's economic well-being. Employers and foremen, after all, were like teachers in viewing attempts at dialogue as evincing ingratitude. This might spark shop floor retaliations ranging from verbal humiliation to being fined, given bad assignments, or even fired, the most feared outcome. The power to hire and fire provided a much more compelling incentive to conformity than the prospect that one of their children might not graduate from primary school, for which working-class parents could always console themselves with the knowledge that not everyone had "a head for school" and that they would gain, in the short run, another small income stream as their school-leaving children took menial jobs.[21]

How "Politics" Touches Daily Life

Lula in the early 1960s had everything to learn in what workers called the "University of Life."[22] In this regard, his trajectory illustrates the challenges facing workers in this industrializing metropolis as it emerged from an unprecedented boom. Yet Lula's storytelling about this period is less likely to involve authoritarian bosses, who were a given, than inadequate pay for the work done, as judged in relation to the prices paid when shopping. Lula's priorities were typical of the immediatism of paulista factory workers, whose basic problem, in their view, began and ended with wages. Grumbling about salaries had led to Lula's departure from the Marte Screw Company and Metalúrgica Independência, and it also figured in his discontent with Fris Moldu Car, a factory of one hundred where he worked for eleven months in 1964–65. The factory, he complained, "was too far away, we earned little, and the money wasn't enough" to even cover bus fare. He sometimes had to walk for well over an hour from the Ipiranga factory to his new home on the border of São Paulo and São Caetano. There were times when he would stop in an empty field to "cry, cursing the day I'd been born."[23]

Yet after foolishness cost Lula his job at Fris Moldu Car, the naive twenty-year-old faced an unexpected crisis: five to six months without a salary. He was stuck "in a jam [*pendura*] so large and so disastrous" because of the "very heavy" unemployment accompanying the 1965–66 national economic recession. "It was a very difficult situation with much misery," Lula recalls, as he searched desperately for a job while scrambling to cover expenses for a household in Ponte Preta that included two sisters and an unemployed brother. As Lula has noted about his early privations, he and his family sometimes had "nothing to eat"—clarifying that rice and beans alone (*arroz e feijão puro*) did not count as a real meal without at least a scrap of beef or chicken on the plate. Lula's other recollections about hunger (*fome*) are equally insightful. Those who have never experienced it, he observed, don't understand that going hungry does not necessarily mean having nothing to eat; one might have something, but not "what you have the desire" to eat. Hunger's relative nature was illustrated by a story about his early life in Vila Carioca, when they rarely ate meat—sometimes a roll of mortadella lifted by a brother—and survived mostly on "bean soup with macaroni." Dona Lindu's kids complained vocally about not having rice to mix with their "bean soup," Lula says, but the same meal was judged "marvelous" by newly arrived relatives from Pernambuco, given "the misery from which they were coming."[24]

A compelling concreteness also marks Lula's account of his fruitless job hunting in 1965: He "would leave home at 6 A.M. to catch the opening of factories at 8 A.M., walking along the Via Anchieta highway on foot" because he lacked bus fare. Nothing, he adds, was more humiliating than "return[ing] in the afternoon, your working papers [carteira] all sweaty, without having landed a job." Sometimes he walked ten kilometers, his "carteira in a deplorable state," to wait for hours at a factory gate for a man to finally glance at the carteira and inform him that "lamentably we have no openings, lamentably the opening was filled, lamentably we don't need that." He felt even more demolished (*arrasada*) when the man took his carteira inside and returned to say they had nothing available.[25]

Lula's extended unemployment revealed something infinitely worse than being poorly paid or badly treated. Being jobless spoiled everything, including one's psychological and emotional well-being. Interviewed in the 1990s, a lifelong São Bernardo metalworker, Adilson, explained that having a job was important because it allowed you "to organize your life. It's your point of reference"; providing "for your own survival gives you satisfaction and credibility. 'I am working, I'm developing something.'"[26] But when unemployed, as an ABC metalworker wrote in 1972, one "finds himself totally at odds with his surroundings. He feels demoralized in relation to his own family (he, the man of the house, unable to do anything), in relation to his neighbors (not working, half bum [*vagabundo*]), as well as in relation to society (a pariah, a useless person)."[27]

A man without a job, Lula explains, is "without money, without cigarettes, without being able to drink a little beer"; "the first thing you lose," he goes on, "is your friends," because "everyone thinks you're a great guy [*cara legal*]" when you've got the job, but without one you're a hindrance, an obstacle (*um estorvo*), and an embarrassment. Joblessness also undermines one's dignity: when Lula ran into his employed friend Osmar at the Mercedes-Benz factory gate, he jealously watched him smoke a cigarette, thinking only about how much he wanted Osmar to go in so that he could smoke his thrown-away cigarette butt. By the time Osmar went in, the butt had burned out. The wait for a job ended four hours later, again in disappointment. Getting ready to leave, Lula faced an added indignity: after taking a shoe off because his foot was aching, he could not get it back on because of swelling.[28]

Unemployment, Adilson observed, inevitably leads to a loss of "confidence in yourself. You think the whole world is accusing you of being a bum [vagabundo] . . . even when people aren't saying that." And if they ask if you had any luck, he continued, it feels like "they are calling you to account [*cobrando*]. So life without a job is super complicated because you are not [socially] recognized."[29] Lula cites an especially traumatic episode from this period, a day that "really marked me very, very much," when, returning from job hunting, Frei Chico called him "a bum" (vagabundo). "Suffering like an unlucky wretch [*desgraçado*]," Lula recalls how he "hit him in the face with my shoe; there was really no work, what was I going to do?"[30] Yet it might well be, as Adilson suggests, that Frei Chico's teasing was misinterpreted given the powerfully stigmatizing nature of the word *vagabundo* as the negation of male self-worth and respectability. This was well illustrated in a 1978 story by Roniwalter Jatobá, a Bahian migrant metalworker turned writer, about a newly arrived migrant who was ten days behind on the rent for his room in Brás. When kicking him out, the boardinghouse owner humiliated him by yelling, "Get out of here you bum [vagabundo]"; to restore his honor, the man returns later, newly employed, to pay the rent owed.[31]

Lula's half year of unemployment dramatically upended illusions that were shared by tens of thousands of other first-generation factory workers, whether skilled or unskilled.[32] Yet the impact of unemployment and how it was processed at the level of individual consciousness varied widely. On the one hand, the recession revealed a situation of economic vulnerability that didn't spare individuals because of their occupation, skill level, or willingness to work reliably and obediently. Whether skilled or unskilled, all manual workers faced a new insecurity during the recession as coveted industrial jobs became harder to land, but the psychological impact was felt most powerfully by those with credible expectations of future prosperity. The situation was especially galling for those with certified skills because they did not judge themselves against the lower end of the manual factory labor hierarchy. In a revealing offhand observation, Lula talked about peons (*peões*) like himself—referring to all manual workers—who had to hit the streets to find work, as opposed to those with a "real profession," like salaried employees, who could look "for a job in the newspaper or by telephone." "I sometimes would stop in the middle of the road and cry," Lula recalls, while reflecting on how much worse it would have been if he had been married.[33] Moreover, workers without an up-to-date carteira do trabalho lacked "evidence of good conduct with the police," noted an ABC metalworker in 1972, and were liable to harassment as "marginals, vagabundos."[34]

When examined in terms of Lula's life course, the years after 1965 were a turning point, when he abandoned the foolhardy behavior of his first years on the job market. Although never explicitly articulated, obvious lessons were learned by Lula after quitting two jobs, getting himself fired from a third, and then suffering sustained unemployment. A more mature Lula would maneuver more cautiously around those in power, whether in the factory or, after 1969, the trade union. After experiencing the rough edges of the industrial world, Lula had to abandon the feeling of indispensability held as a newly trained machinist whose SENAI degree had gone to his head. Luckily, his nightmare would come to an end in January 1966, when he was hired as a machinist at Indústrias Villares in São Bernardo, although it would take a while to recover from his dire economic situation.[35]

It is hardly surprising that Lula's behavior began to be shaped by a more conservative calculus as married life loomed on the horizon. Yet not every individual experiences a process of maturation linked to life cycles in the same way or at the same age. Frei Chico continued to hector his brother about exploitation, capitalism, the bosses, and the state, but Lula did not share his quixotic rebelliousness—premised on the possibility, not the reality, of collective action. Yet unlike many others, even after getting his life back on track Lula retained a vague feeling that something was amiss, unfair, or perhaps even wrong with the industrial world he had embraced with such enthusiasm only a few years earlier. When Villares carried out a large layoff that didn't affect him, Lula perceived it as unfair; the government's 1967 decision to end job tenure (estabilidade), a privilege for which he was not yet eligible, would lead to his first trip to the São Bernardo union headquarters, although the encounter, as we have seen, left a negative impression.[36] In the end, it was precisely this inchoate discontent that prevented Lula from dismissing out of hand the invitation to run for union office. Without quite knowing why or how, he already perceived the trade union as something that addressed an "out of sorts" feeling (*mal estar*).

7 YEARS OF LIVING DANGEROUSLY

Lula's experience in the mid-1960s shows how national political developments could directly affect even the most apolitical of workers. His travails in 1965–66 stemmed directly from the new military government's ambitious modernization of Brazil's macroeconomic policies, governmental institutions, and financial markets. The Government Program of Economic Action, introduced in November 1964, aimed to put the nation's economic house in order by checking inflation and ending the balance of payment disequilibrium. The new economic team believed that inflation was "caused by an excess of demand," Regis Bonelli observes, and that "the inflationary process was [best] attacked by harsh monetary and fiscal measures."[1] This led to a powerful economic downswing, with a contraction of demand that, while dampening inflation, brought mass layoffs, factory closures, bankruptcies, and the buying up of Brazilian manufacturing firms by foreign competitors.[2] Many workers in São Paulo's factory districts were left scrambling in an ever more competitive labor market in a city that was still drawing tens of thousands of new migrants.

Yet the negative impact of the government's policies reached well beyond the unemployed. Those still employed in São Paulo's factories and workshops endured an unprecedented salary squeeze (*arrocho salarial*) "through the utilization of an ingenious formula of salary adjustments that included a (frequently underestimated) estimate of future inflation."[3] As a top Labor Ministry official later explained to US labor attachés in a confidential May 1968 briefing, the squeeze was meant to avoid "compensat[ing] workers for past losses in purchasing power due to inflation," the practice of weak elected governments before the coup.[4] Rather than restoring a previous real wage level quickly corroded by inflation, centralized national wage setting would calculate increases in light of the "anticipated declining inflation rate" for the following period plus a productivity factor to be determined by the government's policy makers.[5] Between its restrictive fiscal policies and the "salary squeeze," by 1966 the new military regime had brought annual inflation down to 20 percent, its average in the late 1950s. This achievement did speak to a key worker grievance before the 1964 coup, when surging inflation and the high cost of living (*carestia*) militated against the appeals for mass mobilization by leftists and labor activists, enamored as they were with the political opportunities they saw in the short-lived Goulart government.

While Jango's 1964 ouster may have barely registered at a mass level, it is equally clear that grumblings grew over the following three years among São Paulo's workers. The reason was obvious, as a Labor Ministry official explained: "The [wage] formula, in practice, resulted in . . . sizable downward trends in real wage rates to 1967"—albeit with some variation by industrial sectors—due mainly to a "decline in the real minimum wage [*salário mínimo*]" by over 20 percent from 1964 to 1967. The government's regional minimum wage system affected "around half of Brazilian urban workers," whose earnings were "based principally on minimum wage adjustments."[6] This even affected metalworkers in big firms, whose higher salaries were nevertheless calculated in reference to the salário mínimo.

By 1968, US observers had identified an "accumulation of resentment and frustration," which led the US consul in São Paulo to believe that the military government was unwittingly fostering the Left's return. But the labor and student agitation of that tumultuous year would not be most visibly associated with the Communists, whose influence fell precipitously due to internal divisions as much as persecution.[7] During Goulart's presidency, the illegal PCB enjoyed an unusual level of public toleration; a generation of Communist labor leaders rose to local, regional, and even national prominence. While several Communists elected in São Paulo in 1962 were barred from taking office, some were seated in other states (under other party labels), and there was good reason to believe that the party's request for legal recognition would be granted.

This de facto legality was a drastic turnaround for a party that in 1947 was outlawed under a constitution it had helped draft in 1946, two years after its presidential candidate had won 10 percent of the national vote. Optimism on the left had grown since 1961, when divisions within the army combined with regional and popular resistance prevented military commanders from vetoing Goulart's accession to the presidency; two years later, a national referendum overwhelmingly restored his full presidential powers.[8] The PCB's new prominence was on display during Goulart's speech to a massive rally in Rio on March 13, 1964, with Osvaldo Pacheco, a Communist labor leader from Santos, standing at the president's side in support of his proposed Reformas de Base.

Despite right-wing attacks, Communist leaders were now living and operating openly, which necessarily shaped their political outlook and psychology. After spending twenty-one of the previous thirty years either in prison (1935–45) or in absolute clandestinity (1947–58), the PCB's longtime secretary-general and former senator, Luis Carlos Prestes, could now speak publicly, be interviewed on TV, and meet and negotiate with other politicians, which explains why he accepted the Goulart camp's reassurances that the president had deep military support.[9] Prestes's abrupt return to the underground was an embarrassing and sudden move, forcing him to leave Rio and preventing him from retrieving from his São Paulo home notebooks (*cadernetas*) with details on party affairs, including names. These eighteen cadernetas served as the centerpiece for the new military government's "show trial" indicting seventy-four national and state PCB leaders, most already clandestine. Prestes received the harshest sentence (fourteen years in prison) in 1966 having already had the honor, on April 9, 1964, of being one of the first three individuals—along with ex-presidents Goulart and Quadros—to lose their political rights for ten years under Institutional Act #1 (AI-1). The following day, one hundred more lost their rights, including forty deputies.[10]

Leftist illusions about the Brazilian revolution's inexorability were widespread before the coup, but the PCB's misjudgments were more consequential because it was the largest leftist party and a point of reference for the Left as a whole. The coup also shook Brazilian Communists' confidence in their leaders at a moment when the Cuban Revolution seemed to demonstrate an alternative path to power. Since Khrushchev's revelations about Stalin in 1956, the PCB had formally renounced its insurrectional past, abandoned the "dictatorship of the proletariat," and begun speaking of a "peaceful road to socialism," a "revisionist" stance that led to the creation of the tiny but orthodox PCdoB (Communist Party of Brazil) in 1962.[11] The PCB's post-1958 strategy was premised on acting openly within the established system, which involved papering over internal differences in emphasis. The resulting compromises were subject to diverse interpretations, whether "rightist" or "leftist," in Communist jargon. The PCB alternated between pushing President Goulart to the left or defending him against opponents, even if this meant him moderating his policies. The disastrous coup brought demands for accountability for these strategic decisions from within the ranks of even the PCB's Central Committee. The most prominent "leftist" critic on the Central Committee was the charismatic fifty-two-year-old Bahian mulatto Carlos Marighella (1911–69), a former deputy (1945–47) who gained admirers for his combativeness after being shot while resisting arrest in 1965.[12]

Thus a mix of festering disagreements, radical disappointments, and unresolved frustrations—often focused personally on Prestes—shattered the party that had anchored the Left, for good or bad, since the 1930s.[13] ABC was not exempt from the general disarray. When twenty local Communists met in Santo André on June 30, 1965, "severe criticisms" were lodged against the national leadership for placing "too much confidence in the *dispositivo militar* [military backing] of the João Goulart government and underestimating the forces of reaction."[14] Yet the party in ABC was divided, with the region's top (though clandestine) Communist labor leader, Andreotti, siding with Prestes's policy of organized retreat. In contrast, his longtime political counterpart Rolando Fratti (1912–91), a worker in local PCB leadership since 1945, was an early ally of Marighella, whose faction won leadership of the São Paulo PCB at a clandestine meeting in June 1966.[15] For Marighella, this was the first step in a plan for armed resistance; he stepped down from the national leadership in December 1966 and formally resigned—in a letter written from Havana—the following August from the party he had joined in the 1930s as a radical student.[16] In São Bernardo, the dissident Communists included four young machinists recruited into the PCB and the union by Orisson Saraiva between 1961 and 1963. Ranging in age from eighteen to twenty-six, the four Carvalho brothers were energetic offspring of Methodist migrants from Minas Gerais who broke with the PCB in 1965 to make their own path to armed struggle—initially through the PCdoB. All but one would be killed by 1973.[17]

While the mainstream PCB, although much diminished, did retain influence in key unions, it was no longer the only leftist group active in a labor movement characterized by a swirl of competing leftist forces. The PCB's primary post-coup goal was to prevent unions from being hijacked by direct agents of the bosses and the police (*agentes patronais e policialescos*), a problem that bedeviled them after the union interventions following the PCB's outlawing in 1947. The remaining PCB-aligned activists sought to draw together "honest" elements, even if this meant supporting non-Communist slates that included former opponents. Thus the metalworkers' slates elected in 1965 to replace Communist leaders like Andreotti and Saraiva were drawn from the pre-1964 union opposition linked to the "Worker Bishop," Dom Jorge Marcos de Oliveira. A reformist outlier within the postwar Brazilian church, this bishop, appointed in 1954 to the newly created diocese of Santo André, had championed certain strikes in the late 1950s while working to foster internal opposition within local Communist-led trade unions. During the reformist euphoria of the Goulart years, the Worker Bishop's highly visible activism attracted a remarkable constellation of Brazilian and foreign-born priests, including worker-priests, who rallied to Goulart's Reformas de Base and proceeded to play a highly visible political role in the late 1960s, especially in Santo André and Mauá.[18]

Once in office, the post-1965 leaders of ABC's metalworkers found themselves in an uncomfortable situation. Whatever their political inclinations, they quickly saw through government rhetoric about a "new laborism" that would end *peleguismo* and the Left's instrumentalization of unions. As the recession cut employment, these new leaders watched the government undermine established rights and understandings by revoking job tenure (estabilidade) and making work stoppages nearly impossible through a new strike law. In addition to such "atavistic" antiunionism, the government's wage squeeze laid bare an "aversion" to the reivindicações (demands or claims advanced) of workers, shared by emboldened employers.[19] Unlike most of their constituents, including Lula, those directly involved with the labor movement understood that national politics was central to advancing working-class and union interests. Yet there was no clarity on what was to be done, since illegal leftist parties, opposition politicians, and the left-leaning minority of São Paulo's intellectualized middle class all lacked a clear understanding of the new military regime, its goals, and its trajectory. It quickly became clear, however, that the "revolution," as the military called its coup, was not another temporary intervention, as such coups had been as in the past. No one would have guessed that the regime of exception would last a remarkable twenty-one years.

To contend with these challenges, the post-1964 Left drew on impoverished, highly politicized analytical and rhetorical tools focused primarily on meta-notions of "strategy," epochal thinking, and a form of stylized "class" analysis. For many leftists, the government's economic policies, especially during the 1965–66 recession, proved that a "government of national treason" had betrayed the project of national development and thus condemned Brazil to economic stagnation.[20] This could easily be framed as a "selling out" to imperialism, as heightened nationalist rhetoric had become common currency in national politics since Vargas. Or perhaps national development was impossible under capitalism, a belief held by the Cubans and an emerging "revolutionary" Left. This would negate Marxist-Leninist theory that spoke of "revolutionary" change as unfolding in stages in developing or semicolonial countries, each with its own alignment of classes at any given stage. This approach allowed Communists political flexibility by according a progressive role to a vaguely defined "national bourgeoisie," whether in curbing "feudal" agrarian relations or contesting "imperialist" domination. In 1964, the up-and-coming USP sociologist Fernando Henrique Cardoso made a big splash academically by forcefully attacking this idea. His critique paralleled the thinking of São Paulo's most famous Marxist intellectual, Caio Prado Júnior (1907–90), a former PCB deputy of an older generation whose 1966 book *The Brazilian Revolution* vigorously attacked his former party on several fronts.[21]

The political terrain was even murkier for the coup's opponents, because the overwhelming majority of civilian politicians, including most governors, had supported the ouster of President Goulart in violation of the 1946 constitution. The coup's first military president, Humberto de Alencar Castelo Branco, was "elected" by Congress on April 11, 1964, with 361 out of 475 votes.[22] Additionally, the military regime canceled the scheduled 1965 presidential elections and in 1966 replaced the multiparty political system with a duopoly consisting of a pro-government National Renewal Alliance (ARENA) party and an ostensible opposition party (*oposição consentida*), known as the Brazilian Democratic Movement (MDB). Marking the Populist Republic's definitive end, the key political debate on the left through 1968 was between those defending electoral participation—despite the dictatorship allowing elections only for legislative, not executive, positions—and those advocating an electoral boycott.

Now persecuted as dangerously "revolutionary," the PCB sought to strengthen oppositional sectors in the new MDB, an artificial party (a "bag of cats," in Brazilian parlance) without an oppositional vocation. The PCB refused armed struggle, for which other leftists, including dissident Communists, attacked the party as foolishly or traitorously "reformist." Yet the PCB's posture was hardly surprising, especially in São Paulo, where the party was a recognized and respected, if minor, political actor before 1964. Indeed, the PCB benefited from a network of ties, influence, sympathy, and even membership among a minority of well-placed middle-class professionals, cultural figures, USP professors, politicians, and trade unionists. Although most MDB officeholders were inconsistent opponents of the government, the resolutely oppositional minority shared the PCB's goal of building the broadest possible coalition, with untrustworthy allies if necessary, to restore electoral democracy and enable future progress.

By late 1967, the military's hegemonic pretensions alienated more and more civilian political elites, and former presidents Juscelino Kubitschek and Jango Goulart joined their former bête noire Carlos Lacerda to demand direct elections. Some hoped that the three men's September 25, 1967, joint statement would bridge the historic divide between getulistas and anti-getulistas in defense of democracy.[23] Supported by the PCB, the Frente Amplio was announced in São Caetano at a March 23, 1968, rally with Lacerda, attended by 1,800 to 3,500 people, "mostly working class," according to US consular observers. DOPS noted license plates and attending politicians, radio personalities, religious figures like Bishop Dom Jorge, and trade union leaders like Santo André metalworkers' union president Benedito Marcílio and Pedro Daniel de Souza, the Communist ex-president of the São Caetano Civil Construction Union. Placards included protests against the arrocho and the government's "new starvation-level minimum wage" as well as demands that "not a single Brazilian soldier [be sent] to Vietnam"; one even averred that "the Amazon is ours!"[24] The Frente Amplio never progressed beyond an ephemeral alignment of personalities too easily dismissed as powered by personal pique on the part of Lacerda, who proved incapable of galvanizing the Right on behalf of democracy. The Frente Amplio was outlawed on April 5, 1968, without significant protest, and after AI-5 Lacerda was arrested and lost his political rights alongside Prestes, Goulart, Quadros, and Kubitschek.[25]

The Rebels of '68: Courageous but Divided

Yet 1968 was also powerfully shaped by the radicalizing impulses of a surging student movement. A highly visible group of middle- and even upper-class students, young but lettered, boldly condemned the hypocrisy of well-placed fathers complicit with a military regime that violated the values for which they claimed to stand.[26] The prevailing spirit of indignation fed a youthful disdain for the ineffective top-down maneuvering of opposition leaders, trade unionists, and the Partidão (the big party), as the PCB was sarcastically known. Like Marighella, the students deemed the common front with Lacerda, an architect of the 1964 coup, futile opportunism. They equally disdained the MDB, which they saw as a phony opposition party, and the elections that granted the dictatorship a democratic facade: for them, the only principled response was to call for a null vote in protest.

Although simplistic, the youthful insurgents' rhetoric could be compelling. For instance, a September 28, 1966, protest led by Father Rubens Chasseraux (1939–2019) in Vila Palmares derided "an unjust world of dominant minorities and false progress" and the "hunger, misery, persecutions, beatings, the lack of freedom, the betrayals, lies and attempts to fool [*tapeações*]" under the dictatorship. As workers and voters, the protesters wanted to elect "representatives of the common people [*povo*]" rather than have representatives chosen for them. "If today we have no such candidates," their statement went on, "it is because neither ARENA nor the MDB represents the povo," both parties being "impositions of a regime" deserving "total repudiation at the ballot box."[27]

Like Chasseraux, ABC's most vocal leftists were *igreijeros* (church people), as their secular opponents in the metalworkers' unions dubbed them.[28] Whether lay or clergy, most Catholic activists were linked, directly or indirectly, to Ação Popular (AP), founded in 1962 by Catholic University Youth, whose leaders comprised the elected leadership of the National Union of Students (UNE) between 1963 and 1968.[29] By the time it formally committed to Maoism in 1968, the AP had with its increasing radicalism and sectarian behavior alienated even trade unionists with Catholic roots such as Afonso Monteiro da Cruz and Maurício Soares, that year the São Bernardo metalworkers' union's president and lawyer, respectively.[30] Yet the AP had won the fierce loyalty of a number of priests and several dozen activist workers, including José Nancy, vice president of the Santo André metalworkers' union; José Barbosa Monteiro, a member of the São Bernardo union *diretoria* (directorate) in 1965–67; the high school–

educated metalworker Aparecido de Faria, author of a 1972 account of the AP's labor activities in ABC; and Raimundo Eduardo da Silva, a young black worker from Mauá who in 1971 was dragged from a hospital bed, taken into custody, tortured, and died.[31]

The working-class Left's pluralization, with its generational overtones, went well beyond ABC. In Osasco, similarly insurgent youngsters—close to the student movement but not linked to the AP—won unquestioned control of that industrial suburb's metalworkers' union in 1967 via a slate that included Catholic worker-activists supported by priests. The short, much-mythologized strike and factory occupation they led on July 16–18, 1968, produced iconic images of labor conflict especially dear to the new "revolutionary" Left; in the aftermath of the strike's defeat, several of the union's leaders, including President José Ibrahim and the black metalworker José Campos Barreto (Zequinho), joined the Vanguardia Popular Revolucionária (VPR); the latter died in 1971 in rural Bahia at the side of the legendary military rebel Carlos Lamarca.

This spirit of defiance and youthful rebelliousness generated the heated confrontations Lula witnessed when entering union life in 1968–69. Opposition labor activists in ABC's metalworkers' unions, whether Communist, Catholic, or independent, had found common ground in 1965–66 but diverged sharply by the second half of 1967, at the moment when the leadership of São Paulo's various unions formed a loose coalition known as the Interunion Movement against the Squeeze (Movimento Intersindical Anti-arrocho, MIA), whose successive public events were marked by sharp clashes between a more radical opposition minority and mainstream union leaders supported by the PCB's remnants.[32] The Santo Andre metalworkers' headquarters, for example, hosted a MIA rally on December 11, 1967, that was disrupted straightaway when those presiding tried to take back the microphone from a leftist speaker, a defeated candidate in a recent union election, who denounced the dictatorship and the MIA's union sponsors as tools of the bosses. The tumult involving his 150 supporters did not escalate to physical blows (*pancadaria*), DOPS noted, but the meeting of 1,000 had shrunk to 200 by the time the protesters left to march in the city streets.[33]

The symbolic centerpiece of this fratricidal clash within labor and the Left was the 1968 May Day rally, held in the Praça da Sé in downtown São Paulo. Organized by the city's trade unions, the rally against the arrocho, attended by at least 5,000, was legally authorized by the state's indirectly elected civilian governor, Roberto Costa de Abreu Sodré, a savvy politician from the União Democrática Nacional (before the coup abolished parties) eyeing future electoral gain (he refused in 1968 to ban student marches across the board). Although called by the MIA unions, the demonstration rallied regime opponents: students, politicians, intellectuals, religious figures like Bishop Dom Jorge, elected union leaders like Paulo Vidal, labor activists like Frei Chico, and even some rank-and-file workers. In an unpleasant surprise for the organizers, the crowd also included several hundred from a variety of new "revolutionary" vanguards: the State Union of Students, Marighella's Agrupamento Revolucionário (soon renamed the Ação Libertadora Nacional), the AP folks from ABC, and Osasco's young Turks. Their plan was to shatter a murky "opposition" unity that they saw as too conciliatory. Even twenty years later, the legendary 1968 São Paulo student leader José Dirceu, a Marighella supporter, was blunt: Governor Abreu Sodré's presence at the rally "was a provocation, a farce," so they "wanted to give a thrashing to that crew [the rally organizers and the PCB] in order to teach them to never do something like that again: we couldn't passively accept that agents of the dictatorship could appear posing as politicians linked to popular causes."[34]

Before the rally got going, students and young workers stoned the governor, seized and burned the stage, and raised a poster of Che Guevara, followed by denunciatory speeches and a small march. The São Paulo metalworkers' newspaper reported on the action negatively: "The boos increased second by second and, when a group in attendance tried to impede the continuation of that protest, the strangest objects began to be thrown . . . [and] a stone hit the head of Mr. Abreu Sodré. What followed were scenes of vandalism, carried out by agitators, infiltrated among the demonstrators, . . . [which included] student leaders, intellectual agitators, leftists, and opponents of the current diretorias of the respective unions."[35] This diverges drastically from how the AP covered the May Day action in its clandestine journal *Libertação*. The rally—which they claimed was attended by 6,000, "the majority workers" but also "many students"—revealed the "unity of various sectors" when they together "expelled the dictatorship" from the Praça da Sé, although admitting that not everyone in the crowd rejected the MIA's little May Day party (*festinha*). The article celebrated the flight of Governor Abreu Sodré, "a banker representing employers and imperialism" who had come "to fool the people," and of his allied "pelegos and politicians serving a dictatorship of national betrayal," replaced onstage by "real workers" who grasped, unlike the PCB revisionists, that ending the arrocho required defeating the US imperialists who, at that very moment, were under siege in Vietnam and by the "Black people" of the United States.[36]

Among the "real workers" offering full-throated denunciations of the more moderate MIA forces was São Bernardo's José Barbosa Monteiro, a black migrant from Ceará affiliated with the AP whose church-related union activism began in 1963.[37] Interviewed from exile in the mid-1970s, Barbosa explained that the forces disrupting the rally aimed to unmask the farce being mounted by the government, union leaders, and the PCB. He predicted the consequences of such action: "I could foresee that I would be persecuted by the police after appearing and participating in the rally. And so it happened." Thus he went underground and fled to foreign lands. In the rally's aftermath, the police brought in dozens from ABC for interrogation, laymen as well as clergymen, including Father Chasseraux. Some were tried in military courts.[38]

As ABC's two big metalworkers' unions saw it, the disruption undermined their hard work, having mobilized fifteen busloads of workers from Santo André and nine from São Bernardo. Santo Andre's union president Benedito Marcílio was especially furious, he told reporters, because some of the agitators "had come with us on the bus" and had "not only taken advantage of the ride but cursed [*xingam*] us" as pelegos.[39] The MIA's official manifesto of amends (*desagravo*) after the rally expressed its "most profound revolt at these lamentable events." Signed by all the MIA's major unions except Osasco, the desagravo reiterated the legitimacy of the coalition's demands, the peaceful methods through which they pursued them, and the maturity, serenity, and sense of responsibility that characterized workers and their leaders when dealing with the authorities. As for the long-planned rally's disruption, they condemned "the riotous action [baderna] and disorder promoted by irresponsible persons disguised as students who did not, and never will, have the support of workers who, despite being unjustly treated under a rigid economic-financial orientation, would not—even then—reach [such a] level of personal desperation, political sectarianism, and total irresponsibility."[40]

May Day in the Praça da Sé pitted the *porra-loucos* (crazies) against the pelegos, in the terms of mutual abuse recalled by Lula from the clashes he witnessed in 1968–69. Yet the square's young working-class rebels also included many like Frei Chico—who would join the PCB in 1971—and most who witnessed the clash were unaffiliated or unaligned. Impressions of what happened naturally varied. As an attending Santo André metalworker told a USP researcher in 1970–71, "There were a lot of students at the gathering and they took charge. Workers started it but then students took over. The revolt was carried out by some workers and students opposed to the unions."[41] An adolescent worker from Mauá reacted differently, as he explained in a 2012 interview. "I was sixteen but I had always been like this, a little idealistic and rebellious," when someone invited him to the Praça da Sé demonstration. As he recalls, "When I arrived there I saw so many police, bombs, arrests, dogs, horses. You know?! The policemen with swords hitting people. It was crazy." Much as Lula reacted to his first boisterous union meetings, this worker from Mauá "was impressed with all that"; he joined the AP and carried out routine clandestine tasks until the organization was liquidated in Mauá in 1971.[42]

If the PCB erred in failing to anticipate the coup, the "revolutionary" Left—including Marighella—were equally misguided in their conviction that in 1968 "the revolution was there, within reach of our hands."[43] Those who argued for armed resistance did so because, as Marighella articulated it early on, the dictatorship could "*only* be overturned by the violence of the masses given that *no* more space exists for political action."[44] By February 1968, his Agrupamento Revolucionário's founding manifesto flatly declared that "*nothing* can be done against the dictatorship without firepower and armed men."[45] AP militants followed similarly pessimistic assessments when they began to work to develop a following among ABC metalworkers. In a 1967 leaflet of "enlightenment for metalworking companheiros," the AP argued that "the trade union, under the current military regime, lacks the force to fight for workers' rights because the current union leaders are tools of the bosses [patronais]." Since DOPS had to clear any union election candidate, no "authentic" leader could be elected; the leaflet suggested instead that members write "Down with the regime of fear" on their union ballots. It ended with the slogan "Hurray for the worker-peasant-student struggle."[46]

The anger of the young 1968 "revolutionaries" was directed against the PCB as much as Abreu Sodré or the forces within the military, which at the time was undergoing a radicalization that would lead to the crushing of regime opponents after December 13, 1968. In rhetoric and practice, the Far Left had its own version of "revolution by stages," and the necessary first step was to "unmask" the PCB, trade union leaders, and more moderate regime opponents to dispel the illusions that prevented the masses' inevitable radicalization. Speaking in the name of the nation and the workers, this energetic leftist minority of students, ex-students, and clergy was searching for the common people (povo). In their earnest activism under adverse conditions, they did find rebellious workers willing to join their revolutionary vanguards, although never enough to change their organizations' overwhelmingly non-working-class social composition. Yet this vanguard of middle-class radicals was also characterized by a certain "ventriloquism," in the words of Marcelo Ridenti, speaking in the name of, and even proposing to direct, the subaltern classes.[47] This was well illustrated when, on the eve of May Day 1968, the State Union of Students distributed leaflets to workers traveling by train to and from industrial suburbs like ABC that repeatedly employed the first-person plural to elide workers and students as a unified subject. For example, the leaflet denounced the MIA pelegos and their useless petitioning while boldly proclaiming that "*our* best arm against the arrocho is the strike." The leaflet then attacked union leaders who whined that "conditions for such a strike" did not yet exist or "that *we* lack consciousness" for such an action. Rejecting these arguments for inaction as pathetic excuses, the leaflet boldly declared that the students would lead such a strike if the union leaders were unwilling.[48]

But the us-versus-them rhetoric of these youthful revolutionaries obscured the immense distance separating members of the lettered classes, however radical, from the workers in whose name they claimed to speak and act. Immature and bookish ideas about Marxism-Leninism and revolutionary "theory" also blinded them to the bruised feelings and festering resentments of those workers who did belong to their organizations. It was only on the eve of these New Left organizations' defeat that their worker members voiced their sharp criticisms.[49] The AP's self-righteous actions and words in the late 1960s also left a legacy of anger, suspicion, and bitterness among elected union leaders and activists.

Yet as we saw with Lula at this time, these political debates, so preoccupying labor leaders, leftist priests, radical students, and disgruntled politicians, had little meaning for the working class's nonpoliticized majority, who were most concerned about a sustained, perceptible drop in real wages. The chasm between the competing "vanguards," whether pelegos or crazies, and the working masses would be starkly revealed during the last week of May, when festering discontent produced a remarkable flurry of section stoppages in São Bernardo factories, including Willys-Overland (Ford), Mercedes-Benz, Volkswagen, Fendt Tractors, and Chrysler. Driven by immediatist concerns, these shop floor combustions were characterized, as historian Negro notes, by an "ebullient mixture" involving the "return and recycling of older militants, the emergence of new activists, government hostility, a disbelief in officialdom, and the discrediting [*desgaste*] of union leaders." "Beaten down and poorly represented, the workers showed a 'marked tendency to take problems into their own hands without consulting the unions.'" As the US consul saw it, workers had moved into action "with or without their present leaders," whom they deemed "prisoners of a system that did not permit them to exercise any basic union function."[50]

The May 1968 stoppages would prove humiliating for the leaders of the São Bernardo metalworkers' union, reduced to hopelessly pleading for the government to change its wage policy while disclaiming responsibility for stoppages that they had not instigated but whose justice they fully recognized.[51] While it fell to Second Secretary Paulo Vidal to lead the union's apologetic response, the excruciating pressures of the situation also led union president Afonso Monteiro da Cruz not to seek reelection in 1969, which opened the way for Vidal's presidential candidacy on the slate that included Lula as an alternate. Monteiro da Cruz had been away at an international trade union meeting when the stoppages began. When interviewed on his return in early June by ABC's daily newspaper, the mixed-race Pernambuco-born leader appeared disgruntled and ill at ease as he criticized the labor minister (not the government as a whole), referred to the freedom enjoyed by trade unions in Western Europe (without directly criticizing the Brazilian labor system), and called for unspecified change in Brazil. When asked directly what he would do if a big strike were to happen, he answered clearly though hypothetically: if such a "movement were to occur (note, if it were), since the union is an organ of defense for workers and if the workers were disposed for such a fight, we would have to support it because the union is the workers' own house [*própria casa do operário*]."[52] Neither Vidal's disclaimers of responsibility nor Monteiro da Cruz's veiled dissent should be taken as expressing their "real" views given the repressive framework within which they operated in 1968: speaking with Laís Abramo in the 1980s, a union director recalled how at a São Bernardo strike the Military Police (Polícia Militar), armed with machine guns, surrounded the factory at the bosses' request and threatened to arrest Monteiro da Cruz and intervene the union if he tried to interfere.[53]

The public performance of helpless passivity, however understandable, validated the union's internal leftist opponents. Yet these leftist labor dissidents were, in late May 1968, no more capable than those whom they denounced of offering a credible path to success for these scattered stoppages involving thousands in local factories. When push finally came to shove, the several dozen union activists affiliated with the AP and other "revolutionary" organizations were themselves reeling from the post–May Day repression. Neither the elected union leaders and their supporters nor their "revolutionary" opponents, with their paper allies in the student movement (itself under siege), had the power in May 1968 to force substantive negotiations in the affected factories. General Moacir Gaia, the government's labor delegate in São Paulo, took a hard line, not only publicly defending the government's wage policy but also forcefully condemning the stoppages as "illegal strikes with concealed [*inconfessáveis*] objectives" of a subversive sort.[54]

The Praça da Sé May Day rally was emblematic of the Brazilian 1968, as were the June 26 "March of the 100,000" in Rio and the hundreds of workers arrested after the July 16–18 factory occupations in Osasco. Yet despite these vivid images, the underlying tragedy of 1968 was that Brazil's courageous rebels and oppositionists—whether students or workers, crazies or pelegos—were locked in fratricidal combat precisely at the moment when an upswing of discontent, reaching well beyond leftist ranks, offered the most serious challenge to military domination since 1964. Despite their aversion to useless risk-taking, members of the national civilian political class were deeply frustrated by the military, which, despite expectations to the contrary, was refusing to restore elections for executive positions—especially the presidency—even after Congress had agreed to amend the constitution according to the military's wishes in 1967. In a sense, it was the centrist military leadership who miscalculated in the fall of 1968 when they demanded that the legislators of the pro-government ARENA party strip a fellow deputy of congressional immunity for making statements that offended "military honor."[55] While most judged the statements in question immature and reckless, legislators ended the momentous year of 1968 with a courageous vote to reject the military ultimatum. With this act, national politicians finally stood up to the military they had bowed to since 1964. This brave act convinced the military that ARENA was a "phony" pro-government party and led to the regime's definitive radicalization, reflected in the passage of AI-5, which closed Congress, abolished habeas corpus, adopted prior censorship, and led to a more aggressive, centrally coordinated, and highly efficient system of repression that used torture far more widely than ever before.

This was the much gloomier situation facing the twenty-four-year-old Lula on his inauguration as part of the union diretoria in April 1969. At the same time, not all had changed since 1968, as the AP continued to declare that it had "nothing to do with the Diretoria of the Union," now headed by Paulo Vidal, and called for mobilizations "in union assemblies and elections to defeat the traitorous pelegos."[56]

PART II
FROM LUIZ INÁCIO INTO LULA

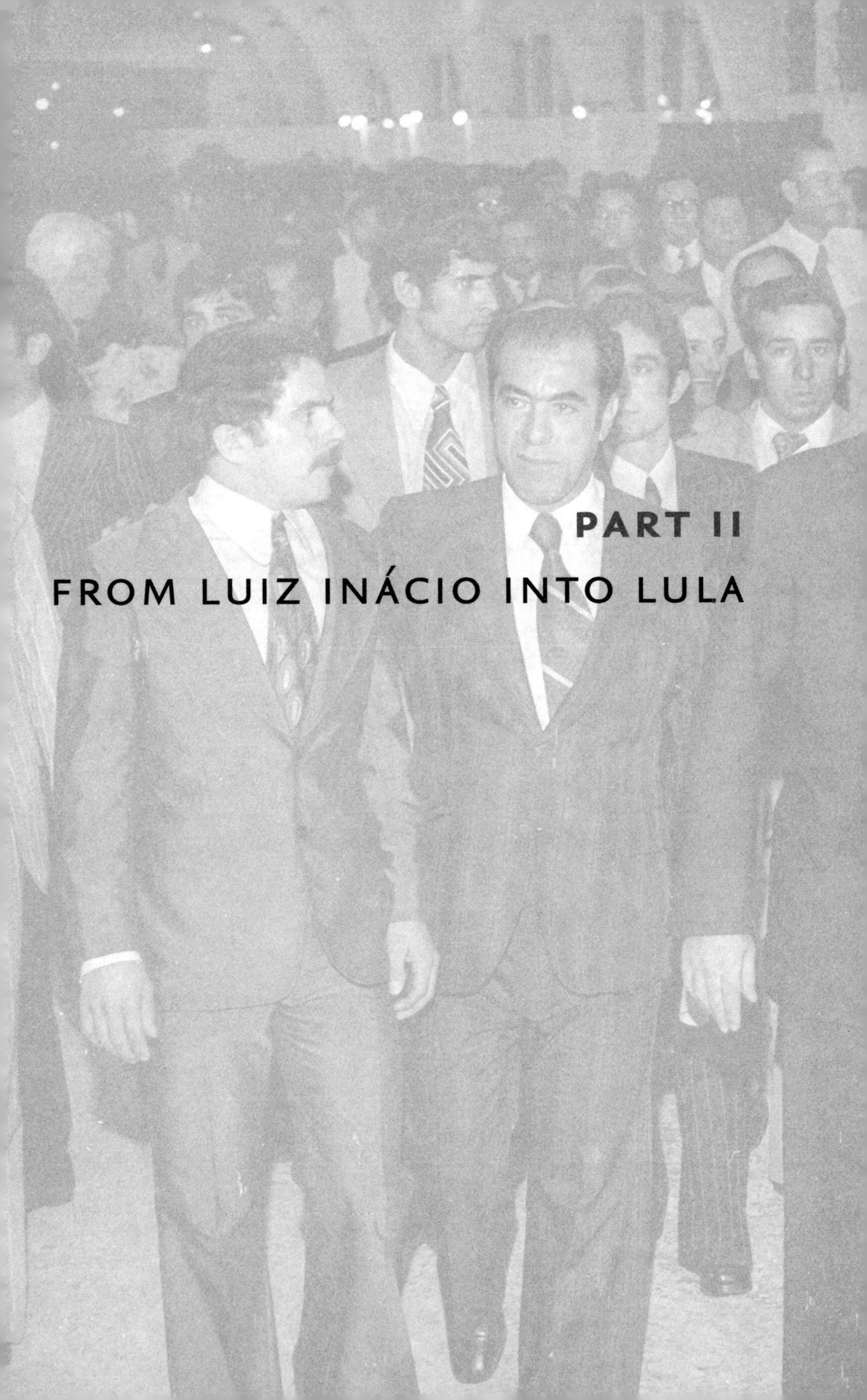

8 BOOMERS / BUILDING MODERNITY

Two buildings marked Lula's trajectory from adolescence through his twenties: the Escola Roberto Simonsen of SENAI, inaugurated in 1954 in the downtown industrial district of Brás, and the impressive headquarters of the metalworkers' union of São Bernardo do Campo and Diadema that opened in October 1973. The Escola Roberto Simonsen, with its quality training and decent treatment, launched Lula as an apprentice and then as a practicing machinist. A decade after graduating, Lula began a second apprenticeship from 1972 to 1975 as a newly elected full-time director under the capable guidance of union president Paulo Vidal. Both men joined in the inaugural festivities of the new six-story "palace of metalworkers" built at 121 Rua João Basso in downtown São Bernardo. If SENAI decisively shaped his outlook and self-conception, the São Bernardo union would prove a spectacular school for politics in what would be a crucial decade in Brazilian political and labor history.

As concrete manifestations of modernity, the buildings housing the Escola Roberto Simonsen and the São Bernardo metalworkers' union expressed the bold ambitions spawned by São Paulo's postwar industrial boom. Both the school and the union were government-sponsored institutions, projects initiated from above to anticipate, shape, and control transformations being unleashed by industrialization. For Roberto Mange's SENAI, the goal was a generation of skilled shop floor collaborators: educated citizen-workers toiling for national development in concert with employers and the state. Government-sponsored trade unions, created under President Getúlio Vargas, aimed to foster a working-class elite inspired by not class struggle but social peace as Oliveira Viana dreamed of in his most utopian moments.

The São Bernardo headquarters was a tribute in concrete, glass, and steel to the grandeur of the rapidly growing metalworking categoria in a South American Detroit, a veritable city within a city, where Volkswagen alone employed 38,979 of the município's estimated 85,000–90,000 metalworkers in 1974.[1] The headquarters also broadcast the union's arrival, flaunting its financial prowess as one of the richest labor organizations (though not the largest) in Greater São Paulo.[2] The building's construction was tied to the Brazilian "economic miracle" from 1968 to 1974, during which São Bernardo and Diadema experienced unprecedented economic growth that transformed their industrial, demographic, and urban realities.

As the country transitioned to full-fledged dictatorship after AI-5, São Bernardo stood out for its epic factories and as the country's largest producer of modernity's icon, the automobile. This chapter provides a bottom-up view from this município of the experience, aspirations, and self-understanding of a generation of working-class baby boomers during the presidency of General Emílio Garrastazu Médici (1969–74). Retrospective storytelling is combined with the voices of ABC's metalworkers in the early 1970s, recorded prior to the famous strikes central to Brazil's new industrial revolution. Focusing on the politics of the everyday, this chapter shows how the tens of thousands who entered São Bernardo's giant factories defined and pursued their objectives during the most authoritarian years of the Brazilian military regime.

ABC's metalworkers faced formidable obstacles to collective mobilization during this moment of large-scale industrial expansion. Effective representation of workers' interests was impeded by across-the-board repression of free speech, free press, and political opposition, in addition to employer and government repression. This chapter innovates by analyzing how the immediatist politics of everyday life inflected workers' views of the military regime, laying out the baseline understandings—inherited from the past but not frozen in time—that informed the cunning (*astúcia*) and dissimulation through which workers navigated metropolitan São Paulo.

Like Lula, ABC's skilled workers were restless strivers, hungry for knowledge and eager to harvest the economic miracle's bounty of progress. By focusing on the shop floor at Indústrias Villares, which employed Lula between 1966 and 1980, as well as Lula's 1969 marriage to Maria de Lourdes Ribeiro and subsequent 1971 purchase of a house, this chapter sheds light on workers' actions and aspirations both within and beyond the factory walls. Concentrating on private lives, this chapter centers on ambitions aroused and fulfilled, not on poverty endured or exploitation survived; the gestalt of the boom years was less about what was left behind than the obstacles that most expected would soon be vanquished.

ABC as Ground Zero

The early 1970s were bleak years for the military regime's opponents in São Paulo: labor activists, student radicals, opposition politicians, and the liberal and leftist sectors of the intellectualized middle classes.[3] The AI-5 bombshell in December 1968 was followed by the second wave of repression since 1964, breaking up the opposition networks that had come to the fore in ABC, São

Paulo, and elsewhere. When a purged Congress was finally reopened in October 1969, politicians operated within rigorous limits given the threat of losing office, a new regime of prior censorship, and the suspension of habeas corpus. The government-favored ARENA party would sweep elections in 1970, a year that saw Brazil exult over a third World Cup victory. Triumphalist patriotic advertising, especially through the newly influential medium of TV, propagated a bold, optimistic vision of Brazil as an emerging "great power" that "no one could hold back."[4]

Following the tumultuous 1968 came public conformity with—if not adherence to—the government, fostered by the startling success of the Brazilian "economic miracle."[5] Economic chaos, high inflation, and severe recession yielded to the first signs of renewed economic dynamism in 1967, followed by 11.3 percent annual real GDP growth from 1968 to 1974, with inflation at postwar levels (under 20 percent). Fueled by foreign direct investment, rapid industrial expansion—at a yearly rate of 12.6 percent—drove the Brazilian boom, with machinery, transport, and electrical equipment production seeing the largest growth.[6] The industry and mining workforce increased from 1.6 million in 1960 to 4.9 million by 1976; half of national industrial production and employment originated in São Paulo state, especially the capital's metro region, including ABC.[7] The number of Brazilians employed in manufacturing, mining, construction, and transportation almost tripled from 4.5 million in 1960 to 12.5 million in 1980.[8] The promise of 1964 seemed finally realized, the military having put the country on the path to the future.

Brazil was now fully committed to a future based on the internal combustion engine, whatever the long-term implications for energy consumption, urban development, or the environment.[9] The auto industry was well positioned due to earlier import substitution policies that forced international companies to build in the country or effectively be barred from the Brazilian market. Five of the top ten international vehicle producers had opened assembly plants in Brazil by 1963, each with at least one plant in ABC. Yet the consumer market for cars was still small in Brazil and the rest of Latin America, so the newly built factories were modest compared to those in the developed world.[10] Prior to the boom, the factories struggled to run anywhere close to maximum production levels, which made it easy to scale up production after 1968 without significant new investments.[11] Production tripled from 279,715 units in 1968 to 930,235 in 1974, increasing at annual rates from 18 to 25 percent between 1968 and 1973 and thus sharply outpacing the growth rate of GDP or overall industrial manufacturing.[12] The motor vehicle industry, including assembly plants and associated auto parts producers, were the leading sector of a larger metal-mechanical industry in Brazil that was booming during these years. By the second half of the

1970s, Greater São Paulo metalworking enterprises employed 650,598 workers: 421,277 in the município of São Paulo, 191,792 in ABC, and 37,529 in Osasco. Sixty-five percent of ABC's metalworkers (126,000) fell within the legal constituency of the São Bernardo and Diadema metalworkers' union.[13]

While São Paulo município had the most metalworking firms, the large-scale factories were concentrated in ABC. Only 33 percent of São Paulo's metalworkers were employed in factories of more than five hundred workers, compared to 61 percent in Santo Andre, 74 percent in São Bernardo, and 86 percent in São Caetano do Sul (which hosted a large General Motors assembly plant).[14] Metalworking firms of more than 1,000 workers employed 86 percent of the metalwork force in São Caetano, 67 percent in São Bernardo, and 49 percent in Santo André, compared to 21 percent for São Paulo município.[15]

When the new factories began to arrive, the ABC region—other than the cities of Santo André and São Caetano—was rural, and the new job opportunities quickly attracted a flood of settlers. ABC's population would double between 1960 and 1970, when it reached 1 million inhabitants; it would rise by 50 percent by 1980. Home to Lula's employer, Indústrias Villares, São Bernardo was vast but still sparsely settled in 1966, divided by the Billings Reservoir. Now it began to experience the full impact of cheap land and easy access to the Via Anchieta highway. From 1960 to 1980, São Bernardo would increase its population from 82,000 to 426,000, Diadema from 12,000 to 229,000.[16] This was driven by the 400 percent growth in industrial employment between 1960 and 1975, at which point metalworking likely employed three-quarters of the residential industrial workforce.

What happened, recalled a VW worker hired in 1966, "was like when it rains on São José's day in the Northeast. The people gather in the street. The implantation of the auto industry was like that: an explosion. They were hunting [for people to work] with lassos." Demand was such, he added, that "I didn't choose VW, it chose me."[17] Another recalled how "the bosses [*homems*, men] were so hungry for production that the peons [*a peaozada*] didn't even have time to go to the bathroom."[18] The excitement was captured in a 1978 autobiographical short story by Roniwalter Jatobá, who worked at the Karmann Ghia auto plant in São Bernardo from 1970 to 1973.[19] Searching for work, the story's new migrant frequented the old industrial region of Brás, the site of the Escola Roberto Simonsen, and queried passersby about jobs. Hearing about São Bernardo, he took the bus there and ventured fearfully across the Via Anchieta and through unknown streets, full of cars. Cold and hungry, he jingled his last coins and entered the doubled line along the factory fence that stretched the street's length. This hungry young man in search of opportunity ended his day exultant: once "all the [health] exams were signed and notarized, and the firm's stamp affixed to it," he would finally be able to "walk into bars with his head held high without needing to fearfully run away at the slightest sign of a police car." He overhead others in his rooming house commenting, "That guy is a lucky bastard; an automobile firm, that's a lot of luck!"[20] São Bernardo, soon to be world famous for its unexpected strikes, was inseparable from the world of flux that was Greater São Paulo. At least a third of those working in São Bernardo and Diadema's factories lived elsewhere in ABC or São Paulo. Likewise, a smaller but still substantial number of metalworkers resident in São Bernardo worked outside that município.[21]

This growing commuter workforce in Greater São Paulo depended on mass transportation to take advantage of new job opportunities or to cope when family members lost the jobs for which they had originally moved. Yet as settlement sprawled outward, municipal governments could neither regulate the chaotic development spurred by the metropolitan region's real estate industry nor create an effective mass transportation system. To deal with lengthy and unpredictable commutes, the largest factories—especially the auto assembly plants—eventually contracted with bus fleets to deliver their workers, an option not available for smaller firms.

All of this meant that São Bernardo and Diadema's metalworkers did not possess a deeply rooted common culture or a preexisting class identity that might unite them as a factory proletariat. The distance between their residences and the commuting difficulties were only a few of the cleavages, which also included birth region, race, color, gender, and education. Even their commonalities did not seem a compelling basis for mobilization as an industrial working class in formation. Though they all earned a wage—some more than others—their unity was threatened by differences in skill levels and rivalries between factory shifts and sections.

Yet these workers did share commonalities. Ninety percent of the industry's workforce was male and overwhelmingly young. They came from Brazil's agrarian and hinterland regions, although the rural economies of these regions varied sharply and there was always a small but not insignificant contingent of foreign-born and first-generation immigrants, usually of diverse European origins, and native-born paulistas, who distinguished themselves from the baiano migrants from the Northeast.[22] The third commonality was the unprecedented concentration of ABC's metalworkers in the auto assembly plants, among Brazil's largest factories.

From a distance, the collective representation of workers' interests should have been facilitated by the presence of international auto companies such as VW, Ford, and Chrysler, all of which were powerfully unionized in their home countries, and by Brazil's well-established system of government-sanctioned trade unionism. Yet the post-1964 government had reduced collective bargaining, already weak, to a formality by adopting a national across-the-board formula that fixed annual wage increases, at a rate inevitably less than inflation. The Ministry of Labor encouraged trade unions to expand their provision of social services, which might, in the case of a rich union like São Bernardo's, be administered from grandiose new headquarters.

Barred from the shop floor and hemmed in by government, trade unions also faced hostile employers in new factories whose very scale—and the anonymity of those laboring in them—made effective, large-scale labor mobilization more difficult. These vast factories also had an enormous turnover (*rotatividade*), only some of which was voluntary; workers, especially the unskilled, were hired at entry-level wages and laid off before they could advance in the pay scale through seniority, thus minimizing the company's wage bill.

Workers also faced a well-developed repressive system aimed at preventing protest. In a secret meeting on November 11, 1969, top leaders of many of ABC's big factories—including GM, VW, and Chrysler—met with DOPS and the army to create a formal coordinating center for surveillance that, with financing from industrialists, would evolve into Operation Bandeirantes and, eventually, the Departamento de Operações de Informações—Centro de Operações de Defesa Interna (DOI-CODI), which became infamous for the torture and death of suspected subversives and revolutionaries.[23] Despite the military regime's insistence that Brazil was a "guided democracy," daily life in ABC saw little respect for even the most narrowly defined civil and democratic rights. Those running for office, most of them middle class, were forced to submit a certificate of their *antecedentes políticos-sociais* from DOPS. Local police chiefs routinely checked schoolteacher rosters for subversives and passed mimeographed student newspapers on to DOPS, which even investigated a local high school student whose class essay—preserved in the police records—had been denounced as subversive by his teacher and principal. When someone tied leftist leaflets to fences near a factory entrance, the police scrambled to capture the suspects and reported to DOPS headquarters in São Paulo. Armed DOPS agents also made periodic visits to factories to "investigate" subversion and detain suspects; less visibly, both companies and the police recruited and cultivated informants (*dedo-duros*) in the workforce and among unionists.[24]

Ever Striving

ABC's working people were mostly apolitical, driven by the material improvements and enhanced well-being of those years. In their immediatism, they saw much to celebrate in terms of lots bought, homes built or expanded, consumer durables purchased, and more education. This progress fed into an enhanced feeling of national belonging, central to government propaganda, that could lead to patriotic identification with the nation or its leaders, although the military discouraged personalist cults around its various generals turned presidents. With intense economic growth and a silenced political world, many working-class voices expressed admiration for the government's grandiose public works and faith in Brazil's future as a great industrial power.[25]

The majority of São Bernardo's workers in the late 1960s, recalled a revolutionary AP activist, "came from the interior and were in a process of economic ascension and professional afirmation. It was a period where there wasn't much unemployment." While "there were serious problems in local factories," he added, "a good part of the people didn't think that they had to fight precisely because of the economic improvement" that they were experiencing.[26] The region's metalworkers enthused over São Paulo as the "axis" or "heart" of Brazil, a "place of progress" where even the unskilled, if courageous, could eventually "buy a lot and construct their house."[27] A similar point was made when the emissary of an armed struggle organization offered their support to Catholic labor militant Waldemar Rossi in 1970. Recalling his rebuff thirteen years later, this São Paulo metalworker—who would be arrested and tortured—told them that their path had nothing to do with his fellow workers, who wanted above all "a job, a wage, and to acquire a little house."[28]

The huge demand for land among migrants fed a booming low-end real estate industry that sold tiny lots on an installment plan. The activity of *loteadores* (those who break up land for sale) was profitable, speculative, and sometimes illegal; land titles were often unclear and in some cases fraudulent, and fly-by-night operators made off with hard-earned down payments, leaving would-be owners in the lurch. However sleazy the market, the net result was an amazingly high level of homeownership among even the city's poorest workers: a 1974 survey of districts with the lowest average income showed that three-quarters of residents were homeowners. The lots where workers lived usually fell well below the legal minimum lot size: in 1974, 45 percent of São Bernardo's *terrenos* were clandestine in legal terms.[29] Self-construction in poorer areas could make up as much as half the housing stock. Only families with higher incomes could afford an existing home, especially one with two bedrooms, so many bought a terreno and erected a shack, likely not much worse than their home in the countryside. The savings on rent and any future windfalls could then support an ongoing and creative, if often haphazard, process of household construction and improvement.

This drive for landownership was interpreted by some in the 1960s as evidence of a residual "peasant consciousness."[30] Yet empirical research quickly established such behavior as part of the compelling logic of the "proletarianization of space under the aegis of industry."[31] In purely economic terms, buying a lot and building oneself on the city's ever-expanding outskirts was best given low wages and the absence of enough rental housing to keep rents low for a surging population. Moreover, the only cheap rental units—the degraded older tenements (*cortiços*) in the dying central industrial districts—were far from the new factories springing up in places like ABC. The results would prove both enduring and destructive for the future of Greater São Paulo, a metropolitan region already on its way to becoming the world's third-largest metropolis.

For those living on the periphery, the urban frontier was full of aggravation and frustration, but a home of their own—however makeshift—not only guaranteed a better future but offered evidence that they were indeed winners. Outsiders might view their neighborhoods as decrepit, but they improved their homes from year to year as they built what they called their simple little lives (*vidinhas*). Like other strivers, Lula's family believed that paying rent was throwing money away, something that only fools or the poorest of the poor would do. When Lula married in 1969, four of his eight siblings already owned pieces of land or houses. Typically, family members pooled resources, as Vavá and Marinete did in 1964 and again in 1969. And any windfall—like the proceeds from a lottery won by Frei Chico and his cousin Zé Graxa in 1966—was invested in land. In 1964, even the nineteen-year-old Lula became a landowner, buying a lot with the indemnification for losing a finger at Metalúrgia Independencia, though the Vila Oliveiro property was never built on because it lacked a bus route.[32]

Yet the biggest Silva family conquest, a tribute to dona Lindu's wisdom, came when Lula landed a dream job at Indústrias Villares, a new, dynamic metalworking firm in January 1966.[33] At age twenty-six, Lula had moved on from irregular *bicos* in the informal sector, work as an office boy, and employment in three small metalworking firms that had low pay and dangerous working conditions and lacked the resources, technological sophistication, and profitability of the bigger companies. Despite working nights for a 25 percent differential, he had barely been able to get by while employed at such "fabriquinhas." His level of pay at Villares, by contrast, allowed him within his first year there to pay off the debts accumulated during his bout of unemployment.[34]

During his seven years at Villares, the young machinist earned more than anyone else in his family, even without the forty hours a month of overtime that he sometimes worked to accumulate savings. Lula's retrospective description of his aspirations in the late 1960s would ring true for his fellow workers: "I wanted to be a good professional, to earn my salary, to live my life. To have children."[35] In 1967, the twenty-two-year-old was ready to contemplate settling down, as his brother Frei Chico had done at twenty-four.[36] By his own account, as well as those of Tiana and Lambari, the teenage Lula had always been crazier about soccer than about girls and preferred work and study to flirting (*trouxa*, in Lambari's words). He had grown up in a boisterous gender-segregated street culture and describes himself as timid and simple (*bobinho*) with girls.[37] Of course, even the simplest interactions between girls and boys was difficult, as Frei Chico explained: "You couldn't [even] touch the hand of your girlfriend [*namorada*]" in those days, and even to imagine kissing her "was the most difficult thing in the world."[38] Growing up working class in 1950s São Caetano, José de Souza Martins recalled the prevailing Catholic social mores, in which sex, a source of "shame and apprehension," was never "a subject of conversation between children and adults."[39] As for sexuality more broadly, boys learned about masturbation from each other in the nearby empty fields that were the "true democratic redoubts" of their privacy.[40]

Such experiences held true for Lula as well. Asked in August 1979 by a female reporter for *Nova* (the Brazilian edition of *Cosmopolitan*) about his sexual initiation, a thirty-four-year-old Lula replied that a brother-in-law took him to a "house of prostitution where I did the whole thing [*fiz a festa*]," a story that he occasionally repeated.[41] A month earlier, a *Playboy* interviewer asked whether his first sexual experience was with a man or a woman. Lula replied that it was of course with a woman, before observing that "at that time a boy [*moleque*], with 10, 12 years already had sexual experience with animals"; his childhood world, he went on, was far freer than that of today's kids, and people did more "sacanagem," a term that "refers to sexual acts that, however common they may be, carry a hint of the forbidden."[42]

If marriage was the unquestioned ideal, the time from courtship (*namoro*) to engagement (*noivado*) was often truncated, and pregnancy quickly followed marriage. Discussing his decision to marry in 1981, Lula humorously suggested pragmatic reasons: living with his mother and sister and paying the expenses, he figured that if he already had "the life of a married man, it was better to get married because at least then you have a woman."[43] So one fine day, the timid Villares worker discovered that he was interested in the sister of his best friend, Lambari: Maria de Lourdes Ribeiro, who had long been a close friend of himself, his younger sister Tiana, and Frei Chico. The two families had lived two lots away from each other in Ponte Preta, and the kids were in and out of each other's houses. "It was real friendship" between the two, Tiana recalls, "and then suddenly they were courting."[44] About Lula's height, Lourdes was pretty, with chestnut-brown eyes and brown hair.[45] They were soon engaged; the marriage, held on May 25, 1969, "had everything going for it to succeed," Tiana believed.[46]

Lourdes stands out in the memory of her family and Lula's as an especially

Lula and Lourdes cutting the cake at their wedding.
(Courtesy President Luiz Inácio Lula da Silva)

hard-working young woman. Living in the interior of São Paulo state, where her mineiro parents first settled, she failed to complete primary school because she was raising her siblings, between the ages of ten to fourteen, while her mother was hospitalized in Araraquara for a lung problem; her father was ill and disabled. Arriving in São Paulo city in 1964–65, she was hired at the first textile shop that Lambari took her to: a small weaving firm (*tecelagem*) in Sacomã owned by a family of *turcos* (the generic term applied to Middle Eastern immigrants such as São Paulo state's substantial Syrian Lebanese population), where she did miscellaneous tasks (*serviços gerais*) such as sewing and carrying things around. As described by her machinist brother, Lourdes worked like the devil but earned "nothing, nothing, nothing," as was typical for unskilled women workers.[47]

Lourdes's big dream, according to Lula's sister Tiana, was to own her own home, which conforms to the wisdom among São Paulo's poor that "quem casa quer casa" (those who marry want a house).[48] Lula, as a skilled worker, and his wife could achieve this shared objective if they were sufficiently disciplined. The young couple decided to rent for a year and half a one-room apartment with a kitchen to save enough to buy a house near dona Lindu. "Having our own house was the great utopia," Lula said, and it was worth the sacrifice. Taking a loan from Villares, he made a down payment on an already constructed house in Parque Bristol, a neighborhood of unpaved streets and no sidewalks where one could barely walk when it rained due to the mud. Describing its open sewers and the threat of flooding from a nearby creek, Lula nonetheless emphasized that the neighborhood met the fundamental requirements: a bus stop, a nearby bakery, a weekly fair, and a pharmacy. The young couple moved into their new home in early 1971, while awaiting their first child. It had two bedrooms, a living room, and a kitchen; the backyard had a detached room and kitchen where Maria Baixinha and her husband, who were in financial straits, could live.[49]

Learning Machines

A payoff for his hard work and study, Lula's half dozen years at Villares marked the arrival of long-dreamed-of good times. His new factory provided a full array of nonsalary benefits, including medical services, hospital referrals, and a program of loans, and this "job in a large factory earning ten minimum wages" would later be used to underline the fact that "a machinist was an important profession in those days."[50] Working for a well-paying, well-organized firm was a new experience for Lula, and it was here, he says,[51] that he "began to perceive the game [*jogada*] of modern capitalism, a new type of exploitation that one didn't know in a small fabriquinha."[52]

Compared to the more relaxed atmosphere that could reign in smaller firms, at Villares Lula competed against another on a single machine for maximum production at the least cost. An early night-shift partner was the fantastically productive Joe Lizard (Zé Lagarto), who could make eighty cast-iron rings per shift to Lula's thirty. Lula describes appealing to his colleague not to go "beyond the normal production quota," because he would earn nothing more for the effort and the extra profit would go to the boss—in addition to threatening Lula's job, "since any boss will fire the one who produces less if he has another who can produce twice as much."[53]

Reflecting on his work life in 1979 to a journalist unfamiliar with industry, Lula noted that while many workers faced a torturous subordination to the machine, it was "a bit different" for machinists "because their work requires technical knowledge."[54] As Santo André workers noted, skilled jobs required intellectual skills, technical knowledge, and proven competence.[55] Even to be hired, especially at a big firm, affirmed self-worth because, as a machinist told Luiz Pereira, it meant "a better salary" and an "opportunity to continue to progress in my profession"—to sharpen their skills, assume greater responsibilities, and even win promotions.[56] At Villares, Lula returned to his comfortable role as a "good boy," if a chastened one, and eventually rose to a semisupervisory post as a *contramestre* (a type of foreman).[57]

Flexibility and versatility were fundamental for those operating milling and grinding equipment such as the metal lathe on which Lula specialized. Their job required extensive training and continuous improvement "in the course of their professional practice." They were "highly prized in the labor market," even more so during the post-1968 industrial boom.[58] A Santo André worker named Edísio explained to a USP researcher that the skilled, even without the right to strike, could always "ask for a raise, and if they don't give it, they can leave"—unlike "a helper asking for a raise," whom employers could simply "fire . . . and hire another."[59] Unskilled workers confirmed this to the researcher.[60]

Those who operated universal machine tools in Brazil valued their ability "to plan and to dictate the pace of their own activities" with little interference by supervisors. Drawing on his early 1980s field research, José Tauile described how these workers, after "receiv[ing] the drawing of the part to be machined," "study and analyze it carefully" and then "decide upon virtually everything, from how to fasten the workpiece to the machine up to determining which tools must be used, in what order and in what manner."[61] Lula illustrated such command of the work process in 1981 when discussing how one year, over several months, the machinists at Villares perfected the production of a new part for an overhead crane by inventing "ways of doing it differently" with the same machine and tools, which led to a fourfold increase in production—though (and this was the point of his story) for the same salary.[62]

Work as a space for self-realization and the perfection of individual craft could also generate resentment about piecework and increased pace of work. Lula remembered how workers would complain about production target times set by someone in an office who couldn't even make the part. Workers would be penalized for missing the target; if they produced the part in less time, the target time would be reset. Regardless of how many parts one made in a day, Lula continued, the worker wouldn't "even receive [in salary] the equivalent of the value of a single one." According to Lula, the skilled worker perceived this unfairness most clearly, as he had been to school and done a course of study.[63]

A perceived lack of recognition for extraordinary efforts could also generate conflict. Villares would sometimes put five or even six metal lathes online at the same time, an experience that, as Lula recalled in 1981, "was really crazy," with "splinters of iron flying, falling in your hair, with no time to do anything more than to knock [them] off with your hand and smell the burned flesh." Lula rued how, of course, no extra money came with the extra number of pieces produced.[64] As these reactions suggest, the skilled felt that they could stand up for themselves, and their relations with foremen, although at times conflictual, were based on their ability to deliver as machinists. They did complain about overseers looking over their shoulder or trying to control what they did, such as going to the bathroom. "That was something that irritated me, it left me feeling nervous," Lula remembered, and "we fought about it"—an example of "talking back" impossible for the common worker.[65]

Lula's experiences resonate with the array of attitudes and outlooks captured in a richly documented and wide-ranging 1973 profile of "the young worker" in São Paulo. Appearing in the newsmagazine *Visão,* the article included the transcribed dialogues of two focus groups of skilled and unskilled workers brought together by economist Paul Singer for a marketing company. Covering everything from family, work, and education to politics, Singer's penetrating analysis established both commonalities and divergences among the participants, none of whom were older than the twenty-eight-year-old Lula. In a world divided between those who command and those who obey, the unskilled felt most comfortable taking orders; as one such worker put it, this caused less worry and meant that when a part got ruined (*peça matada*), its operator was "the only one who has no responsibility" in the matter.[66] "To be the owner of a professional skill," by contrast, meant "to depend less on knowledge emanating from others," which made "the young skilled worker more 'free' to think within his own head and assume full responsibility for what he does."[67] Describing the work process, one machinist sketched out the roles played by those who planned, designed, and laid out a given piece; when his turn came, he "felt greater responsibility than even they do," because "the fulfilment of their jobs now lies in my hands."[68] Another relished the power that flowed from responsibility, even with its associated risks. Responsible for fabricating the most expensive parts, he explained that even those who worked under him couldn't handle the task: "Everything I do is tough [*barra pesada*] since they're big parts. I have the responsibility. If by some chance I ruin the part, the blame falls on me. I could be out of work. It's sink or swim."[69]

Cunning and the Subaltern Art of Maneuver

Although thousands were jailed and hundreds killed during the Emílio Garrastazu Médici presidency, civil and political rights were not a central concern of the urban popular majority. A concern about freedom of speech, the press, and association was felt most strongly by the tiny politicized minority, including labor activists, union leaders, and the middle-class opposition. More ruthlessly realistic Brazilians could easily view those suffering persecution as having unwisely "chosen" to get into trouble with the authorities. This was especially true for rank-and-file workers, who knew little about distant political disputes but had few illusions about the rules governing their world. Notions about citizenship, inalienable rights, and equality for all had at best limited credibility with the popular classes. Those arriving in ABC from rural or small-town worlds had been shaped by the powerful legacies of slavery and the oligarchical First Republic (1889–1930). They and their ancestors had grown up under the social and political domination of the landowners and the local bosses whom they controlled. Like slavery, *coronelismo* entailed a pervasive etiquette of submission and deference; politics for the humble revolved around seeking the favor of big shots, the educated, and the wealthy.

Authoritarianism's legacies were hardly surprising in a country that had never been liberal or democratic in its social mythologies and practice. The interests and opinions of those who were ruled had never counted for much, but they were well aware of the price for frontal opposition. Even in urban areas many had seen neighbors, relatives, and shop mates suffer during the most recent persecutory waves of 1947, 1964, and 1968. Thus, mass consciousness was anchored by a ruthless realism based on a frank recognition that the world was unjust and stacked against the weak. As we know from Luiz Pereira, São Paulo's workers in the early 1960s associated manual labor (*braçal*) with abjectness, a finding confirmed by another USP student, drawn to the Left in 1967. Celso Frederico's rigorously empirical 1975 master's thesis, published in 1978, adopted a phenomenological approach based on a careful exegesis of hundreds of quotes by individually identified workers at a small Santo André metalworking firm in 1970–71, male and female, skilled and unskilled.[70] Probing ideal types, Frederico asked them to define the boss (patrão) and the worker (trabalhador). In doing so, they highlighted the distinction between those who command and the worker, who must be "submissive." The boss, they suggested, enters with the money, while the worker provides only the labor (braços). They did recognize that workers were different from the "poor," whom they defined as miserable persons (*miseráveis*) who didn't work, begged, or lived under bridges. Those poor souls had nothing; the worker, while doing better, exists just to survive and "can't aspire to anything for the future."[71]

For Frederico's interviewees, being a trabalhador was a sad fate "because it takes nothing to become a worker," and anyone punching a time clock "has to accept whatever appears [in the way of work] to earn their bread." While a lone worker did insist that the "working class" sustained a class of bosses, the rest emphasized that anyone who does not work for themselves (*conta propria*) is a "slave" doomed to "do what the boss orders because, if not, it's the street!" While these statements could be seen as describing "wage slavery," their responses were marked less by grievance than by an overwhelming emphasis on the worker as "a submissive person" who "depends on others."[72]

Given such a bleak view, how did working people navigate a society whose entrenched norms reflected the country's vast differentials in power, wealth, and cultural capital? Here we must examine the interclass etiquette governing everyday interactions between subordinates and superordinates. Luiz Pereira and Leôncio Rodrigues had been oblivious to how the data collected before 1964 had been influenced by these norms. It was Frederico, in his second ABC metalworkers' project, who highlighted the chasms separating those of different social classes and levels of educational attainment. Aligned with the mainstream Communist Party, he had planned to compare class mobilization among assembly-line workers and tool and die makers at Volkswagen.[73] Yet the young Marxist found himself frustrated by workers who consistently avoided "uncomfortable questions, changed subjects, made visibly contradictory observations, and maintained significant silences." Stymied by their "amiable resistance," he eventually came to realize that a "more or less conscious dissimulation" was at work in relation to a strange and distant "other," the "researcher." Acknowledging an "understandable lack of trust [*desconfiança*]," he realized that their cordial but evasive responses were "the very essence of the cunning [*astúcia*] of the dominated, of those who cannot yet expose themselves to the other but who, at the same time, do not want to totally renounce their convictions."[74]

Cunning in the form of veiled talk, disguised discontent, or camouflaged action is amply documented for the time of slavery and beyond in a country characterized by despotic authority and a largely landless peasantry. Well before James Scott's "hidden transcript," French Jesuit sociologist Michel de Certeau had aptly described the "lucid discourse" to be found among rural folk whom he interviewed in Pernambuco's interior in 1974. Given a starkly unfavorable balance of power, they viewed the world as "an immemorial struggle between 'the powerful' and 'the poor,'" "as a field of constant victories by the rich and the police, but also as the reign of mendacity" where "the strong always win and words always deceive." While recognizing this unjust state of affairs as "an order of things that seemed immutable," they accorded it "no legitimacy whatever."[75]

For Certeau, cunning in rural life was "the subtle, stubborn, resistance activity" of those condemned to acting within "a network of already established forces and representations."[76] Their wisdom (*sabedoria*) consisted of stratagems (*trampolinagem*) and trickery (*trapacaria*) through which they insinuated into relations of domination certain "styles of social exchange, technical invention, and moral resistance, that is, an economy of the '*gift*' (generosities for which one expects a return), an esthetics of '*tricks*' (artists' operations) and an ethics of *tenacity*."[77] The weapons of the weak, as they have been described by James Scott, are the traditional resort of "relatively powerless groups" and include "foot dragging, dissimulation, desertion, false compliance, pilfering, feigned ignorance, slander, arson, sabotage, and so on." These ubiquitous behaviors, Scott suggested, usually fall "well short of outright collective defiance" and for the most part avoid a "direct, symbolic confrontation with authority."[78]

Everyday cunning explains, for example, migrant families' responses to their children's mistreatment in the school studied by Luiz Pereira. Faced with abusive authority, most followed a strategy of retraction (*retraçao*), concealing their discontent and minimizing contact with authorities who they knew would not take their concerns seriously. Those who wished to formally lodge complaints were aware of the risks: even when feigning exaggerated deference, they feared that facial gestures, bodily posture, or tone of voice might unwittingly reveal their critical feelings, however muffled, and lead to a humiliating dressing down. The most cunning parents, however, found a way to strike back at minimal personal risk. They availed themselves of Osvaldo Gimenez's booming voice on local radio; while they'd tell those they didn't trust that everything at the school was fine, later they might complain about stuck-up teachers when talking to a neighbor.

Among educated observers, cunning and dissimulation reinforced beliefs in the herdlike passivity of São Paulo's workers, with their opaque words, submissiveness, and apparent fatalism. Looking down on these workers, the intellectuals saw a continuation of the personal dependency and traditionalism that they believed prevalent in a rural Brazil about which they knew little. Yet this ignores how the very elements of stasis that characterized swaths of rural life were being undermined in the new, more anonymous urban milieu that lacked the "already established forces and representations" cited by Certeau for rural Brazil. With fathers losing sway, the young (especially but not limited to men) were developing radically new individualistic behaviors in relation to the opportunities around them.[79] Living in an urban world in flux, their use of cunning was increasingly shaped by the competitive dynamics of an emerging urban and industrial social order that provided new chances to advance and a greater degree of freedom for individual and family maneuvering.

Cunning was central in the fight to "win at life" among Lula's generation. For instance, in one of Singer's 1973 focus group dialogues, workers agreed with the observation that men are prone to rascally things ("todo homem so faz a coisa na malandragem"), which the others identified with the *sacana*, a word connoting a scoundrel, trickster, or jokester, which "a person often has to be . . . in order to win at life."[80] This simply reflected the fact that "many want to get ahead by climbing on the shoulders of others like us [subir às costa da gente]"; as one of the workers concluded, "You have to use others" if you want a nice apartment, a car, or a house, because no one gets ahead except at the expense of someone else.[81]

The vision underlying this exchange recalls the zero-sum postulate, found among peasants and ABC's working people, that anthropologists have called the "image of limited good": that the "desired things in life . . . exist in finite quantity and are always in short supply," and thus those who get ahead do so at the expense of their fellow peasants and workers.[82] This is not to say, however, that workers did not admire cunning when well-executed and successful. "In these combatants' stratagems," Certeau observed in Pernambuco, "there is a certain art of placing one's blows, a pleasure in getting around the rules of a constraining space" characterized by a "tactical and joyful dexterity" through which "even the field of misfortune is refashioned by this combination of manipulation and enjoyment."[83]

Cunning was ubiquitously deployed in Lula's world to maneuver both vertical and horizontal relationships. As a weapon of the weak, it could be deployed defensively and even offensively, for many ends, and with both good and bad consequences. As a veil, disguise, or camouflage, cunning concealed true motivations and feelings ranging from class resentment to selfish and antisocial individualism. A purely predatory example of cunning is found in the 1979 novella *Children of Fear* (*Filhos do medo*), by the former metalworker Roniwalter Jatobá. Living in São Miguel Paulista, the "capital of northeasterners" in metropolitan São Paulo, a young migrant named Jacinto is hired as a helper in the stamping department of a metalworking shop in Brás; Felipe, the older worker in charge of the machine, teaches him the ropes. When Felipe loses a finger in an accident, Jacinto sees his chance. He leads the bosses to believe that Felipe intentionally injured himself to receive an indemnification, leading to the older man's firing and the promotion of his cunning helper, which otherwise might have taken years. The desperate Felipe, unaware of what Jacinto has done, repeatedly implores his former helper to make clear to the bosses what had happened; Jacinto ignores him.[84]

Jacinto's story reminds us that cunning and dissimulation are involved in far more than a war of maneuver between us and them. They just as often are deployed against fellow workers, and such self-serving behavior was common in ABC's workplaces. The untrammeled pursuit of individual gain can be seen in the universally repudiated figure of the dedo-duro (informer), who used dissimulation to gain the information that he passed secretly to the employer or the police. The ubiquitous shameless wheedler (puxa-saco), by trumpeting his loyalty to higher-ups through shameless flattery, was often rewarded through patron-client ties with authority figures. These social types violated the minimum in-group norms regulating when dissimulation edged over into betrayal of the most basic sense of group membership and a recognizable if minimal sense of mutual obligation. The dominance of cunning and dissimulation is also clearly linked to the conviction among workers that as a group they were submissive and weak, which thwarted open defense of group interests. Collective mobilization requires not only that tens of thousands of individual workers decide to act against their immediate self-interest but also that they believe that others will be willing to do the same.

This chapter has focused on the silent years of the industrial boom and the transformations of ABC during the Brazilian economic miracle. While the unskilled rank-and-file also benefited from the boom, the benefits were most reaped by the tiny minority of skilled workers. Skilled workers like Lula possessed a powerful drive for individual achievement along with a sturdy professional pride. Beyond a certain esprit de corps, these men were veritable learning machines, impatient with social and cultural subordination and given to a nagging suspicion about how the welcome bounty of economic growth was being shared between employers and employees.

Even as it grew by leaps and bounds, ABC seemed an unlikely and inhospitable terrain for collective mobilization, given its industrial, community, and political structures under the dictatorship. These were in addition to the subjective obstacles internalized by the region's metalworkers, who accepted society's stigmatizing judgments and the discouraging inheritance of past defeats. Cunning and dissimulation typified both interclass etiquette and life strategies, an inheritance from the rural world reformulated for new circumstances.

None of this would suggest that in just a few years ABC's workers would offer "outright collective defiance" and "direct symbolic confrontation with" the most powerful international and domestic capitalists backed by a military dictatorship, behavior that is the very opposite of the "weapons of the weak."[85] It was even less predictable that such efforts would be led by the workers who were the boom's greatest material beneficiaries. Yet despite workers' bleak assumptions about power and injustice, at the very heart of cunning existed, as Certeau realized, a "*utopian* space in which a possibility [of change], by definition miraculous in nature, was affirmed."[86]

9 THE APPRENTICE

On April 19, 1975, Lula was sworn in as president of the São Bernardo and Diadema metalworkers' union, after serving as its first secretary since 1972. Held at the São Bernardo convention center, the ceremony drew thousands of workers, friends, and relatives as well as reporters, state and federal deputies, and São Bernardo and Santo André's ARENA party mayors. The event was covered on the *Diário do Grande ABC*'s front page, although in the published photograph the thirty-year-old Lula, dressed in suit and tie, was cropped out.[1] The region's daily newspaper focused on outgoing president Paulo Vidal Neto and his featured guest, Paulo Egydio Martins, São Paulo's indirectly elected governor, who had entered office a month earlier, on March 15. An engineer, businessman, and minister of commerce and industry after 1964, the forty-seven-year-old Egydio played a small, unplanned role in Lula's swearing-in ceremony, offering on invitation "a few purely symbolic words" that had "no legal effect."[2] The union's *Tribuna Metalúrgica* highlighted his presence on its front page: "The metalworking family comes together for the swearing-in ceremony. Honored [*prestigiada*] by the governor, the celebration . . . was a demonstration of our leadership."[3]

Egydio's attendance—along with other ARENA politicians—followed the precedent set by the governor's predecessor, Laudo Natel, who graced the October 1973 opening of the union's splendid new headquarters. That these civilian allies of the regime met no protest demonstrates the political shift since 1968, when Governor Abreu Sodré had been stoned at the union-sponsored May Day rally in São Paulo. Yet during the subsequent, harshly repressive Médici years, no politician, even in a restricted electoral regime, could fail to be impressed that 14,608 workers—87 percent of union's paid-up membership—had voted in the union's 1975 election, although its members constituted only 16 percent of those employed in the categoria.[4]

Although first elected to union office six years earlier, Lula was preoccupied in the weeks preceding the ceremony by his lack of public speaking experience. He had his speech written in advance—by the union's indispensable attorney, Maurício Soares—but when he rose to read he "was trembling so much [that he] wasn't sure" whether his knees or the papers in his hand were shaking

View of the stage at Lula's 1975 inauguration as union president. (Courtesy DGABC [João Colovatti])

harder. Getting someone else to hold the text, Lula read a speech full of blatant flattery (*bajulação*), praising outgoing president Vidal's "audacious rhythm," "administrative sagacity," "ostentatious dedication," "breadth of knowledge," and "grandiosity of purpose." It would be difficult, he insisted, "to replace companheiro Paulo," but he knew that he could count on the "experience, dedication, and idealism" of the ex-president, who, although Lula did not mention it, was continuing in the union's other top position, secretary-general.[5]

Lula's inaugural performance showed none of the decisive influence or personal magnetism that would lead observers, just a few years later, to use the word "charisma." Despite having served as a full-time union official since 1972, Lula still displayed the shyness and timidity that had made him a terrible street hawker in Santos. This should place into question lazy narratives that invoke Lula's charismatic appeal to explain later events in lieu of asking under what circumstances charisma might emerge and take hold. To answer this question, we must examine Lula's time as first secretary as an apprenticeship in learning the union machine under the unusually demanding Paulo Vidal.

This chapter, drawing on new sources, advances an original interpretation of the union's dominant leader before Lula by navigating the vagaries of internal union politics, with its mix of the idealistic and pragmatic, principled and opportunistic. By contrasting Vidal's personality, behavior, and aspirations with those of Lula, I suggest a sociocultural interpretation of what drove this generation of young male union leaders. Treating the union as a working-class public sphere, I shed further light on Lula the "good boy" as he handled the social welfare needs of members (*assistencialismo*), oversaw a high school equivalency course (*curso de madureza*), and positioned himself within the union after a hotly contested 1972 election. Discarding artificial boundaries between public and private, I examine Lula's interpersonal interactions and shed new light on how in 1971 the twenty-six-year-old expectant father became a grieving widow. I also interpret his subsequent frantic womanizing as illuminating the masculine sphere of working-class sociability.

This chapter goes beyond self-interested accounts offered by Lula, a master storyteller, to examine cunning, whether in union politics or romantic relations, as a two-sided process of calculation and performance in which individuals maneuver within webs of power. The mass strikes to come required the involvement of hundreds of thousands of quintessentially modern women and young men like Lula.

The Widowed Bachelor

By 1971 everything had come together for the twenty-six-year-old Lula and his wife Lourdes, three years his junior. Unlike her older brother Lambari, Lula's best friend, she only faintly remembered the small settlement of Morro Agudo in northern Minas Gerais from which she moved before she was three years old. Her life was shaped by the family's moves through São Paulo's interior, including nine years as a tenant (*meiro*), before settling in the small town of Biriri, where she finished a sewing course while working in a vegetable oil factory; her parents were itinerant harvest workers (*bóias-frias*). They moved to São Paulo city in 1964–65 at the invitation of a cousin, an assistant to a construction worker (*pedreiro*), and became neighbors of the Silvas. Friendship between Lourdes and Lula turned to marriage; the couple awaited their first child in their own house, which they were renovating to include a room for the arrival.

The mother-to-be was in an enviable position because her husband worked for a modern factory with medical services and even guaranteed hospital care. This was "one of the best things" about such firms, an enthusiastic metalworker observed in 1976–77; an unskilled recent migrant to São Paulo, who couldn't afford meat because of the low wages at his factory, still preferred it to work on the farm because it provided "a fixed salary, medical assistance, and school."[6] Lourdes appeared for each monthly prenatal checkup, as a Villares nurse recalled, and was seen by the obstetrician Fausto Farah Baract, later an eminent cancer specialist.[7] Lula and Lourdes had every reason to believe that she would escape the fate of their mothers and grandmothers, whose medically unattended pregnancies included multiple infant deaths.[8]

This is why the death of Lourdes and her son in the seventh month of pregnancy was so shocking. Over the prior weeks, Lourdes had experienced severe stomach pain and vomiting, causing her to stay home from work, but she was still able to talk when visited by Tiana and dona Lindu, who suspected hepatitis. She was taken to a local doctor and sent to Hospital Modelo, which admitted her under pressure from Lula; the costs were covered by an agreement with Villares. In extreme pain and increasingly desperate, Lourdes was visited repeatedly over the weekend by, among others, Lula and her brother, mother, and sister-in-law. As Tiana suggests, "it was the lack of a correct diagnosis" that caused her death; as Lula recalls, the doctor insisted that the pain had nothing to do with hepatitis. Lula left on Sunday night. He returned with baby clothes on Monday, June 7, 1971, to learn that she and the child were dead. Putting his head against the wall, Lula swayed and retched; the shock was tremendous.[9]

All who knew Lula agreed that this trauma reverberated over the years. How did she get hepatitis, Lula asked, with running water and a clean house? His sisters wondered how dona Hermínia missed the seriousness of what was happening until one of the Silva women pointed it out.[10] But the specifics of a traumatic episode do not exhaust its meanings. Tragedy and joy are both part of medical practice, observed the doctor overseeing her prenatal care, when interviewed by journalist Eliane Brum. He noted the overwhelming number of cases for which he was responsible at Villares: thirty a day in four hours, plus cases in the hospital. "We were caught with our shorts down" (*pega de calças curtas*), the Villares nurse admitted, although she denied that anyone was personally responsible and mentioned the limited technology at the time.[11]

Yet personal tragedy also takes on meaning in the context of a person's life. Lula could not help but remember the doctor whom he suspected had needlessly cut off his whole finger or how, after a factory accident, doctors operated on the wrong finger of his brother Vavá. Talking to Paraná in 1993, Lula called Lourdes's death medical negligence and still had "certain reservations" about the doctors' behavior. When she was screaming for help, they responded to Lula's pleas by putting him in his place, although, he added, this might have reflected their inexperience.[12] Contemporary voices from ABC elucidate the health care available to the relatively privileged metalworkers employed by big companies. Those who gained access to medical care for the first time were immensely appreciative. "You are attended to as if you were paying for the consultation," one woman insisted, "as if you were *gente* [real or important people]." More worldly and experienced working-class women knew that the doctors were often inexperienced, that doctors with private practices tended better to those patients, and that the good doctors often left. Yet all agreed that the care was better than that offered in the "very bad" public hospitals.[13]

Regarding the death of Lourdes and her infant, the larger truth may have been best stated by the head of the maternity ward: "You know how it is, the poor we treat well," but no one goes out of their way.[14] In his interview with Paraná, Lula converted personal tragedy into social critique. Lourdes's fate showed how hard it is for a poor person (*desgraçado*) to be admitted to hospitals, "to be attended to, or [even to] get a doctor's appointment"; even burying a loved one depends on class, as "those who have money can do anything and those who don't nothing." Thirty-one years later, when her brother was elected president, Tiana noted that what happened to Lourdes "continues to happen every day, at all hours, and in all hospitals."[15]

Yet Lula was hardly poor in 1972, and he noted with appreciation how Villares's social work department covered the cost of transporting the bodies to his house, where they were placed together in a single coffin in the living room. The house quickly filled with neighbors, relatives of the two families, Lula's union friends (the union covered some of the expenses), and even the ambulance driver, who stayed for the wake. Dona Hermínia was so overcome with emotion that she had to be sedated by a doctor, while their cheap wooden floor cracked from the weight, a detail recalled by both Lambari and the Villares social worker. Moreover, tension among the Silvas ran high because the well-meaning Vavá had, per accepted mores, arranged for Aristides to come up from Santos; this horrified one of Vavá's sisters and dona Lindu, both of whom refused to see Aristides during his visit. Throughout the emotionally charged wake, the metalworker Nelson Campanholo never left Lula's side, a protective stance he had also taken when they went to identify the bodies. Born in 1951 in the São Paulo interior, Nelson had become tight friends with Lula after they both entered the diretoria as alternates in 1969. Other unionists at the wake included the former president Afonso Monteiro da Cruz and a union accountant.[16]

For the first half year afterward, Lula was depressed, sluggish (*borocoxô*), thinking of Lourdes constantly; it was especially hard for him to sleep in the house that they had bought together. Dona Lindu and a sister moved in and slept in the couple's bed, while Lula used the living room. "It was a difficult time for him," Tiana observed, but disaster, tragedy, and loss—including repeated floods that cost Marinete and Vavá their hard-won home—were the stuff of life. What mattered most, she said, was that Lula overcame this setback, a sentiment echoed in Lula's odd, offhand comment when recounting the tragedy to Paraná: "You can't spend your whole life mulling it over [*se remoendo*]."[17]

The twenty-six-year-old widow, once again a bachelor after two years of marriage, was better off financially than in the mid-1960s, when he was supporting his mothers and sisters as best he could.[18] That financial pressure had prevented him from devoting as much time to "farra" (partying) as he would have liked. It's not that he had had no fun. He had learned to dance, if only at seventeen, and had served as an occasional manager for two brothers-in-law who played country music (*música sertaneja*); paid in snacks and cachaça, they returned home, half drunk, to get up at 6 A.M. for Sunday mass, where they would "wait for the girls to leave to see if they could flirt [*paquerar*] with them." Even the repeated floods in Ponte Preta, where the Silvas and Ribeiros lived, were welcome because one ended up in shelters after frantically raising everything in the house above water level; when it came time to sleep, "everyone [was] already thinking of sacanagem," and Lula was looking forward to being with his new girlfriend Lourdes.[19] But over the next year the depression lifted and Lula enjoyed unparalleled personal freedom, with no wife and child to support and no one expecting him home at day's end.[20] In a 1979 interview with *Nova*, he passed over the 1971 tragedy quickly, after which the female interviewer asked if he had been a happy widow. Noting that he "already had some experience" and was less inhibited, Lula observed that he became "somewhat shameless" (*meio sem vergonha*), dedicating his life to "work and womenfolk [*mulherio*]." As he recalled, "I would leave my job and go straight to the *gandaia* [*cair na gandaia*, painting the town red]."[21]

Within a year of his wife's death, Lula had become a paid full-time union official, as had his bachelor best friend Nelson. Their new jobs gave them control over their time unknown to a factory worker while expanding the space for male camaraderie, which included having a drink (*tomando uma birita*), usually cachaça, the cheapest alcoholic beverage. At the week's end, as Nelson recalled in 2014, they would leave union headquarters for drinks at a nearby barbecue restaurant (*churrasqueria*): "We would each have two or three and leave happy." The union crowd would also go to the nearby, now famous Bar de Rosa to chat and socialize.[22] If drinking was central to the masculine union world, the organization did also sponsor events, dances, and parties to bring together wives, girlfriends, and single folks to dance and eat on the union's dime. A particularly big event, like a new building's inauguration, might involve thousands and a two-page spread in the union newspaper.[23]

Marrying a well-paid skilled worker was an attractive prospect to young women, given the strength of the male breadwinner ideal.[24] Especially attractive was the funny (*brincalhão*) and engaging Lula, a veritable people magnet. Even the mother of his first child, disaffected by 1989, still described the Lula of 1972 affectionately as "only a peon [*peazao*] but a handsome one [*neguinho bonito*], a hotty [*gatinho*, a little cat]." In her early twenties at the time, Miriam

Cordeiro was a nurse's assistant at a union-affiliated medical clinic. She met Lula when he brought in the sickly twins of his sister-in-law; their relationship involved going to movies and parties and even had, she claimed, the discreet support of union president Vidal. Lula recalled walking to her home from the union and returning there on foot before midnight to take a taxi home.[25]

The details remain sparse for the "happy widow" phase of Lula's social life. A union lawyer, Antônio Possidônio Sampaio, described Lula then as a bohemian, a flirt, and a "lady's man" (*galã*); a few secondhand reports call him an incorrigible womanizer (*mulherengo*).[26] Lacking evidence regarding the degree of deception in his dating life, we can parse Lula's words carefully for what they may conceal and for macho exaggeration aimed at his male counterparts. "I turned sacana and wanted to go out with a woman every day," he told Josué Machado during a three-day May 1979 interview with *Playboy*, published two months later, in which he playfully joked about posing nude. "I wanted to chase girls [*namorar*] every day," he later told Paraná, "preferably different people"—although his romantic exploits likely fell short of Lambari's. When Lula was *namorando* Lourdes, his boastful, womanizing best friend was doing the same with Lula's sister Ruth, which dona Lindu ended because she suspected that Lambari was seeing someone else (she was right, he admitted later nonchalantly; I was "shameless").[27]

Lula frames being a *namorodeiro* as a restlessness after being shaken to the core (*abalado*). As a widow he "had no perspective on life," and three years of craziness passed before meeting the woman who would become his second wife. He may even have been troubled by his behavior, since he heeded the union's Catholic lawyer, Maurício Soares, and attended a church retreat in 1973. The lay lecturer, Lula recalls, went on about Pharisees and sinful betrayals, which left him feeling that he "had committed some sins"; this dissipated, however, after he learned that the lecturer had not only left his wife but also had a lover at his workplace.[28]

Miriam Cordeiro's brief 1989 interviews reveal that their relationship was ongoing and did not involve a promise of marriage. Miriam, according to Lula's sister Maria Baixinha, first told her about the pregnancy, swearing her to secrecy. When first interviewed after the child's "discovery" in 1989, Miriam said that her relationship with Lula slowed a bit after she told him about the pregnancy in her third month. Calling herself a "petista but not a Lulista," she said that Lula had paid the hospital expenses and visited his firstborn "but without wishing to assume a greater commitment."[29] Later in 1989, Cordeiro became briefly infamous when she appeared in the final national TV advertisement of Lula's presidential opponent denouncing Lula as an abortionist and racist who had ruined her life (like Lula, she is white).[30] Talking with fellow metalworkers

Front row: Lula (left) and Lambari. Back row from left: Zé Graxa, Toninho, Zé Eron, and Frei Chico. Lula was ashamed to be the only one not wearing shoes. (Courtesy President Luiz Inácio Lula da Silva)

eleven years later, Lula said he understood Miriam's hatred because they had even begun looking for a house together after she had gotten pregnant.[31]

The baby was born on March 8, 1974—International Women's Day, as Miriam noted—and Lula appears as the father on the birth certificate. The mother chose the name Lurian to honor both parents, although Miriam cut off contact between Lula and his daughter. Over the following fifteen years, however, Lurian and Lula remained in contact (Lurian was a huge fan of Lula and the PT in 1989 and still is) because Miriam's mother, dona Beatriz, raised Lurian and found ways for her to see her dad, with the help of Maria Baixinha and Nelson Campanholo. Miriam married in 1981, was widowed a few years after, and raised her other two children separately from Lurian.[32]

The Building Makes the Man: Understanding Paulo Vidal

When Lula began full-time in the São Bernardo and Diadema metalworkers' union, Paulo Vidal was its "big name," even its "strongman."[33] Vidal is routinely described by acquaintances as intelligent, creative, and a capable administrator.[34] Observers have called him the union's most discussed, criticized, and controversial leader, one who, they hint, may have behaved questionably.[35] Yet no one has comprehensively judged his contributions or relationship with Lula. Only thirty-three years old in 1975, Vidal was already a veteran unionist, having served eight consecutive years on the union's diretoria—six as president—with three more to come during Lula's first presidential term. Although both, like all the other union officers, were under thirty-five, Vidal later referred to Lula as a youngster whom he chose as full-time director in spite of Lula's undistinguished stint as an alternate on the union's powerless fiscal council.[36] Vidal and Lula both came to power through the union apparatus, unlike labor militants such as Frei Chico who took their shop floor activism into the union.

Vidal was born in 1942 to a farming family in Mogi das Cruzes, fifty kilometers from São Paulo city. In this sparsely populated município, in the eastern zone of the metropolitan region, Vidal finished primary school and went to work in a shoe factory at age eleven while earning extra cash as a shoeshine boy. By 1961, the nineteen-year-old had achieved professional status as a milling machine operator (*mandrilhador*) with Molins do Brasil, an English company in São Bernardo. He was first elected to the union as second secretary in 1967, the second election held after the 1964 intervention.[37] After a single term, Vidal assumed the presidency during a tumultuous period of leadership instability and sharp divisions within the union's activist core, especially on the left.

Beginning his first term, Vidal already had some prominence beyond São Bernardo as the union's representative in the Movimento Intersindical Antiarrocho in 1968, in which he clashed with New Left labor activists. Profiled in an opposition magazine in 1974, the energetic union president disdainfully described the late 1960s in union affairs as "political, moral, and economic chaos" driven by "political-ideological, personal, and group interests."[38] While Vidal's 1969 slate had been backed by the union's Communists, he quickly emerged as a leftist bête noire, as Frei Chico explained.[39] In opposition leaflets and retrospective interviews they attacked Vidal as a "notorious pelego" and a "camouflaged police agent at the service of the bosses and the dictatorship," responsible for his union opponents' arrest and torture.[40] Frei Chico said in 1981 that he personally "thought Paulo was a shit," but his brother "didn't believe that."[41]

Influenced by this poisonous internal politics, Lula's English-language biographer described Vidal as egocentric, "conservative in his political attitudes," and lacking "courage, consistency, and empathy."[42] Likewise, the commercial biopic *Lula, Son of Brazil* presented Vidal as a corrupt opportunist eventually repudiated by Lula.[43] Yet those most closely allied with Lula, whether metalworkers or scholars, have been more circumspect, referring to Vidal vaguely as "extremely legalistic" and "personalistic."[44] Studying the union's newspaper, Kátia Paranhos contested such sharp contrasts between Vidal and a bottom-up confrontational approach identified with Lula.[45] She demonstrated that the *Tribuna Metalúrgica*, which Vidal founded in 1971, offered critical coverage, highlighted worker grievances, opposed government wage policies, and sought to convince the categoria that if more workers got involved with the union, their problems could be more effectively confronted.[46] This newspaper also launched, in May 1972, the memorable figure of João Ferrador, the rank-and-file metalworker who drafted cheeky letters to authorities and, as we saw in chapter 5, became a visual icon of the metalworker during Lula's leadership.

When elected in 1969, Vidal's slate promised to stabilize the union—by ending administrative chaos, disciplining expenses, and increasing revenue—and "reestablish respect" with employers and the government by showing that the union defended the worker and not other, unspecified interests, a dig at leftists. Finally, the slate spoke of organizing workers at the grassroots, a hard task in the years after AI-5.[47] In the *Tribuna Metalúrgica*'s first issue, Vidal declared that workers needed to make themselves "felt in the national scenario" to win a fair share of "the fruits of progress." Yet Vidal, realistic about the balance of power, argued that union affairs had to be conducted "within the established order" (*dentro da ordem*), a formula that the authorities and his union opponents could take as criticism of those seeking to use the union to overturn the military regime, if not capitalism.[48]

After AI-5, a practical man like Vidal deemed suicidal the courageous AP militants who chanted "Down with the dictatorship" in union meetings full of police informants. He had little patience for gestures of protest that endangered the union; for instance, the moment of silence requested in a 1970 union meeting by ex-director Afonso Monteiro da Cruz briefly resulted in the union's lawyer, Maurício Soares, being detained. Vidal's leftist opponents disdained such "opportunism" as well as his unorthodox idea that those in highly productive modern industries should negotiate independently of the rest of the working class.[49] Vidal willingly paid a political price for such views in the tumultuous union assemblies between 1969 and 1972, which at times devolved into physical confrontations.[50]

Looking back in 1993, Frei Chico could offer a more nuanced analysis. Initially describing Vidal as an ally of employers and the government, he immediately clarified that he "wouldn't say he was a pelego." Lula's brother commended

Vidal's modernizing vision of the trade union and welcomed the new administrative structures and procedures he brought, along with the hiring of technical staff, the creation of new departments and a high school equivalency course, and the construction of the new union headquarters.[51] The enormous increase in the union's patrimony and revenues between 1969 and 1975 left a formidable instrument in the hands of Vidal's successor.[52]

Building a new headquarters required planning and political moxie by Vidal. Internally, everyone recognized that the union's facilities could not meet the legally mandated medical, legal, and social welfare needs (assistencialismo) of the union's nearly 10,000 members. To hold general assemblies, the union had to book space in the Odeon Club or other downtown São Bernardo venues.[53] This is why the plan to build a new headquarters had been embraced since the union's Communist president Orisson Saraiva displayed a model by famous USP modernist architect Vilanova Artigas, a Communist.[54] The headquarters Artigas designed was never to be built. The big challenge was funding, given the union's shaky finances. A key legal mechanism was the "assistencialist discount" that, once approved by a union assembly, could be collected from workers' salary in addition to the legally mandated annual union tax. According to Lula's description of the discount-collecting process, the factory manager would always refuse to pay, claiming to be "defending" his workers' pocketbook; the union would then go to the labor court to force payment. With revenues on the rise during the economic miracle, all union officials had an edifice complex. As Lula humorously remarked, officers carried blueprints under their arms at labor gatherings, eager to show off the imposing new facility that would deliver unprecedented services to their members.[55] Some labor activists saw such new headquarters as a distraction from the workers and their struggles, unconvinced by claims that the "honored task" of building a headquarters would prove that working-class "unity makes strength."[56]

In October 1973, thousands turned out for the formal inauguration of the new headquarters, following by an evening dance with live music. The event's splendor (*brilho*) was enhanced by the multiple authorities whom Vidal had convinced to attend, including São Paulo's indirectly elected governor, Laudo Natel. Directing himself toward Natel, Vidal observed that "while Brazil [was] developing," the worker was "still waiting avidly for the authorities to remember" his need for "some recognition of his participation in productivity [growth]."[57] With such public-facing rhetoric, Vidal and the union newspaper echoed the government's developmentalist rhetoric and hailed workers as patriotic Brazilians and well-behaved collaborators, which might seem to reinforce Vidal's image as the "notorious pelego." Indeed, only a few years later opposition journalists would deem such rhetorical devices "editorials in support of the government and condemnations of extremism." Yet Vidal was employing a well-established rhetorical convention of Brazilian patron-client relations: workers selflessly contributed their skills, hard work, and loyalty to national development and deserved reciprocal reward by the government.[58]

As leaders and staff settled into their new building, Vidal hailed the "new mentality in union life" being pioneered in São Bernardo at a November 23, 1973, meeting. The union, he declared, had a role in promoting the cultural evolution of the "men of the *macacão* [big monkey overalls]," the mandatory factory uniforms worn by metalworkers at big firms.[59] He announced the union's new Tiradentes Educational Center (CET), named after the plebeian independence martyr, which would offer technical training and high school equivalency courses overseen by First Secretary Lula. By enhancing workers' skills and education, the São Bernardo union was contributing to national well-being by improving workers' technical capacity, enhancing productivity, and fostering individual social mobility.

Such self-improvement programs—including educational fellowships—superficially coincided with the government's desire that unions prioritize their educational, social welfare, and medical and dental assistance functions. But how are we to read this public transcript? And can we reasonably assume that the man's outward-directed performance matches his gut reactions, private opinions, or real views? Those like Vidal who occupy official positions face conflicting demands. They must appear to obey and must perform the role of pelego toward those above them. Yet simultaneously they must signal to those below that they are not pelegos selling out the rank and file for individual advantage. This dilemma breeds suspicion and distrust, which, compounded by internal competition, made united union action more difficult.

Yet new evidence exists regarding Vidal's views as a union leader during the Médici years. On July 7, 1972, he was interviewed by a US graduate student, Kenneth Mericle, who took handwritten notes on Vidal's blunt, oppositional answers to forty-two questions. For example, Vidal declared his opposition to *assistencia social* provision by unions because health care was a government responsibility already paid for by workers via taxes. While he nevertheless recognized that assistencia social met a real need given the bad quality of government health services, he lamented that it corrupted by misleading workers as to the union's true purpose.[60]

Belying his pelego reputation, Vidal also excoriated employers, the labor courts, and the government. The labor justice system was a tool of the government, said Vidal, because it lacked the "normative power" to impose itself and refused to recognize the legitimacy of negotiations over nonwage issues. He preferred replacing the system with collective contracts negotiated directly between the union and the company. He described the courts as slow in responding to individual workers' grievances, unwilling to prevent retaliatory firings for filing complaints, and ignoring pressing industrial health and safety problems.

As expected from someone who protested the arrocho in 1968, Vidal was harshly critical of government labor policy. He attacked the new post-1967 job tenure system as a disaster "written to favor foreign capital and the government's housing plans." By making it easier to fire workers, the FGTS established in 1966 placed "severe limitations on militant workplace activity" while fostering "sub- and unemployment" as well as discrimination against union members. Moreover, the government had lowered workers' purchasing power by setting a mandatory nationwide index for annual salary negotiations. While annual wage campaigns were used as opportunities to educate union members, they had no influence on employers or the labor courts, which only "pretend[ed] to discuss the demands" advanced by the unions.

Vidal's private views, as captured in Mericle's contemporaneous notes, are not absolute truths about his beliefs and dispositions, much less his actions. Yet read alongside what we know from other sources, they dispel stereotypes and provide a "hidden transcript" of Vidal's self-perception and the opinions he shared privately with his protégé Lula. On the government's restrictive 1966 strike law, Vidal was succinct: "For those who like shit it is a good plate." Vidal affirmed that unions should strike to win new agreements, address overdue wages, and even demand labor legislation changes. Most surprisingly, Vidal did not reject strikes carried out for "general political objectives," although this was the standard criticism of the pre-1964 labor movement led by the Communists and trabalhistas whom Vidal disdained. Vidal favored "political strikes" if the issues were important and "if a united workers' movement existed with well-defined and articulated political objectives," an apt description of what would crystallize in the 1980s as the New Unionism.

Vidal repeatedly bemoaned the lack of "political consciousness" and "ideological definition among union directors," whose "politics blow with the political winds." Most, he declared, were careerists who placed "personal objectives and career interests above class interests." Vidal also argued for the union tax's eventual replacement by union dues collected as part of collective bargaining agreements. As he had stated publicly, Vidal considered himself in the vanguard of a modernizing Brazil, charged with reforming the country's archaic industrial relations system created in the 1930s and 1940s under Getúlio Vargas.

At the very least, Vidal's private 1972 opinions serve to relativize the denunciations by union leftists of his alleged lies and demagoguery.[61] While we might be unable to determine which provides a truer portrait of Vidal the individual, his oppositional postures were documented in another 1972 survey, of the fifty-three presidents of "the most important and numerically powerful" labor organizations in Rio and São Paulo. Amaury de Souza found that two-thirds of these presidents—including nine out of ten leaders from the most modern industrial sectors, including the auto and metalworking industries—recognized that their constituents' interests clashed with those of state authorities regarding wage and social welfare policy, labor law enforcement, and the right to strike. The prevailing discontent even generated "outspokenly critical" union leaders willing, unlike Vidal, to directly address political repression. Souza concluded that there existed "a more militant breed of labor leaders who compete for the loyalty of the rank and file." Like Vidal, they would openly criticize the government to an outsider, "even under [the] adverse political conditions" of the Médici era.[62] Far from a bedrock of state support, the men holding local union offices were overwhelmingly discontented with employers and the government, even at the high point of economic success and regime popularity among their constituents.

As Vidal and honest trade unionists saw it, workers were denied a legitimate share of the rising employer profits created by the economic boom. This perception was strongest among the skilled, who monopolized the collective representation of their fellow workers through unions. As self-made men, honest union leaders were forced into demeaning tutelage by petty government functionaries and shamelessly self-serving higher-level union figures not directly elected by workers. These proud men had to dissimulate daily to stay on good terms with those whose policies hurt workers and directly aided employers. On a gut level, they resented being treated like peons only tasked with behaving themselves, begging for crumbs, and staying silent. The rewards offered for such conformity—escape from the rigors of daily factory life, travel, and social perks—were not enough. So this ungrateful modern generation of unionists increasingly imagined an escape from the government's authoritarian labor relations system.

The "Good Boy" as Apprentice

Looking back on his 1972 research in São Paulo, Kenneth Mericle recalled the skilled workers with whom he had roomed as very entrepreneurial in their attitudes and unrealistic in their expectations.[63] Brash, self-confident, opinionated young working-class men like Paulo Vidal were common during the economic miracle. In his 1973 profile of these men, Paul Singer noted how their working lives shaped their worldview: inasmuch as the skilled "work with machines, they imagine society as a machine in which individuals are parts [*peças*]," each having a role in its effective functioning. As a union office, skilled workers would have to learn—through study, practice, and improvisation—what Frei Chico called the union's gear system (*engrenagem sindical*).[64] It was the mechanics of the union enterprise that were the focus of Paulo Vidal the operator, a third social type among workers alongside the rebels and good boys introduced in chapter 4. Vidal was a smooth-talking entrepreneur with an eye on engineering power and the drive and vision needed to, following union usage, *tocar a maquina* (literally, to play or run the machine).

As Lula joined the full-time leadership, Vidal was consolidating control after a term in which the diretoria's members had clashed sharply. In 1972 Vidal had finally vanquished his enemies, although his slate won only 60 percent of the 8,200 valid votes cast, a decline from the 75 percent of 6,500 votes received three years earlier.[65] But the union over which he now held sway was far from the powerhouse he wished to build. Forward motion, he realized, would require quelling internal conflicts and a concerted drive to increase worker involvement. Lula learned trade unionism and politics during this moment when São Bernardo tackled the formidable "challenge of being a real trade union," as the Médici years came to an end and the military regime, in late 1974, initiated a controlled process of political opening.[66]

Lula would have to master the mundane aspects of union life, including bureaucratic routines, budgets, services, and preparing union assemblies. Lula would also undergo a gradual politicization through relationships with fellow directors, union lawyers and staff, and activists central to the union's turbulent internal politics. Finally, Lula would need to learn about the repressive dimensions of working-class life under military rule, including close supervision and surveillance by the police, employers, and labor ministry officials.

Lula was rightly thought a "loyal pupil" of Vidal, his "tutor and teacher" (mestre).[67] Vidal was a type of godparent (*padrinho*) to Lula, the president's client (*un protegido*), and Lula would make his career in Vidal's shadow. In retrospective interviews, Vidal underlined the patronage dimension by recalling that he had discovered Lula—whom he refers to by his factory nickname, Taturana—when "still a kid, a big boy and single" (um garoto ainda, um molecão solteiro).[68] As the union's lawyer perceived, Vidal regarded Lula as "a good boy" (*moço bonzinho*) who would be pliable. Frei Chico the "rebel" agreed, describing his brother as a "good boy, timid and 'obedient' [*bem mandado*]," who Vidal believed would serve as his doormat (*capacho*). Even Lula recalls how "everyone thought [he] was an easy-to-manipulate doll" when he accompanied Vidal to meetings. And intelligence agencies, as late as 1976, pointed to then union president Lula's "demonstrative" support for Vidal's city council candidacy as proof of the godparent's decisive influence (*ascendencia*).[69]

When initially included on the 1972 slate as a director linked to production,

Lula believed that the three years of job security that came with the position would make him an effective union representative at his factory. "I thought when I entered the union that I would have a big impact [*lavar a egua*, wash the mare]," he told Altino Dantas in 1981 with comic exaggeration; "I was going to climb up and shit on the boss's desk. . . . The worker at Villares was not going to have any more problems." Yet his naïveté was soon apparent. The boss would claim to be powerless when confronted with the workers' problems; consulting the union lawyers after work went nowhere, too. As formal union representation was illegal in the factory, Lula needed his boss's permission to leave his section to check out a problem. Moreover, confronting management sometimes brought warnings, which led his more experienced union colleagues to suggest that he was being too forceful.[70]

Unlike the Ford or Scania factories, the new Villares factory lacked a well-integrated union membership, and the standard union recruitment pitch, emphasizing assistencia, had less appeal at a reasonably well-paying firm whose benefits approximated those of big multinational auto companies. Lula was also increasingly disillusioned by the union's fractured leadership, marked by "petty politics" (politicagem) over assignments and matters as insignificant as who took the union's car the night before. Internal divergences prevailed over the "uniformity of thought" needed to effectively represent the categoria. With a baby expected, Lula stopped going to the union hall for four months.[71] In Vidal's telling, at this point he brought a bottle of cachaça and sausages to Lula and Lourdes's home. While she cooked, the two men talked and drank into the early morning hours until Vidal convinced Lula not to quit.[72] Over the next year, a newly energized Lula recruited new members who saw the union as a shield and sword; he even led a modest movement to end a 2 percent pay deduction for an unnecessary sick-leave plan and fought for the construction of a cafeteria.[73]

Vidal's visit to Lula was tied to the slate he was constructing for the 1972 union elections. This was of enough concern to Afonso Monteiro da Cruz, a former union president and Vidal opponent, that he discussed it with Frei Chico at Lourdes's wake. As when first recruited to the union in 1968, Lula neither accepted nor declined Vidal's pitch, and the president was savvy enough not to be pushy. Lula would even attend meetings of the heterogeneous opposition, which included Frei Chico and what remained of the AP and the PCB and those over whom these parties still had influence. According to Vidal, he encouraged Lula to reach out to them, and the opposition may even have offered him the top of their slate. In this account Vidal played up his self-confidence to better highlight his victory when Lula decided to run on his slate as first secretary along with friends like Nelson Campanholo.[74]

What did Vidal and his opponents see in the inexperienced young man who had recently considered dropping out of the union? The bottom line of all electoral politics: the perception that an appealing personality might help their side win. Analysts have underestimated the importance of the type of personal popularity that Lula already enjoyed among fellow directors, staff, and the workers who frequented the union. "I captivated many people" at the time, Lula has observed, and his friendships made him attractive as a candidate. This also illustrates Lula's lack of a clear political disposition or polarizing alignment; he "had friends on both *chapas*," as he recalled, which "was a crazy thing [*coisa maluca*]."[75]

The Left's calculation regarding Lula reflected their weakness. Their organizations had been decimated by political repression: the AP disappeared by 1971, and the PCB would be liquidated in a repressive sweep centered at VW by the end of 1972. In the fight against Vidal, the remaining dispersed leftists were allied with Scania's Afonso Monteiro da Cruz and the Galache brothers at Ford, one of whom had been a member of the diretoria under Vidal, with whom he was locked in a poisonous leadership rivalry.[76] Leftists found some reassurance in the fact that Frei Chico was Lula's brother, while the arch "antileftist" Vidal saw an opportunity to broaden his appeal among those who might otherwise support the opposition.[77]

A focus on labels, platforms, and principles obscures how much electoral politics is anchored in personality. Talking to Paraná about his adolescence, Lula recalled a certain preeminence (*ascenção*) that he had enjoyed among his soccer mates. Possessing a broad array of friendships, he was able exercise influence without fighting; his adversaries treated him kindly. "I got along with everyone." This relative openness was attractive in a union whose boisterous political culture featured bitter enmities and harsh condemnations. As a union newcomer in 1969, Lula occupied a status similar to that he had enjoyed a decade earlier when first hired at Marte Screw Factory, where, as Lula recalled, "I got along well with everyone, and they treated me as if I was the *caçulinha* [the spoiled youngest brother]."[78]

As a union team member, the enthusiastically social Lula was a hit with everyone. He was devoted to soccer, dancing, card playing, and farra; one of Vidal's strongest allies, the anti-Communist Janjão (João Justino da Silva), would personally teach the young man to drive.[79] Lula loved talking—as he still did fifty years later—and spoke *with* people, not *at* them. Lula's sociability captured what ABC's metalworkers believed most characteristic about their way of being as peons (*peões*): a distinctive sense of humor, an appreciation of tricks and games (*brincadeiras*), and a love for cheerful, deflating mockery of higher-ups, especially if the mocker didn't take himself too seriously (unlike Vidal). This jovial spirit is captured in Frei Chico's story about Lula at Villares, where he was tight with the "happy kids" (*molecada alegre*) who typically occupied tool shops. The night-shift workers wanted to use the ping-pong tables in the white-collar employees' association; after the guard refused, Lula led the successful fight to let them play and entertain themselves.[80]

In this Lula resembled São Paulo's great midcentury union leaders, who often "emerged spontaneously, even casually," according to the unnamed trade unionist interviewed by Trotskyist intellectual Fábio Munhoz in the early 1970s. Drawing on experience with the São Paulo and Santos metalworkers' unions, this unionist explained that these leaders might even have entered union activity by chance, possessing "absolutely no political consciousness" prior to this. Yet those who evolved into great leaders, he believed, possessed certain innate human characteristics (*indole*), being the "most honest, the most human" individuals, "always ready to share information, to offer a clarification, to resolve some doubt, whether professional or juridical." Munhoz's interviewee insisted that such a young man (*rapaz*) could become a great union leader by standing out and saying what workers wanted to hear. The veteran labor activist pointed to a young man admired by his coworkers "because he liked soccer, liked to play [*brincar*]," danced, and "took care to buy presents for their weddings." After he stood up for his coworkers and was reprimanded, they began bringing their concerns to him. The union recruited him in 1959 as an alternate, although his involvement waxed and waned in his first two years. By 1964, however, he reached the top of union leadership in Santos, the Brazilian city most famous for its powerful union movement and mobilized workers.[81]

Lula's decision to join Vidal's slate spurred a "tremendous fight" with Frei Chico. However, Frei Chico noted with admiration how Lula, having chosen a side, worked energetically to guarantee victory, in the process beginning to become a true trade unionist. Lula was at the factory gates every weekday and even on Saturday. After the opposition slate distributed leaflets, Lula would use a stick capped with a nail to spear them off the ground so that no one else could read them. The brothers would grow more distant in the election's aftermath, but not primarily for political reasons. The married Frei Chico, who had been living with Lula and dona Lindu for two years to save money, moved out around this time.[82]

Union business offered Lula a focus for his life ambitions. Unlike some of the other, more senior full-time directors, who went through the motions, he threw himself into learning his new line of work. As he remembered in 1981, he had "always believed that the only weapon through which you can win at anything" is dedication and hard work.[83] In part, this reflected the drive shared by São Paulo's skilled workers at midcentury. As the sociologist Celso João Ferretti observed, their self-improvement projects were driven by curiosity and personal initiative and fueled by "willpower and hard work." "You always have to be trying to improve and to please in what you do," the onetime machinist Durval told Ferretti.[84] In the early 1970s, the upward trajectory and superb "on-the-job performance" of SENAI graduates like Lula was well-known, although many attributed this to the skills they had acquired in the classroom. The key researcher on SENAI, by contrast, emphasized that noncognitive factors were equally important, especially the "self-discipline, organization, and willpower required to complete a course successfully."[85]

Life in the São Bernardo union, a legally defined collaborative organ of the government, encompassed various administrative, bureaucratic, and legal tasks. Dealing with the lawyers who represented employers, as one paulista union leader noted, was enough to cause someone "with a primary school education" to suffer a heart attack.[86] Union leaders needed both general and specialized knowledge. As a São Bernardo director (likely Vidal) explained to USP doctoral student Luís Flávio Rainho in 1976, his union took in annual revenues higher than most Brazilian municípios. A lack of sufficient technical and administrative staff left all the bureaucratic responsibilities to the seven full-time directors. Over 8,000 different documents were associated with union accounting alone, not to mention the 20,000 contract rescissions (*homologações*) that the president had to sign off on each year.[87]

The São Bernardo official insisted on the importance of hiring accountants and other professionals to handle (*tocar*) such administrative matters, as this left the directors freer to reach out to workers and the broader society.[88] Such hiring of the highly educated by manual laborers, a reversal of social hierarchies, was not unprecedented, since trade unions had long contracted with lawyers and doctors. But to prevent the union from being run by outsiders, directors needed to understand the laws, regulations, history, and politics of trade unionism. This is why Vidal contracted with the Departamento Intersindical de Estatística e Estudos Sócio-Econômicas (DIEESE) for skill-building courses for union directors taught by Walter Barelli, a formidable USP-trained economist and son of a factory worker who would become a regular at the union and, decades later, a national minister of labor.[89]

The São Bernardo union included unusually talented professionals who worked for the union over the long haul. Among these was Antônio Possidônio Sampaio, a self-styled non-card-carrying Communist lawyer who specialized in industrial health and safety cases but whose passion was writing about São Bernardo's workers.[90] And there was the man who had hired Sampaio, Maurício Soares: active in progressive Catholic circles before 1964, he became the union's attorney the following year and remained central to its affairs until 1980; two years later he would become São Bernardo's mayor.[91] And there was the labor lawyer Almir Pazzianotto (whose Vemag exploits figured in chapter 4), contracted to handle the annual salary negotiations; he later became a national labor minister.[92] They all wrote for the union's newspaper.

Freed from the time clock, Lula took innumerable courses at the union on topics including labor-management relations, social welfare (*previdência social*) laws, and the FGTS system. Early on, at the suggestion of both Sampaio and Frei Chico, he also took a course at the Rui Barbosa Oratory Center, associated with the USP's law school. If these courses did not fundamentally transform Lula's public speaking capacity, they did give him "an above-average understanding" compared to other unionists.[93] Lula also helped shape such educational opportunities, since he was responsible for creating and overseeing the CET, inaugurated in December 1973. Those attracted to the center—whether for high school equivalency or technical courses—were precisely those hungriest for knowledge and advancement, ambitious men with sufficient talent and determination to handle the pressures of studying mathematics while working full-time and supporting a family.[94]

But the CET was not Lula's primary assignment as one of the union's directors. Vidal tasked Lula with establishing a new division of the union's legal department dedicated to social welfare benefits and the FGTS. Although union leaders disdained assistencialismo, these legally mandated services brought thousands to the union headquarters on a regular basis and were central to the union's reputation within the categoria. The union already provided legal, medical, and dental care as well as a barbershop but had no department dedicated to the needs of retired, widowed, or laid-off members or those needing help with a government home loan. The case-by-case problem solving and paperwork preparation for these matters would fall to Lula; the lawyer whom he hired, Hélio Manso; and eventually Lula's assistant, Luisinho.[95]

The department's three-member team needed to offer advice on any problem that a worker brought to them, including industrial accident insurance, government house permits, or even dealing with Funrural, a government program for rural workers. The department's bread and butter, however, was retirement pension applications: informing individuals about their rights and the relevant rules and procedures, as well as helping them prepare the forms by counting the years on their working papers or even nailing down a missing document. Beyond the tedious detail work, Lula had to navigate multiple government bureaucracies, with their rules and personalities. Three times a week, he would pick up a union car at 9 A.M. and drive to government offices in nearby São Paulo city to negotiate pensions with the Instituto Nacional de Previdência Social (INPS) or to submit loan requests to the Banco Nacional de Habitação, work that would take until late afternoon.[96]

Only after a few months did Lula realize that he'd been tasked with the chore of "taking care of old people" because no other director wanted the position. Beyond the potential aggravation, the other directors saw few political gains to be had from being buried under paperwork. But Lula grasped that if handled well, this new division could yield political dividends; it was this department of widows and pensioners that made him union president three years later. In a 1979 interview, he was particularly sardonic in criticizing certain doctrinaire opponents of assistencialismo who called for its abolition in their union election platforms: "Do you know when they are going to win elections? Never!"[97]

As Frei Chico observed, assistencia administration was not political, not central to confrontations with employers, but was preeminently electoral. Those coming to the union for help always viewed it as a test, as Lula had when in 1967 he came with a question about the new FGTS and left dissatisfied with President Monteiro da Cruz's handling of the matter. Lula's capacity for empathetic connectedness worked to his advantage. Lula's new job brought him face-to-face with layers of suffering, desperation, and neuroses within the categoria: a worker who had lost his wife because he could no longer maintain sexual relations, another who had worked for thirty days but found no money in his pay packet because of a debt at the company cooperative, or a hopeful northeastern migrant who had arrived to what he expected to be paradise only to find himself living in a shantytown (*favela*) on São Bernardo's outskirts. Lula "was a good union leader at the time," he reflected, because he listened and "felt sorry for the person" in front of him, even when he recognized that he couldn't resolve their problem.[98]

These daily consultations were mostly invisible in the union's formal deliberations.[99] Many years later, Lula observed with satisfaction that those who had thought the assignment would cramp his future "fell off their horse" (*cairam de cavalo*). The seriousness with which the division handled its responsibilities gave it "great respectability" and enhanced the reputations of both Lula and the man who chose him, Vidal. But Lula also gained access to an even larger constituency at the union headquarters, a working-class public sphere. "Do you know how many people pass by the union daily?" he asked a journalist in 1979. "At a minimum, fifteen hundred." Those frequenting the union did so for many reasons: often for various sorts of assistencia but also to complain about work, shoot the breeze, or catch up with friends. Some union directors often arrived late to the headquarters and were always busy when they did arrive. The gregarious Lula, by contrast, maintained an open-door policy, and his office became a gathering point for rank-and-file workers, factory activists, and fellow directors still linked to production.[100]

Building friendships as he went along, the ever-accessible Lula generated good feeling, even among Vidal's opponents. Rather than leaving them isolated and disgruntled in the lobby, Lula would invite them into his office, where he "treated them decently" rather than as enemies. As he has noted repeatedly, conversation flowed because he "always kept a bottle of pinga" in his drawer.[101] Such openness would have been unthinkable for his patron Vidal, always busy and still nursing wounds from years of dishonest slander by the opposition.[102] Yet the breadth of his client's outreach—and the good feeling that it generated—contributed to Vidal's strategic objectives for his second term: to lower the temperature and prominence of internal conflicts; pull into the union the energies of union activists, members, and the categoria; and channel those energies toward finding a means to tackle their shared problems.

A Happy Man

Like Lula, São Paulo's factory workers in 1973 were happy, hard-working young men who saw a clear path to a better future. As the USP-educated economist Paul Singer put it in the biweekly business magazine *Visão,* they were confident because "there was no lack of opportunities to work, no fear of unemployment, [and] the situation was good for those who studied."[103] Life was still hard, but things were immeasurably better—a judgment, Singer emphasized, based on the prevailing national economic model's "concrete effects" on their lives, not on any familiarity with the model as such.[104] A beckoning future, he added, generated feelings of belonging, especially among the unskilled. They credited these positive results to the national authorities under Médici.

Singer's focus group participants, whether skilled or unskilled, were all involved with, planning for, or entertaining fantasies about educational and professional development as well as buying land to escape rent. In the early 1970s, as Lula put it, Brazil was barreling "full speed ahead," flush with money and jobs; large metalworking firms were giving "monthly or bimonthly pay increases" (*antecipações*) so that workers could stay abreast of inflation.[105] Along with the usual scarcity of skilled workers, factory managers faced a shortage of unskilled workers due to a dip of in-migration and a boom in big government construction projects. In addition to lowering hiring standards and increasing pay rates, Ford was offering antecipações in advance of the annual contract negotiations to lure workers, although companies also depended on overtime well beyond the forty-eight-hour legal work week to deal with the labor shortage.[106]

São Paulo's uniquely favorable economic environment strengthened Vidal's confidence as he headed his new leadership team. In October 1973, the union's president was extensively quoted in a national magazine story about successful overtime boycotts by São Bernardo ferramenteiros at VW and Mercedes-Benz.

Criticizing government wage policies and citing unrecompensed productivity, Vidal defended VW's 3,000 ferramenteiros, whose actions had reduced car production from 1,700 to 1,000 vehicles per day before the company surrendered. Brazil was witnessing, the journalist concluded, the emergence of a skilled labor elite who demanded salary increases not for survival but to support their desired standard of living. Describing these tensions with labor as normal, company officials used the familiar excuse of being unable to do anything about wage levels because these were determined by the government.[107]

Although overworked, workers were doing well, and the skilled were unquestionably bem de vida. As Lula would brag decades later, he was the first in his family with a refrigerator, a television set, and a car (an aquamarine Volkswagen TL 72 purchased in 1973).[108] For some São Bernardo labor activists, workers were indulging in a fantasy of "wanting to live like the man [*os homems*—i.e., the rich]." As soon as they got a somewhat better job or a tiny promotion, veteran activist Nego Blaster complained, they dreamed about a car, weekends at the beach, or São Bernardo's famous polenta restaurants, usually beyond their budget. He pointed to the cars parked near the gates of large factories owned by "guys who didn't even have a place to live." Blaster also disapproved of workers' conspicuous consumption. Some who "lived like animals" in favela shacks, he groused, owned TVs, blenders, refrigerators, and floor waxers. His criticism likely reflected his disapproval of the younger generation's willingness to run up debt to buy such items.[109]

Money earned beyond immediate needs was destined for girls (*garotas*), trips to the beach, and, if anything was left over, visits to cabarets. A less-well-off worker, having just turned eighteen, noted a more modest objective: to see all the films that he had been barred from when underage.[110] As his jocular comment suggests, factory workers were given to boisterous, freewheeling conversation whether in the shop, on the bus or train, or in a bar. Cafeteria conversation could range from soccer, women, and food to the day's occurrences, and there was inevitably verbal jousting and brincadeiras. Anything could spur the creative exchange of put-downs: the differences between those born in one or another state always figured prominently with baianos like Lula, a perennial target. When done eating, some played cards or dominos or slept in the bathroom; others watched the office girls returning to work or (at least in one factory) went outside to heckle factory girls entering next door with vulgarities (*palavrões*) and invite them to go out. The disapproving worker who reported the latter noted, however, that some of the female workers even responded in kind. He concluded that workers, whether male or female, were "all adolescents."[111]

An intense sociability was fundamental for those laboring in a world of pounding machines and noisy assembly lines. Yet the internalized ideal for young working-class men, Singer emphasized, was the nuclear family, and this structured their way of being.[112] Indeed, factory workers were either married or soon to be. The young men under twenty-eight years old who spoke with Singer said that they earned money to "conquer women" and "start a family." They all agreed that men were sacana in the competitive race for money and women, though they noted how mothers are always there for their children, while fathers inevitably abandon their kids if they find another woman (which conformed perfectly to Aristides and dona Lindu's story).[113] According to Gonçalves's survey, the top reasons for constituting a family were, in descending order, to avoid loneliness (*vencer a solidão*), because marriage is "everything in life," and self-realization (*realização pessoal*).[114]

Due to reasons beyond his control, the widowed Lula may have gained boasting rights as a flamboyant *namoradeiro*, bragging to male acquaintances about the women he was supposedly having sex with. But he began his full-time union apprenticeship as a less-than-fully-successful man precisely because he was unmarried. Lula spoke of this time as a half-crazy (*meio-doido*) phase that left him without inner peace (*sossego*).[115] As his language suggests, the solution to this imbalance was marriage and constituting a family, which Lula did on May 23, 1974, with Marisa Letícia Casa dos Santos (1950–2017), his life partner for the next forty-three years.

When they met in late 1973, Marisa was a twenty-three-year-old widow with a child under three. She had been born to an Italian-descended family of São Bernardo farmers whose children had become metalworkers. With eleven siblings, she had worked as a live-in caregiver (*babá*) from age nine to fourteen, followed by five years wrapping chocolates in a factory before her first marriage, at nineteen years old. Her husband Marcos Cláudio dos Santos was a truck driver. In 1970, her husband was murdered while driving his father's taxi at night in order to make money for savings; they had married without a house. On February 4, 1971, she gave birth to her first child, Marcos Cláudio, four months before Lourdes died while pregnant; once married, Lula adopted Marcos Cláudio, at his request, at the age of nine, and Marisa would have three children with Lula, all boys, between 1975 and 1985.[116]

Lula's second marriage followed his aggressive whirlwind pursuit of Marisa, an employee at a local school, whom Lula had only met a half year earlier when she stopped by the metalworkers' union headquarters to get paperwork stamped for a pension with the INPS. Lula's storytelling regarding their early relationship has prevailed in the public record, as observers and journalists frame Marisa as the strong, if mostly invisible, woman behind the "great man."

Lula's framing emphasizes events preceding his actually meeting Marisa, which gives their encounter a sense of destiny. He reports how he ordered Luizinho, his subordinate at the union, to alert him when any "pretty little widow" (*viuvinho*) showed up to the headquarters looking for help. Only once has Lula explained this curious order: he "didn't want any more to be married to a virgin," he told *Playboy* in 1979, because he wanted "someone who had passed through the same thing that [he] had."[117] Lula then highlights that he had already heard of the pretty widow Marisa, through her father-in-law the taxi driver.[118] A private person averse to publicity, Marisa has only given a handful of interviews, and because of the strategic demands of Lula's 2002 presidential campaign, the two interviews released that year center on what mattered most to readers: her encounter with and courtship by Lula.[119] Together, the couple's interviews coincide broadly on the details and are filled with Marisa emphasizing her annoyance, resistance to his entreaties, and skepticism about his motives.

To summarize their stories, a "pretty little widow" did show up to Lula's social welfare department. Alerted by Luizinho, Lula held back her paperwork so that he could meet her, during which he lied about changes in the law in order to force another meeting; she describes him giving a spiel about their shared experiences as widows. He even dropped his wallet in order to show her that he was indeed a widow; having recognized the ruse, she responded, "So?" By the time Lula finally stamped her paperwork, he had virtually blackmailed her into providing her phone number. At this point, a story of arbitrary bureaucratic abuse becomes one of harassment, as Lula constantly called Marisa at her workplace to convince her to go out with him. After a few dates, including at a famous polenta restaurant, Lula invaded her family's privacy by showing up uninvited to her house, introducing himself to her mother, and demanding that Marisa send away her current namoro when he arrived to go out with her.[120]

Two journalists have attempted more substantive assessments of what this courtship reveals about Lula. In his highly critical 2011 biography, Nêumanne labels Lula's behavior boorish and despicable (*meio-cafajeste*) and suggests that it could be considered harassment (*asedio*). In this he coincides with the progressive feminist Eliane Brum, an admirer of the Lula government's social policies and author of substantive articles on Lourdes and Marisa. For Brum, the courtship story evinces Lula's sexist coarseness and exhibits lying and blackmailing extensive enough to constitute abuse.[121] Neither Brum nor Nêumanne, however, squares this characterization with the fact that Marisa and Lula do marry and make a life together; moreover, their assessment reduces Marisa to an object of Lula's manipulations. Yet Marisa's own narrative is driven by the need to establish autonomy: she is not fooled and is even resistant to marriage, a point that she emphasizes.

A deeper reading of Marisa's and Lula's accounts would see them as performances directed toward others, framed within the social mores and styles of sociability characteristic of their working-class world, unequal as it was in terms of gender. Popular understandings are not derived from an idealized vision of egalitarian interaction; for working people the world is driven by cunning and calculation, with competitiveness and aggressiveness expressed in conflictual verbal forms. It is more fruitful to place this courtship story within its context of working-class conventions of expression—full of brincadeiras and teasing—which takes us beyond the temptation of reductionist judgments. The dynamic, two-sided nature of Lula and Marisa's conversational exchange is best seen in the actual back-and-forth witnessed by Josué Machado, who spent three days with them for the May 1979 *Playboy* interview, conducted five years after they had met. Marisa enters from the kitchen while Lula is describing their first encounter as "a sleight of hand" in which he began to vex her (*encher o saco dela*). Marisa interrupts with a sardonic, deflating intervention: "First he prepared the terrain for conquering me. But he was very shameless [*sem vergonha*] you know? And one fine Sunday he appeared at my house without warning [*sem mais sem menos*] and started talking with my mother." To Marisa's observation that the courting Lula showed "some nerve" (*cara-de-pau*), Lula interjects, with false humility, that "I lost my timidity." But Marisa goes on to note that she invited him into the house because she could do nothing else.

Seizing the conversational opening, Lula raises the issue of his rival for her attention who also showed up that day, to which Marisa replies "So what?" Asked by Machado how she chose between the two, Marisa says that she initially didn't know and asked for time to think, to which Lula interjects that it took her "only five minutes." Establishing that she was the one who made the choice, Marisa then describes the pros and cons of each man to Machado (and Lula): the one upright, someone she'd known from childhood, almost part of the family; and the other, Lula, for whom she had more sympathies and liked his *jeito* (characteristic style or manner). Lula breaks in to note that they were married within six months, which leads Marisa to sum up the contrast between the suitors and the eventual result: "One had good intentions, and the other bad ones. And I ended up conquered" by the latter. Lula crows in triumph: "The problem with women is to catch them in your hand."[122]

This exchange emphasizes the dialogical nature of Lula's and Marisa's respective accounts of their courtship, which must be placed within the context of their long-term relationship. In the same interview, Marisa at first denies ever fighting with Lula, before in two sentences listing all the reasons that lead her to "break the club" (*quebrar o pau*) fighting with Lula. Returning later to the room where Lula is being interviewed, Marisa hears him declare that a housewife with three kids can't be a feminist, to which she asks skeptically, "A husband can, but a woman can't?" The interviewer immediately asks her if Lula is

Lula with Marisa at home. (Courtesy Olhar Imagem [Juca Martins])

very macho (*machão*), to which she exclaims, "Epa!" This causes both Lula and Marisa to laugh.

Lula's courtship of Marisa has a clear moral: victory goes to those bold and cunning enough to maneuver with aplomb in pursuit of an objective. The words spoken and actions taken do not, in and of themselves, define any given performance; they must be contextualized interpersonally and in relation to the social mores and understandings of those involved. Lula's courtship of Marisa could be seen as arrogant and humiliating, constituting harassment and abuse. (Lula insists that he never participated in "cantando as mocas" [literally, "singing the girls"], propositioning women who enter the union.)[123] But we should read these actions and words in the spirit in which they unfold, which was forward but playful and accompanied by a mischievousness meant to establish a connection. "All of a sudden," after Lula's uninvited appearance at Marisa's house, their "relationship began to go well [*dar certo*]." He returned many times, making friends with her mother and sister. As she recalled, "He makes friends easily, you know. He ended up convincing me."[124] When he decided to run for the top union office, she agreed that he should and proudly watched Lula, now a truly happy man, inaugurated as president in 1975, after Marisa had just given birth to his firstborn son, Fábio. As Marisa and others have observed, Lula is a determined person, and when he knows what he wants, he usually gets it.

10 LITTLE FISH IN A WORLD OF SHARKS

The speech that Lula had read at his 1975 union presidential inauguration was marked by its polished grammar, erudite vocabulary, and elegance of argument. As drafted by the union's lawyer, the speech drew on Catholic social doctrine to depict a world that offered two false and malevolent alternatives. In the Communist world, people were "crushed by the State," "enslaved by Marxist ideology," and denied the right to think and express themselves freely; under capitalism, they were "enslaved by economic power" and denied their dignity due to a fevered search for profit. Structures, Lula read, should be at the service of those who construct the riches of the world but who today live in hovels, die in hospital lines, and dwell in favelas. We must avoid blaming particular governments, he went on, but it is imperative to "prepare today for the victories of tomorrow" because "the future lies in our hands."[1]

Frei Chico was thrilled by his younger brother's debut yet recognized the challenge that Lula faced in speaking to so many people. However haltingly delivered, the text wasn't exactly leftist, in Frei Chico's opinion, but he was certain, as vice president of the São Caetano metalworkers' union, that criticizing Communism and capitalism in front of the authorities was an act of defiance. The hard-hitting words crafted by Maurício Soares reflected the upbeat feelings of the regime's opponents after the electoral earthquake of November 1974.[2] When the dust cleared, a once weak MDB had been transformed into a formidable opposition force in the national and state legislatures. In 1966, the military had replaced a multiparty system with a two-party one in order to guarantee centralization of power in the national presidency that they would monopolize; the downside of this political engineering was revealed in 1974, when the choice between only two parties—the MDB and the pro-military ARENA Party—served to aggregate votes, whether cast vaguely in favor of change or in sharp protest, thus producing a plebiscitary dynamic.[3]

When the votes were counted, the MDB had doubled its representation in the federal Chamber of Deputies, where the party's national vote jumped from 4.8 million in 1970 to 10.9 million four years later; its Senate representation increased from 7 to 20, and in 1974 it beat ARENA by 14.6 to 10 million votes. The economically dynamic state of São Paulo was the tip of the opposition spear. Not only did the MDB win the majority of state legislative seats, but the ARENA senatorial candidate Carvalho Pinto, a well-regarded if sickly former governor, was beaten by a virtually unknown mayor from the interior, the youthful Orestes Quércia, by a margin of 3 million votes.[4] Not even the opposition expected such a "revolution by the vote" at a moment when the government's record of economic success, since Médici, was as yet unbroken, the opposition was cowed, and the mass media was mostly well behaved as well as censored.

The November 1974 election had special meaning for the state's trade unionists, especially metalworkers, because of the election as federal deputy of Marcelo Gato (1941–2011), the former president of the Santos metalworkers' union. One of the highest vote getters among federal deputies, Gato received many of his 100,000 votes from the opposition stronghold of Santos, along with significant electoral support in ABC.[5] That the new federal deputy attended Lula's inauguration, along with Governor Egydio, was duly noted by the intelligence services of the Second Army, which had virtually cogoverned São Paulo under Médici.[6] For Frei Chico, Gato's victory was especially meaningful because he had campaigned for the young lawyer and they were both members of the PCB, the party that Lula's brother had joined clandestinely in 1971 or 1972. All in all, the results—which included the election of another Communist, Alberto Goldman, as MDB state deputy—vindicated the strategy of those leftists, denounced as reformists, who had rejected the path of armed struggle and electoral boycotts advocated by Carlos Marighella and the student New Left in the late 1960s; indeed, the decline of votes cast in protest (*votos em branco e mulo*) explains some but by no means all of the MDB's improved electoral performance in 1974.

The unexpected MDB victory sparked euphoria among those who had been defeated when AI-5 was promulgated on December 13, 1968. The postelection editorial in the PCB's official but illegal organ, *Voz Operária*, was written anonymously by Central Committee member Marco Antônio Tavares Coelho, a former federal deputy from Minas living clandestinely and condemned to a seven-year prison sentence in 1966. Titled "Tighten the Siege," the editorial looked forward to further advances in the coming year in the fight to restore electoral democracy.[7] The sad irony, however, is that 1975 would bring a campaign by the army's Destacamento de Operações de Informação (DOI) that demolished Coelho's organization from top to bottom. Even for an illegal party with a long experience of persecution, the DOI's ferocious 1975 assault was unprecedented, including, crucially, its success in turning several top leaders into informants—in exchange for their lives—while knocking out the PCB's printing operations and patiently mapping its network of leadership and contacts.[8]

To avoid publicity, detainees in 1975 were routinely disappeared—some to reappear later, others executed summarily—while hundreds of rank-and-file militants, sympathizers, and mere acquaintances were relentlessly ground up in the DOI's cycle of torture and information gathering.[9]

The army's DOI and the other related military intelligence agencies were known collectively as the *porão*, literally "the basement of a house" or "the hold of a ship," where old and dirty things are stored. Its closest English equivalent is *dungeon*, but in Portuguese *porão* also figuratively refers to the part of the psyche where indecent and inadmissible memories and secrets are kept. It is the dungeons of the military regime—especially in the years after AI-5—that produced the most emblematic image of human rights violations under the dictatorship: the body of Jewish journalist Vladimir Herzog hanging in a DOI cell, disseminated via an unconvincing photo released by the army to prove the implausible claim that he had committed suicide, not died from torture. Herzog's death in November 1975—brought to public attention through the courageous actions of the city's journalists' union, Archbishop Paulo Evaristo Arns (1921–2016), and a politically conservative but principled paulista newspaper owner, Ruy Mesquita (1925–2013)—was the climax of an orgy of violence that broke through the silence about human rights violations in São Paulo. A heavily policed ecumenical service for Herzog, attended by thousands, marked a turning point in upper- and middle-class opinion, which was sufficient to exacerbate intraregime factionalism and thereby lead to a degree of liberalization that constrained at least unauthorized state violence after January 1976.[10]

It is not surprising that we look away from the pain of others, especially when that suffering occurred in a past moment and good eventually triumphed. This chapter, however, will focus on the politics of 1974–75 and how metalworkers were swept into a whirlwind of terror, including Marcos Andreotti, his wife, and his daughter as well as Frei Chico, his comrades, fellow trade unionists, and his wife and family. Those who have read journalistic accounts of Lula's life are aware that Frei Chico was picked up, tortured, and held for seventy-six days, an event that Lula has claimed was decisive for his future trajectory. Yet no one has explained how this family disaster fits into the decisive confrontation between the dungeon, factions within the military, and organized resistance within civil society that followed the 1974 MDB electoral victory to which trade unionists like Paulo Vidal and the Silva brothers contributed.

While giving the reader a powerful sense of what it meant to live under the Brazilian dictatorship, the chapter also offers a bottom-up take on what it means to live through a human rights violation. It explores the regime's dragnet of annihilation against the PCB that swept up Frei Chico and ended with the martyrdom of Vladimir Herzog and Manoel Fiel Filho as well as two officers of the São Paulo Military Police. In narrating Frei Chico's kidnapping and torture, the chapter eschews a sensationalism that highlights the most spectacular, "evil," and perverted elements of physical coercion and human degradation. Treating torture as a bundle of practices, I explore the experience as something that must be parsed, weighed, and analyzed, through an exhaustive examination of accounts by the Silva brothers and others as well as newly released national and state intelligence agency documentation.

Understanding what happened to Lula's brother will help us better understand the Brazilian popular classes, who have, from time immemorial, been subjected to arbitrary violence and torture. It will also help us understand how a working-class individual like Frei Chico comes to take political risks, and why such risk-taking is so discouragingly rare. Establishing these points not only helps to underline how extraordinary were the collective struggles that would soon unfold in ABC but also sheds light on the decisions made by the hundreds of thousands who participated in those defiant mass actions.

When interviewed in 2014 by Brazil's National Truth Commission, Lula's brother observed sarcastically that "I was a privileged tortured one you know!" Frei Chico explained that his privilege was to have not "been penetrated by a billy club" or had his "teeth broken." It "didn't reach that point," he explained, because "I was a, I was a"—hesitating before completing his thought—"a so-called little fish." His self-identification as a "little fish" refers most immediately to his level of party responsibility: a member of the PCB's tiny São Caetano municipal committee, as opposed to the state and national leadership whom the DOI was prepared to torture to death to find out what they knew. But the image of small prey reflects a recurring emphasis in Frei Chico's accounts of his detention: that those abducted and held with him included "famous" and "middle-class" people such as lawyers, architects, journalists, Jews, and Masons. Unlike workers, he observed, such people were "rooted in high society," and he was emphatic that no one would have heard anything about what happened in the state's detention centers if the suspected Communists were only from "the so-called lower half."[11] That there were middle-class figures among his fellow prisoners, he suggests, was lucky for him.

The DOI detainees' common leftism and shared experience of terror and abjection could not erase the distinctive life trajectories and subjectivities separating those on the upper floor of Brazilian society (*andar em cima*) and those on the bottom. First-generation workers like Frei Chico and his family retained from the rural world, as Certeau suggested, a vision of society as "organized by an immemorial struggle between 'the powerful' and 'the poor,'" marked by "constant victories by the rich and the police."[12] For these "sons and daughters of fear," to allude to the title of the short novel by worker turned writer Roniwalter Jatobá, the world was divided between the weak and the strong, predators and their prey. This brings us to the image of the greedy and unscrupulous shark (*tubarão*), deeply rooted in popular culture and ubiquitous in the political language of an emerging mass electoral politics in postwar São Paulo.[13] Studying the city's metalworkers in 1957, Juarez Rubens Brandão Lopes recorded their unvarying response to any change in the factory's functioning: "The benefit is theirs [the owners] and never the workers'." This revealed, he correctly notes, "a sentiment of antagonism, a consciousness of a shared situation among those who work, in opposition to the rich, the 'sharks,' the factory owners, or the 'capitalists.'"[14]

The image of the shark reflects the popular wisdom that unscrupulous and predatory forces—often blamed for inflation and the high cost of living—abuse the poor and the weak with impunity. While registering moral disapproval, such a conviction was highly conducive to reproducing the existing distribution of power because it counseled a life strategy that we have called, following the sociologist Pereira's study of the Santo André primary school, withdrawal (*retração*). A man interviewed in the 1970s in a working-class neighborhood (*loteamento*) in Osasco evokes exactly this strategy in deploying the shark metaphor:

> I don't know any rich guys round here. Sharks just live in the ocean, if not they die. Because the little fish can't go in the ocean, the little guys can't go in there. So the sharks stay in charge in the ocean. Anybody goes in there, they eat them, right? And coming over here, well sharks can't do that, otherwise they die, because the water is shallow, ya see?[15]

Despite having a wife and two children under five, Frei Chico not only refused to stay in the shallows but had plunged into the ocean of politics, ruled by sharks. Driven by a fierce rebelliousness, he insisted on the right to his own ideas and opinions, even when they were deemed subversive by a dictatorial capitalist government. In this sense, the horror and suffering visited on Frei Chico, his family, and his fellow trade unionists was eminently predictable. What they could not know, however, was the impact that this personal disaster would have on Frei Chico's brother, the good boy, and the cunning path that he would take in the future as an agile and cool-headed performer.

Stasis and Restlessness in a Brazil on the Move

When General Ernesto Geisel (1907–96) was indirectly elected as president on March 15, 1974, the sixty-seven-year-old was confident about the regime's prospects and accomplishments. Looking back at a decade of military rule, he was proud that the armed forces had maintained enough internal cohesion and respect for hierarchy to have parried efforts to institute a straight-out dictatorship. Moreover, the regime's ambitious economic and institutional reforms had produced extraordinarily high growth rates from 1968 through 1974. It was true that 1969 and 1970 had seen screaming headlines about politically motivated robberies, shootings, and the kidnapping of foreign diplomats in exchange for political prisoners. Yet this threat had been ruthlessly eliminated by a repressive apparatus that came to be anchored in the army's DOI; December 1973 saw the elimination of the very last of the small guerrilla groups that had resorted to extralegal violence.

Having just served as head of Petrobras, Brazil's national oil company, Geisel was aware of the significant challenge that the country faced, given its overwhelming dependence on imported oil, with the Organization of the Petroleum Exporting Countries (OPEC) price increase of October 1973. Yet GDP growth in 1974 was still high, and even the modest rise in inflation seemed unlikely to change the electoral pattern set in 1970 and 1972, when ARENA easily beat the MDB. Yet the one political headache that tormented Geisel went back to the very origin of military rule. Supported by the United States, the 1964 removal of President Goulart had been a collaboration between the military and the civilian economic, political, religious, and media elites, with substantial support from the middle and upper classes. The civilian political class quickly gave parliamentary assent to the transfer of power to a military president and did not oppose the purging of Goulart's partisans from elective office and the state apparatus; the decapitation of "Communist" and "subversive" organizations such as trade unions, student groups, and peasant associations was entirely uncontroversial, since they had been among Goulart's noisiest supporters.

As part of this alliance with civilian forces, the regime's first military president, Humberto de Alencar Castelo Branco (1900–1967), preserved electoral forms of political representation.[16] This allowed the coup to be presented as a defense of democracy and distinguished the new government from the outright military dictatorships and crude caudillos of Spanish America. The postcoup government also shared the well-established rhetoric of Brazilian liberalism that had characterized the dominant classes since the advent of independence in 1822. Across a century and a half, military and civilian elites had cherished the conviction that the country's common people—overwhelmingly composed of slaves, ex-slaves, and descendants of slaves—were not yet prepared for full citizenship. Although racist, Brazil's rulers felt no need to formally proclaim the inferiority of the masses on explicitly racial grounds; they could instead paternalistically point to them as poorly educated, ignorant, and dependent subjects who were easy prey for demagogues and subversives like those ousted in 1964. In this regard, the top of Brazilian society understood the vote as playing a largely rhetorical role as the source of government legitimacy. The peculiarities of Brazil, they believed, made necessary an extended period of tutelage, a "guided democracy," in order to prepare the populace for an eventual transition to a more perfect democracy with security.

The political challenge that bedeviled Brazil's military rulers and its civilian administrators stemmed not from those on the bottom but rather from the fact that the military as an institution, once in power, was simply unwilling to return to the barracks. Influenced by a messianic rhetoric going back to antioligarchic military rebels in the 1920s, the armed forces saw no reason to hand the government back to a corrupt political class whose venality, shortsightedness, and unprincipled search for votes generated backwardness, chaos, and subversion. The military's sense of mission, combined with the imperative of institutional unity, led them to proclaim their movement a self-legitimating revolutionary regime. While the political class might acquiesce rhetorically to the military's dubbing of the coup as the "Revolution of 1964," they could not ultimately accept any claim to legitimacy other than the votes that they themselves received.[17] The right-wing politician Carlos Lacerda, Rio's governor in 1964, was a central figure in Goulart's overthrow. Within three years, as we have seen, Lacerda was radicalized by the military's unwillingness, once the emergency passed, to return power to a directly elected president, whether civilian like himself or a military man (if they had the votes, which was doubtful).

That the military regime survived for twenty-one years demonstrates both the ruling group's willingness to use force and its capacity to exercise societal leadership through tactical blows, feints, and dodges. That the regime preserved elections for legislative office no doubt contributed to its success, as this provided space for disparate losers (such as the MDB) and allowed the pro-government party, ARENA, to attract a host of opportunistic and unprincipled politicians whom the military themselves often disdained. Elections, even if restricted, allowed expression of clashing if often parochial concerns at the local and state level driven by individual, family, group, or regional self-interest. In this regard, the conduct of politics within the military was permeated by the same personalist patron-client dynamics that prevailed among their civilian counterparts; Geisel, for example, froze out Médici and his closest ministers and aides as soon as he took office.

Yet the political problems inherited by President Geisel were made more intractable by the military's response in 1968 to the congressional rebellion by MDB and ARENA politicians. The post–AI-5 legal regime heightened the contradiction between the government's rhetoric about democracy and its unprecedented violation of fundamental liberal norms including habeas corpus and freedom of the press. As his term began, the new president was a bit bolder than Médici in hinting at an eventual political transition; the evolving formulations offered by Geisel and his advisers included decompression, détente (*distensão*), and eventually opening (*abertura*), with the implied threat that it might close (*fechamento*).[18] In early 1974, in other words, the political scene was bifurcated, with a static group of older military men ruling over a society in restless commotion.

The November 1974 elections would dramatically reveal the existence of new actors, ambitions, and sensibilities at play nationwide. Most importantly, there was a new generation—men such as São Paulo's Orestes Quércia and Paulo Vidal—who chafed at the monopolization of power by their elders and sought their own place in the sun. While the MDB vote surged throughout urbanizing Brazil, the party made its biggest impact in São Paulo state, which had proven an enduring problem since Getúlio Vargas ousted the state from control of the national government in 1930. Over the intervening half century, those in control of the presidency could always depend on the politicians from the country's poorer regions, but São Paulo remained a necessary but difficult partner in national government and a potentially formidable challenger. Not only was the state the hub of the national economy, but its self-regarding upper class had a history of regionalist particularism.

In 1970 the MDB had been all but wiped out in São Paulo, so its rebirth there in 1974, Célia Melhem notes, depended on adapting to the changes occurring in the state's economy, society, and polity. The economic miracle had not only radically "altered the composition of economic elites" but also expanded its middle classes while diversifying a growing industrial working class. Accelerating urbanization in the interior had produced new cities with more complex local power structures like Campinas, home to a new state university. An old political dichotomy was thus slipping away in which an urbanized and politicized capital was juxtaposed with the electoral "grottos" of the interior, where local politics was monopolized by powerful families. New industrial regions, above all ABC, were another vector for change, given the vast increase in the number of workers with high levels of income and skill.[19]

The Second Army in São Paulo was keenly aware of ABC's strategic significance and noted, in a confidential October 1975 report, that ABC's annual municipal revenue was projected to reach the lofty sum of 2 billion cruzeiros (90 percent from the three biggest municípios: Santo André, São Bernardo, and São Caetano). The chief concern of the report's authors, however, was that São Bernardo trade unionists—in other words, the metalworkers' union—were attempting to put an end to ARENA's local hegemony "in favor of the MDB."[20] Indeed, the union's leadership group—of which Vidal had been a part since 1967—was central to the local MDB. Union director Mário Ladeia served as

MDB city councilman from 1969 to 1976, and another union director, Antenor Biolcatti, joined him in 1974, the same year when one of the union's lawyers, Almir Pazzianotto, was elected MDB state deputy. Ladeia would be elected as vice mayor in 1976, when the MDB won local elections and Vidal became city councilman.

Other than during a few moments in his childhood, the young Lula had shown little interest in electoral politics until serving under Paulo Vidal on the union's diretoria; from this point on, he would find politics exhilarating. In the national senatorial race for São Paulo, ARENA had nominated the stuffy Carvalho Pinto, who in the past had been a governor, senator, and minister. As Lula recalls, no one knew anything about Carvalho Pinto's thirty-six-year-old opponent, Orestes Quércia, but Lula's fellow director Biolcatti, a delegate to the MDB convention, was impressed by this young lawyer and ex-mayor of Campinas. Invited to meet with the union's diretoria, Carvalho Pinto was taken aback by their aggressive interrogation and had little of substance to offer in reply; the assembled union leaders told him straight out that he was not getting their votes. Retrospectively, an impish Lula remembers running a politician out of union headquarters as our "first collective action" as a diretoria; and best of all, to the diretoria's surprise, Quércia won.[21]

As vice president of the local MDB, Paulo Vidal was a man on the move. When he initially became the São Bernardo union's president, Vidal had no intention of simply administering what already existed. From the very start he demonstrated a willingness to shake things up, and he has been aptly described as "a restless figure" (*irrequieta*) by DIEESE director Walter Barelli, who worked closely with him. As an example, Barelli cites Vidal's attempts to escape from the collective agreements negotiated by the state metalworkers' federation. Controlled by pelegos, the federation claimed and exercised the legal right to represent the metalworkers' unions of the interior, most of them tiny and weak, but their remit also included the three big unions in ABC. In his first year, Vidal attempted a separate *dissídio* with a percentage wage increase demand that did not coincide with DIEESE's cost-of-living calculation. In a huff, Vidal withdrew his union from the organization, although Barelli, after much talk, convinced him to rejoin a little over a year later. By 1973, Vidal had hired Barelli to offer leadership courses for his diretoria, and the relationship with the DIEESE director continued under the Vidal and Lula presidencies.[22]

Like Quércia, Vidal was driven by a desire to move up and make his mark on the world. Unlike the lawyer Quércia, however, Vidal's social origins and limited education were an obstacle to social mobility in most spheres of activity.[23] And while these were not as formidable an obstacle to success in electoral politics, both participation in party affairs and municipal administration required mastery of the spoken and written word, along with a certain refinement of manner. As the *Tribuna Metalúrgica*'s editor explained, when Vidal founded the paper in 1971 he was distinguishing himself from the average trade unionist, who, usually "lacking in their level of culture and without a habit of reading," placed a very low priority on written communication compared to something concrete like a new medical clinic. Yet Vidal always had a very "real passion" for the newspaper, contributing a presidential column every month and participating fully in the general camaraderie, as the union lawyer and *Tribuna* contributor Antonio Possidonio Sampaio notes.[24] When the first issues appeared, Nunes reports, Vidal was anxious about the disinterest shown at the factory gate when they were handed out. Pondering what could be done to make workers less likely to throw the paper away after glancing at the front page, the *Tribuna* launched what would be its most popular feature across the 1970s: the always critical and often humorous letters written by the fictional João Ferrador, the irreverent peon.[25]

With a splendid new headquarters as a personal calling card, the voluble Vidal emerged after 1973 as a go-to source for journalists, who regularly quoted the union president in São Paulo–based and national newspapers and magazines. He possessed a sui generis discourse that was not leftist, populist, or peleguista, and he always spoke proudly about the modernity of São Bernardo's industries, the productivity of its workers, and the wealth they produced. Keeping to the straight and narrow of economics, he nonetheless offered well-articulated criticism of employers, the labor relations system, and the government's interventionist role. Rhetorically, he differed from other trade unionists who used the CLT defensively to criticize employer violations of the law while appealing to the government to act as an honest broker. Vidal, by contrast, expressed skepticism about the labor law drafted in 1943, which he judged archaic in relation to his categoria. Eschewing discussion about the "working class," he emphasized the specific issues facing metalworkers; his indictment of employers was that they refused to fairly share the profits that stemmed from the industry's high level of productivity. The ideal solution, he argued, was direct negotiation between labor and capital without harmful state intervention. Such themes would remain elements of Lula's later discourse.

Two months before the November 1974 elections, Vidal pulled off his most notable achievement in bringing together several hundred local metalworkers to assess their industry, their categoria, and the labor relations system. Held on September 6–8, 1974, the First Congress of the Metalworkers of São Bernardo and Diadema was a tribute to the creative drive of Vidal and his diretoria and their collaboration with DIEESE's Barelli and, through him, with opposition circles within the intelligentsia. A unique initiative in terms of the trade union scene, it was held despite pressure from the director of the Labor Ministry's Regional Labor Delegacy (DRT); this made the meeting, as Pazzianotto and Lula confirm, an act of courage.[26] In terms of the categoria, it was also a step forward in Vidal's avowed objective of deepening worker involvement and beginning to unify a badly divided membership. It was also of vital concern to Vidal that there be written documents that formulated the issues intellectually; these would serve as a calling card for his leadership. Drafted by Barelli and the DIEESE team, the congress documents reflected far more serious empirical research than demonstrated at other state or national union gatherings of the day. The congress also adopted a manifesto called the "Declaration of São Bernardo," which Vidal would later call the union's distinctive "doctrine."[27]

DIEESE was a small operation of at most a half dozen, often irregularly paid, employees, but Barelli's investment of time and energy cultivating Vidal was a strategic decision that would pay off handsomely. Moreover, Barelli spanned the worlds of the trade union and the university—he had been a bank worker after his college AP activism—and was thus well-known within a leftist but mostly non-Communist intellectual milieu associated with USP and the Centro Brasileiro de Análise e Planejamento, the public policy think tank founded by FHC. Many of the graduate students and professors who comprised this milieu were Marxists, and their engagement with labor was intellectual but by no means purely academic. For those USP students who attended the congress at Barelli's invitation, Vidal "was the one who impressed" the most, observed the carioca Communist student Luiz Werneck Vianna, due to his "vivacity, intelligence, eloquence and rhetoric. He was a man, it was said, of American[-style] unionism."[28] This impression would find formal expression in a widely influential and still useful 1975 article by Vianna's USP colleague Maria Hermínia Tavares de Almeida. Quoting extensively from Vidal and the union's written documents, the article linked the dynamic sectors of large-scale modern industry to a new type of trade unionism that might, she suggested, be the nucleus of a style of "North American business unionism: combative, 'apolitical,' solidly implanted in the factory, and technically prepared to confront and resolve the general and specific problems of those they represented."[29]

Heavily covered in the press, the São Bernardo union congress offered clear evidence—two months before the surprising MDB vote—that something new was happening in Brazilian trade unionism. This further enhanced Vidal's growing reputation among an intellectualized opposition milieu in São Paulo that found its voice in *Opinião*, a serious news magazine much persecuted by the censors (it ceased publication in 1977). Intrigued by the congress, *Opinião*'s September 1974 profile of Vidal—including a sketched portrait—described him as the most original trade union leader since the late 1960s. Aware of the stereotypes of their highly educated audience of nonworkers, the magazine began by noting that, unless forewarned, one would never imagine that Vidal was a working-class trade union leader. Highlighting Vidal's bushy mustache and refined manners, the article described the thirty-two-year-old as "an easy and agile speaker with a culture rare in his environment." While the article's authors hinted that they would prefer from him a more overtly political stance, Vidal was judged on his own terms as a man who—in statement and deed—was truly independent of existing political currents.[30] After the November 1974 MDB landslide, Vidal could easily be seen as the right man for a new day. He might even seem the trade union movement's Quércia, a political operator of great energy who, as even leftists at the time noted, lacked ideological rigor. A new world was emerging in São Paulo that generated such ambitious men from within well-established political and trade union systems.

The Dragnet

Voting was mandatory for literate Brazilians, but most were spectators on election day as *cabos eleitorais* (electoral corporals) hustled on behalf of the candidates who hired them to turn out votes. In the run-up to November 15, 1974, Frei Chico was helping to line up people to leaflet in exchange for a small payment, a free lunch, and a soda. The campaign material was delivered to São Caetano before election day; a sixty-three-year-old retired construction worker, Pedro Daniel de Souza, picked up the expense money from a certain "Ivo" in São Paulo. Meeting early at Pedro Daniel's house, Frei Chico helped organize the twenty-one adults and five minors for delivery to polling places by a volunteer with a car. Frei Chico had earlier arranged for one of the candidates whom he supported, trade unionist Marcelo Gato, to meet the diretoria of the São Caetano metalworkers' union, for which Frei Chico had been elected vice president.[31] When the results came in, all three MDB candidates backed by Lula's brother had won: Quércia for senator and Alberto Goldman and Gato for state and federal deputy, respectively.

Tens of thousands were getting out the vote on election day in São Paulo, but we know details, including how much each leafleteer was paid (ten cruzeiros), only for Lula's brother and his friends. Pedro Daniel's account fills two pages of an air force intelligence agency report, filed a year after the election, laying out findings from "the first phase" of the DOI's "dismantling" of the PCB in São Paulo. The individuals featured in the report were picked up by the DOI during an October 1975 dragnet (*arrastão*) and were tortured before eventually being turned over to the police for prosecution. In a secret intelligence report from that month, the Second Army explained that the earlier "extermination" campaign against terrorist groups had allowed the mainline Communists to gain strength. "In addition to not being harried [*fustigado*; literally, "whipped"]," the PCB "had managed to prove to the country's Left that the taking of power must be undertaken through the 'peaceful path.'"[32] Inadvertently, the document underlined the fact that Frei Chico and his comrades were simply exercising their rights as Brazilian citizens to participate in an election under the government's rules. While Goldman and Gato were indeed PCB members, they had been duly registered by the electoral justice system, which did not find proof of disqualifying social or political antecedents. Moreover, there was no law barring even members of an illegal party, like the PCB, from exercising their right to vote or to support a candidate.

The political objective of the dungeon, as reflected in the anti-Communist dragnet and air force intelligence report drawn from it, had nothing to do with Marxism-Leninism or Communism. A modest level of activism sustained by a tiny persecuted minority was a pretext to attack the MDB's resounding electoral victory in November 1974. The drama that characterized Geisel's first two years in the presidency originated six years earlier with the executive branch's seizure of unlimited power through AI-5.[33] Under its rules, the military president could eliminate elected officeholders and close any legislative body at will. The act even further nullified liberalism's separation of powers by allowing the central government to legislate by decree and to fire or retire government employees, including any judge and prosecutor who might not bend to the military regime's will. Adopted in the face of opposition in the streets and the suites, AI-5 allowed for the declaration of a state of siege without the restrictions found in the military regime's 1967 constitution. AI-5 also exempted crimes against national security from that constitution's guarantee of habeas corpus, the right to legal recourse for someone "suffering or thinking that they are threatened with violence or coercion" due to "illegalities or abuses" by the state.[34] Such crimes against national security were to be adjudicated exclusively by the military justice system, and the government was granted the right—apparently little used—to confiscate private property as punishment for subversion or corruption.

The military was aware of the criticism that AI-5, used to temporarily close Congress, would face from the political class and elite public opinion. Although circulation was small, the print media were important because they shaped the middle- and upper-class opinion that was so decisive politically. This led the government to double down on press censorship, with the Federal Police issuing guidance as to what could or could not be covered; violations led to seizures of publications and a financial loss to publishers. Censors could also be directly installed in the editorial offices of recalcitrant publications. The most notable case involved the conservative but stubborn Mesquita family, who owned the *Estado de São Paulo*, the country's most influential newspaper.[35] Having supported the 1964 coup but opposed AI-5, the paper refused to exercise self-censorship; when the government censored articles prior to publication, the paper would publish poems or recipes where the banned articles would have appeared. Zealous in defense of São Paulo, property rights, and liberal principles, the Mesquitas won the admiration of the opposition through their defiance, and the newspaper's longtime Brasília correspondent remained a stone in the military's shoe.[36]

Most Brazilians did not read the *Estado de São Paulo*, the *Folha de São Paulo*, or the small-circulation magazines, such as *Opinião*, read by a left-leaning intellectualized middle class.[37] The emerging medium of television was far more influential, and here the government exercised decisive sway by supporting the expanding Rede Globo television empire of their businessman ally Roberto Marinho. Protected from criticism and enjoying broad support, the Médici government had ignored the political difficulties dividing the military, its civilian allies of convenience, and dissident factions within the dominant classes. That this was the regime's Achilles' heel only became fully apparent after the MDB's stunning 1974 triumph. As President Geisel settled into the presidency, his group within the military saw the strategic importance of winning back civilian elites marginalized in 1968, especially in São Paulo. This was his aim in appointing Paulo Egydio Martins as the state's governor and tasking him with opening dialogue—whether with the Mesquitas, the Catholic Church, or the São Bernardo metalworkers—and thus diminishing sources of tension. As a gesture of goodwill, censorship of the *Estado de São Paulo* was lifted in January 1975, on the newspaper's hundredth anniversary.[38]

When they meet confidentially on January 20, 1975, the armed forces' high command was still coming to terms with the bad election news. Two months earlier, Geisel had ruled out using AI-5 to overturn the results, as suggested by the military men allied with the dungeon. We can live with the results, the president now told his fellow officers, but the truth is, he went on, that "we don't know what's happening down below."[39] For too long, Geisel argued, the regime had been self-satisfied, and he warned unnamed critics that the worst possible path forward was to "dream of a dictatorship." He even broached the question of whether the Left was perhaps "no longer engaged in outright subversion," specifying that he meant armed subversion. While criticizing ARENA, he noted that the MDB campaign championed the rule of law and "the rights of the human person." Geisel argued that the regime need not fetishize the rule of law but that the issue could boomerang on the government if not at least confronted. As for the opposition's demand to end AI-5, the president reassured his top commanders that while it might at some point be possible, he would always choose the maintenance of order over "the rule of law in its fullness."[40]

As Geisel spoke with his colleagues, the government's repressive apparatus was making giant strides in taking down the PCB's top leadership. This progress reflected the modernization and professionalization of repression compared to the late 1960s, when dozens of suspects might be investigated to nail a single target. This professionalization was epitomized by the army's DOI, a body formally created on June 27, 1969, that unified command of repressive activities, combined sustained surveillance with the rapid extraction of information (i.e., torture), and "followed the chain" of connections to strike "down political leaders who could play the role of catalyst of revolts." As a bureaucratic machine, the DOI relied as much on white-collar analysts as on street operatives and in-house torturers; the institution was implacable in its drive to "locate and annihilate the enemy."[41]

While the armed Left was being smashed, the much-diminished mainline PCB remained relatively unscathed even as several Central Committee members, most famously Marighella, opted for armed resistance, taking with them many of the PCB's student adherents. Unlike the new revolutionary groups, the Partidão possessed an apparatus for resisting repression, with professional cadre, safe houses, and secret printing presses that enabled the uninterrupted production of a national newspaper for ten years. By 1972, the PCB's top ranks suffered their first serious security breaches, and desperation mounted in the run-up to what would be the last Central Committee meeting held in Brazil, in November 1973. While recognizing the looming threat, a resolution to send the rest of the committee's top leadership into exile was narrowly defeated. Over the next two years, ten of the Central Committee's thirty-one members—along with more than a dozen other full-time party cadres—would be disappeared, tortured, and executed by the DOI, with their quartered bodies disposed of in Rio and São Paulo.[42] For all their accumulated experience, the PCB's veteran leaders had never really "imagined being the target of [such] an offensive of assassinations."[43]

Leading the campaign, the São Paulo DOI used the information from its Communists turned informers, along with whatever they could extract from each comrade who was arrested (a "fall," or *queda*, in clandestine jargon), to carry out sustained, patient surveillance. Composed of a mix of police and military men, the paulista DOI referred to its Rua Tutóia headquarters in various ways: the "general clinic" (when they were talking on the police radio), the "butcher shop," or "Grandfather's house" (as DOI officers explained this slang to reporter Godoy, "That's where things were good"). In their slang, surveilling enemies was "flirting" (*paqueira*), and those whom they picked up were "patients," the most important of whom either "traveled" (were executed) or became "dogs" (informants). The killings were mostly carried out at the "night club" in Itapeva.[44]

From 1974 to 1976, the São Paulo DOI realized its full potential under its second leader, Lieutenant Colonel Audir Santos Maciel, and far outshined its less-disciplined rival in Rio. The anti-Semitic and virulently anti-Communist Maciel had been personal friends, since the military academy, with General Ednardo d'Avila Melo, appointed head of the Second Army in January 1975. Maciel also inherited a legendary head of the intelligence subsection, army captain Ênio Pimentel da Silveira, known as Doctor Ney or Little Ney (Neyzinho). Popular with his male and female subordinates, Ney had interned with the infamous Sérgio Fleury at DOPS and proved to be an energetic leader who "in person commanded the kidnapping, torture, and death of at least four dozen people in São Paulo." As the vanguard of the dungeon's forces, São Paulo's DOI was further empowered in 1975 by the support of army chief of staff Sylvio Frota, an aspirant for the national presidency already engaged in an unsubtle rivalry with those aligned with Geisel.[45]

Keeping the dungeon under control while loosening repression was going to be difficult. The dictator as arbiter, as journalist historian Elio Gaspari suggests, is easier to maintain when a government is moving to restrict public liberties but hard to execute while controls are being loosened.[46] While the opposition responded positively to the loosening, they remained uncertain about how much they could trust in Geisel's goodwill, as his power ultimately derived from a military that zealously shielded its rivalries and disagreements from public scrutiny. To succeed, his enlightened master plan required not only finesse but a level of internal military agreement that was hard to achieve despite the routine invocation of the armed forces' monolithic unity. The Revolution of 1964's war on subversion offered internal military dissidents ample room for maneuver as they executed the agreed-on plan to eliminate the PCB, allowing the dungeon to attack the opposition that Geisel was trying to woo discreetly.

Unlike his rivals, Geisel recognized that defense of the rule of law and the "rights of the human person" was a potentially powerful platform for the elite opposition. With torture as the wedge, the emerging human rights discourse targeted practices that figured centrally in the destruction of armed opposition movements, whose members were overwhelmingly university-educated children from middle- and upper-class families.[47] Since the time of slavery, those on the upper floors of Brazilian society had always aspired to do away with—at least on paper—the violence and "backwardness" that marked their country as uncivilized in North Atlantic eyes. Thus, the 1824 constitution of newly independent Brazil, bequeathed by its first king, outlawed "whippings [*açoites*], torture, and branding with a hot iron, and all other cruel punishments" (slaves and poor free people continued to be whipped, tortured, and abused). When the monarchy gave way to the republic, the liberal constitution of 1891 offered guarantees, such as habeas corpus, to those "in imminent danger of suffering violence or coercion" or other abuses of power; this language was still found in the military's 1967 constitution, which also required that authorities "respect the physical and moral integrity" of those it detained or imprisoned (a rule routinely ignored for the subaltern).[48]

Geisel's strategic vision was for the regime to change so that things would not have to change at all. While seeking to enhance the government's political standing among relevant civilian elites, Geisel was by no means opposed to extralegal repressive tactics, including the execution, without legal proceedings, of 104 individuals in the year or so before he came to power. Authorizing the continuation of this practice on April 1, 1974, Geisel's concern was twofold: that such decisions be authorized at the top of the chain of command, thus curbing the DOI's de facto autonomy; and that such extralegal executions should be reserved for "only dangerous subversives." In other words, he favored just enough repression to sustain military rule, executed carefully, discreetly, and with enough sensitivity to minimize political fallout beyond the military.[49]

The AI-5's denial of habeas corpus in national security cases facilitated the disappearing of suspects, which served the interests of Geisel and the DOI. While leaving relatives, friends, and coworkers in the dark, the failure to acknowledge a person's detention allowed torture to proceed unimpeded, and those who survived, if and when it was judged convenient, could be eventually transferred to the police for prosecution.[50] Ideally, the suspect was grabbed off the streets with no witnesses or lured from their place of work under false pretexts. Two days after Frei Chico's kidnapping, Lula's economic adviser at the union, a former ferramenteiro named Osvaldo Cavignato, was visited at the union headquarters by men who told him that his elderly dad was doing poorly and that they'd been sent to get him.[51] Cavignato, along with fellow "little fish" Frei Chico, was kept by the DOI and tortured before surfacing at the DOPS headquarters on October 20. (A military court the following year would find them innocent.)[52]

For the forces of the dungeon, Geisel's "softness" caused things to "go awry," giving victory to the revolution's enemies. A case in point was the seizure in Rio of PCB Central Committee member Coelho, a well-connected former deputy in charge of the underground PCB's political articulations (*articulações*). He yelled out when seized on January 18, 1975, and his disappearance came to public attention through MDB federal deputies approached by his courageous wife. With public pressure, she was able to see her husband at Rua Tutóia on

February 20, and she described his ravaged condition to publisher Ruy Mesquita. In an act of courage, Mesquita not only made inquiries but also, three days later, published her letter to President Geisel, which ended with a dramatic plea: "Kill my husband but do not torture him! Do not degrade him, for the love of God."[53] A month later, the *Estado de São Paulo* published yet another letter to Geisel, this time from a very small fish: the daughter of Marcos Andreotti, a married mother of two children. She appealed for a guarantee of her family's safety after DOI agents threatened to detain them if her Communist father did not give himself up.[54]

Such defiance by the press—and a loosening of self-censorship in other papers—heightened the tensions between Governor Egydio and Second Army general d'Avila Melo. While the PCB appealed to some members of the working-class intelligentsia, Communism in postwar São Paulo had also attracted a visible minority of respectable liberal professionals, including lawyers, doctors, intellectuals, journalists, and cultural figures. While the PCB was electorally insignificant after its post–World War II heyday, it stood out as the strongest organized force of protest and contention before 1964. The PCB had even attracted some members and sympathizers in the poorly paid Civil Guard, having supported their strikes in the 1950s; the party retained some support after the Civil Guard merged into the Military Police. For the DOI, Communist "infiltration" of a police force directly subordinate to the state governor offered an ideal target, and July–August 1975 saw four dozen or more members of the Military Police, including officers, delivered to the DOI; for the crime of reading and discussing the Communist newspaper, the Military Police officers were brutally tortured to implicate those "higher up."[55]

As the clash unfolded, the Second Army commander and the DOI were pitted against Governor Egydio and his state security authorities, which included hard-liners, like Erasmo Dias, who resented the DOI's incursions into their jurisdictional turf. The conflict's broad outlines appeared in the now freer print media, whose journalists—most of them opposed to AI-5 and some of them Communist—were increasingly prepared to push boundaries. At the turning point in mid-August, political pressure had built to the point where the Second Army had to send an officer to visit the DOI headquarters to check on the condition of a detained officer. This outsider was so shocked by the detained officer's physical destruction—his head had been kicked repeatedly a week earlier—that he ordered the man's immediate removal. In all, one suspected policeman had died at Rua Tutóia, and another was doing so badly that the DOI, in order to avoid more controversy, sent him by taxi to his family in Campinas, where he died in a hospital a few days later.[56]

Kidnapped

The thirty-three-year-old Frei Chico was aware of the *Folha de São Paulo* article on the arrests among the Military Police, where the PCB had support. The subject even came up during a two-hour lunch on Saturday, October 4, with his friend Afonso Monteiro da Cruz, Vidal's non-Communist predecessor and opponent in the São Bernardo metalworkers' union. Eating at a bar next to the São Caetano union headquarters, Frei Chico and Monteiro da Cruz "were discussing that imprisonment [of Military Police officers], how difficult things were, [and] how risky" their work as trade unionists was, Frei Chico recalls. Getting home at around 3 P.M., he caught his wife Ivenê as she was leaving, with their five-year-old son, to pick up their toddler at her mother's house nearby. Before leaving, she queried him about men who had come by looking for the family of Pedro Antonio Bernardino, who had been in an accident and whom Frei Chico had just replaced as union vice president on Monday, September 29. Mulling over his wife's comments while taking a shower, he decided to throw away a compromising publication in a nearby empty lot. Wearing sandals and a T-shirt, he had just left the house when a Chevrolet Veraneio pulled up and two men, carrying machine guns, threw him in the back. His wife wasn't home, and his neighbors saw nothing. The kidnapping took no more than thirty seconds.[57]

With this fateful event, Frei Chico joined the ranks of the 3,400 individuals detained by or passed into the custody of Second Army DOI since it began operations in 1969.[58] What made his kidnapping all the more traumatic was that it occurred just five days after he had finally assumed the union vice presidency. He had been elected to the position in 1974, but, as accommodating as ever, he had agreed to hold off on assuming the office in order to protect the outgoing vice president, Bernardino, gifting him the job tenure afforded to union leaders so that he might reach retirement age (much like when in 1968 he held off on joining the union slate to protect an older worker). After being fired in São Bernardo in 1969, Frei Chico had moved his activism to São Caetano, where he was hired at CONFAB Indústrial SA, a Brazilian metalworking firm that was far from a model of modern labor relations. Despite employing 3,000 workers, the factory did not have a single drinking fountain, and its workers suffered an abundance of health problems and easily preventable industrial accidents. CONFAB failed to provide adequate safety clothing, the company doctor came only once a week, and the factory lacked an ambulance to take injured workers to the hospital. "There was a lot of sacanagem" going on, Frei Chico observed. He transferred his union membership to São Caetano and won a place on the union diretoria in 1971 and again in 1974, this time at a higher position.[59]

Created in 1958, the São Caetano metalworkers' union had 25,000 workers in its categoria by 1975, which put the union on par with Santo André's, which represented 30,000 workers. Both unions were dwarfed by the São Bernardo union, which had 107,000 in its categoria and an annual budget four times greater than the two smaller organizations' combined revenues.[60] Both the São Bernardo and São Caetano metalworkers' unions had been spun off from the ABC-wide union directed by Andreotti, and the São Caetano union's early leaders were Communists. After the 1964 intervention, that union's politics had been far less riven than those in São Bernardo's: the non-Communist president Manoel Constantino had served in the top leadership for ten years by 1975.[61] Known as Manezinho, this former maintenance mechanic had been one of the union's founders and was popular with the membership. With six children (one of them adopted), the outgoing Manezinho was at the union headquarters so much that people joked that he lived there.[62] Practicing the basics of trade unionism, Manezinho did not stand out for his militancy or sport a distinctive discourse, as Vidal did. Although both were enthusiastic about the MDB, Manezinho differed from Vidal insofar as he was respectful of Communists and viewed them as legitimate participants in union life. In 1975, Manezinho was a delegate to the MDB's national convention and was planning a run for São Caetano city councilman (*vereador*) in 1976, the same year Vidal was elected to that position in São Bernardo.[63]

Frei Chico's intellectual horizons reached well beyond the local metalworkers' union offices that defined Manezinho's world. Unlike Lula, Frei Chico read widely, although at the time it was dangerous to even be seen with a book about Lenin and Marx. During his adolescence in Vila Carioca he had been impressed by a Communist neighbor, the son of Bulgarian immigrants, whom he described in 2015 as a "marvelous figure, an amazing intellectual, [and] a worker." At Frei Chico's first factory, there were militants active in the illegal PCB, some straight off the farm, who could defend the Cuban Revolution while explaining why imperialism had to be defeated.[64] When kidnapped in 1975, Frei Chico was carrying a pamphlet that reflected his breadth of interest: a European Communist Party's view of contemporary European workers' movements. As he observed, having it in his possession "really said everything" when he was picked up; in his signed interrogation he acknowledged receiving "documents" from Ivo with "instructions to later destroy them."[65] Like Lula's brother, many of the 3,400 who passed through São Paulo's DOI learned the hard way that certain thoughts and books were illegal and dangerous.

There were many young people—of various social classes—who became politicized during the reformist ferment of the late 1950s and early 1960s. One of them was the future journalist Vladimir Herzog, a Yugoslav immigrant who entered USP in 1959. Both he and Frei Chico had long associated with leftists, and their hopes had been crushed in 1964 and again in 1968. Favoring the path of democratic mass resistance, each made the consequential decision to join the PCB in the years after AI-5. Frei Chico did so, around the time of entering union leadership in 1971, in a VW with his Communist contact and the PCB state committee assistant in charge of ABC.[66] Herzog's decision came later, probably in early 1975, after four years as cultural editor for the business magazine *Visão*. Long a critic of the Soviet bloc, Herzog surprised his Communist friends with the decision, and he only told his wife a few months before his death. "The political situation was grave," he told her, adding a touch of humor by claiming that only two organized groups were capable of combating the dictatorship: the Catholic Church and the Communist Party. "I'm a Jew. I only had one option."[67]

Detained a little over six weeks after Frei Chico, Herzog was aware of the risks, as was his working-class counterpart. Both felt somewhat protected because they were not living clandestinely, unlike the PCB party assistants and São Paulo state committee cadre. Both were regularly employed, lived with their family at a known address, and were exercising their democratic rights through public activities that were in no way illegal. It was clear in the second half of 1975, Frei Chico recalls, that Communists were facing a wave of persecution, but "I didn't have any idea of what imprisonment would be like. I was innocent [*puro*] in this regard." While he had read about torture, he thought it foolish (*babaca*) talk with each leftist faction, "pushing the sardine to their side of the plate" (puxando a sardinha para seu lado), offering puffed-up stories meant to advertise the exemplary heroism of their comrades. Nothing prepared him for how he felt when he arrived, hooded, at Rua Tutóia, with no idea of "what's going to happen. It's terrifying, a crazy business."[68]

After mug shots and paperwork, Frei Chico was told to strip—in the presence of others—and given to wear a filthy army uniform from a previous prisoner. The DOI operated twenty-four hours a day on the principle that time was of the essence in extracting information, so the prisoner was plunged immediately into physical torment—a type of shock and awe—designed to stoke terror and intensify disorientation.[69] Taken to a soundproofed cell, Frei Chico was strapped naked to a chair referred to in São Paulo as a "dragon chair," the centerpiece of the DOI's torture practices. As Frei Chico recalls, "They tie your arms to the arms of the chair and your legs to the legs of the chair, and they put a stick in between the legs" so that the soles of your feet are exposed. Frei Chico has detailed memories of this experience:

> Then they cripple [*aleijar*] your hands with blows [*pancadas*] . . . in such a way that they get all swollen up. And they give blows to the soles of your

> feet as well. Sometimes they break a few fingers, but that's not the aim, not at all. It's a very scientific thing with them. You end up in such a state that you can't pick up a pack of cigarettes. You can't close or move your hand. It's completely hard. [And down below], everything beneath your feet is all swollen. It cripples you and that's it. You remain that way for a good period. This they did to everyone who passed through there. No one was saved from it.[70]

Standard operating procedure also involved electrical shocks—of varying intensity—to different parts of the body. "They would pour water on you, put salt in your mouth . . . and then they'd shock you. And on the penis," Frei Chico recalls. He told a story about his friend Zé Cabeludo (Hairy Zé), a sixty-year-old retiree and PCB member who, as Frei Chico remembers, had a sense of humor and was a bit of a simpleton (*simplezão*). When they moved to shock his genitals, he joked, "Now this shit is going to get hard." For this comment, Frei Chico notes, "they gave him a devil of a beating."[71]

The torture teams for a prisoner rotated during different sessions; some overseers were somewhat better, while others were real "sons of whores" (*filhos-de-puta*), according to Frei Chico. The torture workers—as many as eight at a time—demonstrated teamwork and practiced dehumanizing styles of abusive verbal interaction that Frei Chico described as sarcastic, even hateful, including yelling, cursing, and name-calling. The sound of the blows—along with the victim's voluntary and involuntary vocalizations and the torturers' questions—were drowned out by the radio; Frei Chico powerfully associates his travail with the popular daily country music show of Zé Béttio. Periodically a medical doctor would check the tortured individual's blood pressure and decide if the torturers could keep going. When a session was over, the torturers sometimes tied the individual's hands to hooks in the hallway, where one could hear muffled screams, moans, and yelling and see people being brought in and out of the cells.[72]

Each torture session was a violent assault that left the body in shock and the mind reeling. To keep captives destabilized, the DOI regimen included sleep deprivation, which might include a guard banging on the cell bars at night or, in one case, a bizarre form of collective torture in which prisoners were moved into a classroom and their heads covered with plastic bags. Under regular conditions, it was even hard to nap because one never knew when one might be called back to the torture chamber. The food was terrible—and sometimes the victim's mouth was so torn up from salt and electric shocks that he or she couldn't even eat. When coffee and a piece of bread was delivered, it tasted delicious, although sometimes torturers reinforced feelings of helplessness by taking a prisoner away before he or she could enjoy the food.[73]

Physical and verbal abuse alternated with aggressive questioning: the key to the DOI's operations was the data extracted and passed on to the white-collar analysts who created the individualized scripts for each prisoner's next torture session. Electric shocks and blows continued for the first four or five days until the prisoners told the DOI all they knew or confirmed what the DOI already knew. This constituted a key part of the moral and psychological torture facing the prisoner: how to navigate the boundary between survival and what one owed one's comrades, with an impractical ideal of revolutionary comportment hovering in the background. Raimundo Lopes da Silva, the forty-six-year-old Santo André metalworker known to Frei Chico as Raul, was particularly tough (*valente*), and he was tortured mercilessly because he refused to confirm anything. Frei Chico himself was lucky to have had a quick exchange—on the third or fourth day of imprisonment—with Central Committee member Coelho (whom he knew by a code name as Virgulino from Minas), who told him to confirm what the DOI already knew; as Frei Chico recounted, Coehlo said that it was "'stupidity' [*besteira*] to take beatings for nothing" when everyone had fallen.[74]

Those who carried out the brutalizing of helpless prisoners were mostly policemen in their early twenties. The DOI gave them a pay raise and allowed them to escape the rigid dress and disciplinary codes to which they were otherwise subjected. While justifying themselves through the language of saving Brazil from international Communism, these rank-and-file torturers were fulfilling their societal role of providing brute manual labor under bad conditions in a foul-smelling workplace splattered with blood, sweat, urine, and pus, and sometimes even excrement and vomit; the job of cleaning up fell to humble cleaning ladies.[75]

The DOI facility during Frei Chico's sixteen days there got more and more crowded, with forty to sixty people on average on a given day, with eighteen to twenty per cell. The DOI had swept up eighty-eight people between October 1 and October 22; smaller waves of detentions would follow from late October through January 17, when the paulista metalworker Manoel Fiel Filho died in custody. Among the eighty-eight were two party cadre members who lived in ABC and three who worked closely with the region's Communists, including "Ivo" (Emílio Bonfante Demaria). Ten ABC residents were also among those kidnapped, six of whom were politically active in São Caetano, three in São Bernardo, and one in Santo André. Lula's brother was among those detained in the first week starting on October 1, along with his comrade and veteran São Caetano Communist and union leader Pedro Daniel de Souza, two low-level rank-and-file members or sympathizers, a market person who lived next to a Communist, and the non-Communist president of Frei Chico's union, Manoel Constantino.[76] As small fish they were all tortured, but none of the São Caetano group were subjected to the most extreme forms of torture in the DOI's repertoire.[77]

Shortly before the end of his first week of imprisonment, Frei Chico was pulled out of his cell, hooded, and taken upstairs, where he met sympathetic army officers indignant at what had been done to him by "filhos-de-puta." They offered coffee and water and hinted that they might be able to help as they tried to get him to confirm that the São Bernardo union president, his brother Lula, was linked to the PCB. They said that Lula was in Japan for a congress and repeatedly asked whether Lula was carrying a letter there to the PCB secretary-general, Luís Carlos Prestes; not only did Frei Chico not know that his brother was traveling, but the whole idea of the letter did not make sense to him, especially as Prestes was now residing in Moscow. This "psychological torture" went on for three or four hours, with Frei Chico denying any connection between his brother and the PCB. In the end, the officers saw that they had gotten nothing and sent Frei Chico back down for another session of torture.[78]

A few days later, the prisoners were made unwilling witnesses to the torture of women in a brutally sexual manner. Frei Chico's friend Ana, an assistant to the São Caetano PCB, was tortured in front of him and her husband, whom Frei Chico knew as Guilherme.[79] The torture included forcing objects such as a broom and an electrified baton (*bastião*) into her private parts. In recounting this story Frei Chico rises to indignation, as he does remembering the utterly gratuitous violence against a young comrade from Santos known as Cebola (Jaime Estrela), who was forced with another prisoner to "swim" naked on a bare concrete floor or low wall onto which they threw water. Done at least twice in the view of those in the cells, this torture went on for hours; then the youngsters, bloodied, were assaulted "with blows, with beatings, and socks to their noses and mouths."[80]

Frei Chico and his comrades Pedro Daniel and Manezinho were moved from DOI custody to DOPS five days before Vladimir Herzog voluntarily reported to the DOI on the morning of October 25. He turned up dead by late afternoon. His death under torture was officially dubbed a suicide, a claim whose absurdity was attested to by the eyewitnesses to the torture who testified in the case filed by Herzog's wife, Clarice, against the central government (which she won in 1978). As a matter of course, those held by the DOI were never allowed anything that could be used for self-harm—especially, as Frei Chico observed, when one was being tortured, during which one sometimes dreamed of dying as a way out. Frei Chico matter-of-factly suggests that Herzog likely died from a mistaken blow by a torture worker, perhaps drugged, who hit too hard out of hatred.[81]

After arriving at DOPS on October 20, Frei Chico was no longer tortured, although one nasty official, he recalls, threatened to send individuals back to

DOI. It was here that the paperwork for Frei Chico's military indictment on the crime of subversion was finalized. After this, he was transferred to a regular prison, where visits and gifts of food from family were possible. He was finally released a week before Christmas, almost three months after being kidnapped from his home in São Bernardo.

Pedro Daniel de Souza, Frei Chico's older comrade and fellow prisoner, was a militant trade unionist, devout Communist, and fervent Protestant—so much so that, to Frei Chico's surprise, he asked for a Bible at DOI. Speaking publicly about his torture for the first time in 1979, he offered the following wry explanation of his experience: "You ask why was I arrested? They said that I was a communist and therefore they took me to the DOI. Was I tortured, beaten? Ah, my son, even Jesus Christ if he was taken there would have been tortured."[82] Pedro Daniel was just one of the 2,000 people nationwide swept up in the DOI's 1975 operations against the PCB. Of these 2,000, 240 were eventually "adopted" by a young international NGO not yet famous worldwide, Amnesty International.[83]

The first round of the anti-Communist blitz reflected a consensus between Geisel and those allied with the dungeon. The blitz targeted the MDB indirectly through some of its lower-level elected officials, local leaders, members, and supporters, some of whom were Communists. From the dungeon's perspective, these limited initial steps were precursors to the "extreme measures" against the MDB sought by those wanting "to guarantee the continuity of the revolutionary process."[84] The controversy over the paulista DOI's indiscriminate arrests grew between July 1975 and January 1976, when three consecutive deaths—none of them clandestine revolutionaries—occurred under torture at Rua Tutóia. To the DOI, such work accidents were inevitable in the war to annihilate subversion, but each successive death tried Geisel's patience further. While a military investigation cleared the DOI of Herzog's death, it was the death of a rank-and-file Communist metalworker, Manoel Fiel Filho, on January 17, 1976, that brought things to a head. Angry at General d'Avila Melo's incompetence, Geisel abruptly replaced him as Second Army commander, which led to Maciel's resignation as the São Paulo DOI head. With Governor Egydio's victory over General d'Avila Melo, São Paulo was henceforth spared the uncontrolled disappearances and terror that had hit Frei Chico and his family, friends, and comrades. But earlier that month—on January 5—in order to make a gesture to the dungeon, President Geisel used AI-5 to order the cancelation (*cassação*) of Marcelo Gato's congressional mandate.

11 CHILDREN OF FEAR

Those who have read journalistic accounts of Lula's life know that he has described what happened to his brother as a turning point. In a way, this turning point was emblematic of a broader national shift as the DOI dragnet in São Paulo, in highlighting torture, moved elite public opinion toward a more substantive political opening than that planned by Geisel. But no one has pondered how Lula—who as a child, we have seen, was too timid to even hawk goods on the street—could muster the courage to face down a murderous state apparatus by seeking his brother's release. How did this child of fear, to again evoke Jatobá's short novel, act in a context in which ABC's metalworkers became targets of the state through treachery and *policialismo* (police manipulation) in São Caetano? How did he face the fear, also traced in this chapter, endured by the families of those caught up in this dragnet—especially acute for those recent migrant families resident in ABC, long disdained by those on Brazil's upper floors?

To answer requires us to ask a question ignored to date: Why wasn't Lula himself targeted by DOI, as was the non-Communist president of the São Caetano metalworkers' union? It is known, after all, that Lula was of interest to Frei Chico's DOI interrogators and that in August 1975 Lula had hired Osvaldo Cavignato, another DOI victim, to work with him in the São Bernardo union. Indeed, a February 1976 army intelligence profile described Frei Chico as "the brother of union leader Luis Inácio da Silva—'Lula'" and noted that both were under ongoing investigation.[1] By understanding the seemingly arbitrary choice to persecute the São Caetano metalworkers' union president and not Lula, we will understand the political and personal relationships that shape the repressive actions so feared by active trade unionists and workers of all sorts. And in tracing Lula's actions in the face of this repression, we will get a glimpse of how the subaltern sojourners of ABC would end up entering national consciousness during the courageous strikes of 1978–80.

On the Ground

On Saturday, October 4, 1975, the day of Frei Chico's kidnapping, he was to meet with his wife, Ivenê Ferreira da Silva, at her parents' home. He never arrived. When his longtime friend Lambari showed up to their house that night, invited for dinner, he found only Frei Chico's slippers and his wife in a desperate state; no one in the family even knew he was a Communist, Lambari remembered later. Ivenê's parents and the Silva family were mobilized to check nearby fields, hospitals, and police stations; Maria Baixinha's husband, Antonio, spent a whole night searching. As Maria recalls, they soon realized that Frei Chico might have been detained; a few days later, they learned that Manezinho and Pedro Daniel had gone missing as well. The only reason Frei Chico was not killed, she insisted, was because of a denunciation of the mass arrests by the MDB's Youth Department, published six days after his arrest in a Mesquita family newspaper that included the names of those missing. Over the following weeks, press coverage would swell as national MDB officeholders joined their party's São Paulo state deputy, Alberto Goldman, who was the first to denounce the arrests, on October 9.[2]

While recording Frei Chico's testimony in 2014, the truth commission interviewers invited his wife to speak. Haltingly, Ivenê described herself as a naive (*inocente*) person at the time of Frei Chico's kidnapping who, like most spouses, knew nothing about her husband's activities; "for those like us, it was a very great shock, something that messed with the whole family." While searching for him, her terror grew as she met others and learned that torturers sometimes brought in wives and children to pressure detainees; for this reason, as her oldest boy recalls, the family moved out of their house. As Ivenê sums up the experience, it was "thirty days of horror."[3]

Teaming up with Manezinho's and Pedro Daniel's daughters, Ivenê spent three weeks seeking acknowledgment of Frei Chico's detention. While checking on the well-being of the father of her kids, a sanctified female responsibility, Ivenê was subjected to verbal abuse by officials who mocked her claim that she knew nothing about what her husband was doing; the whole thing was "very, very shocking," Ivenê said, and it took a long time for her to recover from it. On the twentieth day after Frei Chico's disappearance, the three women ran into a relative of Ivenê's mother outside the DOPS headquarters, where he worked. After they explained why they were there, the relative went inside and came back out to unofficially confirm that Frei Chico, Manezinho, and Pedro Daniel had arrived a few days earlier. They were not tortured at the DOPS headquarters, although Frei Chico received a face-to-face "inspection" by the notorious Sérgio Fleury, who killed many in the armed opposition movements during the late 1960s and trained Dr. Ney. It would be a month after the kidnapping before Ivenê would see her husband, the circumstances of which were distressing. While waiting with the mass of fathers, wives, and children outside the DOPS headquarters, Frei Chico was marched past her with other prisoners, handcuffed, to be transferred to his final detention site, the Hipódromo jail, where he could receive visits. Both Ivenê and Frei Chico recall this first encounter after his kidnapping as, in the latter's words, "a tragedy" for her.[4]

While contending with terror, Frei Chico's wife also had to feed her family. When he was eventually released in the third week of December, after seventy-six days of imprisonment, he found that no money had come in for three months because the São Caetano union refused to pay the vice president's salary, on the orders of its new president, João Lins. On his own initiative, the union treasurer did give the family a little under-the-table help, but Ivenê's parents (rather than the Silva siblings) were the ones who did the most to meet the family's needs. And once released, Frei Chico found out that CONFAB didn't want him back on the job. The labor lawyer Almir Pazzianotto worked out a solution (*jeitinho*, a trick): Frei Chico would step down as the union's vice president while keeping the job guarantee that came with the position, preventing CONFAB from firing him until his term would have ended.[5]

Ivenê and Maria Baixinha were horrified when they first visited Frei Chico at the Hipódromo, because his whole body still showed the marks of torture. Yet physical recuperation may have been easier than dealing with the psychological and emotional trauma. Shortly after his release, Frei Chico was shocked, while walking to his in-laws' house on Christmas Eve, to discover that a DOI torturer lived nearby. His military court case also generated anxiety because, when he renounced his signed statement as exacted under duress, he confirmed that his nickname was Frei Chico. An ill-disposed military judge took that as confirmation of a PCB code name, which forced Frei Chico and his lawyer José Carlos Dias, arranged by Lula, to scramble to collect signed testimony from Paulo Vidal, Maurício Soares, and Mário Ladeia explaining that the nickname originated from when he was active in São Bernardo union affairs.[6]

Frei Chico also faced challenges given his responsibilities as a breadwinner and protector who had endangered his family's well-being. "I was very foolish," Frei Chico told the truth commission interviewers; his wife had been demolished (*arrasada*) by the experience, and his family "suffered a great deal." Withdrawing from activism for several years, Frei Chico continued his job as a welder while repairing relations with his wife and children, her parents, and the Silva family (some of whom disapproved strongly of his political activities). As someone burned (*queimado*) by the police, Frei Chico found some individuals reluctant to deal with him given the risks.[7] And perhaps the ultimate source of anxiety came from the fact that Frei Chico was still living under a dictatorship, with a functioning DOI. He was startled every time he saw a Chevrolet Veraneio—especially when it drove by his house—or whenever, as he waited at a bus stop, a police car drove past and then circled back.[8]

Four decades after his kidnapping and torture, Frei Chico was not given to heroic posturing about the catastrophe that had ended his career as a full-time union official after only five days in office. After this event, he could never imagine power as an abstraction; its brutal exercise had been so deeply internalized that at times it took control of his "inner being" (*intímo*).[9] This did not mean that Frei Chico abandoned his political beliefs or his activism, to which he returned in the late 1970s, getting arrested with Lula in 1980. But from then on Frei Chico was acutely aware of his vulnerability—perhaps the defining characteristic of being a peon. And this awareness would necessarily shape this decided rebel's future actions. In torturing all who fell into their maw, the DOI implanted an enduring message that at any given moment life and death hung in the balance. It communicated that the state was powerful and omniscient and exercised its power with impunity; the individual being tortured, and those like them, were nothing. As Frei Chico notes bitterly, there had been absolutely no need to torture the two São Caetano union leaders because the DOI already knew everything through its surveillance operations (*paqueira*). In the run-up to their kidnapping, a retired army colonel had become a regular visitor at the union—chatting with Manezinho and going out to lunch. Another, less frequent visitor, also not a metalworker, would be one of the DOI agents who picked Manezinho up on October 5.[10]

Reverberations

The logic behind the unjust, illegal persecution suffered by Frei Chico was to punish, demoralize, and dissuade those foolhardy enough to rebel or foolishly drawn to those who did. This logic undergirded all the DOI's actions relating to the metalworkers' unions of ABC. In his October 17 report on the arrests of Manezinho, Pedro Daniel, and Frei Chico, the US labor attaché described the first as "an outspoken opponent of the military government" who was "forthcoming and friendly" in his dealings with the US representative. The union's lawyers had also initially told the attaché that they expected their two officers, Manezinho and Frei Chico, to be released in a few days. By November 5, however, the US consul in São Paulo was reporting deepening tension and nervousness among the labor leaders in São Paulo who were not "pelegos." The Santo André union president, Benedito Marcílio, had even told the US labor attaché that he feared for his "personal freedom," given the "almost weekly summonses" he faced from the security apparatus. If it could happen to Manezinho, president of the São Caetano union, it could happen to him. Even Manezinho's release on October 31 did not tamp down the fear and resentment felt by "São Paulo's deeply divided, frustrated and intimidated labor movement."[11]

Yet Manezinho's disappearance also highlighted treacherous political battles within the labor movement that fall under the term *policialismo*. That two of the São Caetano union's three top leaders went missing overnight created an opening for the union's ambitious secretary-general, João Lins Pereira, a Pernambucan migrant like Lula, as well as for Argeu Egydio dos Santos, the longtime boss of the São Paulo state metalworkers' federation.[12] Classified by the government as a Communist and agitator before 1964, Argeu kept his cushy job by becoming an instrument of DOPS, and he now saw an opportunity to take control of the São Caetano metalworkers' union, the state's third largest.[13] As the attaché noted, all three of ABC's metalworkers' unions opposed Argeu, if for different reasons.[14] The São Bernardo union's grievances, for instance, included Vidal's attempt (discussed earlier) to withdraw from oversight by the state metalworkers' federation in favor of negotiating a separate dissídio for his union.[15] Santo André and São Caetano, by contrast, were clearly aligned with a bloc of large leftist metalworkers' unions in São Paulo state headed, until 1972, by Marcelo Gato of Santos. In the clashes between this leftist bloc and the federation's leadership at meetings and congresses, Vidal positioned himself ambiguously and even voted at times with the latter, whom he privately viewed with contempt.[16] Given the heavy police influence in the state and national union leadership, union meetings and labor congresses sometimes saw violent clashes between Left and Right during those years. Lula recalls the first such meeting he attended, in Salvador, Bahia, in 1970, where "there was almost a massacre" when "the pelegada expelled" the Santo André delegation from the hall after it introduced a resolution in favor of agrarian reform.[17]

Talking with the US labor attaché, Argeu described Manezinho as a man of "affable demeanor" who was not a Communist. Yet Argeu followed these admissions by claiming that a man of such "limited leadership talents" could only have maintained "control of such an important union" through the PCB's support. While Argeu referred openly to his contacts in the military, this dedo-duro was also cozy enough with the national labor ministry's São Paulo state delegacy to pull off his takeover of the São Caetano union. While it is possible that Argeu and the DOI coordinated before Manezinho's arrest, it is more likely that Argeu simply seized the opportunity when it arose. In exchange for release (six weeks before Frei Chico) and dismissal of his pending military court case, Manezinho would turn over the São Caetano union presidency to João Lins, who would hold on to this position, with DOPS and DOI assistance, into the 1980s, well after the metalworkers' strikes that began in 1978.[18] Proud of his artful maneuver, Argeu would brag that his extended absence from Brazil on a November junket in the United States had allowed him to avoid "having to say no" to the call of the federation's "more militant affiliates" for a public stand on the arrests.[19] Argeu was always very clever in union maneuvering, Lula observed, and even more deeply committed to the struggle against the Left.[20]

Despite the deal, Manezinho was still forced to sign a statement at DOPS in which he expressed regret about participating in two meetings arranged by Pedro Daniel, an acquaintance with whom he had worked twenty years ago at the massive Industrias Reunidas Francisco Matarazzo rayon factory in São Caetano. He also "admitted" to giving small donations to Frei Chico—though he thought they were intended for the families of political prisoners—and said that he had received the PCB's newspaper, though he threw it out.[21] The most damning admission was that he had participated in two meetings, which he thought had been called to discuss labor matters, that included Ivo, the PCB code name for Emilio Bonfante Demaria (1923–98), a fifty-two-year-old former merchant marine pilot and captain born in Santa Catarina. As leader of a famous 1953 merchant marine strike in Rio, which pitted him against then labor minister and future president João Goulart, Bonfante was a prominent Communist trade unionist who lost his political rights in 1964 and was condemned, in absentia, to four years in jail in 1969.[22] Well after Frei Chico had been transferred, Bonfante was still in DOI custody, and he was sentenced to four years' imprisonment, the stiffest penalty among the nine found guilty in July 1976 of violating the National Security Law; the other sixty-five defendants in the military trial were absolved, including Frei Chico, Pedro Daniel, Zé Cabeludo, and Osvaldo Cavignato.[23]

Before his release from the Hipódromo, Frei Chico was anxious for his brother. Bound to secrecy about his PCB affiliation, Frei Chico had at various points invited Lula to events that may or may not have been related to PCB activities or proselytism, meetings that Lula refused to attend. Frei Chico had, however, succeeded in convincing Lula to meet with Bonfante, a man on the regime's most-wanted list, by describing him as a fascinating figure, a "real student of the labor question"; Lula later noted Bonfante's fame for having led the 1953 merchant marine strike. Meeting in a public square (*praça da matriz*) in downtown São Bernardo around the election in 1974, the two men sat back-to-back, each reading a newspaper, and talked for a half hour—mostly about the election—after which Ivo got up and left, followed shortly thereafter by Lula.[24]

From the Hipódromo, Frei Chico sent Lula a message that he should deny ever having met Ivo, because neither he nor anyone else had confirmed such a meeting while at the DOI. As Lula noted, he was never asked about it, which raises the question of why. He was spared thanks to his patron Paulo Vidal, an operator who calculated his actions and alignments, which included his refusal to automatically vote with the leftist federation affiliates. The person who informed Lula of his brother's detention was Sebastião de Paula Coelho, a good friend of Vidal's and a lawyer for the state metalworkers' federation headed by Argeu. Trusted by the powers that be, Coelho would be chosen by São Paulo governor Paulo Maluf, an ARENA party member indirectly elected in 1978, to serve as state labor secretary, a post he held during the dramatic ABC strikes of 1979–80. Coelho relayed the news via phone, as Lula was 11,000 miles away on his first international trip, a twenty-day excursion to Tokyo as guest of the Toyota autoworkers' union. Whether he received the call in Japan or during his short stopover in the United States is unclear, but we do know that Lula decided to ignore Coelho's advice to delay his return to the country to avoid risk of arrest. Retrospectively, Lula presents the decision variously, as humorous ("I'd rather be imprisoned in Brazil than stay in this goddamned [*porra*] country"), defiant ("If they arrest me, fuck it!"), or matter-of-fact ("I'll return and see what happens"). Arriving at the São Paulo airport with the dragnet in full swing, Lula was met by union lawyers and associates, but nothing happened. He went home and attended his sister-in-law's wedding over the weekend. After consulting his sisters and touching base with Vidal, Lula and union vice president Rubão went to the São Paulo DOPS headquarters to find out more about what was happening to Frei Chico and Osvaldo Cavignato.[25]

This decision was a bold one, particularly because the visit occurred before the DOI's belligerence had begun to be challenged after Herzog's October 25 death. And Lula was aware of the risk: "I went to look for my brother trembling, that's the truth." "It was a delicate matter to go to look for information on political prisoners," he recalls; "either you were a lawyer, or you were crazy [*doido*]!"[26] The interaction with the DOPS official, a Dr. Campanela, was carefully staged to put the intrepid little fish in their place. First, they were made to wait for hours, taking "tea in a chair" (*chá de cadeira*), as they say in Brazil, a nineteenth-century expression about authorities who, as a sign of their power, made petitioners wait while serving them tea.[27] Once they were received, the *delegado* told Lula and Rubão to sit down, a disconcerting invitation because there was only one empty chair in the room. After Lula asked about his brother, Campanela dramatically picked up the phone to check on whether that "communist son of a whore [filho-de-puta]" was being held.

Controlling his fear, Lula didn't take the bait and deployed the deferential language appropriate to the circumstances. "Doctor Campanela," he reports himself saying, "I want to thank you. I also want to ask about another friend of mine," Osvaldo Cavignato. This elicited yet another tirade from the delegado: "That filho-de-puta of a communist who spent two years studying in the Soviet Union and they haven't killed him yet?" As Lula later emphasized, Campanela said this right to his face, "and you can imagine the fear."[28] Thus Lula continued responding with deference: "No problem, doctor; how generous you are, doctor; how good you are, doctor, to provide us with information."[29] Lula left the meeting angry, all the more so because the insults were "right in my face, really offending me." In his male working-class world, as José de Souza Martins explains, a vicious fight would likely ensue if one called a man a filho-de-puta, and someone might even end up "badly hurt if there was a difference in age, force, or size." Yet Lula kept his cool in response to the official's tirade. "There was nothing I could say, I only managed to respond: 'Well doctor, he erred, huh?'"[30]

Holding all the cards, the DOPS official lorded over these two less powerful men through a quintessentially Brazilian performance of *prepotência*, the overbearing, abusive, and arrogant assertion of unquestionable power. It was this type of aggressive performance—likely excluding the obscenities, because she was a woman—that so terrified Ivenê when she was petitioning for information about her husband. In dealing with the petitioning Lula, Dr. Campanela demonstrated the flip side of paternalist magnanimity, dramatizing the power differential to frighten and terrify. Such loud, abusive, and sarcastic performances were routine for the prisoners seized in the October dragnet, when DOI and its members, no matter how lowly, felt untouchable.

Reflecting the current balance of power, Delegado Campanela also made mocking allusions to those who would criticize the regime: "You see, Lula, what a democratic country this is. A communist is jailed, and his brother is here to ask for information." In 1975, of course, Brazil was not even a reliable electoral democracy, but elections had long provided a facade concealing an entrenched authoritarianism that divided the world between those with rights (*homems de bem*) and those deserving none (*vagabundos, bandidos, comunistas*). Campanela directly invoked this when referring to union employee Cavignato: "And you have a relationship of friendship with this person? You should break it! You're an homem de bem." Lula always ends his narration of this intimidating exchange by exposing the tendentiousness of this false dichotomy camouflaged in anti-Communist rhetoric. His story's conclusion suggests that what distinguished a Communist from an homem de bem was only one's perceived power, influence, or fame: when Lula met Campanela at the DOPS headquarters next, in 1980, after being arrested for violating the National Security Law, the delegado proved a most cordial host, treating Lula like a son and even competing with other DOPS officials to win his favor, because by then Lula was a proverbial "big fish," though not a shark.[31]

In July 1976, a Second Army military court finally judged those swept up in the October dragnet for "communist subversion," including the São Bernardo union employee Osvaldo Cavignato. But who was the thirty-year-old Cavignato, and how did he end up working from an office at the São Bernardo union, next to Lula?[32] Born in the same year as Lula in Duartina, in the São Paulo interior, Cavignato was raised in Santo André and went to work as a SENAI-trained metalworker as an adolescent. He would become politicized in the late 1960s while working as a ferramenteiro at VW, where a small group of Communists was active, including Lúcio Bellantani (arrested, tortured, and tried in 1972). Recruited for a two-year training course in the Soviet Union, he returned in August 1972 after his comrades at VW were arrested and tortured, and he passed the college entrance exam the following year, studying economics while working full-time in industry.[33]

The court's consideration of Cavignato's case acknowledged the factious nature of much of the evidence and its lack of legal credibility. The judges recorded his claim that his signed statement stemmed from physical torture (*sevícias fisicas*) while also noting that the written testimony produced against him by the prosecutors from a certain Marino Trotta not only failed to specifically mention Cavignato but also contained a statement by Trotta that he had been beaten (*espancado*) and coerced into lying.[34] Coming six months after the DOI's wings had been clipped following the Herzog scandal, the judges to their credit recognized that torture vitiated even a minimal understanding of the rule of law and opened the way to total arbitrariness. It's not that these military judges were "soft on Communism"—when judges found the evidence convincing, defendants were found guilty, as in the case of Bonfante and eight others—but the judges refused to divide the world between those with rights (homems de bem) and those without rights (i.e., anyone charged). To do so would hand unprecedented power to those commanding the physical savagery leading to the coerced signed statements deployed in turn by security officials for their own self-interested or factional ends.

Such abuse was common practice. In 2007, ex-governor Egydio explained that the various intelligence agencies in the 1970s so routinely circulated accusations about Communism against a wide variety of individuals, including Lula, that it was impossible to judge the credibility of any such accusation, clearly a tool for persecution and elimination of rivals. Looking back, this Geisel appointee asked the big question pertinent to the cases of Frei Chico, Pedro Daniel, and Cavignato (who we now know were members of the PCB) and many others from the time: "What possible problem for national security" did reading or distributing a Communist newspaper really present, especially if one ostensibly believed in freedom of the press?[35] As more and more people asked such tough questions over the decade following the October 1975 dragnet, nonleftist Brazilians increasingly rejected DOI-style anti-Communism as a threat to themselves and public liberties.

Fear's power among the peons of Brazil went beyond the threat of the brutal exercise of state power on individual bodies; it reflected the already existing wisdom of the children of fear. Speaking to Paraná two decades before his truth commission interview, Frei Chico explained why he "never told the story of [his] imprisonment and torture" to his mother. "She was traumatized when she found out" about his disappearance, he said, and he "never told her the details" because "she was very afraid of this. She feared that something would happen to Lula as well."[36]

12 BECOMING LULA

In 1975 the up-and-coming journalist José Nêumanne Pinto, assisted by USP sociology professor Leôncio Rodrigues, got to know Vidal and Lula while preparing a profile of the contemporary Brazilian worker, published the following year in *Jornal do Brasil*.[1] As Nêumanne recalled in 1989, the union's new president failed to impress even at his own inauguration, sporting a thick mustache and the same shiny suit he wore when marrying Marisa. It was the "interminable but well-articulated" speech of the union's secretary-general that drew visitors' attention; the discreet Lula, "a man of few words," stood in the shadow of his patron's "dominating and personalistic style," which raises the question of how Lula ever became president to begin with.[2] Yet not all outsiders attending ignored the novice president; São Paulo's newly appointed governor, Paulo Egydio, was intrigued by Lula and cultivated him over the following years, seeing in him proof that an "authentic" trade unionist had finally emerged from the corruption, demagoguery, and subversion of the getulista system.

This chapter demonstrates that the essential elements of Lula's discourse and leadership practice were present before the May 1978 strikes that made Lula famous. I begin with the maneuvers that got Lula unexpectedly named presidential candidate on the 1975 slate coordinated by Vidal, investigating the diretoria's small-group politics and examining Lula's relationship with the union's leftists. I then show how Frei Chico's travails, rather than "radicalizing" Lula's political outlook, functioned as an episode in a critical period of personal growth and self-discovery, which had intensified after the February 1975 union election. With ambition and energy, Lula broadened his intellectual and political understanding and deepened relationships with fellow directors, union activists, and members as he struggled to become de facto, not merely de jure, president.

Through creative self-invention, Lula in this period crafted an enduring self-representation as free and independent, employing a distinctive discourse whose appeal would eventually reach well beyond organized labor and the working class. Yet when we situate the São Bernardo union within the wider power networks of this moment, the Lula who emerges in the mid-1970s can be understood as expressing the hopefulness unleashed by Geisel's discourse of change, especially after the DOI had been tamed. By late 1977, Lula and his union would join a civilian upwelling with roots in different social classes, strata, and organized interest groups. The fast-changing world above and beyond São Bernardo was thus crucial during Lula's explorations of the cracks created by the regime's internal contradictions as they intersected with a society in motion.

To understand this, I adopt an embodied approach to the political, going beyond the cliché of politics as public performance to also examine Lula's backstage work in 1975–78 and the crucial, often-neglected existential dimension of political life, the dyadic self-other relationships between individual actors. I examine Egydio's indispensable role during the "battle of São Paulo" and in Lula's rise to prominence both before and after the May 1978 strikes. In doing so, I bear in mind the limits of the politics-as-theater metaphor, given how even the paying audience includes those who pay little attention, others who at best catch the drift, and only a small group of fans knowledgeable enough to appreciate the fine points; most of all, one must never forget the vast population that doesn't frequent the theater at all.

Lula's mental revolution between 1975 and 1978 had wide-ranging ramifications: he declared independence from Vidal and Frei Chico, assumed full command in the union, and crafted a bolder articulation of workers' interests that placed them on the public agenda. Having faced fear and uncertainty head-on, Lula shed his inhibitions to emerge as the intriguing personality whom millions would eventually know and admire: the fearless self-made man, with no strings attached, a US expression for someone who says what he thinks without having his "rabo preso" (tail caught).

Reaching the Top

Lula first assumed the presidency as a figurehead, a fact reflected even in the union offices' physical layout. Vidal, officially Lula's secretary-general, took the office next to Lula's, so that he might observe everyone who came to see the new president. For instance, for Lula's very first interview, conducted in May 1975, the nineteen-year-old journalist Maria Alzira de Melo Rodrigues, hired two weeks earlier by the *Diário do Grande ABC*, was ushered in to Lula's office by Vidal, who answered all but two of the questions, the new president limited to commenting on plans to improve medical services and affirming that the union's day-to-day operations would not change. As Rodrigues told the author of a 1981 Lula profile, she found the new president timid, uncertain, and unresponsive.[3]

It's not hard to explain why the gregarious Lula behaved thus. If the desire for self-advancement could lead to union office, those on the lower rungs could be expected to toady to higher-ups in hopes of career promotion, never mind the presidency. Lula had learned this pragmatic lesson after, as recounted in chapter 6, his overconfidence resulted in a painful spell of unemployment. Once Lula became a full-time union officer, he kept his head down and avoided making waves or showing untoward ambition. The young apprentice knew his place when accompanying Vidal to the countless meetings at DIEESE, the state union federation, and state labor congresses or on a visit to Centro Brasileiro de Análise e Planejamento (CEBRAP); Lula was supposed to watch and listen carefully, learning how it's done.[4] Lula makes clear that catering to Vidal, a self-satisfied big shot, could be irritating, but Lula's apprenticeship as a machinist had taught him that showing deference to one's mestre was about paying one's dues in order to eventually achieve equivalent status.

Lula has likened his first term to entering a soccer game as Pelé's substitute, knowing that the "king of soccer," "in good physical and technical form, was on the bench." Vidal, he emphasizes, was an expert in trade unionism and an experienced public speaker, while Lula dreaded being put on the spot at a union meeting or being asked a question he couldn't answer. He thus seemed destined to preside over the union for Vidal rather than take his place, given how, as an AP metalworker observed in 1972, the union president must always "speak with great confidence" and establish his authority (*affirmer-se perante*) in union assemblies lest he be fatally judged cowardly by the crowd. Thus Lula "went to every meeting feeling really bad" in his first year, especially given the implicit comparison with Vidal, described admiringly by Lula and his brother as a commanding orator who could vanquish aggressive opponents before a demanding union audience.[5]

But if Vidal exercised such overweening power, why did he relinquish the presidency in the first place? As the union election of February 24–27, 1975, approached, those in power (the situação) had to assemble a slate of candidates; the task naturally fell to President Vidal, basking in the heightened attention brought by the union's well-received September 1974 congress.[6] The union was experiencing a real if modest upswing in member involvement, driven by the energetic young directors recruited by Vidal in 1972. It thus seemed inevitable that Vidal would run for a third term. The oft-repeated explanation for why he did not is that the firm where he worked, Molins, was transferring its operations to Mauá, which would place him in the Santo André union's legal categoria and thus disqualify him for the São Bernardo union presidency. If this were the reason, though, Vidal should not have been on the slate at all, much less for one of its top three positions, with his name listed first on all leaflets and ballots. It was equally curious that Lula, then a lowly first secretary, would be the slate's nominee for president, when three other directors, including the two-term vice president Rubão, were more logical choices.

Understanding this requires grasping the political game inside the seven-person diretoria. By examining commentary from half a dozen participants and knowledgeable observers, we can glean the subtleties of politics as embodied experience, a dimension routinely lost when analysts depend on reductive generalizations.[7] Each union leader participated in the organization's shared emotional life as an individual, even when a particular union seemed united or placid—which was not the case in the São Bernardo union. Still, those in leadership could not contemplate opposing Vidal, because that would lead to the warfare that had poisoned the diretoria between 1969 and 1972, when Vidal struggled with the leftist union faction led by Luciano Galache.

Such political realities explain why the planned move by Vidal's employer factored into the 1975 slate's construction. Vidal himself introduced the matter—in the hope that his fellow union directors, afraid of losing their indispensable leader, would draft him to remain or approve a fictitious registry (*registro frío*) listing him as working in São Bernardo or Diadema. Over the course of successive slate-planning meetings, however, they did not; in conversations among themselves, the other directors agreed that there should be a new nominee for the presidency. Rebuffed, Vidal conceded the point; yet when the diretoria's next three most senior members, starting with Rubão, were asked to run, they all declined (as agreed to in ex-parte discussion). This left Lula and another director, Lulinho (Luiz dos Santos), in the mix. When asked, Lula requested a week to think it over. Afterward he agreed, but only on the condition—in Vidal's version, which in this regard is trustworthy—that the current president be on the slate to help him and that, after one term, Lula would be succeeded by Lulinho, a talented and well-regarded electrician at VW (who a few years later would die in a car crash). Like a chess game, this nomination struggle unfolded slowly, with time taken between each move to carefully consider the next option—and with the question of electoral appeal hovering over each decision.

To grasp what happened requires avoiding the simplistic assumption that Vidal lost the presidency because of a predictable waning of support over years in office—"desgaste," in Brazilian political parlance. After all, Vidal in 1975 "still maintained much of his force and prestige," as Laís Abramo reminds us, and Lula only emerged as the union's "principal figure" two years later.[8] But as early as 1974, there had been signs of subterranean discontent with the union's "golden boy"; the highly favorable *Opinião* profile that year noted that some close collaborators described Vidal as "a little dictatorial . . . with union activity, at all levels, centralized around him."[9] The struggle over the 1975 union slate, however, was not driven by an abstract desire for more democratic decision-making within the diretoria. While they might sometimes deploy democratic-sounding rhetoric, these workers turned union leaders did not base their actions on idealistic "democracy talk" or reject power differentials across the board. What drove the six union directors below Vidal was an accumulation of slights, irritations, and resentments caused by his willful blindness toward others and excessive self-regard, which deepened into arrogance as he gained recognition in the wider world into which he aspired to escape.

"Paulo Vidal generated a lot of jealousy because he was very intelligent and not very humble," Lula said; his politics consisted of "me and me," Frei Chico suggested dryly. While praising him, Lula noted that Vidal was not given "to speaking with others as equals" and pitted individual directors against each other. This generated ill feeling that transformed into personal indignation when, with sufficient trust established, the subordinate directors spoke frankly with one another.[10] The collaboration among these six directors was encouraged by their sense that things were coming together for the union; they avoided direct contestation, however, to avoid endangering their reelection chances by spurring a thwarted Vidal to run against them, with unpredictable results for both sides. For the other directors, nominating Lula for president placed someone at the top of the slate who was energetic, popular with members, and a supporter of their emerging project for a more aggressive and participatory union. That he wasn't comfortable speaking publicly was far less important.

Each actor in this offstage drama had distinct impressions of what was unfolding, in addition to different versions that they shared with interested third parties. Lula took advantage of his credibility with the union's leftist opposition, activists from the PCB, PCdoB, and AP who, in his words, were among his friends. Their organizational networks had been destroyed during the Médici years, but these anti-Vidal labor activists were present in individual factories yet unrepresented in the diretoria. By engaging with "those to the left in the Union, linked to the Partidão," the progressive church, and other organizations, Lula had gained a measure of trust and goodwill because such behavior contrasted sharply with the antileftism of his patron Vidal.[11]

This trust is typified by Lula's relationship with Cavignato. A PCB member, Cavignato had opposed Vidal's faction within the union but found himself drawn into the informal seminar of chatting and drinking that had sprung up around the gregarious Lula. Earlier in 1975, Cavignato had told Lula that he was leaving his job because it interfered with finishing his degree. Instead Lula hired him as his economic adviser to draft the statement that Lula would give on his visit to Toyota in Japan, with the idea of eventually creating a freestanding DIEESE section at the union. Cavignato started on August 25, 1975, and was not fired after his disappearance; he was still working in the position in 2017. Talking to metalworker interviewers in 2000, Lula said that he had hired

Cavignato "because he was the first ferramenteiro, the first peon, to have a university diploma while still working in the categoria." Lula claimed to learn much from this cosmopolitan young man, who "trusted me so much that I was even the godfather at his wedding," "because he was really politicized, we talked a lot."[12] His December 18, 1975, release papers revealed something of Cavignato's character: while expressing regret for the activities that led to his detention, he added that, "as a question of morality," he would not inform the police if approached again by subversives.[13]

During the slate's composition, Lula privately urged various leftist friends, including Cavignato, not to run an opposition slate, assuring them that he would be the current situação's presidential candidate. They didn't believe that Vidal would agree to this, but when Lula was announced the nominee, he had already defused potential opposition, as he puts it, and paved the way for them to become part of his base of support independent of Vidal. Looking back in 2010, a disapproving Vidal described this as how "the lefts took power over Lula and absorbed him," although from a certain leftist vantage it might seem that the opposite had happened.[14] In 1999, Lula insisted that he had not catered to leftists "promiscuously" in courting them; rather, he welcomed their participation on an equal basis but demanded, up front, that they agree to respect the decisions made by the majority in union assemblies, over which he would eventually hold sway.[15]

Those who knew or met Lula in 1975 were aware of his discomfort in a public, official role but appreciated his ability in small-group politics, the pleasure he took in the political game, and his ability to reach unengaged members. Despite his later harsh criticisms of Lula, Nêumanne recalls Lula at the time as standing out for his nimbleness, "extraordinary intelligence," and proven capacity to "absorb lessons and to adapt to new situations."[16] But what resources did Lula draw on in these first years as union president? As we have seen, when Lula joined the diretoria Vidal had made him the first overseer of the CET, which operated from the union headquarters and had an enrollment by 1975 of 1,742 students, 80 percent of them union members (an additional 254 union members took professional training courses); their teachers were mostly leftist students, some having been active in clandestine organizations. Lula himself studied there to prepare for the first-degree state education exam, as did Rubão, Lulinho, and Djalma Bom, the union treasurer with a skilled job (as a quality inspector) at Mercedes-Benz. Even after Lulinho took over, Lula regularly dropped in to strengthen his bonds with this swath of the union's membership.[17]

Lula has described the mid-1970s as when he learned that the world was far "larger than just metalworkers, that there were other categorias, and that society is very complex."[18] Like Vidal, Lula possessed a curiosity uncommon among union leaders. For example, this would lead him, at Cavignato's suggestion, to attend a guest lecture in a fourth-year college economics class on political economy and wealth distribution offered in Santo André by Eduardo Suplicy, a São Paulo professor. This future PT founder and longtime senator recalls how an administrator asked the outsiders attending to leave; when Suplicy finished, he found Lula and his fellow director Devanir Ribeiro waiting with questions, which led them to invite Suplicy to speak at their union.[19]

While respectful of academics and their knowledge, Lula primarily fueled his social, intellectual, and political growth through intense engagement with the broad array of people who crossed his path. During what he calls "another apprenticeship," Lula interacted personally with as many workers as possible, often informally over a cachaça. "I would leave the union and go to a bar with 10, 12, 14, 15, 20, or 30 companheiros, and we would sit around talking," he recalled, and "this business of talking a lot, of listening a lot"—"from Saturday to Sunday, from Monday to Monday[,] . . . whether it was raining, or sunny, or a holiday"—was the basis of his learning. The key, he went on, was "to be attentive so that you can take advantage of the essence of what you hear. What's not worthwhile, you throw out, but what is, you keep as part of your apprenticeship."[20]

From these rambling conversations, Lula learned far more than trade unionism or politics. A great conversationalist, Lula strove for total engagement with the individual worker, his life, and that of his family. His approach illustrated a lesson hard-earned by an AP metalworker while organizing in 1960s ABC. As Aparecido de Faria wrote from exile, we revolutionaries were too "puritan in our politics," filling up our time with political "meetings and contacts," and thereby failed to "participate in the life of the workers outside the factory." "A mass leader must participate in the lives of the masses, in their happiness and sadness," Faria learned; "you cannot restrict your political work" to the factory but have to bring it to "soccer games, worker's parties, neighborhood dances, and bars."[21] Unlike Vidal, Lula forged individualized self-other connections with fellow workers, which contributed to his grasp of their diversity, commonalities, and dispositions. He learned their travails and triumphs, their adventures, jokes, and tall tales—about payday mishaps, bad bosses, and the price of beans as well as worries about kids and, of course, soccer and drinking, with maybe some trade unionism or politics thrown in along the way. In adopting this capacious approach, Lula accorded special value to the "least important" of those with whom he spoke, which would characterize the millions of conversational exchanges through which Lula, across four decades, engaged with the populace while crisscrossing all of Brazil.

No Strings Attached

The November 1974 election that encouraged regime opponents led to the sprawling anti-Communist dragnet and sparked the intraregime battle won by Geisel in January 1976, which ended the DOI's autonomy in São Paulo. Frei Chico's detention violently forced national politics into the lives of the extended Silva family, and with it shock, anguish, and suffering. Frei Chico was the other Silva brother who appeared in the newspaper in 1975, even if only on a list of detainees published by a freer press reporting on the dungeon's unfolding campaign against Egydio, Geisel, and the victorious MDB.

Though the full details of Frei Chico's imprisonment would only be revealed twenty years later, through Paraná's 1996 book on Lula and the National Truth Commission's interview, his trauma was known to a national and even international audience long before then, because Lula, who suffered no damage to his body, psyche, or union career from it, made it a prominent part of his life story. He first publicly addressed his brother's arrest in a celebrated July 1978 profile by Ruy Mesquita published in the Brazilian men's magazine *Senhor Vogue*. In this and later autobiographical narratives, his brother's detention and torture was for Lula a personal turning point. Casual observers and biographers have assumed that it radicalized him.[22] They echo Frei Chico, who claims that his imprisonment crucially formed Lula's politics (his *formação política*, in leftist terminology). Until then, according to Frei Chico, Lula had lacked "a vision of what power really was" as well as the true nature of "the regime." This implicitly equates Lula's newfound consciousness with Frei Chico's own politics as a member of a vanguard party.[23]

Yet there are good reasons to doubt these claims of radicalization, which often rely on the impoverished political language employed by the sort of ideologically disciplined Marxist parties to which Lula never belonged. For one thing, it grossly exaggerates the naïveté of Lula, who by 1974 had a solid understanding of the nuances and practice of politics, including its various leftist options within the labor movement. Nor was Lula an apolitical bystander during the struggle for the return of democracy in 1974. As we saw in chapter 10, Vidal's whole leadership team was deeply committed to the MDB in the mid-1970s.[24] And Lula was aware of the regime's repression, having seen the union's lawyer Soares detained in 1970 and Communists like Bellentani at VW tortured in 1972. Torture also came up during his 1974 meeting with twenty-five VW ferramenteiros who wanted to organize a stoppage. Then-president Vidal, invited to join the meeting and offer advice by an uncertain Lula, told the discontented workers about the antistrike law and warned that they could be arrested or even tortured with electric shocks to their genitals. His comments scared the men into backing off and further damaged his reputation with more militant workers.[25]

While these points all counsel against assuming that Frei Chico's detention radicalized Lula, we ultimately lack contemporaneous evidence for how his thinking, feeling, and speaking about the crisis evolved over the eighteen months leading to the mid-1978 *Senhor Vogue* profile. Yet by examining comprehensively Lula's observations about Frei Chico, we can gain a far more complicated story about the range of Silva family reactions to the event.[26] First, Frei Chico's pushy and self-righteous advocacy had long irritated Lula and other family members, as we learned in chapter 4. Second, the family clearly expressed anger at Frei Chico for his actions, including endangering Lula by inviting him to meet Ivo and harming his wife and extended family through his secret life as a Communist. Third, some blamed his arrest on his foolish devotion to nonsense (*bobagem*) and association with stupid people (*babacas*); as a grown man of thirty-two, he should have known better.[27] Yet finally, and perhaps most hurtful, some family members saw Frei Chico as a coitado, a sorry case to be helped as a family obligation. After his release, some family members distanced themselves, as if in exasperation that he would never learn his lesson.

Yet despite these traces of anger, resentment, and blame Lula is on the whole positive about his brother in the aftermath of October 1975 and indignant about the injustice done to him. This is confirmed by Frei Chico, who stresses Lula's bravery in his remembering of the ordeal. The "average Joe would have tried to hide" when hearing the news. Yet Lula not only refused to delay his return to Brazil from Japan but went to DOPS to inquire about his brother and his employee Cavignato. Sounding quite different when speaking in a personal rather than a political register, Frei Chico praised his brother's "outspokenness and courage in confronting the crisis." When Frei Chico, after his release, told Lula what had been done to him at the DOI, his brother suffered and felt anger and indignation. Summing up, Frei Chico perceptively describes Lula's response as being driven by "innocence and courage." Lula could respond thus, Frei Chico suggests, because São Bernardo's new union president, using a favorite expression of Lula's, had "no strings attached" (não ter o rabo preso) to any clandestine political group.[28]

Lula repeated such language during the four-hour interview conducted by Ruy Mesquita, a critic of the military, at Mesquita's mansion in June 1978, the basis for the *Senhor Vogue* profile. This piece, interspersed with excerpts from the interview, made a big splash when published the following month. Lula here first publicly describes his brother's arrest as a "subversive, and I don't know what else." Curiously, he does so in response to a question about the labor movement's unexpected revival, heralded by the strikes in São Bernardo that had begun the previous month. "After my brother was released, he told me what had happened in jail, and I decided to take a position," Lula said, because "what happened to my brother could happen to any Brazilian citizen." This remark was bound to please Mesquita, a conservative who combined a resolutely pro-capitalist outlook with a devotion to the rule of law that, as discussed in chapter 10, led him to place DOI torture on the national agenda through his newspapers, which were also the first to publish the list of those picked up in the October dragnet that had snared Frei Chico.

Highlighting the personal effects of a human rights violation was therefore smart politics for Lula in dealing with Mesquita. Yet instead of going on to discuss workers, democracy, or the rule of law, Lula next speaks in what sounds like a mostly personal register: "At that moment, I lost the worry I had about displeasing others, of offending someone, and began to say what I wished to say." "My objective is to say what I think," he said, because he was not owned by anyone — "I usually use the word rabo preso," he went on, because "things are easier when a man's only obligation is purely and simply to his own conscience or those he represents." With no strings attached and nothing to hide, Lula "decided to open [his] mouth to say what any worker would wish to say if he were placed in front of a microphone." "And I never expected," he concluded, "that these truths, coming from a worker, could possibly have had the repercussions that they have," bringing himself and his union to political prominence.[29]

Three years after the *Senhor Vogue* interview, Lula, recently ousted as a union leader by the government due to his actions during the 1978–80 strikes, reiterated to another journalist that "the keynote of my life is to not have my rabo preso," as a man "can only truly be himself if he is free," having no secrets to hide from the public eye and no hidden patrons with whom to curry favor. "For that reason," he added emphatically, "I will never give up my right to be Lula."[30] He thus proclaimed the ideal of the self-made man: an autonomous individual in a world where people, especially the subaltern, are constrained by others' power and opinions. It was a declaration of independence, a veritable mental revolution, linked to the transformations Lula was undergoing after his brother's torture and his breaking free from Paulo Vidal, a man to whom he had catered relentlessly. This aspiration would have appeal well beyond the working and popular classes, especially among the young and educated, who were even more closely bound up with, and sensitive to, the demeaning relations of dependency associated with patron-client ties.

Lula's public discourse has framed Frei Chico's fate in a variety of ways at different times and for different audiences, in pursuit of distinct objectives. To neutralize workers' distrust of "subversives," Lula described his brother as having been "seized because they said he is this or that, but the 'bad' that he did was really to have fought to earn a little bit more" to secure a better future for his kids. On trial in 1981 under the infamous National Security Law, Lula told Altino Dantas, a former leftist student jailed under the dictatorship, that his brother "was arrested because they said he was a communist" but quickly proceeded to describe him as a working-class guy like any one of us, "a welder earning twenty thousand a month . . . who started working at ten years of age, worked hard his whole life," a man "who had nothing except his family and his ideas." Turning to the case of PCB member Cavignato, he asked, "What harm did he ever do to Brazil" other than wanting everyone to have a job and eat and live well? As he would note in later years, the injustice visited on his brother and friend was "bad for their bodies in terms of the blows [porradas] they received" but "extremely good for my head," contributing to an "extraordinary leap in the quality of my political activities"—although he did not elaborate further.[31]

Lula has also used Frei Chico to express his disagreement with workers active in clandestine organizations, whose legalization he supported. As a self-styled child of a mass movement and not of the traditional Left, Lula has expressed respect for ideologically equipped workers while noting that not all the politicized workers who got arrested, at least among those whom he knew, were actively mobilizing their fellow workers, even if some had in the past.[32] In his judgment, a well-founded fear of "political persecution" led his brother to prefer "tiny meetings with two people in a backyard" or even in a dark room at night; indeed, the PCB meetings listed in Frei's Chico's DOPS interrogatory usually included two to three people and never more than six. If Frei Chico had broken with this "hallucinatory clandestinity," Lula argued, he might have been able turn out 500 or even 2,000 workers at the São Caetano union hall and "harshly and rudely attack whatever needed to be criticized" openly, because if something happened, at least "everyone would know why you were being arrested."[33] Lula generally framed his objections to the clandestine Left in terms of whether it had helped or hindered workers' struggles, not in abstract terms. Only once does Lula take up and criticize the "vanguard party" model hegemonic within the Left at the time. Workers who joined the Communists, he complained, ended up representatives of the party *to* the workers, rather than vice versa.[34]

By publicly disclosing what had happened to his brother, Lula also gained a mark of authenticity with the broader middle-class opposition that had spearheaded the courageous public protest against Vladimir Herzog's death at the hands of the DOI. The legendary Audálio Dantas, president of the journalists' union, was representative of this opposition and had lamented the lack of solidarity by blue-collar unions with his organization, which risked nightly meetings as the head of democratic resistance to the DOI's atrocities—even the São

Bernardo metalworkers' union was absent, which was all the more remarkable because Antônio Carlos Felix Nunes, editor of the union's newspaper *Tribuna Metalúrgica*, was also on the journalists' union's diretoria.[35] Lula's references to his brother's torture would also be significant for another key middle-class constituency that had mobilized around the Herzog case: college students at the University of São Paulo who two years later would take to the streets and raise the temperature of the fight for democracy for the first time since 1968.

The Governor and the Trade Unionist

The November 1974 elections and their aftermath ended the political quietism of the Médici years and led Geisel's incoming administration to promise a slow, gradual, but secure political transition. The ensuing factional conflicts within the military have been memorably described in 2007 by one participant, São Paulo governor Paulo Egydio, as "a fight with scythes in a dark room": "You could hear the swish but didn't know where it came from or whose hand was wielding it. It was a violent struggle, so much so that it caused deaths."[36] Once the DOI's wings had been clipped, civilian elites were increasingly confident that a predictable path to civilian rule lay ahead, which led to heightened activity by politicians, lawyers, journalists, and church officials followed by the begining of mobilization, first by students in 1977 and then workers in 1978.

An engineer by profession, Egydio had risen to the top of the UNE during the early 1950s, part of an anti-Communist slate that ousted a leadership supported by the illegal PCB. Egydio's anti-Communist and anti-getulista politics overlapped with the oligarchical liberalism of the Mesquita family, owners of the *Estado de São Paulo*. As politics swung to the left in the early 1960s, Egydio actively conspired against Goulart and received high-level appointments under President Castelo Branco, including minister of industry.[37] Unlike the Mesquitas, Egydio supported AI-5, remained close to his patron Geisel, and saw his loyalty rewarded with an appointment as São Paulo governor in 1975–79. This pleased neither the local ARENA nor the state's businessmen, industrialists, and bankers, who had lobbied for fellow paulista Antônio Delfim Neto, Médici's powerful economy minister whose unbridled ambition was distrusted by Geisel.[38] Egydio, the businessman turned politician, was tasked with strengthening the state's ARENA by resolving its crippling internal divisions, although he had greater success sounding out opposition sectors, including politicians, intellectuals, the Catholic Church, and even trade unionists, a long-disfavored interest group. In terms of class analysis, Egydio was not only pro-capitalist but a manager of factories and director of companies, including what would become Alcoa of Brazil. Judged in political terms, Egydio was a bourgeois politician who epitomized the post-1964 "civil-military" dictatorship. As governor, he not only rejected demands for ending AI-5 but also assumed responsibility, in a 2007 interview, for a truculent police intervention on September 22, 1977, that dispersed a student congress, being held at the Pontifical Catholic University of São Paulo, to reconstitute the outlawed UNE, his first political home.[39]

As the state spearhead for Geisel's controlled transition, Egydio displayed political dexterity by combining inflexibility on AI-5 with a softer liberalizing rhetoric. In July 1976, an entire article in the opposition *Opinião* summarized Egydio's statements without polemic, starting with his affirmation that "the MDB is not something that should cause anyone fear," a welcome contrast with those who denounced the party as a tool of Communist subversion. Egydio assured the mainstream opposition that federal deputy Marcelo Gato's cassação six months earlier was aimed at "action by the PC[B], purely that, nothing more." His MDB opponents were also pleased that he recognized as legitimate their complaints about civilians' loss of decision-making power after 1964. Regarding the path forward, he urged the political class to forsake a "utopian idealism" that dreamed of ending military rule outright and instead trust that Geisel's government was continuing with "profoundly liberalizing" measures, although he admitted that the transition might take four to even twelve years.[40] Beyond mollifying a far-from-radical MDB, his words also expressed his own hope as a civilian who had, despite ostensibly liberal principles, supported military rule and now saw light at the end of the tunnel.

As a multilevel game, politics includes a moral and ethical dimension in which lines are drawn to delineate friend and foe. Yet neither moralism nor class analysis can explain Egydio's role in defeating the dungeon in January 1976. On taking office, the new civilian governor received a public broadside by General d'Ávila Melo, who underestimated both Egydio's combativeness and his closeness with Geisel. Without Egydio's emergency phone calls about the DOI's actions, it is unlikely that Geisel would have chosen to pay a political price within the military over one or another death by torture at the DOI's hands. His man in São Paulo, however, was a good enough client to deserve reciprocity; after the fourth death at the DOI in six months, Geisel knew that allowing Egydio's definitive humiliation would diminish his own power. Hence the unprecedented replacement of the Second Army chief.

With the passage of forty years, we can now better grasp the battle of São Paulo's backstage and offstage politics. A sophisticated man of power, Egydio reacted viscerally to the dungeon's disrespect and anti-intellectualism, with its marginal media allies who outrageously dubbed as subversive several distinguished businessmen and intellectuals whom he had appointed to top positions.

He was capable of indignation and explosive anger in the face of DOI atrocities and even cried when he heard of the death of Herzog, a man whom he had defended a few months earlier when hired at TV Cultura. That the governor's repudiation of the DOI was sincere is suggested by how he quietly facilitated a pension from the state legislature for Lieutenant Vicente Silvestre, a Communist military police officer barbarously tortured by the DOI. On December 28, 1975, when Geisel consulted with Egydio about canceling the electoral mandates of MDB federal deputy Marcelo Gato and a PCB-affiliated state deputy, the decision to proceed stipulated that neither would face "interrogation" by the DOI, which was still brutally torturing its victims.[41]

Confident in both his own judgment and Geisel's support, Egydio was willing to take risks avoided by other top ARENA appointees, who spent more time looking over their shoulders. Take, for instance, the relationship he pursued with the São Bernardo union's new president. In a long autobiographical interview published in 2007, Egydio spoke extensively about his friendship with the young torneiro mecânico who by then was Brazil's president. Given the questions posed to Frei Chico about Lula by the DOI, it is plausible that, as Egydio claimed, Geisel spoke with him about the intelligence community's belief Lula was a "communist." Asked by the president why he was giving Lula prestige, the governor told Geisel that Lula had "defeated the communists" in his union and that the intelligence services in Brasília should update their information. Looking back in 2007, Egydio was emphatic that "Lula wasn't a communist [then]—just as he is not [today]. I would dare to say that . . . he doesn't have an ideological matrix." Without strings attached to clandestine groups, Lula was, Egydio insisted, "always someone devoted to looking after the interests of the workers."[42]

That Egydio gave President Lula the benefit of the doubt is not surprising. The security forces and DRT in São Paulo knew that the victory of Vidal's 1972 slate, with Lula as first secretary, was a hard-fought victory over the São Bernardo union's leftists, including the PCB, which violently opposed Vidal. And the 1975 diretoria lacked the "card-carrying" leftists of its counterparts in São Caetano (where Frei Chico served) and Santo André (which had a well-established reputation for being "on the left"). As Frei Chico explained, a single Communist diretoria member gave a union a reputation as Communist-controlled, which "burned" it with the police, employers, and the Labor Ministry and made it a target of ruthless police agents like Argeu dos Santos.[43]

Taking his cue from Vidal, Lula publicly avowed an "independent attitude in relation to the left," which gave him credibility on Brazilian society's upper floors between 1975 and 1978.[44] He insisted that clandestine party militancy was harmful and rebuffed leftist students as "bosses of the future," in his conversation with Mesquita.[45] In November 1976, he even publicly criticized the MDB as indistinguishable from ARENA ("two sacks full of cats") and declared as misplaced the hope of workers "that by voting for Quércia he would save Brazil."[46] While continuing his predecessor's criticism of earlier trade unionism, Lula avoided Vidal's explicitly antileftist rhetoric regarding a trade unionism in thrall to "political and ideological interests," code for the Left.[47] Instead, Lula's critique used the language of "não ter o rabo preso" to affirm his independence from employers, the DRT, and the government as well as political parties, students, and the church, not to mention the union movement's upper levels.

Like Vidal, Lula declared as his top priority the unfailing defense of the workers' economic interests. When asked what workers wanted, Lula always answered with a straightforward "more": more salary, more dignified conditions, more consumer durables, more time with their family, and so on. To this end Lula sought contact with ARENA politicians, government ministers, and even Geisel, to whom he passed a message (with Egydio's help) during a 1976 presidential visit to São Bernardo. After a decade in which unions were denied recognition as legitimate interlocutors, Lula followed Vidal's lead and pursued any prospect for addressing workers' long-festering complaints and demands. Leftists and PCB union presidents also met with government officials, of course, but they assumed a priori that a capitalist dictatorship would not meet workers' legitimate demands, using such encounters instead as set pieces for educating their followers about the need for democracy's return and an end to government policies biased toward employers.

When the May 1978 strikes began, Lula also unprecedentedly requested a meeting with the Second Army's commander, and he was always willing to meet privately with national government emissaries sent to assess São Paulo's novel political situation, which by then included Lula and his union.[48] With a consistent message to all audiences, Lula and his diretoria welcomed the national civil society dialogue the regime launched in early 1977, under the direction of ARENA senator Petrônio Portella.[49] After meeting with this senator for ninety minutes in Brasília on February 16, 1977, Lula went on to spend four hours that night with Delfim Neto at the apartment of the MDB federal deputy (and Lula's erstwhile lecturer) Eduardo Suplicy.[50] Lula's remarkable openness undermines any notion that he was definitively radicalized by his brother's torture. Indeed, his participation in Portella's project of national dialogue was vocally opposed at lively union assemblies by those "in the categoria who thought it was a surrender"; as Lula recalls, he responded that discussing a return to "democracy was in everyone's interest."[51]

Egydio played an important role in Lula's sounding out of the dictatorship. After first meeting in 1975, Egydio saw Lula at the governor's palace several times, and *Tribuna Metalúrgica* thanked Egydio in July 1976 for helping the union build a holiday colony on the coast; Egydio even claims to have dined with Lula and Marisa, along with his own wife.[52] In turn, Lula invited the governor to a session of the São Bernardo's metalworkers' second congress, in September 1976. While union leftists boycotted in protest, the visit by São Paulo's highest authority was conducted quite differently from similar past visits, such as Laudo Natel's attendance at the union headquarters opening in 1973 or Egydio's own presence at Lula's inauguration in 1975.[53] As Lula announced the visit in the August 1976 issue of *Tribuna Metalúrgica*, the São Bernardo union would not ring the bells "for the authorities, as other leaders do. Here the governor will hear hard truths, just as he can tell us his."[54]

The *Estado de São Paulo* noted with surprise how "a simple courtesy visit by Paulo Egydio . . . to the hall where the Second Congress was being held" became "an unexpected dialogue between the governor and the workers," who interrogated him about why their lives were so difficult, complained about living conditions, and talked about the advantages of collective bargaining agreements.[55] Egydio recalls an afternoon spent "answering questions and debating," with which he had much experience from his UNE days. The session brought him and Lula closer, he adds. Its distinctive choreography is captured in a photo of Lula, dressed informally in white and tieless, standing between the more formally dressed Egydio and the São Bernardo ARENA prefeito, all standing on the floor, rather than on the raised stage behind them, facing the seated workers.[56] Such a freewheeling exchange highlights Egydio's novelty among bourgeois politicians and military supporters.

This event also highlights the complicated relationship between politics' public and private dimensions. Lula was simultaneously strengthening ties with Egydio, parrying the internal union opponents attacking the invitation as a sellout, and reassuring those on the left who were moving toward Lula and yet worried about seeming continuities with Vidal's approach. Least important among Lula's opponents were the far left college students and ex-students in the union who were issuing an ongoing barrage of leaflets critical of him. While these opponents are sometimes accorded significance in scholarship because they produced materials preserved for subsequent researchers in the DOPS archive, they had no substantial support or presence in the categoria.

The second congress's organization also illustrates the creativity of Lula's collaborators and his diretoria's emphasis on building and maintaining trust by dispelling rather than dismissing doubts. First, the governor did not speak from the raised stage or offer the typical stiff ceremonial speech and official platitudes. Second, there was a real exchange of views, with union members, especially activists, empowered to directly question the governor about their grievances, hear his response, and offer their thoughts in turn. In other words, the event was not the theater of deference that characterized prior visits by the state's "august authorities." Placed on the same level as Lula and his members, the governor was the one on the spot, even if standing next to his supportive host.

Yet the episode also reminds us that we cannot ignore the politics of patronage, as can be seen with a surprising editorial in *ABCD Jornal*, a leftist newspaper newly launched by survivors of the armed struggle organization Ala Vermelha (Red Wing). It might be expected that such a leftist group would have criticized the union for cozying up with the dictatorship. Curiously, it did not do so, which was not unconnected to the fact that it received paid advertisements from the union and would become its unofficial organ during the 1978–80 strikes. The paper's editorial praised the governor's "very engaging" style of interaction, offering only one critical note: that Egydio was hoping to improve ARENA's prospects in the November 1976 election. Yet when the results came in, the union had achieved a long-term strategic objective, getting the MDB's Tito Costa, a lawyer, elected as São Bernardo's prefeito; Mário Ladeia, a former union director, as his vice prefeito; and Vidal as the newest trade unionist on the city council.[57] MDB control of São Bernardo's wealthy prefeitura would prove extraordinarily helpful during the big strikes of 1979 and 1980.

Notwithstanding these results, the relationship between the ARENA governor and Lula strengthened. For instance, in 2007 Egydio recalled a barbeque organized by the newly elected prefeito Costa, whom Egydio deemed part of the "hard-line" MDB. Egydio learned indirectly that he was only invited because Lula threatened to not show up otherwise. Whether or not this is true, the ex-governor's willingness to believe it indicates a level of trust in Lula, with whom he had frank exchanges and never, Egydio insists, directly discussed politics. "I felt he was a person you could have confidence in," Egydio recalls, because, unlike during his earlier experience with the São Paulo metalworkers' union, "I didn't feel [in Lula] what they call malandragem," a propensity for hustling. When he was a director of Byington, Egydio had to grapple with a failing subsidiary that might go out of business if an ongoing strike there continued. Egydio recalls meeting the São Paulo union's president, a "big pelego" (pelegão), who assured him that the subsidiary's problem could be resolved easily in exchange for what Egydio took to be a bribe. Angered, Egydio rejected the proposal and ended the strike by attending the workers' assembly that evening—he had never been "afraid of an ugly face by anyone"—and explaining the looming threat of bankrupcy.[58]

In cultivating Lula, Egydio took more seriously than most ARENA politicians the modernizing rhetoric typical of the economic miracle. For the governor, Lula represented the most modern sector of Brazil's manufacturing industry and seemed the antipelego incarnate. As noted in chapter 5, Brazilians had spent decades searching for an honest, "real" trade unionist. Egydio would never have supported someone he considered a pelego (like the São Paulo metalworkers' president Joaquim dos Santos Andrade, known as Joaquimzão) or a rebel (like Frei Chico or Arnaldo Gonçalves, the Communist president of the Santos metalworkers' union). And he wasn't taken with Paulo Vidal, the calculating operator who put on airs and aspired to escape his social position, in addition to being involved in opposition politics. It was Lula, the unashamed worker, who won his favor precisely because this straight-talking "good boy"—no doubt channeling the lessons learned at SENAI—was forthright in his "honest defense of the interests of workers" and his devotion to the country's development in the spirit of President Juscelino Kubitschek.[59]

1968 Redux?

Radical students and opposition intellectuals in 1968 had idealized workers and the power they possessed as a class. When their illusions dissipated after AI-5, they reverted to skeptically judging these barely known "others" as sellouts; only a few Marxist diehards, like Celso Frederico, continued to believe in the working class's "leading role" in fighting the dictatorship. In May 1978, the country was surprised by a sequence of strikes by tens of thousands of workers that originated in São Bernardo and spread to Santo André and the capital. The left-leaning middle class was electrified, once again idealizing workers as powerful, organized, and mobilized. To many associated with USP, the strikes also appeared to vindicate the influential leftist political scientist Francisco Weffort, a future PT leader, who argued in a celebrated 1972 essay that the 1968 strike in Osasco marked the birth of a new labor movement ready to cast off its populist and Communist past.

As a union leader unlike any seen before, the thirty-two-year-old Lula began to receive extensive media coverage, including his first television interview—on TV Cultura, where Herzog had worked before his death. The station's director, Roberto Muylaert, invited Lula to appear on the show *Vox Populi*, a first for a trade unionist. As the show was to go live on May 12, 1978, a colonel from the Serviço Nacional de Informações (SNI) arrived with orders to stop the broadcast; Muylaert called Egydio, who told him to air it anyway, which Muylaert did.[60] With this decisive action, Egydio provided his friend Lula, just inaugurated for his second term as union president, a unique opportunity that made him even more famous among the highly educated. It also raised the political price that the security forces would pay if they arrested Lula, insulating him

Lula's inauguration celebration, 1975. Lula is front left, Egydio is second from right, and Vidal is on the far right. (Courtesy DGABC [João Colovatti])

from the fate of the two less famous São Caetano trade union directors seized by DOI in 1975.

During this first extended, high-profile exposure to a broad public, Lula, although trembling, let it rip. His TV debut was a hit, attracting forty-seven questions from the audience, some of them phoned in—including one each from the state labor secretary, Jorge Maluly Netto, and secretary of public security, Erasmo Dias, both of whom had served until recently under Egydio, and one from General Dilermando Gomes Monteiro, the Second Army commander who had met Lula a few weeks earlier. The appearance generated newspaper coverage the next day and led to many more interviews over the following year, including the one conducted a month later by Mesquita, who had been intrigued by Lula's performance.[61]

In facing off on *Vox Populi,* Lula discovered that many asking questions had 1968 on their minds and were not shy about pressing their opinions. One female interviewer asked Lula why he had not participated in the recent May

Day events, including "an independent rally in Osasco" that she described as "the first joint workers' rally" since 1968 or even the officially sponsored event, instead of leaving "on a trip when you could have met with other workers to discuss important questions." Lula deemed it "a legitimate decision by my diretoria," though he had no objections if other unions decided differently. He then went on "to disagree" with her claim that "a large number of companheiros participated"; if she had gone to the Osasco event, he pressed, she would have seen that it was attended by "many more nonworkers than real workers," primarily "the class of students." Answering her irritated follow-up as to whether an alliance with students was not valid, Lula responded firmly: "I am looked on badly by some students because I don't believe in a student-worker alliance. The student has little to lose and the worker a great deal, and their respective demands are totally different." "I am certain," he went on, "that the movement of the working class is far more serious" and that, if the workers were to decide to fight seriously, "they also would have much more to gain." In answering another question, he answered sarcastically that perhaps it was his "low level of culture," his possession of only a primary school education, and his lack of a high school degree (*curso ginasial*), having only studied to become a torneiro mecânico, that led "to the way I see things, but I think the best way for students to help the working class is for them to stay in their universities."[62]

Lula was then asked about the booing of MDB senators Orestes Quércia and André Franco Montoro at a May Day event sponsored by the Santo André metalworkers' union—an event that recalled the 1968 Praça da Sé May Day rally, when labor's invited speaker, Governor Abreu Sodré, was driven from the stage.[63] Lula made it clear that he would not have booed the MDB senators and criticized those who did, counseling those discontented to express their feelings by voting against them, as was their right. He also insisted, however, that he didn't think the booing came from the workers, who were typically far too polite; in his own union, he said confidently, "I follow the principle that no one boos at even my worst enemy. Once they're invited, they merit respect not only from me" but also from everyone else in the audience. But he added that politicians should be criticized, because they had not done much for workers.[64]

Lula responded aggressively when challenged by a questioner for having been seen wearing a three-piece suit: "Wouldn't it be better," the questioner pressed, "if you dressed more adequately [to represent] your class?" Lula pointed out the implicit assumption here that workers had to be miserable and go hungry to be authentic. "If it were up to me, I would . . . always [be] well dressed because I like it," he insisted, before giving the price of the suit in question, which he had bought at the VW workers' co-op. "The working class doesn't like misery," he went on, and his hope was that in the near future workers would be able to buy everything they produced. One's authenticity, he hammered home, is determined by one's actions, not clothing.[65]

Lula's *Vox Populi* interview was a first for a prestigious television show whose guests usually occupied the upper floors of Brazilian society. The questions to Lula also clearly revealed how many highly educated leftists thought they knew more than the manual worker in front of them. They also displayed a curious lack of attention to the recent unprecedented "arms-crossed" strikes, in which tens of thousands of workers clocked in and then refused to start work. No one asked about the weeks of hectic meetings that Lula had held with those workers to clarify their demands and attempt to negotiate solutions. The audience's dominant viewpoint, whether government representatives or those who identified with the 1968 rebels, was unquestionably middle- or upper-class.

Lula used his *Vox Populi* appearance to make clear that workers' 1978 struggles would not be a repeat of the ill-fated encounter, a decade earlier, between workers, students, and radical intellectuals. Here was a worker expressing himself boldly, chafing at condescension, and rejecting tutelage by "daddy's little boys" (*filhinhos de papai*), a label that workers attached to college students and the children of the rich.[66] Projecting confidence and power, Lula made clear that he was hewing to his own independent path, styled as "owing nothing to anyone," "no strings attached"—which would soon enough attract a section of São Paulo's oppositional middle class, especially among students. When they did join forces with Lula to found the Workers' Party, nonworkers would be forced to act in a more horizontal fashion and with greater sensitivity in their relations with trade unionists and working people. What was needed, Lula already seemed to suggest in 1978, was more truth telling and less deference by those below; Marxist intellectuals were asked to abandon bookish formulas that accorded them pride of place as the vanguard and guardians of "revolutionary theory."

By offering an emphatic declaration of self-worth and autonomy, Lula was contradicting the seemingly eternal subjection of Brazil's peons to their supposed superiors' tutelage. As Lula told Ruy Mesquita, it's much easier to be an instrument of someone else than to be independent, because "defending a point of view" creates enemies—which, he added with equanimity, was a good thing. His credo, he explained, was that "the working class should never be an instrument"; it should instead be "a living force with a real voice because, as the majority [of the country], it should never be treated as if it were a minority. At another point in their conversation, Mesquita asked prophetically what Lula would do about the minimum wage if he were president. Dismissing this hypothetical scenario as utopian, Lula first noted that he didn't "like to talk about the minimum wage" because he was a skilled metalworker, and only those forced to try to live on such an inadequate wage had the authority to speak about this. He then reiterated his firm conviction, expressed on *Vox Populi*, that all workers "must earn enough money to buy a nice suit, to have a car [and] a color television, so that he can finally possess all that he produces." When this happens, Lula said, "we will really have a rich Brazil because it will be a country with a reasonable internal power of consumption," a theme he would often propound during his presidency a quarter century later.[67]

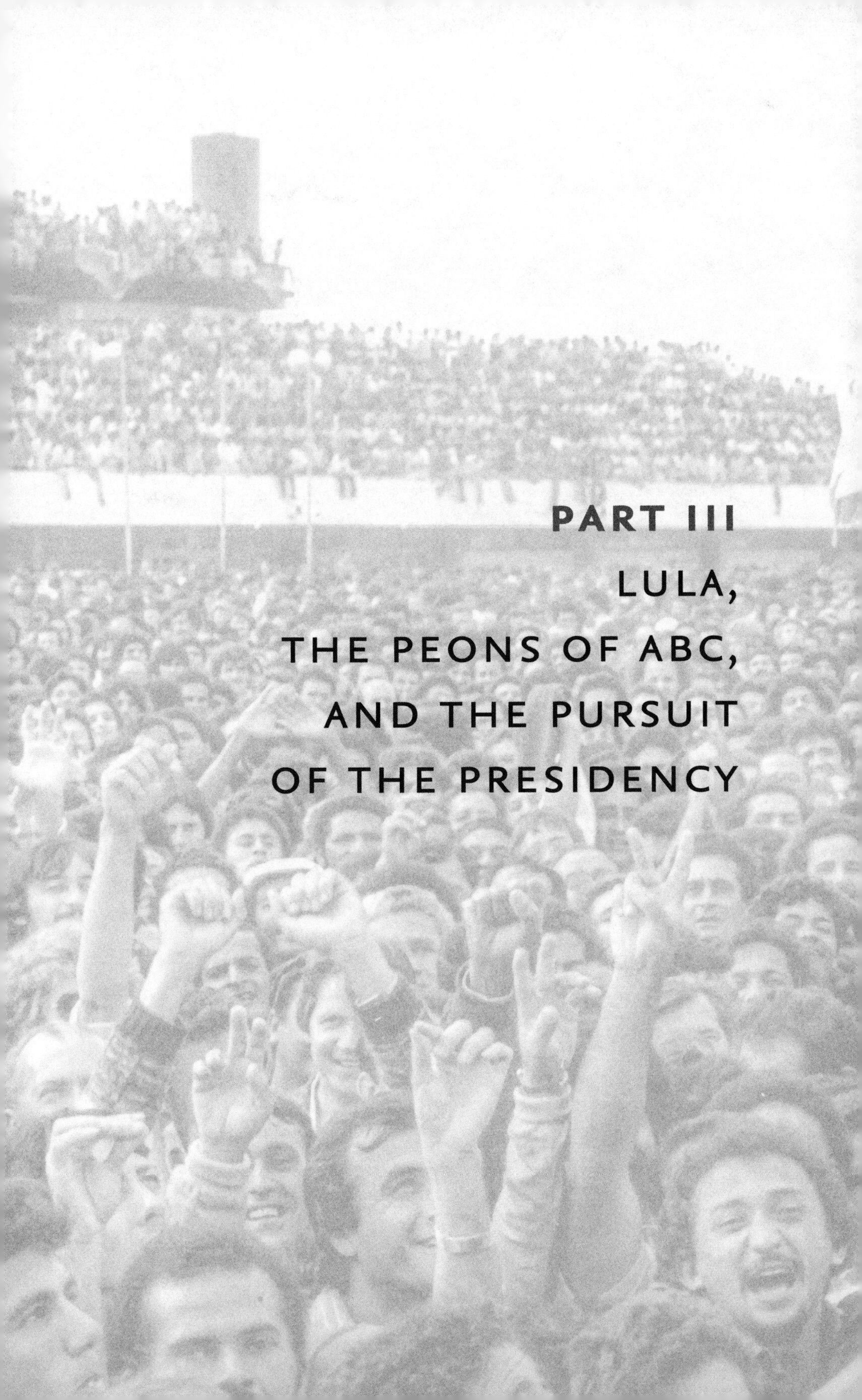

PART III
LULA, THE PEONS OF ABC, AND THE PURSUIT OF THE PRESIDENCY

13 PEONS AROUSED

The ABC metalworkers' strikes of 1978–79 would bring dozens of reporters to an industrial suburb that they would not have otherwise visited. Their mission was to discover what was going on with ABC's workers, many of whom were from states viewed as backward by the highly educated. The crowds of strikers that gathered in the Vila Euclides soccer stadium in 1979 offered a human landscape quite different from their own world on Brazilian society's upper floors. The large number of black, brown, and mestiço workers demonstrated internal migration's impact, as did the stadium rallies' background music, nordestino genres "that made many peons remember their home states with nostalgia [*saudades*]."[1] Here were working-class people whose speech, in a multitude of regional accents, mannerisms, and gesticulations, deviated from middle- and upper-class norms (*norma culta*). Like the earthy Pernambucan Lula, many of these workers' leaders were born elsewhere. This represented a sea change in union leadership since 1964, when paulistas predominated and a good many of them, like Marcos Andreotti, were of European ancestry.

Observing the buoyant strikes of 1979 and 1980, contemporary journalists and academics picked up on the word "peon" among the rural vernacular overheard in everyday speech and crowd harangues. This redolent word, dating back to the era of colonial slavery, when it referred to commoners, aptly dramatized a Brazil turned upside down by a completely unexpected mobilization from below.[2] As a self-referential term, *peão* (as well as *peões* and *peaozada*, in its plural and augmentative forms, respectively) seemed dramatic evidence of a preexisting identity. It also marked the social distance felt by these outsiders in relation to these "poorly educated peon[s], treated with disdain by society" and entrapped in an alienating "culture of poverty."[3] Although not in common usage before 1964, the word "peon" would become powerfully identified with this generation of São Bernardo metalworkers, before losing prominence. Almost four decades later, the well-known journalist Elio Gaspari, in his 2016 study of the military regime, marveled at the emergence of Lula on the national stage, describing him as a man without "an owner [*dono*]," who lacked not only "a political project" but also connections to anyone other than "the peons [peaozada] of São Bernardo," a group whose motivations remained opaque in

Crowd of metalworkers in the Vila Euclides stadium, 1980.
(Courtesy DGABC [Banco de Dados])

his narrative.[4] This chapter begins with the union president's higher cunning in 1977–78, followed by an in-depth analysis of how workers' use of the word "peon" illuminates the nature of worker consciousness on the eve of the great strikes. It ends with an examination of the union's 1977 wage recovery campaign, which, having aroused a sizable group of workers, set the path toward the first strikes in May 1978.

Piercing the Veil: An Exercise in Higher Cunning

As we saw in chapter 12, Lula had already demonstrated his political capacity when maneuvering, dissembling, and persuading his way to the union presidency, in the course of which he perfected an outward-directed image as an independent actor with no strings attached. From the start of his term, Lula had been assiduous in cultivating superordinates from government, industry, the military, police, and the media. Lula approached such cross-class interactions with what I call a "higher cunning," a blend of craft, skill, and expertise that included—as in the original meaning of "cunning"—a form of intelligence, learning, and even magic applied to dealing with superordinates. When asked what workers wanted, Lula was consistently down to earth, while his discourse, in terms of labor relations, operated from the assumption that all parties acted in good faith and fulfilled legitimate roles. Lula would be neither a begrudging petitioner who viewed the system as fixed nor a shameless toady engaged in degrading puxa-saquismo. His style was to put his cards on the table while acknowledging differences between the parties, the only path, he believed, to mutual understanding and an accommodation of interests. While this was premised on the inevitability of conflict, Lula thought such conflict need not be irreconcilable if framed in light of a shared goal: economic growth, just and honest treatment, and well-being for all Brazilians.

The stage was set for Lula to demonstrate this capacity in front of a wider audience by 1977. This was an effervescent year for the opposition, as Lula recalled in 1990, because "society began to shout" for change.[5] Such demands had been percolating over the three years since the MDB's 1974 victory, as more and more restless individuals and aggrieved interest groups joined the debate about a future transition even as the military, retaining its monopoly of power, used AI-5 to close the Congress in April 1977 in order to issue new electoral rules designed to thwart the MDB's advance. Geisel's successor as president, selected from the ranks of the military, was announced in July 1977—the same month in which Lula enjoyed a significant dinner at the Golden Lion restaurant, near the VW plant, with friends from the PCB: the ex-MDB federal deputy Marcelo Gato, whose parliamentary mandate had been canceled in 1976 under AI-5, and Lula's counterpart in the Santos metalworkers' union, Arnaldo Gonçalves dos Santos.[6] All three agreed that things were moving along politically: the students were in motion, and even businessmen were complaining, but these unionists wondered "when would the working class go onstage" and enter the fight (briga) with full force. The dinner seemed almost fateful to Lula in retrospect, as two days later a World Bank report revealed that the Brazilian government had in 1973 falsified the inflation rate used to calculate salary increases. "That was the hook that led" Lula to talk that Monday with fellow union directors about launching what came to be known as the wage recovery or restoration (*reposição*) campaign. According to DIEESE's calculations, São Bernardo's workers were due for a 34.1 percent wage increase to make up for their cumulative losses.[7]

Lula's energetic leadership of the campaign brought him to the forefront for the politicized and highly educated. He made the cover of a national news magazine in February 1978, followed by an extended interview a month later in the counterculture tabloid *Pasquim*.[8] The elites and the media, regardless of political affiliation, found him eminently practical, straight-talking, and trustworthy. Here was a labor leader who, unlike pelegos and "subversives," was not "manipulating" workers' grievances for some unacknowledged end. Lula incarnated the hope, long held by men of power—including, as we have seen, current São Paulo governor Paulo Egydio—that a legitimate, non-Communist trade union leadership might one day emerge to free the employers and government officials from dishonest men whom they did not respect but could not live without in the face of the "Communist" threat.[9]

Yet not everyone in government thought that Lula was "conducting his Union along a reasonable path." In an unattributed labor ministry assessment from 1977, Lula was described as a publicity hound with "utopian ideas" who repeated the tired old slogans of trade unionists critical of the state. In a revealing formulation, the assessment declared Lula "not even a shadow of the model of the union leader deserved by the CLT," the national labor system that these ministry officials thought had given so "many benefits" to metalworkers. Yet the report lacked the usual allegations of ties to the PCB or other clandestine organizations, although it slyly noted that some unnamed state authorities "avid for news coverage" (Egydio) seemed convinced that listening to Lula would have political benefits.[10] Yet not all upper-class actors, who had their own complaints about excessive government meddling, would have agreed that the government's labor relations system was above legitimate critique. Moreover, a group of younger, progressive-minded industrialists and businessmen were prepared to recognize that workers and employers could have divergent interests.[11] These proud paulistas were convinced that their home state, more modern than the rest of the country as always, could handle the honest "bread-and-butter" trade unionism typical of North Atlantic countries like the United States, where organized labor was an ally in the fight against Communism.

Lula's proclaimed ideal of person-to-person engagement and honest communication also spoke to something widely perceived as lacking in the mid-1970s. A dozen years of dictatorship had made Brazil's long-standing "social and cultural barriers between the dominant elites and subordinates"—to borrow from James Scott's more general elaboration in *Domination and the Arts of Resistance*—even more acute. As Scott noted, "It is one of the ironies of power relations that the performances required of subordinates can become, in the hands of subordinates, a nearly solid wall making the autonomous life of the powerless opaque to elites."[12] In seeking to break down such barriers, the loquacious Lula opened a window onto the popular world, and many were intrigued by his autobiographical storytelling. Lula's higher cunning thus played to both the curiosity and disinterested self-image of his highly educated partners in speech, who, suspecting that their subordinates were merely feigning agreement, longed for a more "authentic" connection.

Lula's practice of higher cunning was based on his recognition that abstractions like labor, capital, and the state were necessarily embodied by actual people with idiosyncratic backgrounds, characters, and styles who meet in physical spaces—be it his union's auditorium or Governor Egydio's mansion—that encode social relations. The outcome of such encounters depended on the conversational exchange, shaped by dispositions, moods, and insecurities. Possessing unusual interpersonal skills, Lula set out to disarm the "other side" through friendly, warm engagement, with the goal of escaping the stifling conventions of patron-client relations. Describing his negotiating practice from this time, Nêumanne notes that Lula was "always looking for points in common with the person" with whom he had "the greatest divergence." In doing so, he occupied the pivotal "role of finding convergence in an environment where divergences predominated. . . . without giving up his own position."[13] No door was jammed shut so hard that it couldn't be opened, even if just a little bit, and he avoided poisoning relationships, even with enemies, that might yield benefits down the road. And if agreement was impossible, as it often was, at least a residue of personal good feeling remained.

The best example of Lula's high cunning can be found in his meeting with General Dilermando Monteiro, the Second Army's commander in São Paulo, during the May 1978 factory stoppages. Lula decided to pursue an interview after hearing that Monteiro had met with the industrialist Luís Eulálio Bueno Vidigal, while other unionists immediately assumed the worst: the army was "going to put an end to the strike." Lula cheekily requested a chance to explain their side. After a three-hour talk, the general encouragingly described the stoppages to the public as "a strike without violence, agitation," or "external interventions," one that posed "no national security problem." Monteiro thus ruled out intervening in this legitimate labor dispute, adding that it was "necessary to trust in the spirit of these people."[14]

For the opposition intelligentsia, especially students and the "organized Left," such favorable declarations—and Lula's treatment by the press—made him suspect, leading to rumors that he was Geisel's stooge or perhaps a CIA agent. Seeing such interactions and media courtship as merely an attempt at bourgeois manipulation, the Marxist Left lacked Lula's faith that a "heart-to-heart" connection was possible with individual superordinates who were, at the time, caught up in a crisis of confidence and conscience—just as this faction of the Left lacked Lula's understanding of the potential for such media exposure to bring their message to millions.[15] By refusing to prejudge them, Lula built trust through exchanges experienced by participants as a form of freedom from Brazil's rigid roles and entrenched stereotypes.[16] Remarks such as those offered by General Monteiro, whether the ruling elites came to regret them or not, contributed to the drift toward democracy gaining strength in 1978.

Change was also unfolding in the trade union movement, whose mainstream, which included such figures like Vidal, was criticized for their accommodationism and routinism by Lula.[17] As men of goodwill, most unionists knew that employer greed, backed by the government, caused the workers' difficulties. Yet these same men stoked fears of AI-5, government intervention, and arrest in order to excuse their willingness to play their assigned role in the farce that was the labor relations system. While many unionists deployed a rhetoric of righteous "protest," their words had no teeth and would change nothing. Lula's rabo preso rhetoric thus drew a sharp contrast between such inaction and the declared commitment of São Bernardo's youngsters to act boldly in intransigent defense of their categoria, whether union members or not. To deliver on this promise would demand an unprecedented grasp of the baseline and broad currents of mass consciousness within the categoria, including its divisions, if workers were to be moved into action.

Peons as Working-Class Heroes? A Word of Ambivalence

The word "peon" would appear in the titles of three foundational works on the events of 1977–80: Antonio Possidonio Sampaio's well-informed novella *Lula and the Peons' Strike* (finished in 1981), Luís Flávio Rainho's excellent book *The Peons of ABC* (finished in late 1978), and Eduardo Coutinho's 2004 documentary *Peons*.[18] The first work, written by one of the union's lawyers, vividly captured the day-to-day drama of the 1979 strike based on his contemporaneous diary.[19] This eyewitness account depicted the courage of São Bernardo's peons, whether a rank-and-file worker, a union activist, or Lula, Sampaio's longtime friend and drinking buddy.[20] This celebration allowed the lightly fictionalized novella to show how the pejorative term "peon" could be mobilized as an emblem of self-assertive militancy. But Sampaio also unravels the nuances of this word, with its highly negative connotations. For instance, the novella depicts early on a non-working-class character nicknamed Juiz de Fora, a thin young "doutorzinho" (diminutive of "college graduate") with delicate hands and an upper-class manner (*grão-fino*), who "apprenticed" with São Bernardo's workers in 1976–77—laboring in an auto plant, interviewing everyone, showing interest in everything, and making friends before disappearing. On his return, one of the novella's working-class characters notes that Juiz de Fora had gotten "a doctorate in peon" at USP.[21]

The real Juiz de Fora was the mineiro Luís Flávio Rainho, who had been born in 1943 in the city that provided his fictional nickname. In 1972, four years after completing his bachelor's degree, he ended up in the dungeon for his association with the AP.[22] After being absolved by the military courts, Rainho entered USP's sociology program, conducting his fieldwork in São Bernardo from March 1976 to January 1977. Adopting a phenomenological approach that was becoming common among those studying popular movements at the time, Rainho would produce the single most comprehensive study of the lives, experience, and culture of unskilled autoworkers and their spouses.[23] Two-thirds of his October 1978 thesis consisted of interview excerpts—unique for being transcribed in dialect—and when he published the thesis, unchanged, as *The Peons of ABC* in 1980, Lula provided the back-cover blurb, praising the book for letting workers speak about their lives in their own language, even when they "used words incorrectly" and didn't follow standard written Portuguese (*norma culta*)—errors that, Lula thought, paled in comparison to the "absurd" ones made by those who, unlike Rainho, studied workers in a "totally intellectualized" fashion.[24]

The Peons of ABC opens with two workers explaining, without authorial intervention, that "our class" created the term "peon." "You won't hear any other word" when workers talk with each other, they explain. One of them notes that the term was in use when he first arrived from the countryside (*interior*), where it referred to those who, unlike small farmers, "work for others and are subordinated." While usage varies by state, the rural peon is one who does tough jobs, like breaking wild animals or herding cattle, or a vulnerable laborer, without a family, who moves from place to place to work for landowners, hired and paid by a labor contractor (*gato*, or cat).[25]

For Rainho's informants, "peon" refers to "everything related to the hourly paid worker [*horista*]," who is stuck in a bad situation, mistreated and paid poorly. They also offer examples of the term's everyday usage, the phrase "peons never get a break" (*peões num tem veiz*) used for situations as varied as bad food at the cafeteria or being skipped over in line at the factory infirmary by office workers (*mensalistas*). Attentive to the etiquette of interclass relations, one of the informants adds that those in "elevated" positions at the factory, while they did not generally address workers as peons, used the term when talking among themselves.[26]

A systematic review of oral speech preserved from Lula's generation of metalworkers confirms the role of "peon" as a vector for feeling and emotion that sheds light on workers' consciousness and behavior. In its broadest sense, being a peon described a suffering existence marked by an unfair share of pain, shame, and humiliation, feelings accompanied mostly by resignation, demobilizing anger, and repressed rage. Lula's family used "peon" for those mistreated and victimized, people who never got a break and suffered while being looked down on.[27] A peon, according to a Santo André metalworker, is someone "who punches in, is ordered around by others, and gets up early, . . . a person who has no schooling and has to accept what is offered in order to earn his daily bread."[28] A female metalworker confirmed this point while noting the term's gendered component: the person "who punches a time card is a peon if he's a man, and a woman who does so is a *piorra*," both paid by the hour and bossed around.[29]

Metalworkers' use of "peon" involved a recognition that being one meant being deemed worthless, useless, ignorant, and stupid by the wider society. It meant belonging to a group judged so uncivilized they could not command respect from their bosses and had nothing to say worth hearing by their social superiors.[30] In gesturing toward suffering and powerlessness, peon talk illuminates a historically rooted ambivalence. As we have seen, the interiority of Brazilian society's subordinate strata was decisively shaped by multiple internalized stigmatizations based on differential valuations of worth. As Erving Goffman notes, stigma involves judgments about the inferior population's inherently "spoiled" character, and this societal disdain—how they are seen by others—affects how those stigmatized see themselves as individuals and a group.[31] As an external assault on self-worth, stigma can leave a person feeling besieged, as in the case of an insecure nineteen-year-old metalworker profiled in 1966. Ashamed of his situation, Zé Carlos vowed never to return to the interior until he could do so in a new suit and with money in his wallet. His pretensions invited mockery from fellow workers, who would say, "in jest, that we are all peons," which led to his angry reply: "I am not a peon. I am a bookkeeper [*escriturário*], okay?" In truth, Zé Carlos worked "on a stamping press [*prensa*], a heavy type of work," his claim to white-collar identity resting on having worked in the office briefly, where the employees complained that they couldn't read his numbers because of poor handwriting.[32] Zé Carlos had adopted what I would call a mistaken identity response to stigma by verbally affiliating with those who rejected him and labeling his fellow workers ignorant peons.

The psychic pain occasioned by stigma was captured in the 2004 documentary *Peons*, in which Eduardo Coutinho interviewed rank-and-file participants in the 1979–80 São Bernardo strikes, located with the help of union veterans. In the moving final scene, a worker is reminiscing about his youthful companheiros when he blurts out that he had never wanted his child to be a peon like himself. This triggers an uninterrupted, thirty-two-second silence before the man recovers by asking Coutinho, "Have you ever been a peon?" For this onetime striker, the stigma remained even after the election of his former union leader and fellow worker to Brazil's presidency.[33]

How workers used "peon" depended on what they did, where they fit in the production process, and how they interpreted their position in the world. The willingness to self-identify as such depended on whether one swept the floors, worked on the assembly line, or spent one's day as a ferramenteiro. Many workers, especially the skilled, rejected "peon" as a group moniker, preferring more dignified terms like "metalworker." "Sometimes they call us peons," a master's student in psychology was told by a worker in the late 1970s, who went on to explain that "for me *pião* [top] is that toy that the kids play with in the street"; he personally preferred "the serious name" of "operário," an even more class-specific term than *trabalhadores*.[34]

Yet most unskilled workers combined debased manual labor (trabalho braçal) with other markers of difference and inferiority. Analogous to how, as we have seen, Brazilians distinguish between the povo—the common people—and the povão—the really common people—these unskilled workers could be called the "really peon."[35] A poignant example of how hard it was for those thus identified to stand up for themselves is provided by a nordestino first hired as a cleaning staff helper at Mercedes-Benz. Ricardo was "given" a lucky break to work as a machine operator in the milling department (*usinagem*), but his working papers failed to reflect the change, and he did not receive the salary for this better position. After years of meekly asking his foreman to correct this, he finally approached the plant manager (*gerente*), who brutally rebuked him: "You should go back to sweeping the floor because that's your place! We gave you a chance and now you are trying to pressure us!" After this blow, the manager gratuitously violated interclass etiquette while unequivocally affirming his authority: "Bosses are not required to give explanations to a peon!" As Ricardo remarked laconically, this humiliating incident "marked me profoundly."[36] That such crude bullying was common enough is reflected in the popular story of an outraged foundry worker who threw himself into a furnace at Volkswagen, causing an explosion that disrupted production.[37]

All this peon talk thus reveals both generalized dissatisfaction among ABC's metalworkers and the hidden injuries of stigma. As a term of group self-identification, "peon" could indeed be "a symbolic form of insubordination," as two scholars of Bahia have suggested, but it did not denote a purposeful, collective identity linked to resistance.[38] Peon talk was mostly a grumbling lament, not a call to arms, and it also revealed the vast chasms and profound dissensus characterizing the categoria. The shop floor lives of the really peon, after all, were characterized by unrelenting rivalry, the favor of despotic foremen curried to gain advantage or escape layoffs (*façāo*, knife).[39] Far from united, the unskilled lived in a grueling factory world of "one snake eating the other," full of puxa-sacos and dedo-duros, where every peon hoped to see the "death head" (*caveira*) of his fellow worker.[40]

An even more consequential divide separated peons from skilled operários, precisely those more likely to oppose the bosses or enter the union. As a VW activist commented, the skilled and the unskilled often had competing interests; every time a quality control inspector rejected faulty parts, for instance, he screwed the peons (*ferrar o peão*).[41] The skilled also displayed an ambivalence regarding the stigma against manual labor. If their individual achievements as skilled workers contested insulting stereotypes of workers as peons, did their repudiation extend to all workers who were labeled as peons or only to themselves as skilled workers, as opposed to the really peon? Based on his experience in ABC, an AP organizer concluded in 1972 that his prospects for success were inversely related to the "number of peons" in a given factory or section, due to their low cultural level.[42] Gabriel, a Santo André metalworker and self-declared rebel (revoltado), likewise claimed that while the skilled used their breaks to talk about serious things, such as the union and laws, peons only chatted about radio shows and listened to country music (*música caipira*).[43]

Such condescension tinged with prejudice would not have gone unperceived by those whom the skilled deemed peons, even as the latter knew better than to disagree with superiors, at least publicly. On the eve of the first ABC strikes, VW ferramenteiros were complaining to the USP sociologist Celso Frederico about peons, newly arrived from the countryside, who thought that everything was marvelous. When they did realize that they were being scammed (*sacaneado*), peons more often responded with flight than with fight. Dependent on their foremen, they were spectators, not participants, in resistant activity, sheep (*carneirinhos*) who swallowed abuse from horselike bosses (*chefes cavalhos*), only to futilely curse their tormentor afterward. Lacking self-respect, the cowardly peon "put up with everything, and [even] allow[ed] their boss to mount him without opposition."[44]

So even some class-conscious activists openly lamented the flawed human material at their disposal. Moreover, the very aspirations that brought such skilled workers into conflict with the superordinate—in the factory and beyond—coexisted with values, shared by nonworkers, that led them to treat those below pejoratively. Nor was it unusual that characteristics attributed to the really peon tended to reflect racially tinged regional prejudices against baianos.[45] For example, Frederico's VW ferramenteiros, when discussing those occasions when nordestinos finally struck back by physically attacking foremen, didn't "hide their disdain for those 'baianos' who, following a hallowed nordestino tradition, resolve their problems individually with a knife [*peixeira*] in their hand."[46]

Prior to 1978, the atomized components of the categoria in São Bernardo were in a state of seriality, to use Sartre's terminology, riven by diverging interests and loyalties and lacking a unity of consciousness or purpose.[47] Their most meaningful ties were often cross-class ones. These included participation in communities of faith—be it Catholicism (the most important in ABC), Protestantism, Spiritism, or Communism—or loyalty to their state of origin and its distinctive music or culture. Some forged ties to local merchants and neighborhood associations, such residence-based sociability being central to local electoral politics. And there were still others who derived recognition from an exchange of loyalties with social superiors, perhaps even a foreman, while rebels like Frei Chico found meaning through unions and leftist politics, whose horizons reached beyond the working class proper. And finally, some—like Lula and Vidal—were married to the idea of industrial progress: a better life based on the promise of economic growth and modern technological advances.

"We've Been Robbed!"

Defending their self-worth was never high on the agenda of São Bernardo's really peon, 85 percent of the categoria, who were focused instead on their six-day-a-week jobs in noisy and accident-prone factories.[48] After they got home, they slept poorly and worried about paychecks that did not reliably satisfy their needs. What affected them most in the mid-1970s was seeing their hard-earned pay diminished due to increasing inflation when the glory years from 1970 to 1972 came to an end. From the historically low level of 16–20 percent, inflation had increased to 30–34 percent by 1974–75, 46 percent in 1976, and 39–41 percent in 1977–78, destined to leap to 77 percent in 1979 and 110 percent in 1980.[49] As a skilled worker at Molins recalled, "The salary question" was the primary focus for "the guy who was a peon," although even the skilled could become anguished ahead of government-determined salary adjustments (*reajuste*) due to the sheer uncertainty, with pressing bills awaiting payment.[50] Discontent over pay was shared by floor sweepers and ferramenteiros, nordestinos and urban-born paulistas, supporters and opponents of the military. Such a common denominator might seem to favor mobilization, but the unskilled were dissuaded from collective action by their ease of replacement. Struggle was risky, the price for failure high, and hope usually in short supply. After 1975, the skilled, for their part, also felt the gradual narrowing of the differential between their salaries' real value and those of the unskilled.[51]

The rising inflation and salary issues shared by the categoria went hand in hand with continued, if no longer "miraculous," economic growth, financed increasingly with loans from international banks recycling the petrodollars accumulated by OPEC nations. The production of automobiles, trucks, and buses continued to increase, as did the number of those at work in São Bernardo's factories. But by 1973, Brazil's miraculous boom was under pressure from economic imbalances and raw material and even some labor shortages. Deriving legitimacy from economic success, neither Médici nor Geisel was prepared to give up the government's ambitious goal of accelerating Brazilian "economic development at a rhythm and for a duration" sufficient to overcome "underdevelopment" by the year 2000.[52] Thus, in its heyday, the military regime's highly interventionist policy-making was driven by an untrammeled executive branch, free of legislative oversight and protected from outside scrutiny by censorship. Many at home and abroad credited Delfim Neto, a larger-than-life paulista who served as treasury minister from 1967 to 1974, with the brilliant technocratic management of the economy.

Much like the military, the solid institutional facade of their regime concealed a far less disciplined, rational, and bureaucratic governance process than suggested by its modernizing rhetoric. Due to backbiting rivalries, the ambitious Delfim set an unrealistically optimistic goal of 12 percent annual inflation for 1973, burnishing his image as a stern inflation hawk and enhancing his political prospects. When Delfim realized that inflation would be much higher, he tried to reduce it by manipulating imports and exports, flexibilizing regulations, and managing prices for state-produced steel. When this failed, he ordered the Getúlio Vargas Foundation, which calculated the cost-of-living statistic, to distort the inflation numbers by using wholesale rather than retail prices for certain items.[53] The official figure of 15.5 percent annual inflation in 1973 thus radically diverged from the actual rate of at least 22.5 percent, if not more, as the trade union–backed DIEESE had demonstrated in its independent calculation published in 1974. It would thus be a lie about inflation that ultimately fomented the May 1978 strikes.[54]

Delfim's sharp elbows and outsize ambition made enemies during his years as the economy's czar. Geisel and his men were especially put off by the ruthlessness of this civilian intellectual of modest immigrant origins. Their group even collected allegations about possible corruption and shared stories among themselves—assisted by the older, well-placed rival economist Eugênio Gudin—about Delfim's falsification of the inflation rate, a charge substantiated by a later study conducted by one of Geisel's economic ministers. This backstage gossip would have a political impact when businessmen lobbied Geisel to appoint Delfim governor of São Paulo. Convinced that the "dishonest" Delfim was positioning himself to become the first civilian president of the "Revolution," Geisel squashed his pretensions by sending him to the Brazilian embassy in Paris. It was this that led to the governorship of Brazil's wealthiest state being assigned to the carioca Paulo Egydio.[55]

Until 1977, only those in the highest circles of power knew that the country's single most important economic statistic had been falsified. In July of that year, an enterprising Brazilian journalist in New York discovered a World Bank publication in which the government admitted that the actual inflation rate for 1973 was higher than the reported official rate.[56] With the easing of censorship, this news could not be suppressed, and the effects of the scandal extended well beyond the issue of wage determination. It also gave legitimacy to the union-supported DIEESE, although its poorly paid social scientists would continue to face harassment by security agencies and the labor ministry. As Lula's friend and DIEESE director Walter Barelli recalled, the government was forced to "try and shut the union movement up in a more noble fashion, by seeking dialogue." An unprecedented meeting was called in Brasília between labor leaders, including Lula, and the government's two top economics ministers; that the meeting was held at all further legitimated trade union criticism. The emboldened Chamber of Deputies, after their temporary closure to pass the April package, kept the matter in the news by opening an investigation.[57]

São Bernardo's union was among the first to take up the issue, and they set the pace with their energetic, boldly conducted wage recovery campaign. Along with Santo André's unionists, they took the creative, conflictive step of mobilizing to demand direct negotiations with employers, without government mediation, in order to make up for lost salary. São Bernardo's union leadership, unlike those in charge of other unions, was not content with simply sounding off or hailing MDB politicians eager to exploit the scandal for votes. Nor were they interested in simply "educating" their members about yet another "injustice" while leaving the fight, as the São Paulo union would, to their lawyers in government-controlled courts, where the issue was destined to linger and eventually die.[58] To veteran trade unionists like Paulo Vidal, this strategy seemed foolhardy and naive; some leftists saw it as a false and demagogic enticement (*engodo*), given that justice would never be achieved while a pro-capitalist dictatorship ruled the country.[59] This widely shared opinion about the government would lead some, like Vidal, Manezinho, Frei Chico, and the PCB, to prioritize the fight for democracy and deepen their commitment to the MDB, even though labor and the Left's influence in the party was slight and the MDB had no control or sway over wage setting.

São Bernardo's youngsters, of course, had no experience conducting a large-scale campaign aimed at reaching the entire categoria but found an enormously persuasive slogan in the DIEESE study that highlighted the cumulative loss in the real value of their wages: "We are fighting for the 34.1 percent that we lost because of the government." The union's message as it spread allowed more and more workers to understand the pocketbook pressures they were experiencing and to imagine what they would do with the windfall when the injustice was finally righted.

As the campaign took off, the union's established routines were rigorously reconsidered by the leadership. They stopped handing out leaflets with a lot of words, since they knew that peons were not used to reading, and replaced them with comic strips, for which they recruited the talented cartoonists Henrique de Souza Filho (Henfil) and Laerte Coutinho.[60] This move was enthusiastically received by workers and became standard.[61] A thirty-six-member mobilization commission was formed, and 70,000 leaflets were distributed calling for a milestone assembly on September 2, four days before the Brasília meeting with the government's economic ministers; 2,700 signed the attendance rolls, with more milling about outside the meeting.[62] Working dynamically for a common goal also allowed Lula and his allies to bring the leftist opposition into the mainstream of the union's growing activist core, leading to their full assimilation the following year.[63]

The wage recovery campaign also proved personally transformative for Lula, who finally shed completely his earlier reticence about public speaking. "I headed it alone," he recalled in 1981. "I talked and I yelled whatever I wanted to. Until then I was constrained"—because someone was at his side—but this campaign "was where I managed to take a leap and really be myself."[64] Seizing the moment, Lula would storm, stomp, and make a fuss at factory gates, in small-group meetings, and one-on-one with rank-and-file workers. The goal was to fan the workers' existing sense of grievance into anger, with an eye on a possible strike at some point in the future. By the following February and March, Lula would be warning authorities that a strike might happen if concrete steps were not taken, although at the time this seemed an idle threat.

At least at the outset, Lula was not burning all his bridges with the state authorities. He framed his argument in a language of well-grounded reproach that shaded into legitimate but respectful anger. Quoted early in the fight, on July 4, in the *Folha de São Paulo*, Lula made clear that workers had zero interest in riotous behavior (baderna) or creating a fuss. He emphasized that they were patriots who had always done their bit "when called on," having even given "gold for the good of Brazil," a reference to a procoup publicity campaign in 1964. "But there comes a time," he added, "when a citizen wants to live with dignity. We want to recover what was taken from us during the era of the so-called economic miracle. I even admit that there was a miracle, because I believe in God. But I do not believe that you can have one by stealing from those who have nothing."[65] Beyond the touch of religiosity, his statement's moral force derived from the most basic notion of injustice: the violation of the asymmetrical pact of reciprocity binding superiors and inferiors.[66]

In framing the issue, Lula and his team touched on the mixed logics structuring workers' consciousness. On the one hand, Lula's acceptance of the good faith of the government and employers evoked the idea that those who provided jobs were benefactors, the government the protector of workers. In line with this idea, they initially referred to the incorrect inflation numbers as a mistake rather than a purposeful lie; with the error identified and responsibility accepted, simple justice clearly demanded that the authorities rectify it and make good on the workers' losses. On the other hand, Lula invoked the peons' perpetual suspicion that the game was fixed against them, which this scandal proved. Peons hated more than anything else the idea that they were suckers and fools (*otarios e bobos*) taken in by a lying government to the unfair advantage of their employers. Lula blended these discourses when he told a left-wing monthly in November 1977 that "we have entered with a plea for what we have lost" because "this time the government has recognized its error." With "the official word of the government" on the false inflation data, Lula went on, the union could show "workers the extent to which they have been abused. We are using the word robbery, we have proven that we were robbed."[67]

The union's leadership knew that it was highly unlikely that the government and employers would agree to do the right thing. When not even a modest recompense to the workers was offered, Lula preached that this was the moment when, chagrined by dishonesty, shock necessarily gave way to legitimate anger and even righteous indignation. The workers had been cheated, and they wanted what was rightly theirs.[68] On the eve of the annual salary negotiations with the government for 1978, Lula and the union leadership saw an opportunity to expose both the existing system of collective bargaining and the government's ostensible neutrality. The union voted unanimously on March 12, 1978, to not participate, instead demanding direct negotiations with employers.[69] This seemed to many a suicidal gesture, and factory workers feared that they would lose their chance for even a minuscule salary increase to keep up with inflation. But in the end, the labor courts gave São Bernardo the same government-fixed figure received by all the other unions, thus confirming their leader's prediction and proving that the existing process of negotiating salary demands was meaningless.[70] With this point made, Lula and his team were ready to up the ante.

"Letting the Dogs Loose"

Lula was reelected unopposed in February 1978, and the new diretoria's inauguration was held on April 21, 1978, in the sprawling facilities that used to house the Vera Cruz film studios. The festive celebration, with live music, beer, and sandwiches, was attended by 7,000 workers and their wives and children. As in Vidal's heyday (he was left off the new diretoria), representatives from the local, state, and federal government, along with the Second Army, attended—though São Paulo state metalworkers' federation president (and DOPS asset) Argeu dos Santos, feuding with the São Bernardo union, was a notable absence. Union leaders from beyond São Paulo state also attended, including the gaúcho bank worker Olívio Dutra, a future PT founder, which attested to Lula's national stature in the labor movement.[71]

Surveying the crowd, Lula could only be proud. The union had gained members — in the just-held elections, 25,324 workers had voted, an increase of 10,716 voters since 1975 — and hundreds of new workers were coming to meetings and spreading the word at their workplaces. The diretoria, the staff, an augmented core of activists, and a good swath of its membership shared an increasing sense of mission and a sturdy confidence in their president.[72] Lula won reelection on a slate that he was fully responsible for composing and that was launched with a substantive manifesto in late January 1978.[73] Vidal and some of the old-timers were displaced without unseemly controversy, replaced by energetic young workers who had shown determination (garra) during the wage recovery campaign. "It was a diretoria," as Lula affectionately put it in 1981, "of companheiros who drank cachaça and talked nonsense" but were, "above all else, men and responsible persons who, at the factory gate, knew how 'to hit the target.'"[74] Lula valued such gifts above the political and theoretical training they lacked.

As in 1975, Lula stood onstage with a prepared speech, "but when my turn came," he recalled, "I left the speech on top of the table and let the dogs loose."[75] With his "strong and thunderous words," the authorities on hand "began to feel ill," Lula recalled. "One bit his nails, another passed his hand over his face, others whispered, and one could not sit straight."[76] Speaking honestly, with no strings attached, Lula explained that workers had "put up with the conditions" they faced "because we believe in Brazil." He also highlighted his own belief in the much-ballyhooed dialogue between union, employers, and government over the past year. Yet after eight months of such meetings, he had concluded "that nothing has changed and nothing will change." This was because, lamentably, "the employer class does not want to negotiate but only to take the physical force of their workers to the last drop of sweat." "For that reason," Lula concluded, "the time [has] come to put dialogue aside and start making demands without fearing anything."[77]

"We are the majority," he declared, "and can't allow ourselves to be treated like a minority. This is a democratic principle, and we have to fight to impose ourselves as the majority. The new diretoria is disposed to face the ultimate consequences to achieve our aspirations." Speaking to the rank and file, Lula said that the leadership team "awaits for you to join our fight, which is the fight of all of us, even if it may result in the sacrifice of our jobs, our family, and . . . our lives."[78] Lula and the union hammered home the message that nothing had ever been handed to peons on a silver platter. The government was too beholden to employers while politicians, who talked a good game, seldom delivered anything concrete. With a fresh mandate, Lula and his diretoria were ready to push the message that the workers needed to stand up for themselves, because the powerful, even those who were today sympathetic, respond only to pressure. As Lula recalled of the speech in 1981, "We were fed up [*saco cheio*] with authorities who speak nicely but don't feel the pain in our stomach. . . . It's come time for us to raise a club [*soltar o pau*]."[79]

14 THE BIRTH OF LULA'S CHARISMA

Over the course of the São Bernardo wage recovery campaign, workers' optimism, born of faith in the authorities, transformed into righteous indignation, fanned by the union's impressive outreach and messaging.[1] The fruits of this indignation came on May 12, 1978, less than a month after Lula "let the dogs loose" at his second inauguration speech, when an in-plant stoppage began at São Bernardo's Scania factory and spread to Ford and Mercedes-Benz, eventually encompassing 235,000 paulistas over the course of four months.[2] In the end, the strikers received raises that slightly exceeded the government-imposed percentage for such pay increases, flummoxed employers paid workers for the days that they were on strike, and the government had finally lost its ironclad control over wages. The union would subsequently call two categoria-wide strikes over the next two years, convinced that the time had come, as Lula told 40,000 workers in 1980, for "the jaguar to drink water," a popular saying that refers to hunters awaiting the animal's appearance at a watering hole. As Lula would gloss the reference later, it meant that the union would be "going all the way to the very end, whatever the consequences."[3] Convinced of their own strength, São Bernardo's metalworkers, having lost their fear, now had hope.

That the union was able to get workers to commit to a general strike in 1979 was due in good part to a crazy idea that came to Lula and his union buddies while watching the soccer team Corinthians play in São Paulo's Morumbi Stadium. Surveying his surroundings, Lula hazarded that "when we can call an assembly that is half the size of this crowd, we'll be able to turn the world upside down."[4] Up for the challenge, the union scheduled the opening rally for its first general strike at a soccer stadium in the Vila Euclides neighborhood of São Bernardo on March 13, 1979. Twenty thousand workers appeared despite rain, according to a DOPS report. A speakers' platform was hastily improvised out of wooden desks; Lula remembers wobbling as he addressed the crowd because the legs of the desks kept sinking into the muddy ground. Lacking a sound system, Lula spoke to those at the front of the crowd, who in turn would repeat what he said to those behind them. At first, as Lula told Paraná, the peaozada who had filled the flooded field didn't seem interested, and some left; he tried to rally the crowd by yelling that "no one here is made of sugar." But Lula also

Lula at the first assembly at Vila Euclides. [Courtesy Olhar Imagem [Juca Martins])

remembers encouraging words from those at the front of the crowd: "Be calm, no one's in a hurry. Go slowly, Lula, don't be nervous." Somehow the situation turned around (*se virou*); Lula continued speaking, and the experience had a very strong impact: "It was a lot of confidence, a lot of faith."[5]

Vila Euclides would become the iconic hub from which São Bernardo's metalworkers made history by paralyzing Brazil's industrial heartland in 1979 and again in 1980, the first two years of the first military president since 1968 to rule without AI-5. Eyes and imaginations were drawn repeatedly to this neighborhood stadium named in honor of one of Brazil's dictators following the 1964 military coup. At least eighteen rallies would be held at the stadium there during the 1979–80 strikes. According to DOPS, twelve of these were attended by 40,000 to 70,000 strikers, family members, and spectators; the other six attracted turnouts of 15,000 to 35,000. Lula's fame would become inextricably linked to his performances in this stadium—or, when its use was denied, at rallies held in and around São Bernardo's main Catholic church downtown and the local city hall.

The ABC strikes were courageous—some would even say foolhardy—actions at a moment when the personnel of the dungeon were violently resisting the country's move away from dictatorship. ABC's strikers faced police violence, union intervention, large-scale arrests, detention of its leaders, the military occupation of the region, and the firing of tens of thousands. A mas-

The overflow of workers at an assembly at the main Catholic church in downtown São Bernardo. (Courtesy DGABC [Fernando Ferreira])

sacre was avoided only due to the good judgment of military leaders and a government labor minister who sought to moderate rather than radicalize the conflict. While generating a vast literature, scholars of the strikes have evaded the question of how Lula, the gifted organizer, emerged as a recognizably charismatic figure.

This chapter will explain when and why this happened, and the impact that such extraordinary attention and adulation had on a leader whose decisions affected the well-being of hundreds of thousands. It traces the grassroots dynamic of these defiant mass mobilizations during which a charismatic bond was forged in which the union's rank and file would famously carry its president on their shoulders. In the end, over 100,000 stigmatized, fearful, self-doubting "peons" would constitute themselves as a locally articulated social actor, a group in fusion, whose boldness and creativity led to extraordinary feats of organization and mobilization. Together they would prove themselves—along with their wives and families—to be powerful *cabra machos* (tough men) capable of bringing immense factories to a stop, at a high cost to those who had for so long disdained them and trampled their interests.

Becoming Charismatic

In January 1979, Lula decided to grow the beard, against his wife's wishes, for which, along with informal dress, he would became iconic.[6] It was a year in which he acquired "an almost mythical aura" as the whirlwind in ABC transformed Lula "into a national figure with thousands of workers hanging on his every word."[7] It was during these events that Lula became known for his "charismatic command" of crowds that would be invoked to explain his meteoric political rise.[8] Three decades later, for example, the Brazilian historian Lilia Schwarcz would note "his seductive rhetoric, his command of populist language and his personal charisma," for which he was "sometimes compared to saints and miracle-workers."[9]

Lula's charisma would remain a commonplace in journalistic, political, and academic commentary even as the actual events of 1978–80 faded from public memory. In casual use, charisma is generally taken to be something someone either has or hasn't. It is sometimes confused with media-manufactured fame and celebrity, or even with the aura that surrounds those who hold power.[10] Yet the concept has had a technical, sociological sense since Max Weber first introduced the term, which literally means "gift of grace," into the social sciences from historians of early Christianity.[11] In an unfinished manuscript published posthumously, Weber offered the following tentative definition: "'Charisma' is the personal quality that makes an individual seem extraordinary, a quality by virtue of which supernatural, superhuman, or at least exceptional powers or properties are attributed to the individual: powers or properties that are not found in everyone and that are thought to be the gift of God or exemplary, rendering that individual a 'leader.'"[12] Yet scholars continue to disagree over the concept's "meaning, content and potential," in large part because Weber's ruminations were "frustratingly abstruse," often diffuse, and even contradictory.[13] Thus, the concept has been applied promiscuously to a bewildering array of individuals across a gamut of societies and epochs. The problem was worsened by careless readers who missed Weber's disclaimer that charisma is "an analytical construct" that "in its conceptual purity . . . cannot be found empirically anywhere in reality."[14]

If judged by Weber's core definition, Lula in 1978–80 certainly possessed qualities that contributed to miraculous deeds. It undoubtedly takes special talent for any union to pull off a massive, illegal strike that led, predictably, to the ouster of the union's diretoria. But there is something almost magical about the political savvy demonstrated during the ensuing negotiations that ended with that labor minister's surprising decision to return the union to Lula, something that had never happened in thousands of earlier government interventions. And when the union was intervened again, in 1980, Lula pulled off another one of "his great feats," in the recollection of union treasurer Djalma Bom. Facing a hostile interventor, Lula secretly approached Joaquimzão, the president of São Paulo's metalworkers' union. This move surprised Djalma because Joaquimzão was hated by many as a pelego. But Lula had maintained ties with this government-trusted unionist, whom he was able to convince to advocate with the labor minister for the naming of a junta to normalize the situation. When asked to name men in whom he had confidence, the sly Joaquimzão offered the names provided by Lula, which facilitated the efforts of the ousted leadership to regain control in the 1981 union elections.[15]

Lula's "outside-the-box" intuition could thus be seen as evidence of a metaphorical "gift of grace" and evidence of his charisma. Indeed, in a 2005 interview recounting Lula's negotiations during the strikes, Djalma Bom twice described him as charismatic, a term that rarely appears in worker interviews.[16] Yet that would be to misunderstand Weber, who insisted that charisma was neither innate nor a quality that adheres to a person, even though followers might believe this.[17] The true source of Lula's success can be approached via Alan Bryman's clearer reformulation of the concept of charisma, which he argues is best seen as "a particular kind of social relationship between leaders and their followers."[18] As Weber puts it, charisma is "validated through the recognition of a personal proof," the result of which is "voluntary dedication," "hero worship," and "absolute trust in the leader" and his or her mission.[19] Weber himself emphasizes that charisma is proven not by an objective metric but by "how this quality is actually judged" by those who become followers.[20]

Lively admiration for an inspirational leader could be celebrated as evidence of healthy civic engagement. However, Weber's views of charismatic leadership would seem to many—as its use spread—to be a threat, not a boon, to democracy, even though all recognize its often-transformative impact. As Weber described the skewed interdependence that this type of leadership establishes, if those to whom the charismatic leader "feels *sent* do not recognize him, his claim collapses," but "if they recognize it, he is their *master*," because his claims derive not "from the will of his followers, in the manner of an election," but rather from "their duty to recognize his charisma."[21] Their supporters were thus said to act out of blind obedience because "the masses are irrational and emotional."[22]

The antipopular valence to Weber's ideas reflected his ambivalence as a liberal nationalist under pre-Weimar Germany's authoritarian monarchy. Fearful of the masses when not properly guided, Weber was utterly convinced that "'democratic' politics is synonymous with oligarchy," which he meant positively as rule by an elite acting rationally according to modern legal-bureaucratic rules, as opposed to traditional authority, with its patrimonialism.[23] "As every experience teaches," Weber wrote, the masses are "always exposed to direct, purely emotional and irrational influence" because they lack the "cool and clear mind" on which "successful politics, especially democratic politics depends."[24] These views explain why many readers of Weber saw charismatic appeals as potentially dangerous; when faced with a charismatic leader, the masses, susceptible to unscrupulous manipulation, act out of personal loyalty, not as free and rational participants in society's political deliberations. In this sense, the prevailing stereotype of charisma echoes the deep fear of the appeal of demagoguery to the masses held by Brazil's highly educated going back to the country's formation under a constitutional monarchy only abolished in 1889.[25]

Taking the entire package into account, charisma in its negative sense clearly does not apply to Lula. Fundamentally, this is because the 1978–80 strike movements in which he first acquired his charisma were firmly rooted in the trade union, a highly organized, government-financed bureaucracy that exemplifies the rationality Weber believed to be incompatible with charismatic authority.[26] As an elected union president, Lula was committed to defending the material interests of those he legally represented, in the name of which he and the union leadership provided intellectually coherent educational materials designed to persuade multiple audiences of varying sophistication.[27] Rather than imposing his will, Lula reached decisions collaboratively with his diretoria while relying on appropriate counsel from the highly educated, including lawyers, economists, and other specialists. And finally, his rhetoric and practice were aimed at strengthening the trade union while encouraging active participation by its members. The mobilization committee recruited to manage the 1980 strike, for example, consisted of four hundred workers who provided nodes of decentralized, neighborhood-level leadership that allowed the strike to continue after the union was intervened and its diretoria and other key activists jailed.[28]

Throughout his career, Lula has consistently been an institutionalist—whether for the union or the political party. He never sought an unmediated relationship between atomized individuals and an anointed savior that is considered central to "charismatic" or "populist" leadership.[29] During the strikes Lula preached the gospel of organization by the subaltern to advance their interests and gain a respect they were denied. What happened in 1979 was that a remarkable mobilization led to a surprising love affair between the masses and Lula, followed by a lasting marriage between organization and charisma. In rejecting top-down salvationism, Lula echoed the views of his US analogue, Eugene V. Debs, who was prosecuted after leading a strike of 100,000 railway workers, a strike crushed by federal troops in 1894, and who became a socialist after his release. Two years before receiving 6 percent of the national presidential vote in 1912, Debs explained emphatically, "I do not want you to follow me or anyone else; if you are looking for a Moses to lead you out of this capitalist wilderness, you will stay right where you are. I would not lead you into this promised land if I could, because if I could lead you in, someone else would lead you out. You must use your heads as well as your hands and get yourselves out of your present condition."[30]

1978: "A Warning to the Big Shots"

When focusing on the union, it is easy to forget that Lula in 1978 was still unknown to the vast majority of the categoria outside of its unionized minority. Six months after the relatively successful wage recovery campaign, a plucky reporter from *Pasquim* approached 112 workers at three São Bernardo and Diadema factories to ask about Lula. The overwhelming majority refused to be interviewed; described as "withdrawn, suspicious, quick moving, and preoccupied," they were likely put off by an outsider with a tape recorder. But even the small group willing to comment, mostly supporters of unionism even if not themselves union members, knew little about Lula. "He supports the firm and those who work" here, said one, while others said he was going to "do things for us." Only one person—a ten-year veteran of the union who was born in Rio—mentioned the wage recovery campaign, only to say that the diretoria would have to push hard to get the government "to release that money to us." The only class-conscious response came from a VW worker enrolled in the company's SENAI program, who explained that his fellow students resisted naming a company big shot (*um grandão*) for their graduation speaker (*paraninfo*) and instead voted for Lula. In retaliation, shortly thereafter some of these 150 skilled workers in training were fired by VW.[31]

Lula's name recognition in the categoria, however, spiked during the in-plant stoppages that began on May 12, 1978, which were, as one striker recalled, "a warning to the big shots."[32] Lula was in an early morning meeting with fellow union directors Rubão and Devanir Ribeiro as well as DIEESE's Barelli when they got a call informing them that Scania's 3,000 employees had stopped work under the leadership of union directors Severino Alves da Silva and Gilson Menezes, the latter a twenty-five-year-old African-descended worker just elected to the union's fiscal council.[33] While they were aware that a strike atmosphere was building, "it happened even earlier than we had expected," Barelli recalled, and they wondered whether they were "going to lose their positions [*cassados*], be punished, perhaps expelled," as had happened to so many before them.[34] No union director at the time had any experience handling a strike, and Lula was particularly exposed, having all but called for strike action less than a month earlier during his inauguration. On top of this, Lula received news within the hour that his father had died. When Lula's brothers went ahead to Santos on receiving news of their father's death, they learned that Aristides had died two weeks earlier, buried as an indigent, after ending his life in alcoholism and mental disturbance while squandering his meager pension on drink and prostitutes.[35]

As for the stoppages, Lula's union officially disclaimed responsibility but did nothing to impede its spread. The initial in-plant stoppage at Scania was paralleled by work actions at Ford and Mercedes-Benz; by the end of May, the stoppages encompassed twenty-eight firms with 62,000 workers in São Bernardo and Diadema.[36] Workers would show up each day and punch in; then they would stand by their machines, silently rebuffing pressure from foremen. Though this work action was organized by skilled workers, the tactic's simplicity lowered the barrier for participation for the unskilled while avoiding police repression, because it took place inside the factory. As the movement spread within and beyond ABC, it was described as a wave, a contagion, or even a contamination, upending the expectations of employers, the military regime, and many sectors of the union leadership. Caught with their pants down, as Brazilians say, employers did not know how to react in a political atmosphere of official liberalization; this confusion was only compounded when the Second Army's commander, Dilermando Monteiro, declared after meeting Lula that these spontaneous actions had not been instigated by Communists or political subversives.

Discussions of the May 1978 strike, the best studied of the three labor actions that took place in ABC between 1978 and 1980, often leave the impression that the "really peon" were champing at the bit for a confrontation, although all scholars recognize that workers and the union both avoided the dangerous word "strike." In truth, this action—not too aggressive, all things considered—reflected a long-standing ambiguity in rank-and-file behavior described as "unconscious adhesions" by Lula's predecessor, Marcos Andreotti, in describing the 1957 mass strike of 400,000 workers in São Paulo, a movement the twelve-year-old Lula, newly arrived, had witnessed. Workers in 1957 would show up at the factory gates and silently linger to see whether anyone else was going to go in. If some did, they all went in; if none did, they dispersed and would nonetheless insist that they had not struck. In this way, the workers cautiously expressed discontent while avoiding risk, which was quite different from the bolder minority who, in Andreotti's words, "consciously" chose to adhere, precisely what would happen during the strikes of 1979 and 1980.[37]

The roiling stoppages in May 1978 dismayed employers and the government, who turned to the leadership of Lula's union for help in resolving the problem. The first to do so was the management of Scania: on the fourth day of the strike, they invited Lula, along with Gilson and Severino—who had initiated the stoppage—and the union's lawyer, Maurício Soares, to conduct an unprecedented meeting with the firm's workers inside the factory. DOPS transcribed the back-and-forth during the May 16 meeting. The transcripts show Lula positioning himself respectfully vis-à-vis the firm while praising the workers for offering "the country a lesson." The union, he insisted, was only an intermediary to facilitate dialogue—no one should ever be afraid "of conversing with anyone"—and he pledged that their formal vote, on that day, was sovereign in approving their demands (*pauta*) and deciding to go back to work while negotiations advanced.[38] In the first of many such meetings, Lula showed some timidity and uncertainty regarding what to say and how to act; according to the recollections of a Scania worker present at the meeting, he was at that point far from the battle-hardened leader who would later show a remarkable capacity to directly and courageously challenge the bosses.[39]

Lula's oft-commented-on moderation in 1977–78, which could veer toward deference at times, served to lessen the suspicion felt by the more cautious unskilled workers, whose disposition to go along with management had long been disdained by the militant and the skilled. Lula was also sanctified as the employer's guest during the May factory meetings and came off as a thoughtful person (*ponderado*) who cared for the workers but didn't cause anxiety by directly attacking their employer. His respectful posture toward the company also undermined the denunciations, whether from their foremen or family members, that trade unionists were dangerous Communists. A good many of these unskilled workers would become supporters after May 1978, but even those who only shifted to a slightly more neutral stance helped the union's drive to pull off a categoria-wide strike in 1979, conducted outside the factory, that would thus require conscious adhesion.

A unique glimpse into the subterranean stirrings within the categoria in late 1978 and early 1979 can be found in a neglected thesis by an USP psychology student who interned at a São Bernardo auto parts factory. She was told that some workers had been fired after the May stoppage, although not all of them were activists, according to her informants; some had merely talked too freely about the strike. Among those interviewed was an eloquent young worker who captured the democratizing transformation of consciousness that was well underway. "The union provides the peon with security," he said, and when at a union meeting "you feel freer.... In the factory you don't elect the foreman, or the leader [*líder*], or the overseer [mestre]; all of them are chosen by the manager [gerente]. In the union, you feel like a human being. The leaders of the union are elected by the peons. The President speaks in our name," which is why we take our problems to the union.[40]

Lacking not only charisma but even name recognition, Lula the individual was responsible for neither the May 1978 stoppages nor the success of the union's aggressive pro-strike messaging in 1979. Rather, more and more workers had become receptive to strike action, frustrated, as we have already seen, in their desire to better their families due to the stagnation of their salaries. One rank-and-file São Bernardo metalworker explained the situation to an interviewer in 1975 by using a metaphor he credited to a friend: "If you take a little dog and put him in a fight with a big bulldog, there's no chance [*não tem graça*]." But, he went on, it "is something entirely different" when 20,000 little dogs unite to confront the bulldog.[41]

Collective Effervescence and Group Formation

Holding rallies in Vila Euclides created a space of convergence where subterranean stirrings among workers could surface and find public expression. Having escaped peremptory dispersal in 1978, a localized process of group formation could broaden and deepen over the following two years in strikes marked by exhilaration, fear, and even terror. By April 1980, the region would fall under military occupation, with armed helicopters flying over the rallies, increasingly violent skirmishes, and hundreds of arrests, as workers stopped buses and tried to prevent strike breakers from reaching the factories.

In terms of Weber's core insight, the origin of Lula's charisma is to be found in the minds, culture, and emotions of those who applauded, booed, and cheered during these rallies. The audience's attention varied according to who was speaking onstage, but Lula always spoke last and was listened to attentively. The rallies were crucial to an ongoing contest over workers' loyalty and obedience between powerful employers and the union, both of whom were new to this kind of conflict. A categoria-wide strike, after all, would collapse unless a solid plurality of workers joined and stayed committed, and this was tested each day the strike continued. In 1979, few among employers, the government, and even veteran trade unionists believed that the region's peons had it in them to hold out as they did for fifteen days.

As in all strikes, the propaganda fight from the start involved statistical claims by each side regarding how many had not shown up to work. Until now, historians have had to rely on guesstimates regarding participation numbers because we lack access to company payroll records or the archives of employer sindicatos. Luckily, however, among the materials compiled by SNI in its surveillance of the strike was a two-page handwritten table of data collected from company officials, organized by município, that included factories by name, total workforce (efetivos), and the number of strikers between 4 P.M. on March 16 and 8 A.M. on March 17, 1979.[42] This document, while it misses many factories affected by the strikes, offers the first decisive evidence of the strike's robust success. The three ABC metalworkers' unions accounted for 90 percent of the 124,000 strikers listed statewide (the dissídio for ABC also included some small metalworkers' unions in the interior). This meant, remarkably, that 111,600 workers—three-quarters of the 146,000 metalworkers listed for ABC—had joined the strike, and Lula's union accounted for 60 percent of those participating.

The table reveals that only in four São Bernardo and Diadema factories did a majority of workers report for work: Chrysler (2,350 workers; 56 percent of workforce), Borg Warner (1,000 workers; 66 percent of workforce), and two other small companies employing 311 and 110 workers, respectively. In sharp contrast, the município's four biggest factories saw two-thirds or more of their workers join the strike: Volkswagen (74 percent of 39,000 workers employed), Mercedes-Benz (76 percent of 17,500 workers employed), Ford (66 percent of 12,000 workers employed), and Gemmer (89 percent of 11,060 workers employed). For the union, success at VW was especially satisfying because management had decisively crushed the in-plant stoppage that had been attempted in May 1978. Finding safety in numbers, workers in 1979 were clearly ready for a fight even before the movement had endowed Lula with charisma.

According to DOPS, the strike's first Vila Euclides rally was attended by 20,000, while two subsequent rallies were each attended by 60,000 each, just under the 66,000 São Bernardo metalworkers listed as having been on strike in the first week. Not all of those attending the rallies were strikers; family members were encouraged by the union to attend, and some nonmetalworkers showed up out of curiosity or solidarity. Yet the extraordinary attendance at the rallies by strikers suggests the remarkable unity that had been achieved among Lula's constituents. Held at 10 A.M. so workers wouldn't arrive after drinking, the rallies saw people trickle in and catch up with shop mates, friends, relatives, and neighbors; those with cars parked in the streets around the stadium.[43] It was a welcome contrast to workers' regimented workday and a moment for the "little people" to strut a bit after having shown gumption and won the country's undivided attention. As recalled by one worker, a migrant from Minas Gerais, when he first saw a picture of Lula amid the massive rally in a clipping from the *Folha de São Paulo*, "it gave me goose bumps. I said, 'Holy shit [*puta merda*], look at that beauty! We succeeded. We've made the greatest leader in the history of the union. No one has ever brought together as many people as he has.'"[44]

Beyond pride, the rallies also brought comfort in numbers. As Lula later observed, "Individually everyone has their fears," but by uniting repeatedly in Vila Euclides, rain or shine, "the courage of each one" was joined to the rest, allowing workers to achieve "what they individually understood to be impossible."[45] It was this collective mobilization that generated the charisma that Lula came to exercise as the commander of an army of peons. The 1979 strike represented one of those "revolutionary or creative epochs" in which, as the French sociologist Émile Durkheim reminds us, a collective effervescence can arise in which "men [can] see more and differently . . . than in normal times"; "changes are not merely of shades and degrees; men become different."[46] In São Bernardo, most of the categoria would come to see themselves in and through their identification with Lula as they forged a boldly audacious collective identity: "We are all peons! We are all cabra machos! We are all Lula!"

Before this moment, the metalworkers, despite being a legally recognized social category, had not been a group in terms of mass mobilization, collective struggle, or a purposive shared identity. To understand this distinction, it is helpful to turn to Pierre Bourdieu's 1987 critique of "realist interpretations of the construction of classes," which drew on Sartre's critique of mechanistic social theories in Marxism and mainstream sociology during the 1950s. Bourdieu emphasized that "these 'classes on paper,' these 'theoretical classes,' constructed for explanatory purposes are not 'realities,' groups which would exist as such." The challenge, he went on, is to understand "the limits (or the probabilities) of any attempt to turn theoretical classes into real classes," attempts that depend on the "political work of group-making (whose specific logic must be analyzed)."[47]

Even if one granted that the destiny of the working class was immanent, in the teleological sense suggested by Marx, the class can only be constructed via politics, the embodied work done with words. Making an agglomeration of individual workers into a class, in Bourdieu's language, is possible only if the leader's discourse "is true, that is, adequate to things." Only in that way can we "creat[e] things with words." "In this sense," as Bourdieu puts it, "symbolic power is a power of consecration or revelation, a power to conceal or reveal things which are already there."[48]

The creation of a collective subject had long been the goal of working-class activists and leaders; as they chatted with fellow workers in factory bathrooms, on the buses, at the union, over a cachaça, or at the factory gate, they were engaged in "class-making" praxis. The carnivalesque atmosphere during strikes—heightened during the exhilarating Vila Euclides rallies—was particularly fruitful in allowing workers to rethink their place in the world. With work stopped in its tracks, the individual experienced a feeling of freedom. As the Ford worker and trade unionist Alberto Eulálio (known as Betão) recalled, it was thrilling to see 20,000 people in the stadium time after time, including those who would never be seen at the union's headquarters. These nonengaged workers would show up to the rallies, perhaps with their wife, son, or daughter, and everyone got to liking the movement.[49]

Highly motivated individuals like Betão were the foot soldiers of the army of peons that Lula came to command during the 1979–80 strikes. As mobilization intensified, the number of such purposeful activists grew exponentially as individuals found personal recognition and fulfillment in the categoria's collective struggles. In their factories and neighborhoods, these men and some women provided top union leaders with a read on the diversity of industrial environments; cultural, sociological, and psychological understandings; and preexisting forms of organization—reflected in configurations of consciousness—that linked and divided potential group members who prior to the strike were collectively in a state of seriality.[50]

A mass struggle on the scale of that occurring in ABC cannot be explained simply by referring to the charismatic Lula's relation with "masses" in Vila Euclides. Rather, leadership occurred from the top to the bottom by multiplying spaces of convergence and constructing ensembles of new horizontal and vertical relationships. When assemblages of grassroots activists successfully formed, they served—to adopt a metaphor from metallurgy—much like a flux, something mixed with a metal to facilitate melting. But the complex, multilevel project of group-making can only be understood by identifying its mechanisms and linkages, which are distinct from an institutionally designated voice. The group's actual constitution involves connecting the consciousnesses of individuals to each other based on recognition of a linked fate and shared hope.

This can only occur through concerted action, involving physical and speech acts, as the individual assumes the consequences of these acts in the presence of others—what Sartre calls the pledge or oath, the exercise of individual agency that is the foundation of group affiliations.[51] In the case of ABC's workers, this pledge meant assuming the long-feared identity of a "striker" and becoming one of the now (in)famous rebel "peons of ABC."

Contending with Lula's Charisma

The unprecedented images of Vila Euclides were projected worldwide by Brazilian newspapers that had recently escaped censorship as part of the new liberalizing measures that included a general amnesty, the return of exiles, and the ending of two-party rule. Many Brazilians were riveted by what they perceived as a veritable "theater of democracy," with the thirty-three-year-old São Bernardo metalworkers' president playing the lead. The more they heard, the more they became convinced that Lula epitomized their desire for political participation and the end of military tutelage. The scruffy torneiro mecânico seemed to personify the new in what Richardo Kotscho dubbed the "Republic of São Bernardo," the only free territory in a country ruled by a stifling dictatorship that many believed had long outlived its time.[52] Lula's celebrity reached such heights that the industrialist Cláudio Bardella, at the end of the 1979 labor negotiations, asked Lula on behalf of his son for an autograph.[53]

Early- to mid-career journalists and editors guaranteed that ABC's metalworkers were not relegated to the newspapers' inside pages, which would have likely prevented the strikes from entering the social and political imaginary of the highly educated. The legendary Italian-born editor Mino Carta put Lula on a magazine cover in February 1978 and assigned Kotscho the Lula beat in 1979. "Ah, one more bearded little USP intellectual to bug me [*encher o saco*]," Lula gruffly responded after Kotscho explained his assignment. By 1980 Kotscho was an expert on ABC and was invited to write about the "thickset, decided, and courageous" trade unionist for the *Folha de São Paulo*'s cultural insert. As Kotscho—who would go on to be a founding member of the PT and Lula's spokesperson—noted in his memoir, it was easy because Lula loved to recount his life saga. Here was a man who "was his own hero, [someone] without idols or models," Kotscho reflected. What most impressed the journalist was the rapport between Lula and São Bernardo's peons, who would roar his name during the Vila Euclides rallies.[54]

This emblematic rendering of the strikes—epitomized in photos of Lula and the crowd—distorts our understanding of the movement as our eyes are inevitably drawn to Lula, the man onstage, which exemplifies how, in Pierre Bourdieu's words, "the signified, that is, the group, is identified with the signifier, the individual, the spokesperson."[55] This is the "social magic" at the heart of "the charismatic illusion in which, in extreme cases, the spokesperson can appear to himself or herself and others as *causa sui*." As described by Bourdieu, this form of "political fetishism" is what we have come to know as "charisma, a mysterious objective property of the person, an impalpable charm, an unnamable mystery," but one that conceals far more than it reveals.[56]

Personifying this social fiction, Lula came to be endowed by São Bernardo's metalworkers "with full power to speak and act in the name of the group," which lifted these workers "from the state of [being] separate individuals" and "enabl[ed] them to act and speak" through Lula while granting him the right "to speak and act as if he *were* the group made man."[57] The heart of charismatic representation, as described by Bourdieu, is when "the individual who represents the group, . . . and expresses it verbally, names it, [and] acts and speaks in its name," becomes its "concrete incarnation" who "by making the group seen, by making himself seen in its place, and above all, by speaking in its place, makes it exist."[58]

Well before the strikes, just after being elected union president in 1976, Lula drew this very distinction between a *dirigente*, "who is there to fulfill the legislation, to administer the union according to the statutes," and a *líder*, "who is born within a class and has the capacity to guide those he leads." Unfortunately, he went on to tell the interviewer, "this does not [yet] exist."[59] In July 1979, after Lula's rapturous embrace by workers, another interviewer asked him whether he still felt this to be true. There were moments, Lula admitted, when "I felt like a real leader. Especially when the workers carried me on their shoulders, when they made songs for me." But he insisted that he still had a bit further to go before becoming "a real leader, the guy who is incarnated in the workers and with whom the workers are incarnated."[60] Such adulation, as he told another interviewer two months before, also caused apprehension "because it increased my responsibility, and I knew that I could end up being hurt [*machucado*] on the day when I couldn't give the workers all they wanted."[61]

Over the course of 1979, Lula's appeal transcended the union as he came to be embraced by a healthy plurality of nonunion metalworkers. The sense that he was uncommon and marvelous would be felt even among the broader public, by people who did not necessarily support him. This is the essence of charismatization: it enhances the power of the one so blessed, the group in the making that bestowed it, and the individuals and institutions tied to the blessed one. The emergence of Lula's widely recognized charisma would also affect the calculations of employers and the government, which increased Lula's influence and capacity for successful maneuvering.

As a practical man, the union's longtime attorney Maurício Soares saw the benefits of having someone so "authentic" and "full of charisma" as the leader of ABC's peons.[62] However, the primacy of charisma in Lula's appeal was more troubling for those committed to a collectivist philosophy of working-class self-emancipation. Like liberalism, Marxist traditions tend to valorize "rational" action — coded male — over the "spontaneous," "emotional," and "intuitive" — lesser, feminized spheres to be brought under the control of "conscious" thought. This explains why those who studied the ABC strikes tended to minimize the Lula phenomenon. In 1987 the Mexican labor sociologist Victor Manuel Durand Ponte implausibly suggested that Lula's "charisma" derived from "the strong identification of the [union] leadership with the rank and file," which allowed the rank and file to identify with the leadership.[63] And in 1992 Ricardo Antunes, while he "unequivocally" recognized the positive value of Lula's "personalized and charismatic leadership," thought it fell short of offering the conscious leadership needed by the workers.[64]

These issues were taken up most directly by two founding PT members, the sociologist Luís Flávio Rainho and his skilled metalworker collaborator Osvaldo Bargas, a then Marxist elected in 1981 as general secretary of the São Bernardo union's diretoria. Their 1983 book, an analytical tour de force, fully recognized the Lula phenomenon that emerged in 1979, the year he was first "carried on the workers' shoulders and called 'father' by them." Undertaking Marxist-style criticism/self-criticism, they wrote that both workers and the diretoria had shown "excessive dependence" on Lula's leadership. Rank-and-file workers, they said, came to believe that if they "faithfully" followed Lula, "their problems would be automatically resolved, independently of the role that is theirs to play."[65]

Having lived the strike from the inside, Rainho and Bargas even acknowledged in passing a religious dimension to the popular response when they reprinted, without comment, "Our Father Lula," a rewrite of the Catholic prayer by a Mercedes-Benz worker.[66] Along with singing the national anthem, workers often prayed the standard Catholic "Our Father" during rallies, at one point at the prompting of a worker's wife speaking onstage. At least some handmade banners also directly equated Jesus and Lula, while some members of the mobilization committee showed their banners to photographers, one proclaiming that "Jesus too was a worker, which is why he is on our side," and another simply stating, "First God, second Lula, and third, unity."[67]

When these books came out in the early 1980s, ABC's metalworkers were still hot topics as the Workers' Party made its first incursions into the political-electoral arena. Writing for an educated audience, these analysts were fighting the idea "that the working class in the region *is what it is* due exclusively to Lula," which suggested theories of mass manipulation by Lula. While keeping charisma at a distance, all four authors reduced Lula's appeal to a reflection of or conduit for unspecified worker aspirations. Thus Rainho and Bargas awkwardly described the union president as the "'son,' 'fruit,' and 'expression'" of the São Bernardo metalworkers' "combativity, political maturation, and deepening of consciousness."[68] Another spoke of how Lula, with his "workers' intuition," had "faithfully synthesized and systemized the spontaneous aspirations of the masses," ideas that Lula, in the words of a third, "translated" into an oral form "accessible to them."[69] Only Durand Ponte, without elaboration, fruitfully suggested that, "at least in part," Lula's popularity might be due to workers' identification with him: "seeing in him the human being" they would like to be.[70]

If São Bernardo's workers themselves had been asked, they would have echoed a striker from 1979 who, years later, recalled the truth of his wife's frequent refrain that "you love Lula more than you do your family."[71] During the strike "Lula was all that [the workers] talked about" in the factories, one ferramenteiro recalled, because they needed "someone who spoke more loudly, was braver [*peitudo*], [and] more willing to go to the mat [*pro pau*]."[72] As another remembered, Lula thrilled the youngsters because he "spoke the language of the peaozada, recently arrived from the North." At the peak of this enthusiasm, "Lula appeared like a God," and there was "an enormous fanaticism within the factories. Whatever Lula ordered to be done, we did it."[73]

Durand Ponte's insight would be developed twenty-five years later by a lifelong popular educator inspired by Sartre. Mauro Iasi suggested that Lula's leadership stemmed from his ability to speak both what the workers wanted to hear and what they wished to make heard. This was possible only because of Lula's "authenticity": "He is not a populist leader trying to pass himself off as a suffering worker but rather a migrant worker" who had also worked in the factory, "living on the same salary, speaking with the same accent, dressing in the same manner, [and] making use of the same values and expressions." But while sharing this background with average peons, Lula also embodied what they wished they could be, the one who "confronts, fights, speaks, imposes himself, has confidence in himself and us." The irony of this, Iasi underlines, is that the leader also doesn't possess these wished-for characteristics; rather, he is the means for their expression by the group. In this way "a horizontal identity [is created] that permits the group to realize what a serial individual alone would see as impossible."[74] What emerges is an asymmetrical but truly reciprocal relationship between group and leader.

That the alleged "personalism" of the rural world might explain the behavior of ABC's peons bothered intellectuals, whether nonmanual or manual (the skilled). Could Lula, as commander, be understood as a patrão under the traditional patron-client system typical of the countryside? Intellectuals rejected any suggestion of such a wellspring for the ABC strikes based on a schematic stereotype about the nature of the rural patron-client system. But it is hardly farfetched to assume that some of the peaozada, especially those "recently arrived from the North," might have seen Lula as a good patron, one who served as an intermediary because of his ability "to know, interpret, and manipulate the external world." Yet the authority of such a patron, often a landowner or political boss, existed only "to the degree to which he participates in the universe of the community," as the anthropologist Eunice Durham had commented in reference to São Paulo's migrants in 1973. If he met their expectations, the weak reciprocated by according respect and repaying him with loyalty, although this made them a party to his internecine battles with rival landowners or officials. Under this dyadic system of paternalistic domination, it was also not uncommon for the "bad" patrons to prey on those they had pledged to protect, usually at minimal cost to themselves given the weakness of their clients.[75]

Yet there is another, oft-neglected horizontal dimension of rural life that had a more direct bearing on Lula's relationship with ABC's peons. As Durham notes, rural communities often accord informal leadership to certain individuals who, because of "personal qualities" and the "richness" of their experience, had the "capacity to express the collective consensus." The community solidarity behind this informal leader grew out of "physical proximity, personal sympathy, and the shared experience of mutual assistance."[76] As a leader, Lula thus expressed both the rural ideal of horizontal leadership—in his capacity to produce a consensus—and aspects of the role of a patron—as mediator with powers above—although Lula had little power to offer jobs, material favors, or influence with the police. Those who followed Lula were embarking on a path of struggle that pitted them, as a group, against immensely powerful enemies. Learning as the struggle unfolded, many would undergo a broadening and reconfiguration of their view of the world that intellectuals would label consciousness-raising.

Yet it is a mistake to think that only rural migrants were "susceptible" to Lula's charisma, which was felt just as strongly by city-born workers and the skilled. Moreover, a significant swath of the highly educated, especially students and the vanquished "revolutionaries" of 1968, were powerfully attracted to Lula as the fulfillment of Marxist fantasies about the working class's leading role or for his decisive contribution to ending military rule. This could be seen at the May Day rally held in São Bernardo in 1979, which was attended by 150,000, according to the local police delegado. He reported that many attendees were of "middle-class appearance," including a contingent of "stereotypical university" students, male and female, wearing jeans and distributing leftist newspapers. According to his report, applause met "all the orators," but Lula was received with a "total and indescribable delirium." "The man really is a charismatic leader," he concluded breathlessly.[77] In a very real sense, Lula's PT, founded in 1980, would become a multiclass alliance of the generation of 1968 and the new generation of the late 1970s as they came to unite around Lula as a unifying icon despite their differences.

Vila Euclides: The Man at the Microphone

Those gathered in Vila Euclides in 1979 were by no means an anonymous "mass" of strangers, afflicted with anomie and awaiting a savior. The crowd included 10,000 or more workers already actively involved with this union of 25,000 members. As we saw in earlier chapters, Lula had continually expanded his support with diverse sectors of the union since 1972. Trust was built among the rank and file by Lula as a dedicated problem solver who zealously handled mundane social welfare and pension problems. Intelligent, hardworking, and funny, he won the respect of skilled workers like the ambitious Djalma Bom, who had met Lula while enrolled in the union's high school equivalency course created and first overseen by Lula.[78] And it was from among the skilled, as Frei Chico observed, that an intrepid activist core was recruited made up of men, willing to go for broke, during a hot labor market in which there was little fear of losing their jobs.[79]

Within the union, Lula was admired as an untiring, selfless, and energetic leader who didn't dump the grunt work onto lower-level folks. When someone had to address a 4 A.M. shift change at the VW factory gates, Lula was on the scene, and he never shied away from "telling it like it is."[80] In February 1977, for example, he was applauded by those attending a union meeting for expressing exasperation that only 570 workers had turned out for a union assembly on the dissídio. Reproaching the categoria, he even spoke of punishing those who failed to meet their responsibilities.[81] While tens of thousands of workers, even nonunionized ones, had seen or heard of Lula by the start of the 1979 strike, he became an even more familiar figure as an acquaintance, if not a friend, whom strikers encountered at union-sponsored rallies, pickets, and mobilizations. If they stopped by the headquarters—as thousands did every day during the strikes—they might cross paths with Lula, who was always disposed to take a few seconds to chat. And the strikers could even join him at one of the bars downtown, where Lula regularly held court before, during, and after the strikes.

This familiarity would spread further throughout the region (though TV coverage of the strikes was minimal) while stories and testimonials circulated—whether true, false, apocryphal, or exaggerated—that emphasized Lula's cease-

Lula sitting on newspapers for factory distribution, 1979. (Courtesy DGABC [Banco de Dados])

less dedication, incorruptibility, humor, and warmth. Much loved, Lula was described retrospectively by one striker as a remarkable person "who knew how to unite people" and had "a gift for talking."[82] Those drawn into the mobilizations also credited Lula as their teacher; some would cite his lessons years later.[83] A key activist, José Arcanjo (known as Zé Preto), contrasted Lula's consultative leadership style with a president who simply "pulled something from his head" and gave orders, like Vidal. Lula met daily with the other union directors and militants and allowed each to have their say, whether right or wrong, as they arrived at a consensus as to what was to be done next. Like so many others, Zé Preto intertwined his comments with sentimental characterizations of Lula's simplicity, humility, and loving nature.[84]

The Vila Euclides rallies allowed Lula to expand these interpersonal bonds in a distinctive way. When Lula spoke to the crowds of striking workers—in the stadium or elsewhere—the social dynamic being fostered was not that of the leader-follower dyad that stands at the heart of the negative caricature of charisma. Rather, it was of a triad composed of Lula, the individual worker, and the rest of the workers in the stadium as a third.[85] Lula assumed his place in this triad even prior to his performance, as the news of his arrival created a stir. As Lula passed through the crowd, there were countless exchanges of touches and words as part of a canvassing process that continued backstage, where the so-called "important" people—other directors, staff, advisers, key activists, and outside guests—were to be found.

If, as Lula has explained, he "never bring[s] set ideas" to such rallies, this did not reflect a failure of preparation by Lula or his staff.[86] Frei Betto recalls driving him to an immense assembly in 1980, briefing him on the way. "Lula kept it all in his head," Frei Betto observed, "because he detested reading speeches; his approach was to improvise." "How many times have I seen an advisor prepare a speech," he went on, only for Lula to disregard it and take "an entirely different path with greater success." Significant for our discussion, Frei Betto chalks this up to "charisma that doesn't have an explanation."[87] As for Lula, he explains his ability to hit the sweet spot with the audience as deriving from his practice, onstage, of surveying the whole crowd in an attempt "to sift out" the workers' reactions by using their body language and verbal cues to guide his remarks.[88]

As part of this receptiveness, Lula was also acutely attuned to the heterogeneous array of workers in motion during the strikes, ranging from combative, politicized rebels to previously accommodationist workers now upset at being ripped off. This is why Lula in 1979 insisted—even at moments of peak conflict—that the strikers were not disrespecting the government and were not linked to any ideology it deemed subversive. Indeed, he criticized the circulation at the rallies of leaflets by leftist outsiders, especially students, and occasionally even had them removed. Given the diverse outlooks, Lula represented himself as a thoughtful, righteous man who disparaged riotous behavior (baderna) as unworthy and counterproductive. Like all honest workers, he called for the strikers to be disciplined and counseled against clashes with the police; he continually framed their fight as one with the companies, not the government or policemen.

Lula's speeches were powered by an apparently simple moralism based on a rhetoric of reciprocity, fair treatment, and decency rather than fighting a system, whether economic or political, much less calling for an entirely different society or polity. In Lula's rendering, the strikers were petitioning for simple justice to meet their legitimate material demands. As events unfolded between 1978 and 1980, more and more of the peons of ABC, the group-in-formation, would see themselves as opposed to those who, by their actions, had been revealed to be enemies: the greedy managers of Brazil's most profitable factories and a government that had violated its paternal responsibilities by failing to assist the weak against those who took advantage of them.

Yet even as the conflict sharpened, Lula maintained a tone of moderation and openness to dialogue that created a bridge with the church, the opposition, the university intelligentsia, and much of the print media. In doing so, he also sought to blunt the deeply suspicious and often-hostile views of Brazil's conservative men of property and power (homems de bem) who still supported the dictatorship. General Milton Tavares, a man directly involved with the Médici-era program of targeted disappearances and executions, was now in charge of the Second Army. Unlike his predecessor, General Monteiro, who had publicly signaled the benign intentions of the stoppages in May 1978, this new commander repeatedly denounced Lula's advisers as Communists. This rhetoric would escalate during the 1980 strike, when another military spokesperson warned that "when words are not enough, force is often the path to peace because pacifism should never be confused with weakness or . . . goodwill with cowardice."[89] To men like Otávio Medeiros, SNI's head, the strikes were evidence that the country was descending into "'tolerated illegality'—disorder, in straightforward Portuguese."[90]

In addition to their moderate tone, Lula's speeches were anchored in the ordinary, the domestic, and the functional as opposed to the more elaborate, even monumental, dimension found in oral speech patterned on the written word. Hewing to the vernacular, including at time coarseness, his bread-and-butter speeches used simple language without flights of fancy or theory while studiously avoiding the specialized vocabulary that allowed leftists to quickly achieve political if not analytical clarity.[91] When need be, Lula could cite facts, figures, and statistics—company profits, the real value of wages—but his core message was anchored in emotion. Interviewed by a leading Latin American leftist, Lula once explained that he most valued his intuition because it allowed him "to put a little heart" into political work. "Doing politics without heart," he went on, "leaves us hard" and "excessively realistic," not an ideal way of moving people to act.[92]

These speeches elicited a range of reactions as heterogeneous as their audiences. One of Lula's signature slogans provides a good example of how different listeners might have had alternate, even contradictory understandings of his words: "Let no one ever again doubt the capacity of the working class to fight." While the line was overtly aimed at bosses, the government, and other nonworkers, the unskilled heard their bravery being lauded while the skilled heard their long-held doubts being assuaged by proof that the "really peon" did have the courage to fight back. One might also cite the differences in response by male workers versus their wives and children who were actively encouraged to attend by Lula and the union (some even brought picnics for the outing).[93]

Another key element of Lula's discourse was the reshaping of the meaning of "peon" to further cohere the group-in-the-making. In his usage, the term brought under one umbrella quite different groups who saw Lula in distinct ways. For the "really peon," Lula was one of them in that he had fulfilled an aspiration they too had once had to become a skilled worker. For the skilled, he exemplified their ideal in being rational, hardworking, and self-confident, while seeking to improve himself and increase his knowledge of the world. For this manual intelligentsia, Lula's adoption of the term "peon" took hold because it revealed a truth they had long chafed against: they might enjoy middle-class incomes and use their minds in their work, but as manual workers they would always be seen by the highly literate as uppity peons, never as equals. Lula's use of the phrase "we peons" discursively equalized the two groups, both of which idolized him, while his national stature and fame generated pride by demonstrating the worth of each one of them to a society that saw them as inferior.

It was thus helpful that a flesh-and-blood human being bound the categoria together, because no similar degree of unity could have been achieved in 1979 around militant unionism or abstract ideas like "democracy"; that would come later. Lula not only served as an anchor in uncertain times but his decisive sway curbed divisiveness and personal and political rivalry within the union. That his charismatic relationship solved a crucial collective action problem was dramatically demonstrated when the union was intervened in 1979, after which the diretoria decided that Lula should step aside leaving Djalma Bom in charge. The crowd that gathered the next day in front of city hall was smaller and ignored Djalma's attempt to lead, angrily demanding Lula's return; breaking into small groups, they debated how to proceed, as skirmishing with the police erupted. Although the confrontation was defused by the MDB prefeito Tito Costa, a chaotic end of the strike seemed imminent. It was only the announcement of Lula's return on the following day that allowed the strike to regain cohesion and avoid public disorder.[94]

Thus, one won't understand what *really* happened in Vila Euclides unless one thinks *with* the crowd and recognizes that leadership is above all an oral art. Lula's performances at Vila Euclides worked to mobilize his audience in much the same way that, in a different time and context, Martin Luther King Jr. galvanized his Afro–North American listeners in the Jim Crow South, as innovatively glossed by the US sociologist Jonathan Rieder. As anti–status quo agitators, both Lula and King faced dilemmas "common to all mobilizations: shaky commitment, the pull of family life, the power of state repression, fear of being fired."[95] This dictated "the functional dynamic at work" in their mass meeting performances. "The rallies did not just reflect the growing audacity" of their audiences; "their purpose was to generate and sustain it."[96] It was precisely "because talk is cheap," as Rieder observes, that "verbal art" provided the

Police clash with workers in São Bernardo during the 1979 strike.
(Courtesy Olhar Imagem [Juca Martins])

Workers at the reopened Vila Euclides with a newspaper headlined “He Returns.”
(Courtesy DGABC [Banco de Dados])

most "powerful weapon for the movement leaders in managing these vulnerabilities."[97] "To mobilize bodies and prevent defections," both Lula and King had to reshape their "audience's appraisals of the rationality of protest" by employing a "rhetoric of assertion" that "sought to turn wish into reality."[98]

"We Are Men. We Are Family"

"In lifting ancient restraints" on subaltern anger, the rallies led by Lula and King could sometimes take on a "wild spirit" because they unleashed "dangerous emotions—the humiliation of silence, the longing for payback." In essence, both men were appealing to their listeners to exorcise the "demons of debilitating inferiority, ingrained passivity, and paralyzing fear," which explains why the meetings could become "psychic cauldrons that unleased the powers of the self."[99] In this regard, Lula evoked a working-class masculine ideal that a man must *make himself respected* by imposing himself in a violently, hierarchical world that threatened his manhood. The stigmatizations inflicted on ABC's workers, traced throughout this book, built up layers of resentment that found expression in Lula's underlying message that can be paraphrased as follows: "We've been fucked over! We're going to apply the rod [*metendo pau*] to the bosses and the government! We're going to bring them to their knees!"[100] This aggressive stance repudiated everything that had reduced ABC's male workers to "children of fear," as seen in chapter 11, while leading them to defy the very real threat—referenced publicly more than once by Lula—that they might even suffer bodily harm or death.

The self-presentation by Lula and his fellow union directors as fearless men came at a price to their families, who were subject to constant and highly visible government surveillance of their homes. Their public appearances were frequented by uniformed and plainclothes policemen, police informants, and undercover company security agents—often a source of wry humor—while daily clashes occurred between workers and aggressive factory guards and police. Lula's strong-willed wife Marisa, despite initial fears, would often accompany her husband—sometimes with their young children—because even then she "never had the inclination to play a Penelope" awaiting the return of Odysseus, as one journalist recalled.[101]

The regime's coercive power was on full display, with armored personnel carriers (*brucutus*) in ABC's streets—along with cavalry, riot police, tear gas, and dogs—while armed helicopters repeatedly passed over the crowds in 1980. With bombs being set off around the country, his family, as Lula recounts, had to worry about explosives being planted in their car. One day, his suspicions aroused by its unlocked door, Lula asked Marisa to get out with the children;

Lula and Marisa with striking workers, March 30, 1980.
(Courtesy Olhar Imagem [Juca Martins])

"she turned to me, and said, 'you leave the car, I'll turn it on because I'm less important. This had a big impact on me."[102]

To turn "the page at the end of the 1970s," Lula and his fellow directors had to not only embody "fearlessness" but also inspire it in their listeners.[103] Like King and his fellow organizers, their objective was "to shift not this or that preference" among their constituents but their "entire way of approaching the question of worth, value, and meaning."[104] The goal was "to fortify the powers of the self. Rather than hector or shame," they would "coax, inspire, cajole, argue, and even proclaim . . . listeners into feistiness."[105] In doing so, Lula had to contend with the stigmatization workers had internalized in an authoritarian environment that demanded submission, humility, and deference from the subaltern. This effort entailed, as it did for King and his supporters, "emphatic assertions of 'Olympian' . . . manhood" expressed through a martial identity.[106] As each day in 1980 brought dozens of arrests and beatings, Lula would repeatedly emphasize that "prison was made for real men [machos], not effeminate ones [*bichos*]."[107]

Such commitment forced an individual participant to view himself "as a powerful person able to control" his own fate, which was reflected in a rhetoric about the "resgate da dignidade" (the rescue or ransom of dignity).[108] From his first cover story interview to the presidency, Lula consistently emphasized the vital importance of self-esteem for the stigmatized and subaltern: workers, women, blacks, the disabled, homosexuals. This rhetorical leitmotif is always expressed in the simplest of terms: one must always walk with one's head raised high (*cabeça erguida*), unashamed, and offering deference to no man or woman—advice he always credited to his mother dona Lindu, who would die of cervical cancer while he was in jail during the 1980 strike.

With little formal education, Lula employed in his speeches during the strikes a more limited cultural repertoire than King, who had at his command, as a holder of a PhD and the son of a preacher, not only a body of erudite culture but also a deeply rooted tradition of black preaching, with its arsenal of biblical imagery. Lula, by contrast, had recourse to an idealized rhetoric about the family—nuclear, extended, the neighborhood, or even the union—common to the lay Catholic world in which he had been raised. For São Paulo's poor and working class, the family was the privileged locus of emotion, a safe haven in a hostile and uncertain world. It was all the more important as an ideal precisely because their actual family lives so often fell far short, especially in the case of fathers.[109] In 1979, some São Bernardo metalworkers had begun to call Lula "father," and he tapped into this fatherly ideal. As emphasized by Renato Tapajós, who filmed the 1979 rallies for the union, Lula "speaks to the individual [and] always repeats that business of 'think of your house, your wife, your children.' It's the rhetoric of a father giving advice, and the population likes that."[110] As the leader of ABC's peons, Lula would take on the idealized features of the good and wise father—the opposite of the abusive and tyrannical Aristides.

Such a paternal ideal may discomfit intellectuals by seeming to evoke the negative caricature of charismatic leadership as patriarchal. But what type of "father" did many workers dream Lula to be? Certainly not one who, despite failing to fulfill his duties or meet his responsibilities, acted imperiously (*prepotencia*). Rather, Lula exemplified the "good father" who brings home his entire paycheck, honors his wife, and loves all of his children despite their differences. He was the father who meets his primary duties of providing for, protecting, orienting, and guiding his children as they move into adulthood. But most pertinently in light of the potential critique, the idealized paternal image projected was not that of a violent imposition of will but rather that of a father—or the mestre of an apprentice—engaged in an ongoing back-and-forth as his children or apprentice matured and became independent. The "good" father portrayed by Lula thus fulfilled the popular ideal of maintaining harmony in the family through reaching consensus.

What Lula frontally rejected was the all-too-common form of top-down paternalism in which "big shots" proclaimed themselves the "saviors" of the weak. "Whenever a union director assumes the paternity of the working class," Lula explained, "he is lying if he says he will resolve" the workers' problems, because only the working class can do so.[111] Only bad union leaders, Lula's Communist predecessor Andreotti insisted, would claim personal credit for something gained by the categoria. If they do, they are encouraging working-class passivity by propagating the idea that someone else can solve the workers' problems for them when "the ultimate responsibility is that of the working class itself."[112]

The back-and-forth between the group-in-the-making and Lula can be illustrated in several emotionally charged high points of the 1979 strike. For instance, the March 22 assembly voted against the agreement that had been negotiated between the diretoria and the government. As it became clear that the crowd would not accept the agreement, Lula bowed to their will and moved for its rejection, to general acclaim; the union's intervention would follow.[113] According to a sensitive reporter, Lula at the same time added that he would be the first to speak up "the moment I see the cow going in the ditch . . . [and] ask you to vote a return to work." According to the reporter, the ecstatic crowd cried in response to the vote, "Lula you are not alone. We will fill the union [to prevent an intervention] and you won't leave there." Lula responded with his characteristic emotiveness and dried his tears as he formally brought the assembly to an end. After describing Lula being "embraced many times by women and men who cried with him," the reporter then ends with a revealing vignette: "He left running . . . but didn't go far. . . . As if it were the end of a football game, he was lifted up by the multitude like a striker in soccer would be and carried from one extreme of the stadium to the other with cries of 'Lula, Lula.'"[114]

Another genuine interchange between the group-in-the-making and their charismatic leader came on March 27 during a Vila Euclides rally of 70,000 that was to consider an agreement to return to work during a truce of forty-five days in which negotiations would take place and his diretoria would be restored to the union. Lula recalls this as the hardest day of his life, because it wasn't clear that the workers could be convinced that the diretoria was not selling them out in order to return to their cushy union sinecures; speakers preceding him at the rally had been booed. Lula spoke deliberately and then, improvising onstage, asked for a vote of confidence and acceptance of the return to work.[115] Although a minority booed and left the rally, the majority of the workers agreed, and the nature of this assent, as Lula would describe it, suggests the complex relationship between Lula and the rank and file: "They accepted, but I could feel, from up there, that they did so like a son accepts a tap on the rear end [*tapa na bunda*] by their dad. The son is revolted, angry, and has the desire to grab him and punch him, but then he says 'Whoa! That's my dad, he must be right.'"[116] When Lula left the stadium that day, he was battered, and neither he nor the diretoria were even sure if the workers would actually honor the vote and show up for

One of the occasions when workers carried Lula on their shoulders during strikes. (Courtesy DGABC [Banco de Dados])

work. After an exhilirating fifteen days, this resolution to the 1979 strike was a blow to Lula's prestige and that of his diretoria.[117]

What happened next reveals how Lula's command of his army of peons flowed not from "magical" charisma but from a complex dialogical exchange with this group-in-the-making. After the government did return the union, Lula began the first assembly by offering the diretoria's resignation, which was rejected, leading Lula to cry along with many of those present.[118] Lula would devote the next half year to winning back the categoria's trust and unity by challenging the rank and file. If they felt that the workers could have gained more by staying on strike longer in 1979, then he pledged the diretoria would prepare the best-organized strike ever and carry it through to the bitter end, whatever the cost. This would become the amazing forty-one-day strike held in 1980, an illegal movement carried out without access to the union's material resources. This strike saw a resolute and independent engagement by the mass of workers, who no longer displayed the "excessive dependence" on Lula and his fellow directors, almost all of whom were imprisoned. "The union," the slogan went, "is us, not the building!" Although the strike ultimately went down in defeat, it would startle everyone with its length and intensity and would lead to, as its sequel, the CUT and the PT.

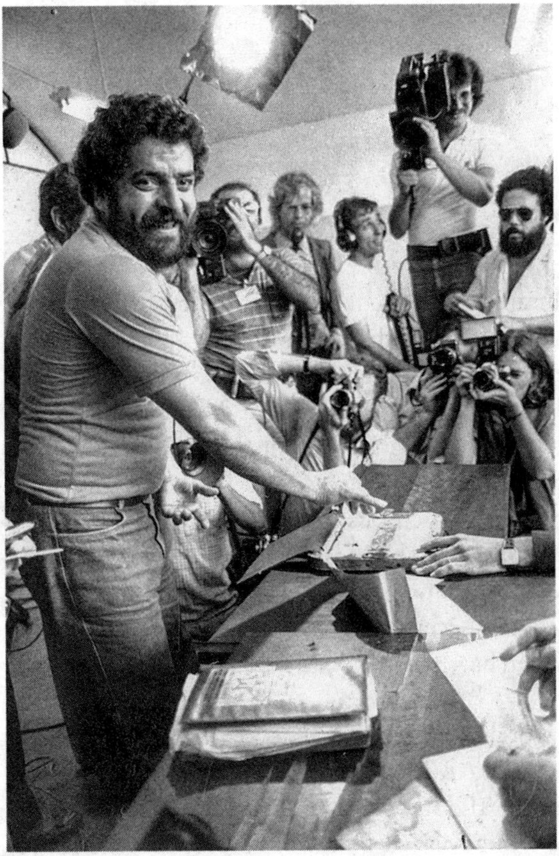

Lula voting in the 1982 election, when he ran for office for the first time. (Courtesy DGABC [Katia Dotto])

In the aftermath, Lula spoke about the military government's decision to crush ABC's metalworkers as having expanded the political understanding of the rank and file. Framing himself as a father, he later compared the experience to a kid who has to fall off his bike and hurt himself in order to learn.[119] Released from jail after thirty-one days, Lula and all his fellow directors—most of them under indictment—returned once again to the factory gates, running a shadow union, and assisting the many thousands who had lost their jobs, which had happened to Lula and his diretoria as well. When the union election was held in 1981, the Lula-supported slate won 90 percent of the vote, while the local PT took off with a bang in ABC. In 1982, the leader of the Scania stoppage, Gilson Menezes, was elected as prefeito of Diadema, while Lula ran for governor and lost with only 9 percent of the statewide vote. Yet his candidacy in that election had the support of 51 percent of the hourly workers at Ford in São Bernardo and even a respectable 23 percent among those who worked for Ford in São Paulo.[120] The link between Lula and the metalworkers of ABC had not been broken.

15 WITHOUT FEAR OF BEING HAPPY

Lula acquired a remarkably durable charisma during the titanic battles of 1978–80. Under his leadership, ABC's peons achieved an "incredible mobilizing force" and an unprecedented "politicization of the daily life of the subaltern." To everyone's surprise, including their own, workers had decided "the path of their own lives" in Vila Euclides via a mass movement that sought to universalize their collective and individual demands as a social class and as dignified, rights-bearing citizens.[1] After this momentous occurrence, the leadership of this emerging working class—symbolized by Lula—threw their weight behind a "reformulation of the democratic political system, out of order since 1964."[2] Much as Lula had predicted at the soccer match during which the idea for the Vila Euclides rallies had first been hatched in 1979, the country was going to be changed "from top to bottom."[3]

The tens of thousands of workers who amassed at Vila Euclides highlight the direct connection between the ABC strikes and the larger societal insurgency against military supremacy. The stadium had only been available to the union because São Bernardo was governed by an MDB prefeito, the lawyer Tito Costa, whose election in 1976 was the fruit of a long-standing effort by the union's leaders. As we have already seen, Costa helped defuse dangerously explosive moments of confrontation during the strikes. When the national government banned the strikers from using the stadium in 1979, the prefeito not only authorized them to use the plaza in front of the city government offices but also worked courageously, in liaison with the union, to support the strike as well as when Lula's mother died while he was in jail.[4] Despite such ties, those who struck in 1979 were not initially fighting for the "democracy" touted by their social superiors; indeed, even Lula was skeptical about so-called political causes—such as amnesty for political prisoners—championed by students and the university-educated middle class. Lula viewed these causes at first as a distraction from single-minded pursuit of workers' material interests and labor's freedom of action.

But the trajectory of the ABC strikes was powerfully dependent on ties forged with other powerful institutions and non-working-class interests. The strikers' most decisive ally was the Roman Catholic Church under the leader-

Lula brought from prison to attend his mother's burial, 1980. (Courtesy DGABC [Reinaldo Martins])

ship of São Paulo's Archbishop Arns, a progressive who, as we saw in chapter 10, was a courageous critic of the dictatorship's abuses.[5] Prior to the 1979 strike, unionists like Lula were openly skeptical of outsiders, including ABC's Catholic Church, meddling in labor's affairs. Such skepticism stemmed from unionists' negative judgment of the role that leftist students and clergy had played in 1968–70. But this suspicion began to wane during the 1979 strike, culminating in the May Day workers' mass attended by 40,000. The church would take an even more central role during the following year's strike.

When 70,000 metalworkers gathered in Vila Euclides on March 30, 1980, to affirm their decision to strike indefinitely, ABC's Bishop Cláudio Hummes pledged the full resources of the diocese to support the strikers' cause and led the crowd in praying the "Our Father." During the strike, local parish churches served as neighborhood nuclei for workers to maintain contact with one another. The downtown church became the site for regular union meetings and

Lula, Marisa, Frei Chico, and Mayor Tito Costa at Lula's mother's burial, 1980. (Courtesy DGABC [Reinaldo Martins])

major mobilizations—the largest, on May Day, attended by well over 100,000—while the strike's headquarters was relocated next door to the church after the government intervened the union. The strikers would be assisted by Frei Betto, a Dominican liberationist and a future founder of the PT, who moved to São Bernardo in early 1980 and would become close friends with Lula and Marisa, living with the family during the strike. When Lula was picked up to face charges under the National Security Law, Frei Betto was the one who called Archbishop Arns to alert him, given fears that something might happen to Lula in custody.[6] Bishop Hummes used his speech at the March 30 rally to place ABC's fight within a wider Latin American context of struggle against murderous dictatorships; less than six days earlier, he noted, the archbishop of El Salvador, Oscar Romero, had been gunned down by right-wing assassins in the cathedral of his nation's capital.[7] Frei Betto, in July 1980, would accompany Lula, one month after his release, to Managua to celebrate the victory of the Nicaraguan Revolution, the first but by no means last time that the young trade unionist would meet with Fidel Castro.[8]

Acting decisively, the categoria in 1980 had defiantly eschewed caution. While the strike ended in decisive defeat, it marked a radicalization of con-

Lula greeted on his release from imprisonment in 1980.
(Courtesy DGABC [Banco de Dados])

sciousness by tens of thousands of workers who had kept the strike alive, against all odds, far longer than anyone could have ever imagined. With Lula and other top union leaders in jail, it was these activists—assisted by church folk and other local supporters—who conducted decentralized guerrilla skirmishes in the neighborhoods.[9] Something new had been born for these tens of thousands of activists who saw their leader Lula emerge as a universally recognized icon of the opposition to military rule. His fame would come at a price, as he told an interviewer in 1979; as a father with a family, he lamented the loss of personal tranquility and privacy. Yet he marveled at how this fame signaled a reversal of the past tendency to view labor leaders as "either subversive or corrupt." Now unionism was being discussed by the bourgeoisie at fancy cocktail parties and among workers at the corner luncheonette.[10]

By 1980, when Lula was ousted from the union where he had earned his spurs, strike participation had reached into the millions nationwide, and the charismatic Lula personified the combative grassroots-oriented New Unionism that would emerge as the majoritarian current in the Brazilian labor movement. In addition to helping constitute Lula's charisma, these strikes shifted the balance of power at the core of Brazil's industrial economy. The ABC strikes were analogous to the militant mass strikes in the 1930s United States that finally broke employer and government opposition to the unionization of basic industry.

Honest Brazilian union leaders had always known that, without the capacity to mobilize workers, their potential for real power and influence would be stymied by "those who wrote the laws and gave orders to the police."[11] From Andreotti to Lula, these leaders sought to free labor relations of the authoritarian encumbrances (*entulho autoritário*) that fostered bureaucratized leadership teams who left workers at the mercy of capital and the state.[12] Like his predecessors, Lula realized along with his companheiros that "there was no way to make a genuine union movement without wrenching from employers the recognition of the union's presence as something indispensable. . . . They could only escape . . . from the marginal position in which they found themselves if the workers rose up alongside them."[13]

After 1980, the militant New Unionism would sweep blue-collar and white-collar organizations and finally put an end, after titanic conflicts, to employer dictation and heavy-handed government intervention in industrial and labor relations. With the onset of the Brazilian debt crisis in 1982, the country embarked on a lost decade with no significant economic growth and severe economic instability: inflation reached a 1,038 percent annual rate in 1988, rising to 1,783 percent in 1989. At the same time, the country struggled to complete the transition from military rule; the 1988 constitution, dubbed the "citizen's constitution," finally guaranteed union autonomy and enhanced collective and individual rights.[14] During the turbulent 1980s, the newly dynamized unions proved capable of conducting truly national general strikes for the first time in Brazilian history. An estimated 2 to 3 million workers and employees participated in the general strike held in 1983, the same year in which the emblematic institution of the New Unionism, the CUT, was founded. Ten million participated in both the 1986 and 1987 strikes. On the first day of the 1989 general strike, participation reached 22 million—a startling 37 percent of the urban waged labor force. Ten million still stayed out of work on the strike's second day.[15] As these numbers suggest, trade unions had successfully demanded recognition of their force in the labor relations sphere in the 1980s, laying the foundations to win recognition in the realm of politics in 1988–89.

"The PT Is a Very Practical Thing"

In addition to being wary of outsiders, Lula had early on been skeptical as well, if not explicitly opposed to, the politicians and political parties participating in the dictatorship's electoral charade. Indeed, the very spirit of the ABC strikes had been opposed to such politics. Of course, Lula and his predecessors did support political candidates—including Quércia in 1974 and future president FHC in 1978—and sometimes received help from sympathetic politicians like

Costa, but on the whole deemed what is known as the "political class" to be both refractory to popular input and driven by individualistic interests. This reflected the fact that even the "opposition" party, the MDB, was a dubious ally given the tendency of individual politicians to switch parties for personal gain. Moreover, no existing party formation—despite election-year promises and paper resolutions—wholeheartedly embraced the demands, priorities, and outlooks of trade unionism; the real game of politics and the exercise of power was judged by trade unionists to be monopolized by a highly educated elite.

In the wake of the ABC strikes, a plethora of clandestine leftist parties formed in Brazil. However, even the strongest of these, the PCB, was not an actual political machine with a mass base. The proliferating labor insurgencies, by contrast, had launched an entirely new generation of leaders, with heightened ambitions and new demands, who felt the need for a political instrument directly under their control in order to act beyond the sphere of labor relations. As Betão recalls, it was during the 1979 strike that Lula began, in small union meetings, to suggest that "we have to have a political party," although he recognized that most didn't want to hear that. "The union doesn't change society," he would explain; they needed a political party so that they could stop supporting politicians who didn't prioritize the union's demands. Trying to demystify politics in those early discussions, Lula would patiently observe that even a mother and father, without knowing it, are doing politics when they deal with a child wanting candy or money.[16]

The movement to create the Workers' Party, as a political arm of the New Unionism, began in 1979 and was completed in 1980, with a preeminent role being played by Lula and other allied union leaders. In August 1980 Lula gave some insight into the motives behind the party's creation. "The PT is a very practical thing," he said then. "We need an instrument, a tool, that opens space for political participation by workers. And that's what the PT is!" Since workers knew their own needs and aspirations best, they had "not only the right but the duty to act politically," in order to not leave politics "in the hands of the powerful." "We need to organize now," Lula exhorted, "in the union but also in our Party."[17] The same practical sense informed Lula's capacity to act decisively to guarantee his faction's ongoing control of the union in the early 1980s, something admired even by the losers. In putting together the slate for the 1981 election, Lula excluded two exemplary activists during the strikes, Osmar Mendonça and Enilson Simões de Moura (Alemão), because they were affiliated with clandestine leftist parties. Instead, Lula chose less prominent but combative workers who lacked political sophistication but had potential, he insisted, to rise and learn with his support. The slate won with more than 90 percent of the votes cast, and a good many of its members, most prominently the union's new president Jair Meneguelli, would go on to become top CUT and PT leaders. Osmarzinho and Alemão, who ran against Lula, faded into political insignificance.

The PT was both fruit of and key actor in the most profound and durable process of democratization yet seen in Brazilian history, in which Lula would play an especially prominent role during the 1984 Diretas Já (Direct Elections Now) movement.[18] After initial skepticism about the party's viability as a national political force, the PT became a place of convergence for a broad array of forces on the left.[19] The party progressively incorporated leftists—individuals and even groups—of diverse ideological orientations, which began to reverse the fragmentation of the Left (traced in chapter 7) that had begun in 1962 with the creation of the Maoist PCdoB and the Catholic student–dominated AP and only intensified after the military coup weakened the PCB's hegemony.

The 1970s had seen polarizing conflict between the military and civil society, which had precipitated the rise of mass antisystemic social movements—involved with struggles over housing, the cost of living, and rights of women, blacks, and gays. Many of these movements were linked organically or in spirit to the "popular church" and liberation theology, which fared less well in the 1980s as the Catholic Church increasingly turned to the right internationally. In its heedless radicalism, the PT occupied the far left of the political spectrum in the lead-up to restored civilian electoral rule in 1985 and in its aftermath. The party would be the natural home for both those who sought radical sociopolitical rupture with the country's past and those who rejected the seamless top-down transition of rule from military to civilian elites that marked the 1985 return to "democracy." Based on a "logic of difference," in the words of Margaret Keck, the PT was a movement uneasily turned party that exemplified the tension between rejection and participation, running for government office while adopting a militantly leftist stance in party documents—except for rejecting the Soviet model (though sympathetic to Cuba and Sandinista Nicaragua).[20]

At its founding, the PT rejected all established Left models, including revolutionary vanguardism and European-style social democracy, and the socialism it formally adopted as its goal in 1981 would be, it said, defined by the masses in struggle. Like the São Bernardo union under Lula's leadership, the PT would be a preeminently pluralistic space containing militant bread-and-butter trade unionists, Marxist-Leninist revolutionaries, practitioners of liberation theology, social democrats, New Deal–style social reformers, and even classic liberals with a social conscience. Yet this "remarkable—and probably unstable—ideological identity" (as the Marxist petista Emir Sader described it in 1987) allowed the PT to thrive as a space of *convergence* that tolerated difference while its internal dynamics were driven by the contest for influence among its various organized factions.[21] Lula well captured his approach as the PT's most prominent member in remarks to a gathering of leftists in 1996 in El Salvador: "We must place much less importance on our ideological differences and much greater emphasis on united action. We must abandon the sectarian spirit that so often has dominated and divided us. That means ending the traditional arrogance that has characterized the left."[22]

Yet despite the PT's plurality of voices and bottom-up participatory politics, it would not be entirely untrue to say that the PT was founded on an event, a personality, and an image. Maintaining this heterodox confluence of forces, tendencies, and ideologies depended on forging bonds of group belonging, a shared story, and a partisan petista identity, if not project. Though usually ignored out of leftist orthodoxy, these bonds, and the party's strengths, lay in its leader. As a sociologist eloquently put it in 2014, Lula wielded throughout the 1980s the "legitimating mechanism" of "mobilization" (*mobilismo*), using "the force of the streets as an element to impose values and demands" and thereby demonstrate that it was "possible to be powerful without being government." Such mobilization across diverse ideologies and constituencies was facilitated by Lula's remarkable ability to link such a leftist project to the worker, the lower middle class, and the povão through "identity and empathy."[23]

Having consolidated hegemony on the left, Lula's broad appeal and nonabrasive behavior would eventually make possible relatively stable electoral alliances among the parties of the Brazilian Left as well as with social movements eschewing explicit political affiliation. By 1989, the interparty alliance backing Lula even came to include those Communist groups that had long operated within the orbit of the old MDB, the opposition party legally allowed by the military regime and reconstituted under civilian rule as the Party of the Brazilian Democratic Movement (PMDB). This growing interparty unity on the left helped to partially overcome the rifts that had led to particularly sharp battles during the administration of President José Sarney (1985–89), a longtime civilian ally of the military who succeeded the indirectly elected Tancredo Neves after his death; Sarney was supported by the PCB and the PCdoB and vigorously opposed by the PT. As he had done as union leader, Lula worked to forge alliances to unite organized leftists in a common front during his presidential campaigns from 1989 on. As a leader with nationwide recognition, Lula seemed to personify the antidictatorial sentiments of Brazil's increasingly visible mass mobilizations, marked by a desire for participation and the end of elite tutelage.

The New Republic and the 1989 Presidential Election

This left Lula and his party in a good position as Brazil held its first direct presidential election since 1960, with 70 percent of the electorate having never voted for the top post in what was traditionally a strongly presidentialist political system. The number of registered voters and turnout in 1989 soared in what was—until today—a unique "unmarried" election, as they call those held without any other races on the ballot.[24] While only 61.8 million were registered in 1985 and 69.3 million in 1986, 82 million (out of a population of 150 million) were by 1989, a sharp rise compared to the only 15 million (out of a population of 70 million) registered in 1960. When Brazilians voted on November 15 (the centenary of the First Republic's proclamation), an impressive 72.3 million went to the polls.[25]

The 1989 contest also stood out as the first national race under new rules requiring a runoff for executive posts if neither of the top two candidates got a simple majority of the vote. The result was an unpredictable presidential election in which the established political parties, who overwhelmingly controlled the national, state, and local legislatures and executives, failed to produce even a single viable candidate. The electoral environment in the first round, Keck noted in her 1992 book on the PT, favored those "seen as the most viable outsiders." The "disastrous electoral performance" of then president Sarney, the candidate of the PMDB, the country's largest party, showed "the degree to which the electorate voted against the status quo."[26] Lula, a one-term socialist federal deputy, barely beat Leonel Brizola, then governor of Rio and a well-known opposition politician, to reach the second round. A defender of Getúlio Vargas's trabalhista heritage, Brizola was the only candidate in 1989 who had been a political figure of national prominence before 1964, a leftist firebrand who boldly made a name for himself as governor of Rio Grande do Sul and federal deputy from Rio de Janeiro. Frustrated at being beaten by a political upstart, Brizola slyly suggested privately to Lula that they both drop out and endorse a third candidate in the runoff; although a newcomer, Lula was by no means that naive. In the speech in which he endorsed Lula, Brizola famously endowed Lula with a new nickname: "Wouldn't it be fascinating to make the elite swallow Lula, that bearded toad?" Brizola's powerful sway among his voters would be demonstrated when the entirety of his popular vote—centered in the two states where he had influence—went to Lula in the second round, thus launching the PT's candidate on the marathon that would take him to the presidency in 2002.[27]

It would also launch, as many Brazilian and US political scientists have noted, a unique second-round campaign, as it brought "into dispute two candidates with quite singular careers." Lula, a marginal figure without status, wealth, or education, would face the first round's top vote getter, Fernando Collor de

Mello, a forty-year-old former mayor, deputy, and governor (serving one term in each case) from the poor, tiny state of Alagoas (1 percent of the national economy and population). Though educated, rich, and well connected, he was "an unknown politician on the periphery of Brazilian politics." Together their candidacies appeared "to generate a paradox": Collor, "victorious, [was] without any party base or defined support in civil society," while Lula, "the loser, [was] anchored in a political party—the PT—with a relatively clear programmatic-ideological profile and characterized by relatively strong links with social movements."[28]

Backed by a coalition of the PT and Communist and socialist parties, Lula began the runoff with support among 17.2 percent of the electorate from the first round but would finish the stirring second round with a surprising 47 percent of the valid national vote (a good share of which he would keep in his next two runs for the presidency). As Lula gained ground, the opposing candidate shifted toward explicitly anti-Communist attacks, which he had earlier avoided when running as a candidate of the center-left.[29] Collor attacked Lula for his dangerous leftism and purported plans to confiscate private property. Such attacks might seem to lend credence to retrospective scholarly accounts of the election as an episode in the global shift toward neoliberalism in a world in thrall to the gospel of Ronald Reagan and Margaret Thatcher.[30] Yet such accounts forget, as Emir Sader and the leftist US journalist Ken Silverstein noted in 1990, that a "free-market" or neoliberal discourse was never "the centerpiece of Collor's campaign," even if the advent of neoliberal policy was the substantive impact of his short time in office.[31] Rather, the most powerfully neoliberal note in the 1989 election was sounded by the presidential candidate of FHC's party, Mário Covas, who in a June 28 Senate speech called for "a fiscal shock . . . a capitalist shock as well, a free enterprise shock"—though even Covas quickly traded in this message for an anodyne "shock of morality" during the campaign, probably in part because of his own past leftist trajectory and that of some of his party's other leaders.[32]

Rather, as Keck notes, Collor succeeded not by parroting neoliberalism but by portraying himself—as did Lula and Brizola—"as an implacable opponent" of the Sarney government. Possessing "impeccable establishment credentials," Collor nevertheless promised "to root out corruption and incompetence at the highest levels" and singled out the "maharajas," the overpaid officials and civil servants who were "cynically and systematically defrauding the country." This apparently uncompromising anticorruption message—a traditional theme of the anti-getulista União Democrática Nacional before 1964—contrasted with the pressure Lula faced during the tough second-round campaign, when he needed to shake his image as dangerously radical. Since the ABC strikes

Lula had been framed as a courageous and fearless warrior, the angry man who frontally negated military rule and incarnated the rage that followed as newly democratic Brazil was ravaged by hyperinflation, unemployment, and political paralysis. This uncompromising reputation allowed Lula to eke past Brizola, who also suffered from his past associations, but now worked against Lula in a race against an energetic, well-funded, and media-supported opponent who combined right-wing rhetoric with an extravagant oppositional posture. In the first debate, the ever more confident Collor, with his support on the rise, even went so far as to fish for support among those inclined toward Lula by criticizing his opponent as unprincipled because of the alliances he was seeking with the "traditional" politicians the two men had defeated in the first round.[33]

Lula's image problems were compounded by his opponent's facility with the modern image-making mediums, long a focus of Brazilian sociologists, communication scholars, anthropologists, and journalists.[34] Collor was not identified with the Left, and his campaign made adept use of polling in developing appeals for "an electorate of whom a majority were less than 30 years of age."[35] This telegenic upper-class messiah found his perfect runoff foil in the "scruffy, bearded figure" of the proletarian Lula, who was not at all slick.[36] Collor, by contrast, used TV to cement Lula's radical image, airing ads that showed the yellow, green, and blue of the Brazilian flag fading into the red of the PT's symbols amid photos of the Berlin Wall and Tiananmen Square. Collor's campaign also scandalously impugned Lula's honor by paying his ex-girlfriend Miriam Cordeiro—the mother of Lula's legally recognized but born-out-of-wedlock child Lurian—to attack him on TV for allegedly wanting her to abort the child, adding that Lula disliked black people.[37] Her unfounded charge that Lula disliked *negros* can be juxtaposed with a verified comment from the mother of her candidate, Collor, who suggested that her son make broad access to dentistry a campaign promise because, as she explained, they've now "put on television that laughing toothless black [*preto*]," a reference to the Brazilian comedian Tião Macalé, whom she went on to call disgusting (*nojento*).[38] As one mineiro petista remarked in retrospect, "We were from Woodstock and they [Collor's campaign] came from Chicago to clobber us."[39]

This deft combination of medium and message allowed Collor, a "formidable illusionist," to craft a "direct, populist, anticorruption and anti-institutional appeal" that was, Keck observed, "particularly effective among poorer and less educated segments of the population."[40] As Leslie Bethell and Jairo Nicolau noted, the "political and economic elite" supported Collor, "a relatively unknown politician . . . with no significant party behind him," because they lacked a viable candidate of their own. But Collor won, they emphasized, because of his support among the "poorest sections of Brazilian society in the so-called grottos [*grotões*]," whom Lula proved "unable to attract"—an assessment shared by most scholars, whatever their outlooks or political allegiances.[41] In the end, Collor won with 53 percent of the total vote, becoming the first Brazilian president to be democratically elected in the fullest sense.

While middle- and upper-class Brazilians were relieved that Lula lost, Collor's victory nonetheless discomfited many well-educated Brazilians, and not just because he was driven from office in 1992 for corruption. Their more general concern was with his oppositional negativity and unprincipled and demagogic rhetoric, which seemed to reach the poorest and least educated Brazilians, including many newly enfranchised illiterates. These concerns can be grouped under the long-standing fear of "populism" or "personalism" in Brazilian electoral life.[42] For instance, a US Brazilianist described Collor's "brilliantly orchestrated" TV attacks as "especially influential among the 50–70 percent of the electorate . . . [who were] insufficiently informed to make 'rational voting decisions.'"[43]

This irrationality has always been an obsession among the educated across the political spectrum. We heard it from former military president Ernest Geisel in chapter 10, and echoes of such elitist views were even expressed in 1989 by some frustrated petistas when they bemoaned the ignorance and lack of class consciousness that led voters to fall for Collor. This matched the view among North Atlantic observers that Lula and the PT, while novel and intriguing, would ultimately fail nationally due to the deficiencies of poor and rural Brazilians, who "were neither members of unions nor of social organizations and . . . voted more heavily for the right-wing Collor de Mello than for Lula," plagued as they were by "the renewed—not merely residual—strength of co-optative clientelism and patronage populism."[44]

This populist critique was mapped onto Brazil's geography, with the PT's emphasis on grassroots activism (basismo) making it a quintessential expression of a modern, organized Brazil that existed only in the country's highly developed Southeast and South. This supposedly explained why the PT's modest electoral support in its first ten years was restricted almost exclusively to its birthplace, urban São Paulo, which produced almost three-quarters of the PT's low vote total in its disappointing first electoral foray in 1982; in the Northeast that year, by contrast, PT candidates received, at best, less than 0.7 percent of the vote. In 1988, polling data indicated that only 5 percent of the voters in Salvador, Bahia, and Recife, Pernambuco—the Northeast's two largest cities—preferred the PT, which had even less support in the region's rural areas and small towns. As late as 1990, the number of PT state and federal deputies in the Northeast could be numbered on two hands.[45] This geographical distribution was a serious problem for the PT, given "the gross underrepresentation of São

Paulo [in the federal government] combined with the extreme overrepresentation of the smaller, essentially agrarian states."[46] This helped to maintain, in Sader and Silverstein's words, "the national power of the reactionary elite of the more conservative and sparsely populated north and northeast."[47] Indeed, the North and Northeast had been the electoral bulwark of the military regime fought by Lula, the PT, and the wider opposition, which was centered in industrialized urban hubs like São Paulo and ABC.

Looking back, these assessments reveal little interest in the millions of people who were actually voting. Instead they reveal—as the dean of Brazilian political sociologists, Gláucio Soares, noted—an enduring "elitist iluminismo" among the highly educated in Brazil, through which "the 'blame' [for election results they dislike] is thrown on the shoulders of the less educated, who are also the poorer: they don't know how to vote." As the first sociologist to study the electoral dynamics during the Populist Republic, Soares emphasized that elitist iluminismo speaks to well-worn anxieties among the highly educated about the Brazilian populace's capacity for citizenship. While "the Right reacted by putting up obstacles to the vote of the poor," Soares notes, the Left was "made desperate by the poorest because they don't vote like they want them to"; as a result, "many, privately, will admit that the less educated (read in its place: poorer) don't know how to vote or allow themselves to be fooled."[48] Implicit in "the argument of those who overemphasize personalism," Soares notes, is the assumption that

> only the "*povo*" is susceptible to charismatic leadership, to "demagoguery," to "bourgeois manipulation." The middle class, the elites, and certainly the intellectuals are protected by the antidemagogic vaccine provided by their class situation, by their education, or by their superior knowledge. Even those who defend the existence of an extreme form of social determinism [Marxism]—which, by the way, has never been empirically demonstrated—open a clause of exception for themselves.[49]

Such elitist iluminismo misses the essence of politics as an endeavor through which leaders learn about and engage with currents of mass consciousness in all their diversity, located as they are in certain places at certain times and potentially subject to change. The analytical abstractions often deployed in understanding politics—"charisma," "programmatic parties," "civil society"—distance scholars from the specific actions of talented activists, seeking to lead, as they strove to learn how to mobilize votes. These diagnoses of the 1989 election thus missed the process by which activist intellectuals, whether of working-class origin like Lula or products of USP, were learning from their intense party engagement with both social movements and electoral politics. By its very na-

Lula as elected federal deputy, 1986. (Courtesy DGABC [Wilson Magão])

ture, a big electoral campaign is actually a social movement; even its relatively short duration does not distinguish it from social movements and episodes of protest that arise, flourish, and fade away unless they acquire a ready source of funding, in which case they become institutions, not movements.

It was this sort of learning that Lula and others in the PT demonstrated in the lead-up to and aftermath of the 1989 election. For example, in a hitherto-neglected 1988 interview, conducted sometime between March 23 and July 1988 by three intellectuals, at least two of whom were petistas at the time, Lula condemned the National Constituent Assembly, in which he was participating as federal deputy, charged with creating new state institutions and the formal structure of constitutional rights to replace the unilateral constitution imposed by the military in 1967: "The povo that's outside does not have the slightest idea what goes on there, and yet folks want them to believe in this."[50] (The results of the assembly's deliberation would fall so far short of the radical Left's demands that the PT's deputies refused to sign the final document.)

In 1988 Lula was powerfully struck by how "disbelieving of everything" Brazilians were, an impression culled from his contacts with those far from Brasília. As a seasoned striker, he pointed to a recent picket of teachers and government employees in Porto Alegre where he witnessed an unprecedented "degree of revolt, a degree of disbelief [*discrédito*]," driven primarily by a recent arrocho (produced through uncontrolled inflation, not by government economic policy, as in the past). Turning to the current electoral scene, Lula presciently diagnosed both Collor's empty anticorruption rhetoric and why the povo might vote for him. Lula recognized that "in an electoral process, not even the Left, full of reason, necessarily wins"; but unlike analysts concerned about "personalism" or "populism," Lula insisted that a loss by the Left meant not that the povo are gullible but that we have not yet convinced them "that our ideas are more just and legitimate." Furthermore, he recognized that a rightist winning a direct election could nevertheless assist in the povo's politicization: "A rightist candidate chosen by the people has to publicly assume certain commitments, and for this reason is more vulnerable to being held to account."

Lula's engagement with the povo was based on his absolute belief that they could be educated politically, as he had been. It also explains why he deemed socialism more a practical than a theoretical matter, given how socialist politics required one "to take into consideration the reaction of the people," which sets limits. "Since we cannot stay fixed in time and wait for socialism to happen," he noted, "we also can't bet on misery as the way of making the povo revolt and make socialism; we have to go on presenting solutions that give the people a chance to begin believing in us, that give them a chance to eat, to work, to live, to give them a chance to go along advancing step by step." "That is why I am not afraid," Lula concluded.

This helps explains how Lula and many of the PT's leadership team came to terms with their defeat in 1989, after having gotten so close. As Lula's campaign manager, Wladimir Pomar, noted in the PT's official election postmortem, the campaign had dismissed Collor as a "simple marionette of Rede Globo" and "also looked down on the need to analyze the groups who sustained" him. "Collor did not have hegemony over the political parties and articulations," Pomar continued, but "did possess the fundamental hegemony over the common values of the broad mass" of the povo. Pomar also warned that "the religious sentiment of our povo, and its national sentiment as expressed in our flag," should never be underestimated by the PT.[51]

Likewise, Lula urged the PT to recognize that "the symbolism of the image, [which] many times touches more deeply," was worked very well by Collor's campaign. The PT, he insisted, ran its campaign with "the head of a politicized person," which prevented the party from responding promptly enough to low blows—like charges that the PT threatened non-Catholics—because the party did not recognize that such charges might be believed by those "in the least politicized strata." This intellectualism explained, he went on, why "we didn't manage to use a language adequate for that most vulnerable sector of our society." As Pomar suggested in his acute campaign postmortem (ignored by all but one of the authors who has published on 1989), Collor "used a populist rhetoric that sounded radical," while the PT was surprisingly "timid and elitist." "It's impressive," even paradoxical, Pomar went on, "how the spirit of vengeance of the poor against the rich appeared most clearly . . . precisely among those who voted for Collor."[52]

In this frank assessment of their own shortcomings, Lula and his companheiros never blamed those who did not vote for him for a lack of reason or education. Rather, the key distinction that Lula and PT leaders drew was between those already politicized and the overwhelming majority who were not and who needed to be reached. Collor had "played on the depoliticized imaginary" of "the low-income strata, those without education, unemployed or semi-employed, [and] socially disorganized, as well as among the lower middle class, whether living as residents in the peripheries of the large urban centers or in small cities in the interior, who together make up 70 percent of the Brazilian electorate." Those in this group "sought a hero who would incarnate their opposition to everything that irritated them: maharajas, public employees, Sarney, the 'political class,' parties, the rich, elites."[53] Along these lines, Lula noted in February 1990 that while his candidacy had received ample support among sectors of the middle class, government employees, intellectuals, and trade unionists, the party now needed "to go directly to those people who are less favored[,] . . . to reach the segment of society that earns the salário mínimo[,] . . . to go to the periphery, where one finds millions of people who allow themselves to be seduced by easy promises of housing and food."[54]

Herein lay the central challenge that Lula and his party took up over the next two decades—in the face of considerable internal resistance within the PT. The Left's "cultura principista" had always missed the deeper logic behind Lula's willingness to talk with everyone, including industrialists: "When one of these people seek me out, they could even be attempting to fool me. But if I am not at least open to conversing with this citizen, even if only to obtain information useful for us, then I am not doing politics. I am locked up in my own world, I become the owner of absolute truth and no one else is worth anything."[55] "The grandeur of politics," Lula observed in a 1990 interview, is learning "how to administer problems, to live with your adversaries and to live with adversity" in order to focus on the central challenge: "that we live in a country so miserable, the needs of the people so great, that the people want immediate results."[56]

This understanding of politics also explains the rhetorical choices made by Lula during the 1989 election. In a radio interview, the PT candidate dodged abstract questions about "savage capitalism" to talk of "a capitalism that bites and one that doesn't bite, that which is bad and that which is good." Rather than the need to "make socialism," he emphasized the problems of "the humble housewife, the humble worker, the worker who lives off his salary, who earns 180,00 new cruzados, 120,00 new cruzados, the unemployed."[57] This was because, as he already recognized in 1988, "the Brazilian povo is in such need, even just of hope, that anyone who presents even a minimum of hope, that makes the povo feel that they can achieve something, will have already gained their confidence. The people [have to] begin to believe [again], and I think we have to bet on this."[58]

This same hope infused the iconic theme song that appeared in Lula's 1989 appearances on the "horário eleitoral," a system of TV advertising allotted free to all candidates under regulations enacted by the military in 1974. The campaign's advertising man, Paulo de Tarso Santos, invited the well-known composer and lyricist Hilton Acioli to produce a jingle for the campaign. A native of the northeastern state of Rio Grande do Norte, Acioli was best known for his collaborations in the late 1960s with Geraldo Vandré, the Brazilian Bob Dylan of the rebel year of 1968, whose antimilitary anthem "Walking" affirmed the belief that "flowers can defeat cannons." Acioli produced a song—recorded by three giants of Brazilian pop music, Chico Buarque, Djavan, and Gilberto Gil—whose memorable title became the de facto slogan of Lula's second-round campaign: "Without fear of being happy" (Sem medo de ser feliz).[59] This enigmatic slogan was married to an infectious melody with words that boldly projected an infinite hopefulness in an election where there were so "many people working for so long" who could now "clearly see who we can trust": Lula, "our growing hope."[60]

Relentlessly positive, the song was sung collectively by hundreds of thousands in 1989—and in Lula's two subsequent presidential campaigns—and created indelible positive associations that continue to be invoked to this day. Asked to explain the slogan's meaning in August 1990, Lula observed that "people are afraid to be happy . . . to believe in the new, to try things that are untested. And we'll never move forward without political will, without audacity, without daring. I hope the slogan leads people to fight for their own happiness."[61] It was a long march through institutions and elections over the next thirteen years, including two more defeats, before Lula and his party would finally win the presidency.

How the PT's Lula Finally Reached the Presidency

So how did Lula finally get elected in 2002 after twice losing in the first round in 1994 and 1998? While circumstances and events can never be discounted in analyzing elections, it is clear that Lula's victory was above all a triumph of politics—not popular insurgency or social movement activism—and a defeat for neoliberalism, but not a conscious repudiation of neoliberalism. In the wake

Lula in 1989 after the presidential campaign. (Courtesy DGABC [J. B. Ferreira])

of the Asian financial crisis that hit Brazil in 1998, Lula's support among voters gradually increased as social conditions and confidence in the government deteriorated. Yet it was neither natural nor inevitable that disgruntled voters would turn toward Lula. It occurred in good part because of Lula's personal choices and persistence, strategic decisions by his party, and the positive impact of the PT's increasing success in running local and state governments.

After being defeated by Collor in 1989, Lula had taken an unusual path for a Brazilian politician: he would seek no office besides the presidency. Addressing the geographical imbalance in the PT's base of support, he traveled constantly, crisscrossing Brazil from one end to the other—most memorably in the "citizenship caravans" of 1993–94—and talking with anyone who would talk with him. In doing so, he acquired unmatched knowledge of the country's socioeconomic, cultural, and political realities, which made it possible for him to offer concrete and relevant examples for any issue. He had also founded the Citizenship Institute, a small think tank for debating and producing public policy guidelines that was mostly autonomous from the PT.

Driven by personal ambition and mission, Lula campaigned for the presidency in the 1990s with the same disciplined and unrelenting application of energy, political skill, and good humor by which he became the de facto as well as de jure president of the São Bernardo metalworkers' union. His practice of leadership involved the ceaseless building of relationships—whether based on identification, friendship, curiosity, respect, or need—as he rose ever higher in the political stratosphere. For the dozen years following 1989, Lula broadened and deepened his engagement with individuals from the top to the very bottom of Brazilian society. This involved tens of thousands of rallies, marches, and public meetings as well as problem-solving sessions with local activists, courtesy visits with big shots, newspaper and TV interviews, and a constant flow of less formal chitchat with those with whom he stayed and those who drove him to his destinations, served him meals, or even cut his hair.

An engaging conversationalist, Lula was equally at ease in the tiniest backland village eating poor peoples' *pirao* (gravy with manioc flour) or chatting up "movers and shakers" over whiskey and *salgadinhos* (hors d'oeuvres) at cocktail parties in São Paulo or Brasília.[62] Even as he spent more time with the rich and well-educated, Lula continued to nurture a bond with the little people, the povão; it seemed that no place was too small and no person so unimportant as not to be worth a visit, a talk, or a touch. Drawing on these experiences, Lula contrasted his approach with those politicians and government officials who knew neither their country nor its people in all their diversity.

Enjoying a wide freedom of movement lacked by officeholders, Lula became a nationally recognized symbol of concern for social justice as well as a synonym for perseverance. Unlike his 1982 campaign for São Paulo governor, Lula was no longer presented as a victim of "the system" who had been unfairly arrested—someone "just like you," as his 1982 campaign slogan went. Lula was now presented to voters as a self-made politician, internationally acknowledged but still proud of his origins. Here was a man who displayed a responsible awareness about the country's critical situation while continuing to urge Brazilians to discard defeatism and never give up their dream of being happy. Or to put this message in more philosophical terms, Brazilians had to do something new "with what's been done to you," as Sartre defined freedom. Of course the gifted political marketing wizard Duda Mendonça was also vital in consolidating this new image in 2002, and the high-quality, pasteurized way in which it was broadcast was decisive to its success, but the message fit the candidate very well—at least better than the orthodox Marxist outlook that many intellectuals and left-wing groups would like to have seen adopted by this unmistakably individual expression of working-class consciousness.

At the same time, local experiences of municipal administration had proven the PT capable of conducting government honestly while taking steps to reorient public policies to the benefit of majorities. The PT had made its first electoral breakthrough at this level in 1988, when its candidates won the municipal governments in Brazil's largest city (São Paulo), two other state capitals (Porto Alegre and Vitória), and several medium-size cities, including the port of Santos, which brought 15 million Brazilians, about 10 percent of the population, under PT administration. Although the experience was not universally successful, the following decade saw enough municipal and state success to give substance to the slogan about a "PT way of governing," although the claim to govern completely differently than other parties was in great measure propagandistic. Yet it worked because it was rooted in something real, including practical policies that expanded access to education, health, and housing and that improved the quality of services and goods provided; programs of popular credit; and, even more important, initiatives such as participatory budgeting aimed at raising the levels of popular participation in governance. These initiatives became the trademark of many PT local governments and generated increased popular support as well as a disproportionate number of international "good government" awards. Taken together with the decline in FHC's popularity, these local experiences contributed to the PT's exceptional performance in the 2000 municipal elections, the first conducted under a new policy that allowed, on a case-by-case-basis, alliances with non-leftist political parties. That this had long been advocated by Lula without success in the PT suggests the limitations of viewing him as a charismatic party leader who had merely acolytes as opposed to comrades and collaborators to whom he had to defer.

The 2000 elections saw the PT emerge as the big winner, with spectacular wins in capital cities across the country—including Porto Alegre, Recife, Belém, Curitiba, Salvador, Aracaju, and São Paulo. As political scientist Alberto Carlos Almeida notes, these victories, especially in São Paulo, also increased the party's capacity to raise campaign funds, which had long been its Achilles' heel in Brazil's byzantine multiparty system, where big money played an enormous role.[63] The PT's expanded power base would prove critical in the presidential race two years later, with Lula being viewed ever more positively, his party's leadership becoming more pragmatic, and its local governments more innovative in public management.

Yet the previous fifteen years had also seen a sharp decline in the PT's original social movement base. For example, the size, composition, and bargaining power of workers such as metalworkers and bank employees, who had done so much to change Brazilian unionism in the 1980s, declined dramatically. The world of big factories—like the 40,000 employed at VW—now seemed part of a remote past. The combined effects of economic stagnation, the reduction of tariffs, and productive restructuring drove unions into retreat. The situation was somewhat different in the countryside, where landless workers (as organized in the MST along with other groups) expanded their actions, although political disagreements at times cooled their relationship with the PT. Inside the Catholic Church, progressive groups had been suffering harsh setbacks at the hands of Vatican conservatives since the 1980s, while also losing followers to Pentecostalism and the conservative charismatic movement within the Catholic Church. And although the PT had always been critical of "really existing socialism," the intellectuals of the Left were deeply affected by the fall of the Soviet Union and the Eastern European regimes. They faced intense difficulties as they sought to articulate a renewed socialist theory that might provide conceptual tools capable of linking day-to-day political activities with some kind of utopian perspective.

Thus, when the PT's electoral strategy for the 2002 presidential election was outlined, the PT was stronger in the institutional field but weaker in its organic base; the problem was made even worse by the brain drain from social movements into public administration, a problem that would become even more pronounced after 2002.[64] The party had managed to become a major collective actor in national politics but could not rely on a magical surge of activism to propel it to the presidency. A broader set of alliances would be necessary, which is why the PT turned to the small center-right Liberal Party to provide its vice presidential candidate. José Alencar, the owner of the country's most important textile group, was a more traditional kind of self-made man than Lula but would prove helpful in calming his business colleagues and gaining votes for Lula in the key state of Minas Gerais, which had elected Alencar senator in 1998.

Likewise, Lula's 2002 presidential campaign consciously aimed to broaden his political, social, and regional base of support, given the weaknesses revealed so starkly in 1989. Lula and his marketing team went out of their way to moderate the campaign's written and visual messages so as not to stoke unnecessary conflict. This strategy was often sarcastically referred to as selling "Lula Light" and included the defining campaign slogan "Lulinha, paz e amor," which combined the diminutive of Lula's name with "peace" and "love."[65] On economics, the PT offered a vague claim that the country could do better economically and in terms of equity than it had during FHC's second term, when the country was hard hit by the Asian and Russian financial crises and ended up under an agreement with the International Monetary Fund (IMF).

The pragmatic logic driving the campaign could not have been more transparent, but its success was far from guaranteed because their candidate and party were sharply defined in terms of protest, insurgency, and radicalism. To be convincing, the new message would have to be delivered without embarrassment by its standard bearer, and once again Lula demonstrated his capacity for remarkable performances. Rather than a retreat from radicalism, Lula would declare that this was his "first professional campaign. I want to win this election and not embark any more on the craziness" of the past. The PT, he declared, "is not ashamed to have changed positions," and "I have realized that the PT which needs to be constructed is broader than the PT of macacão [factory uniforms] that I dreamed of constructing." In the midst of an exchange of insults among his rivals, he serenely assured the public, "This little Lula doesn't want to fight, this one is about peace and love." Asked if his party had become bourgeois, Lula used a family metaphor: "The grandfather is more loving with his grandson than the father is with his son" not "because the love of the grandfather is more than that of the dad, but because the grandfather is more mature."[66]

On the rise, Lula's campaign would also benefit from the defensive stance taken by the incumbent PSDB's candidate, José Serra, who was minister of health under departing president FHC. When Serra and financial market operators attempted to use the specter of international speculative risk to frighten voters, Lula's campaign issued the "Letter to the People of Brazil," which abandoned the party's emphasis on "rupture" with the prevailing economic model, an emphasis that had still appeared in the PT's December 2001 electoral platform. The letter stressed that a "new model cannot be the product of unilateral decisions by the government" but can only come as "the fruit of nationwide negotiation, which should aim toward an authentic alliance for the country, a new social contract, capable of insuring growth with stability." Lula publicly vowed to respect "the country's contracts and obligations"—a reference to Brazil's agreement with the IMF—and to maintain the primary surplus in public finances "as long as necessary."[67]

It is unlikely that the letter attracted a significant new bloc of voters, as Lula's chief of staff José Dirceu notes, but it did rob the Serra campaign of a trump card, as intended, and allowed the PT to advance a winning message of "hopes of a better day, without fear of the future."[68] Promising a pact on behalf of Brazil, Lula declared that if there were to be sacrifices, they would be sacrifices made by all, unlike in the past, when the benefits were only for the few and the sacrifices for the many. It was Lula's tactical brilliance to give this economic message concreteness immediately after being elected with his "guiding phrase: 'at the end of my government every Brazilian will have three meals a day.'" Dirceu in passing offers three possible explanations for this unexpected statement from his candidate: that Lula had "said it all or had an awareness of our limitations or that this was [in fact] his universe."[69] In the end, Lula received 52.8 million votes in the runoff, 61.3 percent of the nationwide vote, and won all but one state; he narrowly missed outright victory in the first round, receiving 46 percent of the vote and carrying twenty-four of twenty-seven states.

For some critics of Lula's first term, the Left had ignored an alternative path to the presidency, whose viability was suggested by the fact that Lula twice won over a quarter to a third of the national electorate while adhering to leftist principles and rejecting spurious alliances. But for petistas concerned with exercising power, the bottom line of the 1994 and 1998 electoral results was that FHC and his center-right coalition had won in the first round and had done so in every region of the country, doing especially well among the poor, the lower middle class, and those outside the big cities where the PT's traditional electorate among the educated was strongest. Most leftists had also come to recognize the truth stated in 1989 by PT economist Paul Singer, a voice in the wilderness at the time, who suggested that a reckless challenge to the IMF and the Brazilian and international capitalist system, with no credible prospects of success, would not only plunge the country into economic crisis but would also immiserate the mass of the population while killing the Left's credibility for generations. His own "enthusiasm in relation to Lula," he had said, was the modest hope that he might, as president, prove capable of implementing capitalism "in a form more favorable to the poor."[70]

Lula was focused in his campaign and first term, as Dirceu observes, on "the social: hunger, the minimum wage, health, education, agrarian reform, and family agriculture." In Dirceu's view, the challenges facing the PT-led government—operating under tight budget constraints—was "how to reform and advance social, economic, political, cultural transformations under capitalism."[71] This sober assessment would prove applicable for all the new Left-led Latin American governments that rose to power after Hugo Chávez's election in 1998 and Lula's in 2002. If neoliberalism was "no longer the only game in town," it could not be denied that the emerging era of policy and governance during Latin America's turn to the Left was best characterized as *post*-neoliberal—that is, coming "after" neoliberalism, as opposed to replacing it tout court. As Laura Macdonald and Arne Ruckert suggest, this involved "a search for progressive policy alternatives arising out of the many contradictions of neoliberalism," which points to how "neoliberal policy has lost its dominance but is not [yet] annihilated," the emerging alternatives themselves "contain[ing] remnants of the previous neoliberal model." In its ambiguities, the term "post-neoliberalism" thus captures the prevailing "discontinuity within continuity"—the latter "predominantly in the realm of macroeconomic policy," the former in the fight against international asymmetries, efforts to deepen democracy, and the steps taken to rebuild state capacity while carrying out a real but modest degree of redistribution.[72]

What Victory Meant for the Left and for the Povo

For the Latin American and European Left, the Lula presidency was an unprecedented development, in the words of Eric Hobsbawm, with Lula "probably the only industrial worker at the head of a Labour Party anywhere"; the story, Hobsbawm went on, could only "warm the cockles of all old red hearts."[73] But the first years of Lula's presidency saw a growing discontent and even disillusionment among the intellectualized leftist middle class in the country's biggest cities and richer states, a core part of Lula's constituency since 1989.[74] They were frustrated with Lula's adherence to the previous administration's macroeconomic policies and its willingness to ally with the oligarchical parties whose corruption the PT had denounced so strongly and for so long. In 2004, this would lead a group of prominent PT intellectuals and a few, but not many, of its politicians to found the Party of Socialism and Freedom (PSOL), critical of the PT in power. It was one of many responses to the challenges that came when the PT finally "reached the presidency, which had been its strategic obsession from early on," but was no longer "the party founded twenty years earlier," in the words of Mauro Iasi. Even those who spoke of the party having matured were "obliged to confess that the PT has changed a lot," the doubt plaguing many of the PT's middle-class members and voters being that perhaps "the PT didn't manage to change the world [but instead] the world had changed the PT."[75]

Founded as a political instrument, in Lula's words, the PT had come a long way in a very short time. Born from a coming together of activists and movements, the PT had become an institutionalized party characterized by a degree of personal and partisan commitment far exceeding that of its competitors. Whether for a few years or decades, hundreds of thousands had devoted parts of their lives and a great deal of energy to opening a new path to a very different Brazil through the PT. Whether members, militants, or sympathizers, activists from organizations like the PT, CUT, and MST faced a powerful narrative challenge after Lula's ecstatic January 2003 inauguration: how to bridge the gap between a heroic past, when the struggle was clear, and a present full of ambiguities, unseemly compromises, and manifest temptations as its leaders settled in to occupy the very top of the political—though not the economic—superstructure of one of the world's eleven largest capitalist economies. In 2003, not a single one of these activists would have even dared to anticipate that their party might win the next three presidential contests and maintain their hold on the presidency for thirteen years.

Looking back, Ricardo Kotscho, Lula's press officer for the 2002 campaign, recalls the euphoric multitude gathered on São Paulo's impossibly crowded Avenida Paulista to hear Lula speak after his victory. Lula would describe his election in simple terms: "Hope defeated fear, and the electorate decided on a new path for the country."[76] Twenty-five years earlier, a young trade union president had spoken boldly about a country deeply tilted in a different direction, toward fear. In numerous interviews, the struggle against fear had always been a part of Lula's distinctive posture as a man beholden to no one (não ter o rabo preso) and free to say exactly what needed to be said. Now, finally, so many people working for so long could begin to live without fear of being happy.

The popular reaction in São Paulo to Lula's election was captured with ethnographic sensitivity by US anthropologist James Holston, who had decades of experience, along with his wife Teresa Caldeira, of working closely with the city's urban housing movements. He described the 2002 results as a "massive, ecstatic victory under the red banners of 'citizenship,' 'democracy,' and 'social justice.'" People voted for Lula, Holston observed, "not only to demand future change but also to acclaim as emblematically theirs a life story about what has already changed." Their country had finally elected to the nation's highest office "a man who campaigned explicitly as a nonelite—not merely as 'the Brazilian equal to you' . . . but as a man who had triumphed without becoming elite, who had succeeded through his experience of the common, and who presented his individual success as expressly collective."[77]

What most impressed Holston was "how many people, mostly working-class," openly wept on the streets of São Paulo and on national television after Lula's victory. "The tears of tough working-class men and women," Holston explained, "sprang from their painful, passionate longing for Brazil to *dar certo*, to 'succeed and become right,'" as well as from "what it meant to them that such a man could become president." Lula's story had "touched the deeply messianic nerve of Brazilian popular imagination" and spoke directly to an enduring "frustration among laboring Brazilians" who longed "for their nation to make good after so many misses, for their work to be valued, accomplishments recognized, and injustices righted," and "for a just share in their country's immense resources, forever monopolized by a habitually disparaging, pampered, and immune elite who always seem relentlessly in control of Brazil's destiny."[78]

Thus, the democratic triumph of the 2002 election stemmed from a mature and considered vote accepted with little fear or controversy by the losers. The popular mood was hopeful but not soaring, and the mass of the PT's voters were not displeased by the "responsibility" shown by the new government, which pledged to guarantee the country's economic stability. The formal transition ceremonies were overseen with elegance by outgoing president Fernando Henrique Cardoso, who passed the presidential sash to his companheiro from the struggles of the late 1970s. Indeed, the overall atmosphere in Brazil during the second-round campaign seemed at times like a society-wide blessing of the new; in some major cities, like Rio and Salvador, Lula won 80 to 90 percent of the vote. At the same time, Lula was acutely aware, as he declared constantly throughout his presidency, that a heavy responsibility rested on his shoulders: "Any other president could fail, but I can't." But what would constitute failure? Or success, for that matter? And how would success be defined by the PT's militants, sympathizers, and repeat voters, or by the many voters who had, for the first time, voted for the PT?

16 COACH, PLAYER, AND STATESMAN

Lula became well-known after the ABC strikes, but it was his near victory in the 1989 presidential elections that made him a leftist icon, dwarfed only by his friend Fidel Castro. Far less controversial than his Cuban counterpart, Lula appealed beyond the political Left to many who simply cared about democracy in the wake of the region's dictatorships. When elected twelve years later as president of a country twenty times the size of Cuba, Lula would kick off what has been called Latin America's "Left turns" or "pink tide," which ended a decade of triumphant neoliberalism, unchallenged US hegemony, and Washington Consensus policies.[1] This had been reflected in the famous declaration "There is no alternative" by the UK's Tory prime minister, Margaret Thatcher, in the 1970s, a cry taken up in the late 1980s by center-left politicians including US president Bill Clinton, UK prime minister Tony Blair, and presidents of Mexico, Argentina, Brazil, and Venezuela, the last three of whom had historic ties to Left, center-left, and popular camps in Latin American politics. With patience, humor, and persistence, Lula had rallied the Latin American Left to oppose this neoliberal juggernaut through both the Forum of São Paulo (FSP), which first met in July 1990, and, starting in 2001, the World Social Forum (WSF), founded in Porto Alegre with PT support after the antiglobalization protests that met the 1999 Seattle World Trade Organization meeting.[2] The WSF would adopt a slogan whose power lay in its very modesty: "Another world *is* possible." It would prove prophetic over the next decade, with sweeping leftist electoral victories in Latin America accompanied, in 2008, by the election of an unlikely US president: Barack Obama.

Brazil's PT-led government stood at the very heart of Latin America's Left turns between 2002 and 2016, and this chapter examines Lula's approach to democracy as the region emerged from a prolonged experience of antipopular dictatorship. It shows how Lula deployed his authority and prestige to bring beleaguered leftists together, serving both as supportive coach and as star player who inspired confidence because he didn't let fame go to his head. This chapter explores the period's mantra of many Lefts following one path by comparing Lula with another outstanding personality arguably to his left, Venezuela's Hugo Chávez. In doing so, I explain the nature of their alliance and distinguish between their leadership styles, discourses, and approaches to organization and mobilization, focusing on socioeconomic and institutional origins, life trajectories, and distinctive national histories. This alliance across difference guaranteed important victories as oil-rich Venezuela bolstered leftist governments throughout Latin America and guaranteed socialist Cuba's survival. Finally, I show that this generation of Latin American leftists had unprecedented success due to an antineoliberal politics, still poorly understood, that was reinforced by interpersonal bonds forged during the 1990s between leftist leaders.

Resisting the Neoliberal Tide: From the Forum of São Paulo to the World Social Forum

Speaking in 2005 to his counterparts at the FSP's fifteenth-anniversary meeting, an ebullient Lula hailed how much had changed since their first meeting, when "we were a continent marked by military coups and the absence of democracy." By 2005, as Lula highlighted, "the Left ha[d] once and for all taken the extraordinary step of betting that it is fully possible to reach and exercise power through the democratic path."[3] This change would, a year after Lula's remarks, be the focus of a celebrated polemic by Mexico's ex–foreign minister Jorge Castañeda about "Latin America's Left turn," published in the US foreign policy establishment's journal. A Communist in his younger years, Castañeda had written an influential 1993 book on the crisis of the Latin American Left but subsequently supported the conservative businessman Vicente Fox, who won the 2000 presidential election that ended one-party rule in Mexico.[4] Castañeda was rewarded with a ministerial appointment, and his *Foreign Affairs* article would be widely read along the Washington–New York corridor and much debated in the ivory tower. The piece had the air of a fairy tale. Glancing back to the neoliberal 1990s, Castañeda asserted that "just over a decade ago, Latin America seemed poised to begin a virtuous cycle of economic progress and improved democratic governance." Yet this hopeful prospect had dissipated, and the region was "swerving left" in a backlash "against the predominant trends of the last fifteen years: free-market reforms, agreement with the United States, . . . and the consolidation of representative democracy." Castañeda dates this shift to Hugo Chávez's 1998 presidential victory, but he sees a "veritable left-wing tsunami" following Lula's 2002 victory, after which "a wave of leaders, parties, and movements generically labeled 'leftist' have swept into power." Most of them, he lamented, were drawn from the region's "nationalist, strident, and close-minded" Left, which had long embraced "macroeconomic folly" and the "virulent, strident nationalism" of Latin America's "populist" past.[5]

The vigor of Castañeda's disdain reflected how badly things had worked out by 2006 for the left-of-center Latin Americans who had opted for neoliberalism when it seemed the wave of the future. Indeed, Castañeda was forced to admit that he had been "at least partly wrong" in believing that Latin American governments would have to adopt "social democratic" policies as the necessary complement to the free-market reforms vigorously denounced as neoliberal by the "old, radical, guerrilla-based, Castroist or communist left," a category to which he consigned Lula and the PT. For Castañeda, the two most successful examples of "social democracy" were the post-Pinochet Concertación in Chile, a Socialist–Christian Democratic coalition, and the government of FHC, the neo-Marxist creator of dependency theory who served as Brazil's president from 1994 to 2002. Yet Castañeda noted ruefully that only Chile had succeeded, and very few Latin Americans accepted that country as the "true model for the region."[6] As for Brazil, the 2002 election had seen José Serra, the presidential candidate for FHC's political party and an extremely competent administrator with a US PhD, beaten by a candidate from the "bad" Left.

The Latin American intellectuals and politicians, like Castañeda and FHC, who had set out to create a third way were aware of how "unrealistic" and "incongruous" their venture seemed in a region "besieged by apparently triumphant neoliberalism and weakened by the criticism and death of real socialism." As the editor of a 1993 programmatic collection noted, the European construct of social democracy was "not viewed very positively" in Latin America. The most straightforward and combative contributor to this collection was FHC, who identified the tasks ahead: to criticize past Lefts, reduce the state, restrict redistribution associated with corporatism (such as wage increases), and move away from nationalist flag waving. Social democrats, he emphasized two years before his presidency, needed to foreground efficiency and "the rational aspects of accumulation, productivity, and investment" slighted by the regressive critique of wealth associated with the "egalitarian utopia" of Christian socialism.[7] FHC's target was the PT, which Marcelo Cavarozzi, the collection's Argentine contributor, dubbed "the most dramatic example" of the "grass-roots Left" linked to liberation theology, labor, and mass protest, a tradition he criticized for deeming "political representation, at its best, as a distortion of true and real democracy, which . . . is associated with modalities of direct participation."[8]

While Castañeda's leftist faith was waning, Lula and the PT were working with Fidel and the Cuban Communist Party to bring the region's leftist parties together for a meeting in 1990 that gave rise to the FSP, which survives to this day. This 1990 gathering in São Paulo was unprecedented because the few regionwide leftist meetings that had been held in the past had been restricted by ideological affiliation, such as the 1975 Havana meeting of Soviet-aligned Communist parties or the clandestine Coordinadora Revolucionaria, which united armed organizations in the Southern Cone. Between 1990 and 2001, the FSP would grow from forty-eight to eighty parties, although those numbers reflect how more than one party from a given country can attend. Brazil, for example, fielded six parties at the outset; at one point, thirteen showed up from Argentina, the only thing uniting them, in Lula's words, being "Maradona's goals in the 1990 World Cup."[9] The largest and most influential groups in the FSP, however, were formidable political forces, each of which would sponsor a forum meeting in the group's first ten years: the PT, the Cuban Communist Party, El Salvador's Frente Farabundo Martí para la Liberación Nacional (FMLN), Mexico's Partido de la Revolución Democrático (Mexico), Nicaragua's Frente Sandinista de Liberación Nacional, and Uruguay's Frente Amplio. The Left's entire ideological spectrum could be found in the FSP, according to one of its Cuban founders; its "anti-imperialist and antineoliberal definition" provided a space where all the region's leftists could meet and debate as well as a mechanism for communication, coordination, and solidarity.[10]

At the forum's beginning, Lula recalled, "we were few, discredited, and talked a lot" because we "didn't think in the same manner [jeito] and didn't believe in the same prophecies." Looking back in 2011, Lula emphasized the depth of division, wariness, and distrust on the left; "many times the divergences were greater than the [areas of] agreement." There were ideological divisions—some parties were Marxist-Leninist, others were not—as well as differing international alignments, although all shared a basic sympathy for Cuba. Perennial leftist disputes were also lurking in the background, including reform versus revolution and armed struggle's role in achieving power. The FSP taught the Left "to act like companheiros, despite our diversity," Lula said in 2005, but this required "a group that played midfield to contemporize, to seek the right word" so as to arrive at a final declaration at any given meeting. According to Lula, it took time for the Latin American Left to learn a lesson taught by Brazilian educator Paulo Freire: "Unite the different in order to defeat the antagonistic."[11]

When the FSP met for the fourth time, in Havana in 1993, Latin American leftists were feeling besieged, and its Cuban hosts faced possible national collapse after the gigantic drop in GDP that followed the loss of the country's markets and assistance from the Communist bloc. Moreover, not only was Latin America shifting rightward in terms of policy—with the privatization of state enterprises, deregulation, and austerity measures affecting health, education, and the general welfare—but some of those carrying out this policy shift were also "betraying" former party alliances. Feeling besieged, leftists could have chosen to "wait out the storm," cultivating purity of principles at a remove from the bourgeois world they disdained. Instead, those who shared the PT's views focused on the electoral battle ahead, even as they recognized the electoral order's flaws and distortions. Elections provided the Left with its most important opportunity to move beyond the noisy protests and ritual denunciations that accompanied the neoliberal reshaping of state-society relations.

Lula straightforwardly laid out his personal opinions in Havana in 1993, though not all PT leaders agreed. "The Left isn't united even when they're in jail together," he joked, noting the Left's inflexibility even when making alliances with other leftists. According to Lula, Latin America's electoral systems were dominated by money and corruption, its democracies as unstable as its economies. Simply maintaining a democratic constitutional order, he insisted, required a successful distribution of wealth, and that was possible only via electoral alliances beyond "the limits of the Left itself," including "sectors of the center left" and nonaffiliated actors. Having a credible shot at winning the presidency in 1994, Lula added that today the urgent questions were whether the Left parties "have the competence to consolidate the popular will and reach power" and whether, once elected, these parties could effectively govern from the left, actualizing the hope of "distributing wealth more justly to end the social backwardness of our countries."[12]

That the FSP eventually overcame its divisions to implement such a project reflected how much had changed since 1980, when Lula discussed unifying the Left on first meeting Fidel Castro, in Managua, Nicaragua, at a celebration of the Sandinista's victory.[13] This unity, as Lula reflected in 2005, came when those on the left learned to be patient and "to build and to bring [forces] together" as part of a search for ways to "banish the fear of so many of the common people [who are] frightened when they imagine the Left winning an election."[14] As Lula explained at the seventeenth FSP, held in Managua in 2011, he had originally believed—as had many others—that a socialist "metalworker could never reach the presidency through the vote." In 1985 he was quoted by the *Folha de São Paulo* saying as much, prompting the PT's opponents to denounce him for disrespecting Brazil's nascent democratic order, but it was the thrilling 1989 presidential race, Lula added, that led him to shed such pessimism.[15]

Yet between then and his eventual ascent to the Brazilian presidency, during the tough and discouraging 1990s, the Latin American Left developed an antineoliberal politics distinct from the previous three decades' anticapitalist and anti-imperialist politics. The Left's very deployment of the term "neoliberalism," along with its popularization in political and policy debates, reflected a strategic shift that contributed decisively to the Left turns a decade later.[16] At this point, regional opposition to neoliberalism, not capitalism, marked the fundamental boundary defining the Left—which, if viewed in orthodox Marxist terms, could be said to obscure the essential capitalist and imperialist enemy. Yet the emphasis on neoliberalism was especially appropriate in Latin America, where autonomous or semiautonomous national development (whether capitalist or socialist) has long been a shared goal across the political spectrum. While anticapitalism has had a place in the Latin American Left's discourse, the practical emphasis had more often been on capitalism's incapacity to achieve autonomous national development and the bourgeoisie's continuing failure to spark a democratic revolution or deliver prosperity to the masses.[17]

As first popularized in Latin America, "neoliberalism" brilliantly delineated an opposing camp in a vague and shifting manner that deeply frustrated those who favored the political forces associated with the Washington Consensus. The term's slipperiness was especially irritating to the English journalist who had, since 1996, served as the Latin American bureau chief for neoliberalism's most ideologically rigorous publication, the *Economist*. In his 2007 book, Michael Reid recognized that the Washington Consensus was "indeed an irrevocably 'damaged brand,'" although some of "its central tenets—of macroeconomic stability and open, market economies—had endured." "That this is not more widely perceived" or convertible into political capital, he said, "owes much to the baleful influence of a meaningless term: 'neoliberalism.'" Reid did not deny its association with the discredited Pinochet dictatorship or ignore that the exemplary neoliberal presidency of the 1990s, under Carlos Menem, had ended in disaster for Argentina in 2001. But Reid did seek to rescue neoliberalism from the Left's obloquy by praising Chile's center-left Concertación coalition and, more importantly, claiming President Lula as a "social democrat," "a convert to this consensus." Yet the Englishman had to admit that Lula was at best "an ambivalent" convert—that he and his party fell far short of being assimilable to neoliberal orthodoxy.[18]

Castañeda followed a similar strategy in fighting back against the discourse of antineoliberalism, inducting some of the newly elected leftist leaders into what he dubbed the "right left" in Latin America. While praising Tabaré Vázquez and the Frente Amplio in tiny Uruguay, Castañeda was most eager to claim Lula for a purported "social democratic" camp. Like Reid, though, Castañeda struggled to pull off such a reappropriation of the Latin American Left: his language was tinged with uncertainty—the PT had "*largely* followed [Lula] on the road *toward* social democracy"—and he could not ignore that Brazil's ruling leftist party maintained a "lingering emotional devotion to Cuba," its members burning "the US president in effigy" across the street from the presidential palace when Lula hosted George W. Bush in Brasília in November 2005. As Castañeda was forced to conclude, "The conversion is *not complete*."[19]

Reid's and Castañeda's failures here are testament to how the Brazilian and Latin American Left creatively developed the language and practice of antineoliberalism over the course of the 1990s, so that it was possible, at the dawn of the new millennium, to take the term to the global level. The WSF Charter of Principles was the product of dialogue in the late 1990s between Brazilian social movements—mostly, but not entirely, hegemonized by the PT—and France's Association pour la Taxation des Transactions Financières et pour l'Action Citoyenne.[20] In its basic principles, the 2001 charter disregarded past ideological disputes and current rivalries within the Left to create a space of convergence in which a vast array of forces, projects, and currents could come together around a lowest common minimum (armed groups and political parties were explicitly excluded). Indeed, the charter's first principle was to bring together "groups and movements of civil society that are opposed to *neoliberalism* and to domination of the world by capital and *any form* of imperialism, and [who] are committed to building a planetary society directed towards fruitful relationships among humankind and between it and the earth."[21] In other words, the WSF and the Latin American Left defined themselves by opposition not necessarily to capitalism per se but to neoliberalism and to "domination . . . by capital." Likewise, the unequivocal statement of opposition to "any form of imperialism" avoids asserting that all capitalist countries are necessarily imperialist.

As a result, the WSF would come to encompass countless celebrities, French cabinet ministers, intellectuals, and even some businessmen. In ideological terms, the body attracted anarchists, socialists, Communists, social democrats, and liberals, not to mention the vast array of unaffiliated labor, environmental, women's, black, LGBT, and indigenous groups. Under such circumstances, those obsessed with defining the Left in terms of "revolution" or "social democracy" seemed caught in a mid-twentieth-century past whose relevance had faded in the face of twenty-first-century challenges.[22]

Chávez, Lula, and the Origin and Politics of Latin America's Left Turns

"I never know where to begin [when] speaking to events as beautiful as this," Hugo Chávez told an overflowing crowd in the Caracas Poliedro on January 27, 2006. The Venezuelan president began his address to the sixth WSF by citing "the grand emotion" he felt facing an audience "overflowing with passion." Thrilling the crowd, he seized the occasion to deliver a message to "Mr. Danger," his term for the US president whom he would label the devil in a UN General Assembly speech eight months later, in September 2006. While citing martyrs, condemning crimes, and promising inevitable retribution, Chávez attacked Castañeda and others who failed to understand that the Latin American Lefts that had come to power were all moving along "the same path, in the same direction." "Intellectuals of diverse origin and the media," he went on, "have spent two years promoting the divisive idea that . . . several lefts exist: Fidel and Chávez are the crazies — and now they include Evo [Morales] too; and others, like Lula, [Ricardo] Lagos, Tabaré, and [Ernesto] Kirchner are 'statesmen.'" "Call us what they will, but we are going to give the right the greatest defeat ever on this continent, which will be remembered for 500,000 years!"[23]

By 2006, Chávez had completed eight years as Venezuelan president, during which he had bequeathed to his country a new name — the Bolivarian Republic of Venezuela — and an entirely different constitutional structure. In 2002, a US-supported civil-military coup had briefly imprisoned Chávez before falling apart; the reinstated Venezuelan president went on to decisively defeat a recall referendum and an opposition-led national oil company strike. In an era of rising international oil prices, Chávez achieved vast personal popularity — consistently winning just under two-thirds of the country's vote — while delivering concrete benefits to the impoverished majority. Of the leaders of Latin America's Left turns, Chávez attracted the most sustained and visceral international disdain, epitomizing, in Reid's words, "populist autocracy." "Strip away the verbiage," Reid continued, "and Chávez looks a lot like a typical military *caudillo*," a charismatic and messianic savior directly bonding with the masses through the media, a president who, lacking restraint, carries out a policy of unsustainable redistribution among a polity made up of clients, not citizens.[24]

By the time of the Caracas WSF, Chávez had arrived at a forceful anti-imperialist, antiliberal, and socialist rhetoric that he would come to call "twenty-first-century socialism." Those "who have lifted the flags of revolution," Chávez thundered to the forum, are on "a victorious offensive against the empire," with battles looming in Latin America, Asia, and Africa. "Representative democracy," he went on, "always ends up being a democracy of the elites and therefore a false democracy." He thus called for a new model, a "people's democracy, participatory and protagonistic," rather than one defined by "an elite that represents the 'people.'"[25] Indeed, his soaring radical rhetoric — which stood at the far left among those holding elected office — sounded less like a revival of Latin American populism, the eternal bête noire of the enlightened, and more like a rebirth of the Tricontinental Third Worldism espoused by the Cuban Revolution at its most radical point, in the 1960s.

By 2006, Chávez was a leftist hero to those seeking a more militant anti-imperialist and anticapitalist champion. He had also won admiration both for his role in founding the Bolivarian Alliance for the Peoples of Our America — an organization that served as a pole for those leaders of the pink tide further to the left, including the presidents of Bolivia, Ecuador, and Nicaragua — and for his bold advocacy of socialism. With his polarizing verbal polemics, Chávez sharply contrasted with the down-to-earth Lula, who eschewed braggadocio and flights of grandeur for carefully chosen words that often aimed to placate and neutralize, if not convince, those with whom he disagreed.

The assumption that Chávez was more "leftist" than Lula, however, is undermined if one goes back their first encounter, at the sixth FSP in El Salvador in 1996. Chávez described this earlier forum in his 2006 WSF speech, noting that its organizers voted to expel him and barred him from speaking. It is easy to see why Chávez's official participation was problematic for many of the leftists gathered in El Salvador. After all, the cashiered young military officer, who had recently been released from jail, had become famous as the head of two failed coup attempts against a democratically elected government, something bound to trouble those who had fought for a quarter century against military rule. Even if only in rhetoric, leftists traditionally idealized bottom-up mass organizing, representation of popular interests, and collective mobilization over the clandestine small-group politics of military conspiracies and the personalized exercise of leadership. His early rhetoric, directed against "corruption" and "oligarchical" elites, was a well-worn political language in Latin America used to justify intervention by the military—the incarnation of the "true" national interest—against discredited civilian rulers. The skepticism of the 1996 FSP attendees, in other words, reflected the Left's unhappy history of contending with any number of "messiahs of national salvation," often of uncertain loyalties, whose "populist demagoguery" won support that the Left felt should have been theirs. As Chávez himself put it at the 2006 WSF, they viewed him "with trepidation" as "a colonel who led a military coup. A caudillo."[26]

Since it first emerged in mid-twentieth-century Latin America, the political phenomenon that came to be known as populism was met with antipathy by liberals and Marxists. The paradigmatic populist was Argentina's Juan Perón, a colonel elected president in 1946 after cultivating workers and unions as a member of a military regime that had refused, for most of World War II, to declare war on the Axis powers. Both the country's socialists and Communists took the principled stance of rejecting a man they dubbed fascist, not entirely without justification. Allying with "oligarchical" liberals and conservatives in the 1946 election, Argentina's leftists made a tragic miscalculation at a historical turning point. By refusing to accept Peronism as an expression of working-class grievance and the popular will, the Left was condemned to electoral irrelevance over the following decades, their support reduced to a sector of the middle classes (the social group from which Che Guevara hailed). Thus Chávez's surprise FSP appearance in 1996 put an old issue on the table for a "New Left" generation in Latin America, including the PT, that had strongly condemned both the populist past, associated with Vargas and Perón, and an "older" Communist Left that had resigned itself to working within a world of popular politics decisively shaped by getulismo and Peronism.

Indeed, Chávez in the early 1990s was not a leftist in any ideological sense, his early ties to Venezuelan leftists limited to conversations with a few isolated survivors of a guerrilla force defeated in the five years after the 1959 Cuban Revolution. But his 1992 coup could only be understood as a sequel to the 1989 Caracazo, a wave of countrywide protest against the lifting of price controls by the newly elected president, Carlos Andrés Pérez, who during his earlier presidency, in the 1970s, had been a center-left friend of Fidel. The Caracazo was a massive repudiation of Pérez's "Grande Virada" toward neoliberalism and the IMF. The protests were ended in Caracas by a massacre in which at least 275 were killed, an event that shook the country's "model" democracy to the core. Chávez's bold military protest—for which he would be jailed—was met with broad approbation by diverse sectors of society, and even the political class would find it expedient to be sympathetic: Pérez was impeached, Chávez and his fellow rebels amnestied.

Chávez showed up in El Salvador committed to a virulent rejection of the status quo, and he saw the FSP as representing resistance in Latin American politics. Although known for his powerful emotional outbursts, Chávez described his response to the FSP rebuff humbly in 2006: "That's fine; I didn't come here to talk to the assembly. I came to see what this is all about, to learn, to learn . . . about movements, political parties, and leaders, to listen to speeches, to take good notes, to learn to integrate myself."[27] Lacking a leftist formation, Chávez was willing to accept a humiliation in 1996 in pursuit of the legitimation that he would eventually receive from the FSP.

Chávez's appearance was exactly the type of opportunity that Lula had anticipated at the FSP's 1993 Havana meeting, when he argued for the vital importance of alliances, "above all [with] the middle sectors of society who have no links to any political party" but are searching for solutions to neoliberalism.[28] To form such alliances, the Left had to overcome its obsession with leftist authenticity and sectarian distrust of nonleftist politicians and political forces. The actual practice of politics, after all, consists not of working out principles or ideologies on paper but, rather, of continually assessing forces and personalities as they emerge, unexpectedly and unpredictably, in the unfolding of events. What is often called pragmatism refers to the clarity that guides decisions when one knows the principal enemy—that is, the antagonists against whom one can unite difference.

In the 1990s, the Latin American Left had arrived at a shared understanding that the construction of a common front against neoliberalism was their primary objective, which allowed them to put questions of style and even, to a degree, substance to one side. Even at the time of his initial rejection by the FSP, Chávez was already a dynamic new factor in Venezuelan politics—a discomfiting one for existing leftist groups—as was the phenomenon of chavismo, which would make him president in 1998. Three years later, Chávez arrived at the 2001 Havana FSP as the first antineoliberal head of state, and the meeting's final declaration hailed the "singular political process" he had spearheaded in Venezuela.[29]

Chávez and Lula: Comparing the Men and Their Words

As Chávez told his WSF audience in 2006, "I always come" to such events "with the desire to reflect on issues and ideas. And there lies the perpetual dilemma—passion vs. reason—but both are necessary."[30] Many of those listening were seeking a more resolute and consequential "leftism" than that which characterized Lula's government. Yet despite the moral authority derived from his "in-your-face" leftist posture and invoked revolutionary political genealogy, Chávez cast a wide net. For instance, in this very radical speech to the WSF the Venezuelan president simultaneously criticized leftists who unfavorably compared him to Lula and his government: "Nobody can ask me to do the same as Fidel does, the circumstances are different; like Lula cannot be asked to do the same as Chávez; or Evo cannot be asked to do the same as Lula." Chávez recalled telling a largely Brazilian audience at the previous year's WSF in Porto Alegre that Lula "is a great man and that they have to work with Lula and support Lula," who like Chávez was seeking reelection in 2006.[31] (Both won with just over 60 percent of the final vote, Chávez in the first round.) How are we to understand his refusal to criticize Lula's moderation?

There is little reason to believe that Chávez, a man who routinely violated diplomatic protocol with harsh comments about the presidents and politicians of other countries, would have held his tongue if he felt betrayed or disappointed by Lula. Nor is it likely that this lack of criticism merely reflected Chávez's personal friendship with Lula or admiration for his history of struggle that links them as insurgents. It is far more plausible that his posture derived from the Venezuelan president's need for the favor of Lula and his government, in which case his position was opportunistic if predictable statecraft. Such a calculus certainly drove the favorable stance toward Lula adopted by US President George W. Bush, famously denounced by Chávez as the devil. Bush had been forced again and again—as late as 2007—to return to Lula for help in the region, just as Lula has repeatedly served as a vital guarantor for both the Chávez government and the Chávez-allied government of Evo Morales, despite the latter's abrupt nationalization of properties held by the Brazilian state-owned oil enterprise Petrobras. Moreover, Chávez was by no means unaware that Lula attracted support in sectors of global politics who were unenthusiastic about Chávez's own policies and discourse. It was this configuration of needs from Chávez and Bush that would allow Lula's government to retain the advantages of apparently incongruous alignments while refusing to allow either of the parties in conflict to force Brazil into a definitive position. In this way, the Lula government became an indispensable point of convergence—between the volatile Chávez and less friendly Latin American governments as well as between Chávez and a more powerful US government eager to see him out of power, each at various political distances to Lula's left and right.[32]

But Chávez's Caracas WSF speech also points to an additional reason for his benevolence toward Lula: the personal and affective. Personal ties had been built over time through one-on-one interactions and in the context of meetings, both before and after this remarkable generation of leftists reached power. The establishment of relations of trust and confidence also encompassed personal affection, which is attested to by all who came to know Lula personally. Writing after a visit by President Lula in 2008, the ill Fidel Castro offered his recollections about the "direct and vibrant" Lula, "astute and quick," who joked with the waiting reporters afterward "in a picaresque fashion and always smiling."[33] With Lula, relations between individuals are never reduceable to political positions or logics, even among "comrades" or "companheiros"; rather, such relationships were between unique individuals who, whatever their differences, could still establish a bond that reached beyond such external factors. In 2011, for example, Lula's improvised speech to the FSP began with a joke about speaking in Portuguese to an audience of Spanish speakers before offering a breezy reference to the early days of the FSP, when he had not a single gray hair and when Tomás Borge, cofounder of Nicaragua's FMLN, had all his hair; he went on to refer to Nicaragua's Daniel Ortega as having lost more elections than Lula had, ending with a wry comment: "As you can see, I have a lot of difficulty making any sort of opposition discourse after eight years in government."[34]

As Chávez observed at the 2006 WSF, while politics is about reason, it is also about passion and emotions, which serve to bind one to those one knows, likes, and respects. The power of personal connection was captured at the end of Chávez's speech to an audience of 15,000 at the 2005 WSF in Porto Alegre, when the Venezuelan president offered a declaration that, in being so human, was all the more deeply political: "I love Lula. I appreciate him. Lula is a good man with a great heart. He is a brother and compañero and I leave him my embrace and my appreciation."[35]

Regardless of such love and warmth, Chávez would unquestionably have preferred for Lula to follow policies more akin to his own and speak in the same tone. In the 2006 Caracas speech Chávez also reveals that hosting the WSF did not mean that he accepted the model of leftist politics implied by the WSF's new global thinking. Chávez clearly accorded status and legitimacy to this Brazilian-identified global convergence of leftists by hosting it in his country, but his speech also differentiated between his politics and those of Lula, the PT, and the largest current within the WSF. The Venezuelan president not only positioned himself to the militant Marxist left of the WSF but explicitly criticized its self-definition as not an organization but a process, "an open meeting place for reflective thinking, democratic debate of ideas, formulation of proposals, [and the] free exchange of experiences," as its charter puts it.[36] Rather than constituting a new leftist international, the WSF aspired to serve as a pluralistic space of encounter by civil society, a movement of movements, with stress on horizontality and autonomy.

While affirming his government's respect—in "an almost sacred way"—for "the autonomy of the social movements" represented at the Caracas WSF, Chávez showed little patience for rules that precluded formal WSF manifestos and plans of action. Making abundant use of military metaphors—offensives, victories, battles, retreats—Chávez insisted on the need both for "perfect strategy for the coming years" and "to link up all our causes." Without "unity, unity, unity," he warned, without "a united work plan, a united, universal plan of action" for the upcoming battles so "vital for the future of the world," the WSF risked becoming simply a "folkloric, tourist encounter." In contrast to the one mention of respect for diversity and autonomy, the word "unity" appears a dozen times in this section of Chávez's remarks, though he offers the revealing "clarification" that "no one is planning to impose anything on anyone, only coordination, unity"—in other words, an imposition. Chávez also signals disagreement with the WSF's ideological pluralism by abruptly ending this section of his speech with "Look, Karl Marx coined the phrase: 'Socialism or death'"—a misattribution.[37]

Chávez was clearly critical of what he deemed the WSF's diffuseness and excessively cautious politics; indeed, he was more openly critical of the WSF than of Lula himself. This explains why Chávez's presence at the 2006 WSF sparked some controversy, as did Lula's second appearance, in 2005, if for different reasons. Although welcome in a personal capacity under the WSF charter, both were elected heads of state when they visited as well as charismatic leaders whose rise to power was based on a relationship—constituted through identification, emotion, and imagination—with a mass base of tens of millions. Both were men of passion as well as reason; Chávez's primary identifier was anger, while Lula was known for his smiles, humor, and moments of tearful empathy.

Yet each leader established this mass relationship in distinctive ways. Beyond differing discursive repertoires, Chávez and Lula most starkly diverged in how they positioned themselves in relationship to their listeners. While Lula touches a "deeply messianic nerve of Brazilian popular imagination," he does so as one of the subaltern, a former metalworker who had "succeeded through his experience of the common" and whose individual success is presented as "expressly collective."[38] Chávez, by contrast, a former military man from a lower-middle-class family of teachers, rose to middling success within a core institution of the state as an officer, not a subaltern. Unlike Lula, his persona was not constructed through a sequence of combative mass struggles in dialogue with hundreds of thousands of followers. Rather, Chávez's political activism originated in the clandestine politics of small groups, and his rise from obscurity came as a revolutionary conspirator, the failed leader of a 1992 military coup against an elected government. The process of identification and the forging of imagined relations with Chávez began with his famous two words televised after his first coup attempt: "For now."[39] After a second failed coup, Chávez discovered his true talent: as a politician with a way with words, who would rise to power through electoral means. Unsurprisingly, Chávez had a very different relationship to the national imaginary, and the structure of feeling surrounding his success is quite different than in Lula's case, in which "one of us" has succeeded.

While Chávez initially aspired (most ineffectively) to a military seizure of power, the twists of history led him to transform his country's politics—for good or bad—through successive elections in tumultuous struggles, near defeats, and triumphs as president. Yet Chávez's "most potent weapon," noted Venezuelan literary critic Yolanda Salas in a 2004 interview, was "his use of language. He is someone who is skilled at wielding discourse and at fascinating the [deprived and excluded] masses. I call him the storyteller of Venezuelan politics. He's always got a great narrative, a great story, something great to say, something that seduces. . . . And if anyone knows the popular imaginary, it's Chávez." Yet Salas quickly deemed this skill a national tragedy, a sign that "Chávez has stolen the popular imaginary from us, because he uses it, he controls it, he manipulates it."[40]

Salas reminds us of the enormous gaps between the analytical vocabularies of intellectuals and the discursive realm of the subaltern as they emerged as a central force in Latin American polities over the past century. As anthropologist Luis Reygadas notes, contemporary intellectuals—and the documents and manifestos they write—prefer a language of liberal "citizenship, equality, inclusion, and intercultural dialogue." Yet these are weak narratives, he suggests, that cannot substitute for the "them-us" logic that structures "subaltern discourses of inequality [that] go back to a long history of plundering, discrimination, and exclusion." The images and tropes of these discourses are, he insists, not "a simple reflection of that history" but, rather, "active constructions that interpret the Latin American condition from the perspective and the interests of the excluded."[41]

To explain Chávez's and Lula's extraordinary trajectories, we must begin with the minutiae of their lives as biographical individuals. But we will understand nothing if we do not grapple with those who have followed, supported, and voted for them at different times across the decades. As Carlos de la Torre has noted, the appeal of populism or any form of mass popular politics cannot be understood without paying "serious attention . . . to the words, communications, and conversations *between* leaders and followers," because "the autonomous expectations, cultures, and discourses of followers are equally important in understanding the populist bond."[42] But even that focus is too narrow to meaningfully explain Chávez's and Lula's successes, whose roots can only be found in the entire spectrum of relationships that these two leaders established with all historical actors around them (whether supporters or opponents) and in how each man acted toward and in response to these actors (including media members and representations).

Chavista discourse, as it emerged, called for an end to the "pillaging, appropriation, and extermination" of the "*pueblo-pobreza*" that originated with the conquest but continued presently under a squalid corrupt oligarchy backed by foreign exploiters.[43] The parallel between Chávez's discourse and the subaltern representations of inequality analyzed by Reygadas are striking. These latter representations, Reygadas observes, "synthesize complex social processes into simple, dramatic images with emotional and ethical elements" by resorting "to the archives of historical memory to recuperate easily identifiable images: the abuse of colonial powers, the mistreatment of indigenous populations, black slavery." Subalterns use these anachronistic images "of another era with little correspondence to the present realities" to "interpret contemporary grievances," and "these temporal imbalances have symbolic and political efficacy: they settle accounts with the ghosts of the past." Given these qualities, as Reygadas goes on to note, such anachronistic rhetoric "should not be interpreted as [signs of] immobility or immutability"; rather, it is a product of "a continuous reconstruction that reclaims many elements of previous configurations but is also open to contingency and change."[44]

In these subaltern representations, Reygadas emphasizes, "the intentional aspects of inequality are generally underscored," and all guilt is attributed to the powerful. Material, moral, and psychological suffering is not represented as resulting from the disembodied processes and abstractions—market failures, globalization, capitalism—favored by intellectuals of all political outlooks. And the government and its leaders are considered most responsible for poverty and suffering, with the expectation that they will "be the chief component in its resolution" and will do so in a direct, immediate, and visible way.[45]

This is how chavismo arrives at its grandiose and direct identification between leader and nation, between leader and pueblo-pobreza, and between comandante and follower.[46] Hence Chávez's enthusiastic embrace of the role of pedagogue, speaking from center stage down to often-adoring audiences. This role thrilled Chávez from early on in his military career, as he relayed in a July 1977 letter to his parents about a patriotic lecture he had given to an audience of five hundred high school students in the name of the nation:

> When I was standing on the stage before beginning, the school choir sang the National Anthem. I then felt a great emotion, I felt the blood surge through my veins, and my spirit burned so much, that I gave one of my best presentations. . . . At the end, the students couldn't stop applauding, and . . . it seemed to me that I was carried away to a future time . . . [and] that it might be that I would achieve what I desired and become happy.[47]

Two years before this speech, Lula had been elected president of the São Bernardo metalworkers' union as an apparent patsy for its former president, rarely speaking publicly in these early years in union leadership. Lula, like the poor and subaltern, first had to fight to gain a voice in a society profoundly characterized by hierarchies and despotic rule, whether in politics, the factory, or the union. As we have seen, the common people (povo) had few illusions about the realities of power that they faced, and they had an acute awareness of their own misery combined with a deeply ingrained sense of being unjustly treated at the hands of the more powerful. The result was that manifest discontent coexisted with high levels of dissimulation within a mass consciousness permeated by a sense that the world was stacked against the poor, the weak, the colored, and the uneducated. "Lula was never a leftist extremist," Fidel observed in 2008, "nor did he rise to become a revolutionary on the basis of philosophical positions; rather he did so as a worker of humble origins and Christian faith who worked hard creating surplus value for others."[48]

A defining feature of these working folk's consciousness was their self-perception as small and weak; hence the cultivation of guile and cunning as their weapon of choice vis-à-vis the powerful. Cunning was also admired in those who wished to be leaders; hence the respect for Lula, who proved a master of being everything to everyone. For working people to achieve their hopes required a leader capable of maneuvering within existing power relations to take advantage of small rifts among the superordinate without being reduced to their power. Since defiance of superiors was immediately punishable, leaders had to be able to relate to and manipulate those antagonistic to one's interests and desires—even more so if one were committed to a transformative or struggle-oriented practice like Lula. At the same time, the price of such maneuvering was that the led might think the leader suspect, so it was essential that they believe in the leader's integrity, commitment, and loyalty. This is why leadership is a relationship and politics embodied work done with words; to lead successfully, as Georg Simmel noted, "all leaders are also led," and this can only occur when the leader is judged to be a reliably worthy recipient of one's faith as part of a pact of reciprocity.[49]

The central thrust of this book's overarching argument has been that leadership, understood as process and relationship (two-way, even if asymmetrical), is the causal link between mass consciousness and mobilization. Lula's practice of leadership shares much with that of Hugo Chávez, both of whom stood at the center of mass political phenomena. Yet Lula adopted a strategy of drawing people into a space for convergence across difference while maintaining a central focus on organizing the popular sectors on a more enduring and autonomous basis. Chávez, by contrast, preferred to attract diversity into a following around him, to act as their "representative," their epitome, their condensation—while conducting a relation between leader and led on a more top-down basis, characterized by individualism and a resort to unity and command, not convergence and persuasion.

An anthropological approach to politics as embodied work done with words by individuals in their relationship with others valorizes the social, cultural, and discursive and offers insight into two distinctive styles of charismatic political leadership within the twenty-first-century turn toward the left in Latin America. Lula's last four decades, in which he rose from trade unionism to the presidency and postpresidency, exemplify his leadership style, a transformative politics of cunning characterized by an additive politics, executed through the creation of spaces of convergence across difference, and carried out via an embodied work done with words in a popular vernacular.

17 THE PRESIDENT, A MAN OF HIS WORDS

Over Brazil's 520 years, the subaltern's fight to be heard has been extraordinarily difficult; for the colonial era's three centuries, less than a half dozen voices from the popular majority, most of whom were enslaved, have been preserved in the archives. A combative Lula, in the run-up to the tough 2006 election, referred to this fight when attacking those who say that "Lula wants to divide Brazil between the rich and the poor." "I was born with it already divided," Lula retorted, "and, unfortunately, I was born on the side of the poor. I could have been born to a sugar plantation owner, but I was born in the slave quarters [*senzala*]. It isn't me who is dividing Brazil. . . . And what I want is to divide up the bread that is produced in a more just way."[1]

From his May 1978 TV appearance on *Vox Populi*, the young torneiro mecânico impressed those he met with his clear capacity to lead and communicate. In April 1979, after his unprecedented feats during the massive fifteen-day strike, the *Folha de São Paulo* marveled, "It cannot be doubted that Lula is gifted with qualities that make of him a great leader: an agile, perspicacious, and adroit intelligence; a capacity and determination that comes close to voluntarism; a great ability to communicate expressed in a fluent and aggressive oratory with short and direct phrases; a great force of will, a lot of determination, and the spark of someone who really believes in himself; [accompanied by] an unequivocal seriousness of purpose that helps assure him a climate of trust and respect based on his authentic and engaged social representativeness."[2]

Three decades later, Ali Kamel, the powerful director general of journalism for the Rede Globo TV network, often critical of Lula, noted how Lula nevertheless is "a captivating person, affectionate, [and] playful," a man who "always has a smile on his lips, makes references to prior contacts, tells one or another joke or recounts a funny situation." Even Lula's physical manner—"small taps on the shoulder, holding his interlocutors' hand"—displays and attracts sympathy, even in the most politically delicate moments. Equally appreciative of Lula were industrialists against whom Lula led strikes, the head of the São Paulo DOPS, Romeu Tuma, who held Lula in jail in 1980, and even his fellow politicians, with whom he might publicly clash but whose private interactions were marked by Lula's grace and charm. As for Lula's communication skills, everyone who has heard him—whether in person, at a rally, or in a TV debate—has at some point found themselves drawn in, even when they disagree; thus, 80 percent of Brazilians gave Lula high marks in 2009–10. "Even among even his most acidic critics," Kamel notes, "no one doubts his immense capacity" to "make himself understood in a simple and efficacious way to both erudite and unlettered listeners."[3]

Kamel's study of Lula's presidential rhetoric emphasizes that Lula's uncommon talents are intertwined with his "concrete life experience, which occupies an absolutely central place in the way in which he sees the world." Kamel, known for criticizing Lula's government, was alone in researching what Lula did with his words as president between 2003 and 2008. Published in 2009, the *Dicionário Lula* crisply arranged Lula's discourse into a comprehensive 566 pages of double-column small-print excerpts, organized by topic for easy reference. As he notes in his ninety-page analytical essay, "Lula deserves to have his thought framed, measured, and evaluated," a task that will face "a battalion of historians and political scientists in the coming decades."[4]

Kamel's book shed more light on Lula's presidency than much of the academic literature, which has been structured around whether Lula's policies in office have broken with neoliberalism. Such arguments were mobilized not only by many leftist and academic critics of the PT government but also by center-right opposition figures, who opportunistically used emotionally powerful tropes of betrayal, disappointment, and lost illusions to provocatively question whether Lula ever was a leftist or whether the PT "can still be rightfully regarded as a party of the Left."[5] Brazilianist historian Joseph Love posed a far more fruitful question in his coedited 2009 book: "In what ways does the Lula government represent a break with the past?"[6]

In answering this, Kamel advances a bold claim: that Lula's life path was "so extraordinary and improbable (in Brazil or in any other part of the world) that he ended up feeling irremediably tied to his past." Lula's trajectory to the presidency was so implausible given where he came from, Kamel says, but it "would have been impossible without that very same origin." As a result, Lula's devotion to his past is presented by the president as "proof of his integrity, of his *ineditismo* [never-before-ness], and his pureness." It would be shortsighted to interpret this as merely opportunistic electoral rhetoric, because Lula's biographical peculiarity is the very basis on which he claims "competency and a commitment to good policies."[7] As Luis Felipe Miguel noted in his study of the 1994 presidential election, Lula had to "fight against the double defect of being 'ignorant' and 'inexperienced'" and did so by invoking lived experience (*vivência*). Along these lines, Haquira Osakabe had earlier emphasized how much Lula's speech as trade unionist was marked not by "formulated wisdom or political slogans" but by his ability to make "felt experience explicit."[8] Lula thus valorized the "empirical knowledge" suggested in a parable he told during his first campaign against sociologist FHC:

> The sociologist asks the fisherman if he knows what "transitory measures are." Or "provisional measures"? Or "budgetary items"? To which the fisherman replies successively, "no, sir." At the end the sociologist says, "How ignorant the common people (povo) are." A little later, the fisherman asks the sociologist: Do you know how I fish with a net? And this fish here, do you know its name? Or that one? The sociologist replied to each question with, "I don't know." Then it's the fisherman's turn to sum up: "It's not that the common people are ignorant. It's that our leaders don't know their people's way of life."[9]

Another reporter covering Lula that year noted how frustration over the dismissal of such knowledge fueled Lula's most emotional campaign speech, in Maceió, the capital of Alagoas: "He spoke from the heart and dreamed of a country without children living in the streets and repudiated the prejudice they foster against him because he doesn't have higher education. 'We are going to show them that a torneiro mecânico can do more for the country than the degree holders [doutores] who have perpetuated themselves in power.'"[10] Or, as he put it as president, "We only won because the Brazilian povo said: 'Wait a minute! These people have been running Brazil since [the explorer] Cabral got here 500 years ago. And . . . we're still in the same *pendura* [jammed up, in a financial bind]. Let's experiment with this peon who came from our environment."[11] This speaks to the gaffes, grammatical errors, and rhetorical infelicities, much exaggerated, that the educated relish in mocking.[12] What is clear, Kamel concludes, is that "Lula knows what he is doing [with his words], why he does it, and when: his objective is to communicate with all but to prioritize the 'povão' who make up the mass" of Brazil's citizenry.[13]

Lula's words also provide an avenue to address debates that had framed discussions during the Lula-Dilma era. To what extent did Lula's popularity reflect substantive achievements by his government? Was Lula's success as president an accomplishment to be hailed by the Left or a dubious deviation from leftist principles? What were the consequences of the shift in the PT's mass electoral base during Lula's presidential administration? And finally, has *petismo*, the PT's doctrinal core centered in the party, degenerated into populism and an amorphous cult of personality—lulismo—accompanied by a weak reformism, the fostering of mass consumerism, and a failure to raise the political consciousness of the millions who benefited from the Lula-Dilma government's policies?

This chapter thus returns to the ongoing fraught dialogue between the intelligentsia and São Paulo's popular classes—including FHC the professor and Lula the worker—while keeping an eye on the real-life consequences of Lula's policies, a point raised by none other than the hardnosed rebel Frei Chico. What his brother had achieved, he noted in November 2015, was "a certain amount of distribution of wealth within the general misery." This might not seem like much to some, Frei Chico went on, but it was a conquest for many other Brazilians—for, as Frei Chico reflected earlier to Paraná, "How many Lulas might there be around us if this country was a different place?"[14] By focusing on those invisible to the well-fed and well-placed, Frei Chico reminds us that Lula's gifts and talents must be seen in relation to the overwhelming majority of Brazilians denied not only a hunger-free decent life but even the opportunity to "be someone" with at least a minimal capacity to change his or her immediate world, however modestly. This will prove central to the assault on the New Republic's constitutional order in the form of a 2016 parliamentary coup against Lula's reelected successor, Dilma Rousseff, which set the country on a spiraling process of socioeconomic and political decomposition that led to the election as president of Jair Bolsonaro, an unreconstructed defender of the military, dictatorship, and torture.

Economic "Orthodoxy," Political Will, and Improving Lives

Facing a deteriorating macroeconomic situation, Lula's first term had been marked by substantial continuity and even austerity, which disappointed many on the left, even in the PT. The PT leadership conducted macroeconomic policy cautiously along the neoliberal lines established in the 1990s. Yet British historian Perry Anderson also notes that this same period, "viewed as a social process[,] . . . marked a distinct break" with Brazil's past.[15] Lula's government emphasized redistribution through what would become its flagship program, the Bolsa Família conditional cash transfer program.[16] Designed to replace his faltering Zero Hunger program and to consolidate existing targeted programs, Bolsa Família was rolled out and scaled up with ruthless efficiency to reach 11.1 million families (45 million members total) by the 2006 presidential election, an estimated 77 percent of those eligible nationally. In contrast to the payments made to the government's creditors or the country's relatively expensive pension system, the program costs an infinitesimally small percentage of the federal budget (2.5 percent).[17] As Lula likes to say, "It's cheap and easy to look after the poor."[18]

At the same time, Lula's government had begun or expanded a variety of programs and incremental initiatives whose impact was increasingly felt as economic growth accelerated in his second term. These included subsidized access to credit for low-income citizens, enhanced support for the elderly and for family agriculture, an ambitious public housing construction initiative, a program to provide universal access to electricity, the expansion of subsidized access to college education, and a vast enlargement of the federal university system. The government's continual increases in the minimum wage—higher by as much as 67 percent in real terms from 2003 to 2010—decisively affected income distribution.[19] During his second term, infrastructure investments also soared through the Program of Accelerated Growth (Programa de Aceleração de Crescimento), while per capita GDP between 2003 and 2009 grew on average by 2.9 percent annually, peaking at 7.5 percent in 2010.[20]

The Lula government was hardly the first administration since 1989 to generate real improvements in well-being. By ending the hyperinflation that especially hurt the poor, the 1994 Plano Real currency stabilization—the economic and electoral anchor of FHC's government—had generated real if discontinuous improvements. And Lula, long before 2002, had acknowledged low inflation and economic stability as a public good. Under Lula, however, the majority experienced continuous and accelerated improvements, including a dramatic reversal of the 1990s trend toward precarious employment due to the informal sector's expansion ("labor market flexibility," in neoliberal jargon).

Despite the inherited economic fragility, Lula's modest first term in office produced striking results, even while maintaining orthodox economic policies. The government's new social policies had by that term's end reduced absolute poverty by 15 percent.[21] These positive results countered the expectations of many scholars—from the right, center, and left—who had doubted the feasibility of reducing inequalities while guaranteeing basic subsistence for every citizen. For neoliberals, short-term suffering from "bitter but necessary medicine" was needed for the economy's long-term health, and "handouts" were deemed pernicious. Yet even many Marxist and leftist economists assumed that, barring structural reforms, the "prospects of material improvement in the short term [we]re not good" for the "fifty million people currently liv[ing] below the poverty line."[22]

Given Brazil's entrenched regional, racial, gender, and class disparities, the second term's results were all the more striking with up to 15 million new jobs created, 23 million people moved above the poverty line, and another 30 million reaching "lower-middle-class" status. This has further legitimated the Left's argument—repeatedly invoked by Lula as a trade unionist and as president—that increased popular consumption provides the best foundation for economic growth and that government-directed redistribution works. Unemployment fell to the lowest levels ever recorded, and the ongoing increase in the minimum wage's purchasing power—which affects remuneration in the formal and informal sectors—improved workers' leverage. With a government favorable to social dialogue and former labor leaders holding key government positions, the bargaining environment for trade unions—in which about a fifth of the formal workforce participates—was favorable, with 78 percent of salary negotiations in 2008 resulting in raises above inflation, 80 percent in 2009, and 89 percent in 2010.[23] Such progress would continue under Lula's successor, as Rousseff's government acted on efforts to guarantee equal labor rights to domestic servants, including retirement and vacation days, through a 2012 constitutional amendment approved by the national Congress (the only opposing vote was from Jair Bolsonaro).[24]

While the Brazilian GDP had grown less quickly than China's, Brazil's growth, unlike China's, brought significant decreases in income inequality. Brazil saw substantial real increases in income by the popular classes since 2003, with the greatest gains for those at the bottom, significant but smaller improvements in the middle, and the smallest increases going to the top 10 percent of earners.[25] In attacking poverty and inequality, Lula's government had also shifted public discourse enough that observers could argue that "poverty reduction is now at the centre of the political debate."[26] By his second term's end, fewer Brazilians would publicly affirm—whether fatalistically or out of convenience—that "the poor will always be with us," although most now believe that Bolsa Família will be, even under Brazil's current far right president. Presidential candidates after 2006 had all declared their allegiance to this program, and it was hoped—despite some prejudice in the middle and upper classes, especially in the richer states—that nonpoor citizens had come to feel good about the significant amelioration of poverty's most extreme manifestations such as endemic hunger, as Lula had promised at his first term's beginning.

By his second term's end, millions of Brazilians would become more fully citizens as waged working people and active consumers, more fully endowed with and assertive about their rights.[27] Perry Anderson rightly deems Lula's second term "a much more confident affair." While Anderson likely exaggerates in dubbing Lula's second term "a radicalisation in government," by its end Lula undoubtedly had fulfilled his pledge to not "repeat what I accomplished in my first term. Now we have to innovate. And for God's sake, do not make the error of using the word development or economic growth without adding the phrase, redistribution of income."[28] The confluence of positive economic developments and credible government initiatives led to extraordinary, sustained personal popularity for Lula. His approval ratings would reach 80 percent on the eve of Rousseff's 2010 victory with 56 percent of the second-round votes.[29] At the campaign's outset, Dilma's opponent José Serra—defeated by Lula in

2002—went out of his way to deny being against Lula, who, he famously declared, "is above good and evil."[30] "By any criterion," as Anderson put it, the outgoing Lula was "the most successful politician of his time," an opinion shared publicly by US president Barack Obama in 2009.[31]

Undoubtedly, the contemporary impact of Lula's success as president was to enhance the popular majority's self-esteem, especially in the Northeast. His rise unexpectedly challenged the internalized prejudices and self-inhibiting behaviors bred by a domineering and paternalistic authoritarian society laced with racism and sexism. Yet the advances of the Lula-Dilma era, while significant and substantial, fell far short of resolving Brazil's social ills (*mazelas socias*), so eloquently denounced by generations of Brazilian reformers. While Brazil did make history by electing a woman president in 2010, the country still was ranked 142nd for the percentage of women in national legislative offices (9 percent, versus a worldwide average of 18 percent).[32] And the government's commitment to broadening opportunity for the popular classes and Afro-descendants will not yield fruit until today's first-generation college students finally rise within the country's political and administrative structures. Even the modest symbolic down payment for Brazil's African-descended majority shows how far Brazil still has to go; after the 2010 elections the percentage of self-identified blacks in the Chamber of Deputies nearly doubled, to forty-three, 8.5 percent of the seats in a country almost half of whose population is African-descended or mixed.[33]

Redistribution, Recognition, and Expanding Opportunity

Since its founding, the PT has been the country's only party with an active mass membership (between 500,000 and 800,000 registered members in 2000) and has enjoyed significant internal cohesion, a powerful advantage for its leader.[34] Moreover, it is the only party with a well-established partisan following among voters. While most express no party identification in national polls, one in four identified with the PT; the 2005 corruption crisis only reduced support to one in five, where it stands today. The only other parties with even a modest degree of partisan identification—the opposition PSDB and the centrist PMDB—were each the declared preference of less than one in twenty voters in 2003, despite together obtaining 46 percent of the national vote in 2002.[35]

Yet one key element of petismo's success traditionally went unexamined until the 2006 presidential elections: its founder's extraordinary appeal, far greater than his party's. The PT, whose membership (as opposed to sympathizers) was largely middle class, unsurprisingly saw themselves in terms of party and campaign platforms, ideology, and principles; their high appreciation of companheiro Lula was deemed "nonpersonalist" on principle.[36] Yet in the presidential contests after 1994, the PT candidates' vote share never came close to Lula's: 35 percent of Lula's vote total in 1994, 41 percent in 1998 and 2002, and 30 percent in 2006, 2010, and 2014.[37]

A purist brand of petismo had begun to fade during the 1990s as party leaders realized that Lula's story, personality, and charisma were key to winning the presidency.[38] Once Lula was elected, his popularity and influence—now dubbed lulismo—far outstripped that of his party and his governing coalition, dwarfing the organized social movements out of which his leadership had emerged. During his first term, the gap between the government's policies and the PT's historic program strained petista identities. When corruption scandals in 2005 felled top PT leaders, deputies, and ministers, Lula's standing with the general population had to carry the day in the 2006 elections. Lula's fate came down to the popular vote because the opposition decided not to seek impeachment, uncertain regarding possible downsides and confident that the cornered president could be defeated electorally. (They would not make this mistake again.)[39]

The 2006 results were a stunning, emphatic victory for Lula and a crushing defeat for his PSDB opponent.[40] Afterward, the discussion of lulismo intensified. Although winning by the same margin in 2002 and 2006, his vote distribution had shifted significantly in terms of region, class, and education level. For the first time in Lula's five presidential races, as Simone Bohn observed, income level was negatively correlated with the likelihood of voting for Lula. Lula "lost ground among college-educated voters" and experienced his "greatest growth among Brazilians with fewer years of formal schooling."[41] The second-round vote also showed disproportionate support for Lula from those who self-identified as black (74 percent) and brown (67 percent) compared to white (52 percent), although Lula's support was only mildly stronger among men than women.[42]

Scholars mainly analyzed the 2006 results via the electoral impact of Bolsa Família. Wendy Hunter and Timothy Power concluded that "a fairly straightforward 'pocketbook' explanation goes a long way toward accounting for Lula's victory."[43] Others argued that Bolsa Família decisively fueled the party's growth in "less populated and poorer municípios" and among populations not traditionally supportive of the PT.[44] Still others framed Lula's new vote as part of a long-established "tendency of poorer regions to support the incumbent [presidential] candidate" for needed federal handouts, thus reflecting textbook clientelism.[45]

Emphasizing simple economic gain in explaining Lula's vote echoes well-established Brazilian ideas about the lack of independence of the country's poorest voters, traditionally seen by their social superiors as ill-informed, easily fooled, and cheaply bought, susceptible to charismatic leadership, demagoguery, and clientelism. As French political scientist Stéphane Monclaire noted in his excellent analysis, in 2006 most voters with four years or less of education (half the electorate) were unlikely to know the political connotations of Left and Right or how to place parties within such a spectrum.[46] It was an analytical flaw, however, to thereby revert to stereotypes about such voters' "lack of a political position, their alienation, or irrationality." Unlike politicized intellectuals, their experience of the political has "to do with the necessary relation between politics and the everyday."[47]

Having led "peons" in massive metalworker strikes, Lula understood that the decisive battle is always for a constituency's mass, not its politicized minority. In a country that originated Paulo Freire's "pedagogy of the oppressed" and liberation theology, the party and social movement Left in Brazil had advanced since the 1970s because it better understood the empirical contours of mass consciousness. The Left had arrived at an ethnographic approach to politics that recognized the integrity and diversity of popular understandings, logics, and discourses.[48] By contrast, intellectuals' political analyses, as one Brazilian anthropologist has noted, are typically rooted in an impoverished "theory of interests" derived from a "muscular and reductionist sociology," a utilitarianism also common to political scientists and many Marxists. Consider the provocative and much-cited 2009 essay by the capable USP political scientist André Singer, a petista who had served as Lula's spokesperson from 2003 to 2007. Singer posits a poorly defined lulismo characterized by "weak reformism," sharply distinct from the PT of 1989. Singer then links this lulismo to an abstract category—the subproletariat—which he defines in terms of weak structural insertion into the labor market and location in the Northeast. Without empirical evidence, Singer then imputes to this amorphous group a passive, conservative disposition and a consciousness—"the maintenance of stability with state distributive action"—analogous to the French peasants supporting Napoleon III in 1848, as described by Marx.[49]

Such economistic structuralism has been rightly rejected by Brazil's political anthropologists, who instead study popular electoral behavior by focusing on "the role of figurative elements of discourse" from both politicians and voters, including the use of "metaphors, ironies, ambiguity, paradox, and hyperbole."[50] The poor and less educated do not simply reproduce inherent dispositions at the ballot box; their votes reflect lessons learned from their own political experiences. Understanding the poor as part of local communities shows how they increasingly changed their minds about Lula, as part of an evolving dialogue going back to 1989 (the elderly poor, for example, were the last group to shift decisively toward Lula in 2006).[51] Like the highly educated, they are independent actors with their own histories; their thinking and decisions change in response to events.[52]

In a deeply divided society like Brazil, the president has always been a vector for popular desires for material improvement, recognition, and inclusion. Thus, rather than pitting a false lulismo against an idealized petismo, we should better understand what lulismo, understood as the societal interpretations of Lula leading to his mass popularity, adds to petismo, seen as a more focused partisan loyalty, and how both have altered the electorate's consciousness. Lula's longtime collaborators, such as his former secretary-general Luiz Dulci, have recognized his personal charisma but have suggested that it is "tied to a collective project of social emancipation, not a personalist one."[53] While true, this should not obscure a striking aspect of Lula's public discourse seemingly unrelated to collective action. From the outset of his political career, Lula has insistently developed motifs and arguments promoting the dominated's self-esteem and affirming their capacity for individual social mobility.[54] For instance, after his defeat in 1989 Lula highlighted the subalterns' lack of self-esteem:

> The worker has a prejudice against the worker. He thinks he can't be anything more than a worker. The black has prejudice against blacks. The woman has prejudice against women. Women don't vote for women, blacks don't vote for blacks, and workers don't vote for workers. . . . People have a cultural formation to think that power is something for really fancy people, that the poor's only job is to work and that's the end of the story.[55]

A living repudiation of the country's entrenched prejudices, Lula's upward mobility and personality empowered the weak by encouraging their pride in sharing, even if vicariously, in the success of one of their own. During Lula's presidency, a young Afro–North American political scientist asked African-descended people in Salvador, Bahia, Brazil's most African-identified and African-descended city, to name a black politician. Unlike in São Paulo, the single most common answer (18 percent) was Lula, especially among respondents who self-identified with the darker "color" category (preto). The responses suggested how Lula's combination of stigmatized features—manual labor, lack of education, and poor command of formal Portuguese—could contribute to his symbolic blackening, a sociocultural dynamic reflected in the fact that Lula and his chosen successor disproportionately received electoral support from people of color.[56] Impossible to glean from election results (and seldom the focus of public opinion polls), Lula's personal success story thus contributed to a "cognitive transformation" among millions of the country's self-identified "little people."[57]

And the government's politics of recognition does not run counter to popular mobilization, as so many who invoke lulismo seem to believe. Even though the Central Bank and the Treasury remained in elite hands, Lula's government most clearly distinguished itself from its predecessor by boldly tackling the hierarchies of worth that so powerfully characterized Brazilian society. Those obsessed with leftist economic developmentalism judged the government a failure for not making a decided effort to transform the socioeconomic order of Brazilian capitalism. But if one focuses on policy arenas made newly important by Lula's administration—and often dismissed by those critics focused on an immediate clash with concentrated wealth—a different picture emerges that highlights the indissolubly related politics of class and color in a country where 53 percent of the population is African-descended. As we have seen, social class, education, and region are all routinely and unconsciously read in racial terms among Brazilians, who despite shifts in recent decades continue to use social class and status as the metalanguage for articulating questions of race and class while obscuring the specificity of these domains.[58]

Unable to massively redistribute wealth through a progressive tax reform, President Lula from the outset frontally attacked racial inequality, discrimination, and racism through gestures that carried powerful symbolic weight. His first cabinet included five black ministers—compared to token representation in previous administrations—and Lula would even name the country's first black Supreme Court justice, Joaquim Barbosa. In his very first year in office, Lula also supported a law long demanded by black movements mandating the teaching of African and Afro-Brazilian history and culture at all schools, private and public. And three months after Lula's inauguration, a cabinet-level Special Secretariat of Policies to Promote Racial Equality (SEPPIR) was established, a long-standing demand of black activists, whether petistas or not. Lula also spoke far more bluntly about race than FHC, who had been much praised as the first president to formally recognize that Brazil suffered from racial discrimination. "At least half of our Brazilian people—the black and overwhelmingly impoverished half—have been seriously harmed by racism and discrimination," Lula declared in inaugurating SEPPIR, as "64 percent of those living in poverty and at least 70 percent of indigents are black. Blacks also number greatest among the unemployed and underemployed populations of our country." Lula further stressed that "this cruel and unjust situation" cannot be explained away simply as "a direct product of our national history" of slavery, which has left "profound and indelible marks on our society." Rather, the main responsibility lay with "the absence of public policies created to ameliorate and eradicate it." The Brazilian government, he went on, cannot "remain neutral on issues of race and racism" but instead must "actively ensure that all Brazilians are granted equal opportunities in the pursuit of a better life."[59]

Nor did Lula's government abandon the drive to enhance popular participation, although its intensity and forms diminished compared to the heroic years of the 1970s. While elite politics had become more central to the government's capacity to produce achievements, Lula as president convened an unprecedented series of national conferences involving nearly 5 million from civil society and public administration around various public policy topics, including women's rights (in 2004 and 2007), the fight for racial equality (in 2004 and 2009), and LGBTQ rights (in 2008).[60] Woefully understudied, this systematic mobilization of civil society has been, as a Brazilian PSDB supporter noted, a strategic move by Lula's administration to encourage "nongovernmental organizations to use national policy conferences and other social-communications methods to pressure Congress."[61]

Such mobilization was also central in the Lula-Dilma government's fostering of the "solidarity economy," a network of cooperatives with central government support. One of the most symbolically powerful and successful of these cooperatives is the one dedicated to the country's estimated 800,000 trash pickers living in and around major garbage dumps. The organization has created a national movement in which these people are celebrated as pioneering recyclers with an exalted environmental mission. During his presidency, Lula spent each Christmas Eve night with the trash pickers, bringing his candidate Dilma along on December 24, 2010, to meet 2,000 attendees from around the country. The hall where they met was bedecked with slogans: "The fight is good, the fight is hard, the fight continues"; "The street picks, the street sings, the street enchants with struggle." In interviews, participants recalled companheiro Lula as the first president who ever cared about them, hailed their individual material gains such as buying their own homes, and insisted that Lula's administration "was better for the poor than others. He gave food and work. The poor are happy with what he has done." Once societal outcasts, they hailed their new autonomy and insisted, "We don't ask for things. We demand that which is ours by right."[62]

Hints that Lula might choose a female successor for president came as early as July 2004, when he addressed the First National Conference of Policies for Women. "Contemporary democracy cannot be limited to economic and political rights," because "gender equality is an inalienable part of social justice in today's world."[63] At the second conference on women's rights three years later, 2,300 feminists and women activists of all backgrounds, colors, and cultures, gathered in Brasília, heard this former metalworker declare that no country can be considered "modern and developed" unless economic growth benefited "all without exclusion and without perpetuating historical inequalities, be they of gender, race, or any other type." Lula hailed Michelle Bachelet's election to the

Lula and Marisa with Dilma at her 2010 inauguration as president. (Courtesy DGABC [Ricardo Trida])

Chilean presidency as "an extraordinary ideological advance," while mentioning by name female presidential candidates in Argentina (Cristina Kirchner, Elisa Carrió), Paraguay (Blanca Ovelar), and the United States (Hillary Clinton). When the country's most popular political leader began to say, "I hope that here in Brazil," he was interrupted by roaring applause, screaming, and shouting at the hint that he might support a woman as his successor.[64]

Less than a year later, Lula began to float the candidacy of Dilma Rousseff, his chief of staff, who had taken over after the mensalão corruption crisis had ousted her predecessor, the powerful PT leader José Dirceu. Although not a lifelong petista, Rousseff was selected as the PT's presidential nominee. Lula's decisive support helped a onetime student guerrilla and PhD-holding technocrat, a woman who had never before run for office, achieve a remarkable political triumph. Yet the election of Brazil's first female president was in keeping with Lula's own rise, which had smashed precedents and rewritten the rules at every step.

Like her predecessor Dirceu, Dilma was from the rebellious student generation of 1968 and had been part of a worker-oriented Marxist group committed to armed struggle.[65] Charged with teaching revolutionary theory to workers, she was subsequently arrested and tortured and spent several years in jail—

experiences differentiating her from her middle- and upper-class peers.[66] "Because of what I went through," she told a reporter from the opposition newspaper *Folha de São Paulo*, "I came to understand many things, [including] the value of democracy." Rousseff refused, however, to apologize for the militant tactics of her youth: "I don't have the same mind-set that I had then. It would be strange if I did. It would even be pathological. People change during their life, we all do. [But] no, I didn't change sides. That's a matter of pride for me. I only changed my methods and vision."[67]

Yet the student movement in which she was active in the 1960s was a tiny and unrepresentative slice of Brazilian society, almost entirely white and overwhelmingly of middle- and upper-class extraction. The broadening of the composition of university students would come only with the expansion of higher education in the early 1970s under the military government, which gave the student movements of the late military period a more representative hue.[68] Once the PT reached power, the Lula government and its successor devoted energy and resources to radically broadening the paths to social mobility through an ambitious higher education expansion and reform that can only be considered a revolution.[69]

This vast expansion of educational opportunity, duplicated for vocational training as well, was accompanied by the implantation of bold affirmative action policies, codified in law for higher education in 2012 and later extended to civil service employment.[70] Unlike the United States, the Brazilian system involves quotas and was constructed so as to be truly intersectional—taking into account color, public school attendance, family income, and disability—and designed to reflect the racial composition of each state. Often inaccurately referred to as affirmative action for race and class, the impact of these policies—which I studied from 2016 to 2019 at a new tuition-free federal university branch in Rio's Baixada Fluminense—vividly illustrates the subversive impact of expanding social mobility among the poor, colored, and stigmatized.[71]

The establishment of a new federal university campus in Nova Iguaçu, the Multidisciplinary Institute of the nearby Federal Rural University of Rio de Janeiro, has had positive repercussions for students and their families as well as local businesspeople and politicians; this wide approval by the local populace has been repeated at each of the new federal universities or campuses established under the Lula-Dilma administration, often located in poor and/or geographically neglected urban and rural spaces. While enrollments expanded sharply at federal university campuses overall, the government's policy of expanding access reached beyond the tuition-free public sector to include an even more rapid expansion of private higher education—accompanied by guaranteed student fellowships with affirmative action—at the lower-quality but ubiquitous for-profit sector. It is also vital that neither increased access nor affirmative action were a "gift" from on high. In the Baixada, there had been an organized mass campaign demanding the creation of a federal university in 2003; in addition, it was precisely the fight for university access for Black and poor students—with a leading role played by the region's Black liberationist Catholics—that placed the demand for quotas on the political agenda in the state of Rio, which adopted quotas in 2001, and that subsequently spread from university to university until codified in national law.[72]

Brazil is not only a starkly unequal country, socioeconomically and racially, but also one averse to recognizing the impact of racism and how far it falls short of its declared ideal of "racial democracy." Not surprisingly, quotas in higher education were widely criticized by the middle and upper classes, and a senator from the conservative opposition Democratas would go on to file a September 2009 Supreme Court appeal against the adoption of admission quotas by race at the University of Brasília. In April 2012, the Brazilian Supreme Court made history by unanimously affirming the constitutionality of affirmative action. The leading decision by Judge Ricardo Lewandowski began by rejecting the "biological notion of race" while emphasizing that "the reduced number of *negros* or *pardos* who exercise high posts" in Brazil was due to "camouflaged or implicit discrimination that still exists in the shadow of a complacent State."[73] As Brazil's chief attorney told the court on July 30, 2009, "[The] principle of equality does not mean that individuals should be treated identically in any and every situation; on the contrary, the realization of equality demands, in certain cases, different types of legal treatment for people who are unequal—like, for example, that which occurs with so-called 'affirmative action.'"[74]

During the Lula-Dilma administration, millions of new first-generation college students of color and working-class in origin would graduate, although their achievements have been largely invisible to—if not criticized by—the established middle and upper class.[75] Like Lula's generation of young skilled workers and SENAI graduates, this minority of college-educated individuals are driven, energetic, and sensitive to their stigmatization by those above.[76] It is these children of Lula and Dilma, along with their families, who have been most visibly on the front lines of recent protests against Temer's and Bolsonaro's regressive higher education policies and in opposition to conservative attempts to turn back the clock. When Lula visited the Multidisciplinary Institute on December 8, 2017, as part of a campaign swing in Rio, the student response was electric, as reflected in the photograph below and on this book's cover. Filmed that day for a short campaign video, one of the five students interviewed recog-

Lula at the Multidisciplinary Institute of the Federal Rural University of Rio de Janeiro in December 2017. (Courtesy Ricardo Stuckert)

nized that these were somber times but declared that they well understood why right-wingers are angry at "the son of the poor being able to study in the same classroom as the son of the executive."[77]

The Professor, the Worker, and the Troll

A year after Lula's inauguration, Brazilian journalist Paulo Markun published a book on the intertwined trajectory of the two "emblematic" figures of the New Republic: Lula the toad, "the first Brazilian of really popular origin to reach the presidency," and his predecessor FHC, the prince described as from a "middle-class family in Rio"—a questionable claim given a genealogy including ten generals, two ministers of war, a president of the Brazilian Central Bank, a senator, and a Rio mayor. As FHC told *Veja* in 1994, "I am from the dominant class. My father and grandfather gave orders [*mandaram*] in this country." By contrast, he suggested, Lula was "radical and unprepared."[78]

Perhaps nothing better expresses Brazil's trajectory over the twenty years separating FHC's 1994 election win and the dubious, ill-advised 2016 impeachment of the democratically reelected Dilma Rousseff than Brazil's newly elected president in 2018. Bolsonaro should force us to recast the opposition between FHC and Lula, the latter convicted and jailed in 2018 with FHC's approval on bogus charges that aimed to knock him out of the 2018 presidential race. The country's current president, the fascistic far right troll Jair Bolsonaro, has long attacked both FHC and Lula equally as "Communists." Indeed, the federal deputy from Rio spent the late 1990s attacking FHC for using human rights to coddle bandits and vagabonds while heading "the most corrupt government in the history of Brazil." In 1998–99, Bolsonaro not only called for the national Congress's closure but repeatedly insisted that President Cardoso should face a firing squad. Asked by a TV interviewer whether democracy was nonsense, Bolsonaro replied that it had "failed in Brazil" because the country simply wasn't ready for it: "Democracy is excellent but only with honest democrats."[79]

Bolsonaro's aggressive, arrogant, and harshly prejudiced rhetoric, which has continued during his presidency, had long been combined with provocations, insults, and threats of torture and death directed at subversives and bandits; this is the arrogant, irresponsible voice of the military regime's dungeon, which tortured Lula's brother and killed hundreds of citizens without mercy or trial. Throughout his career, Bolsonaro has proudly stood outside the New Republic's democratic consensus; his fascist, racist, and sexist posturing has always attracted attention, including ample reproach, but at no cost given his political marginality. Instead, he has continuously given public expression to the authoritarian substratum of Brazilian society while gambling that power could be gained in the end by exploiting the everyday prejudices of fellow Brazilians, especially self-styled homems de bem, against the weak—women, blacks, Indians, gays, northeasterners, manual laborers, environmentalists, and political radicals—as well as politicians (deemed corrupt), the uneducated, and the overeducated.

To understand Bolsonaro's 2018 victory requires a better understanding of the pact that underlay two decades of seemingly successful consolidation of socially aware electoral democracy. It is easy to forget how, coming less than a decade after military rule, even FHC's election was an enormous shock to conservatives like Bolsonaro. FHC not only was a cosmopolitan intellectual, unlike his predecessors, but had also been a young Communist turned independent Marxist theorist in a country whose "conservative classes," including politicians and the military, had long outlawed "subversive agitation" linked to foreign ideologies; even Getúlio Vargas, Brazil's most "progressive" president, was violently anti-Communist and authoritarian.

Yet somehow the leftism of FHC's early decades—from his flamboyance in the 1950s and early 1960s to his maturity in the 1970s—was quickly forgotten after becoming president. In the newly reconfigured polity, the Left came to view FHC as the chief "rightist" political figure, while he was adopted as patron saint by a large swath of Brazil's middle and upper classes. Unlike Lula, FHC did not rise to the presidency via popular appeal. Although twice elected president, FHC was never "good for votes"; his first attempt at an executive position—São Paulo's mayorship—was an epic failure. Even his own pollster in 1994 emphasized that the elegant FHC's major obstacle was his "lack of closeness with the povo," which came naturally to Lula in his manner, vocabulary, and speeches.[80] FHC was not a good student of politics in this regard.

FHC had entered electoral politics in 1978 as an alternate, finally joining the Senate when André Franco Montoro stepped down to become São Paulo's governor in 1983. FHC was widely viewed as the "icon of the combative intellectual of the Brazilian Left"—though he was never as far left as the PT.[81] His new peers, by contrast, were long-term politicians linked to powerful state oligarchies; practical men of power with strong local electoral support, they were at best mildly impressed by FHC's brilliance and intellectual flights of fancy. A man of ambition, FHC got a credible shot at a presidential candidacy after gaining his first ministerial appointment under President Itamar Franco, who had replaced the impeached Collor (FHC had toyed with becoming Collor's foreign minister when his government was in crisis, but wiser minds in the PSDB dissuaded him).[82] In the PSDB's retrospective telling, FHC as finance minister led a small band of economists, smarter than all the rest, and brilliantly solved hyperinflation, in appreciation of which the majority of the Brazilian electorate voted for him twice as president. The Left explains FHC's election as a reward for adhering to US-led neoliberalism, in betrayal of his leftist past. Both are convenient fictions that ignore how both the PT and PSDB were left of center in 1994 and even initially agreed not to savage each other in the first round to allow for cross-party support if one of their candidates advanced to the second round against a right-wing candidate.[83] Indeed, many left-of-center and even leftist voters cast a pragmatic vote for FHC in the first round as the best hope for change.

In truth, FHC's electoral base outside São Paulo in the first presidential campaign came from the conservative mainstream of Brazil's political class, especially the Liberal Front Party (PFL), the old ARENA, and some sectors of the PMDB, the party that FHC had abandoned. It was the great regional political bosses, especially the Bahian caudilho Antônio Carlos Magalhães, who not only delivered votes but also exercised great sway over the political "lower clergy," the rank and file of elected representatives with neither voice nor influence.

Lacking a compelling national candidate themselves, fearing a repeat of 1989's polarized second round, and reeling from the impeachment of Collor, the candidate whom they had backed in that election, conservatives supported FHC in what Lula has called the greatest political pact in Brazilian history. Agglomerating the great regional bosses, especially in the Northeast, the PFL "only assimilated Fernando Henrique Cardoso after May 1994," Lula observed, "when they saw that I had 50 percent in the polls." According to Lula, they found in FHC the perfect candidate, "an intellectual with a tradition of struggle for democracy in the country [and] a good penetration among European intellectuals, the Catholic Church, and the middle sectors." At its root, FHC "was what every middle-class person wanted to be. The intellectual, speaking English, French, and I don't know what else."[84] But the PFL's vital support came at a price for the PSDB, which included top politicians, like São Paulo's Mário Covas, with combative leftist histories going back to 1968. Running as the purportedly sane Left compared to the radical PT, Covas in 1989 had briefly employed the rhetoric of "capitalist shock" to disrupt Brazil's backward economy and patrimonial culture. Building on this, FHC now more forcefully emphasized that the Left could not, after the fall of the Berlin Wall, cling to nationalist and statist dogmas unless they wanted to be "the vanguard of backwardness" in a globalizing world.[85]

Perhaps the main contribution of FHC and the PSDB-PFL pact, rather than curbing Brazil's hyperinflation, was to civilize the Brazilian Right and marginalize its crazies. While embracing a neoliberal economics inimical to the Left, FHC remained faithful to democratic norms during his two terms. While his administration had sharp conflict with oil industry workers, FHC did not set out to destroy Brazil's labor laws or trade unions, and he acknowledged both Brazil's human rights problems, including police torture, as well as the historical injustices inflicted on the black majority while recognizing the need to right the imbalances in the countryside. And most importantly for the Lula administration's success, FHC handled the presidential transition with equanimity as part of the rules of the game rather than polarizing the nation against the new president.

Yet FHC's tolerance of Lula was wearing thin by the end of the latter's first term. At this time FHC published two autobiographies (one of them ghostwritten) revealing how deeply he shared his country's aristocratic fixation on linguistic capital as markers of social class and worth. FHC highlights how Lula's "grammar was atrocious," while graciously attributing this to Lula's lack of education. Likewise, FHC condemns the "two thugs" who briefly interrogated him for DOPS in 1976 (his only experience with police repression) as "barely capable of speaking correct Portuguese."[86] Discussing Lula, FHC strikingly makes no attempt to conceal the sentiments that he shares with those who

Lula and Marisa with President Fernando Henrique Cardoso and Ruth Cardoso, 2003. (Courtesy DGABC [Rivaldo Gomes])

had, by then, become his "natural" constituency as the PSDB's wise man. The distinguished sociologist reports that when he first met Lula in 1973, he treated the then-lowly first-term member of the union diretoria "almost like the subject of a [social] science experiment."[87] He describes his first meeting with Lula at the São Bernardo union headquarters as "shocking, . . . [at least] in terms of the perceptions of a university professor educated within traditional formalities."[88] As he recalled, "I was escorted to a small smoky office where Lula sat, squinting, behind a wooden desk. Several burly men stood menacingly behind him, their arms folded. Lula regarded me for a long moment and then got right down to business."[89] This is a central scene for FHC because during it he receives the support of Lula's union for his Senate candidacy. For twenty months thereafter FHC was in consistent contact with Lula, even leafleting with him, while participating in the discussions that would lead to the PT's founding (FHC did not join).

While FHC's renderings of these cross-class interactions are not entirely credible, it is telling that he depicts a situation in which he, not Lula, is the subaltern. This reversal underlines, as Frei Chico recognized in 2015, how FHC "never had a relationship with workers" because he is one of those who divide their fellow Brazilians into the capable ones and the rest who are "a mass to be maneuvered because they don't have the capacity to solve their own problems."[90] FHC, in other words, reflects the enduring one-sided dialogue, traced in this book, between the highly educated and the workers of ABC. FHC told a US colleague in 1971 that "the intellectuals in Latin America are important because they are the voices of those who cannot speak for themselves." Unlike the "bureaucrats and politicians" who speak for the state, intellectuals can take a broader view and study poor people and their lives with the aim of answering the question "What are the real possibilities for change, seen from the point of view of the people without power?"[91] Such one-sided dialogue also explains his remarkable rebuke of Lula in an August 2006 Brazilian *Playboy* interview, for making "apologies for ignorance":

> You don't have to be a college graduate [doutor] to be the president of the Republic, but you also . . . needn't preach ignorance. It is better to have information, to have the capacity to form good judgments. I think that Brazilian society has had a certain tolerance of rusticity. The coarser [*bruto*] the better. . . . [But] we live in a civilized society. The ideal is not to be coarse. It is the opposite: it is to be polished.[92]

Six years earlier, Lula had anticipated some of FHC's comments in a critique of elitist approaches to politics: "For the Brazilian elite, glued to power, . . . the people are only supposed to be in the audience, . . . down there below. The revolution of the PT was to put them on stage."[93]

Backlash: The Golpe of 2016

The thirteen years of the Lula and Dilma presidential administrations saw economic growth and modest redistribution, which led to international praise and acclaim. This era of center-left government ended after an unrelenting assault. As the impeachment drive against Dilma heated up, her electoral godfather was targeted by the politically driven corruption investigation known as Operação Lava Jato (Operation Car Wash). It was headed by an ambitious lower-tier federal judge in Curitiba, Paraná, named Sérgio Moro, who on March 4, 2016, launched thirty-one raids across several states—including simultaneous ones against Lula's apartment, his nonprofit Lula Institute, and his children's and closest associates' homes and businesses—during the early stage of an investigation in which Lula had already voluntarily testified twice. The media, tipped off by the investigators, breathlessly covered Lula being taken into custody by Federal Police carrying semiautomatic weapons. Such a massive operation was designed to foster the belief that the corruption in Petrobras, which initially spurred Lava Jato, must have extended even to Brazil's ex-president.

As the impeachment battle intensified, the media hyped hyperbolic allegations—spurred by illegal leaks by judges and prosecutors—of Lula as the head of a "criminal gang," his party having looted the Brazilian national petroleum company and singlehandedly "destroyed" the Brazilian economy. Almost overnight, Lula the jovial if slightly folkloric paterfamilias became Lula the criminal mastermind, an illiterate lowlife preying on the masses' ignorance who had ruined his country. As millions went into the streets to support impeachment, visceral hatred was directed at Lula, the PT, and their supporters, symbolized by the large inflated balloons of Lula in prison garb. Very quickly, it seemed, the country had gone crazy, with unprovoked verbal attacks and harassment against PT supporters, especially in big cities.[94] These tensions heightened amid the intensifying judicial investigations against Lula and his allies. The March 4 raids were followed by Moro's release of excerpts from Lula's taped telephone conversations as he spoke with political allies, supporters, and President Dilma. This unseemly spectacle was a bold gamble by Moro to strengthen the impeachment drive—which many doubted—by forestalling Dilma's appointment of Lula as her chief of staff, after which his task, as the man who knew everyone, would be to wrestle votes in Congress against impeachment. Although revealing communications with a sitting president was illegal, Moro defied rebukes by citing the public interest in transparency, claiming that the as-yet-unindicted Lula was being named chief of staff to receive the legal immunity (*foro privelegiado*) accorded to ministers and politicians. A Supreme Court justice barred Lula from taking office. Other wiretap transcripts released by Moro were irrelevant to any investigation and intended solely to prejudice middle- and upper-class public opinion against Lula and his family.

For outside observers, the scale and emotional power of the assault on Dilma, Lula, and the PT in 2015–16 seemed disproportionate given the moderation with which the PT had exercised power. As the crisis grew, Dilma and her top aides seemed paralyzed by the violation of the rules of the democratic game they believed they had mastered. Having foolishly attempted in early 2015 to defeat the PMDB politician Eduardo Cunha, president of the Chamber of Deputies, they made a formidable enemy of this monumentally corrupt operator who, when his Swiss bank accounts were revealed, demanded that the PT representatives on the chamber's ethics committee vote to prevent investigation into his sworn testimony denying such accounts. When the representatives refused, the very next day Cunha accepted the latest of the many impeachment petitions filed with his office, having already bullied and blackmailed the government with votes to blow up the federal budget at a time of falling revenues. Moreover, Dilma's vice president, Michel Temer—also from the PMDB, which was ostensibly allied with the PT—joined the opposition by pledging support for the neoliberal policies of the defeated PSDB presidential candidate Aécio Neves. This cleared the last obstacle to impeachment.

The impeachment drive—now joined by corrupt non-PT politicians in self-defense—reflected a desire to turn back history through a parliamentary coup that did not meet constitutional norms, unlike Collor's 1992 impeachment. The allegations justifying impeachment did not demonstrate corruption by Rousseff. Rather, they referred to technical accounting maneuvers used by all Brazilian presidents and governors, actions falling far short of a "crime of responsibility," the only valid basis for impeachment under the 1988 constitution. Aware of this legal fragility, those voting for impeachment often framed their action as a parliamentary vote of confidence in Dilma, a procedure nonexistent in the Brazilian presidential system.

In truth, the impeachment was part of an unprincipled, no-holds-barred political battle by the dominant class, the PSDB, and its middle- and upper-class mass base, frustrated after losing yet another presidential race. As the "conservative classes" cohered around impeachment, the sprawling Lava Jato provided the silver bullet for those frustrated by the PT's presidential-level electoral hegemony or angry that the country was slipping out of their control. They saw an opportunity to finally disgrace Lula and destroy his national preeminence, which they thought undeserved and pernicious.

Only those ignorant of Lula's biography could have been surprised at how aggressively the seventy-year-old ex-president fought back. Released after a four-hour police interrogation on March 4, Lula gave an electrifying press conference broadcast live on even the national TV networks hostile to him. He ended his comments by making sure that everyone knew that "if they wanted to kill the *jararaca* [a pit viper], they should have struck it on the head. Instead they hit its tail, and this jararaca is as alive as it has ever been."[95] Even at the pinnacle of his prestige, Lula had never fooled himself into believing that he had been honestly, definitively accepted by those on Brazilian society's upper floors. He knew that someone like him would only be seen as a guest graciously welcomed out of his purported superiors' benevolence (or hope for benefits from the power he exercised), always susceptible to being expelled. True to his social, political, and cultural origins, Lula the pit viper was in fighting form following the March 4 raids, campaigning relentlessly and speaking to hundreds of thousands throughout the country until he was jailed in 2018. Lula's decisive response changed the political narrative, though not its outcome, and put his opponents on the defensive with the charge that Dilma's impeachment was really a coup d'état recalling 1964. His inspirational leadership united the Left and the besieged Dilma administration, and inspired a generation of youngsters who all went down together fighting, unlike in 1964, against a right-wing backlash that threatened all that had been gained during the Lula-Dilma era.

Thus, the political maelstrom since 2015—with the unrelenting assault on his personal honor, integrity, and policies—did not silence Lula, although the Brazilian TV and media studiously ignored the hundreds of thousands who turned out for Lula's 2017–18 speaking tours throughout the country; to their surprise, poll after poll showed strong and growing support for Lula as a poten-

Lula "in the arms of the people" during 2017. (Courtesy Ricardo Stuckert)

tial presidential candidate in 2018. After impeaching Dilma, PSDB and Democratas leaders had entered the government of new president Michel Temer believing that victory in 2018 would be easy and proceeded to eviscerate the country's labor laws while slashing funding for education and health. They had not, however, anticipated the resilience of Lula's mass support, nor that Temer and Aécio Neves would be secretly recorded in mid-2017 arranging payoffs by a Brazilian billionaire hoping for leniency from prosecutors. The delivery of suitcases of cash to intermediaries was caught on film; an unoccupied apartment used by another Temer government stalwart was found to contain R$55 million in cash.

Immediately discredited were the claims by PSDB and PMDB politicians, forwarded during the impeachment fight, of being champions of honesty in government against the PT's corruption. These revelations—covered relentlessly as a Rede Globo exclusive—shook the country and led the Left to briefly hope that the scales would fall from the eyes of the tens of millions who had supported impeachment. What the Left did not anticipate, however, was that those disillusioned with the PT due to the media's and the judiciary's narrative would simply extend that narrative to also include the PSDB and PMDB. A significant portion of the electorate sought someone far enough out of the main political game that they could be supported as a protest "against the system." The powerful and wealthy had cynically weaponized corruption; their own corruption, once revealed, produced the energetic core of far right followers for Jair Bolsonaro, a man so unimportant to the rich and powerful that he had always been ignored as irrelevant, crude, and in bad taste. The groundwork had been set for the coming electoral disaster for Brazilian democracy; when the rich and powerful finally tried to cut Bolsonaro down to size, their voters no longer believed them.

As the 2018 elections approached, Sérgio Fausto, a politically well-connected PSDB intellectual, was asked about the lack of charisma of his party's presidential candidate, Geraldo Alckmin, then governor of São Paulo state, an economic powerhouse home to 45 million of Brazil's 210 million inhabitants. As Fausto responded, "Who could you say is a charismatic leader in Brazilian politics today? There's only one, it's Lula."[96] Alckmin, despite reaching the second round against Lula in 2006, consistently polled at less than 10 percent, and he did even worse in the actual election. It was the convicted Lula whom 30–35 percent of voters preferred, leading the two other top competitors (one of them Bolsonaro) by 15–20 points. This meant that Lula would make it to the presidential run-off and likely win.

This was a bitter surprise to the PT's opponents, who had not ousted a legitimately elected president only to lose again to Lula. The Lava Jato crowd led by Judge Moro did their bit to convict Lula and then reject his appeal in record time, thus illegally barring him from the ballot; after Bolsonaro's election, Moro was rewarded with the position of minister of justice. When finally barred (officially but illegally) from running, on the election's eve, Lula named as his substitute Fernando Haddad, a USP professor who had been minister of education and the former PT mayor of São Paulo. The Left thus entered the campaign at the last minute with an unknown candidate—bolstered only by Lula's prestige—in a coalition reduced to only leftist parties, as in the old days before 2002 (Haddad's vice presidential candidate was from the PCdoB). Haddad did make it to the second round but, even after another leftist party (PSOL) added its support, lost to Bolsonaro substantially, by 12 percent of the national vote—results that must be judged impressive given the overwhelmingly negative circumstances. Bolsonaro received the most votes in the richer southern and southeastern states and among the wealthy and highly educated. The poorer and less highly educated Northeast, so long decried as a backward region whose voters were sheep, overwhelmingly supported Haddad.[97] In the second round, the prince of Brazil's intellectuals, FHC, refused to publicly back Haddad against the militantly racist, sexist, and ignorant Bolsonaro (though former admirers hope he did the right thing in the privacy of the ballot box).

Thus, a misguided, unprincipled partisanship among the powerful and highly educated had come to place Brazil's government in the hands of a man who epitomizes the worst of the military regime: the violent, corrupt, and ignorant men of the dungeon who caused such grief for Ernesto Geisel, the military regime's greatest president. If Geisel were alive today, he would be ashamed to see Bolsonaro in the Palacio da Alvorada. And given Geisel's concerns about lines of authority, he would be disgusted that so many generals have accepted appointments from a cashiered army captain, up to his neck in petty graft, with powerful ties to the worst elements in Rio's police forces and their allied criminal gangs known as militias.

CONCLUSION / A VICTIM OF HIS SUCCESSES

Lula and His Politics of Cunning has brought to light the details of the Brazilian president's putatively obscure origins and advanced beyond impressionistic sketches of the early Lula as the suffering migrant, the disrespected nordestino, the exemplar of the "culture of poverty," or even the "exploited" worker. With the laudable exception of Denise Paraná, previous biographers avoided fleshing out Lula's past, surprising given that family background and childhood usually figure prominently in the biographies of the world's mostly wellborn, well-educated, and well-off presidents and prime ministers, even when they are far less successful than Lula. This curious oversight reflects a lack not of sources but of interest, due to a yawning gap that is perceived between the concerns of the literate and affluent—those who write and read books—and the lifeways of illiterate people like Lula's parents, who seldom figure in books, don't read them, and certainly don't write them.

In his 2010 book, subtitled *An Investigation into the Persistence of Inequalities across the Centuries*, Brazilian sociologist Adalberto Cardoso reminds us that this active disinterest has deep historical roots. Brazil's 350 years as a slave society, he explains, has bequeathed to the country's capitalism a stark "irreconcilability between the lifestyles of the dominant social classes and strata" and those of the population below. Even in everyday life, the superordinate are strikingly indifferent toward "the individual or collective destiny of slaves, ex-slaves, and their descendants" as well as the "substantial portion of the rest of the Brazilian population . . . not directly involved in the central economic dynamic" of the society.[1] In other words, there is no need to waste time on insignificant people like the tenants and subsistence agriculturalists of Caetés, Pernambuco, where the Silvas hailed from.

My rigorous detective work reflects forty years of research and engagement with São Paulo's popular and working classes, especially the metalworkers of ABC, their unions, and their most famous native son. As I make abundantly clear, there is nothing unique in Lula's first quarter century that predicts his extraordinary trajectory over the next half century. Even in 1968, there were no signs that Lula, then twenty-three years old, was destined for greatness of any sort. One might have predicted then that Lula would be elected president of the São Bernardo metalworkers' union seven years later, a year after Frei Chico became vice president of the neighboring union in São Caetano. But one would have deemed his Communist brother the Silva most likely to become the militant strike leader, not the apolitical Lula, who had only recently joined the union. Nor did Lula's 1975 inauguration as union president give any hint that, a decade later, he would be the Left's unquestioned national leader, at the helm of a fiery trade union movement that helped finally force the military from power—never mind that he would become the country's president in 2002 and carry (directly or indirectly) the next three presidential elections.

Having explored Lula's origins, roots, and trajectory as a historical actor and public personality across three quarters of a century, I hope this biography's rich granular detail has provided readers a path toward understanding how those on the bottom experienced the processes that shaped their collective well-being and individual prospects as dependent wage earners. I have shown how the people on the bottom maneuvered within a world they did not control but in which they were far from being victims. My tale of two brothers—along with parents, siblings, relatives, adolescent buddies, girlfriends, and shop mates—whose then-anonymous lives were marked by suffering, loss, and nostalgia—is at the same time a story of adventure, joy, and fulfillment.

Working-class life is treated in this book on its own terms, with its own institutions and spaces, and with its own quite varied leftisms. Workers are presented not through abstractions—"cultures of poverty," "backwardness," "class consciousness"—but as vibrant individuals, recounted in terms of what they had to say, how they said it, and when they said it. Discourse, rather than being conceived as a pervasive emanation of power or transparent abstractions, has been shown to be deployed in different ways—in dialogue with others—by fully embodied individuals in their concrete relationships. Through close attention to Lula's siblings, relatives, and wives, I have also explored the gendered cultural norms that governed their world while celebrating the rich vernacular speech that gave their thoughts a homespun eloquence.

A central theme of this biography has been the vexed relationship between politics and everyday life at midcentury. I have explained why only a tiny minority of workers chose the path of union and political militancy by explicating three types: rebels, good boys, and operators. Moreover, I have paid close attention to the dynamics of mass consciousness in order to better understand anti-union and pro-government attitudes among ABC's metalworkers and how tens of thousands of such workers would come to alter their views. I have advanced a radically new interpretation of how workers related to the 1964 military coup and the rebel politics of 1968, in addition to why they turned to militant opposition by the late 1970s. In the process, I have offered a very different history of the Left, especially the working-class Left, while familiarizing the reader with the trade union as the preeminent working-class public sphere, a space that could—as it did in São Bernardo—facilitate the emergence of a collective identity and build power for workers against employers and the state.

Toward this end, the book's second and third parts have examined the politics and culture of ABC's metalworkers' unions, with their rich histories of struggle and an accumulated body of knowledge, customs, and wisdom. Lula's apprenticeship in trade unionism under Paulo Vidal thrust him overnight into a wider world well beyond the community, the factory, and the union. His career began during the Médici era, when self-assertive workers were persecuted in the name of anti-Communism by a regime intolerant of uppity subalterns. I have thus fully explicated both the union's lively internal politics and the state's repressive apparatus, including the murderous DOI-CODI—the proverbial dungeon—that victimized Lula's brother as well as many other working-class and middle-class opposition activists.

As a new union president, Lula took full advantage of the political space opened by the 1974 MDB victory in São Paulo and the ensuing conflicts within the military while developing the political, organizing, and communication skills that, constantly honed and updated, have allowed him to become a courageous strike leader, an inspiring movement and party head, and eventually Brazil's most successful politician. Beyond his sly maneuvering in small-group interactions, chapter 12 has shown how Lula established himself as an intriguing public personality: the fearless self-made man who says what he thinks with no strings attached. His enduring style of leadership and a characteristic vernacular discourse had crystallized by the eve of the 1978–80 metalworkers' strikes, during which, as seen in chapters 13 and 14, he finally acquired the charisma for which he would become famous.

It was in the wake of these strikes that Lula, and a generation of young skilled workers, transformed Brazilian trade unionism and founded the militant confederation CUT. Progress on the political front would take more time—touched on in chapter 15—with Lula and the party he inspired and helmed, the PT, emerging as recognized contenders for national political power in the 1989 election. After this promising start the PT evolved, widened, and extended its appeal to encompass Brazil in its diversity, with Lula further honing a practice of leadership first forged in the trade union movement. As befits the cunning of the weak, however, Lula even at his most combative was always reaching out to those who did not share his party's politics, thus creating a web of relationships within a space of convergence that helped transform (though not overturn) existing social and political relations in Brazil and, as addressed in chapter 16, Latin America as a whole.

Throughout, I have characterized cunning (astúcia) as central to the weak's strategies of maneuver. This way of inhabiting and facing the world is also at the heart of capoeira, the Afro-Brazilian dance and martial art form, where it refers to "a combination of wariness, quick wit, savvy, unpredictability, playfulness, viciousness, aesthetic flare, and a talent for deception." As a great equalizer, cunning makes it possible—though never likely—that "a frail, disadvantaged individual might overcome a more powerful adversary."[2] Dedicated to a transformative politics of cunning, Lula mastered the knowledge, skills, and relationships that allowed him to operate successfully—both publicly and privately—on all levels of the power structure as he rose to decisive national influence. The charismatic Lula mobilized words, interests, and emotion to establish and nurture relationships, while Lula the organizer magnified his influence and impact through a powerful commitment to institution building, through unions, parties, and governing alliances.

In seeking to understand Lula's highly improbable ascent, I have kept in mind, as mentioned at the outset, the characteristic lies of biography—that is, the genre's tendency to recount the individual's past in light of his future. This biography has not only rejected backward storytelling but has also insisted that we must understand an individual's childhood if we are "to discover the whole man in the adult; that is, not only his present determinations but also the weight of his history."[3] If Lula had remained in Caetés or Santos, he would never have escaped the structural rigidities and enduring prejudices that have long rendered the vast majority of the Brazilian population subaltern. It was Lula's arrival in São Paulo that gave him access to a uniquely cosmopolitan space, a city with a vastly heterogeneous population in perpetual motion. It was a dynamic world in flux at a unique moment of unprecedented opportunity that provided an ideal space for self-invention by Lula and the emergent social strata of which he was a part.

Thus, Lula was from an early age a "walking metamorphosis."[4] He may have been rural by birth, but he was deeply urban. He may have hailed from a family of farmers, but he never held a hoe; he was a nordestino but would return to the region only after he became famous and had grown up surrounded by mineiros and paulistas, even Japanese-descended ones. Given all this, it is hard to assert that Lula reasons and feels as a member of the working class because of his socialization into such an identity via his immediate family. Rather, Lula was being perpetually made and remade while partaking of multiple cultures, identities, and outlooks. And he did so with the energy and drive of an ambitious newcomer with a world to conquer, opportunities to pursue, and a sense of dignity to achieve and defend.

The singular defining experience for Lula the individual was his time in a SENAI apprenticeship program, which made him part of a mostly first-generation cohort of skilled metalworkers directly involved with a Third World industrial revolution linked to international capital.[5] Despite working with their hands, these proud skilled workers were never mere escapees from marginality, even though many had been poor as children. Rather, these self-made men were members of a working-class intelligentsia in a manufacturing sector linked to the quintessential icon of international modernity: the automobile. Using universal machine tools, these torneiros mecânicos and ferramenteiros possessed a claim to the mantle of international modernity just as valid as that of the young French-speaking sociologists at the University of São Paulo who set out to study workers in the late 1950s and early 1960s. Yet for the state's stuffy lettered class, such manual workers could never be intellectuals of any sort, only uncultured, uncouth men with little education who spoke inferior Portuguese, wore factory overalls, got their hands greasy, drank too much cachaça, and swore too freely.

This might appear to institute a division between those who studied and published (intellectuals and academics) and those who were studied (workers). And some of the sociologists involved did subscribe to such a monological vision, especially early on, as an expression of class prejudice or self-flattery. But by the 1970s such views were unsustainable as less unequal relationships developed between the ambitious young men on the two sides of the class divide. On one side were the intellectuals, steeped in international disciplinary knowledge at a time when USP was establishing itself as the best university in South America. These were years when the university student movement boldly aspired to be the self-declared "vanguard of national progress." On the other side were the mostly invisible working-class intellectuals such as Lula who used the latest industrial technology and occupied the leadership of ABC's metalworkers' unions, fully aware that their intelligence, knowledge, and skills were essential to the profitability of powerful multinational corporations like GM, Chrysler, Ford, VW, and Mercedes-Benz.

Brought together by a shared rejection of backwardness and state tutelage, the activist minorities in both groups—along with powerful elements in the Catholic Church—would blast a path forward for Brazil, against the odds. In the back-and-forth of events, these groups came to share a goal that eventually assumed the name of democracy—understood, however, in a radically different way than it had been before 1964, when the country's exclusively electoral form of democracy served to protect the privileges of Brazil's "conservative classes." In fighting for change, FHC and Lula helped shift the course of Brazilian history by ending military rule, initiating for this deeply authoritarian country its longest era of democratic governance, and making progress, if still modest, toward a government for all. It must be emphasized that neither FHC nor Lula, around whom the competition for national influence and power in the New Republic would coalesce, would have made it to Brazil's presidency without the other. This was true even though FHC lacked Lula's golden touch at the ballot box, his party's presidential candidates having lost every election after his two terms in office between 1994 and 2002.

Since direct elections for the Brazilian presidency returned in 1989, Lula or his chosen candidate has either won or placed second in eight successive elections. Even the PT's presidential loss in 2018 confirms Lula's continued sway with voters under extremely unfavorable conditions. Barred from running two months before the vote, Lula chose as his last-minute substitute Fernando Haddad, who not only made it to the second round but won 46 percent of the national vote even though Lula was barred from campaigning—jailed, controversially, before his appeals were finished—and denied his legal right not only to give newspaper interviews but even to vote on election day. So whatever else can be said, Lula has undoubtedly demonstrated for forty years a remarkable capacity to remain at the top of the political game in a country of 210 million. Lula is one of the world's most successful politicians—the Pelé of worldwide presidential electoral politics—and the brightest star in Brazil's political firmament.

From Vargas and Kubitschek to Lula and Dilma

Lula's family had arrived in São Paulo at a moment when a profoundly undemocratic society was being reshaped by the daring gambles of Brazil's greatest twentieth-century statesman, Getúlio Vargas. A confident man willing to take risks, Vargas dominated Brazilian politics from 1930 to 1954 with a capacity for cynical maneuver that bitterly frustrated his opponents among the upper and lettered classes. Although authoritarian and anti-Communist, Vargas was Brazil's great modernizer, with a reformist vision of autonomous national capitalist development that took a more inclusive approach to the needs of the masses. Through his social policies and labor legislation, Vargas accorded an unprecedented degree of recognition and citizenship to those employed in the economy's small formal sector and broadly won the support of the popular classes as the "father of the poor."

Having monopolized executive power from 1930 to 1945, when he was ousted by the military, Vargas returned to the presidency in 1950 "in the arms of the people" through a democratic election whose legitimacy was contested by fervent anti-getulistas, both civilian and military. Increasingly isolated, Vargas was besieged during this tumultuous term in office by a virulent opposition that fixated on his links to workers. Depicted as destroying the country through unprecedented corruption, Vargas was unable to galvanize his diffuse mass support until, facing a military ultimatum to step down from power, he killed himself on August 24, 1954, which led the common people in Brazil's cities to pour into the streets while driving his most forceful enemy, Carlos Lacerda, into exile while a getulista coalition won the 1955 election.

Less than three and a half months before this tragic denouement, Vargas gave his traditional May Day speech in a stadium in Petrópolis, in which he offered a remarkably accurate prophecy that few then or since have credited as anything more than populist demagoguery. After announcing a doubling of the minimum wage during a period of high inflation, he directly addressed workers by declaring that while his task was completed, theirs was just beginning. The task that lay ahead for Brazil's workers, he declared, was that of conquering "the fullness of the rights owed to you and the satisfaction of the demands imposed on you by necessity." "There is one right," he emphasized, "that no one can deprive you of: the right to vote"; through this right, he exhorted the crowd, "you can defend not only your interests but influence the destiny of the nation." In the speech's most famous passage, he said that workers, as the majority, had "the decisive force of numbers" and that today you are with the government but "tomorrow you will be the government."[6]

Lula first arrived in Vila Carioca in 1957 during the relatively harmoniuous political interregnum that was Juscelino Kubitschek's presidency, driven by a mildly enlightened reformist vision of inclusion that rejected the polarizing politics of anti-getulismo, anti-trabalhismo, and anti-Communism. Lula's adolescence was thus decisively shaped by a sense, observed by labor sociologist Luiz Pereira in 1965, that a "progressivism that did not negate capitalism" tout court was emerging from São Paulo's rapid industrialization, with the city's industrial working class serving "as the point of encounter between the past and the future."[7] This perhaps explains why Lula has always described the São Bernardo do Campo and Diadema metalworkers' union as where he "was born politically."[8] He still remembers the membership number he received (25986) on officially joining the union on October 25, 1968; as he told an audience in 1990, "When they ask me what I am or where I come from, I always say that I am the result of my class. As my categoria evolved, so have I."[9]

In creating a system of state-supported unionism, Vargas created an institutional structure that helped shelter—as well as control—workers who sought to mobilize their strength. Yet they faced powerful obstacles, and, as seen in part I, many in Lula's family, including his first wife, Lourdes, and his mother, disapproved of his decision to run for union office. As with most of the "children of fear," talk of unionism generated anxiety because, as popular wisdom affirmed, it would inevitably lead to firing, jailing, and stigmatization as a dangerous agitator, thus condemning one's family to penurious instability. It was this fear that Lula remembered in 1993 when discussing his mother's reaction on attending his 1975 inauguration as union president. "I don't know if she was proud of me," he said pensively, before going on, "I think not, basically, because she was afraid. Deep down she was fearful."[10]

This fear remained even after Lula became an international celebrity and successful presidential candidate on first-name terms with businessmen, heads of state, intellectuals, and artists in Brazil and abroad. Ahead of Lula's second run for the national presidency in 1994, his sister Maria Baixinha reflected that "if my mother were alive, she would be doing a lot of pleading with him not to be a candidate," because she was fearful "and only knew what others said." "I think if she were here, she would not be so proud," she emphasized, before sharing her own fears about the prospect that Lula might win.[11] As Lula's brother Vavá told Paraná, many people in Brazil didn't approve of the idea that "a peon, a worker, should get where Lula has gotten."[12]

When the military regime ended in 1985, the economic vulnerability of little fish like the Silvas did not lessen; they suffered intensely from the hyperinflation experienced by the New Republic until 1994, as well as weak economic growth in São Paulo until the twenty-first century. The popular classes, in other words, still lived in a world of sharks, and most remained convinced that it was wisest to stay in the shallows rather than venturing into deep waters, where, as Frei Chico had painfully learned during the dictatorship, the sharks lurked. Most of the povo remained convinced that a price would inevitably be paid by those who embraced an insurgent citizenship and intruded boldly into spaces where they didn't belong.

Lula did, in the end, face a brutal comeuppance from those on Brazilian society's upper floors. There was an unseemly brazenness to the false stories that proliferated about Lula's "billionaire" sons, who actually lost their jobs and businesses as a result of such attacks. When police raids hit Lula and his immediate family in March 2016—one of these raids included the breaking down of a door—it was accompanied by a campaign of ginned-up hatred against a man and his family who had supposedly become rich by looting the state oil company and destroying the Brazilian economy.

Like Vargas in 1954, Lula's chosen presidential successor, Dilma Rousseff, faced a concerted onslaught in 2015 by the middle and upper classes, especially in the wealthiest states, egged on by the mass media and backed by organized economic interest groups. The all-out assault on the Dilma government and her patron Lula included bald-faced lies and unscrupulous actions by the powerful and corrupt politician Eduardo Cunha, head of the Chamber of Deputies, and a slew of illegal actions by prosecutors and judges, now fully revealed by a team of reporters assembled by the Pulitzer Prize winner Glenn Greenwald. If the military was the central actor in 1954, the lead was now taken by sectors of the judiciary, the public prosecutors, and the Federal Police, with the military playing a discreet supporting role. In both the Vargas crisis and the one faced by Lula and Dilma, the pretense of combating corruption allowed for the trampling of constitutional norms. Thus were ousted the governments of two of Brazil's most influential reformers and statesmen of the last hundred years, their overthrow due less to their government's failures and shortcomings and more to their modest successes, which unsettled the comfortably privileged.

For Lula, a man who had rarely made enemies, the plunge from being Brazil's beloved grandfather to public enemy number one was less shocking than the widespread acceptance of lies as simple truth. Not even the failure of a ballyhooed international search for his stolen fortune stanched the proliferation of rumors, allegations, and frivolous investigations and charges hyped up breathlessly in the national media. Yet what was inflicted on Lula and his family happened because he was a man out of place being put back in his place, a foreign body to be ritually expelled from among the high and mighty, where, they now claimed, he had never rightly belonged.

When this assault was launched, Lula was in his early seventies, and it had been six years since he had returned with Marisa to their modest middle-class apartment in São Bernardo. Unlike other politicians, he owned no beach houses, Paris apartments, or rural estates for weekend getaways. He was, however, the unquestioned favorite in the 2018 presidential race, so the Lava Jato task force of prosecutors and judges in Curitiba had to work with what they had: a modest beach apartment he had never owned, and an estate owned by longtime personal friends that he, Marisa, and his grandchildren frequented after his presidency. When the courts rejected his last attempt to remain out of jail until his final appeals were exhausted, as per the provisions of the 1988 constitution, Lula received an ultimatum to present himself in Curitiba to begin serving a thirteen-year sentence on Friday, April 6, 2018.[13]

As Lula well knew, politics can be ruthless in Brazil, and prosecutors and judges often guarantee justice for their friends and the law for their enemies.[14] Although indignant, Lula continued to reiterate his confidence that the judicial system would ultimately right the wrongs being done; he refused the advice of allies, including Frei Chico, that he go into exile to avoid imprisonment. When the order to begin serving his sentence came down, Lula chose to return to his political home: the headquarters of the ABC metalworkers' union in São Bernardo. He arrived on April 5 accompanied by the PT's president, Gleisi Hoffmann, and wearing a jacket that Evo Morales had given him. Lula would sleep for the next two nights on a mattress on the floor while thousands of supporters arrived.[15]

Lula arrived at the union without having decided what his next step would be, so meetings were held with his lawyers and PT leaders and advisers to decide this. At one point, Lula's secretary, Claudinha, recalled that the day after he was due in Curitiba was the birthday of his wife, who had passed away the previous year, her death hastened by the stress (she was a defendant as well). The idea of a Saturday mass in her honor was taken to Lula, who agreed immediately; Judge Moro's order would not be obeyed even though his lawyers worried that the gesture might be taken as *desacato*, a legal charge for disrespect of authority, and hurt his ongoing legal battles. At a fraught high-level meeting, Lula also made clear that he would not forcefully resist arrest—which would endanger his supporters by inviting a police invasion. His surrender to the Federal Police was thus negotiated for Saturday, April 7, after a Catholic memorial mass for Marisa and a last address.[16]

By taking refuge at his union, Lula was once again surrounded by collaborators, friends, lawyers, trade unionists, artists, and admirers who came to show solidarity. In contemporaneous recollections by Hoffmann and others, there was energy in the air but also love, sadness, lots of crying, and even a touch of depression, plus plenty of indignation at the manifest injustices being committed. Over these days, Lula would work the room one-on-one with embraces and words of encouragement, helping to dispel the gloom. One woman recalled him placing her head on his chest to suggest that he'd be fine but that "we need strong people outside"; she had hoped to pass energy and force to him but received these from him instead. While occasionally irritated by the number of selfies taken, Lula also periodically waved from the window to the crowd, the povão, who had gathered in a vigil as rounds of orators spoke from a sound truck provided by the state teachers' union. Another young man, a PT lawyer, noted that Lula could well have been his father, a worker. "Lula is the trajectory of millions of Brazilians," this lawyer reflected. "It's just that he became the greatest president Brazil has ever seen." According to this young man, Lula had overturned the rules as to who was to have a shot at getting ahead in life, "and in the law, the inversion of order is a crime."[17]

Another witness described the Lula he admired as a man who remained "faithful to his principles, without hiding from reality and its contradictions, [and] without living a fantasy of omnipotence or falling into bitterness."[18] Gilberto Carvalho, one of his closest presidential advisers, cited Lula's "teimosia in respecting the institutionality" being violated by imprisoning him while illustrating Lula's fighting spirit and acute realism. "We were few, five thousand, perhaps eight thousand at its peak," Carvalho noted—far fewer than the 40,000–

80,000 in Vila Euclides in the late 1970s. At his side, Lula looked down at the "enthusiastic and generous" militants below and dryly observed, "Gilbertinho, one goes to war with the soldiers you have."[19]

It was a moving scene on Saturday morning as the mass came to an end outside the union headquarters. The inflamed crowd was determined not to surrender Lula to the police, and Carvalho wondered how he would explain his decision to them. But once he started talking, Carvalho observed, it was "the old Lula": he showed defiance, attacking the lies of the prosecutors, the judges, and the media as well as the unprecedented assault on the povo's rights and well-being under the ousted Dilma's replacement.[20] Why, he asked the crowd, was he here today? Because he had dreamed, he said, of a country where child mortality would fall because all children had milk, rice, and beans every day and one where poor and black students from the periphery could go to the best universities so that prosecutors and judges in the future would not come only from elite backgrounds. And what were my crimes? To have helped "the poor to eat meat and buy cars, and travel by plane, to have their small farm or to become a microentrepreneur, to have their own homes."[21] Hailing ex-president Dilma, Lula went out of his way to praise the younger leaders from other leftist parties at his side before explaining, "tamely," in Carvalho's words, why he had decided to obey the imprisonment order.[22]

The rally ended with a collective coming together—a moment of fusion—followed by the final touch—decided on only a few minutes earlier—of Lula being hoisted on the shoulders of the crowd and carried from the stage to the union's entrance. Camilo Vannuchi, the son of one of Lula's close advisers, who had met Lula and Marisa as a child, noted that Lula had in the end succeeded in bringing "the adversary onto his chosen field of battle," politics. His enemies imagined Lula's story ending with "the convicted man, head lowered, alone" abjectly reporting to prison.[23] What they want, Lula told the crowd, was his picture as a prisoner to put on their magazine covers and to broadcast on the Globo TV news, and just the prospect was enough, he joked, to give them "multiple orgasms."[24] What they got instead, in Vannuchi's words, was "the image of an icon, a mass leader carried on the shoulders" of his supporters, something to be exalted in poetry, verse, and a memorable photo shot from a drone overhead by an amateur photographer.[25]

"It does no good," Lula told the crowd, "to think they can put an end to my dreams because, when I stop dreaming, they will still be floating in the air," with "no way of arresting them." Nor would dreams end when he had "a heart attack, that's nonsense, because my heart will beat through your hearts, and there are millions of them." They have never learned, Lula went on, that "the death of a combatant does not stop a revolution" and that there are many Lulas out there,

Lula carried on the shoulders of the crowd at the São Bernardo union, 2018. (Courtesy Ricardo Stuckert)

and many more still to be born. They will be in the streets burning tires, organizing marches, and carrying out occupations in the city and countryside, demanding an end to the "barbarities committed against black kids in this country."[26] The ultimate message of courage, audacity, and struggle was completed when Lula—charismatic and cunning—walked out on his own two legs and into custody, amid an aroused crowd who fought to prevent the Federal Police from taking Lula away from the union. As he told Hoffmann right before leaving, "I am going to complete my destiny."[27]

Five hundred and eighty days later, on November 8, 2019, Lula would walk out of the Federal Police headquarters in Curitiba to await the result of his appeals in freedom; a day earlier, the Supreme Court had by one vote returned to the 1988 constitutional provision to that effect. During his nineteen months in isolation, the seventy-four-year-old widower had his share of grief, including the death of his brother Vavá, at which point he was denied his right to attend the funeral, deemed a possible threat to public order by the judge who took Moro's place. A week later, the same judge—copying verbatim from Moro's earlier sentence—convicted Lula in a case involving a country retreat that was not owned by Lula or his family. The public unease at his perceived mistreatment would force the judge to act differently in early March when Lula's seven-year-old grandson, Arthur, died. While allowed to attend, his family's private mourning was marred by a massive police deployment in the cemetery and the presence of six burly policemen with semiautomatic weapons during the private chapel service.

Lula, alone and imprisoned. (Courtesy Zé Dassilva)

By April 2019, a sea change in judicial circles led the courts (not without criticism) to restore Lula's right to give interviews—a ban in place since the 2018 election—and his inimitable voice was once again heard by Brazilian and foreign reporters. The following June, a cascade of revelations from the leaked internal communications of Moro and the Lava Jato prosecutors started to pour forth from a team led by the Pulitzer Prize–winning journalist Glen Greenwald of the *Intercept*; the Vaza-Jato (leak jet) investigation proved damaging to both the credibility of the Lava Jato task force and the public standing of Moro, much diminished, who was serving as the minister of justice in Bolsonaro's corrupt far-right government. Even while Lula was in jail, more cases were filed against him, many of them this time more quickly dismissed.

When interviewed by *Der Spiegel* reporters in May 2019, Lula was asked whether he suffered from being held in isolation given his outgoing nature. In his reply, Lula shared a story from his early union days—never before told—related to the extreme shyness that made him get nervous even when people simply said his name in a meeting. In confronting that challenge, he explained that he practiced imaginary speeches at home in front of a photo with lots of people. Perhaps, he joked, I'll put photos up on the wall of my jail cell and give speeches to them.[28]

Showing energy and good humor, the ex-president ranged widely in subsequent interviews discussing Brazilian and world affairs. As for Donald Trump and Bolsonaro, he repeatedly cited Mozambican writer Mia Couto, who observed that "in a time of terror, we choose monsters to protect ourselves."[29] Not once did he complain about the conditions of his imprisonment since the poor and unemployed, he insisted, were living far worse than he was. As for himself, Lula continued to affirm his love of life—including for his new fiancé, the fifty-two-year-old sociologist Rosângela da Silva—while eagerly sharing his impressions of the many books that he had read in prison. His favorites were biographies and books that told the story of the Brazilian people's struggles for freedom going back to slavery time.[30] He was, he insisted, a free man without strings attached, all the more so since he has no money in the bank, no patrimony, and no pension investments, all of which have been frozen by the court to pay restitution; the PT has had to put him on a salary.

"Over my 580 days" in isolation, he told a crowd after his release, "I prepared myself spiritually . . . not to have hate . . . [and] not to have a thirst for vengeance . . . [or] to hate my tormentors [*algozes*]." He did so, he went on, to prove that "even being imprisoned by them, I slept with a [more] tranquil conscience" than those who went after him with falsehoods and thus cast a bad light on the rest of the judiciary, the public prosecutor's office, and the federal police whose honest services are vital for an effective democracy.[31] After returning in January 2020 from an hour-long meeting with Pope Francis, he was brought in for an interrogation—ordered by Moro's Ministry of Justice—to determine if his criticisms of Bolsonaro had violated the dictatorship's National Security Law under which he and his fellow trade unionists had been arrested and convicted after the 1980 strike.[32] While Brazil's current president mocks his predecessor as a nine-fingered cachaça drinker, few in Brazil share the bravado of a top Bolsonaro minister who, when asked, insisted that "Lula is a matter for the police, not politics."[33]

AFTERWORD / TOWARD A BIOGRAPHICAL PIVOT

Whether dealing with monarchies, republics, or empires, nineteenth-century writers of history were criticized by the Russian novelist Leo Tolstoy for their tendency to depict "the life of a people" by describing the "activity of individuals who ruled the people"—a tendency true not only for "the ancient historians," he wrote in 1869, but even for those who no longer believed in divinely ordained rulers.[1] In these more recent accounts, "historic personages" exercised power "because they fulfill the will of the people which has been delegated to them... [and] the activity of the leaders [thus] represents the activity of the people."[2] In this famous second postscript to *War and Peace*, Tolstoy noted that many now recognized the implausibility of grafting a veneer of popular sovereignty onto the traditional method of writing history. Their response was to invent "some most obscure, impalpable, and general abstraction" that they then declared to be "the aim of humanity's movement," the most typical abstractions, "adopted by almost all historians," being "freedom, equality, progress, civilization, and culture." In these accounts, those who left monuments behind were to be judged on the extent to which "they have promoted or hindered that abstraction."[3] In rejecting a teleological "great men" approach, the twentieth-century discipline of history could be said to have embraced Tolstoy's insistence that "the life of the nations is not contained in the lives of a few [great] men, for the connection between these men and the nations has not been found."[4]

Having grappled with the narrative challenge of the French invasion of Russia, Tolstoy insisted that "the only conception that can explain the movement of the peoples is that of some force commensurate with the whole movement of peoples." To ask "what causes historical events" is to pose the question "What is power?"[5] In one striking passage, Tolstoy offers a probing dissection of a commonplace in the rhetoric of historical narrative: "Napoleon ordered his men to battle." Beyond noting that Napoleon's power itself was far from absolute, Tolstoy suggested that neither the characteristics of Napoleon the individual nor coercion could adequately explain the execution of such an order. Thus power, he concluded, can only be found "in those relations which the person possessing it stands to the masses."[6] Tolstoy summarized his view as follows: "The movement of nations is caused not by power, nor by intellectual activity, nor even by a combination of the two as historians have supposed, but by the activity of all the people who participated in the events, and who always combine in such a way that those taking the largest direct share in the event take on themselves the least responsibility and vice versa."[7]

In his contribution to the nineteenth-century Napoleon debate, Tolstoy offered a decisive riposte to an approach to history memorably championed by the Scottish polymath Thomas Carlyle, who declared in 1840 that

> the History of the World was the Biography of Great Men. . . . They were the leaders of men, these great ones; the modelers, patterns, and in a wide sense creators, of whatever the general mass of men contrived to do or to attain; all things that we see standing accomplished in the world are properly the outer material result, the practical realization and embodiment of Thoughts that dwelt in the Great Men sent into the world: the soul of the whole world's history.[8]

The most cogent nineteenth-century repudiation of Carlisle was offered by the Marxist materialism that emerged as a critique of liberalism. Sometimes scientistic and positivist in its search for lawlike general causes, Marxism tended to emphasize social determination while minimizing individual agency as part of a systemic theorization of society, a focus on structural features, and an evolutionary societal dynamic, views that would prove profoundly influential well beyond the ranks of its followers.

The classic Marxist formulation on "the role of the individual in history" can be found in the 1898 essay so titled by the Russian Marxist G. V. Plekhanov.[9] In his lively engagement in the debate, Plekhanov posed the counterfactual: Would European history have been different if Napoleon had not lived? While recognizing Napoleon's importance in the events, he judged his indispensability to be an "optical illusion." If the individual named Napoleon had not existed, then some other man of equal talents or attributes would have emerged to fulfill the role of Napoleon, which originated, he argued, in the social and historical imperatives of his age: "The personal qualities of leading people determine the individual features of historical events; and the accidental element . . . always plays some role in the course of these events, the trend of which is determined in the last analysis by so-called general causes, i.e. actually by the development of productive forces and the mutual relations between men in the social-economic process of production." His concern, he said, was with the "deep-lying general causes," not the "casual phenomena and the personal qualities of celebrated people."[10]

Writing in the 1930s, the Trinidadian writer C. L. R. James noted the modern preference for treating individual actors as "a personification of the social forces [in contention, with] great men being merely or nearly the instruments" of larger societal structures, tendencies, and conflicts. At the same time, James signaled his adherence to Marxism by writing that "great men" are at best "instruments in the hands of economic destiny," although in his classic 1938 study of the Haitian Revolution he broke with Plekhanov by giving pride of place to Toussaint Louverture.[11] In doing so, he followed Leon Trotsky, who had pondered, in *The History of the Russian Revolution* (1932), "How would the revolution have developed if Lenin had not reached Russia in April 1917?" Wrestling with his own Marxist orthodoxy, the Russian revolutionary recognized that "the rôle of personality . . . is no unimportant question, although easier to ask than answer." Concluding that Lenin was indispensable, he admitted that it might seem to make the case for "a mechanical contrasting of the person, the hero, the genius, against the objective conditions, the mass, the party." Having a revolution to narrate, however, Trotsky did not elaborate other than to observe that "Lenin was not an accidental element" but a product of the whole of Russian history: he added, in a comment relevant to Lula, that "leaders are not accidentally created . . . [but rather are] gradually chosen and trained up in the course of decades . . . and cannot [thus] be capriciously replaced."[12]

By the mid-twentieth century, the mainstream of history as a professional practice had repudiated the "great man" approach and moved away from a top-down focus on the writings, speech acts, and deeds of individual members of the elites, whether generals, presidents, or diplomats (what Fernand Braudel termed *histoire événementielle*).[13] The search for deeper causal explanation led to a focus on broader socioeconomic and cultural processes. As history grappled with social structures and the constitution of collectivities, interests, and identities (nations, classes, genders), political and diplomatic history began to lose their preeminence within the discipline, and more analytical forms of written expression, rather than strictly narrative ones, came to the fore. Moreover, the Marxist dichotomy between surface appearances, including events and individuals, and deeper underlying explanations would also come to be shared by Western objectivist social science disciplines such as economics, political science, and sociology.

With the rise of social history after the 1960s, the discipline's interest in the geographic, socioeconomic, demographic, cultural, and familial dimensions of human societies loomed large, as did a sharply increased focus on subaltern actors such as workers, peasants, racially subordinated groups, and, eventually, women. While rejecting the elitism of established histories, the social history insurgency had a bias against biography derived from the Marxist social theory, however heterodox, that informed their causal models. To this one might add that "great men" history was also rejected as undemocratic: the division of the world into, on the one hand, geniuses and supermen, always male, and, on the other, average, "common," and inconsequential human beings. For the new social historians, this was tied to an attack on a Marxist-Leninist vanguardism that was often equated with domination of a party by a centralized leadership and a sharp distinction between fully "professional" revolutionaries versus rank-and-file party members and the masses.

While the writing of traditional biographies never disappeared, the status of the biographical faced a new challenge with the rise of structuralism in the 1960s, a diverse current in French intellectual life identified with Claude Lévi-Strauss and Louis Althusser.[14] Eventually relabeled poststructuralism, this complex transdisciplinary body of thought would acquire broad influence after the 1980s within the Anglophone academy, where it was commonly referred to as "French theory." Its emblematic figure, Michel Foucault, would prove the most influential for a new generation of historians.[15] In a stimulating 2013 book, *The Left Hemisphere: Mapping Critical Theory Today*, French sociologist Razmig Keucheyan has aptly described 1960s French structuralism as characterized by "a form of historical determinism and objectivism" that emphasized the "*longue durée* and the 'structural invariants' constitutive of the social world." This was combined with their theoretical "anti-humanism," with its emphasis on abolishing or dethroning an (allegedly) Cartesian subject (often referred to as the "death of the subject"), which they falsely identified with the position of Jean-Paul Sartre and Simone de Beauvoir.[16] As he notes, the limitations of structuralist determinism were dramatically exposed in Paris in 1968, when "the thunder clap of May abruptly altered the perception of politics and history, which obliged structuralists" to shift their self-representation—though not their underlying model of causality—toward what would come to be labeled poststructuralism.[17] A good example of its determinism can be seen in Bourdieu's 1986 essay on "the biographical illusion." Unconsciously echoing Plekhanov, he argued that life history, "one of those common-sense notions which has [now] been smuggled into the learned universe," was based on the false "presupposition that life *is* a history" rather than a point of inflection within a social field.[18]

In *Apologies to Thucydides: Understanding History as Culture and Vice Versa* (2004), US anthropologist Marshall Sahlins took up the challenge of "the acting historical subject." He asked how we are to conceptualize "the relationships between types of historical agency and modes of historical change." Scholars, he suggests, have too long avoided this debate out of fear that they will become "mired in the old epistemic murk of 'the great man theory of history' and the even more ancient quicksands of 'the individual versus society.'"[19] Yet Sahlins reminds us that we need not adhere to the view that people are above all "creatures of some great social machinery," whether created by or through

"Althusserian-derived interpellations, Gramscian-inspired hegemonies, and power-laden Foucauldian discourses," or, one might add, imperatives derived from political economy.[20] Nor need we embrace the opposite extreme, that people are "autonomous and self-moving, society being nothing but the residue . . . of their self-regarding projects."[21] This hyperindividualistic posture, although entirely without influence among historians, is popular among doctrinaire market economists and finds its clearest expression in Margaret Thatcher's repeated declaration that "society" does not exist.

Joining scholars like Emília Viotti da Costa, Sahlins would have us look back to the theoretical terrain from which structuralism emerged as a critique in the 1960s.[22] In *Search for a Method* (1957) and *Critique of Dialectical Reason* (1960), Sartre was engaged in a promising project of combining the insights of phenomenology (existentialism) and Marxism while simultaneously theorizing race, anticolonialism, and homosexuality. Existentialism was to be grounded within society and structures, while the latter was to be freed from determinism and hyperobjectivism.[23] As noted in a 2013 article in *International Labor and Working-Class History,* Sartre and E. P. Thompson are the two most notable proponents of this "submerged tradition within Western Marxist thought that attempted to advance not pure subjectivity but, at least, a 'subject-object dialectic' against the older 'objective' orthodoxy."[24]

Summarizing Sartre's key insights, Sahlins notes that there are in fact no standard interchangeable subjects, "persons who are nothing and do nothing but what their class, country, or ethnic group has made them." Rather, there is only "the concrete individual, whose relations to the totality are mediated by a particular biographical experience in familial and other institutions" and who thus expresses "the cultural universals in an individual form."[25] He suggests, quoting Alexander Goldenweiser, that what we are dealing with empirically is the "biographical individual[,] . . . a historic complex *sui generis.* Neither biological nor psychological, nor civilizational factors exhaust his content. He has partaken of the culture of his social environment, but only of certain aspects of it, and these have . . . [been] received and absorbed by a psyche that was unique. This is the concrete individual of historic society."[26] To paraphrase Sartre, you are not what society has done to you; rather, you are what you do with what is done to you. The freedom to which humans are condemned, as Sartre has suggested, consists in "the small movement which makes of a totally conditioned social being someone who does not render back completely what his conditioning has given him."[27]

While spending my early and mid-career writing about labor, politics, law, and gender, I became increasingly drawn to the biographical as a vital terrain for historians, given our disciplinary "concern with historical totality" and our insistence on, in the words of Charles Bergquist, "the interrelatedness of all aspects of social change."[28] The biographical is important because historians routinely employ a process of abstraction in which we isolate one or another dimension of reality and then deal with it separately under a number of guises. In doing so, we produce a series of abstract representations of reality that may be referred to, for example, as the economic, social, political, intellectual, sexual, or cultural. Simultaneously, we deploy other abstractions to further discipline the unruliness of the phenomenon under examination. We may distinguish levels such as the local, the national, or the global as well as the individual, the family, and the community. And we may use classificatory systems to distinguish class, race, and gender or to mark off the systemic and the structural from the conjunctural.

While necessary, these analytical tools and shortcuts often interfere with our objective of attaining and communicating a holistic and totalizing historical vision.[29] Although inescapable, this problem can be lessened through the judicious use of a biographical approach, all the more so in the modern period where access to sufficient oral sources allows the use of the most sophisticated tools.[30] When done properly, the study of an individual links levels of reality that are otherwise artificially separated. After all, individuals do not experience their own lives as divided into discrete and abstract constituent elements that can be neatly separated and labeled. Rather, the various aspects, levels, or dimensions of that reality are experienced as an integrated part of an organic whole, as a lived experience fixed in a moment of historical space and time. In this sense, individuals are not alienated from one or another of the determining forces that shape their lives; instead they experience them as "of-a-piece," which is, in turn, shaped by their own action (praxis).[31]

Biography's advantages are all the more important when the individual in question is effaced by dominant discourses, mythmaking, and emblematization, whether by their contemporaries or later scholars. In my Andreotti article, for example, I noted how the human specificity of such a Brazilian Communist activist is denied by both the rhetoric of demonization from the right and the grandiose and abstract language of official collectivist ideology on the left. Even in scholarly writing on labor and leftist politics, we too often deal in external labels, ideological markers, and emblematic representations rather than interpreting these abstractions in light of the individuals who made them a real force through their actions. When approached in this fashion, as the historian and PT leader Marco Aurélio Garcia (1941–2017) noted, "concrete historical subjects" are "engulfed by the broad explanatory mechanisms," and individual militants "appear as participants in an impersonal system."[32] In other words, we will never truly understand social and political history if we do not grasp the biographical dimension that underlies the lives of those who, like Andreotti, Frei Chico, and Lula, stood at their center.

Andreotti was largely unknown outside the industrial ABC region, where he made his home from 1925 to 1984. He is in no sense as historically significant as former president Lula, a man of national and global stature who, along with Getúlio Vargas, was one of the two most consequential Brazilian presidents of the last century. The distinction between these two working-class men can best be expressed through Sahlins's idea of the structures of agency. To understand "individual historical agency," he suggests, one must examine "the structures of history that authorize it."[33] To do that requires breaking with "certain received ideas of an unbridgeable opposition between cultural order and individual agency . . . together with the correlated antitheses of the sociological and the psychological, the objective and the subjective, the lawful and the contingent, the universal and the particular."[34] "It is true," Sahlins goes on to say, that

> these contrasting aspects of human existence are irreducible the one to the other, which is one reason why historians and social scientists are often motivated to argue the inconsequentiality of either structures or persons. But what all this manicheanism ignores is the way persons can be empowered to represent collectives: to instantiate or personify them, sometimes even to bring them into existence, without, however, losing their own individuality. Or in other words, what is not sufficiently considered is how history makes the history-makers.[35]

Like Tolstoy, Friedrich Engels emphasized the "innumerable intersecting forces, an infinite series of parallelograms of forces which give rise to one resultant—the historical event." And he always denied, as he did in 1890, that the economic is "the only determining element" in history, an idea embraced by some "younger people" within the Marxism of his day that he deemed meaningless rubbish. Like Sartre, there were multiple determinations and forms through which conflicts were played out, including, he added, their "reflexes . . . in the brains of the participants" and how "traditions. . . haunt the human mind." As for history, its outcome "is made in such a way that the final result always arises from conflicts between many individual wills, of which each in turn has been made what it is by a host of particular conditions of life."[36]

We would do well, in other words, to bear in mind Emília Viotti da Costa's warning in *Crowns of Glory, Tears of Blood*, a study of an 1823 slave rebellion in Demerara, Guyana, that "history is not the result of some mysterious and transcendental 'human agency,' but neither are men and women the puppets of historical 'forces.' Their actions constitute the point at which the constant tension between freedom and necessity is momentarily resolved." As she goes on to observe,

> We have become so habituated to seeing history as a product of reified historical categories, to talking about "variables" and "factors," to dealing with abstractions such as capitalism, abolitionism, evangelicalism, and the like, that we often forget that history is made by men and women, even though they make it under conditions they themselves have not chosen. In the last instance, what matters is the way people interact, the way they think about the world and act upon it, and how in this process they transform the world and themselves.[37]

ACKNOWLEDGMENTS

I have spent forty years grappling with the life and struggles of working people in twentieth-century São Paulo, Brazil, focusing chiefly on the metalworkers of ABC, who drew my attention in 1979 when I entered the Yale doctoral program. At the time, I intended to write a dissertation on Benito Juárez, the Wars of Reform, and the French Intervention in nineteenth-century Mexico, but my adviser Emília Viotti da Costa (1928–2017) asked me, at our first meeting, if I found anything else of interest, because once you choose your dissertation topic, you never escape it. In answering, I mentioned the international headlines about the dramatic strikes in the industrial suburb of greater São Paulo known as ABC. Of my many debts to Emília, I freely admit that I owe my career to her wisdom on that occasion: I signed up for Portuguese and six weeks later wrote my first travel grant proposal.

When I arrived in Brazil as a twenty-seven-year-old in 1980, an even more titanic metalworkers' strike led by the thirty-five-year-old Lula had just gone down to defeat. My eighteen months of doctoral research in 1981–82 was focused on the industrial relations, electoral, and political systems that emerged in ABC between 1900 and 1964. During the same period, dozens of talented Brazilian social scientists, creative artists, and activists—including key foreigners like John Humphrey—were deeply engaged with the study of ABC's remarkable bottom-up challenge to military rule. At the time, I studiously avoided this emerging literature, being all too aware of the temptation of reading the past in light of the present. It was only after submitting my dissertation in 1985 that I began to read what had been published on Lula, the metalworkers of São Bernardo, and the Brazilian New Unionism. At the time I made the plunge, I was living in Logan, Utah, with my wife Jan and our first son, Paul, who was soon to be joined by Elizabeth. The intersection between ABC's past, which I knew so well, and the region's industrial, political, and ideological climate in the 1970s and 1980s was thrilling. After the arrival of the New Republic in 1985, the polemics generated by the fight for hegemony within the Left would fade as Lula, his Workers' Party (PT), and its allied trade union confederation (CUT) consolidated their positions as the leaders of the left and central reference points in the broader fight for democracy.

With support in 1991 from the Social Science Research Council, the American Council of Learned Societies, and the National Endowment for the Humanities, I undertook additional field research while mastering the still-expanding literature on ABC, the CUT, and the PT. During this period, I was lucky to have Jody Pavilack as a research assistant as we plunged into the Sartrean theoretical thickets that have defined my project through today. I also particularly benefited from the ongoing interest, engagement, and feedback from my friend Charles Bergquist, a Latin Americanist social and labor historian, and the Harry Bridges Center for Labor Studies he helped found at the University of Washington.

I continue to benefit immeasurably from the archival holdings of the ever more impressive Arquivo Edgard Leuenroth (AEL) of the Universidade Estadual de Campinas (UNICAMP) as well as the Centro Pastoral Vergueiro, later renamed the Centro de Pesquisa Vergueiro and now incorporated into AEL. I also developed deep friendships with a generation of young labor historians doing graduate work at UNICAMP, including Paulo Fontes, Alexandre Fortes, Antonio Negro, Hélio Silva, and Fernando Teixeira da Silva. An early to mid-1990s project on labor, Mercosur, and NAFTA, codirected with economist Russ Smith, allowed me to establish ongoing ties with the activist intellectual Maria Silvia Portela de Castro of the CUT, while I later benefited from the holdings of the Centro de Documentação e Memória Sindical of the CUT, coordinated by Antonio José Marques. Across the decades, the metalworkers' unions in Santo Andre and São Bernardo have been of inestimable help, and São Bernardo undertook—under the leadership of Osvaldo Bargas—a program of research and interviews that generated the indispensable ABC de Luta website. Having visited the unions on numerous occasions, I appreciate all those I have come to know, including photographer Raquel Camargo, whom I first met in 1991, and Hélio Silva, who made time for me during a December 2018 visit, as did the union's president, Wagner Santana. And a special thanks is due once again to Helena Weiss Gonçalves for her transcription of the eighty hours of interviews I conducted with metalworkers Marcos Andreotti and Philadelpho Braz.

My original plan in the mid-1990s had been to write a traditional labor history monograph titled "The Metalworkers of ABC, 1950–1980," the project that brought me to the National Humanities Center in 1995–96. During that splendid and productive year, my longtime collaborator Daniel James and I finished our 1997 edited volume *The Gendered Worlds of Latin American Women Workers*. My theoretical and empirical engagement with gender was linked to my own turn toward research on Brazilian labor law. My 2004 monograph *Drowning in Laws: Labor Law and Brazilian Political Culture* offered my solutions to the inadequacies of social and labor history in effectively grappling with the cultural, political, and legal dynamics of working people's struggles in the Brazilian case.

A still more radical shift came in the late 1990s, when I left the metalworkers of São Paulo behind in much the same way that Lula did during his presidential runs with ABC as his reference point but never his exclusive focus. In parallel with my wife's field research in the northeastern state of Sergipe, I received a Fulbright-Hays fellowship for a project titled "Translating PT into a Northeastern *Sotaque*: The Social, Political, and Cultural Dynamics of the Growth of Lula's Electoral Support in Four Northeastern States, 1982–1998," based in Sergipe, marked by friendships with Ferando de Araújo Sá and Tânia Elias and Rosemiro Magno da Silva.

In my 1992 book, *The Brazilian Workers' ABC*, I had insisted that electoral and labor relations phenomena are inextricably bound together, and I now began to grapple with Lula's role as a formidable electoral force and a historical personality of the first order. For social historians, the role of the individual in history has always been a vexed question, as discussed in this book's afterword, but Lula's 2002 election would prove to be the turning point in Latin America's shift to the left that had been inaugurated with the 1998 election of Venezuela's Hugo Chávez. In addition to my work with a multiyear project on "left turns" ably directed by Eric Hershberg, Max Cameron, and Jon Beasley-Murray, Lula's rise to power led to two productive residential fellowships over a year and a half in 2005–7. My time at the Woodrow Wilson International Center for Scholars offered intellectual excitement as well as capable research assistants and easy access to the marvels of the Library of Congress and the US National Archives and Records Administration. My DC stay was followed by a semester at the Kellogg Institute for International Studies at the University of Notre Dame, which provided a stimulating interdisciplinary environment; special appreciation goes to Scott Mainwaring, Daniel Brinks, and Nicanor Dominguez.

Since we met in 2003, I have treasured my friendship with neuroscientist Miguel Nicolelis, a man of passion and energy who has made decisive contributions to the world of science and in the fight for progress in Brazil. I appreciate his initiative in arranging for my June 2015 meeting with Lula. It was only the third time I had met Lula since 1991, although I have undoubtedly consumed more of his words, and considered them more carefully, than any other person in the world. On the same trip to São Paulo, I also benefited from the enthusiastic support of leaders turned friends, at two key archives used in this book: Sonia Maria Troitiño Rodriguez (Centro de Documentaço e Memória–UNESP) and Marcelo Antonio Chaves (Arquivo Público do Estado de São Paulo). Going back to the 1997 Brazilian Studies Association conference in Washington, I have benefited from the expansion and maturation of the labor history subfield that now finds its home in the vibrant Worlds of Labor Working Group of the Associação Nacional dos Professores Universitários de História.

After Lula became president in 2003, it was clear—as had been true for Polish trade unionist turned president Lech Walesa—that his biography would be decisively impacted by the balance between the successes and failures of his administration. I was lucky that my inestimable colleague Alexandre Fortes was equally interested in this challenge, and together we directed a three-year international research project that brought together fifteen scholars for multiple panels at the congresses of the Latin American Studies Association in Montreal (2007) and Rio de Janeiro (2009). The project's high point was an international interdisciplinary conference in Durham on May 27–28, 2008, titled "Nurturing Hope, Deepening Democracy, and Combating Inequalities: An Assessment of Lula's Presidency," that received funding from Duke and various Brazilian entities. In its execution, the project benefited from the talents of the conference coordinator, Bryan Pitts, an indefatigable researcher, who met the high standards set by my earlier research assistant and collaborator, Tom Rogers.

Looking back at the challenges of the last two decades, Alexandre and I can be proud of an exemplary collaboration driven by *companheirismo*, an acute realism, and a nuanced understanding of political and academic dynamics; his wisdom and words are reflected throughout this book. As a collaborator, coauthor, and commentator, he combines moxie, attention to detail, and balanced judgment with a depth of knowledge, passion, and insight derived from his own political and intellectual trajectory as a first-rate historian of the Brazilian working class. It was a pleasure to host him as Duke's Mellon Visiting Professor of Latin American Studies in 2011–12, a year in which we cotaught a course titled "Latin American Left Turns" while his wife Cristiani Viera Machado, our dear friend, was on a postdoc at the University of North Carolina at Chapel Hill studying comparative public health policy. My friend Leon Fink, the editor of *Labor*, made it possible for us to twice publish early iterations of that project, while my valued and energetic colleague Wendy Wolford invited me to co-organize an April 2012 Cornell conference on the Lula-Dilma presidencies with a focus on social movements, internal government dynamics, and state-society links, an initiative that became a special issue of *Latin American Perspectives* with the support of its editors.

During the last four decades, I have benefited from the generosity of many Brazilian colleagues, friends, and collaborators, including Paulo Sérgio Pinheiro, Michael Hall, Leôncio Rodrigues, Laís Abramo, Nadya and Antonio Sérgio Guimarães, Salvador Sandoval, Sonia de Avelar, José Ramalho, Iram Jácome Rodrigues, and Patricia Cerqueira and her husband, Cliff Welch, a longtime friend. I also have developed special ties to two now senior historians who specialize in the study of São Paulo's working class. Paulo Fontes, a paulista of energy and creativity, was Duke's first Mellon Visiting Professor and has a rich understanding of the nordestino migration that figures so centrally in this book. My debt also runs deep to Antonio Gino Negro, who first entered into contact with me in 1991, when he was studying strike tactics among São Bernardo's metalworkers for the Centro Ecumênico de Documentação e Informação (CEDI). Gino introduced me to the fear-inducing riches of the newly opened archive of the political-social police (DOPS), while his 2004 monograph offered the first sweeping vision of the trajectory of the region's metalworkers from the 1940s to the early 1970s.

At the earliest stage of this project, I received support from Florida International University in 1991 as well as encouragement from my fellow FIU labor history aficionados Joyce Shaw Peterson, author of a study of Detroit's autoworkers, and Bryan Peterson (1942–2019). Since then, I have received grants from the American Council of Learned Societies and the American Philosophical Society, although my greatest ongoing debt is to Duke's Center for Latin American and Caribbean Studies (CLACS) and its associate director, Natalie Hartman, for its consistent support, along with, on occasion, Duke's Arts and Sciences Research Council and the Trent Foundation. For a dozen years, successive deans of arts and sciences at Duke also supported the annual Latin American Labor History Conference, cofounded at Yale in 1983 with Danny James, where many of the ideas of this book were first presented. Duke's Perkins Library, headed by Deborah Jakubs, has generously supported the acquisition of valuable microfilm collections, while Latin America specialist Holly Ackerman proactively pursued the books that I needed or should have.

I have long grappled with the insights, peculiarities, and puzzles that mark the enormous body of oral testimony from ABC's metalworkers between the early 1960s and the latest interview transcripts found in masters' theses and doctoral dissertations. In doing so, I have accumulated an enormous debt to Daniel James and Lynne DiPietro. With his rich insights into working-class life, populism, and theory, Danny has been my central interlocutor over thirty-six years as a sounding board, critic, collaborator, and close family friend. Danny has generously shared his knowledge of working-class life, which began as the son of a lifelong metalworker, Morgan James, whom Jan and I knew well and interviewed. Danny was among the first to demonstrate the potential of oral historical material when treated with greater methodological sophistication. Consistently inspiring and provocative, the depth of his crystalline assessments of successive drafts have made this a far better book.

Over the decades, I have benefited from dialogue with professional colleagues, including Robert Anderson, Reid Andrews, Idelber Avelar, Joan Bak, Rossana Barragán, Dirk Bonker, Dain Borges, Aviva Chomsky, John Collins, Larissa Correia, Jeff Cowie, Jack Draper, Brodwyn Fischer, Leon Fink, Jim Green, Jeff Gould, Wesley Hogan, Margaret Keck, Victoria Langland, Aldo Lauria Santiago, Michele Lewis, Joe Love, Bryan McCann, Nancy Maclain, John Martin, Bill Mello, Styliane Philippou, Jocelyn Olcott, Sumathi Ramaswamy, Pete Sigal, Steve Strifler, Emília Viotti da Costa, and Barbara Weinstein. My progress has also been shaped by successive cohorts of Duke graduate students turned colleagues, including Mark Healey, Jody Pavilack, Vince Brown, Jeff Cowie, Ivonne Wallace Fuentes, Tom Rogers, Alejandro Velasco, Katharine French-Fuller, Reena Goldthree, Elizabeth Shesko, Danielle Terrazas Williams, Bryan Pitts, Kristin Wintersteen, and, most recently, Gray Kidd and Travis Knoll. For research materials, I thank Robert J. Alexander, Dick Ginnold, John Humphrey, Margaret Keck, Kenneth Mericle, and Cliff Welch, as well as Jack Draper, Alexandre Fortes, Gustavo Furtado, and Bryan Pitts for translation assistance. I owe special thanks to professor Renato Delmanto of Votorantim, who kindly provided the transcript of a key 1978 Lula interview by Rui Mesquita.

Bryan Pitts (Duke PhD, 2013) has been an indispensable coresearcher—sharing as we do the terrain of paulista politics under the military regime—from whom I have learned much and benefited enormously. A generous scholar, he has shared freely from his vast body of research materials and provided rigorous readings of my texts, and he did the on-site research in Rio that allowed me to compile thousands of pages of SNI materials on the ABC metalworkers' strikes. Energetic and decided, Bryan took responsibility for lining up the book's photographic record with extensive assistance from my old friend and fellow researcher Ademir Medici and Cecilia Del Gesso of the indispensable *Diário do Grande ABC*. Photographers Juca Martins and Ricardo Stuckert kindly provided images used in this book, as did cartoonist Zé Dassilva. In lining up Lula's family pictures, we were assisted by Brian Mier, who arranged for Valeska Martins, of Lula's legal team, to get the former president's signature in jail; the images themselves were provided by Luana Soncini, the coordinator of the Centro Sérgio Buarque de Holanda of the Fundação Perseu Abramo.

There is no thinking without writing, and writing takes time and needs deadlines. During academic year 2013–14, a History Department course release was combined with the Douglas Southall Freeman Professorship of History at the University of Richmond where I received a warm welcome from my fellow historians; the department's administrator, Debbie Govoruhk; and its chair, Hugh West. It was also a pleasure to get to know the department's Brazilianist, Manuella Meyer. A concentrated burst of writing during my Richmond semester led to a May Day 2014 book manuscript workshop sponsored by Duke's John Hope Franklin Humanities Institute (FHI), directed at the time by Ian Baucom. I could not have had a better sounding board for what was planned, at the time, to be a two-volume biography: Fuentes, Rogers, Pitts, Olcott, and Wesley Hogan of Duke's Center for Documentary Studies, as well as Jan and Danny and my personal editor, Sean Mannion. My ideas have been shared at the University of Chicago, Cornell, Stony Brook, Princeton, and Washington University as well as the Casa Rui Barbosa, Universidade Federal Fluminense, the Universidade Estadual do Ceará, and at conferences in Liverpool and Linz, Austria.

Although this comprehensive single-volume biography has been long in the making, the writing occurred as a Brazil-focused community was emerging at Duke, an idea that originated with geologist Paul Baker; Paul and his wife, Catherine Rigsby, have become dear family friends. With vital participation by Antonio Arce at CLACS, we won the support of Mike Merson and Eve Duffy of the Office of Global Affairs to create the ongoing provost-level Duke Brazil Initiative (DBI). With that foundation, we acquired substantial additional support for a vertically integrated Global Brazil Humanities Lab, which was funded through the Mellon Humanities Writ Large grant directed by Srinivas Aravamudan (1962–2016) and sponsored over three years by the FHI, at the time directed by Deborah Jenson.

The Global Brazil lab was a splendid environment for thinking with and through Brazilian realities while working side by side with my talented codirectors, Esther Gabara and Christine Folch. The DBI and the Brazil lab became the hub for a remarkable community that includes Brazilian Duke graduate students Marcelo Nogueira and Yahn Wagner as well as visitors from Brazil, including Guilherme Cabral, Carolina Bittencourt Mendonça, Kellen Julio, Júlio Pinto, Cesar Santos, Sales Augusto dos Santos, Marcelo Ramos, Lucas Porto Marchesini Torres, and Silvio Almeida. A group of talented Duke professors have made the DBI a dynamic concern, including Gustavo Furtado, Regis Kopper, Marcos Rangel, Gustavo Silva, Magda Silva, Katya Wesolowski, João Ricardo Visocci, and the energetic new DBI codirector, Kenneth Maffitt of CLACS. As with Rafael Lima and Laura Senna a decade earlier, my work has benefited from bright doctoral candidates visiting on Brazilian

"Sandwich fellowships," such as Leonardo Angelo da Silva and Eduardo Angelo da Silva, the latter a brilliant historian-in training who in 2018 passed away in a tragic loss to his family, his home city of Barra Mansa, the academy, and his wife and many friends. A succession of students enlivened my work—including Kaley Deal, Ruici Ong, and John Victor Alencar—as did my thesis writers Tiffany Lieu and the Brazilianists Andrea Dinamarco, Katie Soltis, Madeleine Roberts, Chloe Ricks, and Courtney Crumpler.

Directing a project on higher education expansion from 2016 to 2019 served as a laboratory for this book's argument about the subversive impact of subaltern ambition among smart young people from a poor and stigmatized urban periphery. An interdisciplinary student-faculty research project, "The Cost of Opportunity," focused on the Baixada Fluminense, outside the city of Rio, with generous support from Duke's innovative Bass Connections program; special thanks are due to Tom Nechyba of the Social Science Research Institute, who led the Bass Education and Human Development track. Codirected with Katya Wesolowski (Cultural Anthropology), Marcos Rangel (Public Policy), and Fortes, seventeen Duke students worked with their counterparts at the Multidisciplinary Institute of the Federal Rural University of Rio de Janeiro (UFFRJ-IM) to study a unique generation who seized the opportunity offered by the democratization of higher education during the Lula-Dilma governments (https://sites.duke.edu/project_duke_baixada_project/).

The surveys, oral histories, and ethnographic observation carried among those I have come to call "Lula's children" sharpened my understanding of the spirited toughness characteristic of Lula and his generation of skilled workers. The US and Brazilian participants each committed themselves fully: I offer a salute to John Victor Alencar, Riley Allen, Joe Beck, Aaron Colston, Mitchell Jacob, Eyram Klu, Jessica Lee, Adair Necalli, and Chloe Ricks, as well as, on the Brazilian side, Douglas Almeida, Sandro Aragão, Luiza Braga, Guilherme Cabral, Carla Castanha, Luanna Lima, Debora Luisa, Juliane Marinho, Rodrigo Monteiro, Bruna Navarone, Louise Queiroz, Barbara Santos, Ana Paula Teixeira, and Yago Vale. Special thanks to the UFFRJ-IM's Renan Aronja and Cláudia de Paula, Felipe Ribeiro, Luis Fernando Orleans, Álvaro Pereira do Nascimento, João Márcio Mendes, Sandra Regina Sales, and the inestimable educator Marcia Pletsch.

The project offered a unique opportunity to dialogue with Stephanie Reist, a vibrant carioca-by-adoption who contributed her wide knowledge, unquenchable curiosity, and acute political sensibility over two years. The remarkable and multitalented rapper and popular educator Dudu de Morro Agudo, from the local Instituto Enraizados, would codirect our project film with Reist, which has been widely used with local high school students. After serving two years as the Brazil lab's graduate coordinator, Brazilianist history doctoral student Gray Kidd did excellent work helping colead our first year's Bass fieldwork and was followed in a similar capacity by his Duke history colleague Travis Knoll and doctoral candidate Andrew Guinn from UNC–Chapel Hill.

The sensibility informing my understanding of Brazil's multiracial and multicultural popular classes has been shaped by what I have learned from the quintessentially "American" history of the Afro–North American people and their role in progressive struggles in my country. In the spirit of Paul Robeson (1898–1976) and Elizabeth Gurley Flynn (1890–1964), this book is dedicated to anthropologist Johnetta Betsch Cole, a professor in the W. E. B. Du Bois Black Studies Department at the University of Massachusetts in the early 1970s, when I was an Amherst College undergraduate. Whether in or out of the classroom or libraries, working with a slew of Afro–North Americans has given me tools to better understand poor and working-class Brazilians of all colors. A tip of the hat to my Duke colleagues John Hope Franklin (1915–2009) and Raymond Gavins (1942–2016), and Duke undergraduates, including Gladys Mitchell-Walthour, whom I taught in the 1990s; and my undergraduate thesis writers—Amelia Herbert and Chloe Ricks—as well as doctoral students Stephanie Reist and Elizabeth Hordge-Freeman.

For almost a decade, I have worked with Sean Mannion, who served as the indispensable managing editor for the *Hispanic American Historical Review*, which I coedited at Duke for five years. Since 2013, he has also been my personal editor and helped me discipline a sprawling story line while discarding scholastic display. At the same time, his contributions go well beyond editorial minutiae: he was a primary partner in the construction of this biography, for which I am profoundly grateful. Since my second monograph in 2004, I have worked with Elaine Maisner, executive editor at UNC Press, who not only pursued this book but also forced me to recognize that a multivolume "total history" was a distraction compared to the analytical and narrative power of a more succinct but substantial one-volume work. Well served by UNC Press since 1992, I am grateful to the four outside readers as well as Christi Stanforth, a first-rate copyeditor; Assistant Managing Editor Jay Mazzocchi; and Paula Durbin-Westby, who produced a compelling index.

My life has been enriched by my family, above all my son and daughter, Paul Joseph and Elizabeth Nora, as well as my brother, Roger Harquail French; his wife, Barbara Brown French; and their children, Henry and Sylvia. In 2016, the warm and formidable Oscar González married Elizabeth, and our lives have since been enriched with the arrival of Lorca Marie González-French on April 25, 2019. Over the past forty-five years, my companheira Jan Hoffman French and I have been engaged in a never-ending conversation that has tested out every hunch and every whisper of an idea found in this book. She is someone from whom I have learned so much and with whom I have lived so hard and loved so powerfully. She is a source of daily inspiration—along with humor and solace—as we confront a twenty-first-century world shamefully lacerated by hunger, lies, suffering, injustice, and loss. As we struggle to better the world, we look back with appreciation to our parents: James Bruce French, a nuclear theorist; the feminist peace activist Helen Harquail French; the unionized Boeing metalworker Edward Hoffman; and Phyllis Hoffman, an enduring font of wisdom and welcome common sense.

NOTES

Abbreviations

APESP	Arquivo Público do Estado de São Paulo
CEDEM	Centro de Documentação e Memória da UNESP, São Paulo
DOPS	Acervo do Departamento Estadual de Ordem Política e Social
SSP	Secretaria do Estado dos Negocios da Segurança Pública
USNARA	U.S. National Archives and Records Administration

Introduction

1. "It's because of his good looks," Obama joked. As reporter Jake Tapper noted, "Lula . . . is hardly the George Clooney of the G20." Jake Tapper, "The Significance of President Obama Praising Lula's 'Good Looks,'" *Political Punch* (blog), ABC News, April 2, 2009, http://blogs.abcnews.com/politicalpunch/2009/04/thats-my-man-ri.html.

2. "Caso clínico—O destino é o ocaso atacado de mania de grandeza." Quintana, "Destino," 66.

3. Nêumanne Pinto, *O que sei*, 90.

4. Lukács, "Narrate," 112.

5. This biography thus addresses the lacunae and mysteries of Lula's development identified with acuity by Florestan Fernandes in "Lula e a transformação do Brasil contemporâneo," 40–41.

6. Payne, *I've Got the Light.*

7. Durand Ponte, *Crisis.*

8. Humphrey, *Capitalist Control*, 154–55, 157–59, 192.

9. Keck, *Workers' Party*, 77.

10. The disposition toward systemic analysis and ideological disputation—disconnected from embodied actors—can be seen in a recent institutional study of the CUT: Sluyter-Beltrão, *Rise and Decline.*

11. For reflections on biographers and biography, see French, "Social History," 122–32.

12. Von Mettenheim, *Brazilian Voter*, 124.

13. French, *Brazilian Workers' ABC.*

Chapter 1

1. Keck, "New Unionism," 266.

2. "Making Trouble on Human Rights," *New York Times*, November 30, 1981.

3. Stepan, "Introduction," xiv.

4. Keck, *Workers' Party.*

5. Ibid., 3, 149. Lula received less than 10 percent of the vote in São Paulo state.

6. Kinzo, "Consolidation of Democracy," 139, 148.

7. Di Tella, *Latin American Politics.* On the FSP and the historiography on Latin American left turns, see French, "Understanding the Politics."

8. Ginger, *Bending Cross.*

9. Salvatore, *Eugene V. Debs*.

10. Hobsbawm, *Age of Extremes*, 370.

11. Rossana Barragán (Bolivian historian), private communication with author, October 10, 2013.

12. Sartre, *Words*, 136.

13. Bourne, *Lula of Brazil*, 155.

14. The "log cabin myth" is described by historian Edward Pessen as the long-popular and widespread belief that the US presidency "is accessible to, and has in fact been occupied by, men born of modest circumstances" who rose "from relative obscurity to the highest position in the nation." Across two centuries, "politicians, orators, editorial writers, ministers, and scholars have never ceased reminding us that the presidential race has typically been won by ambitious and hard-working men who reached the political heights primarily by their own heroic efforts." While recognizing the "pervasiveness and durability of this belief in the plebeian origins of almost all the presidents," Pessen's research led him to express "grave doubt" as to the accuracy of this "article of American faith." Pessen, *Log Cabin Myth*, 1–3, 7.

15. Bourne, *Lula of Brazil*, 230, 210.

16. Markun, *O sapo*.

17. Florência Costa, "Denise Paraná: Como Lula chegou lá," *IstoÉ*, January 8, 2003; Paraná, *Lula*, 36–37.

18. For an account of the interviews' conduct, see Paraná, *Lula*, 36–42.

19. Paraná, "Da cultura da pobreza."

20. Paraná, *O filho*.

21. Fundação Perseu Abramo, "'Lula, o filho do Brasil': Filme sobre vida de Lula retratará o homem comum," *ADITAL*, March 4, 2009, http://www.adital.com.br/site/noticia_imp.asp?cod=37559&lang=PT.

22. An early compilation of press and TV interviews with Lula, along with some speeches, can be found in Guizzo et al., *Lula*. Interviews with Lula, Frei Chico, and Lula's second wife (along with some collaborators) can be found in Morel, *Lula*. For an extended interview with Lula alone, see Altino Dantas, *Lula*.

23. Paraná, *Lula*.

24. Ibid., 33.

25. Ibid., 484–85.

26. Ibid., 380–81, 486, 333.

27. Ibid., 483.

28. Ibid., 33.

29. Ibid., 482.

30. Ibid., 33.

31. Paraná, *O filho*, 443.

32. Paraná, *Lula*, 33, 486.

33. Bibiano Girard et al., "Osvaldo Coggiola: 'A grande maioria da esquerda foi Comprada, aderiu ou fez negocio,'" *Revista o Vies*, April 17, 2012, http://www.revistaovies.com/entrevistas/2012/04/entrevista-com-osvaldo-coggiola/.

34. Coggiola, introduction, 16.

35. Ibid., 19–20. Claims for the absolute historical novelty of the New Unionism and the PT were rhetorical commonplaces for *petistas* (as members of the PT are called) during the struggle for hegemony on the left in the 1980s. For instance, an important Brazilian pe-

tista and his US collaborator, in an English-language book from 1991, described Brazil as a country with "no leftist tradition," a place where labor and popular movements "had little weight" or "importance in political life." Sader and Silverstein, *Without Fear*, 9, 16. In doing so, they wished away the very real challenges the PT faced from Leonel Brizola in the electoral sphere and from the mainstream Communists in the labor movement, where they were historically predominant.

36. Coggiola, introduction, 19 (emphasis in original).

37. Betto, *Lula*, 65. See also Candido, introduction, 16.

38. Skidmore, *Brazil*, 218.

39. *Lula: A história de um vencedor* (2002), reprinted in Sommariva, *Lula*.

40. For a detailed review by two historians of ABC's metalworkers, see French and Negro, "Politics."

41. Rodrigues and Zalla, *Lula*; Bourne, *Lula do Brasil*.

42. Audálio Dantas, *O menino Lula*. *Retirante* refers to a "person forced off the land by drought." Rebhun, *Heart Is Unknown Country*, 229. Himself a migrant from the Northeast, Dantas became famous early in his career for discovering Carolina Maria de Jesus, a black slum dweller whose diary became a national and international best seller.

43. Audálio Dantas, *O menino Lula*, 13–14, 99.

44. Hunter, *Transformation*, 7.

45. Katie Uva, "Parson Weems," George Washington's Mount Vernon, accessed January 11, 2013, https://www.mountvernon.org/library/digitalhistory/digital-encyclopedia/article/parson-weems/.

46. Dutilleux, *Lula*, 19, 10, 289.

47. Ibid., 83.

48. Ibid., 19.

49. Lamounier, *Da independência*, 183, 185.

50. Fernando Henrique Cardoso, "Challenges," 284–85.

51. Nêumanne Pinto, *O que sei*; Nêumanne Pinto, *Atrás do palanque*.

52. Salatiel Soares Correia, "Lula, um homem atrás do mito," *Jornal Opção* (Goiás), March 17–23, 2013.

53. Nêumanne Pinto, *O que sei*, 111, 83–84.

54. Ibid., 104.

55. He even cites unsourced rumors that Lula's loss of his finger may have been a deliberate ploy to win an indemnification; in a display of fair-mindedness, he doesn't directly endorse this charge. Ibid., 78.

56. Ibid., 76, 81–82, 85, 98, 104, 123.

57. Quoted in Nêumanne Pinto, *O que sei*, front material. The Jabor column appeared in *O Estado de São Paulo* on September 21, 2010.

58. The Mugwumps were characterized by their "cosmopolitan cultural traits and the cohesiveness of their intellectual community, especially in the Boston-Cambridge area." They were "usually old American, white Protestants whose social and political dominance was threatened by immigration, industrialization, and urbanization in the late nineteenth century—a group defined as much by its cultural ties as by its politics. . . . [They] always depended on the power of the pen to offset their weakness in numbers and did so again in the historical record." McFarland, *Mugwumps*, 1, 3.

59. Nêumanne Pinto, *O que sei*, front material. The quote is from an article by a distinguished *paulista* (as residents of São Paulo are called) intellectual of the 1960s, Maria Sylvia

de Carvalho Franco, in the *Illustríssima* section of the *Folha de São Paulo*, September 26, 2010.

60. See Candido's interview in Ferreira and Fortes, *Muitos caminhos*.

61. Costa, *Brazilian Empire*, 24–25.

62. "Gaviões da fiel aposta no carisma de Lula para voltar a empolgar torcedor: Enredo conta a saga do homem que saiu do sertão e chegou ao Planalto. Para carnavalesco, preocupação é manter vínculos com os corintianos," *Globo.com*, January 15, 2012, http://g1.globo.com/sao-paulo/carnaval/2012/noticia/2012/01/gavioes-da-fiel-aposta-no-carisma-de-lula-para-voltar-empolgar-torcedor.html. The winner presented a theme around the life of the Bahian writer Jorge Amado, a nationally and internationally renowned writer also well-known for his quarter century of militancy in the PCB.

63. Costa, *Brazilian Empire*, 25.

Chapter 2

1. *Pau de arara* is commonly thought to refer to a type of torture. Rejali, *Torture*, 307. Estrela, *Os sampauleiros*, 113, cites two nordestino explanations for this phrase from a 1969 study of trucks: that it was common in the backlands to refer to stupid people as parrots, which migrants were considered to be; and that the wooden slats on which they sat in the truck were reminiscent of the perch of parrots tied to a stick (*pau*) in backland homes.

2. Audálio Dantas, *O menino Lula*, 57.

3. Vilmar Faria, "Changes," 143–44.

4. Merrick, "Population," 16, 45.

5. Vilmar Faria, "Changes," 145.

6. Hoffman, "Poverty and Property."

7. Bacha and Klein, "Introduction," 3.

8. Ibid., 1.

9. Estrela, *Os sampauleiros*, 117.

10. Luiz Gonzaga, "Pau de Arara," Letras.mus.br, accessed February 7, 2014, http://letras.mus.br/luiz-gonzaga/261217/. Translation by Dr. Jack Draper.

11. Asked about his early childhood in Garanhuns, Frei Chico in 1981 paused to register the class differences *within* the region of his birth: "Miserable infant, like that of all *nordestinos*. All, no, some of them have a good life [*vida gostosa*]. But I will never forget my infancy." Frei Chico, interview by Mário Morel, mid-1981, in Morel, *Lula*, 63.

12. Paulo Narciso, "Lourdes: O amor mineiro de Lula," montesclaros.com, accessed February 7, 2014, http://montesclaros.com/reportagens/lourdes.asp.

13. Brandão Lopes, *Sociedade industrial*, 31.

14. Clay, "Articulation," 288, 50, 42, 105–6, 116.

15. Ibid., 202, 205, 267, 271–72, 276.

16. Lula, interview by Denise Paraná, June 30, 1993, in Paraná, *Lula*, 57;Frei Chico, interview by Paraná, September 3 and 7, 1993, in ibid., 225; Lula, interview by Morel, mid-1981, in Morel, *Lula*, 21.

17. Clay, "Articulation," 303, 284, 290, 299, 309.

18. Lula, interview by Morel, mid-1981, in Morel, *Lula*, 21.

19. Durham, *A caminho*, 139, listed the discovery that one had seduced a local girl as a motivation for single men to migrate. In Aristides's case, he preempted scandal by leaving and minimized reproach by returning under conditions of his own choosing, as a successful migrant displaying material success.

20. Vavá, interview by Paraná, September 3 and 7, 1993, in Paraná, *Lula*, 194–95; Maria Baixinha, interview by Paraná, April 6, 1994, in ibid., 255–57; Jaime Inácio da Silva, interview by Paraná, April 10, 1994, in ibid., 278–79, 281, 284, 287; Lula, interview by Paraná, June 30, 1993, in ibid., 46, 49; Frei Chico, interview by Paraná, September 3 and 7, 1993, in ibid., 198, 200; Lula, interview, 2000, in "Depoimento de Luiz Inácio Lula da Silva," made available online through the union's historical website ABC de Luta, 2-6 (numeration added by author). Conducted on April 17 and 26, 2000, the full interview transcript with questions was provided to me by Raquel Camargo, "Depoimento de Luiz Inácio Lula da Silva."

21. Jaime, interview by Paraná, April 10, 1994, in Paraná, *Lula*, 275, 281, 288; Frei Chico, interview by Paraná, September 3 and 7, 1993, in ibid., 200; Lula, interview by Paraná, June 30, 1993, in ibid., 48–49, 51, 53–54; Lula, interview by Paraná, July 1993, in ibid., 70; Vavá, interview by Paraná, September 3 and 7, 1993, in ibid., 207, 219; Frei Chico and Vavá, interview by Paraná, September 3 and 7, 1993, in ibid., 206; Marinete Leite Cerqueira, interview by Paraná, March 29, 1994, in ibid., 248; Maria Baixinha, interview by Paraná, April 6, 1994, in ibid., 257, 261; Lula, interview by Altino Dantas Jr., circa the first half of January 1981, in Altino Dantas, *Lula*, 11–12; Lula, interview, 2000, in "Depoimento de Luiz Inácio Lula da Silva."

22. Lula, interview by Paraná, June 30, 1993, in Paraná, *Lula*, 50, 52, 56; Frei Chico, interview by Paraná, September 3 and 7, 1993, in ibid., 202, 212; Frei Chico and Vavá, interview by Paraná, September 3 and 7, 1993, in ibid., 202–3; Jaime, interview by Paraná, April 10, 1994, in ibid., 275; Maria Baixinha, interview by Paraná, April 6, 1994, in ibid., 256–57; Vavá, interview by Paraná, September 3 and 7, 1993, in ibid., 195; Lula, interview by Morel, mid-1981, in Morel, *Lula*, 24; Lula, interview, 2000, in "Depoimento de Luiz Inácio Lula da Silva," 2–3, 8 (quote).

23. Frei Chico and Vavá, interview by Paraná, September 3 and 7, 1993, in Paraná, *Lula*, 202–3, 225; Marinete, interview by Paraná, March 29, 1994, in ibid., 241–42, 245, 248; Maria Baixinha, interview by Paraná, April 6, 1994, in ibid., 258; Lula, interview by Paraná, June 30, 1993, in ibid., 51–53; Jaime, interview by Paraná, April 10, 1994, in ibid., 280; Lula, interview by Dantas, first half of January 1981, in Altino Dantas, *Lula*, 12–13.

24. Tiana, interview by Paraná, April 21, 1994, in Paraná, *Lula*, 301–3; Lula, interview, 2000, in "Depoimento de Luiz Inácio Lula da Silva," 3, 10–13; Lula, interview by Morel, mid-1981, in Morel, *Lula*, 27–28 (quote).

25. Langenbuch, *A estruturação*, 170–71, table 1; 250–51, tables 13–14.

26. José Carlos Pereira, *Estrutura e expansão*, 118.

27. Rodrigues, *Industrialização*, 54.

28. Kahil, *Inflation and Economic Development*, 64.

29. Mercadante Oliva, "Estado autoritário," 3; "O ABC arrecada mais do que 9 estados," *Estado de São Paulo*, July 23, 1968, 74.

30. The numbers, rounded here, are available in Shapiro, *Engines*, 241, table A.6.

31. Assis, *Mercado de trabalho*, 189, 216.

32. Shapiro, *Engines*, 241.

33. Abramo, *O resgate*, 91. As was true in 1958, ABC in the late 1970s was marked by the extraordinary concentration of workers in very large factories. Humphrey, *Capitalist Control*, 51, 137.

34. Durham, *A caminho*, 32, 35, table 6.

35. Ibid., 41.

36. Vavá, interview by Paraná, September 3 and 7, 1993, in Paraná, *Lula*, 200–201; Frei

Chico, interview by Paraná, September 3 and 7, 1993, in ibid., 219; Frei Chico, interview by Morel, mid-1981, in Morel, *Lula*, 63.

37. Graham, "Interstate Migration," 35. As Graham explains, it is hard to get a handle on the statistical realities of "interstate in-migration in the major urban labor markets of the Center-South of Brazil." Not only was there a bungled 1960 census, most of the results of which were never published, but even the much-improved 1970 professional census problematically defined migrants as anyone who lived in a município other than where they were born. Moreover, the interstate migration tables are not "cross classified with industrial or occupational classifications." Graham cross-references 1970 data with the rich statistical data available from the Brazilian Labor Law of Two-Thirds for 1969–70. Ibid., 30, 32.

38. Ibid., 38–41, 43–44.

39. Queiroz, "Classes sociais," 747.

40. Tomizaki, *Ser metalúrgico*, xxx.

41. Vila Carioca was one of the more concentrated areas of nordestino settlement in São Paulo, along with the outlying district of São Miguel Paulista, which grew up around the massive Nitroquimica plant, although it too was never homogenously nordestino in its resident population. See the thorough and sensitive study by Fontes, *Um nordeste*.

42. Lula, interview by Paraná, June 30, 1993, in Paraná, *Lula*, 64; Lambari, interview by Paraná, June 27, 1994, in ibid., 343; Tiana, interview by Paraná, April 21, 1994, in ibid., 306; Lula, interview, 2000, in "Depoimento de Luiz Inácio Lula da Silva," 14, 16.

43. Tiana, interview by Paraná, April 21, 1994, in Paraná, *Lula*, 306; Lambari, interview by Paraná, June 27, 1994, in ibid., 339–40, 347–48; Maria Baixinha, interview by Paraná, June 27, 1994, in ibid., 347; Narciso, "Lourdes."

44. Rural paulistas and other migrants to São Paulo city themselves talk defensively about their shyness ("são tímidos"), often accompanied by self-deprecation ("não sabe muito," "somos ignorantes"), in their interactions with city folks in general, which is intensified further by social class and educational differences. Durham, *A caminho*, 140–41.

45. Ibid., 160–61, 164–66.

46. For citations and a brief discussion of the research findings on working-class household economies in São Paulo in the 1960s and 1970s, see French, "Women and Working-Class Mobilization," 177–79.

47. Lambari, interview by Paraná, June 27, 1994, in Paraná, *Lula*.

48. Lula, interview by Paraná, July 1993, in ibid., 69. Durham, *A caminho*, 166, 169–70, discusses the particular appeal of being a driver, including one major advantage: it was a form of self-employment free from the rigid control of factory life.

49. Durham, *A caminho*, 180.

50. Lula, interview, 2000, in "Depoimento de Luiz Inácio Lula da Silva," 18–19.

51. Lambari, interview by Paraná, June 27, 1994, in Paraná, *Lula*, 340, discusses a job where this happened to him in the early 1960s.

52. Colistete, *Labour Relations*, 23.

53. Lula, interview by Morel, mid-1981, in Morel, *Lula*, 33.

54. Negro, *Linhas*, 309–10.

55. Vavá, interview by Paraná, September 3 and 7, 1993, in Paraná, *Lula*, 206, 233; Jaime, interview by Paraná, April 10, 1994, in ibid., 276, 285, 288; Lula, interview by Paraná, July 19, 1993, in ibid., 79; Tiana, interview by Paraná, April 21, 1994, in ibid., 300, 305.

56. Armando Corrêa da Silva, "Estrutura e mobilidade social," 63, 73. Seventeen percent of the fichas lacked data or were illegible. The districts with more than 100,000 residents

in the município's eastern zones include Ipiranga, where the Silvas lived, as well as Saúde, Penha de França, Tatuapé, Alto da Mooca, and Vila Prudente.

57. Ibid., 73. In ibid., 65, Silva explains that he preserved the documents' terms for classifying occupations and economic activities because they reflected the "consciousness of the mode of production and social processes . . . on the part of the interviewees."

58. Armando Corrêa da Silva, "Estrutura e mobilidade social," 86; Fontes, *Um nordeste*, 198–99.

59. Durham, *A caminho*, 67, 131, 184, 208–11; Vavá, interview by Paraná, September 3 and 7, 1993, in Paraná, *Lula*, 206.

60. Armando Corrêa da Silva, "Estrutura e mobilidade social," 86.

61. Maria Baixinha, interview by Paraná, April 6, 1994, in Paraná, *Lula*, 257 (first quote), 260 (second quote); Marinete, interview by Paraná, March 29, 1994, in ibid., 247; Jaime, interview by Paraná, April 10, 1994, in ibid., 283, 293; Lula, interview by Paraná, June 30, 1993, in ibid., 55 (remaining quotes); Lula, interview, 2000, in "Depoimento de Luiz Inácio Lula da Silva," 3, 12, 13 (quote).

62. Marisa, interview by Paraná, May 6, 1994, in Paraná, *Lula*, 326–27; Lula, interview by Paraná, June 30, 1993, in ibid., 61; Marinete, interview by Paraná, March 29, 1994, in ibid., 245.

63. Maria Baixinha, interview by Paraná, April 6, 1994, in ibid., 269; Jaime, interview by Paraná, April 10, 1994, in ibid., 286; Lambari, interview by Paraná, June 27, 1994, in ibid., 346.

64. Durham, *A caminho*, 172. The sacrifices made to achieve even a primary education for some children are described in Armando Corrêa da Silva, "Estrutura e mobilidade social," 76; the family dynamics are discussed with sensitivity and insight in Durham, *A caminho*, 210, 172–73.

65. Durham, *A caminho*, 210.

66. Lula, interview by Paraná, June 30, 1993, in Paraná, *Lula*, 64–65; Lula, interview, 2000, in "Depoimento de Luis Inácio Lula da Silva," 16.

67. Durham, *A caminho*, 211. The assent by Vavá, the most loyal older brother, to the prioritization of education for Lula is clear (Vavá, interview by Paraná, September 3 and 7, 1993, in Paraná, *Lula*, 201, 230); Frei Chico's assent is likewise clear (Frei Chico, interview by Paraná, September 3 and 7, 1993, in ibid., 231). Frei Chico, interview by Paraná, October 5, 1993, in ibid., 152; Frei Chico, interview by Morel, mid-1981, in Morel, *Lula*, 1981, 64.

68. Tiana, interview by Paraná, April 21, 1994, in Paraná, *Lula*, 303.

69. Durham, *A caminho*, 160.

70. Luiz Pereira, *Trabalho*, 12–13. See Beisiegel, "Os primeiros tempos," 600. I discuss the lacunae in the labor historiography surrounding authority and obedience in French, "Laboring and Middle-Class Peoples," 327–28.

71. Luiz Pereira, *A escola*, 91.

72. Ibid., 83, 111. Pereira's survey of teachers established that the husbands of primary schoolteachers were overwhelming "middle-class" (i.e., nonmanual) (70 percent), with 72 percent having husbands of the same background; even the distribution of the ten most common neighborhoods where his surveyed teachers lived suggested their strong "middle-class" composition. Luiz Pereira, *O magistério*, 141–42, 144–45.

73. Luiz Pereira, *A escola*, 8, 75, 79, 88–91, 111, 114.

74. Ibid., 78, 88–89, 113, 116. On how this seigneurial ethos dated back to slavery, see Luiz Pereira, *O magistério*, 157.

75. Luiz Pereira, *A escola*, 110–12, 114. The teachers' certainty that they could care better

for a child than illiterate parents could helps explain the story that Lula tells about a primary school teacher in Vicente de Carvalho, dona Terezinha, "who liked me a lot." As he recounts, "When my mother went to tell her that we were going to leave the school to go to São Paulo, she hinted to my mother that she would like it if I stayed with her. She wanted my mother to leave me there for her to take care of. But my mother had resolved to take me along." Lula, interview by Paraná, July 1993, in Paraná, *Lula*, 70.

76. Luiz Pereira, *A escola*, 116.

77. Ibid., 117–19.

78. Lula, interview, 2000, in "Depoimento de Luiz Inácio Lula da Silva," 11; Lula, interview by Paraná, July 1993, in Paraná, *Lula*, 71.

79. José de Souza Martins, "A valorização," 115, 124–25, 131.

80. Luiz Pereira, *A escola*, 91. At another point in *A escola*, Pereira offers an illuminating use of the term *pé-rapado* that makes its racially derived associations explicit. Trying to capture the unparalleled opportunities of city life, a home-owning mother in Utinga marveled that "here even blacks [*pretos*] have their own houses! In the interior you don't see that. There, the black is always a *pé-rapado*." Ibid., 29. The folklorist Luís da Câmara Cascudo has documented the term in seventeenth-century Bahia and discusses its origin and meanings. Cascudo, *Locuções tradicionais*, 228–29.

81. Luiz Pereira, *A escola*, 114.

82. Ibid., 120, 122.

83. "O primeiro impeachment."

84. On the controversy caused by the position taken by the Union Council of Santo André, see "Comicio do Conselho Sindical," *O Reporter*, October 29, 1961; "'Falsos lideres sindicais'—O vereador Edson Lazari assim classificou os membros do Conselho Sindical do ABC," *Jornal de Santo André*, November 1, 1961.

85. Lula, interview by Paraná, June 30, 1993, in Paraná, *Lula*, 52. For her version of the romance, see Marinete, interview by Paraná, March 29, 1994, in ibid., 242–44.

86. Quoted in Kamel, *Dicionário*, 428.

Chapter 3

1. Quoted in Kamel, *Dicionário*, 418.

2. The occasion was a 1982 TV debate. Carlos Sambrana, "Torneiros mecânicos: Na era da automação industrial, os antigos colegas de trabalho de Lula fazem parte de uma espécie em extinção," *IstoÉ Dinheiro*, October 30, 2002, 88. On other occasions, Lula cited his profession to answer whether he was a Communist.

3. Fernandes, "Empresa industrial."

4. Luiz Pereira, *Trabalho*, 29.

5. Lula, interview by Dantas, first half of January 1981, in Altino Dantas, *Lula*, 16; Lula, interview by Paraná, July 1993, in Paraná, *Lula*, 74–75 (quotes).

6. Luiz Pereira, *Trabalho*, 7, 302. The *banca* for his *tese de livre docência* was composed of Florestan Fernandes, Octávio Ianni, Cândido Procopio Ferreira de Camargo, and Oracy Nogueira. To capture variation, the study encompassed nine firms from two "traditional" branches of industry (*mobiliario*, textiles) and one modern one (*mecânicas*), as well as choosing within each sector one small (30 employees), one medium (150), and one large (2,000) factory. Ibid., 26.

7. Ibid., 142, 228. Unfortunately, when I interviewed Pereira in 1981, he told me that he had thrown out the original material from his 1958 and 1963 research when he moved to his

present apartment. Perhaps some has survived as copies in the hands of those who worked with him, who included José de Souza Martins, from São Caetano.

8. Referring to rural migrants generically as "nordestinos," one paulista worker complained to Pereira that their arrival "has made the workers' situation worse because they offer to work for any wage." "We don't earn enough," he went on, "to live well or to have a better life." He also noted the two-sided nature of "technical progress, which facilitates the work but leaves many people without jobs." Luiz Pereira, *Trabalho*, 200.

9. SENAI, *De homens*, 131. The foremen were called "thinking and directing arms" (*braços pensante e dirigentes*) in Mange's 1941 scheme, a hierarchical language he would later discard as unhelpful. Ibid., 141; Bologna, *Roberto Mange*, 337.

10. Robert J. Alexander, "Observations on SENAI in São Paulo," April 27, 1956, Papers of Robert J. Alexander, Special Collections and University Archives, Rutgers University Libraries, box 5, folder 48.

11. Colistete, *Labour Relations*, 9. If you include the auto parts industry, São Paulo município accounts for slightly over half the transport equipment industry employment, ABC for a third. Ibid., 5.

12. The director of SENAI-SP offered the following estimates for the proportion of skilled workers (*qualificados*) in relation to total employees (*empregados*) by industrial group: 4 percent in clothing, chemical, and pharmaceutical; 7 percent in textiles, leather, and rubber products; 20 percent in metalworking (*mecânicas, metalúrgicas, e de material elétrico*); 30 percent in printing; and 60 percent in the small sector covering jewelry, lapidating, and related activities. Bologna, *Formação profissional*, 54.

13. Luiz Pereira, *Trabalho*, 226.

14. Luiz Marcondes Nitsch, interview by Robert J. Alexander, April 27, 1956, Papers of Robert J. Alexander, Special Collections and University Archives, Rutgers University Libraries, box 5, folder 48.

15. As for the dire need for ferramenteiros, SENAI dispatched a staff member to France for a four-month internship and in 1962 trumpeted what they called Latin America's first course in the profession, although, ten months long, it was most likely a course to retrain those with other skills to become ferramenteiros. Weinstein, *For Social Peace*, 258, 392.

16. For a discussion of these issues from the 1930s through the 1950s, see French, "How the Not-So-Powerless Prevail."

17. Derived from Colistete, *Labour Relations*, 190, table A-8. The table is based on SENAI-SP reports from 1944 to 1960.

18. Bologna, *Formação profissional*, 37–38. The approximate hours specified before this date—and how they were counted and divided—is not mentioned.

19. Ibid. In 1969, a wide range of metalworking jobs were listed as skilled by SENAI-SP. There was an internal, sometimes-disputed hierarchy between these occupations, so the term "skilled" is always relative.

20. Tiana, interview by Paraná, April 21, 1994, in Paraná, *Lula*, 311; Maria Baixinha, interview by Paraná, April 6, 1994, in ibid., 263; Lula, interview by Dantas, first half of January 1981, in Altino Dantas, *Lula*, 15. Dona Lindu walked to economize on the bus fare.

21. Luiz Pereira, *A escola*, 34, 12–13.

22. Nitsch mentions this in his 1956 interview with Alexander. Such requests regarding underage minors, he said, were sometime accommodated, although it required a judge to waiver the child labor rules.

23. Alexander, "Observations on SENAI."

24. Assis, *Mercado de trabalho*, 189.

25. In his Santo André study, Pereira points out that the entry slots at SENAI "are far below the demand" in early 1959, with only 210 for all courses offered in all of ABC; as a result, he notes, "only rarely" will the primary school's adolescents make it into SENAI. Luiz Pereira, *A escola*, 38–39. He suggests that perhaps if such shortage continues, the parents will realize their limited chances to achieve social ascent via this route (something they had already realized for "intellectual professions").

26. Bologna, *Formação profissional*, 54. The issue is addressed in interviews with workers, quotes from which appear in Luiz Pereira, *Trabalho*, 184–85.

27. Luiz Pereira, *Trabalho*, 185.

28. Cláudio de Moura Castro, "Vocational Education," 624. Not to mention the largely invisible subgroup, most likely rural, who never attended any school and thus didn't show up in government enrollment statistics.

29. Vavá, interview by Paraná, September 3 and 7, 1993, in Paraná, *Lula*, 210, 212–13, 229; Jaime, interview by Paraná, April 10, 1994, in ibid., 282; Marinete, interview by Paraná, March 29, 1994, in ibid., 240; Lula, interview by Dantas, first half of January 1981, in Altino Dantas, *Lula*, 15.

30. Luiz Pereira, *A escola*, 32; Maria Baixinha, interview by Paraná, April 6, 1994, in Paraná, *Lula*, 263.

31. Forty percent failed after this first step of presenting the diploma.

32. Luiz Pereira, *A escola*, 110–12, 114, 131. Brazilianist Joe Love has suggested that Lula "is possibly—I emphasize this is conjecture—the least Caucasian president since Nilo Peçanha (1909–1910)." Love, "Lula Government," 305. In discussing their family's background, both Lula and Vavá use words that touch on appearance, color, rurality, and ethnicity in ways best captured by the word *mestiço*. Lula has described his father's parents as "really *caboclos* . . . [who] must be descendants of blacks [*negros*] or Indians [*indios*] because they're all almost black [*negros*]. My father, in fact, was a little more *moreno* than I am." Lula, interview, 2000, in "Depoimento de Luiz Inácio Lula da Silva," 2. Talking to Paraná, he said, "My father was a *bugre* [an old, indeterminate term used for Indians]. . . . That is to say, he didn't have many features [*traços*] of Indian, but had features of a real caboclo." Lula, interview by Paraná, June 30, 1993, in Paraná, *Lula*, 58. Vavá told Paraná in a separate interview that "my father was a descendant of Indians. But the father of my father was light. He wasn't moreno, no. But my father looked like a bugre." Vavá, interview by Paraná, September 3 and 7, 1993, in ibid., 224. As for Lula himself, he is without doubt white within Brazilian phenotypical conventions, although he is blackened by his origin, early poverty, and engagement in manual labor.

33. Luiz Pereira, *A escola*, 63, 83, 88, 90, 100, 116–98.

34. Cláudio de Moura Castro, "Vocational Education," 623, 628. Santo André's teachers thought their pupils' families lacked "the will to improve their lives" because these teachers disdained even skilled manual professions, valuing only a rise to "'intellectual' professions" through postprimary education. Luiz Pereira, *A escola*, 130. This strong aspiration toward white-collar professions over stigmatized manual occupations was also felt among the popular classes. One survey of "students in *primario* and living in working-class suburbs in Guanabara" found that 43 percent declared that their goal was "to reach the university." Mello e Souza, "Rates of Return," 136.

35. Bologna, *Roberto Mange*, 386–87.

36. This was despite the higher pay for skilled occupations like machinists versus higher-status white-collar jobs, established in several major surveys by economists and students of

vocational education for the late 1960s and early 1970s. Mello e Souza, "Rates of Return," 136; Cláudio de Moura Castro, "Vocational Education," 624.

37. Tomizaki, *Ser metalúrgico*, 126. This is why Vavá says in passing that Lula graduated from colegio, a claim Lula has never made. Vavá, interview by Paraná, September 3 and 7, 1993, in Paraná, *Lula*, 212.

38. Mello e Souza, "Rates of Return," 131. Candidate interviews were a late addition to the admissions process, which Mange adopted because he became convinced that students had to be approached not as "a code, a class, or a type but an individual with his own constellation of attributes to which, often, numerical test results do not apply." Bologna, *Roberto Mange*, 371.

39. Lula, interview by Morel, mid-1981, in Morel, *Lula*, 28.

40. Lula, interview by Paraná, June 30, 1993, in Paraná, *Lula*, 56; Jaime, interview by Paraná, April 10, 1994, in ibid., 286, 280–81; Frei Chico and Vavá, interview by Paraná, September 3 and 7, 1993, in ibid., 213; Frei Chico, interview by Paraná, September 3 and 7, 1993, in ibid., 231 (second quote); Lula, interview by Morel, mid-1981, in Morel, *Lula*, 28 (first quote).

41. Vavá, interview by Paraná, September 3 and 7, 1993, in Paraná, *Lula*, 201, 230–31.

42. Tiana, interview by Paraná, April 21, 1994, in ibid., 303.

43. Luiz Pereira, *Trabalho*, 180; Luiz Pereira, *A escola*, 36 (last quote).

44. Luiz Pereira, *Trabalho*, 181, 184–85.

45. As one worker tells Pereira in ibid., 185, "If you're slow-witted, you won't escape the broom." The same pessimistic assessment was offered by a worker two decades later: "If the guy doesn't know how to do anything, he's going to have to sweep, you know . . . [but] a 'floor sweeper' [*faixineiro*] is not a profession." Ferretti, *Opção*, 82.

46. Ferretti, *Opção*, 94.

47. Lula, quoted in Kamel, *Dicionário*, 422.

48. Lula, interview by Dantas, first half of January 1981, in Altino Dantas, *Lula*, 15 (first quote); Lula, quoted in Kamel, *Dicionário*, 422 (second quote); Lula, interview, 2000, in "Depoimento de Luiz Inácio Lula da Silva," 17; Lula, interview by Morel, mid-1981, in Morel, *Lula*, 29 (remaining quotes). The factory's address is from Luís Eduardo Leal, "Lula muda de endereço à procura de empregos," *Folha de São Paulo*, October 2, 1994.

49. Tiana, interview by Paraná, April 21, 1994, in Paraná, *Lula*, 311.

50. "Happy ones" is how Pereira's informants referred to those accepted to SENAI. Luiz Pereira, *A escola*, 38.

51. Lula, interview by Paraná, October 6, 1993, in Paraná, *Lula*, 88.

52. Ferretti, *Opção*, 79, 94. The distance of the factory from Lula's house comes from Lula, interview by Morel, mid-1981, in Morel, *Lula*, 29; the number of factory workers comes from ibid., 33.

53. Lula, interview, 2000, in "Depoimento de Luiz Inácio Lula da Silva," 16; Lula interview by Morel, in Morel, *Lula*, 29, 33. It is possible Lula got apprenticeship by his family knowing the factory's owner, rather than through the bureaucratic postings or special pleadings at SENAI.

54. Lula, interview by Paraná, June 30, 1993, in Paraná, *Lula*, 51.

55. Lula, interview by Paraná, July 1993, in ibid., 75.

56. The skilled workers at Metal Leve in São Paulo studied in 1959 routinely referred to the unskilled northeastern workers as baianos. Brandão Lopes, "O ajustamento," 428, 435–36.

57. Jacinto Ribeiro dos Santos, interview by Paraná, June 27, 1994, in Paraná, *Lula*, 340. Estrela, *Os sampauleiros*, provides examples of baiano jokes as well as the terms teasingly used among nordestinos in São Paulo. See also Weffort, "Nordestinos," 16.

58. Montgomery, *Fall*, 182. US unions at the time assigned different names to each of these competencies for the members' card, but Brazilian unions did not.

59. Tauile, "Microelectronics," 83.

60. SENAI, *De homens*, 151. Ibid., 179, features a picture of Mange watching a boy at a lathe.

61. Montgomery, *Fall*, 204; Frederico, *A vanguarda operária*.

62. SENAI, *De homens*, 151.

63. Unlike Aristides, in an incident that still stings for Lula: having come home with ice cream bought from a street vendor, Aristides gave some to two of Lula's half-brothers and to others there but refused his youngest son on the pretext that "you don't know how to eat ice cream." Lula, interview by Paraná, June 30, 1993, in Paraná, *Lula*, 51–52. It could be that he didn't know how to lick ice cream, Lula went on—it would have been his first attempt—but if so, that was his problem, and his father had no right to deny him ice cream.

64. Lula, interview by Morel, mid-1981, in Morel, *Lula*, 33; Lula, interview by Paraná, July 1993, in Paraná, *Lula*, 76.

65. Alexander, "Observations on SENAI."

66. Others, Nitsch told Alexander, saw the long-run benefit of this short-term sacrifice. Nitsch, interview by Alexander.

67. Bologna, *Roberto Mange*, 214–15; Mello e Souza, "Rates of Return," 131 (quote). Ibid., 157, summarizes the criticisms to be made of the Brazilian curriculum in its relationship to "lower-class children."

68. Cláudio de Moura Castro, "Vocational Education," 626.

69. Bologna, *Roberto Mange*, 214–15.

70. Nitsch, interview by Alexander (quote); Bologna, *Roberto Mange*, 215.

71. Lula, interview by Paraná, July 1993, in Paraná, *Lula*, 75; Frei Chico, interview by Morel, mid-1981, in Morel, *Lula*, 64.

72. Nitsch, interview by Alexander.

73. Alexander, "Observations on SENAI."

74. Cláudio de Moura Castro, "Vocational Education," 626–27.

75. Nitsch, interview by Alexander, April 27, 1956.

76. SENAI, *De homens*, 141.

77. Bologna, *Roberto Mange*, 376, 378–79.

78. SENAI, *De homens*, 140.

79. Bologna, *Roberto Mange*, 337.

80. Mange, quoted in Bologna, *Roberto Mange*, 386–87.

81. Cláudio de Moura Castro, "Vocational Education," 627.

82. Mange, quoted in Bologna, *Roberto Mange*, 387.

83. Lula, interview, 2000, in "Depoimento de Luiz Inácio Lula da Silva," 16.

Chapter 4

1. Medeiros, *Luiz Inácio Lula da Silva*, 90–91.

2. "Lula quer voltar a dizer 'companheiros e companheiras,'" *Repórter Diário*, November 21, 2011.

3. He most likely received lathe training as a helper in the Vila Carioca metalworking plant where he worked in 1957, since he doesn't mention SENAI.

4. Frei Chico, interview by Paraná, October 5, 1993, in Paraná, *Lula*, 152; Frei Chico, interview by Morel, mid-1981, in Morel, *Lula*, 64.

5. Frei Chico, interview by Morel, mid-1981, in Morel, *Lula*, 65.

6. Ibid., 64.

7. Lula, interview with Paraná, June 30, 1993, in Paraná, *Lula*, 65; Frei Chico, interview by Paraná, September 10, 1993, in ibid., 151; Frei Chico, interview by Morel, mid-1981, in Morel, *Lula*, 64. These points of argument are drawn from my interviews with Marcos Andreotti about how to recruit workers to one's union or party.

8. Frei Chico, interview by Paraná, September 10, 1993, in Paraná, *Lula*, 160, 151; Frei Chico, interview by Morel, mid-1981, in Morel, *Lula*, 64. Although an unreliable narrator, his brother Jaime denies his father knew anything about politics.

9. Adhemar had twice allied with the Communists for a statewide run, although in the early 1960s he aligned with the plotters working toward the 1964 coup that ended electoral democracy and constitutional rule. French, "Workers."

10. Lula, interview by Morel, mid-1981, in Morel, *Lula*, 34, 25. Jânio also gathered support and allies from among trade unionists and leftists, although never from the PCB proper.

11. Lula, interview by Paraná, October 6, 1993, in Paraná, *Lula*, 79–80.

12. Ibid., 80.

13. Ibid., 79–80. The time and place of the violent incident described by Lula has not been identified. In reading through thousands of newspaper articles on strikes in greater São Paulo, I came across an article that most likely solves the puzzle, although the incident occurred in Vila Carioca in October 1957, during the famous "Strike of the 400,000," when Lula, newly arrived, was twelve, not seventeen as he suggested in one account. The pickets arrived and the thirty-three-year-old, unmarried owner of Malhas "Fio-Text," Manuel Dias de Carvalho Pereira, took out a revolver and shot two workers (thirty and fifteen years old, respectively) before even talking with the crowd. When reloading, he was disarmed, hit and kicked by the crowd. There is no reference to a death in association with the incident, but the article notes that three men were charged with stealing typing machines from the enterprise. "Aconteceu na industria de Malhas 'Fio-Text': Resultou em tiroteio a chegada do piquete," *Ultima Hora*, October 18, 1957.

14. For a fuller biographical treatment of Andreotti, see French, "How the Not-So-Powerless Prevail."

15. Marcos Andreotti, interview by John D. French, November 5, 18, and 27, 1982.

16. Andreotti, interview by French, November 5 and 18, 1982.

17. Frei Chico, interview by Paraná, October 5, 1993, in Paraná, *Lula*, 151.

18. Lula, interview, 2000, in "Depoimento de Luiz Inácio Lula da Silva," 20; Lula, interview by Morel, mid-1981, in Morel, *Lula*, 34.

19. Andreotti, interview by French, November 18 and 27, 1982.

20. Frei Chico, interview by Morel, mid-1981, in Morel, *Lula*, 64.

21. Lula, interview, 2000, in "Depoimento de Luiz Inácio Lula da Silva," 25.

22. Stacchini, *Março 64*, 14, 36.

23. General Castelo Branco, quoted in ibid., 70. See statements by the anti-Communist Movimento Sindical Democrático (*Jornal de Santo André*, June 14, 1961) and the conservative Catholic Círculos Operários do Estado de São Paulo (*Jornal de Santo André*, April 17, 1963). The allegation that the unions were dominated by a Communist minority can be found in the March 30, 1964, statement of the Clube Naval: Victor, *Cinco anos*, 504–5.

24. General Mourão Filho, quoted in Stacchini, *Março 64*, xix, 10. This was also the formal

charge lodged against Goulart by the three military ministers during the 1961 crisis that followed the *renúncia* of Jânio Quadros. Victor, *Cinco anos*, 354, 356. See also the statement by the conservative rubber workers' union of São Paulo and Santo André, *Jornal de Santo André*, November 28, 1960.

25. Lowy and Chucid, "Opinões e atitudes," 133.

26. Mestres in a textile and a metalworking factory, respectively, quoted in Luiz Pereira, *Trabalho*, 219.

27. Frei Chico, interview by Morel, mid-1981, in Morel, *Lula*, 65 (first quote); Frei Chico, interview by Paraná, in Paraná, *Lula*, 152–53 (remaining quotes).

28. Frei Chico, interview by Morel, mid-1981, in Morel, *Lula*, 64–65; Frei Chico, interview by Paraná, September 10, 1993, in Paraná, *Lula*, 152–53.

29. This formulation was offered in French and Fortes, "Another World," 16.

30. Corrêa, *Memórias*, 100–102.

31. A future lawyer for the São Bernardo metalworkers' union, Pazzianotto showed courage in meeting with Corrêa, a clandestine Communist sought by the police, in January 1966; Corrêa would be condemned, in absentia, to three years in jail on June 7, 1966. "Pena de 14 anos para Prestes," *Folha de São Paulo*, June 7, 1966. The Vemag plant had about a dozen PCB members, Corrêa reports, and a smaller number from other leftist groups, who collaborated on the stoppage. Corrêa, *Memórias*, 100–102. For more on this and other fights at Vemag, see Negro, *Linhas*, 225–27.

32. Corrêa, *Memórias*, 102.

33. Luís Eduardo Leal, "Lula muda de endereço à procura de empregos," *Folha de São Paulo*, October 2, 1994.

34. Lula, interview, 2000, in "Depoimento de Luiz Inácio Lula da Silva," 24.

35. Frei Chico, interview by Morel, mid-1981, in Morel, *Lula*, 64.

36. Lula, interview by Dantas, first half of January 1981, in Altino Dantas, *Lula*, 19.

37. Andreotti, interview by French, Santo André, July 12, 1982.

38. Philip Siekman, "When Executives Turned Revolutionaries. A Story Hitherto Untold: How São Paulo Businessmen Conspired to Overthrow Brazil's Communist-Infected Government," *Fortune*, September 1964, 147–221.

39. Frei Chico, interview by Morel, mid-1981, in Morel, *Lula*, 64–65; Andreotti, interview by French, Santo André, July 12, 1982.

40. Negro, *Linhas*, 184.

41. Fratti, as the head of the PCB's municipal committee, was demanding that the non-Communists on the union's *diretoria* (directorate) also contribute to the party's finances, a proposal supported by the union's Communist treasurer, Ernesto Corraine. At a decisive meeting between Fratti and two union representatives, Andreotti angrily threatened to end all contributions. According to the police informant present (the union's treasurer), he declared, "I am not here to give money to those who don't work," referring to the full-time professional party cadre. Negro, *Linhas*, 172.

42. Orisson Saraiva de Castro, *Entrevistas*, n.p. For an extensive, sensitive, and highly detailed account of the subterranean struggle to construct the association of metalworkers transformed into a union in São Bernardo, see Negro, *Linhas*, 173–98.

43. Orisson Saraiva de Castro, *Entrevistas*.

44. His conclusion was that this would happen "only by reaching power." "Quem faz o movimento? Orisson Saraiva de Castro: *Inverta* entrevistou Orisson Saraiva de Castro, fundador do Sindicato dos Metalúrgicos de São Bernardo," *Inverta*, February 18, 2011.

45. Cadernos produced by *Novos Rumos*, January 1964, quoted in Vieitez, "Reforma," 4.

46. "Os golpistas são fracos," *O Metalúrgico* (Santo André), December 1963, quoted in Vieitez, "Reforma," 2–3.

47. "A situação foi de calma em Santo André," *Folha de Santo André*, March 4, 1964, quoted in Maria Blassioli Moraes, "A Ação Social Católica," 177; Marcos Andreotti, interview by Fátima Murad, in "Marcos Andreotti: Há 49 anos, o primeiro sindicato do grande ABC," *Diário do Grande ABC*, September 19, 1982.

48. Quoted in Maria Blassioli Moraes, "A Ação Social CatóIicia," 165, 178; "Padre José Mahon," in Cido Faria, *O movimento operário no ABC paulista contado por seus autores*, 67–82.

49. Lula, interview by Ronaldo Costa Couto, April 3, 1997, in Couto, *Memória viva*, 250; Lula, interview, 2000, in "Depoimento de Luiz Inácio Lula da Silva," 24–25.

50. Bergsman and Candal, "Industrialization," 52.

51. Kahil, *Inflation and Economic Development*, 316–17, 329–30.

52. The Santo André March with God for Liberty occurred only on April 28, endorsed by dentists, engineers, doctors, merchants, realtors, and the Lions and Rotary Clubs. And the local press reported that the closure of local shops and some factories contributed to the success of the march welcoming the coup. "Marcha da Família com Deus pela Liberdade," *O Repórter*, April 26, 1964; "Vocação democrática do povo foi amplamente confirmada," *O Repórter*, May 3, 1964, both quoted in Maria Blassioli Moraes, "A Ação Social Católicia," 181.

53. Quoted in Vieitez, "Reforma," 5. See also Maria Blassioli Moraes, "A Ação Social Católicia," 94.

54. Martins, interview by Bosi, May 20 and 27, June 10, 1977, in José de Souza Martins, "Sociologia e militância," 137.

55. Unlike the other paid student researchers, Martins went "every night to the working-class neighborhoods on the periphery to carry out interviews." Ibid., 137–38, 140–41, 160; José de Souza Martins, interview by Daisy Perelmutter, June 5, 2006, Projeto Memória Oral, Biblioteca Mário de Andrade, accessed March 24, 2014, http://www.prefeitura.sp.gov.br/cidade/upload/Depoimento_Jose_de_Souza_Martins_1254343852.pdf, 2–5, 7, 17–20.

56. Ramalho and Rodrigues, "Sociologia do trabalho," 135–37.

57. Rodrigues has told me that the original materials from the study are preserved, but they have not yet been made available to researchers. For a historian's engagement with the original study, see Negro, "Ford Willys."

58. Rodrigues, *Leôncio Martins Rodrigues Netto*, 24.

59. Adalberto Cardoso, "De volta," 185–219; Juarez Brandão Lopes, interview, in Bastos and Fernandes, *Conversas*, 101–2.

60. Brandão Lopes, "O ajustamento," 397, 400, 398 (italics added). Luiz Pereira, at least in part, dissented from this emphasis.

61. Rodrigues, *Industrialização*, 39, 52.

62. Ibid., 62, 126.

63. Ibid., 136.

64. This class consciousness scale was a four-part typology that ranged from those who viewed the union solely as a "social charitable assistance institution" to the small minority who saw it as "an instrument of struggle and defense of the workers' social, economic, and occupational interests." Ibid., 102, 109–13.

65. Ibid., 139–40.

66. Ibid., 90. Both Rodrigues's and Brandão Lopes's studies would come to be widely

criticized for creating a negative image of the working class. See Paoli, Sáder, and Telles, "Pensando a classe operária." The wider interpretive framework derived from the earliest of these studies was given international currency in 1960–61 by Brazil's future president Fernando Henrique Cardoso and French sociologist Alain Touraine, as well as in the early works of Francisco Weffort in the 1960s. Fernando Henrique Cardoso, "Le proletariat Brésilien"; Touraine, "Industrialisation"; Weffort, "Política de massas."

67. Luiz Pereira, *Trabalho*, 104; Martins, interview by Bosi, May 20 and 27, June 10, 1977, in José de Souza Martins, "Sociologia e militância," 153–54, 160.

68. Rodrigues, *Industrialização*, 28–31, 33.

69. Ibid., 28–31.

70. Ibid.

71. Cláudio de Moura Castro, "Vocational Education," 624.

72. For example, his data on claimed newspaper readership—even if we discount the figures as an attempt to claim an educated status—suggests that ferramenteiros were three times as likely as common workers to claim to read newspapers three times or more a week (60 percent to 20 percent), while only 4 percent said they rarely or never did (versus 28 percent for common workers). Rodrigues, *Industrialização*, 14. In fact, as Rodrigues notes, consumption of newspapers even by the middle classes was notoriously low, as shown by the papers' small print runs.

73. Ibid., 31–33, 35.

74. Ibid., 32.

75. Andreotti, interview by French, November 3 and 18, December 10, 1982.

76. Andreotti, interview by French, November 3 and 18, 1982. In her study of Nova Lima, Yonne de Souza Grossi reports that 50 percent of all local PCB members in 1954 were plumbers (*encanadores*), an additional 45 percent were from other skilled sectors, and only 5 percent were from the ranks of the least skilled manual group, the carters (*carreiros*). Grossi, *Mina de Morro Velho*, 135.

77. Rodrigues, *Industrialização*, 103–4.

78. Frederico, *Consciência operária*, 60.

79. Lula, interview by Morel, mid-1981, in Morel, *Lula*, 33; Lula, interview, 2000, in "Depoimento de Luiz Inácio Lula da Silva," 17.

80. Luiz Pereira, *Trabalho*, 231.

81. Andreotti, interview by French, November 3, 1982.

82. Miglioli, *Como são feitas*, 36–39.

83. Andreotti, interview by French, November 3, 1982.

84. Andreotti, interview by French, November 3 and 5, 1982.

85. Andreotti, interview by French, December 7, 1982.

86. Andreotti, interview by French, November 3, 1982.

87. Ibid. (emphasis added).

88. Andreotti, interview by French, November 18, 1982.

89. Andreotti, interview by French, November 3 and December 15, 1982. For a brief discussion that places the case discussed here into a broader international comparative dialogue with early twentieth-century developments in metalworkers' industries in the North Atlantic, see French, "Latin American Labor Studies Boom," 294–97.

Chapter 5

1. Lula, interview by Nélson Blecher, June 10, 1978, in Guizzo et al., *Lula*, 91.

2. Lula, interview, 2000, in "Depoimento de Luiz Inácio Lula da Silva," 20.

3. Lula, from a CLT panel with Chico Junior, Luiz Werneck Vianna, Almir Pazzianoto, and João Paulo Pires de Vasconcelos, published as "Consolidação das leis," 252–53; Kamel, *Dicionário*, 424.

4. Lula, interview, 2000, in "Depoimento de Luiz Inácio Lula da Silva," 21. Villares coworkers still referred to Lula as Caterpillar in 2003, after his election. Carlos Sambrana, "Torneiros mecânicos: Na era da automação industrial, os antigos colegas de trabalho de Lula fazem parte de uma espécie em extinção," *IstoÉ Dinheiro*, October 30, 2002, 88–89.

5. Historian Negro's detailed examination of shop floor and union politics among São Bernardo metalworkers, from the union's 1959 founding through 1968, provides an analytical model not yet sufficiently absorbed by the broader scholarship on labor in Brazil. Negro, *Linhas*; French, review of *Linhas*. On the recent development of the labor history field, see French and Fortes, "When the Plumber(s) Come to Fix a Country."

6. Heloisa Helena Teixeira de Souza Martins, *O estado*, 106, 172, 174.

7. Pitts, "Inadvertent Opposition."

8. Lula, interview, 2000, in "Depoimento de Luiz Inácio Lula da Silva."

9. Heloisa Helena Teixeira de Souza Martins, *O estado*, 179–80, discusses the humiliating harassment endured by the São Paulo metalworkers' union leaders. One union president was shown his DOPS dossier with "everything I had said since 1965. They even had taped stuff, which I already knew, because there are always people taping what is said in the assemblies."

10. *Categoria* derives from the legal definition of a trade union as encompassing all the workers represented in a legally recognized activity in a given administrative unit. However, the categoria of São Bernardo do Campo and Diadema metalworkers does not equal the union membership, because categoria members have to join the union and pay dues to enjoy certain benefits (*assistência*) and rights, including voting in union elections. Humphrey, *Capitalist Control*, 130. Nonunionized categoria members are not, however, entirely absent from union life: they are covered by any salary agreement and have money deducted from their wages to support the union's bureaucratic structures. Originally called a union tax (*imposto sindical*) and later a union contribution (*contribuição sindical*), this mandatory financial support has long been controversial. It is possible, for example, that a small group might control a given union and the revenue derived from the categoria while discouraging membership, which produces not only difficulties in providing services but also members whose vote might threaten the group in office. Yet it is wrong to imagine, as many have, that this accounts for most, or even the majority, of the trade unions; it was far less common in industrial manufacturing unions.

11. Nunes, *Além da greve*, 25–27.

12. Heloisa Helena Teixeira de Souza Martins, *O estado*, 99–100. Although the labor minister emphasized that this was only 15 percent of all trade unions, they had the largest memberships and most active leadership and covered the country's most important industrial sectors. And even the nonintervened unions experienced heightened administrative surveillance and control.

13. Ibid., 103–4.

14. Marcos Andreotti, interview by French, November 5, 1982.

15. On the government's considerations in opening the way to elections in 1965, see Heloisa Helena Teixeira de Souza Martins, *O estado*, 103–6.

16. Nunes, *Além da greve*, 27–29.

17. Ibid.

18. Ibid., 29–30.

19. Ibid., 30–31.

20. Ibid., 31–34.

21. Ibid.

22. Ibid., 20–23.

23. Nunes, *Fora de pauta*.

24. For a selection of João Ferrador's notes (*bilhetes*) to authorities, see Nunes and Canabrava Filho, *Bilhetes*, also blurbed by Lula.

25. In 1980 he published a memorable short story collection depicting working-class life and the Communists of eastern São Paulo city in the 1950s: Nunes, *PC linha leste*.

26. See French, *Brazilian Workers' ABC*.

27. Henriques, *Ascensão e queda*, 193.

28. Francisco José de Oliveira Vianna, *Direito do trabalho*, 35, 41–43.

29. French, *Drowning in Laws*.

30. "Depoimento de José de Segadas Viana" (interview from October 6, 1983, in Rio de Janeiro by Valentina da Rocha Lima, Ângela Maria de Castro Gomes, and Plínio de Abreu Ramos), 138–40. This interview was transcribed in 1987 and is held in the archive of the Centro de Pesquisa e Documentação de História Contemporânea do Brasil / Fundação Getúlio Vargas, Rio de Janeiro.

31. Ibid., 153.

32. Segadas Viana lost power in the PTB to Goulart in the early 1950s. His search for vengeance led him, by the late 1960s, to ally with Carlos Lacerda, the fierce bête noire of Getúlio, the PTB, and the Left; he supported the 1964 coup overthrowing Goulart.

33. "Depoimento de José de Segadas Viana," 180–81.

34. Ibid., 153.

35. Gasparian, *O industrial*, 93.

36. Henriques, *Ascensão e queda*, 193.

37. "O imposto sindical é um roubo nos salarios," *Gazeta Sindical*, second half of February.

38. As the political home of choice for pelegos during the Populist Republic, the rightist sectors of the PTB and its union associates often responded defensively about the "Red pelegos," as did one paulista PTB member interviewed in Maria Victoria Benevides, *O PTB*, 47.

39. The two most famous pelegos were Deocleciano de Hollanda Cavalcanti, leader of the CNTI (Confederação Nacional dos Trabalhadores na Indústria, or National Confederation of Workers in Industry) from 1946 to 1961 and again after 1964, and his colleague and sometime competitor Ary Campista.

40. Lula, quoted in "Consolidação das leis," 259.

41. The German scholar Hans Füchtner was the first to narrow the scope of peleguismo to produce a meaningful analytical concept. For him, only those union leaders "who identify *totally* with an intermediary role between the interests of the government and the workers" are pelegos. In broader terms, he sees "the typical pelego as a bureaucrat unconnected to the union rank and file that follows the government's instructions with an eye out for his personal advantages." Füchtner, *Os sindicatos brasileiros*, 100 (emphasis added).

42. Lula, interview, March 1978, in Guizzo et al., *Lula*, 15, 28–30; Lula, quoted in "Consolidação das leis," 259.

43. Lula, quoted in "Consolidação das leis," 259.

44. Ary Campista, interview, August 13, 1978, in Campista, "Todos melhoraram."

45. Romulo Augustus Pereira de Souza, *Memórias*, 187–88, 198.

46. Andreotti, interview by French, November 23 and December 2, 1982.

47. Andreotti, interview by French, November 18 and December 9, 1982.

48. "Entrevistando Rafael Martins," *Folha do Povo*, July 22, 1953. See also articles in *Noticias do Hoje*, July 16, 1953; *Folha do Povo*, July 22, 1953.

49. Andreotti, interview by French, December 7 and 15, 1982.

50. Andreotti, interview by French, December 7 and October 28, 1982.

51. Philadelpho Braz, interview by John D. French, Santo André, August 30, 2004. Andreotti lost his job at Indústrias Sul Americana de Metais after the 1964 coup and two years before his death was barely scraping by, facing difficulties in meeting the monthly payment on his rented house (his tiny pension was inadequate).

52. Andreotti, interview by French, October 28, 1982.

53. Andreotti, interview by French, December 2, 1982.

54. Brandão Lopes, "O ajustamento," 397, 400, 398.

55. Andreotti, interview by French, December 7, 1982.

56. Vera Maria Candido Pereira, *O coração da fábrica*, 217. "We did not," Pereira went on, "observe mention of any link with the government or the Ministry of Labor that could be interpreted as a suggestion of co-optation, except for the fact that the 'pelegos' use the post of union leader or of *vogais* [class judges] in the Labor Courts in a particularist fashion."

57. Lula, interview, March 1978, in Guizzo et al., *Lula*, 28–30.

58. Lula in 1976 linked the invitation to attend the meeting to the offer to join the slate: Rainho and Bargas, *As lutas operárias*, 49. Lula, interview by Dantas, first half of January 1981, in Altino Dantas, *Lula*, 20, confirms that the slate was being put together in August 1968.

59. Tomizaki, *Ser metalúrgico*, 79, notes that city-raised children of migrants must be distinguished from rural migrants in general, based on her extensive oral history interviews in the early twenty-first century with successive generations of workers at ABC's Mercedes-Benz factory, twenty-seven of whom arrived in the 1950s.

60. Lula, interview, 2000, in "Depoimento de Luis Inácio Lula da Silva," 20.

61. Cláudio de Moura Castro, "Vocational Education," 627.

62. Armando Corrêa da Silva, "Estrutura e mobilidade social," 88–89.

63. Ibid., 88–90.

64. For a rich anthropological treatment of the multifaceted roles and disputes associated with mandatory uniforms in a Minas Gerais steel plant, see Farias, "Entre a igualdade e a distinção."

65. Guizzo et al., *Lula*, 182.

66. Tauile, "Microelectronics."

67. Kamel, *Dicionário*, 424.

68. Vavá, interview by Paraná, September 3 and 7, 1993, in Paraná, *Lula*, 199.

69. Lula, interview by Paraná, June 30, 1993, in ibid., 56.

70. Luiz Pereira, *Trabalho*, 260.

71. Frei Chico, interview by Paraná, October 5, 1993, in Paraná, *Lula*, 153–54; Frei Chico, interview by Morel, mid-1981, in Morel, *Lula*, 66; Lula, interview by Dantas, first half of January 1981, in Altino Dantas, *Lula*, 19–20.

72. Frei Chico, interview by Morel, mid-1981, in Morel, *Lula*, 66.

73. Lula, interview by Paraná, July 19, 1993, in Paraná, *Lula*, 97–98.

74. Ferrante, *FGTS*; Rosa, "A indústria brasileira"; Barros and Corseuil, "Impact of Regulations."

75. Lula, interview, 2000, in "Depoimento de Luiz Inácio Lula da Silva," 25.

76. Andreotti, interview by French, December 2 and 9, 1982. For example, a worker interviewed by Brandão Lopes had once been a member of the Santo André metalworkers' union but eventually quit because "when I needed the union, I didn't find [help]. . . . They said, come tomorrow, and then I went on the other day and the lawyer wasn't there. . . . The ones who did what I needed was SESI [Serviço Social da Indústria]," an organ of the industrialists. This cavalier attitude was typical of the leadership during the intervention era from 1947 to 1956 and damaged the union. Brandão Lopes, "O ajustamento," 399.

77. These interviews were conducted between 1976 and 2008. There is an additional interview touching on Lula's initial invitation to join the slate with a member of the diretoria, Antenor Biolcatti. Ademir Medici, "Coluna memoria: O irmão do Frei Chico," *Diário do Grande ABC*, December 30, 2002.

78. Lula, interview, 2000, in "Depoimento de Luiz Inácio Lula da Silva," 25; Lula, interview by Paraná, July 19, 1993, in Paraná, *Lula*, 90 (quote).

79. Lula, interview by Paraná, October 6, 1993, in Paraná, *Lula*, 109–10; "Lula: Somos o mais importante partido de izquerda no mundo," *Caros Amigos*, November 2000, 1; Lula, interview by Dantas, first half of January 1981, in Altino Dantas, *Lula*, 20–21; Frei Chico, interview by Morel, mid-1981, in Morel, *Lula*, 41. See the detailed discussion of the carteira do trabalho in French, *Drowning in Laws*. One's fate could be negatively affected by an entry denoting firings or too many short jobs (rebels like Frei Chico often racked them up, getting fired in some but not all cases for union activities), or even a claim of having lost one's carteira (employers assumed the worse). Employers who refused to enter a worker's skill on the card—usually to save money by paying less—were a source of endless grievance and even litigation. Ferretti, *Opção*, 82.

80. Lula, interview by Paraná, July 19, 1993, in Paraná, *Lula*, 90; Lula, interview, 2000, in "Depoimento de Luiz Inácio Lula da Silva," 25; Lula, interview by Dantas, first half of January 1981, in Altino Dantas, *Lula*, 20 (first quote); Frei Chico, interview by Morel, mid-1981, in Morel, *Lula*, 41, 66 (second quote).

81. Barbosa Monteiro, "Entrevista."

82. Frei Chico, interview by Paraná, October 5, 1993, in Paraná, *Lula*, 153–54.

83. Frei Chico, interview by Morel, mid-1981, in Morel, *Lula*, 66.

84. Lula, interview by Dantas, first half of January 1981, in Altino Dantas, *Lula*, 20–21 (first quote); Frei Chico, interview by Morel, mid-1981, in Morel, *Lula*, 66; Lula, interview by Paraná, July 19, 1993, in Paraná, *Lula*, 90 (second quote); Lula, "Declarações concedidas," 50. On the gendering of labor activism, see the introduction in French and James, *Gendered Worlds*.

85. Lula, interview by Morel, mid-1981, in Morel, *Lula*, 41; Lula, "Declarações concedidas," 50; Lula, interview, 2000, in "Depoimento de Luiz Inácio Lula da Silva," 26. Lula, interview by Paraná, October 6, 1993, in Paraná, *Lula*, 109–10 (first quote); Lula, "Conf. palestra proferida," 212, Lula, interview by Dantas, first half of January 1981, in Altino Dantas, *Lula*, 20–21 (second quote).

86. Lula, interview by Paraná, July 19, 1993, in Paraná, *Lula*, 90.

Chapter 6

1. Lula, interview, 2000, in "Depoimento de Luiz Inácio Lula da Silva," 25.

2. Ibid., 12–13, 17, 25, 65. On Náutico's formation in 1962, see Moisés de Holanda, "Náutico homenageia Lula," *Jornal do Commercio* (Recife), March 16, 2001.

3. Ademir Medici, "Primeiro de maio de 1969," Memória, *Diário do Grande ABC*, 2001.

4. Andreotti, interview by French, November 7, 24, 27, and December 13, 1982.

5. Lula, interviews from 1990 and 1994, in Harnecker, *O sonho era possível*, 56; Lula, interview by Paraná, October 6, 1993, in Paraná, *Lula*, 110; Andreotti, interview by French, December 9, 1982.

6. Lula, interview by Paraná, October 6, 1993, in Paraná, *Lula*, 110.

7. Lula, interview by Dantas, first half of January 1981, in Altino Dantas, *Lula*, 19–20; Lula, interview by Paraná, July 19, 1993, in Paraná, *Lula*, 97–99; Lula, interview by Morel, mid-1981, in Morel, *Lula*, 39; Lula, interviews, 1990 and 1994, Harnecker, *O sonho era possível*, 56.

8. Lula, interview by Morel, mid-1981, in Morel, *Lula*, 39 (first quote); Lula, interview by Paraná, July 19, 1993, in Paraná, *Lula*, 97–99; Lula, interview by Dantas, first half of January 1981, in Altino Dantas, *Lula*, 19–20 (second and third quotes); Lula, interviews, 1990 and 1994, Harnecker, *O sonho era possível*, 56.

9. Luiz Inácio Lula da Silva, "Esse destemor, carregado de desinformação política, acabou se transformando numa intuição que foi fundamental para aquela virada de página do fim dos anos 70" [That fearlessness, reflecting a lack of political knowledge, ended up being transformed into an intuition crucial to the turning of the page at the end of the 70s]," Fundação Perseu Abramo, last modified April 18, 2006, http://csbh.fpabramo.org.br/o-que-fazemos/memoria-e-historia/exposicoes-virtuais/luiz-inacio-lula-da-silva-1.

10. Lula, interview, 2000, in "Depoimento de Luiz Inácio Lula da Silva," 13.

11. Lula, interview by Paraná, June 30, 1993, in Paraná, *Lula*, 65 (first quotes); Lula, interview by Paraná, July 1993, in ibid., 71 (last quote).

12. Frei Chico, interview by Paraná, September 3 and 7, 1993, in ibid., 210; Lula, interview by Paraná, July 1993, in ibid., 74.

13. Lula, interview by Paraná, June 30, 1993, in Paraná, *Lula*, 64–65; Lula, interview by Paraná, July 1993, in ibid., 73; Lula, interview by Paraná, July 19, 1993, in ibid., 85 (quotes).

14. Andreotti, interview by French, December 7, 1982.

15. Quotes from, respectively, Lula, interview by Morel, mid-1981, in Morel, *Lula*, 134; Lula, interview by Paraná, July 1993, in Paraná, *Lula*, 76; Lula's remarks at Inauguracão do Centro Internacional de Neurociências de Reabilitação-Rede Sarah, December 17, 2003, in Kamel, *Dicionário*, 425.

16. Vavá, interview by Paraná, September 3 and 7, 1993, in Paraná, *Lula*, 232–33 (quotes); Jaime, interview by Paraná, April 10, 1994, in ibid., 285. This is not to say that indignation was nonexistent, especially among the lawyers who dealt with easily avoidable accidents and their traumatic consequences. The São Bernardo union's lawyer, Antonio Possidonio Sampaio, not only specialized in industrial accidents—and wrote about them regularly in the union's newspaper after 1971—but also wrote a novela to dramatize the traumatic individual impact of such accidents: Sampaio, *A capital do automóvel*.

17. Moore, *Injustice*.

18. Sampaio, *Sim senhor*, 11; Romulo Augustus Pereira de Souza, *Memórias*, 137.

19. Cláudio de Moura Castro, "Vocational Education," 627.

20. Luiz Pereira, *A escola*, 108.

21. José de Souza Martins, "A valorização," 119.

22. On the use of such metaphors that erase the boundary between letrados and manual workers, see French, *Drowning in Laws*, 191n36.

23. Lula, interview by Dantas, first half of January 1981, in Altino Dantas, *Lula*, 16; Lula, interview by Paraná, July 19, 1993, in Paraná, *Lula*, 88; Lula, interview, 2000, in "Depoimento de Luiz Inácio Lula da Silva," 21. Fris Moldu Car would later move to São Bernardo, where it expanded considerably.

24. Lula, interview by Morel, mid-1981, in Morel, *Lula*, 26, 36; Lula, interview by Dantas, first half of January 1981, in Altino Dantas, *Lula*, 1981, 14 ("marvelous"), 16; Lula, interview, 2000, in "Depoimento de Luiz Inácio Lula da Silva," 11; Lula, interview by Paraná, July 19, 1993, in Paraná, *Lula*, 83–84; Lula, interview by Paraná, July 1993, in ibid., 70–71 ("desire"; "macaroni"); Lula, remarks at Abertura do Seminário Internacional Bolsa Família, Brasília, October 20, 2005, in Kamel, *Dicionário*.

25. Lula, interview by Paraná, July 19, 1993, in Paraná, *Lula*, 83–84, 88.

26. Sales, *Trabalho*, 52. Adilson was born in Paraná in 1965 to a family of small farmers (*pequenos proprietarios* or *roceiros*). When he arrived in São Paulo, he got a job in a small metalworking shop where his uncle worked. Having completed a social science degree, he was professionalized by the Pastoral Operária before entering VW in the painting sector. Ibid., 26.

27. P. Torres (AKA Cido or Aparecideo Faria), "Uma experiência junto ao proletariado" (undated mimeo), in Eder Sader, *Quando novos personagens*, 70.

28. Lula, interview, 2000, in "Depoimento de Luiz Inácio Lula da Silva," 19; Lula, interview by Paraná, July 19, 1993, in Paraná, *Lula*, 83–84 (quotes).

29. Sales, *Trabalho*, 52.

30. Lula, interview, 2000, in "Depoimento de Luiz Inácio Lula da Silva," 19.

31. Roniwalter Jatobá de Almeida, "Trabalhadores," 36, 37.

32. The recession's social and psychological impact was further magnified by the fact that the overwhelming majority of workers were new to urban wage labor and unfamiliar with capitalism's cycle of booms and busts. Those who had arrived in the mid- to late 1950s had known only rapid and uninterrupted industrial growth, whether directly like Lula and his brothers or indirectly through stories about São Paulo as the land of opportunity.

33. Lula, interview by Paraná, July 19, 1993, in Paraná, *Lula*, 88.

34. Torres, "Uma experiência," 71.

35. Lula, interview by Dantas, first half of January 1981, in Altino Dantas, *Lula*, 16–17.

36. Lula, interview, 2000, in "Depoimento de Luiz Inácio Lula da Silva," 25; Lula, remarks at Inauguração da fábrica de pneus de mineração e terraplanagem da Michelin-América do Sul, Rio de Janeiro, February 26, 2008, in Kamel, *Dicionário*, 424.

Chapter 7

1. Bonelli, "Nivel de atividade," 387.

2. The sharp recession negatively affected the enterprises of large and small Brazilian industrialists and businessmen, which depended on continuous growth and government favors including bank financing. The government-induced recession also fostered industrial consolidation; in the automobile industry, two majority Brazilian-owned firms were bought out in 1967: Vemag in Vila Carioca (by Volkswagen) and Willys-Overland in São Bernardo (by Ford). Joaquim dos Santos Andrade (president of the metalworkers' union

of São Paulo), interview by Robert J. Alexander, New Brunswick, NJ, April 28, 1968, Robert Alexander Archive, Rutgers University, New Brunswick, NJ.

3. Ibid.

4. USNARA, American Embassy in Rio de Janeiro, "Memorandum of Conversation: Labor Ministry Brazilian Wage Policy," May 17, 1968, 1–3. The document was kindly provided to me by labor attaché Richard Ginnold.

5. The problem, the Labor Ministry official admitted, was that the wages they set consistently overestimated how quickly inflation would decline. Only for the period after August 1968, after the problem was clear, did they change their future inflation estimates (calculated at 15 percent versus an actual rise of 8 percent). USNARA, "Memorandum of Conversation," 1–3. On the sequence of laws related to the arrocho, which began first in the state sector before being extended to private employment, see Simões, *A lei do arrocho*, 29–36; Fernando Lopes de Almeida, *Política salarial*.

6. USNARA, "Memorandum of Conversation."

7. Negro, *Linhas*, 226–27, 258, 292.

8. Vinhas, *O partidão*, 192–93.

9. His optimistic long TV interview aired in early 1964 and is reproduced in Dênis de Moraes, *Prestes com a palavra*, 150–81.

10. Dulles, *Castello Branco*, 420. For a description of the cadernetas and a retrospective "explanation" by Prestes, see Moraes and Viana, *Prestes*, 177–80; Vinhas, *O partidão*, 251.

11. See the collection of PCB documents in Nogueira, *PCB*. I follow established convention in using PCB for the Communist Party formed in 1922, whose initials then had been PCdoB (Communist Party of Brazil). The Brazilian Communist Party moniker (PCB) was chosen by the party's leadership in the early 1960s when it sought legal recognition; the dissident leaders who split away in 1962 retained the old acronym PCdoB, on the basis that they were the proper descendant organization given the mainstream party's treasonous revisionism after 1958. A wider array of documents can be found in Carone, *O PCB*, vol. 2; Carone, *O PCB*, vol. 3.

12. Marighella, *Por que resisti*.

13. For a moving personal account of the coup's impact on the party, see the memoir by a Communist deputy from Minas Gerais and Central Committee member who moved to São Paulo immediately after the coup: Coelho, *Herança*, 282–83. Under a pseudonym, Coelho authored an important but unofficial analysis of the coup's causes: "Causas da derrocada de 10 de April," *Revista da Civilização Brasileira*, July 1966, reprinted in Carone, *O PCB*, 3:27–49.

14. DOPS, APESP, Dossie 50-Z-318 3036-3180, Pasta 19 3040.

15. DOPS, APESP, "Prontuário no. 6857: Rolando Fratti," http://www.arquivoestado.sp.gov.br/uploads/acervo/textual/deops/prontuarios/BR_SP_APESP_DEOPS_SAN_P006857_01.pdf.

16. Magalhães, *Marighella*, 334–37; Paulo Cannabrava Filho, *En el ojo*, 111; Rezende, *Suicídio revolucionário*, 73. On his break with the PCB, see Carlos Marighella, "Carta á comissão executiva do Partido Comunista Brasileiro," December 1, 1966, in Nova and Nóvoa, *Carlos Marighella*, 536–46. For his final break, see Nova and Nóvoa, *Carlos Marighella*, 229.

17. "Derly José de Carvalho—parte 1," Centro de Memória Sindical, last modified June 26, 2019, https://memoriasindical.com.br/formacao-e-debate/derly-jose-de-carvalho-parte-1/; "Derly José de Carvalho—parte 2," Centro de Memória Sindical, last modified October 15, 2012, https://memoriasindical.com.br/formacao-e-debate/derly-jose-de-carvalho

-parte-2/; Comissão Nacional da Verdade, *Relatório,* 183; Thainá Siudá and Fernanda Toscano, "Devanir José de Carvalho: Um exemplo de resistência e luta da classe operária," Centro de Documentación sobre los Moveimentos Armados (CEDEMA), last modified November 2006, http://www.cedema.org/ver.php?id=2203.

18. Backed by this bishop, Catholic worker-activists ran in 1962 against the leftist leadership of Andreotti and Braz in Santo André's metalworkers' union. Vieitez, "Reforma," 89–94.

19. Negro, *Linhas,* 298–99.

20. The political errors and intellectual weakness of the late 1960s revolutionary Left's Marxism-Leninism was analyzed by several New Left veterans as part of a volume collecting documents from each leftist organization of the time. Reis Filho and Ferreira de Sá, *Imagens da revolução.*

21. Fernando Henrique Cardoso, *Empresário industrial*; Prado, *A Revolução Brasileira.*

22. Five voted for other candidates, seventy-two abstained out of opposition, and thirty-seven were absent for cause. Even fifty-three deputies from Goulart's PTB voted for Castelo Branco. Dulles, *President Castello Branco,* 425.

23. "Nota do encontro com João Goulart," in Lacerda, *Depoimento,* 459–60.

24. The US consul's four-page report on the rally can be found in "Carlos Lacerda Speech" (telegram), March 25, 1968, Opening the Archives: Documenting US-Brazil Relations, 1960s–80s, Brown Digital Repository, Brown University Library, accessed December 2, 2018, https://repository.library.brown.edu/studio/item/bdr:340928/. On one of the other state deputies involved, see "Joaquim Jácomo Formiga, São Caetano do Sul: Typed Report by Serviço de Informações do 'S.S.' do DOPS," August 1, 1962, in Tribunal Regional de São Paulo, Processo 12n (1962), 202; Dulles, *Carlos Lacerda,* 500–501. On the Frente Amplio as seen by a PCB state deputy aligned with Marighella as well as some detailed description of the São Caetano rally (although exaggerating its size tenfold), see Perrone, *Relato de guerras,* 70–71.

25. Dulles, *Carlos Lacerda,* 508–9.

26. Pitts, "'O sangue.'"

27. "Documento protesto da comunidade paroquial de Vila Palmares," reprinted in Antônio de Almeida, *Experiências políticas,* 140–41. For a profile of this remarkable radical priest from a poor background in Santos, see Cynthia Tavares, "Tive a sensação que eu ia me matar," *Diário do Grande ABC,* April 29, 2013.

28. On ABC's Catholic worker–related activism before 1964, see Heloisa Helena Teixeira de Souza Martins, *Igreja.*

29. On the AP's history, see Ridenti, "Ação Popular."

30. For the AP's contribution to weakening the option for armed struggle in ABC, see Heloisa Helena Teixeira de Souza Martins, *Igreja,* 189. Unlike the Marighella revolutionaries, the AP in 1968 refused to commit to immediate armed struggle, since mass agitation retained a place in their interpretation of the Maoist doctrine of "prolonged popular war."

31. Torres, *Uma experiência*; Portuense de Carvalho, "Experiências." See in particular the profiles of and interviews with key AP leaders in ABC in Maeda et al., *Retratos da resistência.*

32. For more on the MIA, see "Entrevista José Ibrahim para *Unidade e Luta, #1,*" November 1972, in Frederico, *A esquerda,* 215–17; "Los obreros: (Testimonio de) José Ibrahim, dirigente obrero," in Caso, *Los subversivos,* 61–110. On the gradual emergence of coordinated protests against the arrocho in fall 1967, see the article from *O Metalúrgico* (Santo André), March 1968, in Frederico, *A esquerda,* 54–55. On the disruption of MIA rallies by the more radical Left, see the excerpt from P. Torres in ibid., 136.

33. APESP, SSP, DOPS, Pasta 50-Z-318.

34. Dirceu and Palmeira, *Abaixo a ditadura*, 97; Paulo Cannabrava Filho, *En el ojo*, 114–15.

35. "1.o de maio agitado," *O Metalúrgico* (São Paulo), August 1967–July 1968. For photographs of the action taken by the police and extracted from the investigations and military trial records of those involved, see "BNM-AEL: Álbum 01," Flickr, accessed December 3, 2018, https://www.flickr.com/photos/armazemmemoria/sets/72157634614452106/.

36. "Em São Paulo, a ditadura foi expulsa da Praça da Sè," *Libertação*, May 15, 1968, in Frederico, *A esquerda*, 124–29.

37. See Barbosa Monteiro, "Entrevista com José Barbosa Monteiro"; "O 10 de maio de 1968 [Entrevista de José Barbosa Monteiro com Maria Moraes na Suiça Onde Vive Atualmente]," *Cadernos do Presente [Reprinted 2009]*, no. 2 (1978): 23–27 in reprint (34–41 in original); Raimundo Rodrigues Pereira, "Muitos Lulas: Quem é o heroe do sindicato dos metalúrgicos de São Bernardo de Campo e Diadema, que no final da semana passada completou 20 anos?," *Movimento*, May 16–20, 1979, 8–10.

38. "Entrevista com José Barbosa Monteiro," 120, 131. On the police investigation and military court prosecutions, see BNM (Brasil: Nunca Mais), *Processo 424 Praça da Sé, SP 1968 (10 Volume)* (359 pages, 1968); *Processo 424 Praça da Sé, SP 1968 (20 Volume)* (857 pages, 1968).

39. CEDI, *História*, 40–41. Philadelpho Braz, the Santo André metalworkers' union's secretary-general ousted in 1964, was at the Praça da Sé rally and recalls that Marcílio detested the radicals, who included his vice president, José Nanci, linked to the AP. Philadelpho Braz, interview by John D. French, Santo André, August 30, 2004.

40. "Manifesto," *O Metalúrgico*, August 1967–July 1968.

41. Frederico, *Consciência operária*, 101. In a retrospective analysis written from exile in 1972, Cido (Aparecido de] Faria noted that many workers interpreted the radicals' slogans and denunciations as opposition to the unions per se. P. Torres, in Frederico, *A esquerda*, 138.

42. Getúlio Miguel de Souza, interview, December 23, 2012, in Portuense de Carvalho, *A Ação Popular em Mauá*, 95–96. This fine book extensively quotes interviews with other working-class AP members and even Souza's mother.

43. Perrone, *Relato de guerras*, 18. For another example, see Nosella, *Por que mataram*, 38–39.

44. Paulo Cannabrava Filho, *En el ojo*, 101–3, 108, 114–15 (emphasis added). Compare Prestes's assessment, given in the early 1980s interview: "I told Marighella that the conditions for armed struggle didn't exist. He had even been arrested in a movie theater in Tijuca and carried himself bravely in reaction to the arrest. Mário Alves [another dissident Central Committee member] had also been arrested. Both were released. In that period, the dictatorship was still releasing communists." Moraes and Viana, *Prestes*, 185.

45. Lima, "'Trabalhador,'" 40–41 (emphasis added).

46. The leaflet was distributed during the 1967 Santo André metalworkers' union elections. APESP, DOPS, Pasta 50-Z-318, Pasta 20, folha 3276 (31/8/67). Part of the leaflet is also quoted in Antônio de Almeida, *Experiências políticas*, 249.

47. Ridenti, *Em busca*, 55.

48. *Folha da Tarde*, April 30, 1968, in CEDI, *História*, 37–39 (emphasis added).

49. Entrevista com Ze Barbosa, 126, 135–37; Torres, *Uma experiência*.

50. Negro, *Linhas*, 298–99.

51. *Diário do Grande ABC*, May 30–31, 1968.

52. *Diário do Grande ABC*, June 8, 1968.

53. Abramo, *O resgate*, 129.

54. *Diário do Grande ABC*, May 25–27, 30–31, 1968.

55. Pitts, "Inadvertent Opposition."

56. *O Ferramenta (Jornal dos Operários da Volks)* 1, no. 3 (March–April), found in Arquivo BNM, Proceso 6110, 2, 4.

Chapter 8

1. See Humphrey, "Development," 265, table A3.7.

2. Although the neighboring São Paulo's union may have had more members, São Bernardo's union collected $R1,939,000 in gross union tax revenue compared to São Paulo's R$1,860,000, according to budget data gathered from union officials by Kenneth Mericle.

3. The specificity of the generational experience of the intellectualized middle class in early 1970s São Paulo is captured with acuity and sensitivity in Almeida and Weis, "Carro-zero," 319–409.

4. Fico, *Reinventando o otimismo*.

5. Widely used in the international press, the term "Brazilian economic miracle" should be challenged for its invocation of the miraculous. Yet it does suggest the extent and depth of the socioeconomic transformations that the country underwent, well beyond GDP growth. In that sense, the remarkable growth testifies to the wide-ranging program of top-down national developmentalism and capitalist modernization initiated by unelected military governments after 1964.

6. Baer, *Brazilian Economy*, 75.

7. Tomizaki, *Ser metalúrgico*, 77, table 3.

8. Keck, *Workers' Party*, 12.

9. Wolfe, *Autos and Progress*.

10. Jenkins, *Transnational Corporations*, 72, 52.

11. José Almeida, "A evolução," 66–67.

12. Shapiro, *Engines*, 241, table A.6; Abramo, *O resgate*, 58, table 2.

13. Humphrey, *Capitalist Control*, 51.

14. José Carlos Pereira, *Estrutura e expansão*, 118.

15. Humphrey, *Capitalist Control*, 51, table 2.6. There are well-known distortions in these numbers because statistical agencies of the time still included car repair shops alongside factories. Pastore and Lopes, *A mão de obra especializada*, 45. In other words, the figures are of interest only as relative measurements because the actual numbers would be less stark if enterprises were reported appropriately in the industrial statistics. Given its wealth and social diversity, São Paulo is likely to have had more auto repair shops—thus depressing the statistics for large-scale firms—compared to the more purely working-class municípios of ABC.

16. Tomizaki, *Ser metalúrgico*, 63, table 1.

17. The interviewee, Antonio César, was born in 1947 and hired in 1966 at Vemag, later acquired by VW; he entered SENAI in 1970 and stayed. Sales, *Trabalho*, 36.

18. Sampaio, *A capital do automóvel*, 49–54.

19. Roniwalter Jatobá de Almeida, "Trabalhadores," 35–47. For the details of his family background, early 1970 arrival in São Paulo, and employment in São Bernardo, see Carlos Herculano, "Literatura operária: Roniwalter Jatobá, escritor mineiro, é visto como pioneiro em retratar a vida do trabalhador urbano brasileiro," *Estado de Minas*, August 2, 2009.

20. Roniwalter Jatobá de Almeida, "Trabalhadores," 38.

21. Prefeitura do Município de São Bernardo do Campo, *Pesquisa Sócio-Econômica 79.*

22. Luiz Pereira, *A escola.*

23. José Casado, "Repressão no pátio da fábrica," *O Globo,* May 15, 2005.

24. The Communist tool and die maker Lúcio Bellantani was arrested at work by machine gun–toting police and beaten within the VW factory before being taken away to be tortured. His German-born comrade Heinrich Plagge, a quality control inspector, was also detained within the factory before being taken for prolonged torture. See Bellantani's *testimonio* in *Diário Oficial do Estado de São Paulo,* December 20, 2012; Rodolfo Lucena, "Morre o operário Heinrich Plagge, que foi entregue pela VW à ditadura militar," *Tutaméia,* March 6, 2018, http://tutameia.jor.br/morre-o-metalurgico-heinrich-plagge-que-foi-entregue-pela-vw-a-ditadura-militar/. After this was highlighted by the Brazilian Truth Commission, VW authorized an internal investigation, which produced a thorough report: Kopper, *A VW do Brasil.*

25. For a thoughtful discussion by a skilled ABC metalworker about industrialization, Juscelino Kubitschek, and the 1964 military government, see Frederico, *Consciência operária,* 133, 110–11. The existence of working-class sympathy for the regime is recognized in the most thorough historiographical article on the topic: Corrêa and Fontes, "As falas," 412–13.

26. Luiz Antonio Duarte, quoted in Strini et al., *Retratos da resistência,* 60–61, 64.

27. Rainho, *Os peões,* 177.

28. "Waldemar Rossi. Depoimento dado, em 31/5/1983 no curso ministrado por Ralph Della Cava, no Departamento de Ciencias Sociais da USP" (in the author's possession).

29. Maricato, "Autoconstrução," 94, 90.

30. Armando Corrêa da Silva, "Estrutura e mobilidade social," 76–77.

31. Maricato, "A proletarização"; Maricato, *A produção capitalista.*

32. Lula, interview, 2000, in "Depoimento de Luiz Inácio Lula da Silva," 15; Marinete, interview by Paraná, March 29, 1994, in Paraná, *Lula,* 249–50; Tiana, interview by Paraná, April 21, 1994, in ibid., 308–9; Lula, interview by Paraná, July 19, 1993, in ibid., 91; Lula, interview by Morel, mid-1981, in Morel, *Lula,* 34.

33. Lula, interview by Nélson Blecher, June 10, 1978, in Guizzo et al., *Lula,* 91.

34. Lula, interview, 2000, in "Depoimento de Luiz Inácio Lula da Silva," 20; Lula, interview by Morel, mid-1981, in Morel, *Lula,* 37.

35. Lula, interview by Paraná, July 19, 1993, in Paraná, *Lula,* 90.

36. Kamel, *Dicionário,* 424.

37. Tiana, interview by Paraná, April 21, 1994, in Paraná, *Lula,* 306; Lambari, interview by Paraná, June 27, 1994, in ibid., 344; Josué Machado, "A realidade íntima do sindicalista," *Playboy,* July 1979, in Guizzo et al., *Lula,* 203–4.

38. "José Ferreira da Silva (Frei Chico)," September 15, 2014 (transcript of testimony), Comissão Nacional da Verdade, accessed September 21, 2019, http://www.cnv.gov.br/images/pdf/depoimentos/vitimas_civis/vc_Jose_Ferreira_da_Silva_Frei_Chico_15.09.2014.pdf.

39. José de Souza Martins, *Uma arqueologia,* 245–46.

40. Ibid., 328, 211.

41. Angela Ziroldo, "Lula: 'Tudo o que eu queria era ser um torneiro mecânico,'" *Nova,* August 1979, 100, 102–5. Visits to the cheap prostitutes in the red zone near the Estação da Luz in downtown São Paulo were part of working-class adolescence, with the payments made by economizing on sweets and films and hoarding pennies. José de Souza Martins, *Uma arqueologia,* 335.

42. Machado, "A realidade íntima," 203–4; Linger, *Dangerous Encounters*, 141. In reference to sex with animals, Lula would later explain that he was talking not about himself but about boys in general, especially in rural areas. It was never, he told Paraná, laughing, "his passion to have relations with animals." Lula, interview by Paraná, July 19, 1993, in Paraná, *Lula*, 84–95.

43. Lula, interview by Dantas, first half of January 1981, in Altino Dantas, *Lula*, 16–17.

44. Lula, interview by Paraná, July 19, 1993, in Paraná, *Lula*, 89–90; Tiana, interview by Paraná, April 21, 1994, in ibid., 306–7.

45. Marinete, interview by Paraná, March 29, 1994, in ibid., 239; Tiana, interview by Paraná, April 21, 1994, in ibid., 306; Lambari, interview by Paraná, June 27, 1994, in ibid., 344–45, 348.

46. Tiana, interview by Paraná, April 21, 1994, in Paraná, *Lula*, 306–7.

47. Lambari, interview by Paraná, June 27, 1994, in ibid., 345.

48. Tiana, interview by Paraná, April 21, 1994, in Paraná, *Lula*, 308; Sartri, *A família*, 41.

49. Lula, interview by Paraná, July 19, 1993, in Paraná, *Lula*, 90–91.

50. Ibid.

51. Lula, interview, 2000, in "Depoimento de Luiz Inácio Lula da Silva," 20.

52. Lula, interview by Morel, mid-1981, in Morel, *Lula*, 37–38.

53. Ibid. In this regard, Brazilian machinists recall their counterparts in the early twentieth-century United States, who were especially opposed to piecework as an immoral and greedy practice that generated "discord and [made] a perfect hell out of our craft." Montgomery, *Fall*, 208.

54. Lula, interview by Nélson Blecher, June 10, 1978, in Guizzo et al., *Lula*, 2–3.

55. Frederico, *Consciência operária*, 51.

56. Luiz Pereira, *Trabalho*, 183. See also Paul Singer, "O jovem operário e o universo brasileiro," *Visão*, August 1973, 54; Rainho, *Os peões*; Frederico, *Consciência operária*, 51–52.

57. This was Lula's listed occupation on his signed registration to run for president in 1978. A copy was made available to the police and can be found in APESP, DOPS, Dossie 50-Z-341#, Pasta 18, Ordem 01946-02089, 2052.

58. Tauile, "Microelectronics," 83.

59. Frederico, *Consciência operária*, 89. Ibid., 128, suggests that the strong labor market demand for skilled workers meant that they were less affected by the government's salary squeeze than their unskilled fellow workers.

60. Ibid., 54, 71–72.

61. Tauile, "Microelectronics," 84.

62. Lula, interview by Morel, mid-1981, in Morel, *Lula*, 38.

63. Lula, interview by *Manchete*, 1978, in Guizzo et al., *Lula*, 90–91.

64. Lula, interview by Morel, mid-1981, in Morel, *Lula*, 37–38.

65. Lula, interview with Paraná, July 19, 1993, in Paraná, *Lula*, 98.

66. Singer, "O jovem operário," 46, 51.

67. Ibid., 55.

68. Ibid., 46, 51.

69. Ibid., 51–52. Thanks to Macelo Noah for his help in translating this passage.

70. Frederico was careful to conduct the sixty interviews and thirteen life histories outside the factory. Frederico, *Consciência operária*, 15–16, 133. On his background, see Frederico, *A esquerda*, 11.

71. Frederico, *Consciência operária*. See also Rainho, *Os peões*.

72. Frederico, *Consciência operária*, 94–95.

73. Sociologist Ricardo Antunes mentions Frederico as part of a group around José Chasin that was active in the PCB. Bastos and Fernandes, *Conversas*, 437–41.

74. Frederico, *A vanguardia operária*, 18. See also Rainho, *Os peões*.

75. Certeau, *Practice*, 16.

76. Ibid., 18.

77. Ibid., 26 (emphasis in original).

78. James C. Scott, *Weapons of the Weak*, xvi.

79. Mintz, "Rural Proletariat."

80. Singer, "O jovem operário," 44. For the definition of *sacana*, see Chamberlain and Harmon, *Dictionary*, 451–52.

81. Singer, "O jovem operário," 44.

82. Foster, "Peasant Society," 296.

83. Certeau, *Practice*, 18.

84. Roniwalter Jatobá de Almeida, *Filhos do medo*, 55–58.

85. James C. Scott, *Weapons of the Weak*, 27, 29.

86. Certeau, *Practice*, 16 (emphasis in original).

Chapter 9

1. Ademir Medici, "Coluna Memória," *Diário do Grande ABC*, April 19, 2005. As Medici notes, before then Silva had only appeared in the newspaper as part of the lists of candidates for union office.

2. Alberti, Farias, and Rocha, *Paulo Egydio conta*, 481–82. On the governor, see Odair Rodrigues Alves, *Os homens*, 169–71.

3. Markun, *O sapo*, 88–89.

4. Mercadante Oliva, "Estado autoritário," 286, table 1; Paranhos, "Mentes," 54, 71.

5. Lula, interview by Dantas, first half of January 1981, in Altino Dantas, *Lula*, 27 (first quote); Lula, interview by Morel, mid-1981, in Morel, *Lula*, 115; Markun, *O sapo*, 88; Lula, interview by Paraná, July 19, 1993, in Paraná, *Lula*, 102–3; Frei Chico, interview by Paraná, September 10, 1993, in ibid., 161; Rainho and Bargas, *As lutas operárias*, 186 (remaining quotes). Though Lula claimed this was his first time speaking before an audience using a microphone, he is known to have said a few words on several earlier occasions. But his fellow union director Antenor Biolcati is not alone in recalling how fearful Lula was about speaking in public: "He shook like a green cane in the wind in front of a microphone." Ademir Medici, "Coluna Memória," *Diário do Grande ABC*, December 30, 2002.

6. Rainho, *Os peões*, 195–96, 177.

7. Eliane Brum, "Bodas de chumbo," *Época*, March 7, 2003.

8. Marinete, interview by Paraná, March 29, 1994, in Paraná, *Lula*, 242; Maria Baixinha, interview by Paraná, April 6, 1994, in ibid., 258.

9. Paulo Narciso, "Lourdes: O amor mineiro de Lula," montesclaros.com, accessed February 7, 2014, http://montesclaros.com/reportagens/lourdes.asp; Tiana, interview by Paraná, April 21, 1994, in Paraná, *Lula*, 308–9; Lula, interview by Paraná, July 19, 1993, in ibid., 91–92, 94.

10. Lula, interview by Paraná, July 19, 1993, in Paraná, *Lula*, 92; Tiana, interview by Paraná, April 21, 1994, in ibid., 308; Marinete, interview by Paraná, March 29, 1994, in ibid., 239–40.

11. Brum, "Bodas de chumbo."

12. Vavá, interview by Paraná, September 3 and 7, 1993, in Paraná, *Lula*, 232–23; Lula, interview by Paraná, July 19, 1993, in ibid., 92.

13. Rainho, *Os peões*, 196–97.

14. Brum, "Bodas de chumbo."

15. Lula, interview by Paraná, July 19, 1993, in Paraná, *Lula*, 92; Francesc Relea, "Lula hermano presidente," *El Pais Semanal*, December 22, 2002, 55 (Tiana quote).

16. Lula, interview by Paraná, July 19, 1993, in Paraná, *Lula*, 92, 94; Lambari, interview by Paraná, June 27, 1994, in ibid., 348; Frei Chico and Vavá, interview by Paraná, September 3 and 7, 1993, in ibid., 214–15; Frei Chico, interview by Morel, mid-1981, in Morel, *Lula*, 68; Nelson Campanholo, interview by Morel, mid-1981, in ibid., 16; Runilda Riedmiller quoted in Brum, "Bodas de chumbo," 65; Narciso, "Lourdes."

17. Tiana, interview by Paraná, April 21, 1994, in Paraná, *Lula*, 309; Lula, interview by Paraná, July 19, 1993, in ibid., 91.

18. Angela Ziroldo, "Lula: 'Tudo o que eu queria era ser um torneiro mecânico,'" *Nova*, August 1979, 103.

19. Lula, interview, 2000, in "Depoimento de Luiz Inácio Lula da Silva," 14–15.

20. Guizzo et al., *Lula*, 92.

21. Ziroldo, "Lula: 'Tudo o que,'" 103.

22. Hugo Moura, "A história de Lula, segundo a birita," *Cícero*, January 3, 2014.

23. *Tribuna Metalúrgica*, October 1, 1973, 1, 4–5.

24. On the prevailing gender ideals and practice in São Paulo and Latin America, see French and James, *Gendered Worlds*.

25. Luiz Maklouf Carvalho, "Lula tem filha cuja existência nunca revelava," *Jornal do Brasil*, April 26, 1989, 1, reprinted in Luiz Maklouf Carvalho, *Já vi*, 42 (quote); Maria Baixinha, interview by Paraná, April 6, 1994, in Paraná, *Lula*, 265; Lula, interview by Paraná, July 19, 1993, in ibid., 95. Lula's relationship with Miriam Cordeiro is discussed in a posthumous 2020 journalistic profile of his second wife, Marisa, although the account is unfootnoted, uses unattributed speech, and is not based on interviews with Miriam or Marisa. Vannuchi, *Marisa*, 33–34, 42–47.

26. Sampaio, *Lula*, 18, 21; Aloysio Azevedo, "Sindicatos," 27; "Quem faz a cabeça do baiano," *Revista Brasil Extra*, August 1984, in Luiz Maklouf Carvalho, *Já vi*, 21.

27. Josué Machado, "A realidade íntima do sindicalista," *Playboy*, July 1979, in Guizzo et al., *Lula*, 203–4; Lula, interview by Paraná, July 19, 1993, in Paraná, *Lula*, 95; Narciso, "Lourdes," 6 (Lambari quote).

28. Machado, "A realidade íntima," 204–5 (first quote); Lula, interview by Morel, mid-1981, in Morel, *Lula*, 149 (second quote).

29. Luiz Maklouf Carvalho, "A história de Mirian, com paixao e ódio," *Jornal da Tarde*, December 14, 1989, reprinted in Luiz Maklouf Carvalho, *Já vi*, 69–70.

30. For her statement, see Conti, *Notícias do Planalto*, 240.

31. Lula, interview, 2000, in "Depoimento de Luiz Inácio Lula da Silva," 23.

32. Maria Baixinha, interview by Paraná, April 6, 1994, in Paraná, *Lula*, 265; Carvalho, "Lula tem filha."

33. Luiz Werneck Vianna, interview, in Bastos and Fernandes, *Conversas*, 166; Abramo, *O resgate*, 167.

34. Sampaio, "As lutas sindicais," 194; Lula, interview by Couto, April 3, 1997, in Couto, *Memória viva*, 254–55; Frei Chico, interview by Morel, mid-1981, in Morel, *Lula*, 69, 83; "Dis-

curso do Presidente da República, Luiz Inácio Lula da Silva, na cerimônia de comemoração dos 30 anos da sua posse como presidente do Sindicato dos Metalúrgicos do ABC" (speech in São Bernardo do Campo, April 18, 2005), Biblioteca: Presidência de República, accessed September 22, 2019, http://www.biblioteca.presidencia.gov.br/presidencia/ex-presidentes/luiz-inacio-lula-da-silva/discursos/10-mandato/2005/18-04-2005-discurso-do-presidente-da-republica-luiz-inacio-lula-da-silva-na-cerimonia-de-comemoracao-dos-30-anos-da-sua-posse-como-presidente-do-sindicato-dos-metalurgicos-do-abc/; Aloysio Azevedo, "Sindicatos," 27.

35. Raimundo Rodrigues Pereira, "Muitos Lulas: Quem é o heróe do sindicato dos metalurgicos de Sao Bernardo de Campo e Diadema, que no final da semana passada completou 20 anos?," *Movimento*, May 16–20, 1979, 8–9; "Discurso do Presidente da República, Luiz Inácio Lula da Silva, na cerimônia de comemoração dos 30 anos"; Bourne, *Lula of Brazil*, 27; Sampaio, "As lutas sindicais," 194.

36. Jorge Pinheiro, "O Brasil ainda será um grande São Bernardo: Uma entrevista com Paulo Vidal, o metalúrgico que 'criou' o líder Lula," *Folhetim*, May 11, 1980, 5.

37. This profile of Vidal is drawn from " Mandatos: 1967 a 1969," ABC de Luta, accessed August 8, 2018, http://www.abcdeluta.org.br/materia.asp?id_CON=2974; "Um novo estilo de sindicalismo," *Opinião*, September 16, 1974, 3; Pereira, "Muitos Lulas," 8–9; Pinheiro, "O Brasil," 4–5.

38. "Um novo estilo."

39. Frei Chico, interview by Morel, mid-1981, in Morel, *Lula*, 69.

40. Galache, "Apresentacão," 7 (first quote); undated appeal to "companheiros metalurgicos" by Comissao Municipal do PC Brasileiro opposing Vidal's election in 1972, in Arquivo Brasil: Nunca Mais, Proceso 6106 (second quote), http://bnmdigital.mpf.mp.br/pt-br/.

41. Frei Chico, interview by Morel, mid-1981, in Morel, *Lula*, 68–69. Frei Chico also called him a pelego and referenced—without disputing—the charge that he informed on his leftist opponents in the union.

42. Bourne, *Lula of Brazil*, 27.

43. French and Negro, "Politics," 383–84.

44. Rainho and Bargas, *As lutas operárias*, 52; Mercadante Oliva, "Estado autoritário," 282.

45. Paranhos, "Mentes," 70; Paranhos, *Era uma vez*, 65, 111.

46. Paranhos, *Era uma vez*, 40–52, 68–71, 82. On Vidal's founding of the paper, see Paranhos, "Mentes," 29–30; Nunes, *Fora de pauta*, 83–84.

47. Pereira, "Muitos Lulas."

48. Editorial, *Tribuna Metalúrgica*, July 1971, quoted in Abramo, *O resgate*, 149.

49. Pazzianotto, *100 anos*, 204, discusses the physical confrontation that occurred at a union assembly in which the categoria's leftists rejected this idea.

50. Pereira, "Muitos Lulas," 8–9.

51. Frei Chico, interview by Paraná, October 5, 1993, in Paraná, *Lula*, 155. On Vidal's innovative administrative reforms, see also "São Paulo: Os sindicatos viram empresas," *Opinião*, September 26, 1975.

52. "Um novo estilo." These revenue increases are confirmed by the "balanço financeiro" and "balanço patrimonial" for 1970 and 1971 provided to US graduate student Kennethححericle by Vidal in July 1972 (in the author's possession).

53. The *Diário do Grande ABC* ran a story on plans for the new headquarters on February 15, 1970.

54. Paranhos, *Era uma vez*, 37–38.

55. Lula, interview, 2000, in "Depoimento de Luiz Inácio Lula da Silva," 45.

56. Quoted in Torres, "Uma experiência," 130.

57. "Metalúrgicos inauguram sede sindical," *Diário do Grande ABC*, October 7, 1973 (quote); "A sede do Sindicato dos Metalúrgicos de São Bernardo é inaugurada com grande festa," *Tribuna Metalúrgica*, October 1, 1973, 1, 4–5.

58. Abramo, *O resgate*, 138, 140–41, 145, 149; Pereira, "Muitos Lulas," 8–9 (quote).

59. Paranhos, "Mentes," 49.

60. Kenneth Mericle, "Unpublished Questionnaire 6-1 from a 7 July 1972 Interview with Presidente [Paulo Vidal], Sindicato dos Trabalhadores nas Indústrias Metalúrgicas, Mecânicas, e do Material Elétrico de São Bernardo e Diadema, pesquisa sôbre o sindicalismo e o conflito coletivo e individual no Brasil," 9 pages (in the author's possession).

61. Polemical attacks on Vidal can be found in the two leaflets from the opposition Chapa Azul slate in the 1972 election, one untitled and the other titled "Companheiros metalúrgicos de São Bernardo do Campo," in Arquivo Brasil Nunca Mais, Anexo 8879–8880.

62. Amaury de Souza, "Nature of Corporatist Representation," 470, 472, 119–20, 126–28.

63. Kenneth Mericle, telephone interview by John D. French, October 19, 1995.

64. Paul Singer, *Economia política*, 44–45; Frei Chico, interview by Morel, mid-1981, in Morel, *Lula*, 69.

65. Mercadante Oliva, "Estado autoritário," 180–81; "Com os resultados destas eleições todos os trabalhadores lucraram," *Tribuna Metalúrgica*, March 1972, 3.

66. Negro, *Linhas de montagem*, 267, 272–75.

67. Nêumanne Pinto, *O que sei*, 121–22.

68. Carla Delecrode, "O que 'Lula, o filho do Brasil' não contou," *Opinião e Notícia*, March 24, 2010, 35; Pinheiro, "O Brasil," 4–5.

69. Sampaio, "As lutas sindicais," 195; Frei Chico, interview by Paraná, September 10, 1993, in Paraná, *Lula*, 161; Frei Chico, interview by Morel, mid-1981, in Morel, *Lula*, 69 (first quote); Lula, interview by Morel, mid-1981, in ibid., 115 (second quote); "Informe 0234 de 29.09.76 do CENIMAR," included with a Ministry of Labor compilation of materials attached to the "Ficha de distribuição e processamento de documentos" on Lula by the Servico Nacional de Informações, November 16, 1978 (third quote).

70. Lula, interview by Dantas, first half of January 1981, in Altino Dantas, *Lula*, 21–23; Lula, interview by Paraná, in Paraná, *Lula*, 98, 110; Rainho, *Os peões*, 50. Lula expressed the same point to Paraná in 1993 in a far less colorful fashion. Lula, interview by Paraná, July 19, 1993, in Paraná, *Lula*, 98. In 1976 Lula distanced himself from his exaggerated initial illusions. Rainho and Bargas, *As lutas operárias*, 50.

71. Lula, interview by Paraná, July 19, 1993, in Paraná, *Lula*, 99; Lula, interview by Dantas, first half of January 1981, in Altino Dantas, *Lula*, 22; Lula, interview by Morel, mid-1981, in Morel, *Lula*, 113 (quotes).

72. Delecrode, "O que 'Lula'"; "Paulo Vidal começa contar verdadeira história de Lula," *ABC Repórter*, May 14, 2009. Lula does not directly reference Vidal's story but mentions an unnamed diretoria member who talked him into not quitting. Rainho, *Os peões*, 50–51; Luiz Werneck Vianna, *Conjuntura nacional*, 248–49. Frei Chico refers to Vidal convincing Lula to go into the union full-time by suggesting that it would also distract him after his tragic loss of Lourdes and his child. Frei Chico, interview by Paraná, October 5, 1993, in Paraná, *Lula*, 156.

73. Lula, interview by Paraná, July 19, 1993, in Paraná, *Lula*, 98–99; Lula, interview by Paraná, October 6, 1993, in ibid., 110–11; Rainho and Bargas, *As lutas operárias*, 50.

74. Frei Chico, interview by Morel, mid-1981, in Morel, *Lula,* 68; Frei Chico, interview by Paraná, October 5, 1993, in Paraná, *Lula,* 156; Lula, interview by Paraná, October 6, 1993, in ibid., 112–13; Lula, interview by Dantas, first half of January 1981, in Altino Dantas, *Lula,* 23–24; Depoimento de Paulo Vidal Neto, ABC de Luta, accessed August 16, 2018, http://www.abcdeluta.org.br/materia.asp?id_CON=2693; Delecrode, "O que 'Lula'"; Negro, *Linhas,* 270–71, 292–95. Luciano Galache, who headed the opposition slate, claimed that Lula was "an integral part of our *chapa* until the last day of [candidate] registration." Galache, "Apresentacão," 10. See also Pereira, "Muitos Lulas."

75. Lula, interview by Paraná, July 19, 1993, in Paraná, *Lula,* 98, 101 (first quote); Lula, interview by Paraná, October 6, 1993, in ibid., 113 (second quote).

76. Frei Chico, interview by Paraná, October 5, 1993, in Paraná, *Lula,* 156, 158; Galache, "Apresentacão," 10–11.

77. Lula, interview by Dantas, first half of January 1981, in Altino Dantas, *Lula,* 23–24; Lula, interview by Paraná, October 6, 1993, in Paraná, *Lula,* 112–13.

78. Lula, interview by Paraná, July 19, 1993, in Paraná, *Lula,* 85–86 (first quote); Lula, interview by Paraná, July 1993, in ibid., 75 (second quote).

79. Frederico Rebelio Nehme, "Após 30 anos, Lula volta ao sindicato dos metalúrgicos," *Diário do Grande ABC,* August 12, 2010.

80. Rainho, *Os peões,* 77, 79–80, 290–91; Frei Chico, interview by Morel, mid-1981, in Morel, *Lula,* 66.

81. Undated, untitled transcript (44 typed pages) of an interview with "R," born in Ceará, conducted and transcribed by Fabio Munhoz ("E"), CEDEM, Fábio Munhoz Collection, 7–9.

82. Frei Chico, interview by Morel, mid-1981, in Morel, *Lula,* 68 (quote); Frei Chico, interview by Paraná, October 5, 1993, in Paraná, *Lula,* 156.

83. Lula, interview by Dantas, first half of January 1981, in Altino Dantas, *Lula,* 24. For a similar statement, see Lula, interview by Morel, mid-1981, in Morel, *Lula,* 114.

84. Ferretti, *Opção,* 94–95.

85. Cláudio de Moura Castro, "Vocational Education," 626.

86. Heloisa Helena Teixeira de Souza Martins, *O estado,* 173.

87. Rainho, *Os peões,* 221.

88. Ibid. A São Bernardo director made the same point in Heloisa Helena Teixeira de Souza Martins, *O estado,* 167.

89. "Walter Barelli: História de vida," DIEESE Memória, accessed August 28, 2018, http://memoria.dieese.org.br/museu/nossas_historias_menu/walter-barelli.

90. Sampaio, "As lutas sindicais"; Veras and Veras, *Retrato.*

91. Elenice Viera, "Ex prefeito Maurício Soares," *Maurício Soares Jr.* (blog), November 26, 2009, http://mauriciosoaresjr.blogspot.com/2009/11/ex-prefeito-mauricio-soares.html.

92. Pazzianotto, *100 anos.*

93. Lula, interview by Paraná, July 19, 1993, in Paraná, *Lula,* 98; Lula, interview by Paraná, October 6, 1993, in ibid., 112 (quote); Lula, interview by Paraná, December 10, 1993, in ibid., 133; Frei Chico, interview by Paraná, October 5, 1993, in ibid., 159–60.

94. Paranhos, "Mentes."

95. Lula, interview by Paraná, October 6, 1993, in Paraná, *Lula,* 114.

96. Ibid., 114; Lula, interview, 2000, in "Depoimento de Luiz Inácio Lula da Silva," 26, 45; Lula, interview by Dantas, first half of January 1981, in Altino Dantas, *Lula,* 24.

97. Lula, interview by Morel, mid-1981, in Morel, *Lula,* 114; Lula, interview by Dantas,

first half of January 1981, in Altino Dantas, *Lula*, 24 (first quote); Pereira, "Muitos Lulas" (second quote).

98. Frei Chico, interview by Morel, mid-1981, in Morel, *Lula*, 68; Lula, quoted in Rainho, *Os peões*, 51.

99. Notices about Lula's department were infrequent and formulaic. See, for example, Luiz Inácio da Silva, "Departamento Jurídico," *Tribuna Metalúrgica*, February–March 1974, 4.

100. Lula, interview by Paraná, July 19, 1993, in Paraná, *Lula*, 101 (first quote); Lula, interview by Paraná, October 6, 1993, in ibid., 114; Lula, interview by Dantas, first half of January 1981, in Altino Dantas, *Lula*, 24; Pereira, "Muitos Lulas" (second quote).

101. Lula, interview by Paraná, July 19, 1993, in Paraná, *Lula*, 105.

102. "Com os resultados," 3. The struggle with the Left, as Lula noted, weighed heavily on Vidal, and Lula would repeatedly criticize their unrelenting personalized attacks even as he explained why some felt that way; he categorically rejected the charge that Vidal was a police informant. Lula, interview, 2000, in "Depoimento de Luiz Inácio Lula da Silva," 49; Lula, interview by Paraná, October 6, 1993, in Paraná, *Lula*, 114.

103. Paul Singer, "O jovem operário e o universo brasileiro," *Visão*, August 1973, 39–40. It is curious that Singer quoted a worker's observation that Brazil had "no problem of revolution or war nor of differences of color or race." Although Brazil shares a national mythology about the absence of racism, the fact that the worker to whom Singer talked mentions color and race at all is uncommon. Unfortunately, an academic focus on social class and, secondarily, regionalism means that we have very few factory studies from this period in São Paulo that gather data on color or race. For one that did, see Gonçalves, *Máo-de-obra*, 38, 48.

104. Singer, "O jovem operário," 39–40. For a biographical interview with the longtime leftist Singer, a future PT leader, see Vannuchi and Spina, "Paul Singer."

105. Lula, interview by Paraná, October 6, 1993, in Paraná, *Lula*, 111.

106. Humphrey, "Development," 268–70; Lobos, "Technology," 171–72, 222; Gonçalves, *Máo-de-obra*, 89–92.

107. "Operários: A especialização," *Veja*, October 24, 1973, 28.

108. Kamel, *Dicionário*, 418; Luiz Inácio Lula da Silva, "Conf. palestra proferida," 213.

109. Sampaio, *A capital do automóvel*, 76–77. Three-quarters of the one hundred workers surveyed by USP graduate student José Sérgio Gonçalves in 1976–77 owned a television. More than two-thirds owned radios, refrigerators, and blenders, and half owned a floor waxer. Ownership was greatest among skilled and less than half as common among the unskilled. Forty to 70 percent at all skill levels regularly used installment plans to make these purchases. Two-thirds of the skilled and a fifth of the unskilled and semiskilled owned a car. Gonçalves, *Máo-de-obra*, 93–94, 107–9.

110. Sampaio, *A capital do automóvel*, 56, 58.

111. Rainho, *Os peões*, 80–83.

112. Singer, "O jovem operário," 41, 43–44.

113. Ibid., 44, 56.

114. Gonçalves, *Máo-de-obra*, 122–23.

115. Lula, interview with Paraná, July 19, 1993, in Paraná, *O filho*, 95. In the 2002 revised edition of Paraná's text, the quote was changed from "meio-doido" to "muito namorador." Lula, interview with Paraná, July 19, 1993, in Paraná, *Lula*, 95. In his 1979 *Playboy* interview, he called it three years of "craziness" and *gandaia* (painting the town red). Machado, "A realidade íntima," 204.

116. Marisa, interview by Paraná, May 6, 1994, in Paraná, *Lula*, 316–20, 323; Marisa, inter-

view by Cláudio Cerri, October 14, 2002, Fundação Perseu Abramo, last modified May 10, 2006, https://fpabramo.org.br/2006/05/10/entrevista-uma-brasileira-chamada-marisa/; Marisa, interview by Morel, mid-1981, in Morel, *Lula*, 100. An unfootnoted version of their encounter and courtship is offered in Vannuchi, *Marisa*, 34–42, 46–49, although the account offered here hews to attributable sources.

117. Machado, "A realidade íntima," 204.

118. Lula, interview by Paraná, July 19, 1993, in Paraná, *Lula*, 95–96; Lula interview, 2000, "Depoimento de Luiz Inácio Lula da Silva," 23.

119. Marisa, interview by Morel, mid-1981, in Morel, *Lula*, 99–111; Marisa, interview by Paraná, May 6, 1994, in Paraná, *Lula*, 315–35 (not included in the 1996 edition); Marisa, interview by Cerri.

120. Lula, interview, 2000, in "Depoimento de Luiz Inácio Lula da Silva," 22 (quote); Marisa, interview by Paraná, May 6, 1994, in Paraná, *Lula*, 321–23; Marisa, interview by Morel, mid-1981, in Morel, *Lula*, 100–101; Marisa, interview by Cerri, 6–7.

121. Nêumanne Pinto, *O que sei*, 98–100; Eliane Brum, "Lula, o filho do Barretão," *Época*, December 28, 2009. The journalistic sketch offered by Marisa's biographer includes undocumented dialogue and does not characterize the nature of their courtship. Vannucchi, *Marisa*, 36–40.

122. Machado, "A realidade íntima," 205–6.

123. Lula, interview by Paraná, July 19, 1993, in Paraná, *Lula*, 101.

124. Marisa, interview by Paraná, May 6, 1994, in ibid., 323.

Chapter 10

1. Rainho and Bargas, *As lutas operárias*, 187.

2. Frei Chico, interview by Paraná, September 10, 1993, in Paraná, *Lula*, 161–62. Among the tasks assigned to Soares was preparing drafts of speeches given by directors, who might make changes. Described by Lula as "very Christian," the lawyer was "considered of the left at the time," so much so that he was arrested in 1970. As for the speech at his inauguration, Lula says that he liked it very much although he recognized—like his brother—that it might seem "neither here nor there" politically. Lula, interview by Paraná, July 19, 1993, in ibid., 103; Lula, interview by Paraná, October 6, 1993, in ibid., 119.

3. Lamounier, "Authoritarian Brazil Revisited," 62–63.

4. Skidmore, *Politics of Military Rule*, 172–73; Gaspari, *A ditadura derrotada*, 454–55, 464–65; Maria Helena Moreira Alves, *State and Opposition*, 143–47; Sarles, "Maintaining Political Control."

5. "Correndo, antes de andar: Os estreiantes da Câmara dos Deputados (e de política)," *Opinião*, December 13, 1974; "Alberto Marcelo Gato," Centro de Pesquisa e Documentação de História Contemporânea do Brasil, Fundação Getúlio Vargas, accessed September 18, 2018, http://www.fgv.br/cpdoc/acervo/dicionarios/verbete-biografico/alberto-marcelo-gato; "Alberto Marcelo Gato: História de vida," DIEESE Memória, accessed September 18, 2018, http://memoria.dieese.org.br/museu/nossas_historias_menu/alberto-marcelo-gato; Araújo, *Operários em luta*.

6. Ministério de Justiça, Arquivo Nacional, SNI, Ministério do Exército Comando do II Exército 2a Seção, "Relatório Periódico de Informações," #5 (1975). 15–40 (excerpt); included in SNI. E0039652-1980, 18-06-1975 "Relatório Referente a Maio de 1980," 21.

7. Coelho, *Herança*, 360; Godoy, *A casa*, 428.

8. Godoy, *A casa*, 424–25, 428, 433, discusses the evidence that the well-placed Central

Committee member Severino Teodoro de Melo was the DOI's most important informant, despite Melo's denial.

9. Ibid., 129. For the type of information being sought, see the DOI questionnaire in Jordo, *Dossiê Herzog*, 171–74.

10. Godoy, *A casa*; Jordo, *Dossiê Herzog*; Audálio Dantas, *As duas guerras*; Markun, *Vlado*.

11. "José Ferreira da Silva (Frei Chico)," September 15, 2014, Comissão Nacional da Verdade, accessed September 21, 2019, http://www.cnv.gov.br/images/pdf/depoimentos/vitimas_civis/vc_Jose_Ferreira_da_Silva_Frei_Chico_15.09.2014.pdf; Frei Chico, interview by Paraná, October 5. 1993, in Paraná, *Lula*, 183.

12. Certeau, *Practice*, 16.

13. See my discussion of sharks in Veras, "John French."

14. Brandão Lopes, "O ajustamento," 409.

15. Bonduki and Rolnik, "Periferia da grande São Paulo," 146. Thanks to Jack Draper for the translation.

16. The decision not to break definitively with classic representative institutions reflected the need for both "the internal compatibilization of elites" and the "maintenance of cohesion by the armed forces." Lamounier, "O voto," 18.

17. My grasp of the military regime' political dynamics, especially in relation to São Paulo, derives from the research of and many hours of conversation with Bryan Pitts. See Pitts, "Inadvertent Opposition."

18. Gaspari, *A ditadura derrotada*, 252, 255, 459.

19. Melhem, *Política de botinas amarelas*, 20–21.

20. Ministério de Justiça, Arquivo Nacional, SNI, Ministério do Exército Comando do II Exército 2ª Seção, "Relatório Periódico de Informações. Periodo de 01 de out a 31 de out 75" #10 (1975), 8, 15, in 27 November 1975: SNI. E0041403-1980, 27-11-1975, 20.

21. Lula, interview by Paraná, October 6, 1993, in Paraná, *Lula*, 116–17.

22. Chaia, *Intelectuais*, 147; "Walter Barelli: História de vida," DIEESE Memória, accessed August 28, 2018, http://memoria.dieese.org.br/museu/nossas_historias_menu/walter-barelli.

23. Amaury de Souza, "Nature of Corporatist Representation," 95, 99. Souza emphasizes "substantial" social gap separating labor leaders and skilled workers from members of national elites, primarily from the upper and upper-middle classes.

24. Sampaio as quoted in Paranhos, "Mentes," 29–30, 34–35.

25. Nunes, *Fora de pauta*, 83.

26. Pazzianotto, *100 anos*, 105–6; Lula, interview by Paraná, October 6, 1993, in Paraná, *Lula*, 116–17.

27. Rainho and Bargas, *As lutas operárias*, 97–98, 199–203; Jorge Pinheiro, "O Brasil ainda será um grande São Bernardo: Uma entrevista com Paulo Vidal, o metalúrgico que 'criou' o lider Lula," *Folhetim*, May 11, 1980, 4–5.

28. Bastos and Fernandes, *Conversas*, 166–67.

29. Tavares de Almeida, "O sindicato no Brasil," 73. This possible path for São Bernardo's metalworkers was drawn from the ideas articulated by Vidal, which were influenced by Barelli and the intellectuals with whom he was associated. As Tavares de Almeida clarified in 1983, Vidal's position was his as an individual, rather than that of the union as an institution, and was shaped by an internal politics that at the time she did not fully understood. Tavares de Almeida, "Desarollo capitalista," 485–86.

30. "Um novo estilo de sindicalismo," *Opinião*, September 16, 1974, 3.

31. Ministério de Justiça, Arquivo Nacional, SNI, Ministério da Aeronáutica, Centro de Informações de Segurança da Aeronáutica, "Relatório Mensal de Informações #11" (November 30, 1975), SNI, 34–36.

32. Ministério de Justiça, Arquivo Nacional, SNI, Ministério do Exército Comando do II Exército 2ª Seção, "Relatório Periódico de Informações. Periodo de 01 de out a 31 de out 75" #10 (1975), SNI, 19.

33. Maria Helena Moreira Alves, *State and Opposition*, 95–96.

34. "Legislação informatizada-Constituição de 1967-publicação original," chap. 4, art. 20, Câmara dos Deputados, accessed October 12, 2018, http://www2.camara.leg.br/legin/fed/consti/1960-1969/constituicao-1967-24-janeiro-1967-365194-publicacaooriginal-1-pl.html.

35. Anne-Marie Smith, *Forced Agreement*; Aquino, *Censura*.

36. On the Mesquitas, see Gaspari, *A ditadura derrotada*, 212, 245; Chagas, *A ditadura militar*.

37. Directed by Fernando Gasparian, the board of *Opinião* included many top São Paulo intellectuals, including Francisco Weffort, FHC, Celso Furtado, Alceu Amoroso Lima, Luciano Martins, and Paul Singer.

38. Gaspari, *A ditadura derrotada*, 434.

39. Ibid., Gaspari, *A ditadura encurralada*, 29. On Geisel's initial decision and the debate about whether to overturn the elections, see Gaspari, *A ditadura derrotada*, 467, 471–74, 481.

40. Gaspari, *A ditadura encurralada*, 30–31.

41. Godoy, *A casa*, 53–54, 36.

42. For the full story, see ibid., 423–49.

43. Gaspari, *A ditadura derrotada*, 405–6, 438. Based on his insider interviews, Godoy, *A casa*, 433, 436, offer a detailed, graphic accounts of every aspect of the campaign, including the disposal of bodies. For how this campaign looked from the perspective of the hunted, see Coelho, *Herança*, 359–66.

44. Godoy, *A casa*, 34, 36–37, 69, 424.

45. Ibid., 35–37, 39 (quote), 129, 390–91, 431, 435, 437, 453–54, 466–67.

46. Gaspari, *A ditadura encurralada*, 35.

47. The massive Brasil: Nunca Mais (BNM) project used the criterion of educational attainment to arrive at its characterization of the "middle sectors" as the social origin of resistance to the military regime. It chose this criterion given the absence in the legal documents of any reliable information on income or jobs. Rounding the numbers, educational data could be found for 4,500 of the 7,400 individuals (80 percent of them male) who appeared in military court cases; of that group, 2,500 had either entered or completed university. This is a striking finding, as they note, given the "notorious elitism of the educational system," through which only a little over 1 percent of the population had achieved a university degree. BNM, *Projecto*, 11.

48. "Legislação informatizada-Constituição de 1967-publicação original," chap. 4, art. 14.

49. Gaspari, *A ditadura derrotada*, 480; "Memorandum from Director of Central Intelligence Colby to Secretary of State Kissinger," April 11, 1974, Foreign Relations of the United States, 1969–1979, Volume E-11, Part 2, Documents on South America, 1973–1976, doc. 99, Office of the Historian, accessed October 12, 2018, https://history.state.gov/historicaldocuments/frus1969-76ve11p2/d99; Godoy, *A casa*, 389–90.

50. Godoy, *A casa*, 129.

51. Lula, interview by Paraná, December 10, 1993, in Paraná, *Lula*, 128; Lula, interview by Couto, April 3, 1997, in Couto, *Memória viva*, 261; "Luiz Inácio Lula da Silva," August

12, 2014 (transcript of testimony), Comissão Nacional da Verdade, accessed September 21, 2019, http://cnv.memoriasreveladas.gov.br/images/pdf/depoimentos/vitimas_civis/Luiz_Inacio_Lula_da_Silva_08.12.2014_-_ct_rp.pdf, 4.

52. For the dates, see Ministério de Justiça, "Relatório Periódico de Informações," 28, 31; on the innocent verdicts, see "Julgamento do PCB," *Opinião*, July 16, 1976, 2, reprinted from *Estado de São Paulo*, July 9, 1976.

53. Coelho, *Herança*, 369–70, 409, 412 (quote). See also Gaspari, *A ditadura encurralada*, 26, 41–44; Godoy, *A casa*, 444–45.

54. Jurema Andreotti Guidetti, "Carta a Geisel," *Estado de São Paulo*, March 13, 1975.

55. For details, see Godoy, *A casa*, 455–63.

56. Ibid.; Dassin, *Torture in Brazil*, 200–201.

57. Frei Chico, interview by Paraná, October 5, 1993, in Paraná, *Lula*, 177–79 (quote); "José Ferreira da Silva (Frei Chico)," 4–5; CEDI, *História*, 44.

58. APESP, "Relatório de Estatística do DOI/CODIII Ex-Mes de Maio de 1975," in II Army, "Relatório Periódico de Informações #5" (1975), 36. Godoy, *A casa*, 482, cites the cumulative statistics from the DOI in 1977, as active operations were shutting down.

59. "José Ferreira da Silva (Frei Chico)," 13 (quote); CEDI, *História*, 41–42.

60. "São Paulo: Os sindicatos viram empresas," *Opinião*, September 26, 1975.

61. Vieitez, "Os metalúrgicos," 55, 61; "Como estão os sindicatos," *Opinião*, November 12, 1975, 4–5; CEDI, *História*, 44.

62. APESP, Delegacia DOPS, "Informações sôbre a Vida Pregressa do Indiciado Manoel José Constantino," October 29, 1975; "José Ferreira da Silva (Frei Chico)," 9.

63. "Como estão os sindicatos," 4–5; "Apelo dos metalúrgicos ignorado por empresas," *Diário do Grande ABC*, September 16, 1975.

64. Frei Chico, interview, 2015, in "Gravação 2015 11–1 Frei Chico (72 Minutos)-Sudeli," Centro de Memória Sindical, São Paulo, 7.

65. Frei Chico, interview by Paraná, September 10, 1993, in Paraná, *Lula*, 159; Frei Chico, interview by Paraná, October 5, 1993, in ibid., 178–79; APESP, SSP, Delegacia Especializada de Ordem Social do DOPS, "Auto de Qualificação e de Interrogatório: José Ferreira da Silva," October 30, 1975, 4. In this case, I was able to combine an interview account with an interrogation statement. As Victoria Langland notes, caution is essential in dealing with sworn and signed statements generated by DOPS and other intelligence agencies. Noting that these documents often reproduce a "decidedly formulaic narrative," she correctly suggests that such declarations should be understood as "officers' reports of information extracted (usually under torture and intimidation) from prisoners," representing "a combination of the officials' overarching interpretative structure supplemented by personal details about the detaineee furnished under pressure." Langland, *Speaking of Flowers*, 190.

66. Frei Chico, 2015 interview, Centro de Memória Sindical, 7. See also Frei Chico, interview by Paraná, September 10, 1993, in Paraná, *Lula*, 157; "José Ferreira da Silva (Frei Chico)," 4.

67. "Biografia de um jornalista," Instituto Vladimir Herzog, accessed October 12, 2018, https://vladimirherzog.org/biografia/. His wife, Clarice, was surprised when she learned about his decision. See also Audálio Dantas, *As duas guerras*, 89–90; Markun, *Vlado*, 16, 39–40, 44.

68. Frei Chico, interview by Paraná, October 5, 1993, in Paraná, *Lula*, 178–79.

69. The DOI's twenty-four-hour dynamic differed from the less-advanced torture prac-

tices at DOPS. When arrested at VW in 1972, the Communist worker Lúcio Bellantani was beaten up by police and guards before being delivered on a Friday to DOPS, where he was left untouched over the weekend; the brutal torture only began on Monday. Lúcio Antônio Bellantani and Benedito Valdir Taoni, interview by Carmen and Betty, November 9, 1984, Centro de Memória Sindical, São Paulo, 5.

70. Frei Chico, interview by Paraná, October 5, 1993, in Paraná, *Lula*, 179–80 (quote), 186; "José Ferreira da Silva (Frei Chico)," 5.

71. Frei Chico, interview by Paraná, October 5, 1993, in Paraná, *Lula*, 184. Zé Cabeludo was the nickname for José Hortencio, born in Capivari, São Paulo, in 1915. According to the DOI, he had lent his house in Praia Grande for party meetings. On the sexual and scatological dimension of DOI torture, see Coelho, *Herança*, 385.

72. Frei Chico, interview by Paraná, October 5, 1993, in Paraná, *Lula*, 179, 181; "José Ferreira da Silva (Frei Chico)," 5, 8.

73. Frei Chico, interview by Paraná, October 5, 1993, in Paraná, *Lula*, 181–82, 187. For another prisoner's confirmation of enforced sleep deprivation at the São Paulo DOI headquarters, see Jordão, *Dossiê Herzog*, 232.

74. Frei Chico, interview by Paraná, October 5, 1993, in Paraná, *Lula*, 179, 184–85; "José Ferreira da Silva (Frei Chico)," 5. Coelho, *Herança*, 433, confirms that he was held at the Rua Tutóia DOI headquarters until the end of 1975.

75. Frei Chico, interview by Paraná, October 5, 1993, in Paraná, *Lula*, 181; Godoy, *A casa*, 313–14. Coelho, *Herança*, 388, offers a curious description of the "humble little mulata" who cleaned the torture cell when he was left alone between sessions. Always whistling, she would glance obliquely at him strung up and once asked him why he looked at her with anger; he didn't reply. Curiously, a week later she heard him defying a captain and whispered to him between her teeth when they were gone, "Meta o pau nos ricos, doutor" (Give it to them, the rich, doctor).

76. "Relatório Periódico de Informações."

77. Frei Chico claimed not to have been subjected to the parrot's perch, a type of "stress and duress" torture known in English as bucking. "José Ferreira da Silva (Frei Chico)," 16, 584; Rejali, *Torture*, 307. This method gained worldwide recognition due to the late 1960s and early 1970s antitorture campaign about Brazil. Green, *We Cannot Remain Silent*, 198–200, 260–61, 272–73.

78. Frei Chico, interview by Paraná, October 5, 1993, in Paraná, *Lula*, 184; "José Ferreira da Silva (Frei Chico)," 6; Frei Chico, interview by Morel, mid-1981, in Morel, *Lula*, 14.

79. In their early to mid-thirties, the cariocas Fernando José Dias and Ana Maria Maduro Gonçalves Brandão worked as assistants to the PCB municipal committees in São Bernardo and São Caetano, respectively. "Relatório Periódico de Informações," 24–25.

80. Frei Chico, interview by Paraná, October 5, 1993, in Paraná, *Lula*, 186; "José Ferreira da Silva (Frei Chico)," 8. Jordão, *Dossiê Herzog*, 148, quotes fellow prisoners of Frei Chico's who also mention how Estrela's feet were entirely torn up.

81. Frei Chico, interview by Paraná, October 5, 1993, in Paraná, *Lula*, 180; "José Ferreira da Silva (Frei Chico)," 8.

82. "Daniel de Souza: 'O 13 foi uma vitória da luta operária,'" *Diário do Grande ABC*, September 30, 1979. See also "José Ferreira da Silva (Frei Chico)," 24.

83. Maria Helena Moreira Alves, "Formation," 608.

84. Gaspari, *A ditadura derrotada*, 471.

Chapter 11

1. "José Ferreira da Silva, Zé, Frei Chico," February 23, 1976, Arquivo Nacional, Rio de Janeiro, SNI, Ministério do Exército, Informação no. 350/76-CB. Curiously enough, Lula's extensive DOPS *prontuário* has very little for these early years and makes no mention of Frei Chico or Osvaldo Cavignato. This could reflect that the political intelligence function of DOPS, a state organ, had been taken over by the SNI, the army's DOI, and the other military intelligence agencies. What is striking, however, is that Lula's DOPS prontuário references only a few reports from those other agencies. APESP, SSP, Polícia Civil de São Paulo, Divisão de Informações/CPI/DOPS/SP, [Pasta] 52-Z-0-23.128: Luiz Inácio da Silva.

2. Lambari and Maria Baixinha, interview by Paraná, June 27, 1994, in Paraná, *Lula*, 346–47; "Exército explica as prisões no estado," *Estado de São Paulo*, October 10, 1975; "Vinte prisões em dez dias: Denuncia do MDB," *Jornal da Tarde*, October 15, 1975. See also the account of the testimony offered by MDB youth activist Waldir José de Quadros before the São Paulo municipal truth commission: "Verdade e história," *BlogdoCitadini* (blog), November 9, 2012, http://blogdocitadini.com.br/?p=2023. Frei Chico was mentioned in the denunciation offered by Rio's MDB senator Saturnino Braga. "O MDB denuncia mais prisões: A ARENA promete explicar," *Estado de São Paulo*, October 16, 1975. The report by US labor attaché Chapin also mentions Constantino and Frei Chico along with Osvaldo Cavignato (described as a "functionary" of the São Bernardo union). USNARA, Department of State, "New Round of São Paulo Political Arrests Includes Two Metalworkers Union Leaders," October 17, 1975.

3. "José Ferreira da Silva (Frei Chico)," September 15, 2014, Comissão Nacional da Verdade, accessed September 21, 2019, http://www.cnv.gov.br/images/pdf/depoimentos/vitimas_civis/vc_Jose_Ferreira_da_Silva_Frei_Chico_15.09.2014.pdf, 16–17.

4. Ibid., 9–10, 16–17 (quote); CEDI, *História*, 44; Frei Chico, interview by Paraná, October 5, 1993, in Paraná, *Lula*, 183; Percival de Souza, *Autópsia do medo*.

5. Frei Chico, interview by Paraná, October 5, 1993, in Paraná, *Lula*, 183, 188; Frei Chico, interview by Paraná, September 10, 1993, in ibid., 164; Frei Chico, quoted in CEDI, *História*, 45.

6. Maria Baixinha, interview by Paraná, April 6, 1994, in Paraná, *Lula*, 267–68; Frei Chico, interview by Paraná, October 5, 1993, in ibid., 186; "José Ferreira da Silva (Frei Chico)," 6, 11, 17; "Entrevista com Frei Chico (16/4/18)—Irmão do ex-presidente Lula," YouTube video, 1:27, posted by "TV 247," April 18, 2018, https://www.youtube.com/watch?v=dDg97hYI_iQ.

7. A labor activist interviewed by Frederico in 1976–77 talked in detail about how he built close personal relations with his fellow workers, but even he, a team leader at VW, reports that "when I call them for a meeting" on activism-related questions, "they are suspicious: 'Couldn't it be that this guy is a subversive?'" Frederico, *A vanguardia operária*, 142.

8. Frei Chico, interview by Paraná, October 5, 1993, in Paraná, *Lula*, 188; "José Ferreira da Silva (Frei Chico)," 7, 9 (quote), 15.

9. "José Ferreira da Silva (Frei Chico)," 7.

10. Frei Chico, interview by Paraná, October 5, 1993, in Paraná, *Lula*, 177.

11. USNARA, "New Round"; USNARA, American Consulate São Paulo to Secretary of State, "Update on Arrests of São Paulo Labor Leaders," November 5, 1975 (quote). São Bernardo vice president Rubão, who served in the early 1970s, commented on the intensity of the pressure on union leaderships under the dictatorship from 1969 to 1975: "If you opened

your mouth, you would end up dead." Rubens Teodoro de Arruda (Rubão), Antenor Biolcatti, and José Arcanjo de Araújo (Zé Preto), "1975 / Eleições," ABC de Luta, accessed January 11, 2019, http://www.abcdeluta.org.br/materia.asp?id_CON=2696.

12. Humberto Domingos Pastore, "João Lins Pereira"; CEDI, *História*, 42–46.

13. See the signed certification by a top DOPS official on October 21, 1965, judging it in the interest of "national union policy" to maintain Argeu in the leadership, contained in an unmarked confidential file initiated by a May 16, 1974, request by Argeu for a certificate of negative political antecedents (which was granted). "Ordem Politica 137729, Argeu Egydio dos Santos, Fichado," APESP, SSP, DOPS.

14. USNARA, "Update on Arrests."

15. Pazzianotto, *100 anos*, 101; Durand Ponte, *Crisis*, 214; Paranhos, "Mentes," 69.

16. Frei Chico, interview by Paraná, September 10, 1993, in Paraná, *Lula*, 158; Osvaldo Cavignato, interview, February 15, 2005, in André Luis Corrêia da Silva, "'João Ferrador,'" 206; Pazzianotto, "Sindicatos," 114.

17. Luiz Inácio Lula da Silva, "Conf. palestra proferida," 212.

18. USNARA, "Update on Arrests" (quote); CEDI, *História*, 45. That DOPS had collaborators in the federation and even local affiliates was widely known. Percival de Souza, *Autópsia do medo*, 381–82. It is less well known that the DOI in São Paulo also became directly involved with the union movement, through its own agents and through thugs provided to intimidate opponents of DOI allies and to steal voter lists (as happened in the São Caetano union). Godoy, *A casa*, 504–5.

19. USNARA, labor attaché Chapin, American Consulate São Paulo to Secretary of State, "During US Visit, São Paulo Metalworkers' Leader Cautions UAW against Publicly Protesting October São Paulo Labor Arrests," December 15, 1975.

20. Lula, interview, 2000, in "Depoimento de Luiz Inácio Lula da Silva," 49.

21. "Informações sôbre a vida pregressa do indiciado," October 29, 1975, APESP, SSP, DOPS.

22. "Biografia do excepcional Comandante Emilio Bonfante Demaria," *Navegadores de Plantão: O Portal dos Marítimos*, last modified November 12, 2014, http://navegadoresem plantao.blogspot.com/2014/11/biografia-do-excepcional-comandante.html. On the 1953 strike, see Barsted, *Medição de forças*.

23. "Justica absolve 65 no processo do PC," *Estado de São Paulo*, July 7, 1975.

24. Frei Chico, interview by Paraná, September 10, 1993, in Paraná, *Lula*, 157; Lula, interview by Paraná, December 10, 1993, in ibid., 130–31; Lula, interview, 2000, in "Depoimento de Luiz Inácio Lula da Silva," 43–44; "Luiz Inácio Lula da Silva," 7.

25. Frei Chico, interview by Paraná, September 10, 1993, in Paraná, *Lula*, 162; Lula, interview by Paraná, December 10, 1993, in ibid., 128 (third quote); Lula, interview by Morel, mid-1981, in Morel, *Lula*, 116 (first quote); Lula, interview by Couto, April 3, 1997, in Couto, *Memória viva*, 261 (second quote); Lula, interview, 2000, in "Depoimento de Luiz Inácio Lula da Silva," 43–44; "Luiz Inácio Lula da Silva," 4–5.

26. Quotes from, respectively, Lula, interview by Dantas, first half of January 1981, in Altino Dantas, *Lula*, 29; Lula, interview by Paraná, December 10, 1993, in Paraná, *Lula*, 129; Lula, interview by Couto, April 3, 1997, in Couto, *Memória viva*, 262.

27. Frei Chico, interview by Paraná, September 10, 1993, in Paraná, *Lula*, 162. On the origin of the expression "tea in a chair," see "Você sabe o que significa a expressão 'chá de cadeira'?," *Vila Brasil: Lingua e Cultura* (blog), September 27, 2013, https://cursovilabrasil .com.br/blog/voce-sabe-o-que-significa-a-expressao-cha-de-cadeira/.

28. Lula, interview by Dantas, first half of January 1981, in Altino Dantas, *Lula*, 28–29. See also Lula, interview by Couto, April 3, 1997, in Couto, *Memória viva*, 262.

29. Lula, interview, 2000, in "Depoimento de Luiz Inácio Lula da Silva," 14.

30. José de Souza Martins, *Uma arqueologia*, 214; Lula, interview by Morel, mid-1981, in Morel, *Lula*, 117.

31. Quotes from, respectively, Lula, interview by Paraná, December 10, 1993, in Paraná, *Lula*, 129; Lula, interview by Couto, April 3, 1997, in Couto, *Memória viva*, 262; Lula, interview by Dantas, first half of January 1981, in Altino Dantas, *Lula*, 30.

32. Lula, interview by Paraná, December 10, 1993, in Paraná, *Lula*, 128.

33. "Osvaldo Rodrigues Cavignato," in Cido Faria, *O movimento operário no ABC paulista contado por seus autores*, 262–63. His successful defense provided a quite different account, as summarized by the military judge (Processo 3/76–135, pp. 3681–82): An adventurer, he moved to Italy in 1970, where he had relatives, although he took a job elsewhere in the country because of their "rigid customs."

34. Brasil Nunca Mais, Poder Judiciário, Justiça Militar Federal, 2.a Auditório da 2.a C. I. M. São Paulo, "Processo 3/76–135, pp. 3681, 3683.

35. Alberti, Farias, and Rocha, *Paulo Egydio conta*, 486.

36. Frei Chico, interview by Paraná, October 5, 1993, in ibid., 187.

Chapter 12

1. José Nêumanne Pinto and Maria Inês Caravaggi, "Perfil do operário hoje: Educação é o caminho do campo para a fábrica," *Jornal do Brasil*, January 5, 1976, 17. The long piece won the Esso Prize for economic reportage in 1976.

2. Nêumanne Pinto, *Erundina*, 163, 143.

3. Maria Alzira de Melo Rodrigues, "O sindicato metalúrgico, segundo os diretores," *Gazeta de São Bernardo*, 1st week of May 1975; Lula, interview by Morel, mid-1981, in Morel, *Lula*, 156 (quote). Likewise, when Vidal and Lula traveled together to Juiz de Fora, Minas Gerais, to speak to students on trade unionism, the former gave the talk. "Movimento sindical," *Diário do Grande ABC*, May 9, 1975.

4. Vidal was generous in providing opportunities to Lula: to head conference commissions, preside at sessions of the First São Bernardo Metalworkers' Congress, and travel internationally. Frei Chico, interview by Paraná, September 10, 1993, in Paraná, *Lula*, 157; Jorge Pinheiro, "O Brasil ainda será um grande São Bernardo: Uma entrevista com Paulo Vidal, o metalúrgico que 'criou' o lider Lula," *Folhetim*, May 11, 1980, 4–5; Chaia, *Intelectuais*, 148. On the 1973 CEBRAP visit, see Fernando Henrique Cardoso, *Accidental President*, 136–37.

5. Lula, interview by Paraná, October 6, 1993, in Paraná, *Lula*, 117 (first quote); Lula, interview by Paraná, July 19, 1993, in ibid., 100, 104; Frei Chico, interview by Paraná, September 10, 1993, in ibid., 158; Lula, interview by Dantas, first half of January 1981, in Altino Dantas, *Lula*, 28 (third quote); Torres, *Uma experiência*, 6 (second quote). Speaking "without false modesty," Vidal said in 2005 that until halfway through Lula's first term the union's presidency "was exercised by two heads or four hands." "Convite da oposição foi rejeitada em 1972," *Folha de São Paulo*, April 18, 2005.

6. Lula, interview by Paraná, July 19, 1993, in Paraná, *Lula*, 102.

7. Ibid., 100, 115; Lula, interview by Paraná, October 6, 1993, in Paraná, *Lula*, 117; Pinheiro, "O Brasil," 4–5; Carla Delecrode, "O que 'Lula, o filho do Brasil' não contou," *Opinião e Notícia*, March 24, 2010; Lula, interview by Morel, mid-1981, in Morel, *Lula*, 115; Luiz Inácio Lula

da Silva, "Conf. palestra proferida," 212; comments by Rubens Teodoro de Arruda (Rubão), Antenor Biolcatti, and José Arcanjo de Araújo (Zé Preto), "1975 / Eleições," ABC de Luta!, accessed January 11, 2019, http://www.abcdeluta.org.br/materia.asp?id_CON=2696; Ademir Medici, "Lula em Santo André: Um retrato que é uma relíquia," *Diário do Grande ABC*, December 29, 2002; Aloysio Azevedo, "Sindicatos," 27–28. For scholarly discussion of the 1975 election, see Paranhos, *Era uma vez*, 52–53; Paranhos, "Mentes," 53, 71; Rainho and Bargas, *As lutas operárias*, 52.

8. Abramo, *O resgate*, 171.

9. "Um novo estilo de sindicalismo," *Opinião*, September 16, 1974, 3.

10. Lula, interview by Paraná, October 6, 1993, in Paraná, *Lula*, 113; Lula, interview by Paraná, July 19, 1993, in ibid., 99–100; Lula, interviews, 1990 and 1994, in Harnecker, *O sonho era possível*, 58; Luiz Carlos Azedo, "Entrevista com Frei Chico," *Correio Braziliense*, December 1, 2008.

11. Lula, interview, 2000, in "Depoimento de Luiz Inácio Lula da Silva," 47, 27; Lula, interview by Paraná, July 19, 1993, in Paraná, *Lula*, 101.

12. Lula, interview, 2000, in "Depoimento de Luiz Inácio Lula da Silva," 66; Cavignato, interview, February 15, 2005, in André Luis Corrêia da Silva, "'João Ferrador,'" 208.

13. "Alvara de soltura: Osvaldo Cagvignato," December 18, 1975, APESP, SSP, DOPS, prontuário 97600, vol. 4.

14. Delecrode, "O que 'Lula.'" Rainho and Bargas, *As lutas operárias*, 98–99, 207, discuss how some non-PCB leftist militants in São Bernardo's factories came to follow Lula after May 1978.

15. Lula, interview, 2000, in "Depoimento de Luiz Inácio Lula da Silva," 28.

16. Nêumanne Pinto, *O que sei*, 103, 122.

17. Paranhos, "Mentes," 50, 54.

18. Lula, interview, 2000, in "Depoimento de Luis Inácio Lula da Silva," 66.

19. "Eduardo Suplicy responde ao Balaio do Kotscho," *Balaio do Kotscho* (blog), November 23, 2011, https://www.balaiodokotscho.com.br/2011/11/23/eduardo-suplicy-responde-ao-balaio-do-kotscho/.

20. Lula, interview, 2000, in "Depoimento de Luiz Inácio Lula da Silva," 66.

21. Torres, *Uma experiência*, 55.

22. Bourne, *Lula of Brazil*, 29; Paraná, *Lula*, 477–78.

23. Frei Chico, interview by Paraná, September 10, 1993, in Paraná, *Lula*, 164. Suggesting the unreliability of this claim, Frei Chico ends by insisting that Lula read a lot after this supposed political awakening—even though elsewhere Frei Chico has complained that Lula never read.

24. DOPS reports routinely noted union director participation in MDB seminars, talks, and electoral mobilizations in 1975–76 São Bernardo: APESP, SSP, DOPS, Dossie 50-Z-341, Pasta 14, Prontuários 1385, 1377 (November 7, 1975), 1378 (November 12, 1975); Pasta 12, Prontuários 1294 (October 18, 1976), 1305, 1322 (November 1976). Further evidence of his politicization comes from the recollection of a never-published August 1975 interview conducted by two leftist USP students, during which Lula, unaccompanied by Vidal, supposedly said that the union had concluded in 1974 that economic struggle alone was insufficient to achieve their demands; he also rejected tutelage by any political party. Luciano Martins Costa, "O governo mudou e a imprensa não percebeu," *Observatório da Imprensa*, February 3, 2004.

25. Lula, interview, 2000, in "Depoimento de Luiz Inácio Lula da Silva," 44.

26. Ibid., 43; Frei Chico, interview, 2015, in "Gravação 2015 11–1 Frei Chico (72 Minutos)-Sudeli," Centro de Memória Sindical, São Paulo, 11; Lula, interview by Ruy Mesquita, June 1978, in Renato Delmanto, "O barão da imprensa entrevista Lula, o sindicalista," *Na Mídia* (blog), http://delmanto.blogspot.com/2009/01/o-barao-da-imprensa-entrevista-lula-o.html; Lula, interview by Morel, mid-1981, in Morel, *Lula*, 117.

27. "Luiz Inácio Lula da Silva," 4–5, 7–8; Lula, interview, 2000, in "Depoimento de Luiz Inácio Lula da Silva," 43–44; Lula, interview by Morel, mid-1981, in Morel, *Lula*, 114.

28. Frei Chico, interview by Morel, mid-1981, in Morel, *Lula*, 69, 162–63; Frei Chico, interview by Paraná, September 10, 1993, in Paraná, *Lula*, 164; Frei Chico, 2015 interview, Centro de Memória Sindical, 11.

29. Delmanto, "O barão da imprensa." Delmanto had access to the full, 120-page unpublished transcript of this interview, which he kindly provided to me. Edited excerpts from the interview appear in Guizzo et al., *Lula*, 100.

30. Lula, interview by Morel, mid-1981, in Morel, *Lula*, 116.

31. Ibid. (first quote); Lula, interview by Dantas, first half of January 1981, in Altino Dantas, *Lula*, 28 (second quote); Lula, interview by Paraná, December 10, 1993, in Paraná, *Lula*, 129 (third quote).

32. "Luiz Inácio Lula da Silva" (interview by unknown interviewer, n.d., ca. 1999–2000), in Dines, Fernandes, and Salomão, *Histórias do poder*, 333–34.

33. Lula, interview by Paraná, December 10, 1993, in Paraná, *Lula*, 130; Lula, interview, 2000, in "Depoimento de Luiz Inácio Lula da Silva," 44; "Lula: Somos o mais importante partido," 3. For Frei Chico's interrogatory, see "Auto de qualificação e de interrogatório: José Ferreira da Silva," October 30, 1975, APESP, SSP, DOPS.

34. "Lula, retrato de corpo inteiro," *Nova Escrita/Ensaio*, January 1982, 49.

35. Audálio Dantas, *As duas guerras*, 261–68; for his discussion of Nunes and his activities on the insurgent slate that won the journalist's union elections, see ibid., 85, 114, 128. In a 1994 interview, Dantas also recounts attending the union inauguration of Lula, "the beardless boy," in 1975. "Um 'furo' de memoria," Museu da Pessoa, last modified March 21, 2014, http://www.museudapessoa.net/pt/conteudo/historia/um-furo-de-memoria-4583/colecao/97503.

36. Alberti, Farias, and Rocha, *Paulo Egydio conta*, 466.

37. "Paulo Egydio Martins: Verbete," FGV CPDOC, accessed January 11, 2019, http://www.fgv.br/cpdoc/acervo/dicionarios/verbete-biografico/paulo-egidio-martins.

38. Gaspari, *A ditadura derrotada*, 433–34; Velasco e Cruz, *Empresariado e estado*, 215–17.

39. Alberti, Farias, and Rocha, *Paulo Egydio conta*, 478; "Relato da invasão da PUC," *Folha de São Paulo*, November 28, 1977.

40. "Declarações de Egydio," *Opinião*, July 16, 1976, 2.

41. Gaspari, *A ditadura encurralada*, 179, 210; See Teles, Ridenti, and Iokoi, *Intolerância*, 476, for the life story and 1975 DOI experience of the Military Police officer Vicente Silvestre.

42. Alberti, Farias, and Rocha, *Paulo Egydio conta*, 482. While this interview valuably captures how Egydio experienced this moment and its spirit, some details are wrong and some statements need qualification.

43. Frei Chico, interview by Paraná, September 10, 1993, in Paraná, *Lula*, 159.

44. Nêumanne Pinto, *O que sei*, 149.

45. Delmanto, "O barão da imprensa," 5.

46. "As eleições vistas dos sindicatos," *Opinião*, November 12, 1976, 4–5.

47. "Um novo estilo," 3.

48. Nêumanne Pinto, *O que sei*, 128–34. Despite his hostility to Lula, Nêumanne Pinto rejects the ubiquitous fringe conspiracy theories, on left and right, that Lula was an agent of Geisel. He also insists that Lula said nothing at these meetings "that brought discredit" to him as a "legitimate and loyal representative" of ABC's skilled autoworkers. Ibid., 134.

49. Gaspari, *A ditadura encurralada*, 447.

50. Rainho and Bargas, *As lutas operárias*, 59–60, 192–94.

51. Lula, interview, 2000, in "Depoimento de Luiz Inácio Lula da Silva," 29.

52. *Tribuna Metalúrgica*, July 1977, 6, cited in Gaspari, *A ditadura encurralada*, 331; Alberti, Farias, and Rocha, *Paulo Egydio conta*, 482.

53. Rainho and Bargas, *As lutas operárias*, 98.

54. Luiz Inácio Lula da Silva, "Nossa opinião," *Tribuna Metalúrgica*, August 1976, quoted in Paranhos, *Era uma vez*, 117.

55. "Governador visita ABC e dialoga com trabalhadores," *Estado de São Paulo*, September 19, 1976.

56. Zerbinato, "Braços cruzados," 33–34.

57. "Editorial: As palavras do senhor governador," *ABCD Jornal*, October 9, 1976, 2. In the 1980s the newspaper's editor, Julio de Grammont, would become editor of *Tribuna Metalúrgica*.

58. Alberti, Farias, and Rocha, *Paulo Egydio conta*, 284, 483. Egydio might have misunderstood the union official's offer.

59. Ibid., 484.

60. Ibid., 486–87; Roberto Muylaert, "Vox Populi com Lula foi ameaçado pelos militares," *Ícaro*, November 2003. Strictly speaking, this was not Lula's first TV interview, since he had been briefly filmed at his 1975 union inauguration.

61. Lula, interview by Paraná, July 19, 1993, in Paraná, *Lula*, 103; Lula, interview by Paraná, October 6, 1993, in ibid., 119; "O povo perguntou a Lula: Aqui estão as respostas," *Jornal da Tarde*, n.d., May 1978.

62. Guizzo et al., *Lula*, 72–73, 79 (the show transcript is reproduced in this source). Lula specifically mentions that he doesn't accept the government rule that deemed a SENAI apprenticeship equivalent to a high school degree. In his memoir, an AP militant who helped organize the 1978 Osasco May Day event confirms that it was overwhelmingly attended by students and "leftists"—though at one point, he says, an unknown worker got up and told them that they should be in São Bernardo with "this Lula guy" and his union, who were doing "the real thing." Ricardo de Azevedo, *Por um triz*, 209.

63. "Em Santo André, debate livre e entusiasmado," *Folha de São Paulo*, May 2, 1978; "Senadores vaiados," *ABCD Jornal*, April 29–May 6, 1978.

64. Guizzo et al., *Lula*, 74. The comment about invited guests not being booed by his union was likely a mild swipe at Benedito Marcilio, president of the Santo André metalworkers' union, who was unable to get the crowd to stop booing Quércia and Montoro at the May Day celebration. The MDB's two most senior officeholders were invited to coincide with the announcement, distributed at the event, that Marcílio was being nominated by the MDB to run for federal deputy. He was subsequently elected.

65. Ibid., 77, 78.

66. Frederico, *Consciência operária*, 99–101.

67. Delmanto, "O barão da imprensa."

Chapter 13

1. Sampaio, *Lula*, 75, 92, 106, 121.

2. Schwartz, *Sugar Plantations*, 246.

3. Paraná, *Lula*, 22.

4. Gaspari, *A ditadura acabada*, 41–42. Others who share this view of the early Lula as naive and nonpolitical include Bourne, *Lula of Brazil*, 47, 80; Paraná, *O filho*, 436–47.

5. Luiz Inácio Lula da Silva, "Conf. palestra proferida," 213.

6. Fleischer, "Manipulações casuísticas," 175–77.

7. Luiz Inácio Lula da Silva, "Conf. palestra proferida," 213; Harnecker, *O sonho era possível*, 36; Lula, interview by Morel, mid-1981, in Morel, *Lula*, 120–21; Lula, interview by Paraná, December 10, 1993, in Paraná, *Lula*, 127.

8. Mino Carta and Bernardo Lerer, "O antipelego," *IstoÉ*, February 1, 1978; "Lula, o metalúrgico, mete bronca: Qual a classe brasileira que é consciente," *Pasquim*, March 24–31, 1978, 4–9, in Guizzo et al., *Lula*, 9–40.

9. "Depoimento de José de Segadas Vianna," 138, 140, 153.

10. SNI, Ficha de Distribuiçao e Procesamento de Documentos, "Assunto Luis Inácio da Silva," November 16, 1978, passing along Ministério do Trabalho document of the same date including a confidential document, origin unattributed, described in handwriting as "Resumo de conduta quando candidatou-se em 1977" (026-SNIG-AC_ACE_115795_78-2.Pdf). For the SNI in April 1978, Lula was the product of manipulation by "persons external to the unions" who had escaped obscurity to achieve "journalistic stardom." "SNI, Apreciação nº 25, do GAE, de 4 de april de 1978. APGCS/HF," as cited in Gaspari, *A ditadura acabada*, 41.

11. For a compilation of statements by such "liberal" authorities from various spheres before, during, and after the May 1978 factory stoppages, see Abramo, *O resgate*, 196, 251–56; Paraná, *O filho*, 436–43; Durand Ponte, *Crisis*, 230–32; Lula, interview by Paraná, December 10, 1993, in Paraná, *Lula*, 136.

12. James C. Scott, *Domination*, 132.

13. Nêumanne Pinto, *O que sei*, 147.

14. Lula, interview, 2000, in "Depoimento de Luiz Inácio Lula da Silva," 30–31 (first quote); *Veja*, May 24, 1978, 95, 69, quoted in Paraná, *O filho*, 438 (Monteiro's quotes). See also Lula, interview by Paraná, December 10, 1993, in Paraná, *Lula*, 135; *Jornal da Tarde*, May 20, 1978, 22–23; Durand Ponte, *Crisis*, 230; Markun, *O sapo*, 129.

15. Lula, interview by Morel, mid-1981, in Morel, *Lula*, 52. Petistas were still expressing these fears of media manipulation in the early 1990s, in an interview by a Cuban-based Chilean leftist. Harnecker, *O sonho era possível*, 45–47. For a more nuanced examination of these press contacts in 1977–78, see Durand Ponte, *Crisis*, 229–38.

16. "Apoio e restricão a documento sindical," *Folha de São Paulo*, February 18, 1978.

17. Renato Delmanto, "O barão da imprensa entrevista Lula, o sindicalista," *Na Mídia* (blog), http://delmanto.blogspot.com/2009/01/o-barao-da-imprensa-entrevista-lula-o.html.

18. Rainho, *Os peões*; Sampaio, *Lula*; Eduardo Coutinho, dir., *Peões* (Rio de Janeiro: Videofilmes, 2004).

19. Sampaio, *Lula*, 111.

20. Veras and Veras, *Retrato*, 21–22.

21. Sampaio, *Lula*, 15–17.

22. "Sumário do BNM," ação penal no. 22/72, Brasil: Nunca Mais Digital, accessed August 2, 2019, http://bnmdigital.mpf.mp.br/sumarios/700/671.html; Ribeiro, "A subida do monte purgatório," 9.

23. Rainho, *Os peões*, 32; Perruso, *Em busca do "novo,"* 193. Rainho's classic work is often neglected because of its extensive detail, resistance to synthesis, and lack of succinct and singular argument, unlike the books of John Humphrey and Celso Frederico. For the best appreciation, see Krueger, "Abertura/Apertura," 184–87.

24. To date, no one has worked linguistically with Rainho's dialect interviews whose worth is suggested by the study of such transcripts of rural folk by a northeastern sociologist working in the state of Sergipe. Magno da Silva, *A luta dos posseiros*, 237–38.

25. Rainho, *Os peões*, 11–12.

26. Ibid., 11–12.

27. Lula, interview by Paraná, July 19, 1993, in Paraná, *Lula*, 88, 101; Vavá, interview by Paraná, September 3 and 7, 1993, in ibid., 233; Frei Chico, interview by Paraná, October 5, 1993, in ibid., 172; Tiana, interview by Paraná, April 21, 1994, in ibid., 311; Jaime, interview by Paraná, April 10, 1994, in ibid., 292.

28. Frederico, *Consciência operária*, 95.

29. Barcelos, "Raquel," 30. This is the only reference in the works I consulted to the term *piorra*, which refers to a "small top" (*pequeno pião, pitorra*), according to the *Dicionário Houaiss da Língua Portuguesa*. Pião means a "toy top."

30. Rainho, *Os peões*, 244.

31. Goffman, *Stigma*.

32. Hamilton Pereira, "Eu fui um simples operário," *Realidade*, September 1967, 60.

33. Masini, "Em nome do real," 166–67. This interview was originally published in *Revista Trópico* in 2005.

34. Maria do Carmo Reginato Gama de Carvalho, "A fábrica," 82.

35. Ford unionist João Ferreira Passos identifies this category as the "common, average peon" in Vitor Nuzzi, "Centrais querem punições a empresas que foram 'quartéis' durante a ditadura," *Rede Brasil Atual*, February 2, 2014.

36. Tomizaki, *Ser metalúrgico*, 85–86. For more on the demeaning and despotic behavior of foremen, see Rainho, *Os peões*, 239.

37. Frederico, *Consciência operária*, 59; Abramo, *O resgate*, 63.

38. Agier and Guimarães, "Técnicos e peões," 51.

39. Rainho, *Os peões*, 238–39; Frederico, *Consciência operária*, 46.

40. Quotes from, respectively, Tomizaki, *Ser metalúrgico*, 104; Maria do Carmo Reginato Gama de Carvalho, "A fábrica," 67. See also Frederico, *Consciência operária*, 61; Rainho, *Os peões*, 242.

41. Frederico, *A vanguarda operária*, 76.

42. Torres, *Uma experiência*, 9.

43. Frederico, *Consciência operária*, 46.

44. Frederico, *A vanguarda operária*, 58–59.

45. Torres, *Uma experiência*, 9; Frederico, *A vanguardia operária*, 58–61.

46. Frederico, *A vanguarda operária*, 68. See also Frederico, *Consciência operária*, 59.

47. Jameson, "Sartre and History," 248.

48. Rainho, *Os peões*, 249.

49. Lanzana, *Diferenciais de salários*, 20.

50. "Cícero Firmino ('Martinha')," Sítio Polêmico, last modified November 17, 2007, http://www.sitiopolemico.com/?p=47.

51. Lívio de Carvalho, "Políticas salariais brasileiras," 57.

52. Macarini, "A política econômica," 89. In his first ministerial meeting, Geisel declared that maintaining high economic growth was his "number one priority." Gaspari, *A ditadura derrotada*, 437.

53. Macarini, "A política econômica," 85–88.

54. Gaspari, *A ditadura derrotada*, 274–75; Macarini, "A política econômica," 88–89; Rainho and Bargas, *As lutas operárias*, 39; Simões, *A lei do arrocho*, 99; Durand Ponte, *Crisis*, 200.

55. Gaspari, *A ditadura derrotada*, 428–30, 432–33; Rainho and Bargas, *As lutas operárias*, 39.

56. Markun, *O sapo*, 110–11; Rainho and Bargas, *As lutas operárias*, 30.

57. "Walter Barelli: História de vida," DIEESE Memória, accessed August 28, 2018, http://memoria.dieese.org.br/museu/nossas_historias_menu/walter-barelli.

58. Durand Ponte, *Crisis*, 201–5; "Walter Barelli"; Lula, interview, 2000, in "Depoimento de Luiz Inácio Lula da Silva," 29; "Os metalúrgicos tentam um acordo direto com patrões," *Folha de São Paulo*, April 13, 1978.

59. Lula, interview by Dantas, first half of January 1981, in Altino Dantas, *Lula*, 32; Lula, interview by Paraná, October 6, 1993, in Paraná, *Lula*, 120; Lula, interview, 2000, in "Depoimento de Luiz Inácio Lula da Silva," 29.

60. Lula, interview, 2000, in "Depoimento de Luiz Inácio Lula da Silva," 28; Lula, interview by Dantas, first half of January 1981, in Altino Dantas, *Lula*, 32; Lula, interview by Paraná, October 6, 1993, in Paraná, *Lula*, 110; Lula, interview by Paraná, December 10, 1993, in ibid., 131 (quote).

61. Lula, interview by Dantas, first half of January 1981, in Altino Dantas, *Lula*, 32, 34; Lula, interview by Paraná, December 10, 1993, in Paraná, *Lula*, 131–32; Lula, interview by Paraná, October 6, 1993, in ibid., 110.

62. Rainho, *Os peões*, 292–93; Rainho and Bargas, *As lutas operárias*, 40–41. By early 1978, Lula was directly engaged with rebutting the two economic ministers he had met with, according to the following newspaper article clippings in my possession that do not indicate the name of the newspaper: "Sentimos melhorias no dialogo, diz Luis Inacio," March 17, 1978; "Lula refuta tese de Simonsen sobre renda," March 9, 1978.

63. Rainho and Bargas, *As lutas operárias*, 98–101, 207. For Lula's discussion of those in the categoria who were "more ideologically organized," see Lula, interview, 2000, in "Depoimento de Luiz Inácio Lula da Silva," 29, 31.

64. Lula, interview by Morel, mid-1981, in Morel, *Lula*, 116.

65. *Folha de São Paulo*, July 4, 1977, quoted in Paraná, *O filho*, 435–36.

66. Moore, *Injustice*.

67. *Em Tempo*, November 1977, quoted in Abramo, *O resgate*, 194.

68. For a superb early analysis of Lula's and the New Unionism's discursive trajectory along these lines, see Isabel Ribeiro de Oliveira Gómez de Souza, *Trabalho e política*.

69. Rainho, *Os peões*, 280; Rainho and Bargas, *As lutas operárias*, 55–57; "Metalúrgicos de SB tem reunião," *Folha de São Paulo*, March 12, 1978; "Posição contra dissídio," *Folha de São Paulo*, March 13, 1978.

70. Lula, interview by Dantas, first half of January 1981, in Altino Dantas, *Lula*, 36; Lula, interview, 2000, in "Depoimento de Luiz Inácio Lula da Silva," 29–30.

71. Rainho and Bargas, *As lutas operárias,* 61; "'Posse mostrou o prestigio de Lula': Da sucursal do ABC," April 23, 1978 (newspaper article clipping, without the name of the newspaper indicated, in the author's possession); "'Exigir sem medo.' 'Somos maioria,'" *ABCD Jornal,* April 29–May 6, 1978, 1–2. For Argeu dos Santos's attacks on Lula and industrialists who dialogued with him, see "Desnacionalização atinge autopecas, confirma Vidigal," *Folha de São Paulo,* March 21, 1978, 20.

72. Mercadante Oliva, "Estado autoritário," 180–81, 286, table E1; Paranhos, "Mentes," 54, 71; Rainho and Bargas, *As lutas operárias,* 54.

73. "'Manifesto dos Associados,' lancando por Lula em sua campanha a reeleicão," in Rainho and Bargas, *As lutas operárias,* 190–91, 54; "Baixos salários marginalizam, afirma sindicato," *O Estado de São Paulo,* January 31, 1978.

74. Lula, interview by Dantas, first half of January 1981, in Altino Dantas, *Lula,* 75.

75. Lula, interview by Morel, mid-1981, in Morel, *Lula,* 124.

76. Quotes from, respectively, Rainho and Bargas, *As lutas operárias,* 60; "'Exigir sem medo,'" 1–2.

77. Rainho and Bargas, *As lutas operárias,* 61 (quotes); "'Exigir sem medo,'" 1–2.

78. "'Exigir sem medo.'"

79. Lula, interview by Morel, mid-1981, in Morel, *Lula,* 124.

Chapter 14

1. On the reactions of rank-and-file workers to this outreach and messaging, see the transcribed interviews with unionists in André Luis Corrêia da Silva, "'João Ferrador,'" 262–63, 290–91, 309, 322.

2. Abramo, *O resgate,* 209; Rainho, *Os peões,* 269.

3. APESP, SSP, DOPS [Pasta] 50-Z-341-2888, "Assembléia dos Metalúrgicos do ABCD, Estádio de Vila Euclides," April 14, 1980 (first quote); Lula, interview, 2000, in "Depoimento de Luiz Inácio Lula da Silva," 35–36 (second quote).

4. Lula, interview by Dantas, first half of January 1981, in Altino Dantas, *Lula,* 51 (first quote); Lula, interview by Paraná, December 10, 1993, in Paraná, *Lula,* 141 (second quote); Lula, interview, 2000, in "Depoimento de Luiz Inácio Lula da Silva," 31.

5. Lula, interview by Morel, mid-1981, in Morel, *Lula,* 54 (first quote); Lula, interview by Paraná, December 10, 1993, in Paraná, *Lula,* 141 (remaining quotes); Lula, interview by Dantas, first half of January 1981, in Altino Dantas, *Lula,* 54; Lula, interview, 2000, in "Depoimento de Luiz Inácio Lula da Silva," 31. The 20,000 figure is for attendance at its height as recorded hourly by DOPS (APESP, SSP, DOPS 50-Z-341-2371, "Greve dos Metalúrgicos," March 13, 1979). See also Rainho and Bargas, *As lutas operárias,* 124–25, on the first stadium rally and the union discussions about what it would mean to fill the stadium. For memorable photos, see Kotscho, *A Greve do ABC,* and films made on the strike: Silva, "O cinema na greve" (2008).

6. Josué Machado, "A realidade íntima do sindicalista," *Playboy,* July 1979, in Guizzo et al., *Lula,* 206. Lula claims this was a personal choice, although an element of calculation cannot be ruled out; as his union associates noted, he had been criticized by the media and students for being "very well dressed, with a dark coat, tie, and vest" during his April 1978 diretoria inauguration speech. Rainho and Bargas, *As lutas operárias,* 60. His new dress conformed more closely to outsiders' conception of an "authentic" worker.

7. Keck, "New Unionism," 262 (first quote); Bourne, *Lula of Brazil,* 47 (second quote).

8. Keck, "New Unionism," 262.

9. Lilia M. Schwarcz, "Brazil in the Shadow of Lula," *NYR Daily* (blog), *New York Review of Books,* November 19, 2010, http://www.nybooks.com/daily/2010/11/19/brazil-shadow-lula/. Bourne, *Lula of Brazil,* 193, dubs Lula a "messianic figure."

10. Rotberg, "Charisma," 419.

11. Weber, *Economy and Society,* 1:342. On how the term, once secularized, came to play a major—if oft-criticized—role in the modern social sciences, see Joosse, "Becoming a God."

12. Weber, *Economy and Society,* 1:374.

13. Bryman, *Charisma and Leadership,* 23.

14. Weber, *Methodology,* 84–90.

15. Djalma Bom, interview, March 8, 2005, in Ferreira and Fortes, *Muitos caminhos,* 94. In addition to his role in 1980, Joaquimzão also printed leaflets for Lula's union during their strike after they lost their headquarters.

16. Djalma Bom, interview, March 8, 2005, in Ferreira and Fortes, *Muitos caminhos,* 94.

17. Bensman and Givant, "Charisma and Modernity," 28–29. On the transhistorical nature of the concept, see Mommsen, "Personal Conduct," 45–46.

18. Bryman, *Charisma and Leadership,* 50.

19. Weber, *Economy and Society,* 1:374–75. See also Bryman, *Charisma and Leadership,* 42. Rotberg, "Charisma," 419, aptly describes charisma as "the inspirational component of the bond between leaders and their political and organizational followers that allows them to act as if they are genuinely inspired to maximize what they presume, or are led to believe, are their own interests."

20. Weber, *Economy and Society,* 1:374.

21. Weber, *Economy and Society,* 3:1112–13 (emphasis added).

22. Cavalli, "Charisma," 317, 324.

23. Baehr, "'Masses,'" 244.

24. Quoted in ibid., 245.

25. Ibid., 244–45; Bryman, *Charisma and Leadership,* 70, 86.

26. Baehr, "'Masses,'" 244–45.

27. For the union's official statements, proposals, and responses between 1974 and 1979, see Rainho and Bargas, *As lutas operárias,* 175–246.

28. Macedo, "A greve de 1980."

29. Bensman and Givant, "Charisma and Modernity," 28.

30. Reynolds, *Debs,* 71.

31. Chico Júnior, "Operário, vôce conhece o Lula?," *Pasquim,* March 24–31, 1978, 9. See also "Tarcísio Tadeu Garcia Pereira." Sítio Polêmico, last modified November 17, 2007, http://www.sitiopolemico.com/?p=53.

32. Interview with "Adão," in Pogibin, "Memórias," 90.

33. Batista, *Gilson Menezes.*

34. "Valter Barelli," Sítio Polêmico, last modified November 17, 2007, http://www.sitiopolemico.com/?p=61.

35. Lula, interview by Paraná, June 30, 1993, in Paraná, *Lula,* 53; Lula, interview by Paraná, December 10, 1993, in ibid., 133; Frei Chico and Vavá, interview by Paraná, September 3 and 7, 1993, in ibid., 213–14. See also Bruno Merlin, "Pai de Lula morreu como indigente," *PortoGente,* April 10, 2005, https://portogente.com.br/noticias/noticias-do-dia/5191-pai-de-lula-morreu-como-indigente; Luiz Maklouf Carvalho, "Pai acabou como indigente: 'Seu' Aristides era o retrato do brasileiro pobre," *Jornal do Brasil,* May 21, 1989.

36. Abramo, *O resgate,* 210.

37. Andreotti, interview, November 24, 1982, in Santo André; Brandão Lopes, "O ajustamento," 404–5.

38. "Ata da reunião realizada dia 16 de maio de 1978 no patio interior da Saab-Scania do Brazil com todos os funcionários e mais os Líderes do Sindicato," APESP, SSP, DOPS 50-7-341, 2118–21.

39. "João Bosco Arcanjo," Sítio Polêmico, last modified November 17, 2007, http://www.sitiopolemico.com/?p=43.

40. Maria do Carmo Reginato Gama de Carvalho, "A fábrica," 76, 79.

41. Murilo Carvalho, *Estórias de trabalhador*, 94.

42. SNI, "Movimento Grevista das 16:00 hs de 16 Mar 79 as 8:00 hs de 17 Mar 79," in SNI, E0012907-1979 "Movimento grevista dos metalúrgicos do ABC," 71–72, found at the end of "ASP_ACE_1290_79_001.pdf" and the second page in "ASP_ACE_1290_79_002.pdf."

43. Lula, interview, 2000, in "Depoimento de Luiz Inácio Lula da Silva," 31.

44. Interview with "Adão," in Pogibin, "Memórias," 128.

45. Lula, interviews from 1990 and 1994, in Harnecker, *O sonho era possível*, 57.

46. Durkheim, *Elementary Forms*, 210–11.

47. Bourdieu, *In Other Words*, 117–18.

48. Ibid., 138.

49. Alberto Eulálio (Betão), interview, in André Luis Corrêia da Silva, "'João Ferrador,'" 301.

50. Jameson, "Sartre and History," 248. On female activists and metalworkers, see the rich, interview-based study Leite, *A operária metalúrgica*.

51. Jameson, "Sartre and History," 254, 256.

52. Ricardo Kotscho, "Essa estranha terra que fica no Brasil," *IstoÉ*, May 1979, 8–12.

53. Gaspari, *A ditadura acabada*, 146.

54. Ricardo Kotscho, "A terra dos peões," *Folhetim*, May 11, 1980. See also Gaspari, *A ditadura acabada*, 83, 86, 97–98.

55. Bourdieu, "What Makes a Social Class?," 14.

56. Bourdieu, "Social Space," 740.

57. Ibid., 740.

58. Bourdieu, "What Makes a Social Class?," 14.

59. Rainho, *Os peões*, 225–26.

60. Machado, "A realidade íntima," 216–17.

61. Lula, interview by Renato Tapajós, May 22, 1979, in Guizzo et al., *Lula*, 186–91.

62. Maurício Soares, "Prefácio," in Rainho and Bargas, *As lutas operárias*, 7. Soares was named in November 1978 as alternate to Fernando Henrique Cardoso in the future president's run for the Senate on the MDB ticket, a deal that created a bridge between Lula and the key leader of the opposition intelligentsia. Markun, *O sapo*, 120–23.

63. Durand Ponte, *Crisis*, 215.

64. Antunes, *A rebeldia*, 59–60.

65. Rainho and Bargas, *As lutas operárias*, 167.

66. Ibid., 167. It was originally published in the union newspaper. "Vamos Rezar: Pai nosso do Lula," *Tribuna Metalúrgica*, April 1980, 6.

67. "Apesar da violência, um 'pai nosso' a 60 mil vozes," *Diário Popular*, March 21, 1979, 6; "Lula refuta infiltração ideológica no movimento," *Folha de São Paulo*, March 18, 1979.

68. Rainho and Bargas, *As lutas operárias*, 164.

69. Ibid.; Antunes, *A rebeldia*, 59–60 (quotes).

70. Durand Ponte, *Crisis*, 277.

71. Eulálio, interview, in André Luis Corrêia da Silva, "'João Ferrador,'" 300.

72. Garlippe, "ABC," 10.

73. João Raimundo, interview, 1999, in Iasi, *As metamorfoses*, 368–69.

74. Ibid., 370.

75. Durham, *A caminho*, 90–91, 158–59.

76. Ibid., 74.

77. Letter, May 1, 1979, by Delegado of São Bernardo do Campo, in DOPS, Pasta 23, 2904.

78. Djalma Bom, interview, March 8, 2005, in Ferreira and Fortes, *Muitos caminhos*, 85.

79. Frei Chico, interview by Paraná, September 10, 1993, in Paraná, *Lula*, 163, 167.

80. Osvaldo Cavignato, interview, February 15, 2005, in André Luis Corrêia da Silva, "'João Ferrador,'" 219.

81. "So em março a reunião de metalúrgicos," *Diário do Grande ABC*, February 15, 1977.

82. Interview with "Reinaldo," in Pogibin, "Memórias," 135.

83. For example, see interview with "Wilson," in ibid., 157.

84. José Arcanjo, interview, in André Luis Corrêia da Silva, "'João Ferrador,'" 323. See also Rainho and Bargas, *As lutas operárias*, 165.

85. Jameson, "Sartre and History," 242–43.

86. Raimundo Rodrigues Pereira, "Muitos Lulas: Quem é o heróe do sindicato dos metalúrgicos de Sao Bernardo de Campo e Diadema, que no final da semana passada completou 20 anos?," *Movimento*, May 16–20, 1979, 8–10 (quote); Machado, "A realidade íntima," 206.

87. Freire and Sydow, *Frei Betto*, 210.

88. Pereira, "Muitos Lulas," 8–10; Machado, "A realidade íntima," 206.

89. "Délio admite uso de força," *Estado de São Paulo*, April 20, 1980, quoted in Ianni, *O ABC*, 34. See also ibid., 25–38; "General afirma que Lula tem conselheiros comunistas," *Jornal do Brasil*, April 22, 1980.

90. Gaspari, *A ditadura acabada*, 169–70.

91. Lula, interview by Morel, mid-1981, in Morel, *Lula*, 117.

92. Harnecker, *O sonho era possível*, 58.

93. Lula, interview by Dantas, first half of January 1981, in Altino Dantas, *Lula*, 65–67. The direct involvement of women in the assemblies was innovative, since the conflict on the home front, during strikes, traditionally pitted the wives, practical and focused, against their husbands' propensity for risky adventures like drinking, fighting, and striking. On this point, see p. 58 in the undated original 1978 "Depoimento de Lula," to be found in the archive of CEDEM. Part of the interview was published in *A greve na voz*.

94. Rainho and Bargas, *As lutas operárias*, 133–42; Antunes, *A rebeldia*, 48–49; Caetano, *Alguma solidão*, 248; Lula, interview by Dantas, first half of January 1981, in Altino Dantas, *Lula*, 54; Lula, interview by Paraná, December 10, 1993, in Paraná, *Lula*, 144.

95. Rieder, *Word*, 186.

96. Ibid., 182.

97. Ibid., 186.

98. Ibid., 199, 205.

99. Ibid., 219.

100. Fernandes, *O PT*, 76, explains the explosive impact of Lula's discourse, his ability to connect with a "latent rage and uncontrollable nashing of teeth" that lies just under the surface among workers.

101. Nêumanne Pinto, *O que sei*, 152.

102. Angela Ziroldo, "Lula: 'Tudo o que eu queria era ser um torneiro mecânico,'" *Nova*, August 1979, 104.

103. Statement by Lula, "'Esse destemor, carregado de desinformação política, acabou se transformando numa intuição que foi fundamental para aquela virada de página do fim dos anos 70,'" Fundação Perseu Abramo, last modified April 18, 2006, http://csbh.fpabramo.org.br/o-que-fazemos/memoria-e-historia/exposicoes-virtuais/luiz-inacio-lula-da-silva-1.

104. Rieder, *Word*, 244.

105. Ibid., 221.

106. Ibid., 226.

107. Expedito Soares, interview, in André Luis Corrêia da Silva, "'João Ferrador,'" 249–50.

108. Rieder, *Word*, 219; Abramo, *O resgate*.

109. Sarti, *A família*.

110. Renato Tapajós, last modified May 12, 2008, http://zequinhabarreto.org.br/blog/?p=918.

111. Lula, interview by Morel, mid-1981, in Morel, *Lula*, 122.

112. Andreotti, interview by French, December 13, 1982.

113. Pereira, "Muitos Lulas," 8–10.

114. "O protocolo é rasgado: E os metalúrgicos prometem resistir," *Estado de São Paulo*, March 23, 1979.

115. Lula, quoted in Guizzo et al., *Lula*, 316.

116. Lula, interview by Dantas, first half of January 1981, in Altino Dantas, *Lula*, 57, 58 (quote), 60.

117. Lula, interview by Paraná, December 10, 1993, in Paraná, *Lula*, 142–43; Lula, interview, 1978, in *A greve na voz*, 32.

118. Lula, interview by Paraná, December 10, 1993, in Paraná, *Lula*, 143.

119. Lula, interview by Morel, mid-1981, in Morel, *Lula*, 141–42.

120. Rodrigues, *Partidos*, 149.

Chapter 15

1. Negro, *Linhas*, 315.

2. Ibid., 308.

3. Lula, interview by Paraná, December 10, 1993, in Paraná, *Lula*, 141.

4. "Tito Costa," Sítio Polêmico, last modified November 17, 2007, http://www.sitiopolemico.com/?p=57.

5. Ricardo Carvalho, *O cardeal*, 115–16.

6. Betto, *A mosca azul*, 66. On the arrest of key associates of the archbishop, along with ABC's union leaders, see Ricardo Carvalho, *O cardeal*, 242–43.

7. "E veio a greve: Uma decisão aprovada por 82 mil metalúrgicos," *Jornal da Tarde*, March 31, 1980.

8. Betto, *A mosca azul*, 66–70; "Lula retorna e exalta a revolução sandinista," *Diário do Grande ABC*, July 24, 1980.

9. Macedo, "A greve de 1980"; Hummes and Betto, "A igreja"; Martins, Pereira, and Ricardo, "A igreja."

10. Josué Machado, "A realidade íntima do sindicalista," *Playboy*, July 1979, in Guizzo et al., *Lula*, 230.

11. Negro, *Linhas*, 314.
12. Ibid., 216.
13. Ibid., 276.
14. Lamounier and Souza, *Depois da transição*, 25.
15. Sandoval, *Social Change*, 184, 186.
16. Eulálio, interview, in André Luis Corrêia da Silva, "'João Ferrador,'" 306–7.
17. "Trabalhador que se preza toma logo o seu Partido," *Nossa Vez, Nosssa Voz*, August 1980, 1.
18. Kotscho, *Explode um novo Brasil*; Leonelli and Oliveira, *Diretas já*.
19. On the PT's emergence and early history, see Keck, *Workers' Party*.
20. Ibid. See also Cavarozzi, "Left."
21. Emir Sader, "Workers' Party," 100, 97–98.
22. Quoted in "XIII Foro de São Paulo: Something to Celebrate in El Salvador," *NotiCen: Central American and Caribbean Affairs*, February 2007.
23. Rudá Ricci, "Se Lula fosse presidente haveria manifestações de rua?," *De Esquerda em Esquerda* (blog), February 17, 2014, http://rudaricci.blogspot.com/2014/02/se-lula-fosse-presidente-haveria.html.
24. Meneguello, *Partidos e governos*, 111.
25. Bethell and Nicolau, "Politics in Brazil," 237, 246.
26. Keck, *Workers' Party*, 158.
27. Markun, *O sapo*, 229.
28. Kinzo, "1989 Presidential Election," 313. On the election's uniqueness, see also Ames, "Reverse Coattails Effect," 107.
29. Gurgel and Fleischer, *O Brasil*, 156.
30. Meade, *Brief History*, 185; Eakin, *Brazil*, 62.
31. Sader and Silverstein, *Without Fear*, 143. See also Meneguello, *Partidos e governos*, 111.
32. Gurgel and Fleischer, *O Brasil*, 92–93, 97; Markun, *O sapo*, 225–26.
33. Nêumanne Pinto, *Atrás do palanque*, 177.
34. Ames, "Reverse Coattails Effect," 107; Matos, *Jornalismo*, 99. See also the exhaustive book by a former *Veja* journalist, Conti, *Notícias do Planalto*.
35. Joseph Smith, *History of Brazil*, 212.
36. Hunter, *Transformation*, 1; Skidmore, *Brazil*. Lula's discomfort in his borrowed suits was legendary. Markun, *O sapo*, 228.
37. Conti, *Notícias do Planalto*, 132–40, 234–45.
38. Gurgel and Fleischer, *O Brasil*, 143, 123.
39. Sader and Silverstein, *Without Fear*, 143.
40. Keck, *Workers' Party*, 158. For "formidable illusionist," see Dutilleux, *Lula*, 185.
41. Bethell and Nicolau, "Politics in Brazil," 249, 247. See also Sader and Silverstein, *Without Fear*, 120.
42. For an introduction to the phenomenon of, and literature on, populism in Brazil, see French, *Brazilian Workers' ABC*. The issue continues to occupy significant space in Brazilian intellectual production, as suggested by the sharp disagreements in Ferreira, *O populismo*. For Latin America as a whole, see Mackinnon and Petrone, eds., *Populismo y neopopulismo*.
43. Levine, *Brazilian Legacies*, 98. In invoking the weakened rationality of the mass voter, Levine cites a 1985 monograph by a US political scientist, von Mettenheim, *Brazilian Voter*, 5: "A central argument of this book is that immediate and personalistic conceptions of politics are both cause and consequence of the direct plebiscitarian appeals, patronage ma-

chines, and state-centered populist-nationalist tradition, which have prevailed in Brazilian mass politics since the 1930 revolution."

44. Angell, "Left in Latin America," 227–29; Schneider, *"Order and Progress,"* 314–15.

45. Keck, *Workers' Party*, 151, 160–61, 163–64.

46. Schneider, *"Order and Progress,"* 365.

47. Sader and Silverstein, *Without Fear*, 88.

48. Soares, *A democracia interrompida*, 238.

49. Ibid.

50. Lula, interview by Regis de Castro Andrade, José Álvaro Moisés, and Francisco Corrêa Weffort, in Andrade, Moisés, and Weffort, eds., *Visões*. The interview was published in 1989 in mimeographed format as part of two poorly circulated volumes of interviews with politicians conducted by the Centro de Estudos de Cultura Contemporânea in São Paulo. All subsequent quotes from this interview here and in the next two paragraphs come from ibid., 24, 29, 38, 41, 47.

51. Pomar, *Quase lá*, 103–4, 58, 120, 122.

52. Ibid., 45, 112; Lula, interview, February 23, 1990, in André Singer, *Sem medo*, 96, 98–99, 113.

53. Pomar, *Quase lá*, 58.

54. Machado and Vannuchi, "Entrevista," 8. On the socioeconomic profile of Collor's voters, including a discussion of São Paulo, see André Singer, "Collor na periferia." See Lara, *Campanha de rua*, 125–29, for a reporter's explanation of Lula's surprising first-round success in 1994 among the very poorest of the poor in Djalma Bom's home region of Jequitinhonha, in Minas Gerais.

55. Lula, interview by Andrade, Moisés, and Weffort, in Fernando Henrique Cardoso et al., *Visões*, 27, 51.

56. Lula, interview, August 1990, in Sader and Silverstein, *Without Fear*, 166.

57. Lula, radio inteview by Heródoto Barbeiro, ca. June–July 1989, in Barbeiro, *O que pensam*, 6–7, 58.

58. Lula, interview by Andrade, Moisés, and Weffort, in Fernando Henrique Cardoso et al., *Visões*, 47.

59. On the origin of "horário eleitoral" and the support of the massive Rede Globo TV chain, see Miguel, *Mito*, 96, 119–27. Haroldo Ceravolo Sereza, "'Eu nunca falo no PT,' conta compositor da música e da letra do jingle 'Lula-lá,'" *UOL Notícias*, December 11, 2009, https://noticias.uol.com.br/especiais/eleicoes-1989/ultimas-noticias/2009/11/12/eu-nunca-falo-no-pt-conta-compositor-da-musica-e-da-letra-do-jingle-lula-la.jhtm.

60. Nêumanne Pinto, *Atrás do palanque*, 177, reports that the phrase was taken from the TV sports announcer Fernando Vanucci. See also Keck, *Workers' Party*, 277. On the multifaceted dynamics of hope, see French, "Lula's Brazil."

61. Sader and Silverstein, *Without Fear*, 168.

62. How Lula interweaved his engaging sociability and political practice is captured wonderfully in the powerful documentary by João Moreira Salles on Lula's behind-the-scenes meetings and activities between the first and second rounds of the 2002 election. *Entreatos*, dir. João Moreira Salles (Rio de Janeiro: VideoFilmes, 2004).

63. Alberto Carlos Almeida, *Por que Lula?*, 152–53.

64. Wolford and French, "Introduction."

65. Although the slogan is usually credited to Mendonça, campaign official Ricardo Kotscho suggests that it originated in a comment that Lula had heard and liked from a

campaign worker in the Northeast, who used it to describe Lula's serene but determined personal posture in 2002. Kotscho, *Do golpe*.

66. Alberto Carlos Almeida, *Por que Lula?*, 209–10.

67. "Leia íntegra da carta de Lula para acalmar o mercado financeiro," *Folha de São Paulo*, June 24, 2002. The debate around the decision to issue the letter is discussed in detail in Dirceu, *Zé Dirceu*, 325–27. The final text, he adds, was drafted by the important minister Luiz Dulci, who eliminated specialized economic language and numbers as Lula had wanted.

68. Dirceu, *Zé Dirceu*, 326–27.

69. Ibid.

70. Paul Singer, "As doces ilusões," 45–47.

71. Dirceu, *Zé Dirceu*, 357, 315.

72. Macdonald and Ruckert, "Post-neoliberalism," 6–7.

73. Hobsbawm, *Interesting Times*, 382.

74. Hunter, *Transformation*, 114–15.

75. Iasi, *As metamorfoses*, 359, 536.

76. "Compromisso com a mudança: Pronunciamento do Presidente Eleito Luiz Inácio Lula da Silva em 28/10/2002," Fundação Perseu Abramo, accessed July 20, 2009, http://www2.fpa.org.br/portal/modules/news/article.php?storyid=2317.

77. Holston, *Insurgent Citizenship*, 5–6.

78. Ibid., 6.

Chapter 16

1. For an annotated, regionwide review of the relevant literature on neoliberalism and its associated controversies, see French and Lymburner, "Neoliberalism."

2. French, "From the Suites to the Streets."

3. "Discurso do Presidente da República, Luiz Inácio Lula da Silva, no ato político de celebração aos 15 anos do Foro de São Paulo," 2005, Biblioteca Presidência da República, accessed January 17, 2019, http://www.biblioteca.presidencia.gov.br/presidencia/ex-presidentes/luiz-inacio-lula-da-silva/discursos/1o-mandato/2005/02-07-2005-discurso-do-presidente-da-republica-luiz-inacio-lula-da-silva-na-reuniao-do-conselho-de-cupula-do-mercosul/view, 2–3.

4. Castañeda, *Utopia Unarmed*. See my appreciation of the book in French, "Latin American Labor Studies Boom," 289.

5. Jorge G. Castañeda, "Latin America's Left Turn," *Foreign Affairs*, May/June 2006. For his earlier take on populism, see Castañeda, *Utopia Unarmed*, 39–40, 43–45. For an extended exegesis of Castañeda's controversial depiction of the left turns and the place of populism in Latin American history, see French, "Understanding the Politics."

6. Castañeda, "Latin America's Left Turn."

7. Vellinga, "Internationalization," 3 (first and fourth quote); Touraine, "Latin America," 297 (second quote); Fernando Henrique Cardoso, "Challenges," 274–75 (third quote), 284–86 (fifth quote), 289 (sixth quote). For the views of the PT's preeminent international strategist on social democracy, see Garcia, "La Socialdemocracia." A national UNE leader before 1964, Garcia returned from exile in 1979 to become a founder of the PT, occupying a variety of top positions in the party. Profoundly knowledgeable about the Latin American and European Left, Garcia was the top presidential foreign policy adviser for both Lula and Dilma.

8. Cavarozzi, "Left," 154–55.

9. Felipe Moura Brasil, "Conheça o Foro de São Paulo, o maior inimigo do Brasil," *Veja*, February 15, 2017.

10. Regalado, *Latin America*, 249. Regalado is a Cuban Communist Party Central Committee member.

11. Brasil, "Conheça"; "Discurso do Presidente," 2, 4–5.

12. "IV Encuentro," 131–36.

13. Fidel Castro, "Lula (segunda parte)," *La Jornada*, January 30, 2008. Discussion between the two men continued during Lula's first visit to Cuba, in 1985. Fidel Castro, "Lula (cuarta y última Parte)," *La Jornada*, February 6, 2008.

14. "Discurso do Presidente," 4.

15. Brasil, "Conheça." For the *Folha de São Paulo* quote, see Dutilleux, *Lula*, 172.

16. Iasi, *As metamorfoses*, 507, notes how the PT's official documents shifted in the 1990s from anticapitalism to antineoliberalism.

17. This point was discussed in one of anthropologist Fernando Coronil's last publications: Coronil, "Future in Question," 238.

18. Reid, *Forgotten Continent*, 10–22.

19. Castañeda, "Latin America's Left Turn" (emphasis added).

20. Corrêa Leite and Gil, *World Social Forum*, 2005.

21. "Revised World Social Forum Charter," 70 (emphasis added).

22. For a contemporary Cuban Communist perspective that emphasizes revolution and armed struggle, see Regalado, *Latin America*, 222, 232.

23. Hugo Chávez, "Act for the People's Anti-imperialist Struggle: VI World Social Forum, Poliedro, Caracas, Friday January 27, 2006," Hugo Chavez in English, accessed March 15, 2008, http://www.chavezinenglish.org/2006/WSF2006.html. See also Hugo Chávez, "Rise Up against the Empire," *Counterpunch*, September 20, 2006, https://www.counterpunch.org/2006/09/20/rise-up-against-the-empire/.

24. Reid, *Forgotten Continent*, xiv, 13, 12, 79–80.

25. Chávez, "Act."

26. Ibid.

27. Ibid. It was the leading representative of the FMLN's Old Left sector, Schafik Handal, who stepped in when Chávez was excluded. Chávez warmly recalled how the Communist Handal had "the delicacy, the firmness, the courage, the spirit to approach me . . . and he invited me to the table . . . he had coordinated, and offered excuses for the debate that resulted from my surprise appearance in the Assembly." Ibid. For a longtime Communist such as Handal, Chávez would by no means have been a surprising figure, because Latin America's most famous Marxist-Leninist, the Brazilian Communist Luís Carlos Prestes, had begun his political life in 1924 as a rebellious twenty-two-year-old military cadet who turned to armed struggle and won fame before joining the PCB.

28. "IV Encuentro."

29. "Declaración final del X Encuentro del Foro de São Paulo," *Diário Granma*, December 17, 2001, http://www.granma.cu/granmad/2001/12/17/nacional/articulo16.html.

30. Chávez, "Act." See also Hugo Chávez, "Rise Up against the Empire."

31. Chávez, "Act."

32. See Lula's adept handling of this geopolitical challenge in a February 24, 2006, interview: "The Working Man's Statesman Gives a Rare Interview to the *Economist*," *Economist*, March 5, 2006, 2–3.

33. Castro, "Lula (segunda parte)."

34. Brasil, “Conheça.”

35. Hugo Chávez, “Foro Social Mundial: El sur, norte de nuestros pueblos, desde el Gimnasio Gigantinho. Porto Alegre, Brasil 30 de enero de 2005,” Ministerio de Relaciones Exteriores, accessed March 15, 2008, http://www.mre.gov.ve/Noticias/Presidente-Chavez/A2005/Discurso-030.htm.

36. “Revised World Social Forum Charter,” 70.

37. Chávez, “Act.”

38. Holston, *Insurgent Citizenship*, 6.

39. See Moisés Naím’s account of these words’ impact in Hawkins, “Populism,” 1148.

40. Rivas Rojas, “On *Chavismo*,” 328.

41. Reygadas, “Imagined Inequalities,” 504.

42. Torre, “Resurgence,” 392 (emphasis added).

43. Hawkins, “Populism,” 1147.

44. Reygadas, “Imagined Inequalities,” 502–4.

45. Ibid., 503.

46. Hawkins, “Populism,” 1154.

47. Zago, *La rebelión*, 25, as cited and translated in Hawkins, “Populism,” 1147.

48. Fidel Castro, “Lula (primera parte),” *La Jornada*, January 25, 2008.

49. Simmel, *Sociology*, 185.

Chapter 17

1. Kamel, *Dicionário*, 101.

2. *Folha de São Paulo*, April 4, 1979, 3. I thank Bryan Pitts for this citation.

3. Kamel, *Dicionário*, 15, 23.

4. Ibid., 17.

5. Hunter, “Partido dos Trabalhadores,” 16. For examples of these arguments, see Kingstone and Ponce, “From Cardoso to Lula,” 98, 110, 122; Barros Silva, Souza Braga, and Cabral Costa, “Lula’s Administration,” 124, 136. Fortes, “In Search,” assesses the Brazilian Left’s debates over the PT’s role during Lula’s administrations. Empirical studies of the Brazilian national legislators’ political ideology from 1990 to 2005 show a classic left–right alignment, with a moderate drift to the right overall and a far more decided shift by the PSDB from the left to the center-right. Power and Zucco, “Estimating Ideology,” 219–20, 231–32.

6. Love, “Lula Government,” 305.

7. Kamel, *Dicionário*, 48–49, 53.

8. Miguel, *Mito*, 164–65; Osakabe, “A palavra imperfeita.”

9. Barreira, “Um operário presidente?,” 184.

10. Medeiros, *Luiz Inácio Lula da Silva*, 75.

11. Kamel, *Dicionário*, 55.

12. Nêumanne Pinto, *Atrás do palanque*, 86. On Lula’s dominion of Portuguese and how it improved, see the linguistic analysis by his *Playboy* interviewer: Josué Machado, “Lula e a lingua do Povo,” *Educação*, no. 263 (March 2003).

13. Kamel, *Dicionário*, 23, 41.

14. Frei Chico, interview, 2015, in “Gravação 2015 11–1 Frei Chico (72 Minutos)-Sudeli,” Centro de Memória Sindical, São Paulo; Frei Chico, interview by Paraná, October 5, 1993, in Paraná, *Lula*, 189.

15. Perry Anderson, “Lula’s Brazil,” *London Review of Books*, March 31, 2011.

16. The literature on Bolsa Família is vast and ever expanding. For a good introduction,

see Lindert et al., "Nuts and Bolts." For an insider's detailed examination of the planning and implementation, see Fonseca, "Transferência de renda."

17. Hunter and Power, "Rewarding Lula," 19; Amann and Baer, "Macroeconomic Record," 36–37. For the budgetary allotments and trends, see Hall, "From *Fome Zero* to *Bolsa Família*," 692–94.

18. Quoted in Anderson, "Lula's Brazil."

19. Morais and Saad-Filho, "Brazil beyond Lula," 35.

20. Amaury de Souza, "Politics of Personality," 82.

21. Hunter and Power, "Rewarding Lula," 16–17; Pães de Barros et al., "A importância."

22. Saad-Filho, "New Dawn," 5.

23. Marli Moreira, "Ganhos salariais acima da inflação tiveram recorde em 2010, segundo o Dieese," *Agência Brasil*, March 17, 2011, http://agenciabrasil.ebc.com.br/noticia/2011-03-17/ganhos-salariais-acima-da-inflacao-tiveram-recorde-em-2010-segundo-dieese.

24. Roberts, "From 'A Foot in the Kitchen.'"

25. Neri, "Income Policies," 229–31.

26. Zucco, "President's 'New' Constituency," 49.

27. On this increasing self-assertion, see Holston, *Insurgent Citizenship*.

28. Anderson, "Lula's Brazil"; Lula, interview, *Valor*, December 7, 2006, quoted in Leopoldi, "Reforming Social Security," 236. Like many European leftist intellectuals, Anderson's ties to Brazil go back to the time spent he spent there in 1966–67 for a thesis on Brazilian history that remained unfinished "in the student turbulence of 1968." Perry Anderson, *Brazil Apart*, x.

29. Barros Silva, Souza Braga, and Cabral Costa, "Lula's Administration."

30. Laura Lacerda, "'Lula está acima do bem e do mal,' afirma Serra," *Estado de São Paulo*, May 14, 2010.

31. Anderson, "Lula's Brazil," 3.

32. Bittencourt, "Mulheres na política."

33. União de Negros pela Igualdade, *Balanço eleitoral*. Leftist parties accounted for 56 percent of the total.

34. The low figure is from André Singer, "A segunda alma," 92; the higher, from Samuels, "From Socialism to Social Democracy," 1009. André Singer, "A segunda alma," 92, claims without documentation that the PT had 1.2 million members by 2009, a significant finding if true.

35. Samuels, "Sources of Mass Partisanship," 5–6; André Singer, "A segunda alma," 91.

36. Samuels, "Sources of Mass Partisanship."

37. Zucco, "President's 'New' Constituency," 32.

38. Barreira, "Um operário presidente?," 170.

39. Figueiredo, *O operador*.

40. Hunter and Power, "Rewarding Lula," 1–2, 20, 24; Amaury de Souza, "Politics of Personality," 78.

41. Bohn, "Social Policy," 66–68.

42. Hunter and Power, "Rewarding Lula," 5.

43. Ibid., 20.

44. Soares and Terron, "Dois Lulas," 298.

45. Zucco, "President's 'New' Constituency," 35.

46. Monclaire, "Lula II," 26, 31. In 2002, 50 percent of Brazilian voters couldn't even name the party of President Cardoso, who had been in office for eight years. Ibid., 27.

47. Borges, "Tanto azul," 222.

48. Monclaire, "Lula II," 32, 35–37, 43–44.

49. André Singer, "Raízes sociais," 83, 99. Singer's argument continues the 1960s–70s New Left Marxist approach to Brazilian populism closely associated with Francisco Weffort, the PT's first secretary-general, who left the party to become FHC's minister of culture. Weffort, "Raízes sociais."

50. Barreira, "Um operário presidente?," 167–68.

51. For voting behavior reached at the individual level via polling across elections, see Bohn, "Social Policy."

52. Vidal, *La politique au quartier.*

53. "A elite chama de populismo a democratização das decisões," *Carta Maior,* November 11, 2010, http://www.cartamaior.com.br/?/Editorial/-A-elite-chama-de-populismo-a-democratizacao-das-decisoes/23512.

54. French and Fortes, "Another World," 21. For an excellent discussion of the heightened emphasis on these themes in Lula's 2002 television campaign, see Miguel, "From Equality to Opportunity."

55. Quoted in Barreira, "Um operário presidente?"

56. Mitchell, "Racializing Blackness," 116, 130.

57. Monclaire, "Lula II," 31–35.

58. The concept of a metalanguage, which structures the discursive field, was developed in relation to the United States in Higginbotham, "African-American Women's History."

59. Quoted in Santos, "Who Is Black," 33. See Lula's discussion of how "slavery continues in the heads of Brazilians," which explains the disgraceful inequalities suffered by and violence inflicted upon Black Brazilians. "Glenn Greenwald entrevista Lula: 'Bolsonaro é a velha política, eu sou a nova,'" *Intercept,* 21 de Maio de 2019. On impacts, see a preliminary comparison with the United States in Andrews, "Racial Inequality."

60. "A elite"; Bohn, "Feminismo estatal," 92; Sardenberg, "With a Little Help," 125–29; SEPPIR, *Subsídios,* 31; "1a Conferência Nacional"; Luiz Inácio Lula da Silva, "Speech."

61. Amaury de Souza, "Politics of Personality," 81.

62. José Henrique Lopes, "Catadores se despedem de Lula e agradecem por vida melhor: Trabalhadores celebram avanços dos últimos oito anos e esperam continuidade com Dilma," *R7 Noticias,* December 24, 2010.

63. "Anais da I Conferência Nacional de Políticas para as Mulheres," Secretaria de Políticas para as Mulheres da Presidência da República Federativa do Brasil, last modified 2004, http://spm.gov.br/pnpm/anais.pdf.

64. "Discurso do Presidente da República, Luiz Inácio Lula da Silva, na cerimônia de abetura da II Conferência Nacional de Políticas para as Mulheres," Secretaria de Políticas para as Mulheres da Presidência da República Federativa do Brasil, last modified August 17, 2007, http://spm.gov.br/pnpm/discurso-pr-iicnpm.pdf.

65. The most famous action by this group was robbing the safe of a particularly corrupt São Paulo ex-governor. Solnik, *O cofre do Adhemar*; Tom Cardoso, *O cofre do Dr. Rui.*

66. "Na ditadura, Dilma deu aulas de política a trabalhadores," *Folha de São Paulo,* November 28, 2010.

67. Fernanda Odilla, "Aos 19, 20 anos, achava que eu estava salvando o mundo," *Folha de São Paulo,* April 5, 2009.

68. Motta, *As Universidades e o Regime.*

69. Ristoff, *Democratização do Campus.*

70. Guinn, "Embedded Mobility." Poder Executivo, "Lei 12.711." http://www.planalto.gov.br/ccivil_03/_ato2011-2014/2012/lei/l12711.htm. Accessed February 15, 2018; Poder Executivo, "Lei 12.990." http://www.planalto.gov.br/ccivil_03/_ato2011-2014/2014/lei/l12990.htm. Accessed February 15, 2018.

71. For research reports, blog posts, and other coverage of the Duke–Universidade Federal Rural do Rio de Janeiro project "The Cost of Opportunity: Higher Education and Social Mobility in the Baixada Fluminense, Rio de Janeiro," see its website: https://sites.duke.edu/project_duke_baixada_project/. Reist, "'Christ the Redeemer.'" See the subtitled film with interviews with students and parents: Dudu do Morro Agudo and Stephanie Reist, "O Custo da Oportunidade," YouTube video, 31:32, posted by "Hulle Brasil," March 26, 2017, https://www.youtube.com/watch?v=Q_60CIxvLHY.

72. See the forthcoming Duke University history dissertation by Travis Knoll, "Liberate, Inculturate, Educate! Black Brazilian Catholics and Affirmative Action, from Rio de Janeiro to Brasilia."

73. "Acórdão, ADPF 186," *Supremo Tribunal Federal*, 66–67. The Prouni program of fellowships with quotas for private higher education was also judged constitutional in 2012. http://www.stf.jus.br/portal/cms/verNoticiaDetalhe.asp?idConteudo=206553. Accessed February 15, 2018.

74. Advogado Geral da União, "Arguição de Descumprimento de Preceito Fundamental." ADPF 186. *Supremo Tribunal Federal*, 8.

75. Michelle Carneiro, "Pesquisa revela perfil heterogênio de estudantes da UFRRJ: Maioria tem renda baixa, é preta ou parda, e veio da escola pública," *Rural Semanal* 26, no. 6 (July 8–14, 2019); "Pela primeira vez, negros são maioria no ensino superior público," *Carta Capital*, November 13, 2019; IBGE, Diretoria de Pesquisas, Coordenação de População e Indicadores Sociais; "Desigualdades sociais por cor ou raça no Brasil," *Estudos e Pesquisas · Informação Demográfica e Socioeconômica* 41 (2019): 9.

76. Speaking about Lula's generation of upwardly mobile workers, Pastore observed in 1982 that social mobility "is far from being an anesthetic for a dissatisfied society, especially when it is a new phenomenon, as it is in Brazil, and when it begins at an extremely low social level. Mobility is a progressive process which creates satisfactions and dissatisfactions" that induce change by leading individuals and society to organize "to strive for better conditions." Pastore, *Inequality*, 161–62.

77. PT—Partido dos Trabalhadores, "UFRRJ espera por Lula," Facebook, https://www.facebook.com/pt.brasil/videos/1575494249203611/. Accessed February 15, 2018.

78. Expedito Filho, *Fernando Henrique Cardoso*, 71.

79. Saint-Clair, *Bolsonaro*, 72, 76. Even FHC's association with Lula's union was grist to the mill of the DOPS, which in 1978 reported his presence at the VW factory gate with Lula and other union officials and activists. APESP, DOPS, 0-Z-341-2336.

80. Expedito Filho, *Fernando Henrique Cardoso*, 67; Markun, *O sapo*, 124.

81. Ibid., 31.

82. Ibid., 19–21, 23–24.

83. Ibid., 35, 59, 63.

84. Lula, interview, 2000, in "Depoimento de Luiz Inácio Lula da Silva," 61–62.

85. Expedito Filho, *Fernando Henrique Cardoso*, 67.

86. Fernando Henrique Cardoso, *Accidental President*, 137, 117.

87. Ibid., 135–36.

88. Fernando Henrique Cardoso, *A arte da política*, 84.

89. Fernando Henrique Cardoso, *Accidental President*, 136.

90. Frei Chico, 2015 interview, Centro de Memória Sindical, 15.

91. Kahl, *Three Latin American Sociologists*, 179. The author chose FHC's quote about the role of the intellectuals for his book's dedication.

92. "Fernando Henrique Cardoso: Uma conversa franca com o ex-presidente," *Playboy*, August 11, 2006, 73–91.

93. Lula interview, 2000, in "Depoimento de Luiz Inácio Lula da Silva," 62–63.

94. For an *O Estado de São Paulo* reporter's description of the hostile climate, see Vanessa Barbara, "Banging Pots and Beating Dogs in a Polarized Brazil," *New York Times*, March 25, 2016.

95. "De 'jararaca' a 'merda de metalúrgico': Veja frases do pronunciamento de Lula," *GaúchaZH*, March 4, 2016.

96. Mariana Schreiber, "'Não coloco Lula e Bolsonaro no mesmo patamar,' diz cientista político da Fundação FHC," *BBC Brasil*, January 17, 2018, http://www.bbc.com/portuguese/brasil-42713238. Fausto is chief executive of the foundation created by FHC.

97. Hunter and Power, "Bolsonaro."

Conclusion

1. Adalberto Cardoso, *A construção*, 51. The great nineteenth-century Afro-Brazilian engineer and abolitionist André Rebouças defined the enduring challenge facing Brazil as that of abolishing misery. French and Fortes, "Nurturing Hope," 10–11; French, "The Abolition of Misery."

2. Downey, *Learning Capoeira*, 123.

3. Sartre, *Search for a Method*, 60.

4. This song lyric by Raul Seixas was cited by Lula as president. Tiago Pariz, "Lula: 'Prefiro ser considerado uma metamorfose ambulante,'" *O Globo*, May 12, 2007.

5. "It is one thing to leave the rural zone to be a trash collector or shoeshiner in the urban zone but it is quite another to become a lathe operator." Pastone, *Inequality*, 121.

6. Vargas, *O governo trabalhista*, 463–73.

7. Luiz Pereira, *Trabalho*, 299, 132.

8. Lula, interview by Couto, April 3, 1997, in Couto, *Memória viva*, 249–50.

9. Lula, interview, 2000, in "Depoimento de Luiz Inácio Lula da Silva," 26. For the date that Lula joined, see Luiz Inácio Lula da Silva, "Conf. palestra proferida," 212; for his membership number, see "Lula: Somos o mais importante partido de izquerda no mundo," *Caros Amigos*, November 2000.

10. Lula, interview by Paraná, October 6, 1993, in Paraná, *Lula*, 119–20.

11. Maria Baixinha, interview by Paraná, April 6, 1994, in ibid., 267–68.

12. Vavá, interview by Paraná, September 3 and 7, 1973, in ibid., 231.

13. André Shalders, Felipe Souza, Mariana Sanches, Camilla Costa, and Mariana Schreiber, "Lula se entrega para a PF em São Paulo e chega a Curitiba," *BBC News*, April 7, 2018, https://www.bbc.com/portuguese/brasil-43683394.

14. Although by no means new in Brazil, the weaponization of anticorruption charges for partisan ends in the Lava Jato investigation is a serious setback for efforts to improve accountability. It is especially discouraging because Brazil since 2003 had made significant progress in perfecting institutional and legal mechanisms for identifying and going after corruption. See the fine volume by Power and Taylor, *Corruption and Democracy*.

15. Solano, Zaiden, and Vannuchi, *Luiz Inácio*, 20.

16. Ibid., 20–22.
17. Ibid, 58, 60.
18. Ibid., 71.
19. Ibid., 14.
20. Ibid.
21. Luiz Inácio da Silva, "Discurso de São Bernardo," in Secco, *A ideia*, 177–78. Lula, "Discurso no Sindicato dos Metalúrgicos em Abril de 2018," in: Jinkings, *A Verdade Vencerá*, 217.
22. Solano, Zaiden, and Vannuchi, *Luiz Inácio*, 15.
23. Ibid., 67.
24. Luiz Inácio da Silva, "Discurso de São Bernardo," 180.
25. Solano, Zaiden, and Vannuchi, *Luiz Inácio*, 67.
26. Luiz Inácio da Silva, "Discurso de São Bernardo," 181–82.
27. Solano, Zaiden, and Vannuchi, *Luiz Inácio*, 22. For scenes from the union on the day Lula passed into custody, see Costa, *Edge of Democracy*.
28. "Íntegra da transcrição da entrevista de Lula para a Der Spiegel," May 26, 2019. https://lula.com.br/integra-da-transcricao-da-entrevista-de-lula-para-a-der-spiegel/?fbclid=IwARoNEFRbYFunA1NNH-NX9qAqm4ZCo6ioZOvDKFYlPHMQYJJ2ayDmjwaws8M.
29. "Glenn Greenwald entrevista Lula: 'Bolsonaro é a velha política, eu sou a nova,'" *Intercept*, 21 de Maio de 2019.
30. Bia Pasqualino e Nina Fideles, "O ex-presidente evita fazer planos, mas projeta sua saída da prisão ao lado do povo para resistir ao desmonte do Estado," *Brasil de Fato*, October 24, 2019. "Após mais de 40 anos, Lula planeja sair de São Bernardo, *Repórter Diário*, November 10, 2019.
31. "Discurso no Sindicato dos Metalúrgicos em novembro de 2019," in Jinkings, *A Verdade*, 226; Pasqualino and Fideles, "O ex-presidente evita fazer planos."
32. "Após pedido de Moro, Lula é investigado na PF com base na Lei de Segurança Nacional: 'Ex-presidente ligou Bolsonaro a milicianos em discurso; PF concluiu que não houve Crime,'" *Folha de Sao Paulo*, February 19, 2020.
33. Camila Turtelli, "Entrevista: Onyz Lorenzoni: 'Não há espaço para o centro em 2022,'" *Estado de São Paulo*, December 20, 2019. Criticizing the conditions of Lula's imprisonment in a BBC interview, Bolsonaro's vice president, Hamilton Mourão, doubled down on the class-based prejudice that unites the Far Right. The general insisted that Lula really belonged not in the Federal Police headquarters but "in a common prison" because he lacks the university degree that, by law, provides its holders with privileged accommodations when jailed. Felipe Corazza, "Bolsonaro presidente: General Mourão diz que temor pelo futuro da democracia é 'choro de perdedores,'" *BBC News Brasil*, October 30, 2018.

Afterword

1. Tolstoy, "Second Epilogue," 1313.
2. Ibid., 1325–26.
3. Ibid., 1326.
4. Ibid., 1328–29.
5. Ibid., 1328–29, 1321.
6. Ibid., 1322–23.
7. Ibid., 1335.
8. Carlyle, "On Heroes, Hero-Worship, and the Heroic in History," 102–3. The irony, of course, is that Carlyle was not a "professional historian," and this celebrated essay was an

attack on the intellectual trends that were birthing history as an academic discipline, which he deplored.

9. Plekhanov, "On the Role of the Individual in History."

10. Ibid., sections 7–8; Sartre, *Search for a Method*, 56.

11. C. L. R. James, *The Black Jacobins*, xi. David Scott offers a useful discussion of James's project, subject to criticisms in recent years, while also challenging poststructuralism (*Conscripts of Modernity*, 37–38).

12. Trotsky, *The History of the Russian Revolution*, vol. 1, *The Overthrow of Tzarism*, 329–31.

13. That Tolstoy's nineteenth-century critique of the cult of great men and big ideas anticipated trends in the discipline in the twentieth century does not figure in the most celebrated essay on Tolstoy's second postscript (Berlin, *The Hedgehog and the Fox*).

14. Dosse, *History of Structuralism*, vol. 1, *The Rising Sign, 1945–1966*.

15. Cusset, *French Theory*.

16. Keucheyan, *The Left Hemisphere*, 44–45.

17. Ibid., 48.

18. Bourdieu, "The Biographical Illusion," 7.

19. Sahlins, *Apologies to Thucydides*, 138.

20. Ibid., 139, 145.

21. Ibid., 139.

22. Costa, "New Publics, New Politics, New Histories," 17–31.

23. Sartre's project in *Critique of Dialectical Reason* was immediately subjected to powerful attack by France's pioneering structuralist, anthropologist Claude Lévi-Strauss, that centered on Sartre's pernicious privileging of history ("History and the Dialectic," 257–58). For Annales historian Fernand Braudel, by contrast, Sartre was an ally whose "research moves from the surface to the depths, and so links up with my own preoccupations," which were to connect the "teeming reality of events," a characteristic of biography, with the "deep-seated structural context" (Braudel, "History and the Social Sciences," 50).

24. Burgmann, "The Multitude and the Many-Headed Hydra," 172. The second powerful attack in the 1960s on Sartre's "humanist" Marxism came from Louis Althusser, the advocate of the hyperstructuralist version of Marxism as pure science that was targeted in 1978 by Thompson in a now mostly neglected polemic (E. P. Thompson, *The Poverty of Theory and Other Essays*). For further evidence of the kinship between Sartre and the pioneers in the US labor history field, see Gutman, "Labor History and the 'Sartre Question.'"

25. Sahlins, *Apologies to Thucydides*, 151.

26. Alexander Goldenweiser, quoted in ibid., 151–52.

27. Sartre, "Itinerary of a Thought," 45. See also Jopling, "Sartre's Moral Psychology."

28. Bergquist, "In the Name of History," 168; French, "How the Not-So-Powerless Prevail," 110–42.

29. Daniel James and I have criticized the impoverished logic of "abstraction through subtraction" advanced by Latin American history's most 'orthodox' Marxist. See French and James, "The Travails of Doing Labor History," 95–116.

30. For a complex example of the theoretical and methodological issues involved with oral history, see Daniel James, *Doña María's Story*. For more on his trajectory, see French, "Laboring and Middle-Class Peoples of Latin America and the Caribbean," 310–18.

31. Sartre, *Search for a Method*.

32. Garcia, "The Gender of Militancy," 50.

33. Sahlins, *Apologies to Thucydides*, 155.

34. Ibid.

35. Ibid. These are precisely the challenges that Sartre took up in his mid-1950s engagement with Marxism and biography. Jameson, "Sartre and History," 206–305.

36. Friedrich Engels (London), letter to J. Bloch (Königsberg), September 21, 1890, https://www.marxists.org/archive/marx/works/1890/letters/90_09_21.htm.

37. Costa, *Crowns of Glory, Tears of Blood*, xviii–xix.

BIBLIOGRAPHY

ABC de Luta. Memória dos Trabalhadores. São Bernardo: Sindicato dos Metalúrgicos do ABC, 2003. http://www.abcdeluta.org.br/.

Abramo, Laís Wendel. *O resgate da dignidade: Greve metalúrgica e subjetividade operária*. Campinas, Brazil: Editora da Unicamp, 1999.

Agier, Michel, and Antônio Sérgio Guimarães. "Técnicos e peões: A identidade ambígua." In *Imagens e identidades do trabalho*, by Michel Agier, Nadya Araujo Castro, and Antonio Sérgio Guimarães, 39–73. São Paulo: Hucitec, 1995.

A greve na voz dos trabalhadores, da Scania a Itu. São Paulo: Editora Alfa-Omega, 1979.

Alberti, Verena, Ignez Cordeiro de Farias, and Dora Rocha, eds. *Paulo Egydio conta: Depoimento ao CPDOC-FGC [Centro de Pesquisa e Documentação de História Contemporânea do Brasil-Fundação Getúlio Vargas]*. São Paulo: Imprensa Oficial, 2007.

Almeida, Alberto Carlos. *Por que Lula? O contexto e as estratégias políticas que explicam a eleição e a crise*. Rio de Janeiro: Editora Record, 2006.

Almeida, Antônio de. *Experiências políticas no ABC paulista: Lutas e práticas culturais dos trabalhadores*. Uberlândia, Brazil: Editora da Universidade Federal de Uberlândia, 2009.

Almeida, Fernando Lopes de. *Política salarial, emprego, e sindicalismo 1964/1981*. Petrópolis, Brazil: Vozes, 1982.

Almeida, José. "A evolução da capacidade de produção da indústria automobilística brasileira no período 1957–1969." *Pesquisa e Planejamento Economico* 2, no. 1 (1972): 55–80.

Almeida, Maria Hermínia Tavares de, and Luiz Weis. "Carro-zero e pau-de-arara: O cotidiano da oposição da classe média ao regime militar." In *História da vida privada no Brasil*, vol. 4, *Contrastes da intimidade contemporânea*, edited by Lilia Moritz Schwarcz, 319–409. São Paulo: Companhia das Letras, 1998.

Almeida, Roniwalter Jatobá de. *Filhos do medo: Um romance suburbano*. São Paulo: Global, 1979.

———. "Trabalhadores." In *Crônicas da vida operária*, 35–48. São Paulo: Global, 1978.

Alves, Maria Helena Moreira. "The Formation of the National Security State: The State and Opposition in Military Brazil." PhD diss., Massachusetts Institute of Technology, 1982.

———. *State and Opposition in Military Brazil*. Austin: University of Texas Press, 1990.

Alves, Odair Rodrigues. *Os homens que governaram São Paulo*. São Paulo: Nobel/EDUSP, 1986.

Amann, Edmund, and Werner Baer. "The Macroeconomic Record of the Lula Administration, the Roots of Brazil's Inequality, and Attempts to Overcome Them." In Love and Baer, *Brazil under Lula*, 27–43.

Ames, Barry. "The Reverse Coattails Effect: Local Party Organization in the 1989 Brazilian Presidential Election." *American Political Science Review* 88, no. 1 (1994): 95–111.

Anderson, Perry. *Brazil Apart 1964–2019*. London: Verso, 2019.

Andrade, Regis de Castro, José Álvaro Moisés, and Francisco Corrêa Weffort, eds. *Visões da Transição*. Vols. 1 and 2. São Paulo: Centro de Estudos de Cultura Contemporânea, 1989.

Andrews, George Reid. "Racial Inequality in Brazil and the United States, 1990–2010." *Journal of Social History* 47, no. 4 (2014): 1–26.

Angell, Alan. "The Left in Latin America since c. 1920." In Bethell, *The Cambridge History of Latin America*, vol. 6, pt. 2, *Latin America since 1930: Economy, Society, and Politics*, 163–232.

Antunes, Ricardo. *A rebeldia do trabalho: O confronto operário no ABC paulista, as greves de 1978/80*. Campinas, Brazil: Editora UNICAMP, 1988.

Aquino, Maria Aparecida de. *Censura, imprensa, estado autoritário (1968–1978): O exercício cotidiano da dominação e da resistência, "O Estado de São Paulo" e movimento*. Bauru, Brazil: EDUSC, 1999.

Araújo, Braz José de. *Operários em luta: Metalúrgicos da Baixada Santista (1933–1983)*. Rio de Janeiro: Paz e Terra, 1985.

Assis, Marisa de, ed. *Mercado de trabalho em São Paulo (aspectos gerais)*. Vol. 2. São Paulo: Companhia Editôra Nacional, 1972.

Azevedo, Aloysio. "Sindicatos tem mesmo que ser reformistas." 1989. In Bueno and Faro, *Capital e trabalho*, 25–29.

Azevedo, Ricardo de. *Por um triz: Memórias de um militante da AP*. São Paulo: Plena, 2010.

Bacha, Edmar L., and Herbert S. Klein. "Introduction." In Bacha and Klein, *Social Change*, 1–14.

———, eds. *Social Change in Brazil, 1945–1985: The Incomplete Transition*. Albuquerque: University of New Mexico Press, 1989.

Baehr, Peter. "The 'Masses' in Weber's Political Sociology." *Economy and Society* 19, no. 2 (1990): 242–65.

Baer, Werner. *The Brazilian Economy: Growth and Development*. 5th ed. Westport, CT: Praeger, 2001.

Barbeiro, Heródoto. *O que pensam os presidenciáveis: Luiz Inácio Lula da Silva. Partido dos Trabalhadores*. São Paulo: Harbra, 1989.

Barbosa Monteiro, José. "Entrevista com José Barbosa Monteiro." In *Memórias do exílio, Brasil 1964–19??: Obra coletiva*, edited by Pedro Celso Uchôa Cavalcanti and Jovelino Ramos, 113–43. São Paulo: Editora Livraria Livramento, 1978.

Barcelos, Caco. "Raquel, 'piorra' na indústria de automóveis: São Bernardo do Campo (Grande São Paulo)." In *Mulher: Depoimentos sobre um trabalho ignorado*, edited by Adélia Borges, 29–31. São Paulo: Brasiliense, 1976.

Barreira, Irlys Alencar F. "Um operário presidente? Ideologia e condição de classe no universo da representação política." In Heredia, Teixeira, and Barreira, *Como se fazem eleições no Brasil*, 157–87.

Barreto, Fábio. "Lula, Filho Do Brasil [Lula, Son of Brazil]." Rio de Janeiro, 2010.

Barros, Ricardo Pães de, and Carlos Henrique Corseuil. "The Impact of Regulations on Brazilian Labor Market Performance." In *Law and Employment: Lessons from Latin America and the Caribbean*, edited by James J. Heckman and Carmen Pagés, 273–350. Chicago: University of Chicago Press, 2004.

Barros Silva, Pedro Luiz, José Carlos de Souza Braga, and Vera Lúcia Cabral Costa. "Lula's Administration at a Crossroads: The Difficult Combination of Stability and

Development in Brazil." In Weyland, Madrid, and Hunter, *Leftist Governments in Latin America*, 124–39.

Barsted, Dennis Linhares. *Medição de forças: O movimento grevista de 1953 e a época dos operários navais*. Rio de Janeiro: Zahar, 1981.

Bastos, Elide Rugai, and Florestan Fernandes, eds. *Conversas com sociólogos brasileiros*. São Paulo: Editora 34, 2006.

Batista, Pedro César. *Gilson Menezes, o operário prefeito: Experiências e desafios*. Brasília: P. C. Batista, 2004.

Beisiegel, Celso de Rui. "Os primeiros tempos da pesquisa em sociologia da educação na USP." *Educação e Pesquisa* 39, no. 3 (2013): 589–607.

Benevides, Maria Victoria de Mesquita. *O PTB e o trabalhismo: Partido e sindicato em São Paulo: 1945–1964*. São Paulo: Editora Brasiliense, 1989.

Bensman, Joseph, and Michael Givant. "Charisma and Modernity: The Use and Abuse of a Concept." In *Charisma, History, and Social Structure*, edited by Ronald M. Glassman and William H. Swatos Jr., 27–56. Westport, CT: Greenwood Press, 1986.

Bergquist, Charles. "In the Name of History: A Disciplinary Critique of Orlando Fals Borda's *Historia doble de la Costa*." *Latin American Research Review* 25, no. 3 (1990): 156–76.

Bergsman, Joel, and Arthur Candal. "Industrialization: Past Success and Future Problems." In *The Economy of Brazil*, edited by Howard S. Ellis, 29–73. Berkeley: University of California Press, 1969.

Berlin, Isaiah. *The Hedgehog and the Fox*. Chicago: Elephant Paperbacks, 1993.

Bethell, Leslie, ed. *The Cambridge History of Latin America*. Vol. 6, pt. 2, *Latin America since 1930: Economy, Society, and Politics*. Cambridge: Cambridge University Press, 1994.

Bethell, Leslie, and Jairo Nicolau. "Politics in Brazil, 1985–2002." In *The Cambridge History of Latin America*, vol. 9, *Brazil since 1930*, edited by Leslie Bethell, 231–80. New York: Cambridge University Press, 2008.

Betto, Frei. *A mosca azul: Reflexão sobre o poder*. Rio de Janeiro: Rocco, 2006.

———. *Lula: Biografia política de um operário*. São Paulo: Estação Liberdade, 1989.

Bittencourt, Ana. "Mulheres na política: Entraves e conquistas." *Democracia Viva*, no. 41 (2009): 84–89.

BNM (Brasil: Nunca Mais). *Projecto "Brasil: Nunca Mais."* Vol. 3, *Perfil dos Atingidos*. Petrópolis, Brazil: Vozes, 1988.

Bohn, Simone R. "Feminismo estatal sob a Presidência Lula: O caso da secretaria de políticas para as mulheres." *Revista Debates* 4, no. 2 (2010): 81–106.

———. "Social Policy and Vote in Brazil: Bolsa Família and the Shifts in Lula's Electoral Base." *Latin American Research Review* 46, no. 1 (2011): 54–79.

Bologna, Italo. *Formação profissional na indústria, o SENAI*. Rio de Janeiro: MEC, Diretoria do Ensino Industrial, 1969.

———, ed. *Roberto Mange e sua obra*. Campinas, Brazil: UNIGRAF, 1980.

Bonduki, Nabil, and Raquel Rolnik. "Periferia da grande São Paulo: Reprodução do espaço como expediente de reprodução da força de trabalho." In Maricato, *A produção capitalista*, 117–54.

Bonelli, Regis. "Nivel de atividade e mudança estrutural." In *Estatisticas do século XX*, 383–426. Rio de Janeiro: IBGE, 2003.

Borges, Antonádia Monteiro. "Tanto azul, quanto vermelho: Sentidos e apropriaçoes de um evento político no Distrito Federal." In Heredia, Teixeira, and Barreira, *Como se fazem eleições no Brasil*, 217–41.

Bourdieu, Pierre. "The Biographical Illusion." Translated by Y. Winkin and W. Leeds-Hurwitz. *Working Papers and Proceedings of the Center for Psychological Studies*, no. 14 (1987).

———. *In Other Words: Essays towards a Reflexive Sociology*. Translated by Matthew Adamson. Stanford, CA: Stanford University Press, 1990.

———. "The Social Space and the Genesis of Groups." *Theory and Society* 14, no. 6 (1985): 723–44.

———. "What Makes a Social Class? On the Theoretical and Practical Existence of Groups." *Berkeley Journal of Sociology* 32 (1987): 1–17.

Bourne, Richard. *Lula do Brasil: A história real, do Nordeste ao Planalto*. Translated by Paulo Schmidt and Bernardo Schmidt. São Paulo: Geração Editorial, 2009.

———. *Lula of Brazil: The Story So Far*. Berkeley: University of California Press, 2008.

Brandão Lopes, Juarez Rubens. "O ajustamento do trabalhador à indústria: Mobilidade social e motivação." In *Mobilidade e trabalho: Um estudo na cidade de São Paulo*, edited by Bertram Hutchinson, 360–440. Rio de Janeiro: Centro Brasileiro de Pesquisas Educacionais, 1960.

———. *Sociedade industrial no Brasil*. São Paulo: Difusão Européia do Livro, 1964.

Braudel, Fernand. "History and the Social Sciences: The Longue Durée." In *On History*, 25–54. Chicago: University of Chicago Press, 1980.

Bryman, Alan. *Charisma and Leadership in Organizations*. London: Sage, 1992.

Bueno, Ricardo, and Luiz Cesar Faro, eds. *Capital e trabalho: Os melhores depoimentos do cenário sindical*. Rio de Janeiro: Rio Fundo Editora, 1991.

Burgmann, Verity. "The Multitude and the Many-Headed Hydra: Autonomist Marxist Theory and Labor History." *International Labor and Working-Class History*, no. 83 (2013): 170–90.

Caetano, Maria do Rosário. *Alguma solidão e muitas histórias: A trajetória de um cineasta brasileiro: João Batista de Andrade, um cineasta em busca da urgencia e da reflexão*. São Paulo: Imprensa Oficial, 2004.

Campista, Ary. "Todos melhoraram mas alguns muito mais." In *A história vivida*, edited by Lourenço Dantas Mota, 2:37–56. São Paulo: O Estado de São Paulo, 1981.

Candido, Antonio. "Introduction." In Paraná, *Lula*, 13–16.

Cardenuto, Reinaldo. "O cinema político de Leon Hirszman (1976–1981): Engajamento e resistência durante o regime militar brasileiro." PhD diss., Universidade de São Paulo, 2014.

Cardoso, Adalberto. *A construção da sociedade do trabalho no Brasil: Uma investigação sobre a persistência secular das desigualdades*. Rio de Janeiro: Editora FGV, 2010.

———. "De volta a 'O ajustamento do trabalhador à indústria': Uma homenagem a Juarez R. Brandão Lopes." *Revista Latinoamericana de Estudos do Trabalho* 16, no. 25 (2011): 185–219.

Cardoso, Fernando Henrique. *A arte da política: A história que vivi*. Edited by Ricardo A. Setti. Rio de Janeiro: Civilização Brasileira, 2006.

———. *The Accidental President of Brazil: A Memoir*. With Brian Winter. New York: Public Affairs, 2006.

———. "The Challenges of Social Democracy in Latin America." In Vellinga, *Social Democracy*, 273–96.

———. *Empresário industrial e desenvolvimento econômico no Brasil*. São Paulo: Difusão Européia do Livro, 1964.

———. "Le proletariat Brésilien: Situation et comportement social." *Sociologie du Travail* 3, no. 4 (1961): 50–65.

Cardoso, Tom. *O cofre do Dr. Rui: Como a VAR-Palmares de Dilma Rousseff realizou o maior assalto da luta armada brasileira*. Rio de Janeiro: Civilização Brasileira, 2011.

Carlyle, Thomas. "On Heroes, Hero-Worship, and the Heroic in History." In *The Varieties of History: From Voltaire to the Present*, edited by Fritz Stern, 102–3. New York: Meridian Books, 1957.

Carone, Edgard. *O PCB*. Vol. 2, *1943–1964*. São Paulo: DIFEL, 1982.

———. *O PCB*. Vol. 3, *1964–1982*. São Paulo: DIFEL, 1982.

Carvalho, Lívio de. "Políticas salariais brasileiras no período 1964–81." *Revista Brasileira de Economia* 36, no. 1 (1982): 51–84.

Carvalho, Luiz Maklouf. *Já vi esse filme: Reportagens (e polêmicas) sobre Lula e o PT (1984–2005)*. São Paulo: Geração Editorial, 2005.

Carvalho, Maria do Carmo Reginato Gama de. "A fábrica: Aspectos psicológicos do trabalho na linha de montagem." Master's thesis, Universidade de São Paulo, 1981.

Carvalho, Murilo. *Estórias de trabalhador*. São Paulo: Editora Brasiliense, 1976.

Carvalho, Ricardo. *O cardeal da resistência: As muitas vidas de dom Paulo Evaristo Arns*. São Paulo: Instituto Vladimir Herzog Editora, 2013.

Cascudo, Luís da Câmara. *Locuções tradicionais no Brasil*. Recife, Brazil: Universidade Federal de Pernambuco, 1970.

Caso, Antonio, ed. *Los subversivos*. Havana: Casa de las Americas, 1973.

Castañeda, Jorge G. *Utopia Unarmed: The Latin American Left after the Cold War*. New York: Alfred A. Knopf, 1993.

Castro, Cláudio de Moura. "Vocational Education and the Training of Industrial Labour in Brazil." *International Labour Review* 118, no. 5 (1979): 617–29.

Castro, Orisson Saraiva de. "Entrevistas com Orisson Saraiva de Castro: I gravada pelo Depto. de Jornalismo do Sind. Met. SBC II gravada pelo cedi (20 de maio 86)." Unpublished interview transcript.

Cavalli, Luciano. "Charisma and Twentieth-Century Politics." In Whimster and Lash, *Max Weber, Rationality and Modernity*, 317–33.

Cavarozzi, Marcelo. "The Left in South America: Politics as the Only Option." In Vellinga, *Social Democracy*, 146–62.

CEDI (Centro Ecumênico de Documentação e Informação). *História dos metalúrgicos de São Caetano*. São Paulo: CEDI, 1987.

Certeau, Michel de. *The Practice of Everyday Life*. Translated by Steven F. Rendall. Berkeley: University of California Press, 1984.

Chagas, Carlos. *A ditadura militar e a longa noite dos generais: 1970–1985*. Rio de Janeiro: Editora Record, 2015.

Chaia, Miguel Wady. *Intelectuais e sindicalistas: A experiência do DIEESE (1955–1990)*. Ibitinga, Brazil: Humanidades, 1992.

Chamberlain, Bobby J., and Ronald M. Harmon. *A Dictionary of Informal Brazilian Portuguese: With English Index*. Washington, DC: Georgetown University Press, 1983.

Clay, Jason W. "The Articulation of Non-capitalist Agricultural Production Systems with Capitalist Exchange Systems: The Case of Garanhuns, Brazil, 1845–1977." PhD diss., Cornell University, 1979.

Coelho, Marco Antônio Tavares. *Herança de um sonho: As memória de um comunista*. Rio de Janeiro: Record, 2000.

Coggiola, Osvaldo. "Introduction." In Paraná, *O filho*, 19–20.

Colistete, Renato. *Labour Relations and Industrial Performance in Brazil: Greater São Paulo, 1945–1960*. New York: Palgrave, 2001.

Comissão Nacional da Verdade. *Relatório*. Vol. 2, *Textos temáticos*. Brasília: Comissão Nacional da Verdade, 2014.

Conti, Mario Sergio. *Notícias do Planalto: A imprensa e Fernando Collor*. São Paulo: Companhia das Letras, 1999.

Coronil, Fernando. "The Future in Question: History and Utopia in Latin America (1989–2010)." In *Business as Usual: The Roots of the Global Financial Meltdown*, edited by Craig Calhoun and Georgi Derluguian, 231–92. New York: New York University Press, 2011.

Corrêa, Hercules. *Memórias de um stalinista*. Rio de Janeiro: Opera Nostra Editora, 1994.

Corrêa, Larissa Rosa, and Paulo Fontes. "As falas de Jerônimo: Trabalhadores, sindicatos e a historiografia da ditadura militar brasileira." *Anos 90* 23, no. 46 (2016): 129–51.

Corrêa Leite, José, and Carolina Gil. *The World Social Forum: Strategies of Resistance*. Translated by Traci Romine. Chicago: Haymarket Books, 2005.

Costa, Emília Viotti da. *The Brazilian Empire: Myths and Histories*. Rev. ed. Chapel Hill: University of North Carolina Press, 2000.

———. *Crowns of Glory, Tears of Blood: The Demerara Slave Rebellion of 1823*. Oxford: Oxford University Press, 1994.

———. "New Publics, New Politics, New Histories: From Economic Reductionism to Cultural Reductionism—In Search of Dialectics." In *Reclaiming the Political in Latin American History: Essays from the North*, edited by Gilbert M. Joseph, 17–31. Durham, NC: Duke University Press, 2001.

Costa, Petra. *Edge of Democracy*. Netflix, 2019.

Couto, Ronaldo Costa, ed. *Memória viva do regime militar: Brasil, 1964–1985*. Rio de Janeiro: Editora Record, 1999.

Cusset, François. *French Theory: How Foucault, Derrida, Deleuze, & Co. Transformed the Intellectual Life of the United States*. Minneapolis: University of Minnesota Press, 2008.

Dantas, Altino, Jr. *Lula sem censura: ". . . e aí peãozada partiu pro pau."* Petrópolis, Brazil: Editora Vozes, 1981.

Dantas, Audálio. *As duas guerras de Vlado Herzog: Da perseguição nazista na Europa à morte sob tortura no Brasil*. Rio de Janeiro: Civilização Brasileira, 2012.

———. *O menino Lula: A história do pequeno retirante que chegou à Presidência da República*. Rio de Janeiro: Ediouro, 2009.

D'Araújo, Maria Celina, ed. *Governo Lula: Contornos sociais e políticos da elite do poder*. Rio de Janeiro: Centro de Pesquisa e Documentação de História Contemporânea do Brasil/Fundação Getúlio Vargas, 2007.

D'Araújo, Maria Celina, and Celso Castro, eds. *Ernesto Geisel*. Rio de Janeiro: Fundação Getúlio Vargas, 1997.

Dassin, Joan, ed. *Torture in Brazil: A Shocking Report on the Pervasive Use of Torture by the Brazilian Military Governments 1964–1979, Secretly Prepared by the Archdiocese of São Paulo*. Translated by Jaime Wright. New York: Vintage, 1986.

Dines, Alberto, Florestan Fernandes Jr., and Nelma Salomão, ed. *Histórias do poder: 100 anos de política no Brasil*. Vol. 3, *Visões do executivo*. São Paulo: Editora 34, 2000.

Dirceu, José. *Zé Dirceu: Memórias*. Vol. 1. São Paulo: Geração, 2018.

Dirceu, José, and Vladimir Palmeira. *Abaixo a ditadura: O movimento de 68 contado por seus líderes*. Rio de Janeiro: Garamond, 1998.

Di Tella, Torcuato S. *Latin American Politics: A Theoretical Framework*. Austin: University of Texas Press, 1990.

Dosse, François. *History of Structuralism*. Vol. 1, *The Rising Sign, 1945–1966*. Minneapolis: University of Minnesota Press, 1997.

Downey, Greg. *Learning Capoeira: Lessons in Cunning from an Afro-Brazilian Art*. Oxford: Oxford University Press, 2005.

Dulles, John W. F. *Carlos Lacerda, Brazilian Crusader*. Vol. 2, *The Years 1960–1977*. Austin: University of Texas Press, 1996.

———. *Castello Branco: The Making of a Brazilian President*. College Station: Texas A&M University Press, 1978.

———. *President Castello Branco, Brazilian Reformer*. College Station: Texas A&M University Press, 1980.

Durand Ponte, Victor Manuel. *Crisis y movimiento obrero en Brasil: Las huelgas metalúrgicas de 1978 a 1980*. Mexico City: Universidad Nacional Autônoma de México, 1987.

Durham, Eunice Ribeiro. *A caminho da cidade: A vida rural e a migração para São Paulo*. 3rd ed. São Paulo: Editôra Perspectiva, 1984.

Durkheim, Émile. *The Elementary Forms of the Religious Life*. Translated by Joseph Ward Swain. London: George Allen and Unwin, 1915.

Dutilleux, Christian. *Lula*. Paris: Flammarion, 2005.

Eakin, Marshall C. *Brazil: The Once and Future Country*. New York: St. Martin's, 1997.

Estrela, Ely Souza. *Os sampauleiros: Cotidiano e representações*. São Paulo: Humanitas FFLCH/USP, 2003.

Faria, Cido, ed. *O movimento operário no ABC paulista contado por seus autores*. Santo André, Brazil: Instituto Centro de Memória e Atualidades, 2015.

Faria, Vilmar. "Changes in the Composition of Employment and the Structure of Occupations." In Bacha and Klein, *Social Change*, 141–70.

Farias, Rita de Cássia Pereira. "Entre a igualdade e a distinção: A trama social de uma grande empresa corporificada no uniforme de trabalho." PhD diss., UNICAMP, 2010.

Fernandes, Florestan. "Empresa industrial em São Paulo (projeto de estudo)." In *A sociologia numa era de revolução social*, edited by Florestan Fernandes, 328–64. São Paulo: Companhia Editora Nacional, 1963.

———. "Lula e a transformação do Brasil contemporâneo." In *A contestação necessária: Retratos intelectuais de inconformistas e revolucionários*, 26–50. São Paulo: Editora Ática, 1995.

———. *O PT em movimento*. São Paulo: Cortez Editora, 1991.

Ferrante, Vera Lúcia B. *FGTS: Ideologia e repressão*. São Paulo: Editora Ática, 1978.

Ferreira, Jorge, ed. *O populismo e sua história: Debate e crítica*. Rio de Janeiro: Civilização Brasileira, 2001.

Ferreira, Marieta de Moraes, and Alexandre Fortes, eds. *Muitos caminhos, uma estrela: Memórias de militantes do PT*. Vol. 1. São Paulo: Editora Fundação Perseu Abramo, 2008.

Ferretti, Celso João. *Opção, trabalho: Trajetórias ocupacionais de trabalhadores das classes subalternas*. São Paulo: Cortez Editora, 1988.

Fico, Carlos. *Reinventando o otimismo: Ditadura, propaganda e imaginário social no Brasil*. Rio de Janeiro: Editora Fundação Getúlio Vargas, 1997.

Figueiredo, Lucas. *O operador: Como (e a mando de quem) Marcos Valério Irrigou os cofres do PSDB e do PT*. Rio de Janeiro: Record, 2006.

Filho, Expedito. *Fernando Henrique Cardoso: Crônica de uma vitória*. Rio de Janeiro: Editora Objetiva, 1994.

Filho, Paulo Cannabrava. *En el ojo de la tormenta: América Latina en los años 60/70*. São Paulo: Cortez Editora, 2003.

Fleischer, David. "Manipulações casuísticas do sistema eleitoral durante o período militar, ou como usualmente o feitiço se voltava contra o feitiçeiro." In Soares and Soares D'Araújo, *21 anos de regime militar*, 154–97.

Fonseca, Ana. "Transferência de renda: Continuidades e rupturas na experiência do programa Bolsa-Família." Paper presented at "Nurturing Hope, Deepening Democracy, and Combating Inequalities: An Assessment of Lula's Presidency." Duke University, Durham, NC, May 27–28, 2008.

Fontes, Paulo. *Um nordeste em São Paulo: Trabalhadores migrantes em São Miguel Paulista (1945–66)*. Rio de Janeiro: Editora Fundação Getúlio Vargas, 2008.

Fortes, Alexandre. "In Search of a Post-neoliberal Paradigm: The Brazilian Left and Lula's Government." *International Labor and Working-Class History*, no. 75 (2009): 109–25.

Foster, George M. "Peasant Society and the Image of Limited Good." *American Anthropologist* 67, no. 2 (1965): 293–315.

Frederico, Celso, ed. *A esquerda e o movimento operário, 1964–1984*. Vol. 1, *A resistência à ditadura*. São Paulo: Novos Rumos, 1987.

———. *A vanguarda operária*. São Paulo: Edições Símbolo, 1979.

———. *Consciência operária no Brasil: Estudo com um grupo de trabalhadores*. São Paulo: Editora Ática, 1978.

Freire, Américo, and Evanize Sydow. *Frei Betto: Biografia*. Rio de Janeiro: Civilização Brasileira, 2016.

French, John D. "A abolição da miséria: Desafios do Século XIX no Século XXI." *E-Legis [Centro de Formação, Treinamento e Aperfeiçoamento da Câmara dos Deputados]* 10, no. 24 (2017): 86–98.

———. *The Brazilian Workers' ABC: Class Conflict and Alliances in Modern São Paulo*. Chapel Hill: University of North Carolina Press, 1992.

———. *Drowning in Laws: Labor Law and Brazilian Political Culture*. Chapel Hill: University of North Carolina Press, 2004.

———. "From the Suites to the Streets: The Unexpected Re-emergence of the 'Labor Question,' 1994–1999." *Labor History* 43, no. 3 (2002): 285–304.

———. "How the Not-So-Powerless Prevail: Industrial Labor Market Demand and the Contours of Militancy in Mid-Twentieth-Century São Paulo, Brazil." *Hispanic American Historical Review* 90, no. 1 (2010): 109–42.

———. "The Laboring and Middle-Class Peoples of Latin America and the Caribbean: Historical Trajectories and New Research Directions." In *Global Labour History: A State of the Art*, edited by Jan Lucassen, 289–333. Bern: Peter Lang, 2006.

———. "The Latin American Labor Studies Boom." *International Review of Social History* 45, no. 2 (2000): 279–308.

———. "Lula's Brazil: The Management of Hope." *Labor: Studies in Working Class History of the Americas* 5, no. 1 (2008): 134–36.

———. Review of *Linhas de Montagem: O industrialismo nacional-desenvolvimentista e a sindicalização dos trabalhadores*, by Antonio Luigi Negro. *Tempo Social: Revista de Sociologia da Universidade de São Paulo* 22, no. 1 (2010): 277–87.

———. "Social History and the Study of 'Great Men'? The *Hispanic American Historical Review*, William Spence Robertson (1872–1956), and the Disciplinary Debate about Biography." *Anuario Colombiano de Historia Social y de la Cultura* 40, no. 1 (2013): 99–138.

———. "Understanding the Politics of Latin America's Plural Lefts (Chávez/Lula): Social Democracy, Populism, and Convergence on the Path to a Post-neoliberal World." *Third World Quarterly* 30, no. 2 (2010): 349–70.

———. "Women and Working-Class Mobilization in Postwar São Paulo, 1945–1948." With Mary Lynn Pedersen Cluff. In French and James, *Gendered Worlds*, 176–207.

———. "Workers and the Rise of Adhemarista Populism in São Paulo, Brazil, 1945–47." *Hispanic American Historical Review* 68, no. 1 (1988): 1–43.

French, John D., and Alexandre Fortes. "Another World Is Possible: The Rise of the Brazilian Workers' Party and the Prospects for Lula's Government." *Labor: Studies in Working-Class History of the Americas* 2, no. 3 (2005): 13–31.

———. "Nurturing Hope, Deepening Democracy, and Combating Inequalities in Brazil: Lula, the Workers' Party, and Dilma Rousseff's 2010 Election as President." *Labor: Studies in Working Class History of the Americas* 9, no. 1 (2012): 7–28.

———. "When the Plumber(s) Come to Fix a Country: Doing Labor History in Brazil." *International Labor and Working Class History*, no. 82 (2012): 85–91.

French, John D., and Daniel James, eds. *The Gendered Worlds of Latin American Women Workers: From Household and Factory to the Union Hall and Ballot Box*. Durham, NC: Duke University Press, 1997.

———. "The Travails of Doing Labor History: The Restless Wanderings of John Womack Jr." *Labor: Studies in Working-Class History of the Americas* 4, no. 2 (2007): 95–116.

French, John D., and Matthew Lymburner. "Neoliberalism." In *Oxford Bibliographies: Latin American Studies*, edited by Ben Vinson. New York: Oxford University Press, 2012. https://dx.doi.org/10.1093/obo/9780199766581-0078.

French, John D., and Antonio Luigi Negro. "Politics, Memory, and Working-Class Life in the Commercial Biopic *Lula, Son of Brazil*." *A Contracorriente* 8, no. 3 (2011): 377–94.

Füchtner, Hans. *Os sindicatos brasileiros de trabalhadores: Organização e função política*. Rio de Janeiro: Edições Graal, 1980.

Galache, Luciano Garcia. "Apresentacão." In *A tomada de Ford: O nascimento de um sindicato livre*, by José Carlos Aguiar Brito. Petrópolis, Brazil: Vozes, 1983.

Garcia, Marco Aurélio. "La Socialdemocracia y el PT." In *La renovación de la izquierda latinoamericana*, edited by Augusto de Franco, 75–108. translated by Nils Castro, México: Editorial Nuestro Tiempo, 1992.

———. "The Gender of Militancy: Notes on the Possibilities of a Different History of Political Action." In *Gender and History: Retrospect and Prospect*, edited by Leonore Davidoff, Keith McClelland, and Eleni Varikas, 45–56. Oxford: Blackwell, 2000.

Garlippe, Saulo Roberto. "ABC: Um breve histórico do movimento operário e sindical." In *A CUT nas campanhas salariais de 1985*, 7–10. São Paulo: CEDI, 1985.

Gaspari, Elio. *A ditadura acabada*. Rio de Janeiro: Intrínseca, 2016.

———. *A ditadura derrotada*. São Paulo: Companhia das Letras, 2003.

———. *A ditadura encurralada*. São Paulo: Companhia das Letras, 2004.

Gasparian, Marcos. *O industrial*. São Paulo: Martins, 1973.

Ginger, Ray. *The Bending Cross: A Biography of Eugene Victor Debs*. New Brunswick, NJ: Rutgers University Press, 1949.

Godoy, Marcelo. *A casa do vovó: Uma biografia do DOI-Codi (1969–1991), o centro de sequestro, tortura e morte da ditadura militar: Histórias, documentos e depoimentos inéditos dos agentes do regime*. 2nd ed. São Paulo: Alameda, 2015.

Goffman, Erving. *Stigma: Notes on the Management of Spoiled Identity*. Englewood Cliffs, NJ: Prentice-Hall, 1963.

Gonçalves, José Sérgio R. C. *Máo-de-obra e condições de trabalho na indústria automobilística do Brasil*. São Paulo: Hucitec, 1985.

Graham, Douglas H. "Interstate Migration and the Industrial Labor Force in Center-South Brazil." *Journal of Developing Areas* 12, no. 1 (1977): 31–48.

Green, James N. *We Cannot Remain Silent: Opposition to the Brazilian Military Dictatorship in the United States*. Durham, NC: Duke University Press, 2010.

Grossi, Yonne de Souza. *Mina de Morro Velho: A extração do homem. Uma história de experiência operária*. Rio de Janeiro: Paz e Terra, 1981.

Guinn, Andrew. "Embedded Mobility: Federal Technical Education Reforms and Inclusive Industrial Development in Northeastern Brazil, 2003–2016." PhD diss., University of North Carolina at Chapel Hill, 2019.

Guizzo, João, José Antônio dos Santos, Maria Izabel Simões Gonçalves, and Wilma Silveira R. de Moura, eds. *Lula, entrevistas e discursos*. Guarulhos, Brazil: O Reporter de Guarulhos, 1978.

Gurgel, Antonio de Padua, and David V. Fleischer. *O Brasil vai às urnas: Retrato da campanha presidencial*. Brasília: Thesaurus, 1990.

Gutman, Herbert. "Labor History and the 'Sartre Question.'" In *Power and Culture: Essays on the American Working Class*, edited by Ira Berlin, 326–28. New York: Pantheon, 1987.

Hall, Anthony. "From *Fome Zero* to *Bolsa Família*: Social Policies and Poverty Alleviation under Lula." *Journal of Latin American Studies* 38, no. 4 (2006): 689–709.

Harnecker, Marta. *O sonho era possível: A história do Partido dos Trabalhadores narrada por seus protagonistas*. Havana: MEPLA, 1994.

Hawkins, Kirk. "Populism in Venezuela: The Rise of Chavismo." *Third World Quarterly* 24, no. 6 (2003): 1137–60.

Henriques, Affonso. *Ascensão e queda de Getúlio Vargas*. Vol. 2, *Getúlio Vargas e o Estado Novo*. Rio de Janeiro: Distribuidora Record, 1966.

Heredia, Beatriz Maria Alásia de, Carla Costa Teixeira, and Irlys Alencar F. Barreira, eds. *Como se fazem eleições no Brasil*. Rio de Janeiro: Relume Dumará, 2002.

Higginbotham, Evelyn Brooks. "African-American Women's History and the Metalanguage of Race." *Signs* 17, no. 2 (1992): 251–74.

Hobsbawm, Eric. *The Age of Extremes: A History of the World, 1914–1991*. New York: Pantheon, 1994.

———. *Interesting Times: A Twentieth-Century Life*. London: Allen Lane, 2002.

Hoffman, Helga. "Poverty and Property in Brazil: What Is Changing?" In Bacha and Klein, *Social Change*, 197–231.

Holston, James. *Insurgent Citizenship: Disjunctions of Democracy and Modernity in Brazil*. Princeton, NJ: Princeton University Press, 2009.

Hummes, Cláudio, and Frei Betto. "A igreja e a greve do ABC: Depoimento à comissão de pastoral operário nacional em Nova Iguaçu 14 de junho de 1981." *Revista Eclesiástica Brasileira* 40, no. 160 (1981): 721–28.

Humphrey, John. *Capitalist Control and Workers' Struggle in the Brazilian Auto Industry.* Princeton, NJ: Princeton University Press, 1982.

———. "The Development of Industry and the Bases for Trade Unionism: A Case Study of Car Workers in São Paulo, Brazil." PhD diss., University of Sussex, 1978.

Hunter, Wendy. "The Partido dos Trabalhadores: Still a Party of the Left?" In *Democratic Brazil Revisited,* edited by Peter R. Kingstone and Timothy J. Power, 15–32. Pittsburgh: University of Pittsburgh Press, 2008.

———. *The Transformation of the Workers' Party in Brazil, 1989–2009.* New York: Cambridge University Press, 2010.

Hunter, Wendy, and Timothy J. Power. "Bolsonaro and Brazil's Illiberal Backlash." *Journal of Democracy* 30, no. 1 (2019): 68–82.

———. "Rewarding Lula: Executive Power, Social Policy, and the Brazilian Elections of 2006." *Latin American Politics and Society* 49, no. 1 (2007): 1–30.

Ianni, Octavio. *O ABC da classe operária.* São Paulo: Hucitec, 1980.

Iasi, Mauro Luis. *As metamorfoses da consciência de classe: O PT entre a negação e o consentimento.* São Paulo: Expressão Popular, 2006.

"IV Encuentro del Foro de San Pablo: Discursos de Cárdenas, Fidel Castro, Lula." *America Libre,* no. 4 (1994): 131–36.

James, C. L. R. *The Black Jacobins: Toussaint L'Ouverture and the San Domingo Revolution.* Rev. ed. New York: Vintage Books, 1963.

James, Daniel. *Doña María's Story: Life History, Memory, and Political Identity.* Durham, NC: Duke University Press, 2000.

Jameson, Fredric. "Sartre and History." In *Marxism and Form: Twentieth-Century Dialectical Theories of Literature,* 206–305. Princeton, NJ: Princeton University Press, 1971.

Jenkins, Rhys. *Transnational Corporations and Uneven Development: The Internationalization of Capital and the Third World.* London: Methuen, 1987.

Jinkings, Ivana, Gilberto Maringoni, Juca Kfouri, and Maria Inês Nassif, eds. *A verdade vencerá. O povo sabe por que me condenaram.* Campinas: Boitempo, 2020. 2nd revised and expanded edition.

Joosse, Paul. "Becoming a God: Max Weber and the Social Construction of Charisma." *Journal of Classical Sociology* 14, no. 3 (2014): 266–83.

Jopling, David A. "Sartre's Moral Psychology." In *The Cambridge Companion to Sartre,* edited by Christina Howells, 103–39. Cambridge: Cambridge University Press, 1992.

Jordão, Fernando Pacheco. *Dossiê Herzog: Prisão, tortura e morte no Brasil.* 6th ed. São Paolo: Global Editora, 2005.

Kahil, Raouf. *Inflation and Economic Development in Brazil, 1946–1963.* Oxford: Clarendon Press, 1973.

Kahl, Joseph A. *Three Latin American Sociologists: Gino Germani, Pablo Gonzales Casanova, Fernando Henrique Cardoso.* 1976. Reprint, New Brunswick, NJ: Transaction Books, 1988.

Kamel, Ali. *Dicionário Lula: Um presidente exposto por suas palavras.* With Rodrigo Elias. Rio de Janeiro: Editora Nova Fronteira, 2009.

Keck, Margaret E. "Democratization and Dissension: The Formation of the Workers' Party." *Politics and Society* 15, no. 1 (1986): 67–95.

———. "The New Unionism in the Brazilian Transition." In Stepan, *Democratizing Brazil*, 252–96.

———. *The Workers' Party and Democratization in Brazil*. New Haven, CT: Yale University Press, 1992.

Keucheyan, Razmig. *The Left Hemisphere: Mapping Critical Theory Today*. London: Verso, 2013.

Kingstone, Peter R., and Aldo F. Ponce. "From Cardoso to Lula: The Triumph of Pragmatism in Brazil." In Weyland, Madrid, and Hunter, *Leftist Governments in Latin America*, 98–123.

Kinzo, Maria D'Alva Gil. "Consolidation of Democracy: Governability and Political Parties in Brazil." In *Brazil: The Challenges of the 1990s*, edited by Maria D'Alva G. Kinzo, 138–54. London: Institute of Latin American Studies, 1993.

———. "The 1989 Presidential Election: Electoral Behaviour in a Brazilian City." *Journal of Latin American Studies* 25, no. 2 (1993): 313–30.

Kopper, Christopher. *A VW do Brasil durante a ditadura militar brasileira 1964–1985: Uma abordagem histórica*. Wolfsburg, Germany: Volkswagen Aktiengesellschaft, 2017.

Kotscho, Ricardo, ed. *A greve do ABC: A greve vista por vários fotojornalistas*. São Paulo: Editora Caraguatá, 1980.

———. *Do golpe ao Planalto: Uma vida de repórter*. São Paulo: Companhia das Letras, 2006.

———. *Explode um novo Brasil: Diário da campanha das diretas*. São Paulo: Editora Brasiliense, 1984.

Krueger, Robert. "Abertura/Apertura: A Political Review of Recent Brazilian Writings." In *The Discourse of Power: Culture, Hegemony, and the Authoritarian State in Latin America*, edited by Neil Larsen, 172–93. Minneapolis: Institute for the Study of Ideologies and Literature, 1983.

Lacerda, Carlos. *Depoimento*. Edited by Cláudio Lacerda Paiva. Rio de Janeiro: Editora Nova Fronteira, 1977.

Lamounier, Bolívar. "Authoritarian Brazil Revisited: The Impact of Elections on the Abertura." In Stepan, *Democratizing Brazil*, 43–79.

———. *Da independência a Lula: Dois séculos de política brasileira*. São Paulo: Augurium, 2005.

———. "O voto em São Paulo, 1970–1978." In *Voto de desconfiança: Eleições e mudança política no Brasil: 1970–1979*, 15–80. Petrópolis, Brazil: Vozes, 1980.

Lamounier, Bolívar, and Maria Teresa Sadek Ribeiro de Souza, eds. *Depois da transição: Democracia e eleições no governo Collor*. São Paulo: Edições Loyola, 1991.

Langenbuch, Juergen Richard. *A Estruturação da Grande São Paulo*. Rio de Janeiro: Instituto Brasileiro de Geografia, Departamento de Documentação e Divulgação Geográfica e Cartográfica, 1971.

Langland, Victoria. *Speaking of Flowers: Student Movements and the Making and Remembering of 1968 in Military Brazil*. Durham, NC: Duke University Press, 2013.

Lanzana, Antônio E. T. *Diferenciais de salários na economia brasileira: Uma análise do período 1960–83*. São Paulo: Instituto de Pesquisas Econômicas, USP, 1987.

Lara, Maurício. *Campanha de rua: A cobertura jornalística de uma eleição presidencial*. São Paulo: Geração Editorial, 1994.

Leite, Rosalina de Santa Cruz. *A operária metalúrgica: Estudo sobre as condições de vida e trabalho de operárias metalúrgicas na cidade de São Paulo*. São Paulo: Semente, 1982.

Leonelli, Domingos, and Dante de Oliveira. *Diretas já: 15 meses que abalaram a ditadura.* 2nd ed. Rio de Janeiro: Editora Record, 2004.

Leopoldi, Maria Antonieta P. "Reforming Social Security under Lula: Continuities with Cardoso's Policies." In Love and Baer, *Brazil under Lula*, 221–39.

Levine, Robert M. *Brazilian Legacies*. Armonk, NY: M. E. Sharpe, 1997.

Lévi-Strauss, Claude. "History and the Dialectic." In *The Savage Mind*, 245–69. Chicago: University of Chicago Press, 1962.

Lima, Edileuza Pimenta de. "'Trabalhador: Arme-se e liberte-se': A Ação Libertadora Nacional (ALN) e a resistência operária pela luta guerrilheira." Bachelor's thesis, Universidade Federal do Estado do Rio de Janeiro, 2007.

Lindert, Kathy, Anja Linder, Jason Hobbs, and Bénédicte de la Brière. "The Nuts and Bolts of Brazil's Bolsa Família Program: Implementing Conditional Cash Transfers in a Decentralized Context." SP Discussion Paper No. 0709, World Bank, Washington, DC, May 2007.

Linger, Daniel Touro. *Dangerous Encounters: Meanings of Violence in a Brazilian City.* Stanford, CA: Stanford University Press, 1992.

Lobos, Julio Alejandro. "Technology and Organization Structure: A Comparative Case-Study of Automotive and Processing Firms in Brazil." PhD diss., Cornell University, 1976.

Love, Joseph L. "The Lula Government in Historical Perspective." In Love and Baer, *Brazil under Lula*, 305–15.

Love, Joseph L., and Werner Baer, eds. *Brazil under Lula: Economy, Politics, and Society under the Worker-President*. New York: Palgrave Macmillan, 2009.

Lowy, Michael, and Sarah Chucid. "Opiniões e atitudes de líderes sindicais metalúrgicos." *Revista Brasileira de Estudos Políticos*, no. 13 (1962): 132–69.

Lukács, Georg. "Narrate or Describe?" In *Writer and Critic and Other Essays*, edited and translated by Arthurd D. Kahn, 110–48. New York: Grosset and Dunlap, 1970.

Macarini, José Pedro. "A política econômica do Governo Médici: 1970–1973." *Nova Economia* (Belo Horizonte) 15, no. 3 (2005): 53–92.

Macdonald, Laura, and Arne Ruckert. "Post-neoliberalism in the Americas: An Introduction." In *Post-neoliberalism in the Americas*, edited by Laura Macdonald and Arne Ruckert, 1–18. New York: Palgrave Macmillan, 2009.

Macedo, Francisco Barbosa de. "A greve de 1980: Redes sociais e espaço urbano na mobilização coletiva dos metalúrgicos de São Bernardo do Campo." *Revista Mundos do Trabalho* 3, no. 5 (2011): 136–64.

Machado, João, and Paulo Vannuchi. "Entrevista: Lula—mãos à obra." *Teoria e Debate*, no. 13 (December 2, 1991). https://teoriaedebate.org.br/1991/02/12/lula-maos-a-obra/.

Machado, Josué. "Lula e a língua do povo." *Educação*, no. 263 (2003): 32–39.

Mackinnon, María M., and Mario A. Petrone, eds. *Populismo y neopopulismo en America Latina: El problema de la cenicienta*. Buenos Aires: Eudeba, 1998.

Maeda, Danilo, Antônio Strini, Carlos Eduardo Carlini, Marcio Hasegava, and Vinícius Romero. *Retratos da resistência: História da Ação Popular no ABC*. São Bernardo do Campo, Brazil: Faculdade de Jornalismo e Relações Públicas da Universidade Metodista de São Paulo, 2008.

Magalhães, Mário. *Marighella: O guerrilheiro que incendiou o mundo*. São Paulo, Brazil: Companhia das Letras, 2012.

Magno da Silva, Rosemiro. *A luta dos posseiros de Santana dos Frades*. Aracaju, Brazil: Editora UFS, 2000.

Maricato, Ermínia, ed. *A produção capitalista da casa (e da cidade) no Brasil industrial*. 2nd ed. São Paulo: Editora Alfa-Omega, 1982.

———. "A proletarização do espaço sob a grande indústria: O caso de São Bernardo do Campo na região da Grande São Paulo." Master's thesis, Universidade de São Paulo, 1977.

———. "Autoconstrução, a arquitetura possível." In Maricato, *A produção capitalista*, 71–93.

Marighella, Carlos. *Por que resisti à prisão*. N.p.: Edições Contemporâneas, 1965.

Markun, Paulo. *O sapo e o príncipe: Personagens, fatos e fábulas do Brasil contemporâneo*. Rio de Janeiro: Objetiva, 2004.

———, ed. *Vlado: Retrato de um homem e de uma época*. 1985. Reprint, São Paulo: Círculo do Livro, n.d.

Martins, Heloisa Helena Teixeira de Souza. *Igreja e movimento operário no ABC*. São Paulo: Editora Hucitec, 1994.

———. *O estado e a burocratização do sindicato no Brasil*. São Paulo: Editora Hucitec, 1979.

Martins, Heloisa Helena Teixeira de Souza, Henrique Pereira Júnior, and Carlos Alberto Ricardo. "A igreja na greve dos metalúrgicos—São Bernardo, 1980." *Religião e Sociedade*, no. 6 (1980): 7–68.

Martins, José de Souza. "A valorização da escola e do trabalho no meio rural." *Debate e Crítica*, no. 2 (1974): 112–32.

———. "Sociologia e militância: Entrevista com José de Souza Martins." *Estudos Avançados* 11, no. 31 (1997): 137–87.

———. *Uma arqueologia da memória social: Autobiografia de um moleque de fábrica*. Cotia, Brazil: Ateliê Editorial, 2011.

Masini, Fernando. "Em nome do real." In *Eduardo Coutinho*, edited by Felipe Bragança, 160–69. Rio de Janeiro: Beco do Azougue, 2009.

Matos, Carolina. *Jornalismo e política democrática no Brasil*. São Paulo: Publifolha, 2008.

McFarland, Gerald W. *The Mugwumps, 1884–1900: Moralists or Pragmatists?* New York: Simon and Schuster, 1975.

Meade, Teresa A. *A Brief History of Brazil*. New York: Checkmark Books, 2004.

Medeiros, Alexandre. *Luiz Inácio Lula da Silva: Crônica de um sonho*. Rio de Janeiro: Editora Objetiva, 1994.

Melhem, Célia Soibelmann. *Política de botinas amarelas: O MDB-PMDB paulista de 1965 a 1988*. São Paulo: Editora Hucitec, 1998.

Mello e Souza, Alberto de. "Rates of Return, Occupational Mobility, and the Labor Market for Industrial Workers: A Study of Two Brazilian States." PhD diss., University of Michigan, 1975.

Meneguello, Rachel. *Partidos e governos no Brasil contemporâneo (1985–1997)*. São Paulo: Editora Paz e Terra, 1998.

Mercadante Oliva, Aloízio. "Estado autoritário e desobediência operária: Os trabalhadores metalúrgicos de São Bernardo do Campo e Diadema." Master's thesis, Universidade Estadual de Campinas, 1989.

Mercadante Oliva, Aloízio, and Luís Flávio Rainho, eds. *Imagens da luta, 1905–1985*. São

Bernardo do Campo, Brazil: Sindicato dos Trabalhadores nas Indústrias Metalúrgicas, Mecânicas e de Material Elétrico de São Bernardo do Campo e Diadema, 1987.

Merrick, Thomas J. "Population since 1945." In Bacha and Klein, *Social Change*, 15–48.

Miglioli, Jorge. *Como são feitas as greves no Brasil?* Rio de Janeiro: Editôra Civilização Brasileira, 1963.

Miguel, Luis Felipe. "From Equality to Opportunity: Transformations in the Discourse of the Workers' Party in the 2002 Elections." *Latin American Perspectives* 33, no. 4 (2006): 122–43.

———. *Mito e discurso político: Uma análise a partir da campanha eleitoral brasileira de 1994*. São Paulo: Imprensa Oficial, 2000.

Mintz, Sidney W. "The Rural Proletariat and the Problem of Rural Proletarian Consciousness." *Journal of Peasant Studies* 1, no. 3 (1974): 291–325.

Mitchell, Gladys Lanier. "Racializing Blackness and Politicizing Race: The Significance of Race in Electoral Politics in Salvador and São Paulo, Brazil." PhD diss., University of Chicago, 2008.

Mommsen, Wolfgang. "Personal Conduct and Societal Change." In Whimster and Lash, *Max Weber, Rationality and Modernity*, 35–51.

Monclaire, Stéphane. "Lula II: Un vote de reconnaissance." *Lusotopie* 14, no. 1: 1–68.

Montgomery, David. *The Fall of the House of Labor: The Workplace, the State, and American Labor Activism, 1865–1925*. Cambridge: Cambridge University Press, 1987.

Moore, Barrington. *Injustice: The Social Bases of Obedience and Revolt*. White Plains, NY: M. E. Sharpe, 1978.

Moraes, Dênis de, ed. *Prestes com a palavra: Uma seleção das principais entrevistas do líder comunista*. Campo Grande, Brazil: Letra Livre, 1997.

Moraes, Dênis de, and Francisco Viana. *Prestes: Lutas e autocríticas*. Petrópolis, Brazil: Vozes, 1982.

Moraes, Maria Blassioli. "A Ação Social Católica e a luta operária: A experiência dos jovens operários católicos em Santo André (1954–1964)." Master's thesis, Universidade de São Paulo, 2003.

Morais, Lecio, and Alfredo Saad-Filho. "Brazil beyond Lula: Forging Ahead or Pausing for Breath?" *Latin American Perspectives* 38, no. 2 (2011): 31–44.

Morel, Mário. *Lula, o início: 25 anos depois, o livro-reportagem que mostra como tudo começou*. 3a ed. Rio de Janeiro, RJ, Brasil: Editora Nova Fronteira, 2006.

———, ed. *Lula o metalúrgico: Anatomia de uma liderança*. Rio de Janeiro: Editora Nova Fronteira, 1981.

Motta, Rodrigo Patto Sá. *As universidades e o regime militar: cultura política brasileira e modernização autoritária*. Rio: Zahar, 2014.

Negro, Antonio Luigi. "Ford Willys anos 60: Sistema auto de dominação e metalúrgicos do ABC." Master's thesis, Universidade Estadual de Campinas, 1994.

———. *Linhas de montagem: O industrialismo nacional-desenvolvimentista e a sindicalização dos trabalhadores (1945–1978)*. São Paulo: Editorial Boitempo, 2004.

Neri, Marcelo. "Income Policies, Income Distribution, and the Distribution of Opportunities in Brazil." In *Brazil as an Economic Superpower? Understanding Brazil's Changing Role in the Global Economy*, edited by Lael Brainard and Leonardo Martinez-Diaz, 221–69. Washington, DC: Brookings Institution, 2009.

Nêumanne Pinto, José. *Atrás do palanque: Bastidores da eleição 1989*. São Paulo: Edições Siciliano, 1989.

———. *Erundina: A mulher que veio com a chuva*. Rio de Janeiro: Espaço e Tempo, 1989.

———. *O que sei de Lula*. Rio de Janeiro: Topbooks, 2011.

Nogueira, Marco Aurélio, ed. *PCB: Vinte anos de política, 1958–1979 (documentos)*. São Paulo: Livraria Editora Ciências Humanas, 1980.

Nosella, Paolo. *Por que mataram Santos Dias: Quando os braços se unem à mente*. São Paulo: Cortez, 1980.

Nova, Cristiane, and Jorge Nóvoa, eds. *Carlos Marighella: O homem por trás do mito*. São Paulo: Editora UNESP, 1999.

Nunes, Antônio Carlos Felix. *Além da greve*. São Paulo: Editora Criart, 1978.

———. *Fora de pauta (histórias e história do jornalismo no Brasil)*. São Paulo: Proposta Editorial, 1981.

———. *PC linha leste: Fragmentos da vida partidária*. São Paulo: Editorial Livramento, 1980.

Nunes, Antônio Carlos Felix, and Paulo Canabrava Filho. *Bilhetes de João Ferrador*. São Paulo: Editora Grafite, 1980.

"1a Conferência Nacional da Promoção da Igualdade Racial, realizada em Brasília por reuniu negros, indios, judeus, e ciganos para debater e festejar." *Revista Raça Brasil*, no. 89 (2004).

"O primeiro impeachment do Brasil." Special issue, *Direto da História: Boletim da História do Ministério Público Federal* 2, no. 4 (2009).

Osakabe, Haquira. "A palavra imperfeita." *Remate de Males* (Campinas), no. 7 (1987): 167–71.

The Oxford-Duden Pictorial Portuguese-English Dictionary. Oxford: Clarendon Press, 1995.

Pães de Barros, Ricardo, Mirela de Carvalho, Samuel Franco, and Rosane Mendonça. "A importância da queda recente das desigualdades na redução da pobreza." IPEA Textos para Discussão 1256, Instituto de Pesquisa Econômica Aplicada, Brasília, 2007.

Paoli, Maria Celia, Eder Sáder, and Vera da Silva Telles. "Pensando a classe operária: Os trabalhadores sujeitos ao imaginário acadêmico (notas de uma pesquisa)." *Revista Brasileira de Historia* 3, no. 6 (1983): 129–49.

Paraná, Denise. *A historia de Lula, o filho do Brasil*. Rio de Janeiro: Objetiva, 2009.

———. "Da cultura da pobreza à cultura da transformação: A história de Luiz Inácio Lula da Silva e sua família." PhD diss., Universidade de São Paulo, 1995.

———. *Lula, o filho do Brasil*. Rev. ed. São Paulo: Editora Fundação Perseu Abramo, 2002.

———. *O filho do Brasil: De Luiz Inácio a Lula*. São Paulo: Xamã, 1996.

Paranhos, Kátia Rodrigues. *Era uma vez em São Bernardo: O discurso sindical dos metalúrgicos—1971/1982*. Campinas, Brazil: Editora da UNICAMP, 1999.

———. "Mentes que brilham: Sindicalismo e praticas culturais dos metalurgicos de São Bernardo." PhD diss., UNICAMP, 2002.

Partido dos Trabalhadores: Trajetórias: Das origens à vitória de Lula. 2nd ed. São Paulo: Fundação Perseu Abramo, 2002.

Pastore, Humberto Domingos. "João Lins Pereira: O sindicalista dos anos 50, 60, 70, 80." *Raízes* (São Caetano do Sul) 18, no. 36 (2007): 67–73.

Pastore, José. *Inequality and Social Mobility in Brazil*. Translated by Robert M. Oxley. Madison: University of Wisconsin Press, 1982.

Pastore, José, and João do Carmo Lopes. *A mão de obra especializada na indústria paulista*. São Paulo: Instituto de Pesquisas Econômicas, 1973.

Payne, Charles M. *I've Got the Light of Freedom: The Organizing Tradition and the Mississippi Freedom Struggle*. Berkeley: University of California Press, 1995.

Pazzianotto, Almir. *100 anos de sindicalismo*. São Paulo: Lex Editora, 2007.

———. "Sindicatos, corporativismo e política." In Soares and D'Araújo, *21 anos de regime militar*, 89–122.

Pereira, João Baptista Borges. *A escola secundaria numa sociedade em mudança: Interpretação socioantropológica de uma experiência administrativa*. São Paulo: Pioneira, 1969.

Pereira, José Carlos. *Estrutura e expansão da indústria em São Paulo*. São Paulo: Editora Nacional, 1967.

Pereira, Luiz. *A escola num área metropolitana: Crise e racionalização de uma emprêsa pública de serviços*. 1960. Reprint, São Paulo: Pioneira, 1976.

———. *O magistério primário numa sociedade de classes: Estudo de uma ocupação em São Paulo*. 1963. Reprint, São Paulo: Livraria Pioneira Editôra, 1969.

———. *Trabalho e desenvolvimento no Brasil*. São Paulo: Difusão Européia do Livro, 1965.

Pereira, Vera Maria Candido. *O coração da fábrica: Estudo de caso entre operários têxteis*. Rio de Janeiro: Editora Campus, 1979.

Perrone, Fernando L. *Relato de guerras: Praga, São Paulo, Paris: '68*. São Paulo: Busca Vida, 1988.

Perruso, Marco Antonio. *Em busca do "novo": Intelectuais brasileiros e movimentos populares nos anos 1970/80*. São Paulo: Annablume, 2009.

Pessen, Edward. *The Log Cabin Myth: The Social Backgrounds of the Presidents*. New Haven, CT: Yale University Press, 1984.

Pitts, Bryan. "The Inadvertent Opposition: The São Paulo Political Class and the Demise of Brazil's Military Regime, 1968–1985." PhD diss., Duke University, 2013.

———. "'O sangue da mocidade está correndo': A classe política e seus filhos enfrentam os militares em 1968." *Revista Brasileira de História* 34, no. 67 (2014): 39–65.

Plekhanov, G. V. "On the Role of the Individual in History." In *Selected Philosophical Works*, vol. 2. London: Lawrence and Wishart, 1961. First published in 1898 in *Nauchnoye Obrozhniye*, nos. 3–4. Available at Marxists Internet Archive, accessed April 3, 2014, http://www.marxists.org/archive/plekhanov/1898/xx/individual.html.

Pogibin, Guilherme Gibran. "Memórias de metalúrgicos grevistas do ABC paulista." Master's thesis, Universidade de São Paulo, 2009.

Pomar, Wladimir. *Quase lá: Lula, o susto das elites*. São Paulo: Editora Brasil Urgente, 1990.

Portuense de Carvalho, Sandra Aparecida. *A Ação Popular em Mauá: Resistência e soldariedade em tempos de ditadura*. Jundiaí: Paco Editorial, 2017.

Power, Timothy J., and Matthew M. Taylor, eds. *Corruption and Democracy in Brazil: The Struggle for Accountability*. Notre Dame, IN: University of Notre Dame Press, 2011.

Power, Timothy J., and Cesar Zucco. "Estimating Ideology of Brazilian Legislative Parties, 1990–2005: A Research Communication." *Latin American Research Review* 44, no. 1 (2009): 218–46.

Prado, Caio, Jr. *A Revolução Brasileira*. São Paulo: Editora Brasiliense, 1966.

Prefeitura do Município de São Bernardo do Campo. *Pesquisa Sócio-Econômica 79: Relatório I*. São Bernardo do Campo, Brazil: Secretaria de Planejamento e Economia, Prefeitura do Município de São Bernardo do Campo, 1979.

Queiroz, Maria Isaura Pereira de. "Classes sociais no Brasil: 1950–1960." *Ciência e Cultura* 27, no. 7 (1975): 735–56.

Quintana, Mário. "Destino." In *Mário Quintana: Poesia completa*, edited by Tania Franco Carvalhal, 66. Rio de Janeiro: Editora Nova Aguilar, 2005.

Rainho, Luís Flávio. *Os peões do Grande ABC: Estudo sobre as condições de vida e consciência de classe do operário metalúrgico (sem especialização e semi-especializado) ligado à indústria automobilística*. Petrópolis, Brazil: Vozes, 1980.

Rainho, Luís Flávio, and Osvaldo Martines Bargas. *As lutas operárias e sindicais dos metalúrgicos em São Bernardo (1977–1979)*. São Bernardo: Associação Beneficiente e Cultural dos Metalúrgicos de São Bernardo do Campo e Diadema, 1983.

Ramalho, José Ricardo, and Iram Jácome Rodrigues. "Sociologia do trabalho no Brasil: Entrevista com Leôncio Martins Rodrigues." *Revista Brasileira de Ciências Sociais* 25, no. 72 (2010): 133–79.

Rebhun, Linda-Anne. *The Heart Is Unknown Country: Love in the Changing Economy of Northeast Brazil*. Stanford, CA: Stanford University Press, 1999.

Regalado, Roberto. *Latin America at the Crossroads: Domination, Crisis, Popular Movements, and Political Alternatives*. Melbourne: Ocean Press, 2006.

Reid, Michael. *Forgotten Continent: The Battle for Latin America's Soul*. New Haven, CT: Yale University Press, 2007.

Reis Filho, Daniel Aarão, and Jair Ferreira de Sá, eds. *Imagens da revolução: Documentos políticos das organizações clandestinas de esquerda dos anos 1961 a 1971*. Rio de Janeiro: Marco Zero, 1985.

Reist, Stephanie. "'Christ the Redeemer Turns His Back on Us': Urban Black Struggle in Rio's Baixada Fluminense." PhD diss., Duke University, 2018.

Rejali, Darius. *Torture and Democracy*. Princeton, NJ: Princeton University Press, 2007.

"Revised World Social Forum Charter of Principles, June 2001 Version." In *World Social Forum: Challenging Empires*, edited by Jai Sen, Anita Anand, Arturo Escobar, and Peter Waterman, 70. New Delhi: Viveka Foundation, 2004.

Reygadas, Luis. "Imagined Inequalities: Representations of Discrimination and Exclusion in Latin America." *Social Identities* 11, no. 5 (2005): 489–508.

Reynolds, Stephen Marion, ed. *Debs: His Life, Writings and Speeches, with a Department of Appreciations*. Girard, KS: Appeal to Reason, 1908.

Rezende, Claudinei Cássio de. *Suicídio revolucionário: A luta armada e a herança da quimérica revolução em etapas*. São Paulo: Editora UNESP, 2010.

Ribeiro, Flávia Maria Franchini. "A subida do monte purgatório: Estudo da experiência de presos políticos na penitenciaria regional de Linhares." Paper presented at Anais do I Coloquio do Laboratório de História Econômica e Social, Juiz de Fora, June 13–16, 2005.

Ridenti, Marcelo. "Ação Popular: Cristianismo e marxismo." In *História do marxismo no Brasil*, vol. 5, *Partidos e organizações dos anos 20 aos 60*, edited by Daniel Aarão Reis Filho and Marcelo Ridenti, 213–82. Campinas, Brazil: Editora da Unicamp, 1991.

———. *Em busca do povo brasileiro: Artistas da revolução, do CPC à era da TV*. Rio de Janeiro: Editora Record, 2000.

Rieder, Jonathan. *The Word of the Lord Is upon Me: The Righteous Performance of Martin Luther King, Jr.* Cambridge, MA: Harvard University Press, 2008.

Ristoff, Dilvo. *Democratização do Campus: Impactos dos Programas de Inclusão Sobre o Perfil da Graduação*. Cadernos Do GEA [Grupo Estratégico De Análise da Educação Superior no Brasil] #9. Rio de Janeiro: FLACSO/GEA/UERJ/LPP, 2016.

Rivas Rojas, Raquel. "On *Chavismo*: Interview with Yolanda Salas (Caracas, 7 September 2004)." *Journal of Latin American Cultural Studies* 14, no. 3 (2005): 325–33.

Roberts, Madeleine. "From 'A Foot in the Kitchen' to 'A Foot in the Door': Domestic Service in Transition in 21st Century Brazil." Honor's thesis, Duke University, 2017.

Rodrigues, Leôncio Martins. *Industrialização e atitudes operárias (estudo de um grupo de trabalhadores)*. São Paulo: Editôra Brasiliense, 1970.

———. *Leôncio Martins Rodrigues Netto (Depoimento, 2008)*. Rio de Janeiro: Centro de Pesquisa e Documentação de História Contemporânea do Brasil/Fundação Getúlio Vargas, 2010.

———. *Partidos e sindicatos: Escritos de sociologia política*. São Paulo: Ática, 1990.

Rodrigues, Tony, and Rodolpho Zalla. *Lula: Luiz Inácio Brasileiro da Silva*. São Paulo: Editora Sarandi, 2010.

Rosa, Maria Inês. "A indústria brasileira na década de 60: As transformações nas relações de trabalho e a estabilidade." Master's thesis, UNICAMP, 1982.

Rotberg, Robert I. "Charisma, Leadership, and Historiography." *Journal of Interdisciplinary History* 42, no. 3 (2012): 419–28.

Saad-Filho, Alfredo. "New Dawn or False Start in Brazil? The Political Economy of Lula's Election." *Historical Materialism* 11, no. 1 (2003): 3–21.

Sader, Eder. *Quando novos personagens entraram em cena: Experiências, falas e lutas dos trabalhadores da Grande São Paulo (1970–1980)*. Rio de Janeiro: Paz e Terra, 1988.

Sader, Emir. "The Workers' Party in Brazil." *New Left Review*, no. 165 (1987): 93–102.

Sader, Emir, and Ken Silverstein. *Without Fear of Being Happy: Lula, the Workers Party, and Brazil*. London: Verso, 1991.

Sahlins, Marshall. *Apologies to Thucydides: Understanding History as Culture and Vice Versa*. Chicago: University of Chicago Press, 2004.

Saint-Clair, Clóvis. *Bolsonaro: O homem que peitou o exército e desafia a democracia*. Rio de Janeiro: Máquina dos Livros, 2018.

Sales, Telma Bessa. *Trabalho e reestruturação produtiva: O caso da Volkswagen em São Bernardo do Campo, SP*. São Paulo: Annablume, 2002.

Salles, João Moreira. *Entreatos*. Rio de Janiero: Videofilme, 2004.

Salvatore, Nick. *Eugene V. Debs: Citizen and Socialist*. Urbana: University of Illinois Press, 1982.

Sampaio, Antônio *Possidônio. A capital do automóvel: Na voz dos operários*. São Paulo: Edições Populares, 1979.

———. "As lutas sindicais e as greves: Os trabalhadores do ABC como protagonistas da história política do país—o novo sindicalismo." In *Anais do I Congresso de História da Região do Grande ABC*, 194–98. Santo André, Brazil: PMSA, 1990.

———. *Lula e a greve dos peões: Romance-reportagem*. São Paulo: Escrita, 1982.

———. *Sim senhor, inhor sim, pois não*. 1976. Reprint, Santo André: Alpharrabio Edições, 1997.

Samuels, David. "From Socialism to Social Democracy: Party Organization and the Transformation of the Workers' Party in Brazil." *Comparative Political Studies* 37, no. 9 (2004): 999–1024.

———. "Sources of Mass Partisanship in Brazil." *Latin American Politics and Society* 48, no. 2 (2006): 1–27.

Sandoval, Salvador A. M. *Social Change and Labor Unrest in Brazil since 1945*. Boulder, CO: Westview Press, 1993.

Santos, Sales Augusto dos. "Who Is Black in Brazil? A Timely or a False Question in Brazilian Race Relations in the Era of Affirmative Action?" Translated by Obianuju C. Anya. *Latin American Perspectives* 33, no. 4 (2006): 30–48.

Sardenberg, Cecília M. B. "With a Little Help from Our Friends: 'Global' Incentives and 'Local' Challenges to Feminist Politics in Brazil." *IDS Bulletin* 35, no. 4 (2004): 125–29.

Sarles, Margaret J. "Maintaining Political Control through Parties: The Brazilian Strategy." *Comparative Politics* 15, no. 1 (1982): 41–72.

Sarti, Cynthia Andersen. *A família como espelho: Um estudo sobre a moral dos pobres*. São Paulo: FAPESP, 1996.

Sartre, Jean-Paul. "Itinerary of a Thought." *New Left Review* 58 (1969): 43–66.

———. *Search for a Method*. Translated by Hazel E. Barnes. New York: Vintage, 1968.

———. *Words*. Translated by Irene Clephane. London: H. Hamilton, 1964.

Schneider, Ronald M. *"Order and Progress": A Political History of Brazil*. Boulder, CO: Westview Press, 1991.

Schwartz, Stuart B. *Sugar Plantations in the Formation of Brazilian Society: Bahia, 1550–1835*. Cambridge: Cambridge University Press, 1985.

Scott, David. *Conscripts of Modernity: The Tragedy of Colonial Enlightenment*. Durham, NC: Duke University Press, 2004.

Scott, James C. *Domination and the Arts of Resistance: Hidden Transcripts*. New Haven, CT: Yale University Press, 1990.

———. *Weapons of the Weak: Everyday Forms of Peasant Resistance*. New Haven, CT: Yale University Press, 1985.

Secco, Lincoln, ed. *A ideia: Lula e o sentido do Brasil contemporâneo*. São Paulo: Núcleo de Estudos de *O Capital*, 2018.

SENAI (Serviço Nacional de Aprendizagem Industrial. Departamento Regional de São Paulo). *De homens e máquinas*. Vol. 1. São Paulo: SENAI-SP Projeto Memória, 1991.

SEPPIR (Secretária Especial de Política de Promoção da Igualdade Racial). *Subsídios à II CONAPIR (Conferência Nacional de Promoção da Igualdade Racial)*. Brasília: SEPPIR, 2009.

Shapiro, Helen. *Engines of Growth: The State and Transnational Auto Companies in Brazil*. Cambridge: Cambridge University Press.

Silva, André Luis Corrêia da. "'João Ferrador na República de São Bernardo': O impacto do 'novo' movimento sindical no ABC paulista no processo de transição democrática (1977–1980)." Master's thesis, Universidade Federal do Rio Grande do Sul, 2006.

Silva, Armando Corrêa da. "Estrutura e mobilidade social do proletariado urbano em São Paulo." *Revista Civilização Brasileira* 3, no. 13 (1967): 81.

Silva, Luiz Inácio Lula da. "Conf. palestra proferida por Lula no I Congresso de História da Região do ABC." In *Anais do I Congresso de História da Região do Grande ABC*, 211–18. Santo André: Prefeitura Municipal de Santo André, 1990.

———. "Consolidação das leis do trabalho ou liberdade sindical? Dia 12 de junho de 1978." In Luiz Werneck Vianna, *Conjuntura nacional*, 247–55.

———. "Declarações Concedidas a Luís Flávio Rainho, 5 November 1976." In Rainho and Bargas, *As Lutas Operárias*, 49–51.

———. "Depoimento de Luiz Inácio Lula da Silva, entrevistado por Karen Worcman, Oswaldo Martines Bargas, and Gilvanir Batista, in São Paulo, 17 and 26 April 2000." Part of the Projeto Preservação da Memória dos Trabalhadores dos ABC. Museu da Pessoa.

———. "Depoimento Luis Inácio Lula da Silva." In *ABC de Luta!*

———. "Entrevista-Lula." Ruy Mesquita, June 1978. Original typed manuscript of 138 pages provided to the author by Renato Delmanto.

———. "Speech of the President of the Brazilian Republic at the Opening of the First National Conference of Gays, Lesbians, Bisexuals, Transvestites, and Transsexuals." In *The Politics of Sexuality in Latin America*, edited by Javier Corrales and Mario Pecheny, 265–69. Pittsburgh: University of Pittsburgh Press, 2010.

Silva, Maria Carolina Granato da. "O cinema na greve e a greve no cinema: Memórias dos metalúrgicos do ABC (1979–1991)." PhD diss., Universidade Federal Fluminense, 2008.

Simmel, Georg. *The Sociology of Georg Simmel*. Edited and translated by Kurt H. Wolff. Glencoe, IL: Free Press, 1950.

Simões, Carlos. *A lei do arrocho: Trabalho, previdência e sindicatos no regime militar 1964–1984*. Petrópolis, Brazil: Vozes, 1986.

Singer, André. "A segunda alma do Partido dos Trabalhadores." *Novos Estudos*, no. 88 (2010): 89–111.

———. "Collor na periferia: A volta por cima do populismo?" In *De Geisel a Collor: O balanço da transição*, edited by Bolívar Lamounier, 135–52. São Paulo: IDESP, 1990.

———. *Os sentidos do Lulismo: Reforma gradual e facto conservador*. São Paulo: Companhia das Letras, 2012.

———. "Raízes sociais e ideológicas do lulismo." *Novos Estudos*, no. 85 (2009): 83–102.

———, ed. *Sem medo de ser feliz: Cenas de campanha*. São Paulo: Scritta, 1990.

Singer, Paul. "As doces ilusões da CUT e da direita." In Bueno and Faro, *Capital e trabalho*, 43–48.

———. *Economia política da urbanização*. São Paulo: Brasiliense, 1973.

Skidmore, Thomas E. *Brazil: Five Centuries of Change*. New York: Oxford University Press, 1999.

———. *The Politics of Military Rule in Brazil, 1964–85*. New York: Oxford University Press, 1988.

Sluyter-Beltrão, Jeffrey. *Rise and Decline of Brazil's New Unionism: The Politics of the Central Única dos Trabalhadores*. Oxford: Peter Lang, 2010.

Smith, Anne-Marie. *A Forced Agreement: Press Acquiescence to Censorship in Brazil*. Pittsburgh: University of Pittsburgh Press, 1997.

Smith, Joseph. *History of Brazil, 1500–2000: Politics, Economy, Society, Diplomacy*. With Francisco Luiz Teixeira Vinhosa. New York: Longman, 2002.

Soares, Gláucio Ary Dillon. *A democracia interrompida*. Rio de Janeiro: FGV Editora, 2001.

Soares, Gláucio Ary Dillon, and Maria Celina Soares D'Araújo, eds. *21 anos de regime militar: Balanços e perspectivas*. Rio de Janeiro: Editora FGV, 1994.

Soares, Gláucio Ary Dillon, and Sonia Luiza Terron. "Dois Lulas: A geografia eleitoral da reeleição (explorando conceitos, métodos e técnicas de análise geoespacial)." *Opinião Pública* (Campinas) 14, no. 2 (2008): 269–301.

Solano, Esther, Aldo Zaiden, and Camilo Vannuchi, eds. *Luiz Inácio Lula da Silva: Nós vimos uma prisão impossível*. São Paulo: Editora Contracorrente, 2018.

Solnik, Alex. *O cofre do Adhemar: A iniciação política de Dilma Rousseff e outros segredos da luta armada*. With Antônio Roberto Espinosa. São Paulo: Jaboticaba, 2011.

Sommariva, Marco, ed. *Lula: Storia, idee, speranze*. Rome: Malatempora, 2003.

Souza, Amaury de. "The Nature of Corporatist Representation: Leaders and Members of Organized Labor in Brazil." PhD diss., Massachusetts Institute of Technology, 1978.

———. "The Politics of Personality in Brazil." *Journal of Democracy* 22, no. 2 (2011): 75–88.

Souza, Isabel Ribeiro de Oliveira Gomes de. *Trabalho e política: As origens do Partido dos Trabalhadores*. Petrópolis, Brazil: Vozes, 1988.

Souza, Percival de. *Autópsia do medo: Vida e morte do delegado Sérgio Paranhos Fleury*. São Paulo: Editora Globo, 2000.

Souza, Romulo Augustus Pereira de. *Memórias de um pelego*. Rio de Janeiro: Gryphus, 1998.

Stacchini, José. *Março 64: Mobilização da audácia*. São Paulo: Companhia Editora Nacional, 1965.

Stepan, Alfred, ed. *Democratizing Brazil: Problems of Transition and Consolidation*. Oxford: Oxford University Press, 1989.

———. "Introduction." In Stepan, *Democratizing Brazil*, vii–xvii.

Strini, Antônio, Carlos Eduardo Carlini, Danilo Maeda, Marcio Hasegava, and Vinícius Romero. *Retratos da resistência: Histórias da Ação Popular no ABC*. São Bernardo do Campo: Universidade Metodista de São Paulo, 2008.

Tauile, José Ricardo. "Microelectronics, Automation, and Economic Development: The Case of Numerically Controlled Machine Tools in Brazil." PhD diss., New School for Social Research, 1984.

Tavares de Almeida, Maria Hermínia. "Desarollo capitalista y acción sindical (a propósito de la experiência de los metalúrgicos de San Bernardo del Campo." *Revista Mexicana de Sociologia* 40, no. 2 (1983): 467–92.

———. "O sindicato no Brasil: Novos problemas, velhas estruturas." *Debate e Crítica*, no. 6 (1975): 49–74.

Teles Janaina de Almeida, Marcelo Ridenti, and Zilda Márcia Grícoli Iokoi, eds. *Intolerância e resistência: Testemunhos da repressão política no Brasil, 1964–1985*. São Paulo: FFLCH/USP, 2010.

Thompson, E. P. *The Poverty of Theory and Other Essays*. New York: Monthly Review, 1978.

Tolstoy, Leo. "Second Epilogue." In *War and Peace: The Maude Translation*, edited by George Gibian, 1313–51. New York: W. W. Norton, 1966.

Tomizaki, Kimi. *Ser metalúrgico no ABC: Transmissão e herança da cultura operária entre duas gerações de trabalhadores*. Campinas, Brazil: Arte Escrita Editora, 2007.

Torre, Carlos de la. "The Resurgence of Radical Populism in Latin America." *Constellations* 14, no. 3 (2007): 384–97.

Torres, P. [Aparecido Benedito de Faria aka Cido Faria]. "Uma experiência junto ao proletariado." In Frederico, *A esquerda e o movimento operário, 1964/1984*, vol. 1, *A resistência à ditadura*, 129–38, 283–313.

———. *Uma experiência junto do proletariado*. Lisbon: Slemes, 1977.

Touraine, Alain. "Industrialisation et conscience ouvrière à São Paulo." *Sociologie du Travail* 3, no. 4 (1961): 77–95.

———. "Latin America: From Populism toward Social Democracy." In Vellinga, *Social Democracy*, 297–309.

Trotsky, Leon. *The History of the Russian Revolution*. Vol. 1, *The Overthrow of Tzarism*. New York: Simon and Schuster, 1932.

União de Negros pela Igualdade. *Balanço eleitoral do voto étnico e presença dos negros no Parlamento*. Belo Horizonte, Brazil: Unegro, 2011.

Vannuchi, Paulo, and Rose Spina. "Paul Singer." *Teoria e Debate*, no. 62 (2005). https://teoriaedebate.org.br/2005/04/10/paul-singer/.

Vannuchi, Camilo. *Marisa Leticia Lula da Silva*. São Paulo: Alameda, 2020.

Vargas, Getúlio. *O governo trabalhista do Brasil*. Vol. 4, *Do projeto do instituto nacional de Babaçu (1953) à carta-testamento*. Rio de Janeiro: J. Olympio, 1969.

Velasco e Cruz, Sebastião C. *Empresariado e estado na transição brasileira: Um estudo sobre a economia política do autoritarismo (1974–1977)*. Campinas, Brazil: Editora da Unicamp, 1995.

Vellinga, Menno. "The Internationalization of Politics and Local Response: Social Democracy in Latin America." In Vellinga, *Social Democracy*, 3–22.

———, ed. *Social Democracy in Latin America: Prospects for Change*. Boulder, CO: Westview Press, 1993.

Veras, Dalila Teles, and Valdecirio Teles Veras, eds. *Retrato de um homen livre: Antonio Possidonio Sampaio*. São Bernardo do Campo: Gráfica e Editora FC, 1991.

Veras, Flavia. "John French: Um brasilianista diferente." *Mosaico* 4, no. 6 (2013): 82–108. http://bibliotecadigital.fgv.br/ojs/index.php/mosaico/article/view/64381.

Vianna, Francisco José de Oliveira. *Direito do trabalho e democracia social (o problema da incorporação do trabalhador no estado)*. Rio de Janeiro: Livraria José Olympio, 1951.

Vianna, Luiz Werneck, ed. *Conjuntura nacional: III ciclo de debates do Teatro Casa Grande (17 de abril a 12 de junho de 1978)*. Petrópolis, Brazil: Vozes, 1979.

Victor, Mário. *Cinco anos que abalaram o Brasil (de Jânio Quadros ao marechal Castelo Branco)*. Rio de Janeiro: Editora Civilização Brasileira, 1965.

Vidal, Dominique. *La politique au quartier: Rapports sociaux et citoyenneté à Recife*. Paris: Éditions de la Maison des Sciences de l'Homme, 1998.

Vieitez, Cândido Giraldez. "Os metalúrgicos de São Caetano do Sul: 1957–1984." *Novos Rumos* 1, no. 2 (1986): 49–68.

———. "Reforma nacional-democrática e contra-reforma: A política do PCB no coração do ABC paulista/1956–1964." PhD diss., Pontifícia Universidade Católica de São Paulo, 1986.

Vinhas, Moisés. "Contribuição para o estudo da estrutura e da organização do proletariado paulista." *Revista Brasiliense*, no. 36 (1961): 100–125.

———. *Estudos sôbre o proletariado brasileiro*. Rio de Janeiro: Civilização Brasileira, 1970.

———. *O partidão: A luta por um partido de massas 1922–1974*. São Paulo: Hucitec, 1982.

von Mettenheim, Kurt. *The Brazilian Voter: Mass Politics in Democratic Transition, 1974–1986*. Pittsburgh: University of Pittsburgh Press, 1995.

Weber, Max. *Economy and Society: A New Translation*. Vol. 1. Edited and translated by Keith Tribe. Cambridge, MA: Harvard University Press, 2019.

———. *Economy and Society: An Outline of Interpretive Sociology*. Vol. 3. Edited by Guenther Roth and Claus Wittich. Translated by Ephraim Fischoff. New York: Bedminster Press, 1968.

———. *The Methodology of the Social Sciences*. Translated and edited by Edward A. Shils and Henry A. Finch. New York: Free Press, 1949.

Weffort, Francisco. "Nordestinos em São Paulo: Notas par um estudo sobre cultura nacional e cultura popular." In *A cultura do povo*, edited by Edênio Valle and José J. Queiróz, 13–23. São Paulo: Cortez and Moraes, 1979.

———. "Política de massas." In *Política e revolução social no Brasil*, edited by Octavio Ianni, 161–98. Rio de Janeiro: Editôra Civilização Brasileira, 1965.

———. "Raízes sociais do populismo em São Paulo." *Revista Civilização Brasileira*, no. 2 (1965): 39–60.

Weinstein, Barbara. *For Social Peace in Brazil: Industrialists and the Remaking of the Working Class in São Paulo, 1920–1964*. Chapel Hill: University of North Carolina Press, 1996.

Weyland, Kurt, Raúl L. Madrid, and Wendy Hunter, eds. *Leftist Governments in Latin America: Successes and Shortcomings*. Cambridge: Cambridge University Press, 2010.

Whimster, Sam, and Scott Lash, eds. *Max Weber, Rationality and Modernity*. London: Routledge, 1987.

Wolfe, Joel. *Autos and Progress: The Brazilian Search for Modernity*. New York: Oxford University Press, 2010.

Wolford, Wendy, and John D. French. "Introduction: Deconstructing the Post-neoliberal State Intimate Perspectives on Contemporary Brazil." *Latin American Perspectives* 43, no. 2 (2016): 4–21.

Zago, Angela. *La rebelión de Los Ángeles*. Caracas: Fuentes Editores, 1992.

Zerbinato, Luiz Antonio. "Braços cruzados, máquinas fotográficas: As greves dos metalúrgicos no ABC Paulista pela fotografia (1978–1980)." Master's thesis, Pontifícia Universidade Católica de São Paulo, 2016.

Zucco, Cesar. "The President's 'New' Constituency: Lula and the Pragmatic Vote in Brazil's 2006 Presidential Elections." *Journal of Latin American Studies* 40, no. 1 (2008): 29–49.

INDEX

Page numbers in italics refer to illustrations.